SPECIAL EDITION
USING
Business
Objects® Crystal
Reports® XI

Neil FitzGerald

Kelly Byrne

Bob Coates

James Edkins

Dan Howell

Anthony Krinsky

Eric Liang

Bill Shimp

Michael Voloshko

Previous contributor:

Ryan Marples

Pearson Education

Indianapolis, Indiana

CONTENTS AT A GLANCE

SPECIAL EDITION USING BUSINESS OBJECTS® CRYSTAL REPORTS® XI

International Standard Book Number: 0-7897-3417-6

Library of Congress Catalog Card Number: 2005922653

Printed in the United States of America

First Printing: September 2005

08   07   06   4   3   2

Trademarks

Warning and Disclaimer

Bulk Sales

Que Publishing offers excellent discounts on this book when ordered in quantity for bulk purchases or special sales. For more information, please contact

U.S. Corporate and Government Sales
1-800-382-3419
corpsales@pearsontechgroup.com

For sales outside of the U.S., please contact

International Sales
international@pearsoned.com

Associate Publisher
Greg Wiegand

Acquisitions Editor
Michelle Newcomb

Development Editor
Mark Renfrow

Managing Editor
Charlotte Clapp

Project Editor
Dan Knott

Production Editor
Heather Wilkins

Indexer
Bill Meyers

Technical Editors
Bill Shimp
Bob Coates

Publishing Coordinator
Sharry Lee Gregory

Multimedia Developer
Dan Scherf

Designer
Anne Jones

CONTENTS

II Formatting Crystal Reports

V Web Report Distribution—Using BusinessObjects Enterprise and Crystal Reports Server

VI Customized Report Distribution—Using Crystal Reports' Components

VIII Web Chapters

Neil FitzGerald has 10+ years experience working with information delivery, business intelligence, and enterprise reporting products. He has combined this experience with his Bachelor of Computer Science degree from Queen's University in Kingston, Canada and his MBA from the Ivey School of Business at the University of Western Ontario to help provide information solutions to Fortune 500 companies across North America. Neil is currently based in NYC and is helping Business Objects' clients to understand the potential of the BI suite of products. He can be reached at neil_fitzgerald@hotmail.com.

Kelly Byrne has worked for Business Objects for more than six years, starting with four years in Professional Services where he rose to the position of National Practice Lead focused on enterprise deployments. Currently, he is in Strategic Presales serving some of the larger customers in North America with planning enterprise deployments. Kelly loves to talk about the semantic layer whenever possible. Currently, Kelly is pursuing his MBA part-time in Chicago at Northwestern University's Kellogg School of Management. When not working or studying, Kelly and his wife Kasia are preparing for the birth of their first child in October.

Bob Coates has been an employee of Business Objects (through the acquisition of Crystal Decisions) for nine years. He is currently a member of the presales department and the Public Sector team in the United States. Bob started working with Crystal Decisions as a technical product specialist and team leader in technical support; he moved on to become a consultant in the professional services organization, and finally moved into his current role in presales. Prior to coming to the technology industry, Bob enjoyed diverse roles as an Infantry Officer in the Canadian Forces Army Reserve (Seaforth Highlanders of Canada), a bartender in various bars and restaurants, and a first-aid attendant in a sawmill in Vancouver.

James Edkins is a senior presales consultant for Business Objects. He holds a bachelor's degree in information technology and a post graduate diploma in marketing management. He has been in the information technology sector for more than 10 years and has experience working with Fortune 500 companies in an ERP, product development, and business intelligence capacity.

Dan Howell has been an employee of Business Objects (through the acquisition of Crystal Decisions) for four years. He is based in Vancouver as a Program Manager for the Presales Consulting department. Mr. Howell has worked in the Business Intelligence industry since 1995 as a sales consultant, an implementation consultant, and a project manager.

Anthony Krinsky is currently a pre-sales engineer and solution architect at Business Objects, specializing in Java integration.

Eric Liang was a technical manager in the professional service organization of Business Objects (and formerly Crystal Decisions) for two and a half years. During that period, he led several large BI implementations, especially in the financial services industry. Eric left Business Objects in 2004 and founded BI consulting company Data Compass (www. data-compass.com), which specializes in the design and development of highly customized enterprise reporting systems based on BusinessObjects Enterprise product lines. Eric resides in Princeton, New Jersey.

Bill Shimp has nearly 10 years of experience in information technology supporting business intelligence, billing, and CRM initiatives. He is currently a senior sales consultant at Business Objects in support of strategic accounts in the northeast region of the United States. Prior to that, he supported financial accounts in New York City for Crystal Decisions. Bill holds a bachelor's degree in Engineering from Rutgers University.

Michael Voloshko is a senior pre-sales consultant for the financial services team at Business Objects. Michael has been with Business Objects for five years and is based in New York City.

To my newborn daughter, Maya Grace, and her incredible mom, Arlene.

—Neil FitzGerald

To my wonderful wife Kasia—you continue to make the ordinary extraordinary. Thank you for your steadfast love and support with this book and all things.

—Kelly Byrne

First and foremost to my wife Amanda—you inspire me and you make every day an adventure.

—Bob Coates

To my wife Cristine, who during the writing of the book had our second child. Thank you for picking up the slack during those trying times.

—James Edkins

I would like to dedicate this to the spread of harmony and compassion around the world.

—Dan Howell

Dedicated to Isel.

—Anthony Krinsky

To New Jersey, Singapore, and Mars. Peace out.

—Eric Liang

To my wife Melany, for all her love, support, patience, and understanding.

—Bill Shimp

To all the people throughout the years who have inspired me to continue achieving and advancing in life.

—Michael Voloshko

Neil FitzGerald—Thanks to all the authors for delivering on our joint goals of making this book a reality and for truly applying yourselves in tough times. You are all world-class and it was a treat to work with each of you.

Special recognition also goes to the Crystal Product and R&D teams for delivering this world-standard suite of products and the truly great leaders at Business Objects—you know who you are.

Kelly Byrne—Thanks first to Neil for giving me this opportunity to join the team, it's been fun! I would also like to thank Roxane Edjlali and Michael Thompson who helped provide some feedback on the semantic layer and the Web Intelligence engine. Also, thanks to Paul Hearmon for proofreading and making very good suggestions on structuring. I would also like to thank Charles Killam, who hired me into the company more than six years ago; you changed my life and I won't forget it. I would like to thank all of the customers I have worked with over the years—you have taught me more than I could have imagined. Finally, thanks to my Mother and Father—I hope I am a reflection of your love and compassion.

Bob Coates—To my friends and family; thanks for helping me to grow, and for all the great times. And to my peers and co-workers; every day you make our company great.

James Edkins—To the members of the team, my co-workers, and Neil FitzGerald for making this possible.

Dan Howell—First, and foremost, I would like to thank the Business Objects product development team. Their tremendous talent and commitment to developing the highest quality software is an inspiration. Thank you, Neil, for offering me the opportunity to contribute to this book. Additional thanks and gratitude is due to the entire publishing team— your patience and faith are much appreciated. To the many people I have had the honor to work with through the years, thank you so much for your contribution to the evolution of Business Intelligence. Finally, thanks to my family, friends, Mr. Fleck, Mr. Lenz, Mr. Smith, Ms. Todd, and Pat; your guidance, candor, and encouragement will never be forgotten.

Anthony Krinsky—Neil and Que, thank you for this opportunity to contribute to such an important book! I hope our customers find implementing and using Business Objects software even easier. Special thanks to Deborah and my family for their patience and support during the writing process. I would not have been able to complete the assignment without the incredible support and responsiveness of my friends at Business Objects who contributed to or reviewed my work: Adam Binnie, Alexis Naibo, Blair Wheadon, Bruno Louifi, Chuck Piercey, Corey Wilke, Craig Chaplin, Dan Howell, Dan Kearnan, David Maher, David Marks, Doug Martino, Erik Lemen, Fabien Aubert, Francois Imberton, Frederic Vanborre, Kevin Chan, Iain Cox, Ingo Hilgefort, Johnny Hermann, Karl Kwong, Kevin Chan, Kiet Trang, Kuhan Milroy, Larry Skiscim, Michael Voloshko, Mike Chatfield, Nicholas Short, Oz Greenberg, Radim Bacinschi, Rob Horne, Ryan Marples, Sean Murphy, Terry Penner, Thomas Stoesser, and Tim Weir. At the same time, responsibility for the accuracy and presentation of the content in my work is entirely my own. I would also like to thank my inspiration, friends, and original patrons in computing: Alan Margarella, Arthur Niyazov, Brian Grossman, Craig Teahan, David Unger, Doug Levy, George Jagodzinski, Jeff Tapper, Jeremy Allaire, and Libby Freligh. You can reach me at work using dot notation, or at my full name at hotmail.com.

Bill Shimp—Thanks to Neil for giving me the opportunity to contribute to this book and to all those who have helped me learn and grow throughout my career with Crystal Decisions and Business Objects.

Michael Voloshko—I would like to thank Neil for giving me the opportunity to contribute to this book and the rest of the team at Business Objects for all the hard work that goes into creating great products.

WE WANT TO HEAR FROM YOU!

As the reader of this book, *you* are our most important critic and commentator. We value your opinion and want to know what we're doing right, what we could do better, what areas you'd like to see us publish in, and any other words of wisdom you're willing to pass our way.

As an associate publisher for Que Publishing, I welcome your comments. You can email or write me directly to let me know what you did or didn't like about this book—as well as what we can do to make our books better.

Please note that I cannot help you with technical problems related to the topic of this book. We do have a User Services group, however, where I will forward specific technical questions related to the book.

When you write, please be sure to include this book's title and author as well as your name, email address, and phone number. I will carefully review your comments and share them with the author and editors who worked on the book.

Email: feedback@quepublishing.com

Mail: Greg Wiegand
      Associate Publisher
      Que Publishing
      800 East 96th Street
      Indianapolis, IN 46240 USA

For more information about this book or another Que Publishing title, visit our website at www.quepublishing.com. Type the ISBN (excluding hyphens) or the title of a book in the Search field to find the page you're looking for.

INTRODUCTION

In this introduction

INTRODUCTION TO INFORMATION DELIVERY

Organizations today of all sizes find themselves increasingly awash in data yet hungering for information to help them meet their business objectives. These corporations, from Main Street and Wall Street alike, have spent large amounts of time and money over the past 10 or so years implementing systems to help collect data on and streamline their operations. From monolithic Enterprise Resource Planning (ERP) systems (SAP, PeopleSoft, Oracle, and so on) through Customer Relationship Management (CRM) systems (Siebel, Pivotal, Salesforce.com, and so on) to Custom Data Warehousing projects, these firms are now looking for ways to extract value from that collective body of data to help them run their businesses more productively and competitively. These firms are looking for a strategic *information delivery* or *business intelligence* solution to help them become more productive and ultimately compete more effectively. The products covered in this book are geared toward meeting that challenge.

The information delivery products and solutions that are presented in this book are often categorized under the *Business Intelligence (BI)* banner. BI is the industry of value-added information delivery based on structured data sources—essentially providing meaningful, business-driven value and information to business end-users by connecting them to data with appropriate tools and products. Figure 0.1 highlights the conceptual divide of Information Delivery Solutions into the structured and unstructured world. Although evidence suggests an eventual blurring of the boundaries between these discrete industries over time, the Business Objects products covered in this book most aptly fit under the BI banner.

Figure 0.1
The information delivery industry is broadly divided into structured and unstructured information management.

Information Delivery

Structured Information Management or Business Intelligence

Relational databases,
OLAP databases,
Web logs, Excel files, and so on

Unstructured Information Management or Document Management

HTML documents,
Word or WordPerfect documents,
Email content, and so on

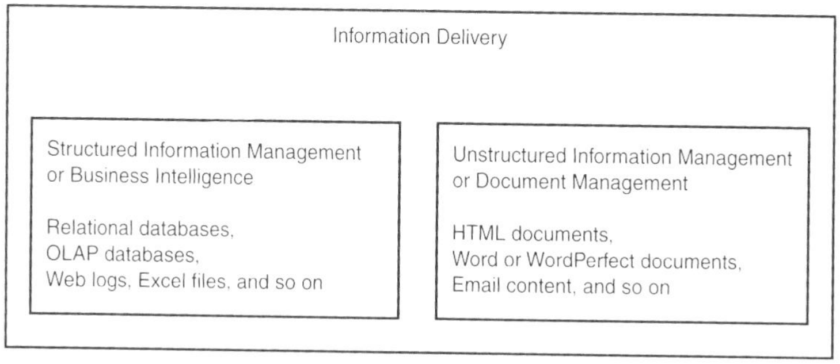

Industry analysts in the information delivery area regularly highlight the impressive adoption rates of BI products in the last few years as testimony to their value. The dynamic double-digit percentage growth rates for industry leaders like Business Objects are especially impressive when the difficult macroeconomic operating environment of recent years is taken into account. Ironically, many suggest, it is this same poor economic environment that has largely driven the increased worldwide demand for BI functionality as firms work to increase their productivity and competitiveness by leveraging existing investments—and doing more with less. This BI industry driver along with a few other drivers are covered in the next section.

SPECTRUM OF BUSINESS OBJECTS PRODUCT USAGE

BI products like those distributed by Business Objects (Crystal Reports, Crystal Reports Server, BusinessObjects Enterprise, OLAP Intelligence, and WebIntelligence) are deployed and used in about as many different ways as there are product implementations—and there are millions. However, as you become exposed to a broad swath of BI clients and their implementations, you can find definite themes to their deployments. Taking a step back, distinctive drivers to worldwide BI product adoption become evident and a few of the most common are discussed in the following sections.

CUSTOM INFORMATION DELIVERY APPLICATIONS

Despite the increasing functionality of turnkey software and Web applications available today, corporations of all sizes still regularly look to custom developed applications to provide them with unique competitive advantage and to meet their proprietary business requirements. These applications run the gamut in size from small business applications through large departmental applications to enterprise intranet and extranet applications. The key component of these custom projects is the integration of BI functionality, such as formatted reporting, ad hoc query, self-service Web reporting, and/or analytic capabilities, within an internally developed application. Table 0.1 highlights some typical examples of custom applications using Business Objects suite of products to help deliver custom applications.

TABLE 0.1   SAMPLE CUSTOM INFORMATION DELIVERY APPLICATIONS

Application	Application Audience	Product Usage
Small retail chain's internal Java-based sales metrics application	Approximately 20 sales employees and managers	Using Crystal Reports Java Engine, the developer provides the sales team with Web access to on-demand metrics reports built into the intranet application.
Large portfolio management firm's client extranet application	10,000+ high value customers of firm	Using BusinessObjects Enterprise, the developer provides access to the scalable reporting infrastructure and facilitates those customers getting online Web access to their portfolio reports.
Asset management firm's report batch of institution scheduling application	50,000+ clients	Using the BusinessObjects RAS server and scheduling engine, the developer's application dynamically creates tens of thousands of customized reports daily and automatically emails them to the appropriate clients in PDF and XLS formats.

A key strength of the Business Objects suite of products is that they lend themselves readily to integration into custom applications. From the inclusion of basic formatted reports within your Java/J2EE or .NET applications through the inclusion of rich ad hoc query and self-service reporting functionality in proprietary information product applications to provision of large-scale enterprise BI analytics, scheduling, and security functionality in a globally deployed application, the Business Objects suite of products can meet your requirements. Table 0.2 provides a jump-point for those looking for each type of application integration covered in this book.

TABLE 0.2   CUSTOM APPLICATION CHAPTERS OVERVIEW

Development Environment	Functionality Required	Section and Chapters
Java/J2EE	Pre-built reports included in custom Java application	Part VI, Chapter 28
.NET	Pre-built reports included in custom .NET application	Part VI, Chapter 29
Java/J2EE/.NET	All of the above and self service or ad hoc report creation in custom application	Part VII, Chapters 33 and 34
Java/J2EE/.NET	All of the above and scheduling, alerting, scalability, enterprise security, analytics, and more in a custom application	Part VII, Chapters 30–32

With the proliferation of BI tools and the acceleration of product adoption around the globe, there has been concurrent pressure for the involved companies to standardize on a single set of products and tools—effectively a BI infrastructure or platform. The main arguments for such standardization include the following:

- Reduced total cost of product ownership
- Creation of Enterprise centers of excellence
- Reduced vendor relationships
- Movement towards a BI infrastructure/platform

As BI products have matured from different areas of historical strength and their marketplace acceptance has grown, end-user organizations have found themselves with disparate and incompatible BI tools and products across or even within the same departments in their organization. To eliminate the costliness of managing such a broad set of tools, many firms are now moving to adopt a single BI platform like BusinessObjects Enterprise (or Crystal Reports Server for smaller businesses). The infrastructure of BusinessObjects Enterprise provides a single architecture to manage all the content and tools required to serve an organization's structured information delivery requirements. Figure 0.2 shows an end-user map of a typical organization. As you can imagine, each of the different types of end-users in a company requires different types of tools to be productive. A common infrastructure or centrally managed center of excellence such as BusinessObjects Enterprise that can meet all the varying end-user and IT requirements has clear organizational benefits.

Figure 0.2
Organizational end-user requirements map from Business Objects.

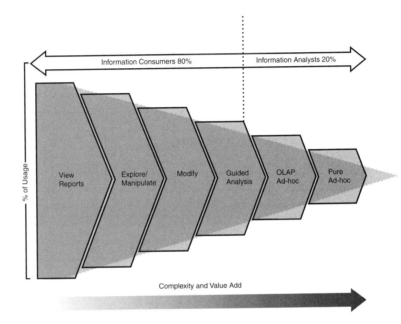

Details of the breakdown of this book are included later in this introduction but to jump-start your learning on this type of BI application, Table 0.3 can point you to the sections and chapters of particular relevance now.

TABLE 0.3   ENTERPRISE BUSINESS INTELLIGENCE CHAPTER OVERVIEW

Enterprise Business Intelligence Focus	Section and Chapters
Out-of-the-box product using BusinessObjects Enterprise	Part V, Chapters 23 and 24
Out-of-the-box product using Crystal Reports Server for small- and medium-sized businesses	Part V, Chapters 22 and 24
Setting up and administering BusinessObjects Enterprise or Crystal Reports Server	Part V, Chapters 25–27
Integrating BusinessObjects Enterprise or Crystal Reports Server functionality into applications	Part VII, Chapters 31–33

ENTERPRISE APPLICATION EXTENSION

In the past two decades, large firms have spent millions of dollars on enterprise applications including ERP and CRM applications such as SAP, Oracle/PeopleSoft, and Siebel. These large organizations are now looking for ways to extract analytic value from these operational data stores to facilitate organizational planning and forecasting through BI products.

The Business Objects suite of products includes a variety of specialized drivers that provide direct connectivity into these enterprise applications. It is important to note that these drivers are provided for use with the BusinessObjects Enterprise infrastructure and are usually released 3–6 months after the product suite is released. Chapter 15 introduces the drivers that were available at the time of publishing for this book for those who have an immediate interest in this topic.

SPECTRUM OF BI TOOL USERS

Across the usage profiles of the thousands of BI scenarios/implementations, there generally exists a consistency in the types of people that become involved. Figure 0.3 provides a relatively high-level yet accurate graphic that shows a typical distribution of the people involved in BI implementations.

Figure 0.3
Average BI implementation user distribution.

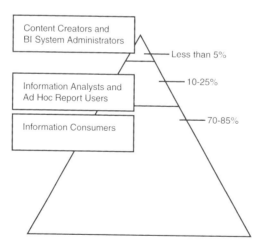

Each of the three communities outlined in the pyramid plays a key role in the ongoing success and operation of any BI implementation. The content creators and system administrators play perhaps the most important role in ensuring the short- and long-term success of any deployment because it is their work to set up the system content and tools from which the other users derive benefit. The information analysts generally come from across an organization's typical functions and are highly demanding users who require rich and highly functional interactive tools to facilitate their jobs as analysts. The last group is by far the largest group and includes employees, partners, customers, or suppliers who rely on the BI implementation to provide timely, secure, and reliable information or corporate truths. This group tends to span the entire corporate ladder from foot soldiers right up to the executive suite—all of whom have the same requirement of simple information provision to enable them to complete their regular day-to-day assignments successfully.

Figure 0.4 provides a schematic highlighting the distinction between the different v.XI content creation tools and the v.XI content delivery tools—BusinessObjects Enterprise, Crystal Reports Server, or Java/.NET Reporting engines. This book is essentially broken down into two halves covering these two themes—content creation (Parts I–IV) and content delivery in all of its possible forms (Parts V–VII) using the Business Objects suite of products.

Figure 0.4
Content creation and content delivery schematic.

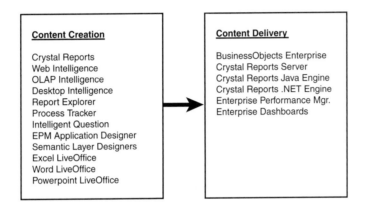

Content Creation	Content Delivery
Crystal Reports Web Intelligence OLAP Intelligence Desktop Intelligence Report Explorer Process Tracker Intelligent Question EPM Application Designer Semantic Layer Designers Excel LiveOffice Word LiveOffice Powerpoint LiveOffice	BusinessObjects Enterprise Crystal Reports Server Crystal Reports Java Engine Crystal Reports .NET Engine Enterprise Performance Mgr. Enterprise Dashboards

CONTENT CREATORS (INFORMATION DESIGNERS)

Content creators provide the foundation to any BI implementation. Using content creation tools such as Crystal Reports, OLAP Intelligence (formerly Crystal Analysis), Web Intelligence, Desktop Intelligence (formerly BusinessObjects) Excel, and so on, this group of users—primarily composed of IT folks but sometimes complemented with technically savvy business users—creates the report content, dashboards, OLAP cubes, and reporting metadata that facilitates system usage and benefits derived from the other system users. Because these tasks are of paramount importance in a BusinessObjects Enterprise suite deployment, the entire first half of the book is dedicated specifically to providing these folks with a comprehensive tutorial and reference on content creation.

After content has been created, it needs to be distributed through an infrastructure such as BusinessObjects Enterprise, the new Crystal Reports Server product, or a custom application; and then, finally, it needs to be managed. Another small but critical group of BI system users—the BI administrators—need to ensure that the system is deployed and tuned correctly to ensure optimal performance for the business end users. Chapters 25–27 provide a detailed guide to enable such administrators to effectively manage a BusinessObjects Enterprise system and the remaining chapters—28 through 34—provide detailed information on deploying Crystal content in a custom home-grown application.

INFORMATION ANALYSTS

Although not the primary group in number, the information analysts in a BI deployment are those who are primarily responsible for the extraction of new business insights and action-able recommendations derived from the BI implementation. Using such analytic tools as Web Intelligence, Excel, OLAP Intelligence, or the Crystal Reports Explorer, this group of users spends their time interrogating, massaging, and slicing and dicing the data provided in the various back-end systems until nuggets of business relevance can be gleaned. These users tend to come from a wide variety of functional areas in a company including operations, finance, sales, HR, and marketing and all work with the provided BI tools to extract new information out of the existing corporate data set. Chapters 19–21 in Part IV provide detailed information on using both Web Intelligence, OLAP Intelligence, the LiveOffice plug-ins, and the Crystal Reports Explorer.

INFORMATION CONSUMERS

This group of users composes the clear majority of those involved with a BI implementation. They are also the most diverse group and come from every rung on the corporate ladder. Executives who view corporate performance dashboards fit into this category as would truck drivers who receive their daily mileage and shipping reports online through a wireless device. The common characteristic of members of this group is that their interactions with the BI system are not indicative of their primary jobs. Unlike the content creators who are responsible for creating the valuable content and tools for the BI system and unlike the information analysts who are tasked with using the system to increase corporate perfor-mance, information consumers have jobs outside of the BI implementation and the key mea-sure of success for them is that the BI system helps facilitate their variety of assignments. Chapters 21 through 23 provide overviews of the out-of-the-box BusinessObjects Enterprise and Crystal Reports Server interfaces. Because the number of interfaces can be as varied as the number of implementations, the final sections of the book (Parts VI–VII) provide you with the customization skills to provide your users with their perfect interfaces.

THE PRODUCT FAMILY FROM BUSINESS OBJECTS

As Figure 0.4 showed, the Product family distributed by Business Objects is broken into two major segments, content creation and content delivery. This book is roughly split in two with each section covering one of the topics in great detail. The primary products in the family that are covered in these sections are Crystal Reports (first section) and Crystal Reports Server and BusinessObjects Enterprise (the second section). The other complemen-tary and specialized content creation products provided by Business Objects are introduced at the end of the first section of the book.

In the content creation section of the book, the following products will be introduced:

- **Crystal Reports version XI**—The world standard for professional formatted reporting across the largest spectrum of data sources. The Crystal Reports Application Designer benefits from more than 15 years of development and provides an unparalleled combi-nation of powerful functionality and report-design flexibility.

- **Web Intelligence XI**—A powerful content creation tool designed to provide interactive, ad hoc querying functionality to users across the end user spectrum. The drag-and-drop end user functionality is intuitive and leverages the best-of-breed semantic layer called Universes.

- **OLAP Intelligence XI (formerly called Crystal Analysis)**—A powerful content creation tool designed to access OLAP datasources and to provide interactive, speed of thought analytic reporting functionality to users across the end-user spectrum. The drag-and-drop design functionality is intuitive and the unique guided analytic functionality enables creation of content that brings the power of OLAP to the masses.

- **LiveOffice add-ins for Excel, Word, and Powerpoint**—Excel is the world's most used BI tool. To enable Excel power users to remain in their familiar Excel interface, the Business Objects family includes a new integrated add-in for Excel, Word, and Powerpoint. These add-ins provide OLAP Cube exploration, powerful ad hoc report creation, and Report Part extraction from existing Crystal Reports. The new XI (release 2) product add-in enables end users to use existing Crystal Reports, Web Intelligence reports, or semantic layers as a data source for new ad hoc reports.

- **Crystal Reports Explorer**—Based on the Report Application Server object model and used with BusinessObjects Enterprise, this application provides designers with a subset of Crystal Reports Design capabilities over the Web in a DHTML interface. All the content created in this interface are Crystal Report files.

- **Universes and Business Views**—The best-in-breed semantic layer (meta-layer) provided by Business Objects enables you to create a data abstraction layer for your report designers and/or business users. These tools provide dynamic SQL generation, access to multiple datasources, row and column level security, and so forth, and are available for use with BusinessObjects Enterprise.

- **Desktop Intelligence XI**—A powerful, client-installed ad hoc query and reporting tool designed to access existing Universes and to provide interactive, ad hoc reporting functionality to users across the end-user spectrum. The drag-and-drop design functionality is intuitive and leverages the best-of-breed Business Objects semantic layer. This product is the legacy BusinessObjects Designer tool. Using this tool is not covered in this edition of the book but BusinessObjects Enterprise XI release 2 will enable distribution of these legacy reporting objects.

In the content delivery half of the book, the following Crystal Products and SDKs are covered:

- **BusinessObjects Enterprise (formerly Crystal Enterprise)**—A complete end-to-end BI and Enterprise Reporting Platform that provides the infrastructure to support a range of implementations from small internal projects to global extranet deployments supporting tens of thousands of users. BusinessObjects Enterprise provides a wealth of Enterprise functionality including scheduling, security, auditing, alerting, and so on through several turnkey interfaces. Additionally, the functionality of BusinessObjects Enterprise can be embedded in your custom applications through use of its completely open Java and .NET object models and UI code.

- **Crystal Reports Server**—New to version XI, Crystal Reports Server provides all the functionality of BusinessObjects Enterprise but is limited to a single multi-CPU server, does not include the ability to distribute non–Crystal Reports content and is aggressively priced for small- and medium-sized businesses. The majority of content in the book discussing BusinessObjects Enterprise also applies to Crystal Reports Server and is a very attractive option for deploying BI and reporting solutions.

- **Crystal Reports Engine for .NET Applications**—The only third-party tool distributed with Visual Studio .NET, this reporting component enables .NET developers to quickly embed limited but powerful reporting functionality into their .NET applications.

- **Crystal Reports Engine for Java Applications**—Embedded in Borland's JBuilder and other Java IDEs, this reporting component enables Java developers to embed limited but powerful reporting functionality into their Java applications quickly.

- **Report Application Server**—No longer a separate product on its own, the Report Application Server (formerly called Crystal Enterprise Embedded in v10), provides a multithreaded object model and scaleable server on the BusinessObjects Enterprise (and Crystal Reports Server) infrastructure. This server provides both Java and .NET developers with access to the power of the Crystal Reports design and modification APIs for integration into their custom applications.

- **Enterprise Performance Management for BusinessObjects Enterprise (formerly called Application Foundation)**—A powerful extension to the BusinessObjects Enterprise, this product consists of dashboarding, scorecarding, and advanced analytic functionality. These tools enable you to deliver aggregated visualizations of your key performance metrics and provide drill-down into associated reports (for instance, Crystal Reports). Using these tools are not covered in this edition of the book but they are available from Business Objects for extending your BusinessObjects Enterprise system.

This book is broken down into several sections to address the varied and evolving requirements of the different users in a BI deployment.

The entire first half of the book (Parts I through IV) is exclusively focused on content creation. Through use of hands-on step-by-step examples and detailed descriptions of key product functionality, you will be able to leverage the powerful report creation capabilities of Crystal Reports v.XI, Web Intelligence, OLAP Intelligence v.XI, Business Views and Universes, the Web-based Crystal Reports Explorer, and the LiveOffice Ad Hoc add-in. Some profiles of people who will find these sections of particular relevance:

- New and mature Crystal Reports designers
- Professional Crystal Reports designers upgrading to v.XI
- Existing and new OLAP Intelligence, Web Intelligence, and Desktop Intelligence (formerly Business Objects) designers and analysts

- Existing and new BusinessObjects Enterprise (formerly Crystal Enterprise) administrators
- New Crystal Reports Server administrators

The second half of the book (Parts V through VII) is geared toward the distribution or delivery of the valuable content created in the first half. Detailed functionality overviews are provided for all the different distribution mechanisms available in the Business Objects suite of products. Additionally, detailed and instructive code samples are provided for all the Software Development Kits (SDKs) that are provided with Crystal Reports, BusinessObjects Enterprise, and the Crystal Reports Server. Some profiles of people who will find these sections of high value:

- New or existing BusinessObjects Enterprise (formerly Crystal Enterprise) administrators
- New or existing BusinessObjects Enterprise (formerly Crystal Enterprise) users
- .NET-based application developers
- Java/J2EE-based application developers
- Application developers looking to integrate report design or modification into their applications
- Application developers looking to integrate report scheduling, security, alerting, viewing, and so on into their applications

PART I: CRYSTAL REPORTS DESIGN

Part I should familiarize you with the foundations of Crystal Reports and get you up and running as quickly as possible. It is critical for someone who is new to Crystal Reports and includes the fundamental report-design concepts that even experienced users will be able to use for the rest of their Crystal Reports writing career. This section also provides powerful exercises and real-world usage tips and tricks that will enable even seasoned reporting experts to become more productive.

PART II: FORMATTING CRYSTAL REPORTS

Part II focuses on some of the more subtle nuances of Crystal Report design: effective report formatting and data visualization through charting and mapping. Improper formatting and incorrect use of visualization techniques can make reports confusing and not user-friendly. This section also provides powerful exercises and real-world usage tips and tricks enabling mature reporting experts to become more productive.

PART III: ADVANCED CRYSTAL REPORTS DESIGN

Part III presents a host of advanced Crystal Report design concepts that involve features such as subreports, cross-tabs, report templates, and alerts. This part also touches on advanced data access methods such as JavaBeans, XML objects, SAP, and Peoplesoft systems. This section also provides powerful exercises and real-world usage tips and tricks enabling mature reporting experts to become more effective in their report-design work.

PART IV: ENTERPRISE REPORT DESIGN—ANALYTIC, WEB-BASED, AND EXCEL REPORT DESIGN

Part IV focuses on a the powerful Web Intelligence and OLAP Intelligence design tools for ad hoc querying and analysis against both relational and OLAP data sources. Chapter 18 also covers the semantic layer (Business Views and Universes), the reporting Repository, and both the Web- and Office-based Crystal ad-hoc reporting capabilities.

PART V: WEB REPORT DISTRIBUTION—USING BUSINESSOBJECTS ENTERPRISE PROFESSIONAL AND CRYSTAL REPORTS SERVER

Part V presents the powerful functionality of the turnkey BI and Enterprise reporting product—BusinessObjects Enterprise (and Crystal Reports Server). In addition to covering the many business benefits of these systems, this part also provides extensive coverage of the end-user interface for end-user training. Extensive architecture, administration, and management best practices are provided for system administrators.

PART VI: CUSTOMIZED REPORT DISTRIBUTION—USING CRYSTAL REPORTS COMPONENTS

Part VI focuses on the Customizable Report Distribution Components that are provided for Crystal Reports Delivery in both the .NET and Java/J2EE worlds. Code samples are provided to help jumpstart your development work.

PART VII: CUSTOMIZED REPORT DISTRIBUTION—USING BUSINESSOBJECTS ENTERPRISE AND CRYSTAL REPORTS SERVER

Part VII provides a detailed look into the object model of the BusinessObjects Enterprise and Crystal Reports Server systems through Java code samples and tutorials (.NET samples also available). All the functionality described in Parts V and VII is included in this rich object model and allows developers to quickly include the powerful functionality of BusinessObjects Enterprise, Crystal Reports Server and Crystal Reports in their custom applications.

EQUIPMENT USED FOR THIS BOOK

You can find various supporting material that will assist you in the completion of the exercises in this book, as well as supplemental documentation on related topics.

WEB RESOURCES

You can find all the source code and report samples for the examples in the book, as well as links to great external content, at www.usingcrystal.com. You'll find report samples to download and code for you to leverage in your report design and sharing efforts. Also, a great deal of additional product-related information on the Business Objects suite of products including Crystal Reports, Web Intelligence, OLAP Intelligence, Desktop Intelligence, Crystal Reports Server, and BusinessObjects Enterprise can be found at www.businessobjects.com.

INTENDED AUDIENCE

This book was written to appeal to the full range of Crystal Reports, OLAP Intelligence, Web Intelligence, Crystal Reports Server, and BusinessObjects Enterprise users. You'll find this book useful if you've never used the Business Objects suite of products before, if you are a mature Crystal Reports user looking for some new productivity tips, or if you want to explore some of the new features found in version XI and their related SDKs.

You don't have to be an expert, but you should have a basic understanding of the following concepts:

- Database systems such as Microsoft SQL Server, Oracle, Sybase, and Informix
- Operating system functions in Windows 2000/2003/XP
- General Internet/intranet-based concepts such as HTML, DHTML, ActiveX, and Java

The first four parts of this book build on each other, so skipping around those parts isn't the best approach unless you have some familiarity with Crystal Reports XI. Even if you are familiar with Crystal Reports, many new features have been introduced in recent versions, so you are encouraged to read the entire first half of the book so that you don't miss anything. The second half of the book is focused on the different forms of content delivery and each part can be approached independently without loss of context.

REQUIREMENTS FOR THIS BOOK

To get the most from this book, you should have access to a computer that has at least a 450 MHz Pentium II or equivalent processor, 128MB of RAM, and Windows 2000, Windows 2003 or Windows XP Professional.

All reports are based on sample data that is installed with Crystal Reports, so you will have access to the same data that was used in this book. You'll need to install Crystal Reports to get the most out of the examples included in each chapter in the first half of the book.

CONVENTIONS USED IN THIS BOOK

Several conventions are used within this book to help you get more out of the text. Look for special fonts or text styles and icons that emphasize special information.

- Formula examples appear in computer type, and they can be found on the Sams Publishing website as well.
- Objects such as fields or formulas normally appear on separate lines from the rest of the text. However, there are special situations in which some formulas or fields appear directly in the paragraph for explanation purposes. These types of objects appear in a special font like this: Some Special Code.
- In some cases, we might refer to your computer as *machine* or *server*. This is always in reference to the physical computer on which you have installed Crystal Reports.

- You'll always be able to recognize menu selections and command sequences because they're implemented like this:

  Use the File, Open command.

- New terms appear in *italics* when they are defined.

- Text that you are asked to type in appears in **boldface**.

- URLs for websites are presented like this: http://www.businessobjects.com.

NOTE

> Notes help you understand principles or provide amplifying information. In many cases, a note emphasizes some piece of critical information that you need. All of us like to know special bits of information that make our job easier, more fun, or faster to perform.

TIP

> Tips help you get the job done faster and more safely. In many cases, the information found in a tip is drawn from experience rather than through experimentation or documentation.

Sidebar

Sidebars spend more time on a particular subject that could be considered a tangent, but will help you be a better Business Objects product user as a result.

Real World sections provide some practical and productivity enhancing usage insights derived from the author's real-world experience designing and deploying hundreds of Crystal Reports.

The Troubleshooting sections provide some quick chapter summary notes and examples that are useful reminders on the product operations.

CRYSTAL REPORT DESIGN

1

CREATING AND DESIGNING BASIC REPORTS

In this chapter

INTRODUCING THE CRYSTAL REPORTS DESIGNER

This chapter takes you through the required steps to create your own basic reports in the Crystal Report Designer. After you've installed the Crystal Reports XI Designer, you are ready to open it and familiarize yourself with the environment. This section briefly introduces the following components of the application interface:

- Report sections
- Application toolbars
- Application menus

If you have already registered your installation, you should be presented with the Getting Started page shown in Figure 1.1. This page provides quick access to existing Crystal Reports files while also enabling you to begin designing new reports via the Report Expert Wizards or from a blank report template.

Figure 1.1
The Getting Started page provides quick access to existing Crystal Reports files as well as the Report Expert Wizards.

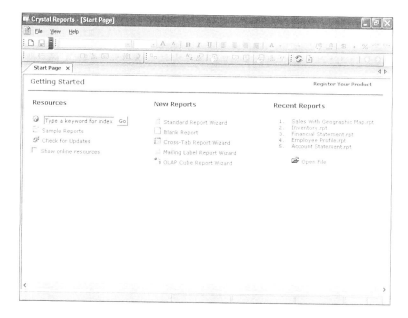

CRYSTAL REPORT SECTIONS

From the Getting Started page, select the Blank Report link (listed below the New Reports heading). You'll see a window labeled Data Explorer; click Cancel. If the Field Explorer window is now displayed on the right side of the new report screen, click the Close button. You will now be presented with a new Report1 Tab beside the original Start Page tab.

On the Report1 tab, you are presented with a blank report template that is divided into numerous report sections. As Figure 1.2 illustrates, report sections are identified by name on the left side of the design area. These sections segment the Crystal Reports design environment into logical areas to facilitate more intuitive report creation—these include the

Report Header, Page Header, Details, Report Footer, and Page Footer sections (if your install displays initials instead of these report section names, go to the File menu, chose options and uncheck "Short Section Names" under the Layout tab). Each of these sections has unique properties and printing characteristics that you can modify. When creating reports, you place objects (such as data fields) into the various sections according to report requirements. If a report object such as an image is placed in the Report Header section, the image displays and prints only once per report, on the first page. If the same image is placed in the Page Header section, the image then displays and prints once per page. The same holds true for custom sections, such as Group Headers and Group Footers. The Details section implies that whatever is placed in this section displays and prints once for each and every row retrieved from the data source.

Figure 1.2
Report sections provide an intuitive way to create and organize your data when designing reports.

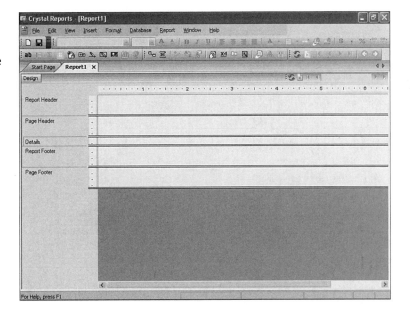

NOTE

Although Crystal Reports is commonly used for Web reporting initiatives, the design environment is built on a paper metaphor with *pages* as a concept to facilitate the presentation of information.

Report sections can contain a variety of different object types, including database fields, text, pictures, charts, and map objects. Additional objects, such as formula and subreport objects, are also positioned within report sections and are covered later in the book in greater detail.

The Section Expert is used to view or modify the properties of the report sections. To access the Section Expert, perform one of the following actions:

- Right-click on the section's label (or name, located on the left sidebar) you want to work with, and then select Section Expert from the pop-up menu.
- Click on the Section Expert button.
- Select the Section Expert option from the Format menu.

> **NOTE**
>
> When designing reports, you should consider the following items when working with report sections:
> - It is good practice to print a validating test page of each report you are designing.
> - Consider keeping all font sizes the same within each section for maximum eye appeal.
> - Print preprinted forms on the same machine to avoid discrepancies in the interpretation of the report layout by different print drivers and printers.

Crystal Reports also provides some more advanced section formatting options, reviewed later in the book, such as underlaying and suppressing sections based on certain criteria (formulas). These features are accessible from the Section Expert dialog.

USING TOOLBARS AND MENUS

Toolbars are the graphical icon bars at the top of the Crystal Reports application environment, containing various buttons that you can click to activate the most frequently used application commands. Toolbars act as shortcuts to access commonly used functions of the design application, and you can enable or disable them to appear or disappear at the top of the application area by selecting Toolbars from the View menu, which is located in the upper-most area of the application. As Figure 1.3 shows, there are five main toolbars that you can use within the Crystal Reports design environment:

- **Standard**—The most commonly used application functions, including New, Open, Save, Print, Preview, Export, Copy, Cut, Paste, and Help.
- **Formatting**—Functions that pertain specifically to modifying object properties with regard to Font, Font Size, Bold, Italics, Underline, Alignment, Currency, and Percentage formats.
- **Insert Tools**—Quick access to the building blocks of all reports including Text Objects, Summary Fields, Groups, Online Analytical Processing and Cross-Tab Grids, Charts, and Maps, and Drawing items such as lines and boxes.
- **Expert Tools**—Functions that enable you to access the main application experts quickly, such as the Database, Group, Select, Section, Formula Workshop, and Highlighting Experts.
- **Navigation Tools**—Functions that enable refreshing of the reports data and navigation through the pages of the involved reports.

Figure 1.3
The five Crystal Reports Design toolbars provide quick and easy access to commonly used application commands during report design.

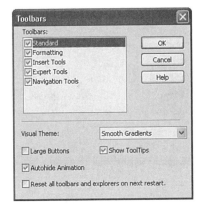

N O T E

> ToolTips are pop-up descriptions that appear when your cursor rests over any of the toolbar buttons. ToolTips are enabled by default. To disable ToolTips on your toolbars, deselect the Show ToolTips check box from within the Toolbars dialog.

In much the same way that the toolbars offer quick and easy access to commonly used commands, the menu items at the top of the application environment provide listings to virtually all the application functions available in Crystal Reports. The menu items act as shortcuts to all the commands within the design application, and they include the following items:

- The File menu includes file-specific commands to create a new report file, open an existing report, close a current report, save a report, save a report with an alternative filename, export to a different file format, and save the current data set with a report. In addition, the File menu contains commands that enable you to send a report to a printer, select a specific printer, modify the page setup and margins add summary information to a report, and set a variety of report options.

- The Edit menu includes commands used to modify various aspects of a report, including commands to undo and redo actions, as well as to cut, copy, and paste report and OLE objects. Additionally, you can edit fields, formulas, summaries, and subreport links.

N O T E

> *Object Linking and Embedding (OLE)* enables you to insert objects (OLE objects) into a report from other applications and then use those applications from within Crystal Reports to edit the objects if necessary. If Crystal Reports did not make use of OLE, you would have to exit Crystal Reports, open the original application, change the object, return to Crystal Reports, delete the object originally inserted, and then insert the newly revised object.

- The View menu includes commands used to customize the user interface of the Crystal Reports application. The View menu commands enable you to navigate between the application's Design and Preview views, access the three main explorers (Field, Report, and Repository Explorers), access the new XI Dependency Checker window, access the new XI Workbench window, access the Toolbars dialog, zoom in and zoom out of a report, as well as to turn on and off the application rulers, guidelines, grids, ToolTips, and group tree from both the Design and Preview views of the report.

- The Insert menu includes commands used to insert text objects, summaries (counts, sums, medians, and so on), field headings, groups, subreports, lines, boxes, pictures, charts, maps, report template objects, and other objects into your report.

- The Format menu provides easy access to a variety of commands useful in formatting your reports for presentation purposes. This menu includes commands used to change the characteristics of the objects in a report. The Format menu provides quick access to commands for modifying font properties (color, size, borders, background color, and drop shadows for example), chart, line height, and hyperlink properties, and formatting for entire sections of the report. The Format menu also provides commands to arrange report objects (move, align, and size) and to specify desired highlighting characteristics via the Highlighting Expert.

- The Database menu includes commands used to access the Database Expert, from which you can add and remove data source tables for use within reports, specify links between data source tables, and modify table and field alias names. This menu also provides easy access to the set database location and enables you to log on and off SQL and ODBC servers, browse field data, and display and edit the report SQL syntax. In general, the Database menu enables you to maintain the necessary specifications for the report with regard to the data source(s) with which the report interacts.

- The Report menu includes commands used to access the main application experts (also referred to as *wizards*), identify the desired records or groups to be included in a report via the Select Expert and Selection Formulas (often referred to as applying report *filters*), construct and edit formulas, create and view alerts, specify report bursting indexes, modify grouping and sorting specifications, refresh report data by executing the query to run against the database, and view report performance information.

- The Chart menu is only visible after selecting a chart or map object and includes specific commands used to customize your charts and maps. Depending on the type of chart you select, the Chart menu includes commands to zoom in and out of charts; apply changes to all instances of a chart; discard custom changes made to the chart; save the chart template to a file; apply and modify template specifications for the chart; change the titles, numeric axis grids, and scales of the chart; and auto-arrange the appearance of the chart. After selecting a map object, the Chart menu then includes additional commands used to configure the overall style of the map, reorganizing the layers of report elements, changing the geographic map, and hiding or showing the Map Navigator.

- The Window menu includes commands used to rearrange the application icons and windows, as well as providing a list of report windows that are currently open and a command that enables you to close all report windows at once.

- The Help menu includes commands used to quickly access the Crystal Reports online help references, commands to register Crystal Reports and locate the Getting Start page, and quick access to the About Crystal Reports dialog and several key Business Objects websites for technical support and product information. Lastly and new to Crystal Reports XI, the Help menu provides online access to Crystal Reports updates, downloaded and installed automatically from the Web. These updates can be set to occur automatically or manually.

REPORT DESIGN EXPLORERS

Several report design explorers, intended to streamline the report design process, compose another key component to Crystal Reports XI. The design explorers are application tools that greatly enhance a report designer's efficiency while working with reports. They are design tools you will use in building reports throughout the remainder of the book.

The report design explorers are dialog windows that display various objects relevant to the report in a hierarchical tree view facilitating quick access to and formatting of each respective object and its properties. The explorers enable you to easily locate and navigate to specific report objects, such as the report header or a corporate logo image, to customize the object for design purposes. All the objects included in a report (report sections, groups, database fields, formulas, parameters, images, charts, and so on) are organized and displayed within one of the design explorers. There are three distinct explorers:

- **Report Explorer**—Provides a tree view of each report section in the report and each of the report objects contained within each section. You can work with each report object directly from the explorer rather than navigating to each object separately in either the Design or Preview tab of the report.

- **Field Explorer**—Displays a tree view of database fields, formulas, SQL expressions, parameters, running totals, groups, and special fields. You can add any of these field types directly to a report from the Explorer dialog. Fields that have already been added to the report or fields that have been used by other fields (such as formula fields, groups, summaries, and so on) have a green check mark icon in front of them.

- **Repository Explorer**—Provides a tree view of each object contained in the Crystal Enterprise report repository. You can work with each report repository object directly from the Repository Explorer rather than locating each object separately for inclusion in the report during the report design process.

NOTE

It is important to emphasize that since Version 10, the centralized Repository is only available for use with BusinessObjects Enterprise. See Chapter 18, "Using a Semantic Layer—Business Views and Universes," for more details on this topic.

LOCATING AND USING THE REPORT DESIGN EXPLORERS

Each of the explorer dialogs can be *docked* in place or used in a free-floating state. By default, the Report and Field Explorers appear docked on the right side of the report design environment. However, you can manually dock each of them in other locations if you prefer. The explorers can also be used in free-floating mode, in which case each of the explorer dialog windows can be dragged to any location within the report design environment and float in place until you either close or reposition them. To view each of the report design explorers, click the View menu and select each desired explorer individually, as shown in Figure 1.4.

Figure 1.4
By default, the design explorers, workbench, and dependency checker are docked on the right side of the report designer application but can be moved about and toggled on and off to facilitate report design.

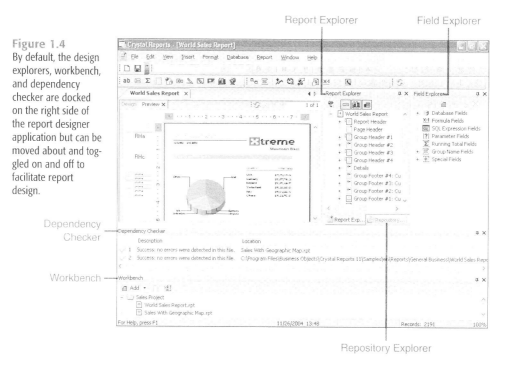

To save space in the design environment, the individual explorers can be dragged on top of each other and provide their functionality through respective tabs in a single dialog. This is the default position for the Field and Report Explorer in a fresh install but note in Figure 1.4 how the Report Explorer has been dragged into its own dialog with the Repository Explorer exposing itself through a tab in that same dialog. Also new in XI is the ability to autohide the explorer windows by clicking on the thumbnail toggle button at the top of each explorer. The explorers will then autohide on the sides of your report until you are ready to use them again.

The report design explorers create an intuitive way for report designers to add and format report objects quickly while constructing reports. As you progress through the remainder of the book, you will be using these explorers on a regular basis, so it's important that you understand the basics of these application features.

THE DEPENDENCY CHECKER AND WORKBENCH

Two new features presented in XI are the Workbench and the Dependency Checker. The Workbench provides a tool within the Crystal Reports Designer that enables the logical grouping and management of reports into projects. The Dependency Checker is another new tool that checks a specified report, or all reports in an existing Workbench report project for several types of errors, including formula compilation problems, database errors, repository object errors (if you're using BusinessObjects Enterprise), and hyperlink errors. You can check for these types of errors and invoke the Dependency Checker from under the main Report menu or from within the Workbench window. Both the Dependency Checker and the Workbench can also be accessed from the main View menu and can be located and locked in the same way as the Report Explorer.

UNDERSTANDING DATA AND DATA SOURCES

The first step in creating a report is always to identify a data source. Today, Crystal Reports supports more than one hundred different types of data sources. These data sources range from traditional databases such as Microsoft SQL Server, Oracle, IBM DB2, and Microsoft Access to other more abstract forms of structured data such as log files, e-mail, XML, COM/.NET/EJB objects, and multidimensional (OLAP) data. Many of the advanced data sources and their specific nuances are covered in great detail in Chapters 15–18.

To determine which database driver to use to connect to a certain data source, it's best to understand the different types of database drivers. The following sections discuss direct and indirect access database drivers.

UNDERSTANDING DIRECT ACCESS DRIVERS

Direct access database drivers are built solely for reporting from a specific type of database such as Oracle. If a direct access driver (sometimes called a *native* driver) exists for the database that you intend to report from, it is generally the best choice. Although they follow the standard model of a database driver, direct access drivers are tailored for that specific database. For example, if you choose the Microsoft Access direct access driver during the creation of a report, you will be prompted for the filename of the Access MDB file. If you are using the Oracle direct access driver, you will be prompted for a server name. Not only is the user experience more specific to that database, a direct access driver often results in better performance than other methods of connecting to the same data. Table 1.1 lists some of the most common direct access database drivers.

TABLE 1.1   COMMON DIRECT ACCESS DATABASE DRIVERS

Direct Access Driver	Description
Microsoft Access	Used to access Microsoft Access databases and Microsoft Excel spreadsheets
Oracle	Used to access Oracle database servers
DB2	Used to access IBM DB2 database servers

UNDERSTANDING INDIRECT ACCESS DRIVERS

As you might guess from the name, an indirect access driver is one that connects indirectly to an actual data source. Indirect access drivers are not built for any one type of database, but rather are built to read data from a variety of data sources via a standard data access mechanism. The purpose of these drivers is to enable Crystal Reports to use data sources for which direct access drivers do not exist. The two major indirect access drivers provided are ODBC and OLE DB.

ODBC, which stands for *Open Database Connectivity*, is a long-standing technology built to connect various applications to various data sources via a common mechanism called an ODBC driver. Just as Crystal Reports has a concept of database drivers that enables data access to report developers, ODBC has a concept of ODBC drivers that enables data access to any application. The Crystal Reports ODBC database driver communicates with an ODBC driver, which in turn communicates with the actual database. ODBC drivers are generally developed by the database vendors themselves and often come bundled with the database software.

OLE DB, pronounced "*OH-lay-dee-bee*," is the evolution of ODBC. Like ODBC, OLE DB has a concept of database drivers, but calls them OLE DB providers. Crystal Reports can read most OLE DB providers. Figure 1.5 illustrates the various ways to connect to your data.

Figure 1.5
The Crystal Reports data access architecture provides unparalleled data access.

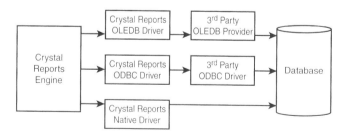

If appropriate, any necessary database client software should be installed and configured prior to installing Crystal Reports. However, if you've installed Crystal Reports before installing the database vendor's client software, follow the directions located in the Crystal Reports Help files to ensure correct configuration of the Crystal Reports system Data Source Names (DSNs) .

INTRODUCTION TO THE DATA EXPLORER

Now that you've got a basic understanding of what database drivers are and an idea of which one you might use to access a particular data source, let's look at the user interface for selecting the data source for a report. Because this is the first step in the creation of a report, it is only natural that this is the first step in the Report Wizard. This is shown in Figure 1.6. The Data Explorer is a tree control hosted inside the Report Wizard that enables you to identify the following:

- Which Crystal Reports database driver you want to use
- Which data source you want you use
- Which database objects you want to use

Figure 1.6
The Data Explorer provides access to the multitude of supported Crystal Report's data sources.

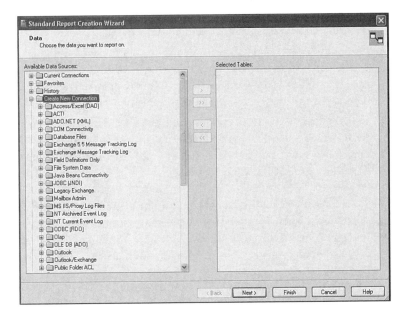

To open the Data Explorer, select File, New and select the type of report you want to create. Selecting Blank Report opens the Data Explorer on its own while selecting any other report type opens the Data Explorer as part one to a multipart wizard dialog. The Data Explorer represents data source connections organized into a number of categories. The following sections describe each of these categories, whereas the Enterprise Repository is discussed in Chapter 18.

CREATING A NEW CONNECTION

To specify a new connection, expand the Create New Connection node in the Data Explorer. As Figure 1.6 shows, you can select from a multitude of data sources in this interface. You will notice a node in this section for each of the drivers selected during the installation process.

One node to take special note of is the More Data Sources node. When this is expanded, it lists all database drivers that are available but not installed. Crystal Reports supports *install on-demand*. This means that various features always appear as being available, even if they are not installed. When you expand one of the database driver's node selections under the More Data Sources node, that driver would be installed on-demand. Then the next time the Data Explorer is loaded, it would list that driver directly under the Create New Connection node.

Now that you understand which data sources are listed where, look at the process of creating a connection. To create a connection, follow these steps:

1. Expand the node that corresponds to the appropriate database driver. An easy one to play with is the Xtreme sample database that comes with Crystal Reports XI. To create a connection to this database, expand the ODBC (RDO) node.

2. Notice that when a node is expanded, a dialog is presented that allows for the specification of connection information. In the case of ODBC, the DSN is the only thing required. In this list of available DSNs, Xtreme Sample Database 11 should be visible. This is pre-installed with Crystal Reports. Select this and click Finish.

3. Focus returns to the Data Explorer, and there should be a node below the ODBC (RDO) node called Xtreme Sample Database 11. Below that node is the list of available tables, views, and stored procedures, as well as the Add Command option for adding a SQL command. (This will be discussed shortly.)

The Xtreme Sample Database could also have been used via the OLE DB or direct Access driver. Note that when prompted for connection information when using one of these drivers, the report developer is asked to provide different information. In the case of ODBC, a DSN needed to be selected, whereas with OLE DB, a provider would need to be specified.

USING CURRENT CONNECTIONS

The Current Connection node lists all database connections that are currently open. In other words, if a report is currently open or was recently open, that connection is listed under the Current Connections node. The first time the Crystal Reports designer is opened, the Current Connection node is empty because no connections have been initiated. This is indicated by a "…no items found…" item shown when the Current Connections node is expanded. This is a quick way to select the same connection as another report currently open.

USING FAVORITE CONNECTIONS

The Favorites node lists all connections that have been designated a favorite. This is analogous to favorites and bookmarks in a Web browser. If you have a certain database connection that is used often, adding it to the favorites makes it quick and easy to find in the future.

To accomplish this, create a connection to a database (you can use the Xtreme Sample Database to try this out), and select Add to Favorites when right-clicking on that connection.

Be sure to right-click on the connection and not the driver or table name. Figure 1.7 illustrates the Xtreme Sample Database connection being added to a user's Favorites.

Figure 1.7
Add the Xtreme Sample Database ODBC connection to the Favorites node to locate it quickly.

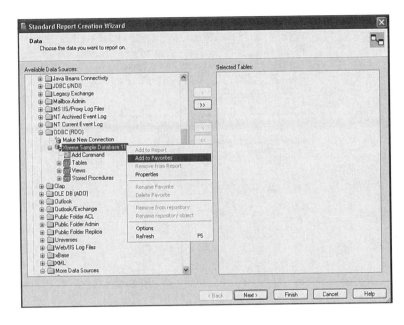

LEVERAGING RECENTLY USED CONNECTIONS WITH THE HISTORY NODE

The History node is situated beneath the Favorites node in the Data Explorer. It lists recent database connections that have been made. This is useful for quickly locating and using a connection that has been recently used, but not added to the Favorites list. The history list stores the last few connections. If you find yourself using connections from the History node frequently, it might be better to add the connection to your favorites list.

ADDING DATABASE OBJECTS TO YOUR REPORT

The term *database objects* is used to describe the various forms of data that can be added to a report. Specifically, Crystal Reports can use the following types of database objects as data sources for a report:

- Tables or system tables
- Views
- Synonyms
- Stored procedures
- SQL Commands

Database objects are listed underneath connections in the Data explorer and are grouped by object type. In Figure 1.8, the various database objects are shown for the Xtreme Sample

Database. In this case, there are tables, views, system tables, and stored procedures. The Add Command node gives you the ability to add SQL commands to this report.

> TIP
>
> You can control the objects that are displayed in the Data Explorer by setting selection, description, and filtering options accessed from either the Database tab of the Options dialog under the File menu or the Options menu option off the database's right-click context menu. This can be particularly useful when you are reporting off databases with hundreds of tables.

Figure 1.8
The Data Explorer presents database objects in their logical categories.

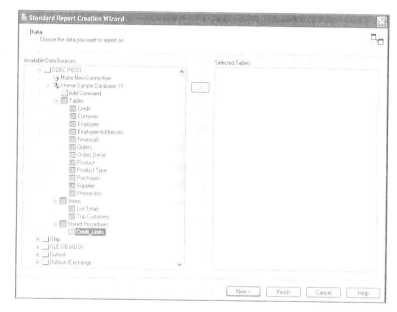

The following sections describe the most common database object types in further detail.

REPORTING ON TABLES

Tables are the most basic form of a data structure. Simply put, a table is a set of fields bound together to represent something in the real world. A Customer table might contain fields that describe all the customers of a given business. An Employee table might store information about a corporation's employees such as name, title, or salary.

To add a table to a report, select the table in the Data Explorer and click the arrow (>) button. The table is added to the Selected Tables list on the right side of the dialog below its corresponding connection. Most database administrators give the tables meaningful names; however, sometimes tables can have quite archaic names, such as RM564_321. A name like this isn't very descriptive, so it would be useful to rename this table to something more meaningful. To rename a table, select it in the Selected Tables list and press the F2 button (F2 is a standard convention for renaming things in Windows). In Crystal Reports, renaming a table is referred to as *aliasing* a table.

REPORTING ON VIEWS

A *view* is a query stored by the database that returns a set of records that resemble a table. Views often perform complex query logic, and good database administrators create them to simplify the job of people (like report developers) extracting data out of the database. For example, the Top Customers view in the Xtreme Sample Database returns all customers who have sales of more than $50,000. From a report developer's perspective, views act just like tables and can be added to the report in the same way.

REPORTING ON STORED PROCEDURES

Stored procedures, in the context of Crystal Reports, are similar to views in that they are pre-defined queries in the database that return a set of records. The major difference is that a stored procedure can be parameterized. This means that rather than having a preset query that returns the same data every time it is run, stored procedures return different data based on the values of parameters passed in.

Adding a stored procedure to a report works much the same way as tables and views. However, if the stored procedure has a parameter, a dialog appears when you attempt to add the stored procedure to the report. This is shown in Figure 1.9. The dialog asks you to provide values for each of the stored procedures' parameters. After you complete this and click the OK button, focus returns to the Data Explorer and the stored procedure is shown in the list of selected tables. At this time, a parameter is created in the report that corresponds to the stored procedure parameter, and any values that parameter is given are passed to the underlying stored procedure.

Figure 1.9
Adding a stored procedure with a parameter invokes the Enter Values dialog.

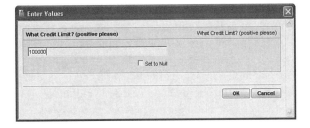

REPORTING ON SQL COMMANDS

When reporting from tables, views, and stored procedures, Crystal Reports generates a query behind the scenes using the *Structured Query Language (SQL)*. This is beneficial because the report developer does not need to understand the complexity of the SQL language, but rather can just drop fields onto the report and get data back that matches those fields. However, sometimes report developers are quite experienced with databases and specifically, the SQL language. Because of this, they sometimes prefer to write their own SQL query rather than have Crystal Reports generate it for them. For an introduction to the SQL language, refer to the Downloads section at www.usingcrystal.com and download the document called "Using SQL Queries in Crystal Reports."

SQL Commands enable you to use your own prebuilt SQL query and have the Crystal Reports engine treat that query like a *black box*. This means that any query, whether simple or very complex, that returns a set of records can be used as a data source for a Crystal Report. To create a SQL Command, select the Add Command item under the database connection, and then click the arrow (>) button. This initiates a dialog that enables the user to type in a SQL query. Figure 1.10 illustrates a typical query.

Figure 1.10
Adding a typical SQL Command to a report.

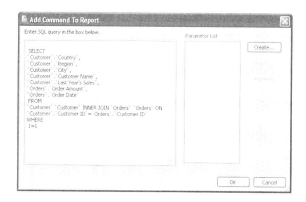

After the query is typed in and the OK button is clicked, focus returns to the Data Explorer, and the newly created command is represented as 'Command' underneath its corresponding connection. As with all database objects, selecting the command and pressing the F2 button enables the user to rename the object.

One key feature of SQL Commands is parameterization. If you had to create a static SQL query, much of the power of SQL Commands would be lost. Fortunately, SQL Commands in Crystal Reports support parameters. Although parameters can be used in any part of the SQL Command, the most common scenario would be to use a parameter in the WHERE clause of the SQL statement to restrict the records returned from the query. To create a parameter, click the Create button in the Modify Command dialog. This initiates a dialog that enables the user to specify a name for the parameter, text to use when prompting for the parameter value, a data type, and a default value. After the OK button is clicked, the parameter appears in the Parameter list. To use this parameter, place the cursor where the parameter should be used in the SQL query, and double-click the parameter name. Figure 1.11 illustrates a simple SQL Command with an 'OrderThreshold' parameter.

When a SQL Command is created with a parameter, the report developer is prompted for a parameter value. This works much the same way as parameterized stored procedures in that a parameter is created automatically in the report that maps to the SQL Command parameter.

CAUTION

> Unlike previous versions (9 and before), SQL Commands can no longer be centrally stored and accessed in a centralized Crystal Repository without the BusinessObjects Enterprise product. In fact, the Repository and all its reusable objects are now only available through BusinessObjects Enterprise. A Repository Migration Wizard is distributed with the Enterprise product to facilitate a quick migration from the V.9 Crystal Reports–based Repository.

JOINING DATABASE OBJECTS TOGETHER

Up until this point, only reports based on a single table, view, stored procedure, or SQL Command have been discussed. However, it is quite common to have several disparate database objects in the same report. Crystal Reports treats all types of database objects as peers, which means that a single report can contain multiple tables, views, stored procedures, and SQL Commands. Because all database objects are treated as peers, the term *table* will be used from now on to describe any of these database objects.

Because of Crystal Reports' inherent basis on relational data, any time multiple tables are used, they must be linked together so that the sum of all database objects is a single set of relational records. The good news is that most of the time, Crystal Reports takes care of this automatically, and the report developer need not worry about linking.

To see this in action, create a connection to the Xtreme Sample Database and add both the Customer and Orders tables to the report. When clicking Next in the Report Wizard, the linking between those tables is displayed as shown in Figure 1.11. Each table is represented by a window. In addition to the name, each field in the table is listed inside the window, and those fields that are defined as indexed fields in the database are marked with colored arrows. Any links defined between tables are represented as arrows connecting the key fields from two tables. Based on general database theory, linking to a field that is indexed generally results in a better performing query, and indexing is highlighted in this dialog through the color-coded icons displayed beside the field names.

Figure 1.11
You can link multiple tables together in the Report Wizard.

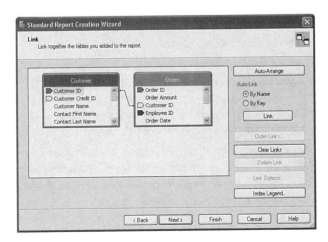

By default, Crystal Reports creates links based on name. In this case, both tables have fields with a name of Customer ID, so a link is already created. To accept this link, simply click Next to move to the next step in the Report Wizard. If there were not a common field name, selecting the By Key option and clicking Auto-Link would attempt to create a link based on the fields defined in the database as keys. If neither of these methods of automatic linking work, the link must be manually created. This is very simple to do: Simply drag the field to link from one table and drop it onto the field from a second table.

After links are created, you can configure them by clicking on the link arrow connecting two tables (it turns blue when selected), and then clicking the Link Options button. Links have two options: join type and link operator. These settings determine how Crystal Reports matches records from both tables. The default join type is an inner join, which means that only records with a matching key in both tables are included. The default link type is equal. For most cases, these two settings do not need to be modified.

UNDERSTANDING THE DIFFERENT JOIN TYPES

In Crystal Reports, the Link tab of the Report Wizard (and Database Expert) provides a visual representation of the relationship between multiple database objects. Defining the appropriate join strategy for any given report should be reflective of the data within the database objects and of how the report needs to read and display that data. Join type settings enable you to control more precisely the query results based on your unique requirements. The following is a list of the most common types of joins and their associated descriptions:

- **Inner**—The resultset includes all the records in which the linked field value in both tables is an exact match. The Inner join is the standard type of join for most reports, and it is also commonly known as the Equal join.

- **Left Outer**—The resultset includes all the records in which the linked field value in both tables is an exact match. It also includes a row for every record in the primary (left) table for which the linked field value has no match in the secondary (lookup) table. For example, if you would like your report to display all customers and the orders they have each placed—including the customers who have not placed any orders at all—you can use a Left Outer join between the Customer and Orders tables. As a result, you would see a row for every customer who has not placed any orders.

- **Not Equal**—The resultset includes all records in which the linked field value in the primary table is not equal to the linked field value in the secondary (lookup) table. For example, if you needed to report on all orders that were not shipped on the same date that they were ordered, you could use the Not Equal join type to join the OrderDate field in the Orders table with the ShipDate field in the OrderDetails table.

- **Full Outer**—The resultset includes all records in both of the linked tables—all records in which the linked field value in both tables is an exact match, in addition to a row for every record in the primary (left) table for which the linked field value has no match in the secondary (lookup) table, and a row for every record in the secondary (lookup, or right) table for which the linked field value has no match in the primary table. The Full

Outer join is a bidirectional outer join, which essentially combines the characteristics of both the Left Outer and Right Outer joins into a single join type.

NOTE

> The capability to enforce links created in a report was introduced in version 10. Enforcing a link between two tables ensures that this link will be used in the report's respective SQL, regardless of whether fields are required from either or both of the involved tables. The default setting is Un-enforced links, meaning that the link will only be used if the report's respective SELECT statement requires it. Access to the different enforcing options is provided by right-clicking on a link and selecting the Link Options menu item.

After a report is created, select Database Expert from the Database menu to return to the Data Explorer. Here tables and SQL Commands can be added, removed, and renamed just as they could from the Data Explorer in the report creation process.

USING THE REPORT CREATION WIZARDS

Now that you have been quickly introduced to the Crystal Reports development environment and reviewed data access, a good place to begin creating reports is with the default report wizards. The report wizards are provided to expedite the report design process for report designers of all skill levels, but they are especially useful for new users of Crystal Reports.

The report wizards, also commonly referred to as *report experts*, provide a simplified interface and guided path to constructing the fundamental elements found within most reports. As a result, designing interactive, professional looking reports can be achieved in a matter of minutes.

This section reviews the various wizards available for different report styles you might require. This chapter also provides a tutorial that walks you through the report design process using the Standard Report Creation Wizard to create a useful, professionally styled report.

TIP

> Using the default report wizards as a starting point for beginners on most reports is a good idea. The report wizards offer a shortcut to establishing the core elements required for most reports.

GETTING STARTED WITH THE REPORT WIZARDS

The Report Wizards are accessed from either the Getting Start page previously highlighted in Figure 1.1 or from the New menu option accessed under the main File menu. The four report wizards facilitate the guided, visual creation of four types of reports.

As Figure 1.12 illustrates, the New menu option from under the File menu serves as the gateway to accessing and using the various report creation wizards. From this menu, you can select from one of the four provided report wizards:

- **Standard**—Used to create traditional columnar-styled reports.
- **Cross-Tab**—Used to create summary styled Cross-Tab reports.
- **Mailing Label**—Used to create reports with multiple columns, such as address labels.
- **OLAP Cube**—Used to create summary styled Cross-Tab reports that are based on an OLAP data source.

Figure 1.12
The Crystal Reports New File menu provides quick access to the various report creation wizards.

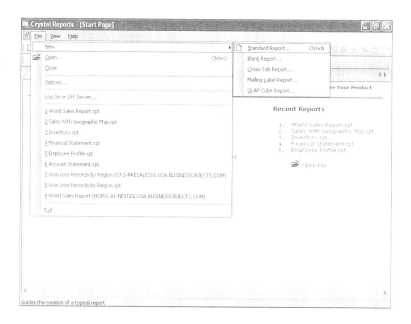

The remainder of this section focuses on exploring and using the Standard Report Creation Wizard. In general, this is the most commonly used report wizard, and it provides a good introduction to the components of the report design process. If your interests lie in either OLAP Cube or Cross-Tab reports, they are covered in later chapters.

USING THE STANDARD REPORT CREATION WIZARD

The Standard Report Creation Wizard is the most frequently used design assistant in Crystal Reports. It provides multiple dialogs common to creating reports that are based on conventional corporate data sources. The Standard Report Creation Wizard guides you through selecting a data source, linking data source tables, adding data source fields to the report, specifying field groupings, identifying summary (total) fields, and setting the desired sort criteria for your report.

Additionally, the Standard Report Creation Wizard walks you through creating chart objects, applying record selection criteria (data filters), and applying predefined templates (layouts) to your report.

> **NOTE**
>
> The term *filter* is commonly used to describe data selection criteria that narrow the scope of the data being extracted by the report from the underlying data source. For example, by using a filter such as Country = USA, you can easily limit your report to include only the information you are interested in extracting.

The Standard Report Creation Wizard consists of nine dialog screens that enable you to specify the criteria mentioned previously to create a professional-looking report quickly. The sequence of the wizard's dialog screens is dynamic and directly associated with the items selected in each of the progressive screens. For example, if you do not choose to identify any summary items for your report, you will not be presented with a Chart dialog screen. In general, charts apply best to summarized data, so if you have not identified any summary fields, the wizard assumes that you do not want to include a chart object in your report.

> **NOTE**
>
> Charts can also be created from base-level data, although to do this you must appropriately specify the On Change Of option and use the Advanced settings with the Chart Expert. Generally, it makes more sense to base chart objects on summary-level data, such as regional sales by quarter—where you are charting the total sales for each quarter rather than each sales transaction in each quarter.

The following exercise steps through the wizard and builds a sales report to display last year's sales by country. By making use of the Standard Report Creation Wizard, you include the country, city, customer name, and last year sales database fields, graphically display a summary of last year sales by country, and apply professionally styled formatting to the report. To create the sales report, follow these steps:

1. From the main File menu, select the New option, and then select the Standard Report Wizard from the wizard list.

2. As shown in Figure 1.13, you should now be presented with the first dialog—labeled Data—as part of the Standard Report Creation Wizard. From the Data dialog screen, expand the Create New Connection node and then expand the ODBC listing as well. This should present the ODBC Data Source Selection dialog.

3. From the ODBC Data Source Selection dialog, scroll to the end of the Data Source Name list and select Xtreme Sample Database 11, as shown in Figure 1.14. Click Next to continue.

Figure 1.13
The Standard Report Creation Wizard begins by requesting a data source for your report.

Figure 1.14
The ODBC Data Source Selection dialog enables you to select a valid connection to access your ODBC data sources.

4. Verify that the Data Source Name is correct and click Finish from the ODBC Connection Information dialog. No password is necessary to access this database.

5. After you have successfully identified and connected to Xtreme Sample Database 11, you should see this item listed under the ODBC node in the Available Data Sources area of the Data dialog screen, as shown in Figure 1.15. Upon expanding the Xtreme Sample Database 11 item, you should see three or four distinct data source items listed: Tables, Views, and Stored Procedures—and possibly System Tables dependent on your options settings (shown in Figure 1.16).

6. Within the Data dialog screen, select the Customer and Orders tables so that they are listed in the Selected Tables area on the right. After these two tables are selected, click Next to continue onto the Linking Dialog.

Figure 1.15
The Xtreme Sample Database is listed under the Available Data Sources area of the Data dialog.

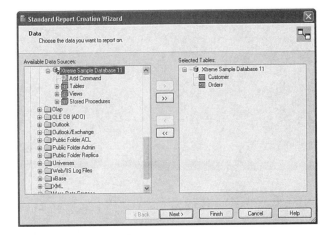

Figure 1.16
Upon expanding the Xtreme Sample Database 11 item, you will notice multiple database items listed.

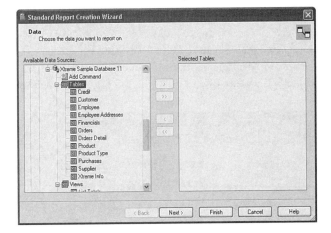

TIP

There are multiple ways to include tables in your report from within the Data dialog screen. From the list of available tables on the left side of the dialog, you can perform any one of the following actions to populate the Selected Tables list on the right side of the dialog area:

- Double-click on each desired table item
- Drag-and-drop each desired table item
- Highlight the table item on the left and click on the respective arrow icons (> or >>) between the two listing areas to populate the listing on the right

7. The Link dialog screen presents a visual representation of the relationship between these two tables and permits you to modify the defined relationship by specifying the exact *Join* links that you require to accurately report on the data within the selected tables. As shown in Figure 1.17, you should now see the Link dialog screen. For our purposes here, accept the default Join condition. Click Next to continue.

Figure 1.17
The Customer and Orders tables are linked together via the Customer ID field.

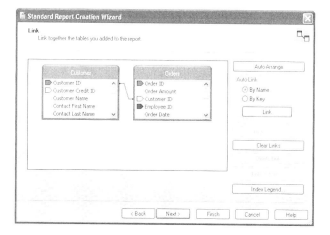

8. After specifying the table linking, you will see the Fields dialog screen, shown in Figure 1.18. Select the Customer Name, Country, and City fields from the Customer table and the Order Amount and Order Date fields from the Order table so that they appear under the Fields to Display area on the right. If necessary, you can use the up and down arrows to modify the order of these fields in the list. Click Next to continue.

Figure 1.18
The Customer Name, City, Country, Order Amount, and Order Date fields should appear under the Fields to Display area.

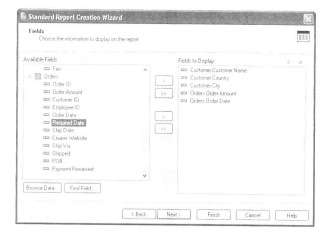

NOTE

If you're not sure of the data contained in any of the respective field items on the left, you can highlight a field name and click the Browse Data button to view a list of values from this field, as shown in Figure 1.19. This can be particularly useful if you are unfamiliar with the database and need to locate a field based on the values it contains, such as account numbers, policy codes, or employee names.

Figure 1.19
The Browse Data button enables you to view a list of values from any of the available database field items.

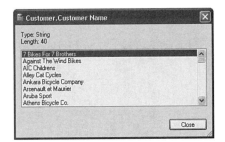

9. You should now see the Grouping dialog screen. This dialog enables you to specify logical groups of information within your reports. For this example, select to group by the Country field only, as shown in Figure 1.20. Click Next to continue.

Figure 1.20
The Grouping dialog enables you to create structured groupings of information within your report.

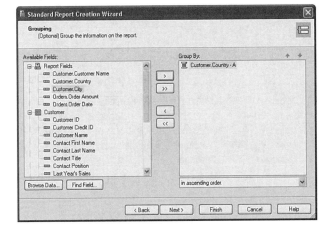

10. You should now see the Summaries dialog screen. The Summaries dialog screen enables you to identify summary values (such as Sums, Counts, and so on) for your reports. If you have not identified any grouped items in a report, the Summaries dialog does not appear because summaries are only applicable to grouped data. To apply a summary object to the report, select the Order Amount field so that it appears under the Summarized Fields list on the right. This is shown in Figure 1.21. Click Next to continue.

NOTE

As you might notice, Crystal Reports automatically chooses a summary for you if you choose to group your report data. It examines the detail information you've specified for the report and builds a summary on the first available numeric field. However, this default summary criteria is easily modified in the wizard.

Figure 1.21
The Summaries dialog screen enables you to create summarized values that are frequently used in coordination with the grouping structure within reports.

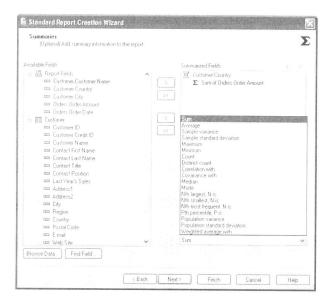

> **NOTE**
>
> By default, the Order Amount field that appears under the Summarized Fields area on the right is aggregated as a Sum of the actual field value. As shown in Figure 1.21, the drop-down list located in the lower-right area of the Summaries dialog screen enables you to select from a variety of summaries, including Sum, Average, Maximum, Minimum, Count, Correlation, Covariance, and Standard Deviation.

11. Now sort the report based on the total order amounts of the top five countries. The Group Sorting dialog screen enables you to sort the grouped fields based on the summarized totals. From the Group drop-down list, select the Country field (the only option in the example here) and select the Top 5 Groups option from the Group Ordering choices. Also, select the Sum of Order Amount item from the Comparing Summarized Values drop-down list, as shown in Figure 1.22. Click Next to continue.

12. Charting can be added through the wizard to visually display the data already selected. From the Chart dialog screen, you can select a chart object to be included in the report based on the group and summary items you identify here. For this example, add a bar chart and select the Country field from the On Change Of drop-down list and the Sum of Order Amounts item from the Show Summary drop-down list. Change the chart title to read **Total Order Amounts by Country**—see Figure 1.23 for additional guidance. Click Next to continue.

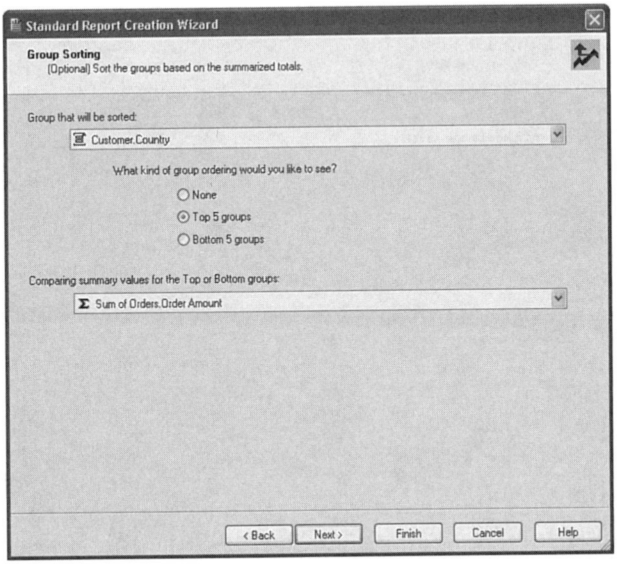

Figure 1.22
The Group Sorting dialog enables you to sort your report based solely on the Group values you want to include in the report results.

Figure 1.23
The Chart dialog enables you to select a chart object for a report based on the previously identified group and summary criteria.

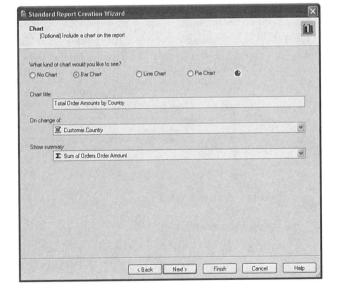

13. Now you'll address the fictitious requirement that you are only interested in customer orders from the year 2003. The Record Selection dialog screen enables you to identify selection criteria, often called *data filtering*, to focus the resultset of the report to include only the information you are interested in returning. To accomplish this, select Order Date as the Filter Field, choose Is Between from the filter operator drop-down list, and select a data range from the newly created date-range drop-down boxes to incorporate all the dates in 2003 (see Figure 1.24). Click Next to continue.

Figure 1.24
The Record Selection dialog permits you to narrow your resultset based on the selection criteria identified here.

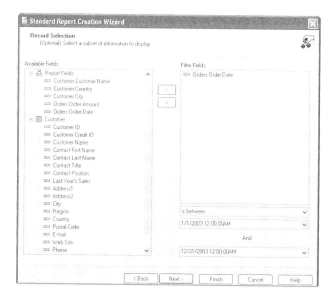

14. Finally, apply a predefined style to your report. From the Template dialog screen, you can select predefined styles to be applied to your report for formatting purposes, as shown in Figure 1.25. The Available Template list includes various sample templates that are included with the Crystal Reports XI installation. However, you can also create your own templates to be used for report formatting. For this example, select the Corporate (Blue) template. For additional details on how to design and implement your own templates, see Chapter 14, "Designing Effective Report Templates."

Figure 1.25
The Template dialog permits you to select predefined styles to be applied to your report.

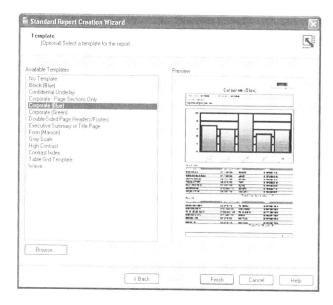

This now concludes the Standard Report Creation Wizard example. After you click Finish, you will execute the report that you have just created and will be presented with the preview of the corresponding resultset. At this point, you can click Finish if you are satisfied with the report design criteria. When you are presented with the preview of your report, save your new report by selecting Save As from the File menu. Name this report **Chap1Wizard.rpt** or anything you would like.

After you select Finish at the end of the Standard Report Creation Wizard process, you will be presented with the executed resultset and a preview of your newly created report. As Figure 1.26 shows, creating a useful and professional looking report is extremely simple when using the Standard Report Creation Wizard. In the preceding exercises, you have connected to a database, identified the tables and fields you wanted to include in your report, linked the tables together, grouped and summarized the data, sorted the data, applied filtering criteria, included a chart object for enhanced visualization of the report results, and applied a report template for quick and easy formatting—all in just a few clicks of your mouse! This process speaks both to the ease of use and power of the Crystal Reports design application.

Figure 1.26
The executed result-set and preview of the report you have just created using the Standard Report Creation Wizard.

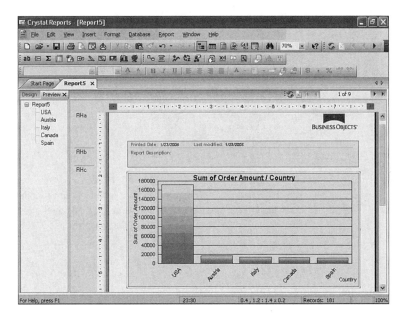

CREATING A REPORT WITHOUT WIZARDS

As with many software tools, educational tools and facilitators like the Report Wizards are often the best way to begin a learning process. They are by their nature, however, limited in functionality and it generally does not take long before maturing students want to roll up their sleeves and discover the raw power and incredible flexibility that lies beneath. This section reintroduces the report just created in the Report Wizard through a manual design process in the Crystal Reports Designer. The beginnings of that same Sales Report are created from scratch with the following steps:

Select a blank report. After opening Crystal Reports, select the New option from the File menu. From the submenu that appears, select the Blank Report option.

Select an appropriate data source. From the Database Expert dialog that comes up, in the Available Data-sources list, browse to Create New Connection, ODBC. As soon as you choose ODBC, the ODBC (RDO) dialog pops up. Scroll until you find the Xtreme Sample Database 11. Select it and click Finish. (There are no other settings to get this database working, so you can ignore the Next button.)

Select the appropriate tables. After choosing the appropriate database to connect to, you need to select the tables for this report. Move down in the left list box and expand the Tables item. Choose the Customer and Orders tables by using the right-arrow (>) button, shown in Figure 1.27.

Figure 1.27
The Data tab from the Database Expert dialog shows the two tables you just added to the report.

Remember that you can choose each table separately and click the arrow button or hold down the Ctrl key to select all tables that you want and then press the arrow button only once. Also, if you want to select several tables in a row, the Shift key helps you with that.

Link tables from the database. Move to the next tab in the Database Expert dialog by either clicking the OK button or selecting the Links tab. Notice that all the tables have already been linked. Crystal Reports attempts to link tables using similar field names and sizes whenever possible. You can optionally turn off this automatic smart linking in the Database tab (accessed from File, Options).

You can enlarge this dialog by using the stretch markers so that you can increase the display area and see more tables at once. The next time you enter this dialog, your adjusted size will be remembered.

You don't need to make any changes at this point, so just click the OK button.

5. Add detail records to the report. First, confirm that the Field Explorer is being displayed so that you can use it to add the fields to the report. If it is not, choose View, Field Explorer. In the Field Explorer that becomes available, open the Database Fields item and then the Orders and Customer tables to expose the fields that you'd like to add. Select each field separately and drag it to the Design tab using your mouse. Place them side-by-side in the Details Section: Customer Name and Customer City from the Customer table, and Order Amount and Order Date from the Orders table. Figure 1.28 highlights the desired result.

Figure 1.28
This is the Design window after you've added all the fields.

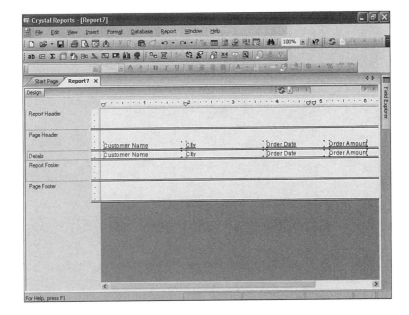

6. Create a logical grouping of data by Country. To accomplish this, choose Insert, Group. When the Insert Group dialog appears, scroll down the first list box until Country under the Customer table is available. Select it, as shown in Figure 1.29, and then click OK.

    Notice that in the Design view of the report, two new sections become available called Group Header #1 and Group Footer #1. Within Group Header #1, the Group Name #1 field is also automatically added.

7. Add a summary value of total Historical Order Amount by Country to the report. Choose Insert, Summary to get the Insert Summary dialog to appear. In this dialog, select the Order Amount field in the Field to Summarize drop-down box. Next, because you plan on finding out how much has been ordered in each country, you need to set the summary operation in the second list box to Sum. Last, because the desired summary is per Country, set the location of the summary to show Group #1, as shown in Figure 1.30. Click OK.

Figure 1.29
The Common tab of the Insert Group dialog with the Country field selected.

Figure 1.30
The Insert Summary dialog with Order Amount summed by Customer Country selected.

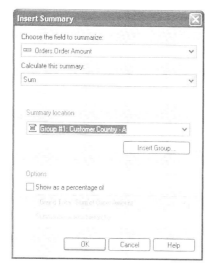

A shortcut to the Insert Summary command (and running total command described later) is accessible for each field on the report by right-clicking the involved field in the report designer.

Notice that in the Design view, in the Group Footer #1, the Sum of Order Amount field has been added.

View the report. Take a look at the report by choosing Report, Refresh Report Data or by either pressing the F5 key or clicking the Refresh button in your Crystal Reports Designer. A report with all the data represented in the last wizard-driven report you created is returned in the Preview tab as shown in Figure 1.31.

Figure 1.31
The resulting report based on steps 1 through 8 in the Preview tab.

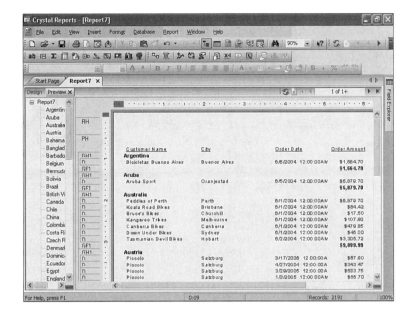

9. Save the report. Choosing File, Save opens the Save dialog. Provide a suitable name for the report, such as Chap1Manual.rpt. You are welcome to explore the charting and report template features now to replicate the Chap1Wizard report but they are covered in detail in Chapter 8, "Visualizing Your Data with Charts and Maps," and Chapter 14.

TIP

If you are concerned about losing work between manual saves of a report, Crystal Reports has an autosave feature that you can enable. Set this option by navigating to File, Options, and then selecting the Reporting tab. The Autosave Reports After option can be set and the length of time in minutes between saves can be specified in the edit box for this option.

TROUBLESHOOTING

I AM HAVING DIFFICULTY ACCESSING THE DATA EXPLORER.

To access the Data Explorer for a new report, select File, New and select the Blank report option or any of the Report Wizards. For an existing and open report, select the Database Expert from the main Database menu.

CRYSTAL REPORTS IN THE REAL WORLD—SQL COMMANDS

Experienced report developers will notice that the sample database is very simple (only a dozen tables) and that all the fields in the tables have useful names. In practice, it's very common for a database to have many more tables with very complex relationships and that the field names are not descriptive. This is where SQL Commands can help. This section explores the advantages of using SQL Commands to create reports. To take SQL Commands for a test-drive, follow these steps:

Open Notepad and type the following lines of SQL exactly as they appear here:

```
SELECT
    'Customer'.'Customer Name' AS Name,
    'Customer'.'City' AS City,
    'Orders'.'Order Date' AS OrderDate,
    'Orders'.'Order Amount' AS Amount
FROM
    'Customer' 'Customer' INNER JOIN 'Orders' 'Orders' ON
    'Customer'.'Customer ID'='Orders'.'Customer ID'
```

This is the SQL statement that will be used in the report.

Select a blank report. After opening Crystal Reports, click on the New option from the File menu and select Blank Report.

Select an appropriate data source. From the Database Expert dialog that opens, in the Available Data-sources list, browse to Create New Connection, ODBC. As soon as you choose ODBC, the ODBC (RDO) dialog pops up. Scroll until you find the Xtreme Sample Database 11. Select it and click Finish. (There are no other settings to get this database working, so you can ignore the Next button. These additional options will be discussed in a later chapter.)

Rather than selecting tables, double-click the SQL Command option. The Modify Command window pops up. Copy the SQL Command from Notepad into the box as shown in Figure 1.32.

Figure 1.32
The Modify Command window with the SQL Command pasted into the text box.

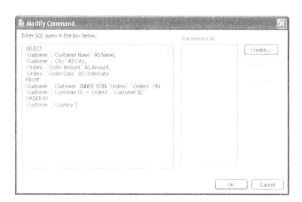

Click OK; notice that there is no need to link the tables because the SQL Command already defines the relationship between the tables. Notice also that there are only four fields to choose from and that the names have been changed.

The SQL Command does four things:

- **Hides database complexity.** Converts many tables into one view with the table relationships defined.

- **Hides unnecessary fields.** Many database fields are ID fields that simply aren't intended to be seen by users. The SQL Command can be constructed so these fields don't pass through.

- **Renames database fields.** Database field names are often unreadable and give no hint about what they contain. The SQL Command can rename these obscure names into something more meaningful.

- **Empowers SQL Experts.** If you are a SQL Expert or have them in your organization, you can leverage their expertise in creating optimally performing SQL through use of SQL Commands.

CAUTION

> SQL Commands cannot currently be created against native connections on Sybase, DB2, or Informix. To leverage the power of this functionality, you can create an ODBC connection against these datasources and then create a SQL Command against that ODBC source.

CHAPTER 2

SELECTING AND GROUPING DATA

In this chapter

INTRODUCTION

The Field Explorer, which was introduced in Chapter 1, "Creating and Designing Basic Reports," provides a quick and easy way to select and display fields on your report and then easily drag and drop them onto the Report Design area. In addition to choosing existing fields from your selected data sources, the Field Explorer enables you to create calculated (formula) fields, parameter fields, running total fields, and group summary fields, as well as choose from a predefined set of default special fields. These additional objects enable a great deal of flexibility and power in the information you can deliver through the reports you create.

In addition to selecting the fields that make up the raw content for a report, it is often beneficial to group base-level data by country, region, or product line. Grouping the data facilitates relevant business user analysis and enables meaningful summarizations in your reports. Crystal Reports provides easy-to-use grouping functionality that enables nested groups, hierarchical grouping, and drill-down analysis into the different levels of grouping selected.

This chapter covers the following information:

- Understanding the different types of field objects
- How to add grouping to your reports
- How to add multiple groups to your report and reorder them
- Hierarchical grouping
- Creating and using drill-down in your reports
- Hiding and suppressing detail records in your reports

UNDERSTANDING FIELD OBJECTS

As described in Chapter 1, the Field Explorer displays a tree view of data fields in your report. It shows database fields, formula fields, SQL expression fields, parameter fields, running total fields, group name fields, and special system fields that you have defined for use in your report. This chapter introduces you to all the standard field types available in Crystal Reports.

To activate the Field Explorer, either select it from the View menu or click on the Field Explorer button in the Crystal Reports Standard toolbar. Figure 2.1 shows the sample Crystal Report created in the last chapter with the Field Explorer activated and docked on the right side of the screen. As previously mentioned, this can be docked on either side of the designer or at the bottom of the screen. Alternatively, the Field Explorer can freely float over any part of the design window by simply dragging and dropping it.

Figure 2.1
Crystal Reports Designer with the Field Explorer docked on the right side.

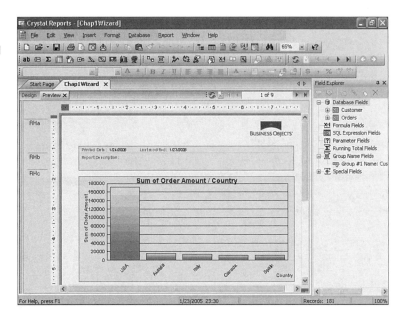

The next seven sections introduce the different types of fields accessible from the Field Explorer and provide ideas on where they might be used in a report. Subsequent chapters in the book cover some advanced uses of these types of fields. Before moving on to explore these different types of fields, here are some common traits shared by all field types:

- Fields that are being used in the report or fields that have been used by other fields (for example, formulas) being used in the report are highlighted with a green check mark in front of them.

- The buttons along the top of the Field Explorer (Insert, Browse, New, Edit, Rename, and Delete) are enabled or disabled based on the availability of the selected Field type.

- Detailed report field formatting, positioning, and resizing are covered in Chapter 6, "Fundamentals of Report Formatting."

ACCESSING DATABASE FIELDS

The Database Fields branch of the Field Explorer tree is used to add database fields to your report. The fields that can be added to your report are those from standard database tables, views, stored procedures, synonyms, and system tables. To add additional tables or other data sources to your report, you would use the Database Expert under the Database menu.

To insert the database fields that are available from the Field Explorer into your report, either click and drag them into the desired location on the report or select them, click the Insert to Report button (or Insert to Report action from the right-click menu), and then select the desired location on the report for the highlighted fields.

> If you are uncertain of exactly which fields to add to your report because of ambiguous (for example, WERKS, MENGE, LEAFS) or similar (for example, District, Region, Locale, Division) field names, you might be able to determine the appropriate field by selecting the respective field and using the Browse button (or the Browse action from the right-click menu) to view the data type and sample values of data from the table.

Multiple fields can be highlighted simultaneously in the Field Explorer and placed in the report designer window at once. Crystal Reports drops the first of the multiple chosen fields in the selected location on the report and places the subsequent fields in order to the right of the initial field. If the report's layout runs out of real estate on the right side of the report, the subsequent fields are placed one line down and the placement algorithm continues.

ACCESSING FORMULA FIELDS

Formula fields provide a means to add derived fields (that is, those not directly available in your database) such as a calculation into your Crystal Reports. Crystal Reports treats derived formula fields in exactly the same manner as it does original database fields. Some examples of where formulas might be used on the sample report from Chapter 1 would include the following:

- **Days Until Shipped**—A date formula determining the difference between the two database fields—Order Date and Ship Date

- **Next Years Sales Projection**—A numeric formula that multiplies the database field Last Years Sales by 110%

- **Custom Name Field**—To include the first letter of a customer contact's First Name (a database field) concatenated with a space and the contact's last name (another database field)

The formula fields branch of the Field Explorer tree is used to add existing or new formula fields to a report. A listing of previously created formulas appears in this part of the Field Explorer tree. Once created, existing formulas are added to the report by either clicking and dragging and dropping or by selecting the formula and using the Insert functionality—available through the right-click menu or Field Explorer action button—and then selecting the location.

> Both simple and complex formulas can be created on any type of field including numeric, date, string, Boolean, or memo fields. This is explored in Chapters 11, "Using Record Selections and Alerts for Interactive Reporting," and 13, "Using Formulas and Custom Functions."

If a new formula is required, it can be created directly from the Field Explorer by using the New toolbar button. You are prompted to name the new formula and then select the method of creation. This dialog is displayed in Figure 2.2.

Figure 2.2
The Formula Name dialog requires specification of a formula name.

Using the Xtreme Sample Database and the sample report created in Chapter 1 (chap1Wizard.rpt), one simple formula you might want to add is a Full Name field that comprises both the first and last name of the customer's contact person (Contact First Name and Contact Last Name in the Customer sample table).

To perform this task, perform the following steps:

1. After opening the **Chap1Wizard** report, highlight the Formula Fields branch of the Field Explorer tree.

2. Select New either by using the New button or right-clicking and selecting New from the fly-out menu.

3. Enter the Formula Name **Full Name** in the Formula Creation dialog and select the Formula Editor using the Use Editor button.

4. Scroll down in the Report Fields window (the top-left window in the main frame) to locate and open the Customer table. Select the Contact First Name field by double-clicking on it. The field displays in the main Formula Editing window.

5. Add a space after the Contact First Name field and then type in + " " +. This concatenates the two fields together and also adds a space between the first name and the last name.

6. Scroll down in the Report Fields window (the top-left window in the main frame) to locate and open the Customer table. Select the Contact Last Name field by double-clicking on it. The field is displayed in the main Formula Editing window.

7. When you have confirmed that the main formula window looks exactly like that shown in Figure 2.3, save the Full Name formula by clicking the Save button and then closing the main Formula Editor window.

By selecting Save in the Formula Editor, you return to the Field Explorer and the new formula, Full Name, is now available to be placed on the report. Finish this section by placing the Full Name Formula Field onto the report beside the Customer Name.

ACCESSING SQL EXPRESSION FIELDS

The SQL Expression Fields branch of the Field Explorer tree is used to add existing or new SQL Expression fields to a report. A listing of previously created SQL Expressions appears in this part of the Field Explorer tree. Once created, existing SQL Expressions are added to the report by either clicking and dragging and dropping or by selecting the SQL Expression—using the Insert into Report button or action on the right-click menu—and selecting the location.

Figure 2.3
This is the Formula
Editor after you cre-
ated a String concate-
nation formula.

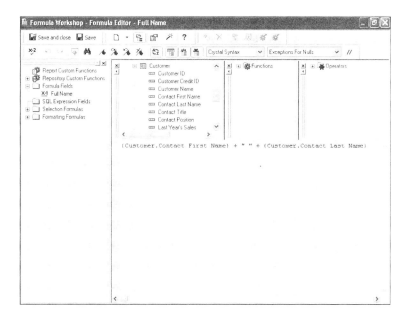

SQL Expressions are created in the same Formula Editor as formulas but use *Structured Query Language (SQL)* statements (rather than the formula syntax). SQL Expressions are used in cases where report-processing efficiency is critical. Using SQL expressions can give report designers greater report processing performance by pushing data processing to the database server instead of the Crystal Reports engine as this is generally most efficient.

> The SQL syntax created in SQL Expressions must be appropriate to the source database. Different databases support various syntactical versions of SQL and even diverse degrees of functionality. This is explored in a document called "Using SQL Queries in Crystal Reports" that is available from the Downloads section of www.usingcrystal.com.

ACCESSING PARAMETER FIELDS

Parameter fields provide a means to create dynamic reports and provide your business users with an interactive method of driving the report content or layout they view. When a Crystal Report contains parameters, it requests certain pieces of information from the business user before processing. The involved Crystal Report can then use those inputted parameters to filter the data that is presented or even suppress entire report sections. Some examples of where parameters might be used include

- A region parameter on a sales report
- A profit center on a financial report
- Beginning and ending dates on a transactional report

- A department on an HR salary listing report
- A salesperson name on a customer order listing report

The Parameter Fields branch of the Field Explorer tree is used to add existing or new parameter fields to your report. A listing of previously created parameters appears in this part of the Field Explorer tree. Once created, Parameter fields are added to the report by either clicking and dragging and dropping or by selecting the Parameter Field—using the Insert into Report button or action on the right-click menu—and selecting the location.

If a new parameter is required, it can also be created directly from the Field Explorer by using the New toolbar button. You are prompted to name the new parameter and enter some supporting information. This dialog is displayed in Figure 2.4.

Figure 2.4
The Create New Parameter dialog enables you to specify a parameter name and supporting parameter type information.

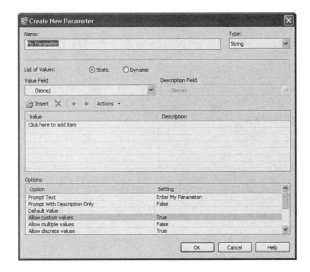

→ For detailed information on parameter creation and use as a means to filter report information, **see** "Creating and Implementing Parameters Fields," **p. 136**.

At this point, it is only important to note the location of this field type.

IMPLEMENTING RUNNING TOTAL FIELDS

Running total fields provide a means to incrementally calculate a total on a report as the records are processed. In contrast to the summary fields you will learn about later in the book, running total fields enable you to control how a total is calculated, when it is reset, and when it is displayed. Some examples in which running total fields might be used include

- Running Total of website hits over multiple Days/Weeks/Months and so on
- Running Total of sales expenses over Weeks in a Quarter or Fiscal Year
- Running Total of average order amount over time
- Running Total of employee count over time

The Running Total Fields branch of the Field Explorer tree is used to add existing or new running total fields to your report. A listing of previously created running totals appears in this part of the Field Explorer tree. Once created, existing running total fields are added to the report by either clicking and dragging and dropping or by selecting the Running Total Field—using the Insert into Report button or action on the right-click menu—and selecting the location.

If a new running total is required, it can be created directly from the Field Explorer by using the New toolbar button. You are prompted to name the new running total. Select the field to calculate the running total on, the type of running total (for example, sum, average, variance, and so on), and some other supporting information about when the running total is to be evaluated and reset as shown in Figure 2.5.

Figure 2.5
The Create Running Total Field dialog enables you to specify a Running Total Name and its supporting information.

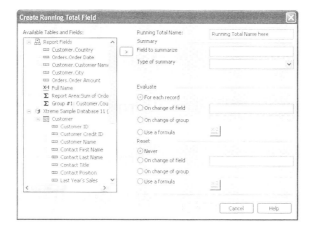

In the sample Customer Order Listing report from Chapter 1, an interesting running total to add would be one on the average order amount over time within each country. This running total tells senior sales management whether the average order size for each country is increasing or decreasing over time. To create this running total, follow these steps:

1. Open the sample report from Chapter 1 (Chap1Manual.rpt). Sort the data by ascending date by accessing the Record Sorting Expert from either the Report menu or the Record Sort icon on the Expert Tools toolbar. Then select Order Date as a secondary sort order after Country.

2. Highlight the Running Total Fields branch of the Field Explorer tree.

3. Select New using either the New toolbar button or by right-clicking and selecting New from the pop-up menu. This opens the dialog shown in Figure 2.5.

4. Enter the name **Avg Order Size** for the Running Total Name.

5. Select the Order Amount field from the Order Table as the Field to summarize by highlighting it in the field selection window and clicking on the Select button (>).

6. Because you want an average summary instead of the default Sum summary, select this from the Type of Summary drop-down box.

7. You want to calculate the average order amount for each order, so select the For Each Record option in the Evaluate section.

8. Because you want to calculate this for each Country, select the Reset On Change of Group option and select the Country group in the Reset section and click OK to finish.

The completed Running Total dialog is shown in Figure 2.6

Figure 2.6
The Create Running Total Field dialog with Average Order Size running total information entered.

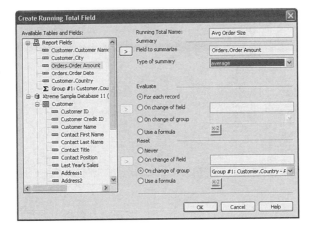

After the running total has been created, it only needs to be dragged onto the report in the appropriate section. In this example, the appropriate section is the Detail section to show a changing average order size for every order. The Updated Sample Customer Order report is shown in Figure 2.7. Notice the changing average order size being calculated for each record. This type of report can now provide increasing value to senior sales management.

> **TIP**
>
> It's not necessary to place running total fields exclusively in the Details Section of your reports. By placing running total fields in different sections of your report, you can receive very interesting results. For example, if you place a running total in a Group Footer section, the running total displays the selected running total up to and including the current group. This can be very useful when analyzing average order size over time and grouping by month or quarter (for example, where you are only interested in some form of aggregated running total).

As highlighted in the Running Total dialog, it is possible to both evaluate and reset the running total fields based on four different options. The first three are self-explanatory—for each record, on the change of a specified field, or on the change of a specified group. The last option, using a formula, is a powerful and flexible option that should be more fully explored after reviewing Chapter 13, "Using Formulas and Custom Functions," on formula creation. In its simplest description, this option enables the creation of a conditional running total or the reset of that running total based on the results of a formula you have created.

Figure 2.7
A sample Orders
report with Running
Average Total on Order
Size for each sales rep.

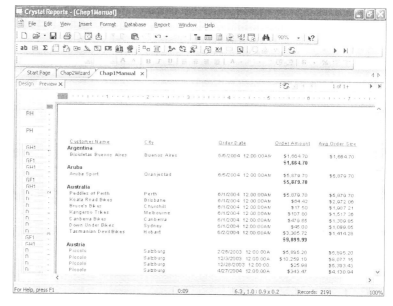

Figure 2.7
A sample Orders
report with Running
Average Total on Order
Size for each sales rep.

A good use of this conditional summing is the creation of a running total that calculates the sum of all orders, but only evaluates (or sums in this case) the running total when the total order amount on a given record is greater than a certain amount (for example, 1,000). This running total, in effect, would provide a running total of only large orders so that business analysts can determine the percentage of revenue derived from large orders. Another common usage of this functionality is for financial statements (such as income statements) where a number of General Ledger transactions compose the rows retrieved from the database and different Running Totals are used to conditionally add the associated transaction value to their total if and only if certain conditions are met (for example, a certain account code is associated with the transaction value). The resulting running totals are then placed in a report to present financial statement–oriented information such as Total Revenue, Operating Costs, Investment Income, Taxes, and so on.

USING GROUP NAME FIELDS

Group Name fields only exist in a report after you have specified one or more groups to add to your report. You will read about that functionality later in this chapter. Group Name fields are created at the same time you add a Grouping to a report. Once created, existing Group Name fields are added to the report by either clicking and dragging and dropping or by selecting the Group Name—using the Insert into Report button or action on the right-click menu—and selecting the location.

SPECIAL FIELDS

The special fields in the Field Explorer are a number of system fields that Crystal Reports provides. These system fields and a brief description of each are presented in Table 2.1. The fields that were new to version 10 are suffixed with a *10 and the fields new to version XI are suffixed with *XI.

TABLE 2.1   SPECIAL FIELDS AVAILABLE IN CRYSTAL REPORTS XI

Field	Description	Valid Locations on Report
Content Locale*XI	The locale setting of the current user—found in the Control Panel under regional settings.	Anywhere
Current CE User ID*10	The ID number of the current BusinessObjects Enterprise(BOE) user (if one exists) .	Anywhere
Current CE User Name*10	The username of the current BusinessObjects Enterprise user (if one exists).	Anywhere
Current CE User Time Zone*XI	The time zone of the current BusinessObjects Enterprise user (if one exists).	Anywhere
Data Date	The date the data in your report was last retrieved.	Anywhere
Data Time	The time the data in your report was last retrieved.	Anywhere
Data Time Zone*XI	The time zone of the data last retrieved in your report.	Anywhere
File Author	The author of the report. This is set in Document Properties (File, Summary Info in the menu).	Anywhere
File Creation Date	The date the report was created.	Anywhere
File Path and Name	The file path and name for the report.	Anywhere
Group Number	An automatically created group numbering field.	Group Header or Group Footer sections only
Group Selection Formula	The current report's group selection formula. This is created by using the Select Expert covered in Chapter 6.	Anywhere

continues

TABLE 2.1   CONTINUED

Field	Description	Valid Locations on Report
Horizontal Page Number*10	The current horizontal page number of a report using either a Cross-Tab or an OLAP Grid.	Anywhere
Modification Date	Date that the report was last modified (in any way).	Anywhere
Modification Time	Time that the report was last modified (in any way).	Anywhere
Page N of M	Indicates current page on report relative to total number of pages.	Anywhere
Page Number	The current page number.	Anywhere
Print Date	Either the current date or a date specified in the Set Print Date and Time dialog under the Reports, Set Print and Date Time option.	Anywhere
Print Time	Either the current time or a time specified in the Set Print Date and Time dialog under the Reports, Set Print and Date Time option.	Anywhere
Print Time Zone*XI	The time zone of the machine where the report printed.	Anywhere
Record Number	An automatically created number that counts the records in the detail section of your report.	Details Section
Record Selection Formula	The current report's record selection formula. This is created by using the Select Expert covered in Chapter 7.	Anywhere
Report Comments	Comments summarizing the report. This is set in Document Properties (choose File, Summary Info in the menu).	Anywhere—but only the first 256 characters are printed.
Report Title	The title of the report set in the Document Properties dialog (File, Summary Info in the menu).	Anywhere
Total Page Count	The total number of pages for this report.	Anywhere

These special fields are added to the report by either clicking and dragging and dropping or by selecting the Special Field—using the Insert into Report button or action on the right-click menu—and selecting the location.

WORKING WITH GROUPS

Grouping data in a report facilitates business user analysis and enables meaningful summarizations. Examples of common and useful groupings in reports include:

- Sales Reports that group by Sales Rep, Product Line, Sales District, or Quarter
- HR Reports that group by Department, Management Level, or Tenure with the company
- Financial Reports that group by Company Division, Product Line, or Quarter
- Inventory Reports that group by Part Number, Supplier, or Manufacturing Plant

Crystal Reports provides easy-to-use grouping functionality that enables multiple types of powerful and flexible data grouping.

INSERTING GROUPS

Taking either the sample report from this or the previous chapter, you can realize the flexibility and power of grouping in a few short steps. Assume that senior sales management in a hypothetical company is interested in viewing customer order information by Employee/Sales representative, in addition to the existing grouping by Country. The following steps will guide you through an example of how grouping can help this company accomplish this task:

1. Select the Group option from the Insert menu or click on the Insert Group button located on the Insert toolbar. This opens the Insert Group dialog shown in Figure 2.8.

Figure 2.8
The Insert Group dialog requires selecting the field to be grouped on and enables specification of some custom grouping options.

2. The Insert Group dialog prompts for the Data field on which the group is based. The field you select can be an existing database field already on the report, a database field included in your data sources (perhaps not yet on the report), a formula field, or a SQL Expression. For this exercise, select the Employee ID field from the Orders Table for the Grouping field.

3. Select Ascending Order for the Sort Order.

4. Click OK, and the report changes to reflect a new grouping on Employee ID.

The results of this new grouping are shown in Figure 2.9. Note that the Employee ID grouping is automatically selected to be the lowest-level grouping. This is the standard and expected behavior when inserting new groups, but based on the sales management's hypothetical request, you will need to edit the grouping order so that Employee ID becomes the highest level and you can view an Employee's sales across countries. You will do that in the next section.

Figure 2.9
Here is a sample report that has been grouped by Country and Employee ID.

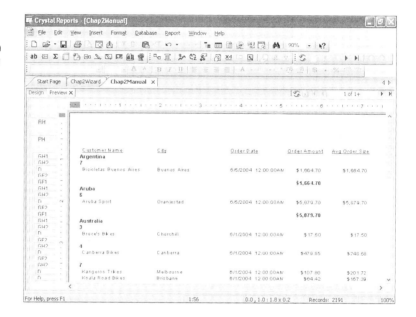

The specified order selection of the Insert Group dialog is particularly interesting because of the great flexibility it provides. With this option, you can dynamically create both groups and a custom order of appearance on the report. A related geographic example would be the creation of a Continent grouping based on the country field in the database with the groupings and order of appearance specified in the Insert Group dialog. Notice that when you select specified order and name the group, two more tabs appear in the Change Group Options dialog (see Figure 2.10). These tabs enable you to specify or create dynamic groupings and also to select a method of handling the other elements that do not fit into your dynamically created groups.

Another custom ordering option new to XI is the ability to conditionally sort a group based on a formula. This option is enabled through the Group Dialog box and the Use Formula As Sort Order check box. A formula can then be entered by clicking on the x+2 box.

Figure 2.10
The Change Group Options dialog displaying the Specified Order tab.

A last note on the Change Group Options dialog is that options around group naming are available for customization. These options are accessed through the Options tab and facilitate the process of making your reports most presentable. For example, in another situation you might want to group on a country code instead of a country name for report processing efficiency (that is, numeric fields are sorted faster than string fields), but you still want to present the actual Country Name in the report. You could perform this customization through the Options tab in the Change Group Options dialog as shown in Figure 2.11.

Figure 2.11
The Options tab of the Change Group Options dialog enables you to set some custom Grouping options, such as the displayed Group name.

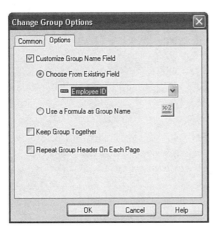

REORDERING GROUPS

As you can certainly imagine, it is quite common to want to group data by different fields within a single report. It is also quite common to receive multiple reporting requests for different views of data by various levels of grouping. Some examples might be

- View sales numbers grouped by product, region, and by sales rep
- View sales numbers grouped by region, product, and by sales rep
- View sales numbers grouped by sales rep, product, and by region

During report design, one of these different grouping orders could be created initially as you did in the last section with the groups Country and Employee ID. If other grouping orders were required, these could be quickly realized through either the Crystal Reports Design window or the Group Expert. Working in the left-most report section area of the Design tab of Crystal Reports (not the Preview tab), the different groups (sections) can be dragged and dropped before or after each other, quickly rearranging the grouping order. To complete the sales management's reporting request from the last section (to group by Employee ID at the highest level and Country below that), follow these steps:

Click on the Design tab of the Crystal Reports Designer if you are not already on that tab.

After double-clicking and holding the last click on either the Employee ID Group Header or Footer, drag that group to the outside of the Country Grouping to dynamically re-sort the order of grouping. A hand replaces the normal cursor image when you have grabbed a group, and blue lines highlight the intended drop location before you release your click and re-sort the grouping order.

To facilitate identification of groups while in the Design tab, hover over a group header or footer section and a descriptive rollover tip temporarily appears.

Click on the Preview tab, and you will see the benefits of your work—the same report with the groupings instantly rearranged. Figure 2.12 highlights your intended results.

Note the change in the Group Tree as you move back to the edited Crystal Report. This Group Tree provides an easy-to-use navigation system for end users of this report as they can drill into the group tree and then link to the exact location and group they desire.

An alternative and powerful method for reordering groups is provided with the Group Expert. It is accessed from the Report menu, and the different groups can be reordered through the up and down buttons within the Grouping dialog. This quick reordering can present your data in completely different ways, serving multiple analysis requirements with very little report development effort. The next section explores the power of the Group Expert.

Figure 2.12
A sample Customer Orders report regrouped by Sales Rep (Employee ID) and then Country.

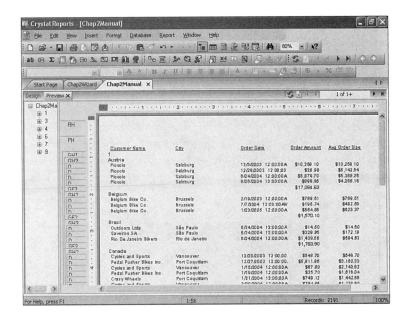

USING THE GROUP EXPERT

Crystal Reports provides an easy method to add multiple groups simultaneously and a central location for accessing all your current groups—the Group Expert dialog. Accessed from the Report menu, the Group Expert dialog, shown in Figure 2.13, enables you to add multiple groups at one time and quickly reorder any specified groups.

Figure 2.13
The Group Expert dialog accessed from the Report menu enables macro-level report group reordering and option setting.

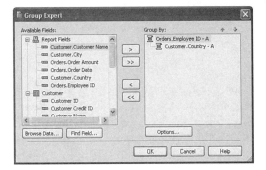

This dialog enables the selection of multiple groups in one location and provides access to the same functionality as the Change Group Options dialog through the Options button. The groups can also be easily reordered from within this dialog through use of the up and down arrow buttons, located on the upper right of the dialog area.

GROUPING ON DATE/TIME FIELDS

One type of grouping that is common across most organizations is date-and-time related grouping. Analysts from all industries want to see how numbers (for example, sales revenue, units shipped, units produced, employees hired, and so on) change over various periods of time. To facilitate this type of analysis, Crystal Reports provides some built-in flexibility around date-and-time grouping. When you are creating a group that is based on a Date or Time field, an extra drop-down box appears in the Insert Group dialog (see Figure 2.14). This extra Print by Section box enables the user to group the detail records in the report automatically by any number of time-related criteria. Examples include By Day, By Hour, By Quarter, or even By Second. These automatic grouping options enable quick time-oriented analysis.

Figure 2.14
The Insert Group dialog with the Date/Time grouping drop-down box expanded.

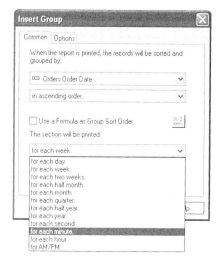

HIERARCHICAL GROUPING

Another type of special grouping that is available in Crystal Reports is hierarchical grouping. This special type of grouping enables your report data to be dynamically grouped on a hierarchy kept within a single table of your database. To enable hierarchical grouping, a group of the base-level data should be created through the standard Group Creation dialogs described previously. The Hierarchical Group option dialog can then be selected from the Report menu. To walk through a quick example, follow these steps:

1. Create a new blank Crystal Report and connect to the Xtreme Sample Database 11.

2. Select the Employee table for the report and Click on the OK button in the Database Expert.

3. Open the Field Explorer, select the First Name, Last Name, Extension, and Position fields from the Employee table, and drop them into the detail section of the report.

4. Insert a Group on Employee ID using the Insert Group dialog (accessed from the Insert menu) and select ascending sort order. Move to the Options tab of the Insert

Group dialog before finishing, click on the Customize Group Name Field check box, and select the Employee Last Name field as the field to display. Now click OK in the Insert Group dialog.

5. Select Hierarchical Grouping Options from the Report menu. You are presented with the dialog displayed in Figure 2.15. Click on the Sort Data Hierarchically option and select either Employee Supervisor ID or Employee Reports To as the parent field with an indent of 0.33 of an inch.

Figure 2.15
The Hierarchical Group Options dialog accessed from the Report menu enables specification of hierarchical grouping options such as parent field and indentation.

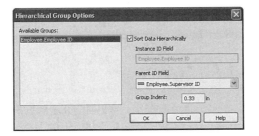

6. Click OK and view your new report. Figure 2.16 displays a report that should be similar and highlights the power of hierarchical grouping.

Figure 2.16
A sample report that highlights the hierarchical grouping and indentation functionality.

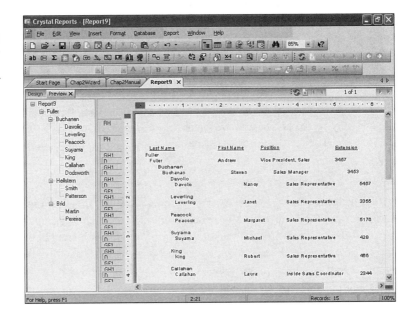

CAUTION

When creating a hierarchical group, the only eligible parent fields are those fields in the selected data source that have the same field type (for example, number, string, date) as the Grouped On field.

As can be seen in Figure 2.16, the value you enter in the Group Indent field affects all other objects in the same report section as your hierarchical group fields. For example, the Position and Extension fields are also indented when you added the Employee field as a hierarchical group with supervisor. With XI, a new function has been added to enable indentation of only the hierarchy records and not the other objects. This is accomplished by leaving this value as 0 (zero) and using the new conditional-X-position feature with the new `HeirarchyLevel()` function. A sample formula is provided in the Crystal Reports help file and a working sample report is available for download from usingcrystal.com.

UNDERSTANDING DRILL-DOWN REPORTS

As you have learned, grouping data facilitates data analysis for business users and enables meaningful summarizations in your reports. Having both the group level and the detail level data available in a view of a report enables the simultaneous analysis of both group level summaries and the supporting detail records (for example, database fields, formulas, and so on). There are situations, however, in which a report consumer or analyst wants to view only aggregated group level information initially and then selectively drill-down into detail records where relevant (that is, drill-down only where the aggregated group level information is interesting, appealing, or stands out). This is easily and quickly accomplished in Crystal Reports through the use of the built-in drill-down capabilities in the product.

When the term *drill-down* is used, it implies that a business user has the capability to move from an aggregated or grouped view of the data (for example, sales revenue for each sales district) to a more detailed level of the data (for example, sales revenue for each salesperson in a selected sales district). In Crystal Reports, this is as easy as double-clicking on the involved group data or aggregated graphic.

CREATING A DRILL-DOWN REPORT

By default, whenever a group is created within Crystal Reports, an automatic drill-down path is created from the respective group headers into the child groups and detail records. The drill-down icon, when the cursor icon turns into a magnifying glass, appears in your Crystal Reports Preview tab as you hover over a group header with drill-down enabled. A sample report with Grouping and associated drill-down on Employee ID and Country is shown in Figure 2.17.

By double-clicking on the involved group header (such as Austria in Figure 2.17), a new viewing tab is opened with only the relevant group header's supporting information. Figure 2.18 highlights one of these views.

Figure 2.17
A sample report with drill-down groups available for end-user navigation/drilling.

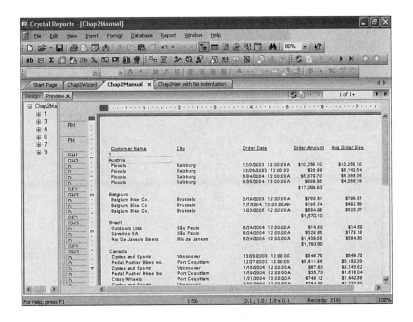

Figure 2.18
The Drill-down viewing tab in Crystal Reports Preview mode highlights the drill-down results.

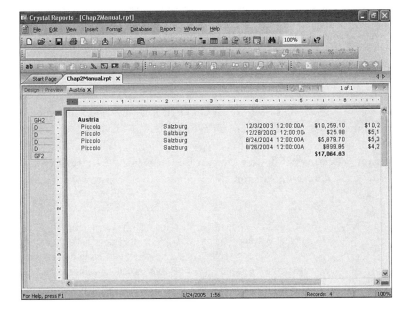

NOTE

An alternative method of navigating through report data is to use the Group Navigation tree that is exposed through all Crystal Report Viewers. The advantage of this is that it does not initiate new viewing tabs like those shown in Figure 2.18. If your report does not have a group navigation tree displayed, click on the Toggle Group Tree button located on the main toolbar. The Group Navigation Tree enables report users to quickly jump to any point in the report by highlighting the group level that they are interested in viewing.

HIDING DETAILS ON A DRILL-DOWN REPORT

To accomplish the task of only displaying the aggregated group level information in our sample report and not the details, right-click on the Details section—either in the Design or Preview window. Figure 2.19 highlights the resulting right-click menu.

Figure 2.19
The Detail Section right-click menu enables hiding (or even suppression) of the detailed section.

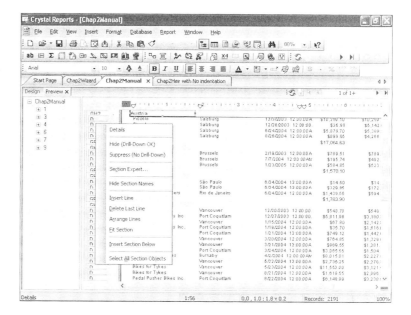

By selecting the Hide (Drill-Down OK) option in this right-click menu, your report now shows the details within the aggregated groups only when a business user drills down into them. Figure 2.20 shows what the report now looks like in Preview mode. From here, the business user can drill-down to the drill-down viewing tabs (refer to Figure 2.18 for an example) by double-clicking on any of the group header rows or data.

> NOTE
>
> The Suppress option from the same right-click menu, shown in Figure 2.19, can provide another viewing option to report designers and essentially turn off drill-down in your report. If the aggregated group level section data is to be viewed by business users but they are not allowed to view detailed section data, this can be accomplished by suppressing the detail section.

Figure 2.20
A sample report with detail sections hidden, but available in drill-down.

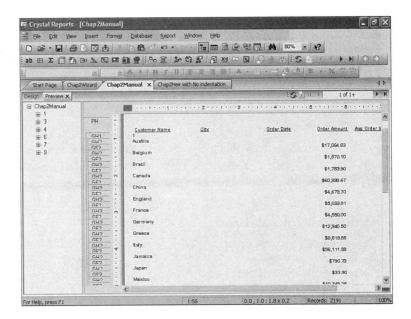

TROUBLESHOOTING

GROUP ON A FORMULA

Sometimes when creating a report, the involved database might not natively contain the data that is specified as requiring a group; that is, the required grouping elements will need to be based on some criteria that is not available in the database. A typical example of this problem occurs when a report design calls for a grouping by a demographic range, such as age or income bracket. In the case of age, the database might have an Age field but the business case calls for some form of market analysis by the age ranges 0–19, 20–34, 35–49, 50–64, and 65 and above. A formula called Date Range similar to that displayed below could solve the reporting problem.

```
Select {@Age}
    Case Is < 19 :
        "0-19"
    Case Is > 19, Is < 34 :
        "20-34"
    Case Is > 34, Is < 49 :
        "35-49"
    Case Is > 50, Is < 64 :
        "50-64"
    Case Is > 64:
        "65+"
```

For the record, this sample is based on the Employee table from the Xtreme Sample Database and uses another formula called @Age that resolves to

```
(Today - {Employee.Birth Date}) / 365
```

In situations such as these, it can be useful to group on a formula as discussed in the next section.

CRYSTAL REPORTS IN THE REAL WORLD—GROUP ON A FORMULA

Sometimes when creating a report, the development database might not be complete or might be in production; there might be a requirement to group elements based on some criteria that is not in the database. In these cases, it can be useful to group on a formula. To explore the benefits of grouping on formulas, follow theses steps:

1. Open the sample report from Chapter 1 (Chap1Manual.rpt). Create a new formula and name it Continent and click the Use Editor button.

2. Type the following text into the code window so it appears like Figure 2.21:

```
WhileReadingRecords;
Select {Customer.Country}
    Case "Canada", "Mexico", "USA":
        "North America"
    Default:
        "Outside North America";
```

Figure 2.21
A sample formula to group information on a formula.

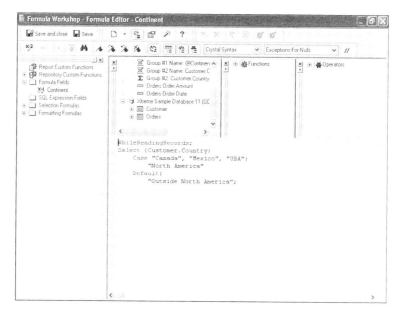

3. With the text entered, click the Save And Close button.

4. From the Report menu, select Group Expert. Find the Group1 formula from the list of Available Fields and add it to the list of Group By fields. Finally, because the Group1 field is a higher level than the For Country field, select it and move it up using the arrow button. The results are displayed in Figure 2.22.

Figure 2.22
The report correctly grouped, highlighting the capability to group on formulas and create increasingly flexible reports.

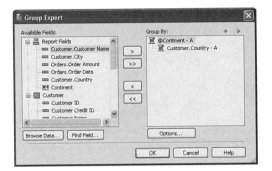

5. Click OK to see the completed report that looks like that presented in Figure 2.23.

Figure 2.23
A report with a group based on a formula highlights the powerful capabilities of custom grouping.

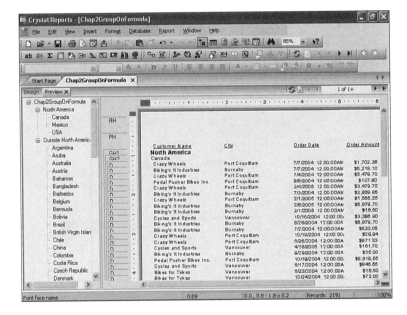

CHAPTER 3

FILTERING, SORTING, AND SUMMARIZING DATA

In this chapter

INTRODUCTION

In the first two chapters, you created reports that display the rows of data in your database onto the report surface with minimal manipulation of that data. The value of Crystal Reports is its inherent capacity to convert those rows of raw data into valuable information. Information will reveal something about the data that cannot be found by simply poring over pages and pages of records. In the last chapter, you began to take advantage of the power of Crystal Reports by applying grouping to a report to organize the data into categorical groups. In this chapter, you build on that by learning how to create reports that perform the following actions:

- Filter data based on a given criteria
- Sort data based on field values
- Summarize and subtotal data

→ For more detailed information on grouping data, **see** "Working with Groups," **p. 65**.

FILTERING THE DATA IN YOUR REPORT

So far, the reports you have created have returned all the records from your database. Sometimes this is appropriate, but often reports need to filter the data based on specified criteria. This is most relevant when you're working with large databases in which there can easily be hundreds of thousands of records returned from a query, especially when table joins are applied.

As with many features in Crystal Reports, there are multiple ways to filter data:

- **Using the Select Expert**—This simple method provides a visual way to specify filtering.
- **Using the Record Selection Formula**—This more granular, yet powerful, method involves creating a custom formula language expression to determine the filter criteria.

Regardless of the method used to filter your report, you should always make best efforts to filter on indexed database fields. By filtering on indexed fields, you realize the greatest performance on the database server. You can determine the indexed fields in a table by using the Crystal Reports Links tab on the Database Expert accessible from the Database menu. Use the Index Legend button and dialog provided to understand the different index markers in your database tables.

WORKING WITH THE SELECT EXPERT

The Select Expert is a design tool that enables you, the report designer, to specify basic yet powerful filters for the current report using a graphical design dialog. Figure 3.1 shows the Select Expert dialog. Let's work through an illustrative example of filtering using the Select Expert. Taking what you have learned so far about creating simple columnar reports, create a new report from the Xtreme Sample Database 11, adding the Customer Name and Last

Year's Sales fields from the Customer table to the details section of the report. Follow these steps to add a filter to this report:

Figure 3.1
The Select Expert provides access to easy-to-use filtering functionality from a graphical interface.

1. To invoke the Select Expert, click its button found on the Experts toolbar or, alternatively, select the Select Expert option from the Report menu.

2. The first step in creating a filter is to choose which field the filter should be created on. Accordingly, the Choose Field dialog is displayed. Both fields that are present in the report and fields from the database are listed. A field does not need to be on the report to create a filter using it. At this point, if you forget which values are stored in any of the fields listed, click the Browse button to see a sample list of values. For this example, choose Last Year's Sales field and click OK. The Select Expert dialog appears, as shown in Figure 3.1.

> **TIP**
> Another quick and directed method of accessing the Select Expert is through the right-click menu available on any data field. This method opens the Select Expert directly with the specified field already selected as the filtered field and bypassing the Choose Field dialog.

3. The Select Expert has a group of tabs—one for each filter defined inside that report. In the case of your sample report, there is only one tab for the Last Year's Sales field and another called <New>, which is used to define additional filters. By default, the filter setting on the Last Year's Sales tab is set to Is Any Value. This means that regardless of the value of the Last Year's Sales field, all records are included in the report. To change the filter in a report, change the value of the drop-down list. For this example, change it to Is Equal To.

4. When this option is selected, another drop-down list appears. If the exact value to filter the field on is known, it can be typed into this list box. However, in this case, you might not know exactly what the values of the field are, so you are provided with the capability to browse that field's values by simply pulling down the drop-down list. Choose the $300.00 value listed in the drop-down list, or type it in and click OK.

> Often when modifying filters and selections in the report designer, Crystal Reports displays a message asking the user if she wants to use the saved data in the report or refresh the data from the database. Using the saved data in the report is usually a good option because it does not incur a new query to the database. However, especially when modifying filters, it can cause some confusing results because the set of saved data in the report might or might not consist of all the records in the database; that is, a filter might have already been applied. So when modifying filters, it's best to refresh the data whenever Crystal Reports asks you.

When returning to the report, you should notice that the report now only displays a single record: the Has Been Bikes company that had sales of $300. A more useful filter would be to show all records that were above or below a threshold. To accomplish this, re-open the Select Expert. This time, change the Is Equal To criteria to Is Greater Than and type **100,000** into the list box. When closing the Select Expert and returning to the report, a small collection of records should be returned (approximately 17). In just a few seconds, you've created a report showing your top customers.

A few more filter types can be applied to a report. Apply these various types of filters with the following steps:

Open the Select Expert again and change the criteria from Is Greater Than to Is Between.

This time, two list boxes are presented, each corresponding to an upper and lower bound. Type in the values **2,000** and **3,000**, respectively (as shown in Figure 3.2), and click OK. The report displays all customers with sales between $2,000 and $3,000.

Figure 3.2
Modify the report to display customers with sales between $2,000 and $3,000.

So far, only the Last Year's Sales field has been used as a filter. However, any field can be used as a filter, although there are slightly different options for various field types. Go back into the Select Expert and, while on the Last Year's Sales tab, click the Delete button to remove that filter.

Add a new filter on the Customer Name field by clicking the New button and selecting the Customer Name field from the subsequent dialog.

To have the report only show a single customer's record, leave the criteria as Is Equal To and choose Alley Cat Cycles from the drop-down list. Applying this filter results in the report only showing a single record.

6. Return to the Select Expert and change the criteria to Is One Of. This option enables you to choose multiple values. Each time a value is selected from the drop-down list, it is added to the bottom of the list box. Select Alley Cat Cycles, Bikes R Us, and Hikers and Bikers and notice how the report now reflects those three records.

7. Next, remove the three values previously selected by highlighting them and clicking the Remove button. Now change the criteria to Is Like and type **Wheel*** into the drop-down list. Click Add or press Enter to add this item to the list. Applying this filter results in the report showing all customers whose names begin with the word Wheel.

> **TIP**
>
> When using the Is Like option, an * acts as a wildcard for any number of characters, whereas an ? acts as a wildcard for only a single character. This can be quite useful when you're searching through textual fields for a specific text pattern.

The last thing this chapter covers with respect to the Select Expert is applying multiple filters. To do so, perform the following steps:

1. Start from scratch and delete any filters you have applied by clicking the Delete button on each tab.

2. Click the New button and add a new filter using the Last Year's Sales field.

3. Change the criteria to Is Less Than and the value to 5,000. This filter would result in showing all customers with sales of less than $5,000, but let's apply another condition.

4. Click the New button and add a new filter based on the Country field. Note that this is slightly different from the previous filters that have been created—not only because more than one filter is being applied at the same time, but also because the filter being created is based on a field that is not present on the report.

5. Change the criteria for the Country filter to Is Equal To and choose Canada from the drop-down list. Clicking OK applies this filter, resulting in a report with multiple conditions: customers from Canada with sales below $5,000. See Figure 3.3 for the filtered output of this report.

> **NOTE**
>
> The two filters that were just added to the report are concatenated together by default with a logical AND statement, that is, All Customers with Last Year's Sales of less than $5,000 AND from Canada. This can be edited in the Formula Editor accessible from the Show Formula button on the Select Expert. This is discussed in the next section.

THE RECORD SELECTION FORMULA

Although the Select Expert is quite powerful, there are certain situations where you need to define a filter that is more complex than the Select Expert allows. Fortunately, Crystal Reports has a built-in formula language that enables custom expressions to be defined as a filter. In fact, this is one of the strengths of the Crystal Reports product: being able to use the formula language to attain a high level of control in various aspects of report creation.

Figure 3.3
A filter is applied to show all Canadian customers with sales less than $5,000.

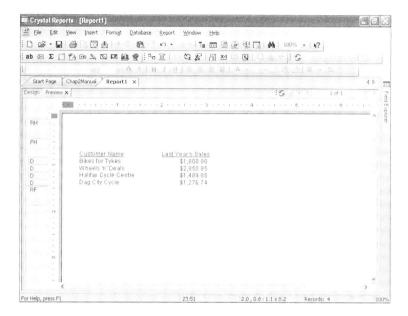

Although you might not have realized it, even when you were using the Select Expert, a formula was being generated in the background that defined the filter. To see this in action, open the Select Expert and click the Show Formula button. This expands the Select Expert dialog to reveal the formula being generated. This formula is called the *record selection formula*. Notice that the formula's value is as follows:

```
{Customer.Last Year's Sales} < $5000.00 and
{Customer.Country} = "Canada"
```

The formula language is covered in more detail in Chapter 11, "Using Record Selections and Alerts for Interactive Reporting," but the following are the key points to learn right now. In formulas, braces denote a field. For database fields, the table and field name are included and are separated by a period. The rest of the formula is a statement that tests whether the sales value is less than $5,000.

Think of a record selection formula as an expression that evaluates to a true or false result. For each record in the database, Crystal Reports applies the record selection formula, plugging in the current field values in place of the fields in braces. If the result of the statement is True, the record is included in the report. If the result of the statement is False, the record is excluded from the report. Let's look at an example. The first record in the Customer's table is that of City Cyclists who had sales of $20,045.27.

For this record, Crystal Reports evaluates the preceding formula, substituting $20,045.27 in place of {Customer.Last Year's Sales}. Because this value is not less than $5,000, this statement is False and the record is not included in the report. To see what other formulas look like, change the filter using the Select Expert to a few different settings and observe how the formula changes.

WORKING WITH THE FORMULA EDITOR

The formula shown at the bottom of the Select Expert is not just for informational purposes: It can be edited in-place. However, a much better editor exists for formulas. It's called the Formula Editor (shown in Figure 3.4), and it can be invoked by clicking the Formula Editor button in the Select Expert or by selecting the Report menu and choosing Selection Formulas, Record. Although the formula language doesn't change, the process of creating formulas becomes much simpler because of a focused user interface.

Figure 3.4
The Formula Editor provides quick access to powerful formula creation capabilities.

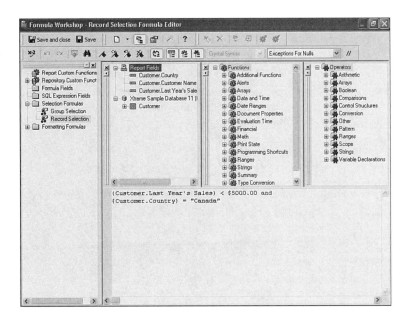

Learn to use the Formula Editor by creating a simple record selection formula. This formula attempts to filter out any customers who owe more than $5,000 in tax. Tax liability will be defined as 2% of the customer's sales figure. To implement this, work through the following steps:

1. To begin, launch the Formula Editor as described previously and delete the existing selection formula.

2. Next, create an expression that calculates the tax liability. To do this, enter the following expression:

```
{Customer.Last Year's Sales} * 0.02
```

The previous expression now represents the customer's tax obligation. To complete the expression to filter out all customers who owe less than $5,000 in tax, modify the formula to look like this:

```
({Customer.Last Year's Sales} * 0.02) > 5000
```

To complete the formula and apply the filter, click the Close button at the top-left corner of the Formula Editor window, and then click OK to close the Select Expert. Focus returns to the report, and when data is refreshed, only a handful of customers should be listed on the report.

Both the formula language and the Formula Editor are topics unto themselves and will be discussed in more detail in Chapter 4, "Understanding and Implementing Fomulas" and Chapter 11, "Using Record Selections and Alerts for Interactive Reporting."

LEARNING TO SORT RECORDS

Although filtering is one of the key components of an effective report, it alone is not enough. Often, to properly see the key pieces of data, a report needs to be sorted. Crystal Reports is quite flexible when it comes to sorting, allowing any field type to be sorted, as well as multiple ascending or descending sorts. Sorting is applied using the Sort Expert.

WORKING WITH THE SORT EXPERT

The Sort Expert is launched from a button on the Experts toolbar, and also via the Record Sort Expert item on the Report menu. Figure 3.5 shows the Sort Expert.

Figure 3.5
The Record Sort Expert dialog accessed from the Report menu.

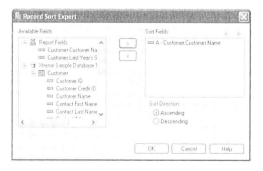

To apply sorting to the report, select a field from the list of available fields on the left side of the dialog area, and click the arrow (>) button to add that field to the Sort Fields list. Note that like filters, sorts can use fields both on the report and fields not otherwise used in the report.

In addition to sorting on report and database fields, you can sort on formula fields. Creating a formula field enables you to sort a report based on a custom expression.

To see this in action, follow these steps:

1. Create a new report using the Employee table of the Xtreme Sample Database and add the First Name, Last Name, and Salary fields to the report.

2. Initially, this report doesn't tell you a lot because the data is in seemingly random order. However, if the report were sorted by last name, it would be more useful. To accomplish this, first launch the Sort Expert.

3. Select the Last Name field from the available fields list and click the arrow (>) button to apply a sort on it. Click OK to return to the report. Notice how the report's records are now sorted in alphabetical order by last name.

The Sort Expert enables you to sort on both alphabetic and numeric fields. To modify this report to sort on salary instead of last name, follow these steps:

1. Return to the Sort Expert and remove the current sort by selecting the Last Name field from the sort fields list and clicking the < button.

2. Now select the Salary field and add it to the sort fields list.

3. Alphabetic fields are usually sorted in ascending order (from A to Z), but numeric fields are often sorted both ways. In this case, select the Salary field in the Sort Fields list and click Descending for the sort direction. This lists the employees with the top salary first. Click OK to apply the sort and return to the report.

Notice that some employees have the same salary level. If you wanted to perform a secondary sort within duplicates of the primary sort field, you can simply add another sort field. These sort fields can be arranged up and down using the buttons near the top-right corner of the Sort Expert.

CREATING EFFECTIVE SUMMARIES

The third key aspect of a good report after filtering and sorting is summarizing. Summarizing creates totals and subtotals that help the viewer of the report understand the data better. The following sections discuss various types of summarizing.

CREATING GRAND TOTALS

The simplest kind of summary is a grand total. This takes a single field and creates a total at the end of the report. To try this out, create a new report from the Orders table and add both the Order ID and the Order Amount fields onto the report.

Initially, this report is more than 30 pages long. A report of this length would make it very difficult to estimate the total amount of all orders, but a summary does that quite easily. Right-click the Order Amount field and select Insert, Summary from the context menu. This opens the Insert Summary dialog shown in Figure 3.6. To insert a summary, the first thing you need to specify is the field to summarize. Because you right-clicked the Order Amount field, this is already filled in for you. The next piece of information to fill in is the summary operation. The default is Sum, which is what you desire in this example, so leave it as is. Finally, Crystal Reports needs to know for which group the summary should be performed. Because there is no grouping in this report, the only option is Grand Total, which is already filled in for you. Click OK to close this dialog.

Figure 3.6
Inserting a summary based on the Order Amount field.

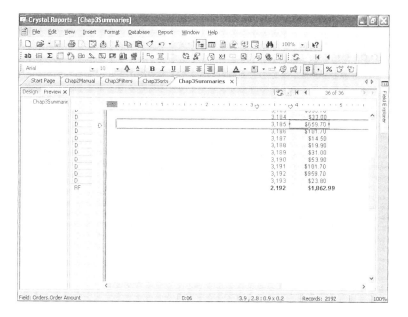

When looking at the end of the report, you see a grand total of the order amount is now visible in bold text. To edit the summary, right-click on it and select Edit Summary from the context menu. This opens the Edit Summary dialog. Try changing the calculation from Sum to Average. This now updates the summary to show the average order amount. There are various calculations to choose from including minimum, maximum, variance, count, deviation and median.

Besides the order amount total, it might be helpful to know how many orders there are. To do this, right-click the Order ID field and select Insert, Summary. Change the calculation from Sum to Count and click OK. Now besides the order amount summary, there is a count of all orders.

CREATING GROUP SUMMARIES

Although grand totals are useful, summarizing starts to become really powerful when it is applied at the group level. This enables totaling for each level of a group and tells more about the data than a simple grand total does because it measures the relationships between the various groups. To apply a group summary, a group must first exist in the report.

Using the same report from the last example with the Order ID and Order Amount fields, insert a group on the Ship Via field. This produces a report showing all the orders grouped by shipping method, for example, FedEx, Loomis, and so on. To compare the different methods of shipment, right-click the Order Amount field and select Insert, Summary. Previously, when you created a grand total, you accepted all the defaults in this dialog. But this time, the summary location needs to be changed. Change Grand Total (Report Footer) to Group #1: Orders.Ship Via in the Summary Location drop-down box, make sure the summary type is Average, and click OK.

Now a summary field is inserted into the report, which acts much like the grand total except that the average is repeated for each group. By examining these summaries, you can determine that the largest average order amount was shipped via UPS. You could also add a group-level summary to the Order ID field to determine the count of orders for each shipping method. Doing this reveals that the most orders were shipped via Loomis. These conclusions would have been difficult to reach without effective summaries.

TIP

When groups have many records inside of them, it sometimes becomes difficult to compare summaries because they aren't all visible on the page at the same time. A good tip for comparing these values is to hide the details section, which contains all the records, and only display the group header and footer that normally contains the group name and its summary. To hide the details section, move to the Design tab, right-click the Details bar on the left side of the screen, and select Hide.

USING GROUP SELECTION AND SORTING

Following closely on the topic of group summaries comes group selection and sorting. These bring together both filtering and summarizing concepts. Group selection and sorting is to groups what record selection and record sorting is to records. In other words, defining a *group selection* or *sorting* defines which groups are included in the report and in which order, respectively. A key point to understand is that whereas record selection and sorting work from values of individual fields, group selection and sorting work from summary fields.

In the example from the previous "Creating Group Summaries" section, you created a report that displayed all orders grouped by the shipment method but to determine which shipment method shipped the highest dollar value of orders, you had to manually browse through the report comparing the numbers. Applying a group sort would provide an easy way to see the rankings. Also, what if you only wanted to show the top three shipment methods? Group selection provides a way to filter out groups in such a manner.

As you might expect, there is an expert for applying group selection and sorting. It's called the Group Sort Expert, and it can be found on the Experts toolbar, as well as from the Group Sort Expert item on the Report menu. When the Group Sort Expert is launched, it displays one tab for each group in the report. In the previous example, there was only a single group on the Ship Via field so that's what you should see. Inside that tab, there is initially only a single list box with a value of No Sort. Changing this list box to All displays a set of options very similar to that of the Record Sort Expert—except instead of having a list of all report fields to choose to sort on, only summaries are listed.

The Group Sort Expert should have initially selected the Sum of Orders.Order Amount summary field and selected Ascending order. In this case, because it's more useful to see the highest dollar value first rather than last, change the sort order to Descending. Clicking OK closes the Group Sort Expert and returns focus to the report, which should have re-ordered the groups from largest to smallest. It's easy to see now that UPS was the method that shipped the highest dollar amount because it is the first group to appear.

There are only six shipment methods, but you can imagine reports that contain many more groups than six. Even if the groups are sorted, sometimes it's just too much data for the consumer of the report to absorb. To solve this problem, you can apply a group selection. To do this, launch the Group Sort Expert and change the All option on the left to Top N. Notice that the options are different from sorting. Applying a Top N selection implies that the groups will be sorted, but enables you to only display a specified number of the top groups in order. The default value is 5: Change this value to 3.

> **NOTE**
>
> New to version XI is the ability to set the N value of a Top or Bottom N sort to a formula. These formulas are created in the Formula Workshop accessed by the x+2 button beside the N value. This new functionality combined with parameters, covered in Chapter 5, "Implementing Parameters for Dynamic Reporting," enables improved report flexibility and allows report viewers to dynamically determine the N value of the Top/Bottom N at report-viewing time.

Another important option is relating to the set of groups that are excluded by the group selection. By default, these groups are all combined under a new group called Others. You might or might not want to include this Others group in your report. If you choose not to, uncheck the option labeled Include Others. Clicking OK returns focus to the report that now should only display the top three shipment methods based on the total order amount.

> **NOTE**
>
> Like the record selection, the group selection also has a formula that can be defined to use a custom expression to determine which groups to include in the report. The group selection formula can be found on the Report menu, under Selection Formulas, Group.

Some other options available in the group sort expert include Bottom N, which is the opposite of Top N, and Top and Bottom Percentage, which allow a filtering of the top x percent of groups.

CAUTION

It is instructive to note that group selection formulas are executed on the second pass of the Crystal Reports Engine. This second pass takes place after grand totals, group sub-totals, and the group navigation tree have been created. To understand the nuances of multi-pass reporting, review the last topic in Chapter 4.

CREATING RUNNING TOTALS

The last kind of summary to be discussed in this chapter is a running total. In some older versions of Crystal Reports, to create a running total, you had to create a collection of for-mula fields, so a feature was added in version 9 just to handle running totals. To create a running total, follow these steps:

1. Create a new report using the Orders table. Add the Order ID, Order Date, and Order Amount fields to the details section of the report. You can reformat the order date to a more user-friendly format if you prefer by right-clicking the field and selecting Format.

2. Add a sort based on the Order Date field in ascending order. This report now shows all orders in the order they were placed. This is a perfect scenario for a running total that would show a cumulative total of orders so that the viewer of the report could see what the current total order amount was at any given time.

3. To add a running total, right-click the Order Amount field and select Insert, Running Total from the Context menu. The Create Running Total Field dialog is shown in Figure 3.7.

Figure 3.7
Creating a Running Total field is quickly accomplished through the Create Running Total Field dialog.

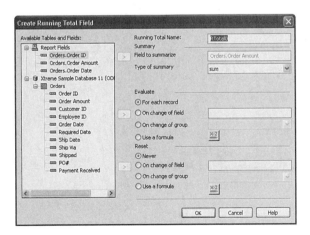

Four pieces of information need to be provided in this dialog, including

- **Name of the running total field**—The default is somewhat cryptic; it's best to give this a more meaningful name.

- **The summary to perform**—The Field to Summarize should be pre-populated for you, but you can change the summary type from the default of sum to other standard summary types. Some of the more useful types for a running total are Count and Average.

■ **When to evaluate the running total**—The default and most common setting here is For Each Record, but this can be modified to only be evaluated when the value of another field is changed or a group value is changed, or you can define a custom formula that defines the evaluation criteria.

■ **When to reset the running total**—This setting determines whether the running total should reset itself. If no groups are present in the report, you'll likely want to keep the default of Never. But if you have groups, you might want to reset the running total for each group or define more complex criteria with a formula.

For this example, give the running total a name of Cumulative Orders and leave all other settings at their defaults. Completing this running total adds this new field to the report next to the Order Amount field and provides a cumulative total of orders. The output of this report is shown in Figure 3.8.

Figure 3.8
A cumulative orders report using a Running Total Field.

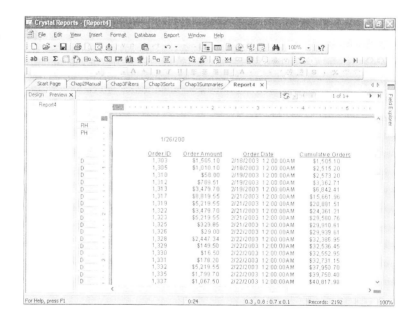

Running totals can also be created from the Field Explorer by selecting the Running Total Field item and clicking the New button or right-clicking and selecting New from the context menu. Creating a field in this way does not automatically add it to the report; you need to place it on the report in a desired location yourself.

TROUBLESHOOTING

GROUP SELECTION FORMULA

Where can I find the Group Selection formula?

The group selection formula can be found on the Report menu, under Selection Formulas, Group.

COMPLEX RECORD AND SELECTION FILTERS

The Record and Group Selection dialogs do not allow me to create the complexity of filter that I would like to use. Is there a way to free-form edit the record and group selection filters?

From the Record and Group Selection dialogs, a Show Formula button is available that enables you to see the current filter and to manually modify it with Crystal formula syntax.

CRYSTAL REPORTS IN THE REAL WORLD—NESTING FORMULAS

It's common for some more complex formulas to be combined to provide specific insight into report data. For example, a user might need to have a report that lists all customers with their total sales, but also show the average value of sales over a given amount. As described previously, there are many ways that a report design expert can approach this; what follows is one method.

1. Open the report Chap3RunningTotal.rpt, or use the report you just created in the last section. Insert a group on Customer ID. Select the running total field, right-click it, and choose Edit Running Total. Under the Reset section, choose On Change Of Group. Now the report is ready for the new functionality and should look like Figure 3.9.

2. Create a new formula from the Field Explorer named Large Orders with the following code:

```
WhileReadingRecords;
If {Orders.Order Amount} > 3000 Then
    {Orders.Order Amount}
Else
    0;
```

3. Add this formula to the report. Right-click on the new formula field and select Insert, Summary and for the section Summary Location change this value to your Group 1 field. This creates the numerator for your average.

4. Next, to determine the value for the denominator, right-click the Large Orders formula and choose Insert, Running Total. Name the running total Large Order Count; for

Type Of Summary select Count; for Evaluate, select Formula and enter the following code:

```
{@Large Orders}>0
```

Under Reset select Group 1. Check your settings against Figure 3.10.

Figure 3.9
This is the starting point for the new functionality.

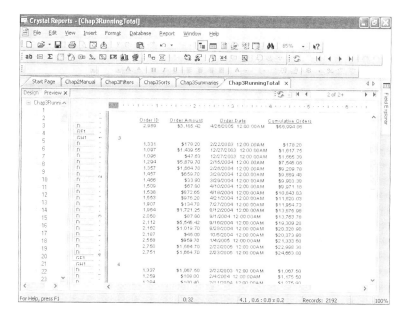

Figure 3.10
Create running totals easily using the Running Total Expert.

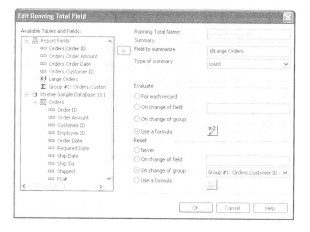

5. Now with the numerator and denominator values defined, simply create a new formula called Avg Large Deal Size with the following code:

```
Sum ({@Large Orders}, {Orders.Customer ID})/{#Large Order Count}
```

6. Insert this new formula onto the Group Footer and the report now has a summary value showing the average of all orders greater than $3,000 for each customer (see Figure 3.11).

Figure 3.11
A report complete with complex formulas.

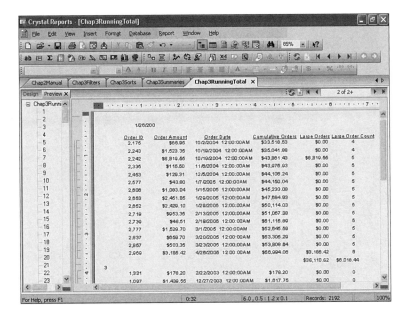

UNDERSTANDING AND IMPLEMENTING FORMULAS

In this chapter

INTRODUCTION

Chapter 2, "Selecting and Grouping Data," introduced the concept of formulas, and you saw how to create them and subsequently drop them into a report from the Field Explorer. This chapter explores the Formula Editor in more detail.

Formulas provide great flexibility and power when creating Crystal Reports by enabling you to create *derived* fields not directly stored in available data sources. Formulas also enable you to create advanced conditional object formatting and use flexible selection formulas in a report.

Crystal Reports has a number of built-in tools that facilitate the formula creation and formula reuse processes, the Formula Editor being a good example. The Formula Workshop provides a single convenient access point to almost all your formula fields within a given report. SQL Expression fields, Record and Group Selection formulas, Formatting formulas, and Custom Report- and Repository-based functions can all be accessed from the new Formula Workshop.

This chapter covers the following topics:

- An introduction to the Formula Workshop
- A review of the Formula Workshop Tree Elements
- Formula Editor
- Arithmetic, Date, and String formulas
- Type conversion
- Variables in formulas
- Formula Expert
- Formula Extractor
- Multi-pass reporting

USING THE FORMULA WORKSHOP

You have already been introduced to the Record Selection and Group Selection functionality of Crystal Reports that each independently leverages the formula capabilities of the product for enhanced flexibility. As you create more advanced reports, you will come across more functional areas that will exploit the formula capabilities of Crystal Reports. Figure 4.1 displays the familiar Formula Editor within the new Formula Workshop interface.

The Formula Editor can be used in the following functional areas of Crystal Report creation:

- Creation of derived fields (Formulas, SQL Expressions)
- Report Section formatting
- Report Object formatting

- Record Selection formulas
- Group Selection formulas
- Running Total conditions
- Formula-based hyperlinks (covered in Chapter 9, "Custom Formatting Techniques")
- Alert conditions (covered in Chapter 11, "Using Record Selections and Alerts for Interactive Reporting")
- Use of Report Variables (covered later in this chapter and in Chapter 12, "Using Subreports for Advanced Reports")

Figure 4.1
The Formula Editor within the new Formula Workshop.

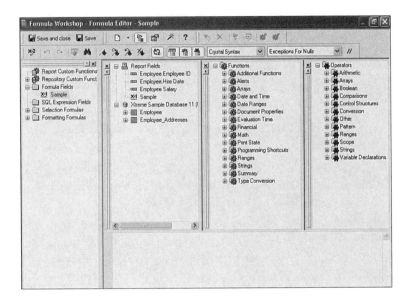

Although the independently accessed Formula Editors for each of these reporting areas provide powerful capabilities, a great new productivity feature introduced in Crystal Reports version 9 is the capability to access almost all the formulas held in a report in a single interface called the Formula Workshop—essentially a one-stop shop for all formulas. At the time of writing, the only exceptions to the rule were Running Total and Alert Condition formulas.

The Formula Workshop consists of a toolbar, a tree that lists the types of formulas you can create or modify, and an area for defining the formula itself either through the Formula Editor or a Formula Expert.

NAVIGATING THE FORMULA WORKSHOP WITH THE WORKSHOP TREE

Figure 4.2 shows some of the new Formula Workshop features you see by expanding the Formula Workshop Tree found in the Formula Editor.

Figure 4.2
The Formula
Workshop with
expanded Formula
Workshop Tree and
the Formula Expert
displayed.

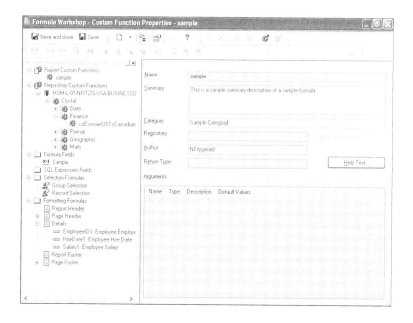

The Workshop Tree is a container for Report and Repository functions, Formula fields, SQL Expression fields, Selection formulas, and Formatting formulas—all of which are explained in more detail in the following sections.

REPORT CUSTOM FUNCTIONS

Report Custom Functions are functions created by Crystal Report Designers that are stored within the current report file. It is important to note that custom functions are accessed from the Formula Workshop along with other types of formulas and functions. New Custom Report functions are created through the Formula Editor by accessing the right-click menu on any part of the Report Custom Function section of the Formula Workshop or by selecting Custom Function from the New menu drop-down list.

→ For more information on custom functions, **see** "Crystal Reports in the Real World—Custom Functions," **p. 314**.

REPOSITORY CUSTOM FUNCTIONS

Repository Custom Functions are functions created by Crystal Report Designers and then stored centrally within the BusinessObjects Enterprise (or Crystal Reports Server) Repository. The repository acts as a central library for these custom functions among multiple other reusable objects. Note that Repository functions are accessed from the Formula Workshop along with the other types of formulas and functions. You upload new Repository functions by creating a Report function and subsequently adding it to the Repository through the Add Repository option accessed by right-clicking any specific Custom Report Function.

→ For more detail on Repository functions, **see** "Sorting Items in the Repository Explorer," **p. 397**.

CAUTION

> Although the Crystal Repository was introduced and made available in Crystal Reports version 9, it is now only available to Crystal Report designers who are licensed for BusinessObjects Enterprise (or Crystal Reports Server) version 10 or XI. When requesting any Repository-related function or activity, a logon prompt for BusinessObjects Enterprise (or Crystal Reports Server) is presented to the designer and must be successfully completed before the functionality is made available.

TIP

> Remember that when you add a custom function to the Central Repository for other report developers to use, you must first create it locally as a Report Custom function and only then can it be added to the Central Repository. Custom functions cannot be directly added into the Central Repository. See Chapters 13 and 18 for more details on Report and Repository functions.

FORMULA FIELDS

As you learned in previous chapters, formula fields provide a means to add derived fields (that is, those not directly available in your database), such as a calculation into your Crystal Reports, as well as provide your business users (report consumers) with additional views of data. Once created, Crystal Reports treats derived formula fields in exactly the same manner as it does original database fields. The majority of this chapter is dedicated to introducing the different methods of creating formulas through two interfaces—the Formula Editor and the Formula Expert. Both of these are discussed next, and Chapter 13, "Using Formulas and Custom Functions," explores some advanced features of formula creation and use.

SQL EXPRESSION FIELDS

SQL Expressions provide a means to add derived fields (that is, those not directly available in your database), such as a calculation into your Crystal Reports, that are based exclusively on *Structured Query Language (SQL)* statements rather than standard Crystal formula syntax. As a reminder, SQL Expressions are used in cases where report-processing efficiency is critical.

Using SQL Expressions facilitates pushing data processing to the database server instead of the Crystal Reports Server, and this is usually most efficient. Like Formulas, SQL Expressions are created in the Formula Editor but provide only a subset of the functionality because of the dependency on the SQL supported by the report's attached data source. A downloadable chapter called "Using SQL Queries in Crystal Reports," provides a good introduction to SQL and is available from www.usingcrystal.com.

SELECTION FORMULAS

As discussed in Chapter 3, "Filtering, Sorting, and Summarizing Data," selection formulas come in two varieties in Crystal Reports—Group and Record. A Record Selection formula provides a filtering mechanism on records to be included in the final report. Likewise, a

Group Selection formula provides a filtering mechanism on the groups to be included in the final report. Each of these selection formulas can be accessed and edited through the Formula Workshop using the familiar Formula Editor component. The Formula Editor will be described in detail in the next major section and in extended detail with respect to selection formulas in Chapter 11.

FORMATTING FORMULAS

Formatting formulas provide flexibility in the presentation of a Crystal Report's report sections and all the report objects contained within report sections. Examples of object and section formatting options include Background Color, Suppression, ToolTip, Border Color/Style, Section Underlay, and so on. All the formatting capabilities available in the Format Editor dialog (see Figure 4.3) and the Report Section Expert (see Figure 4.4) that provide access to an x+2 icon can be set—and be set conditionally—through these Formatting Formulas.

Coverage of the formatting functionality provided through these dialogs is covered in Chapter 6, "Fundamentals of Report Formatting," but you should note that this is accessed and set through the Formula Workshop's Formula Editor. When you select the New Formatting Formula option by either clicking the New button or right-clicking on a Section or Field element under the Formatting Functions tree, you can access all formatting functions that can be modified through a formula.

Figure 4.3
The Format Editor dialog provides access to numerous formatting settings and additional access to the Formula Editor for conditional formatting.

Figure 4.4
The Section Expert provides access to numerous section formatting settings and additional access to the Formula Editor for conditional settings.

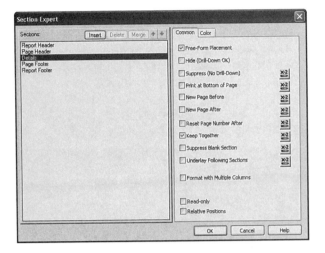

USING THE WORKSHOP FORMULA EDITOR

The Formula Editor, shown in Figure 4.5, is a common tool used across all the different types of formulas accessible through the Formula Workshop. The Formula Editor is composed of five distinct areas:

- The Fields area (at the top-left frame of the Formula Editor) includes all the available report, formula, summarization, and database fields that can be added to the current formula.

- The Functions area (at the top-center frame of the Formula Editor) includes the prebuilt Crystal Reports functions and custom functions that are available to be added to the currently edited formula.

- The Operators area (at the top-right frame of the Formula Editor) includes a number of operators that can be used in the currently edited formula. Examples of operators include +, *, IF/THEN/ELSE, SELECT CASE, AND/OR, and so on.

- The Editing area (the large bottom frame of the Formula Editor) is the free-form text-editing area where formulas are formed through either direct typing or double-clicking selections from the other three Formula Editor frames.

- The toolbar area contains a number of Formula Editor options including toggles on the different frames, a new toggle on the Formula Editor or Expert, some bookmarking options, a formula syntax checking button (x+2), and, importantly, the Crystal versus Basic Syntax drop-down box.

NOTE

Crystal Reports provides two different formula languages for use in creating formulas. Basic syntax is very similar to the Visual Basic programming structure and provides a natural fit for report designers with a Visual Basic programming background. The other

continues

continued

more commonly used syntax–Crystal syntax–has no programming language affiliation, but is highly-evolved and easy to use for nonprogrammers. For the rest of this chapter, the examples are created using the more commonly used Crystal syntax.

Figure 4.5
The Formula Editor provides a one-stop shop for formula development.

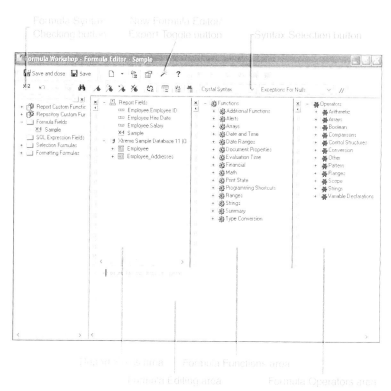

The available elements in each of the top three areas of the Formula Editor vary depending on what type of formula you are creating. For example, when you create a Formatting formula, the Functions frame presents a Formatting section not available while editing or creating other types of formulas. Another familiar example is the limited set of fields, functions, and operators presented when creating SQL Expressions. This is, of course, dependent on the supported SQL for the current report's data source.

To facilitate your understanding of the Formula Editor, the following hypothetical business problem provides a hands-on experience with creating formulas within reports. The CEO of Maple Leaf Bikes is planning an initial public offering (IPO) of his stock to the marketplace. Having recently acquired another company called Xtreme Cycles, he wants to fairly share the success of the overall company with these new employees. As such, he wants to allocate stock options to them based on tenure with Xtreme Cycles (a metric of loyalty) and their current salary (a metric of expected contribution). Therefore, the CEO has determined that a fair allocation would be 100 shares for each year of tenure and 100 shares for each $10,000 in salary, and he wants a report outlining these allocations so that he can present this proposal at the next board of directors meeting. The following steps demonstrate a solution for this problem:

1. Create a new report based on the Xtreme Sample Database ODBC Connection using either the Standard Report Wizard or through the main Report Design menus.

2. Select the Employees and Employee_Addresses tables to be used in the report. They should be automatically smart-linked on their indexed (noted by the Red Icon in the linking dialog) Employee ID fields.

3. Add the Employee ID, Salary, and Hire Date fields into the detail section of the report.

At this point, the design frame (from the Design tab) for the report should resemble Figure 4.6.

Figure 4.6
The Crystal Reports Design window with a sample report.

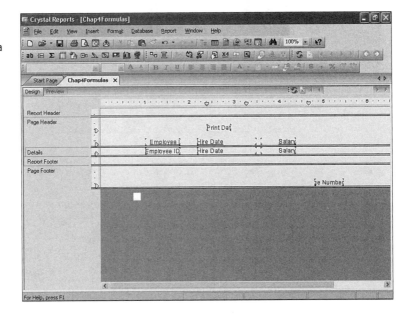

The basic building blocks to the requested report have now been added to the sample report, but there is clearly work to be done to capture the CEO's intent. This report is flushed out through the next few sections as different formula functions are systematically introduced.

ARITHMETIC FORMULAS

Arithmetic formulas are those derived from existing numeric fields (or fields converted into numbers—type conversion information is discussed later in this chapter). These formulas can be simple multiplication or addition operations, or they can be as complex as standard deviations, sums, or correlations. Arithmetic formulas are created within the Formula Editor by selecting any combination of numeric fields, numeric operators, or numeric-oriented functions. Figure 4.7 displays the Formula Editor resized to highlight some common arithmetic functions and operators.

Figure 4.7
The Formula Editor highlighting some arithmetic functions and operators.

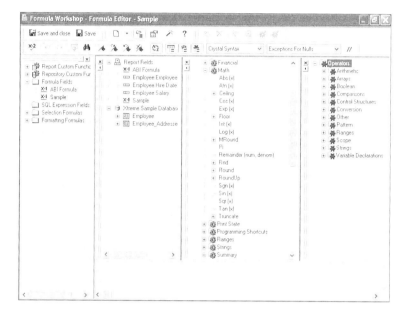

With hundreds of formula functions and operators built into Crystal Reports and the new capability to expand that set with custom functions, it's easy to become overwhelmed with all the available formula possibilities. One very helpful source of information on the many built-in formulas in Crystal Reports is the provided help files accessed through the F1 key. By clicking on the Index tab of the Crystal Reports Help Screen and searching on functions or operators, you can access a detailed description of each of the hundreds of different Crystal Reports functions and operators. Figure 4.8 displays the Crystal Reports Help dialog with an Aging function highlighted.

To create an Arithmetic formula (as any other kind of formula) within the Formula Editor, either double-click on the appropriate elements from each of the Fields, Functions, and Operators frames or select them by single-clicking and dragging and dropping them into the Formula Editing frame. Using either method, a formula begins to be constructed in the Formula Editing Area/Frame. Alternatively, experienced users can create formulas by typing the formula directly into the Formula Editing Area and periodically checking the formula's syntax with the x+2 toolbar button, which provides error-checking functionality.

For users who prefer to work in the Formula Editor and type in their formulas by hand, Crystal Reports provides an Auto-Complete capability accessed by using the Ctrl+Spacebar key combination. A list of formula functions that could complete the most recently typed characters is made available for instant selection.

Figure 4.8
Crystal Reports functions Help—a great reference for understanding the syntax of formula functions.

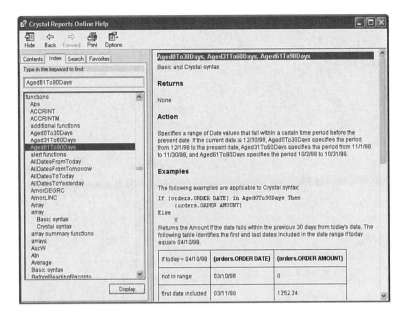

Revisiting the Maple Leaf Bikes reporting scenario, the CEO has designated two criteria for stock option allocation to the Xtreme Sports employees—Tenure and Salary. The Salary component is based on a derivation from a numeric field (salary) and lends itself to the creation of an Arithmetic formula based on the requirements that each $10,000 of salary contributes to 100 stock options. The following steps, continued from the last section, move toward a reporting solution for the CEO and provide exposure to the Formula Creation process in the Formula Editor:

1. If the Field Explorer is not already open in your Crystal Reports Design window, open that now by either clicking on the Field Explorer icon or by toggling to the Field Explorer option under the View menu. Figure 4.9 displays the Crystal Reports Design window with the Field Explorer displayed.

TIP

To maximize report design real-estate in the Design tab, you can shorten the Report Section names by accessing the Show Short Section Names option from the right-click menu accessed over any report section heading. Similarly, to maximize the preview real-estate in the Preview tab, a similar capability exists through the Hide Section Names menu option.

2. Create a new Formula by clicking on the Formula Fields field and either accessing the New option on the right-click menu or clicking the New button in the Field Explorer toolbar. You will be prompted for a Formula Name—call this formula **Salary Driven Options** and select the Use Editor button to create the formula. If you accidentally

click the Use Expert button, have no fear; simply click the Formula Editor/Expert toggle button in the Formula Workshop toolbar. The Formula Expert is explored later in this chapter, but for now, the Formula Editor is your primary focus. The familiar Formula Workshop (as you saw in Figures 4.2 and 4.5) appears.

3. Logically stepping through the CEO's request, the first database field you need to access to determine the Salary Driven Component of stock option allocation is Salary, so find the Salary field in the Fields frame and double-click on it.

Figure 4.9
Maple Leaf Bikes CEO report with Field Explorer displayed.

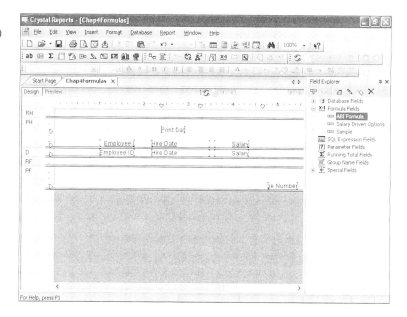

> **TIP**
>
> More than just providing access to those fields already selected for viewing in the report, the Formula Editor Fields frame provides access to all available database fields for those tables selected as report data sources. Additionally, existing formulas, sums, running totals, and so on can be accessed here, which can be included in other formulas.

Because the CEO wants to provide 100 stock options for each $10,000 in existing salary, you logically need to divide each employee's current salary by $10,000 and then multiply by 100. To do so, you could either access the Arithmetic operators (/ for division and * for multiplication) in the Operators Frame and double-click on those or simply type them in.

4. To accomplish this task, you need to type in the numeric constants regardless, so type the following into the Formula Editor so that it resembles Figure 4.10:
{Employee.Salary} / 10000 * 100.

5. Perform error-checking on your report by clicking the x+2 icon. After you confirm that no errors are found and your formula is identical to that in Figure 4.10, save the formula with the Save button and exit the Formula Workshop by clicking Close.

Figure 4.10
Salary-driven options
formula creation
example.

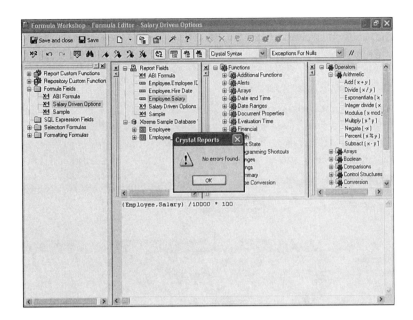

6. Add the new formula into the report beside Employee ID and try to format it to display zero decimals and no currency symbol (hint—right-click on the object and select the Format option or use the shortcut buttons from the Formatting toolbar). At this point, also remove the original Salary and Hire Date fields from the report by deleting them. Note that the Salary Driven Options field can exist without its underlying support fields (Salary) existing on the report. The Preview tab of the CEO's report should now resemble that shown in Figure 4.11.

Figure 4.11
The interim version of
the Maple Leaf Bikes
CEO sample report.

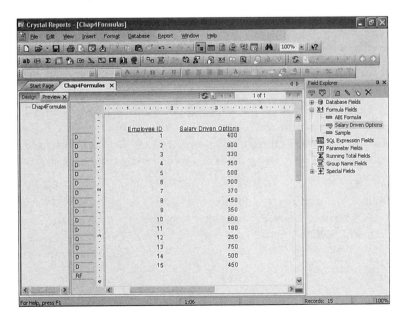

The current version of the report takes the content of the report to about half complete. The tenure-driven component of the CEO's request needs to be taken care of with some date calculations.

DATE AND TIME FORMULAS

Date and Time formulas are those derived from existing date or time fields (or fields converted into dates). These types of formulas can be as simple as extracting a month name from a date field or as complex as determining shipping times in business days (difference between two dates not including weekends and holidays). Date and Time formulas are created within the Formula Editor by selecting any combination of date and time fields, Date operators, or date-oriented functions. Figure 4.12 displays the Formula Editor resized to highlight some common date functions.

Figure 4.12
The Formula Editor highlighting some Date and Time functions.

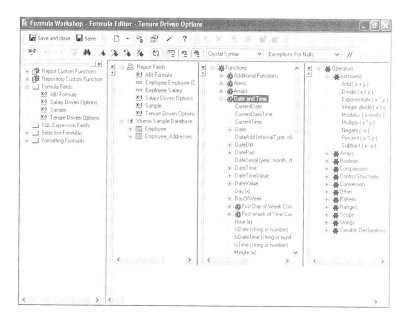

To create a Date/Time formula (as with Arithmetic formulas) within the Formula Editor, either double-click on the appropriate elements from each of the fields, functions, and operators frames or select them with a single-click and drag and drop them into the Formula Editing frame. Using either method, a formula begins to be constructed in the Formula Editing Area/Frame.

Some operators that are commonly used with dates include + and -. Those are displayed in Table 4.1 with some quick examples and their effect. These operators work equally well on time fields and date fields.

TABLE 4.1 COMMON DATE OPERATORS, THEIR FUNCTIONS, AND EXAMPLES

Common Date Operator or Function	Formula Usage Example	Effect
+ operator	`{Employee.Hire Date} + 365`	Returns the one year anniversary date of the given employee in a date format.
− operator	`{Orders.Ship Date}− {Orders.Order Date}`	Returns a numeric field representing the days taken to ship after receiving an order.
− operator	`{Orders.Warranty Expiration Date} − 365`	Returns a date representing the purchase date of the given item.

Common functions that are used with dates include the use of the pre-built date ranges and date type conversion formulas in Crystal Reports.

- Conversion functions are found under the Date and Time section in the Functions frame of the Formula Editor.

- Range functions are found in the Date Ranges section of the same Functions frame and provide a number of built-in date ranges that can be automatically created in Crystal Reports and used in comparisons. Range examples include Aged61To90Days, Next30Days, or AllDatesFromTomorrow. These ranges can be used with the control structures introduced later in this chapter (for example, IF statements) to determine if dates fall within certain predefined ranges.

Revisiting the Maple Leaf Bikes reporting scenario, the Tenure component of option allocation still needs to be created in the report. It is based on a derivation from two date fields (hire date and the current date) and lends itself to the creation of a date formula based on the requirements that every 365 days of tenure will contribute to 100 stock options.

The following steps move toward a final reporting solution for the CEO and provide exposure to date-focused formula creation in the Formula Editor:

1. Create a New Formula in the Field Explorer called **Tenure Driven Options**.

   Because the CEO wants to provide 100 stock options for each year (365 days) of tenure, you logically need to determine each employee's tenure in days by finding the difference (with the - operator) between the current date (with a built-in Crystal Reports function) and the hire date (with a provided database field). This employee tenure measured in days will then need to be divided by 365 to find the tenure in years before being multiplied by 100 to determine the number of tenure-driven options.

2. To accomplish this, add the Current Date function (CurrentDate) to the formula by accessing it under the Date and Time section of the Functions frame in the Formula Editor. You could alternatively add this by typing **Cu** in the editor box, clicking on Ctrl+Spacebar, and selecting the CurrentDate function from the list. Add the - operator (found under the Arithmetic section in the Operators frame) after that, and then add the

database field Hire Date to the formula by double-clicking on it. Finally, add the / 365 and * 100 formula pieces by typing them in and, more importantly, wrap two round brackets around the CurrentDate—{Employee.Hire Date} section of the formula—to ensure the proper order of calculation.

> **NOTE**
>
> The Crystal Reports Formula Editor respects the standard mathematical order of operations. In order this would be brackets, exponents, division and multiplication, and, finally, addition and subtraction.

3. Ensure that your formula resembles what is displayed in Figure 4.13 and save it before closing the Formula Workshop.

Figure 4.13
A Tenure-Driven Options sample formula highlighting some date formulas.

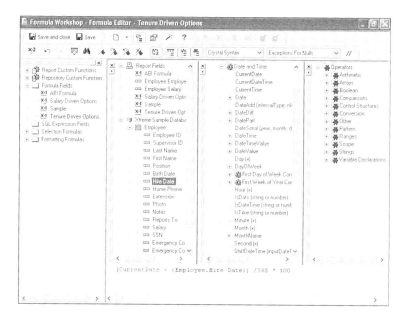

4. Place the new formula on the report beside the Salary Driven Options field and format it to have no decimal places and no currency symbol.

It has likely struck you that most CEOs would not appreciate having to take the two options numbers you have created and add them themselves. It seems like a good opportunity for another formula to sum up those two numbers.

5. Create a new formula called **Total Options** and make that formula be the sum of the two previously created formulas. (Hint: The previously created formulas appear in the Fields frame under the Report Fields Tree node, and you can use the addition operator.)

6. Add this new field to the report, remove the hire date and salary fields, and reformat it to make your sample resemble that displayed in Figure 4.14.

The CEO of Maple Leaf Bikes should be quite happy with the turnaround time on this report. Having created the results so quickly, it might be a good move in career management to spend a little time on the presentation and readability of this report. The next sections and chapters introduce some additional capabilities provided in Crystal Reports and the Formula Editor that increase the presentation quality of this report.

Figure 4.14
Maple Leaf Bikes CEO report with options formulas.

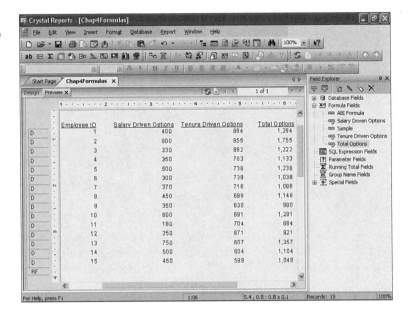

STRING FORMULAS

String formulas are created from existing string fields (or fields converted into strings—type conversion is covered later in the chapter in the section, "Using Type Conversion in Formulas). These formulas can be as simple as concatenating two string fields or as complex as extracting some specific piece of information from a string field. String formulas are created within the Formula Editor by selecting any combination of string fields, string operators, or string-oriented functions. Figure 4.15 displays the Formula Editor resized to highlight some common string functions.

The most commonly created string-based formulas involve the concatenation of multiple existing fields from a data source. This is accomplished through the Formula Editor with either the formal Concatenate function from within the Strings section of the Operators frame or by using the much easier + and & concatenate operators. These last two operators enable the dynamic linking of one or more string fields into one large string field.

TIP

Although the + operator requires all of its arguments to be of the same string type when concatenating, the & operator performs dynamic conversion to text on any non-string fields included in the operation–a nice timesaving feature.

Figure 4.15
The Formula Editor with string-oriented functions expanded.

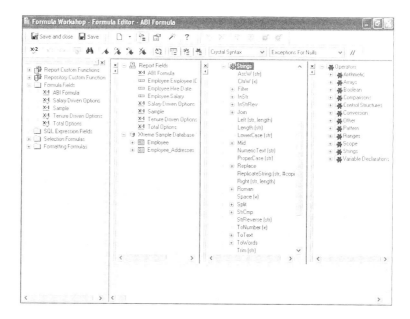

Revisiting the Maple Leaf Bikes reporting scenario and focusing on increasing the readability of the report, Employee ID can be replaced with Employee First Initial and Last Name. To use the string capabilities of the Formula Editor and enhance the report, follow these steps:

> **NOTE**
>
> When creating a string formula that is meant to join two existing strings (for example, First Name and Last Name, or Address 1 and Address 2), the concatenation features of Crystal Reports dynamically resize the resultant formula to exclude any redundant spaces between the end of the first joined field and the beginning of the next. This is an important presentation feature that prevents the requirement to trim all fields before joining them together.

1. Create a new formula in the sample report called **Employee Name**.

2. Because you only want to present the first letter of the employee's first name, you need to use the Left function under the Strings section of the Functions frame. Add this to your formula and note that the cursor is automatically placed in the expected location for the first parameter to this function—a string.

3. Without moving the cursor in the Editing area, find the First Name field of the Employee table and double-click it (you will likely need to expand the Xtreme Sample Database section because this field is not currently added to the report). This adds it as the first argument to the Left function.

4. Move the cursor in the Editing area to the location of the second expected parameter for the Left function—after the comma—and type **1** (the number of characters to

extract). This creates the entry Left ({Employee.First Name}, 1) in the Formula Editor and instructs the Formula Engine to take the leftmost single character from the First Name field.

5. To concatenate this with the Last Name in a nice-looking manner, type + ". " + into the Editing area and then double-click on the Last Name field of the Employee table. Your new formula should resemble Figure 4.16.

Figure 4.16
String formula sample in the Formula Editor.

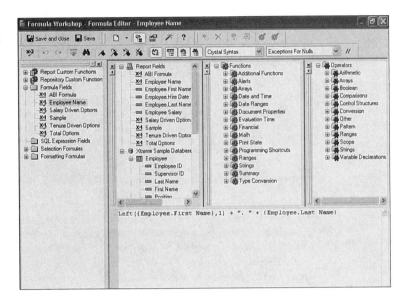

6. Replace the Employee ID field in the CEO's sample report with the new Employee Name formula you just created and re-arrange your report to resemble Figure 4.17.

> **TIP**
>
> If you wanted to continue to provide the CEO with the capability of determining an actual Employee ID but didn't want to squeeze the report real-estate anymore, a clever Crystal Reports feature called ToolTips could be used. This enables a pop-up window to show up with additional information (such as Employee ID) when an end user (in this case, the CEO) scrolls over any Employee Name. This is implemented from the Format Field window (under the Common tab) and the ToolTips Text x+2 button. You can accomplish this by using the following formula: "Employee ID: " + CSTR({Employee.Employee ID},0).

Having covered the primary data types used in strings, it is useful for operating in the real world to know how to move between those data types. The next section discusses data type conversion.

Figure 4.17
Maple Leaf Bikes CEO
report with String
formula.

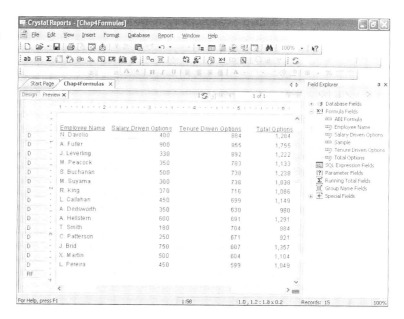

Comments can be added to formula statements to better document the formula. To insert comments, use the double forward slash (//) at the beginning of a line of code to comment out the entire line. Thus, any text on this commented line would not be processed as part of the formula. There is also a toolbar command within the Formula Editor that enables you to add this syntax into formulas quickly, as indicated with the double slash (//) icon. If you're using the Basic Syntax, the apostrophe (or rem) commands can be used for commenting.

USING TYPE CONVERSION IN FORMULAS

Often, data is not accessible in the format that is required for a particular operation. A common example is when numeric fields are stored in a database as string fields and they are required in an Arithmetic formula. For any number of additional reasons, it often happens that data needs to be converted to and from different data types. The Formula Editor provides numerous built-in functions that facilitate this conversion process. These functions are accessible from the Type Conversion section under the Functions frame of the Formula Editor. Figure 4.18 displays the Formula Editor with the Type Conversion section expanded.

A great deal of flexibility is provided with the numerous type conversion functions built into Crystal Reports and these should enable all required conversions. Additionally, Crystal Reports provides some automatic conversions in the following cases: Number to Currency, Date to DateTime, and basic type to a Range Value of the same underlying basic type. Some of the most commonly used Type Conversion functions are

Figure 4.18
The Formula Editor provides you with many different Type Conversion functions.

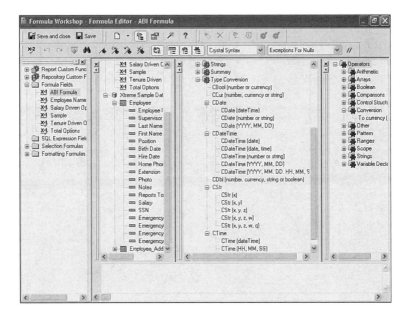

- **CStr()** or **ToText()**—These identical functions convert Numbers, Currency, Date, Time, and DateTime values to text strings.

- **CDbl()** or **ToNumber()**—These identical functions convert Currency, text string, or Boolean values to a Number. Often used in combination with **IsNumeric()** or **NumericText()** to validate input arguments.

- **CDate()**, **CDateTime()**, or **CTime()**—These functions convert their given arguments (numeric, string, and specific fixed formats) to a respective Date, DateTime, or Time value.

A couple of more interesting type conversion options include the following:

- **Roman()**—This function converts a number ranging from 0 to 3999 into its Roman numeral equivalent (for example, Roman(2004) = MMIV).

- **ToWords()**—This function converts a number or currency value to a string representation of that number (for example, ToWords($134.15, 2) = one hundred thirty four and 15/100). This is a nice function for facilitating the delivery of checks.

NOTE

> Barcode conversion functions are also available through a third party, Azalea, at: http://www.azalea.com/CrystalReports/index.html. These enable you to convert numbers to standard barcodes that can be embedded on your Crystal Reports.

CONTROL STRUCTURES—CONDITIONAL AND LOOPING STRUCTURES

The Formula Editor provides additional power in formula creation through a set of control structures made available in the Operators and Functions Frames. Figure 4.19 displays the involved sections of those respective frames that include the provided control structures.

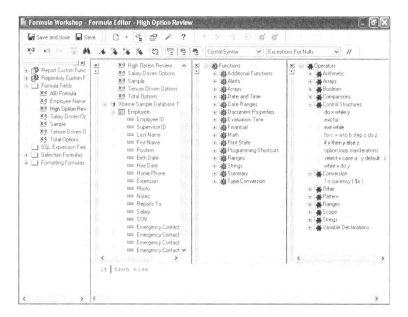

Figure 4.19
The Formula Editor provides several Control Structure functions and operators.

One of the most useful control structures is the If/Then/Else construct. This structure enables the inclusion of conditional logic in Crystal Reports formulas. The If/Then/Else works particularly well when a condition leads to either one of two settings. Although this construct can handle multiple potential settings through nested If statements, creating this type of complicated formula can be avoided with the Select Case operator that allows for multiple settings and multiple potential results.

Revisiting the Maple Leaf Bikes example, assume that the CEO has provided a new requirement specifying that employees with a recommended stock allocation of greater than 1200 stock options need to be highlighted for his personal review. Of course, with Crystal Reports, there are multiple methods of providing this highlighting; to use the If/Then/Else control structure, follow these steps:

1. Create a new formula called High Option Review.

2. Add the If/Then/Else control structure to the formula.

3. Add the condition that the Total Options Formula (the @Total Options field) is greater than 1200 between the If and Then components so that the beginning of the formula text is IF {@Total Options} > 1200 THEN.

4. Now when this condition is met for any employee, you need to highlight that record for the CEO's special review. To do this, add text similar to "** **Review** **" (with the

double quotes surrounding the text) to the area after the Then part of the If statement construct.

5. When that condition is not met, you can simply print a space or dash. Do this by adding "-" (including the double quotes) after the Else part of the If statement so that your new formula resembles that shown in Figure 4.20.

> **NOTE**
>
> Carriage returns (via the Enter key) can be inserted into the construction area of the formula, such as between lines and logical breaking points, to make formulas more readable. If you're using the Basic Syntax, you can extend single code lines over multiple lines for readability by using the underscore character (_) preceded by a space.

Figure 4.20
A sample formula with an If control structure.

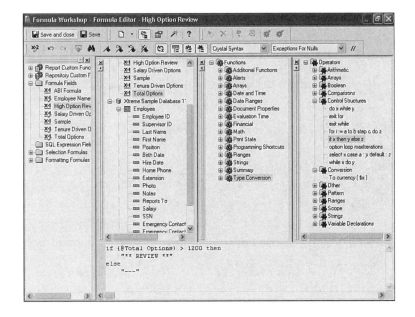

6. Add the new formula to the CEO's report so that it resembles the sample report shown in Figure 4.21.

The conditional logic inherent in the If/Then/Else and Select/Case statements provides clear flexibility in formula creation. Another valuable formula capability that programmers appreciate immediately is the looping functionality. The Formula Editor provides three different looping constructs (For/Step/Do, Do/While, and While/Do), and each of these enable the evaluation of formula logic multiple times for each evaluation of the formula. Table 4.3 describes the most common types of control structures and their usage.

Figure 4.21
The revised sample
report includes a High
Option Review
indicator.

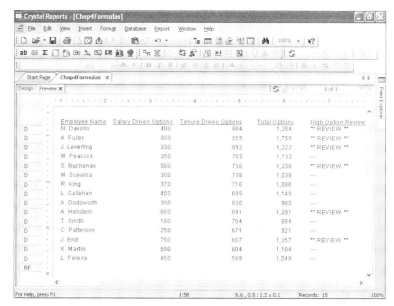

TABLE 4.3   COMMONLY USED CONTROL STRUCTURES

Control Structure	Description	Usage
If/Then/Else and IIF()	Conditional structures that select an execution path based on the evaluated conditions.	This construct is best used when evaluating conditions with a minimal set of potential execution options.
Select Case	Conditional structure that selects an execution path based on the evaluation conditions.	This construct is best used in place of the if/then/else construct when evaluating conditions with multiple potential execution paths.
Switch	Another conditional structure that selects a value from a set of expression/value pairs where the expression evaluates to true.	This is especially effective when creating report selection filters because it allows for the pushing of the results down to the database or faster report execution—this is not possible with the other conditional constructs. It is also useful for compact conditional formula creation.
For/Step/ Do Loops	For loops enable you to evaluate a sequence of statements a fixed numbers of times. An Exit statement can end this looping prematurely.	This construct is best used when you know the number of times that the expressions need to be evaluated in advance or the loops are dependent on a variable in the report. For I = X to Y Step Z Do (*statements*)

Control Structure	Description	Usage
Do/While Loops	Do/While loops execute until the While condition is no longer met. They always execute at least once. The Exit While statement can end this looping prematurely.	While loops can be used to execute a fixed block of statements an indefinite number of times.
		Do statements While condition
While/Do Loops	While/Do loops execute until the While condition is no longer met. It is possible that not a single iteration takes place if the condition is immediately false. The Exit While statement can end this looping prematurely.	While loop can be used to execute a fixed block of statements an indefinite amount of time.
		While condition Do (statements)

CAUTION

The Crystal Reports engine has a built-in safety mechanism that displays an error message and stops processing any formula if it includes more than 100,000 loop iterations. This is important to consider when including any of the loop constructs in a formula. It is also important to note that this built-in governor works on a per formula basis and not per loop. This means that if any one formula contains any number of loops that tally more than 100,000 looping iterations, the formula stops processing with an error. Another control structure function called Option Loop can be used for limiting iterations to a number different than 100,000.

VARIABLES

Crystal Reports has included yet another programming construct, variables, in the Formula Editor to provide even further flexibility in formula creation. Variables give you a powerful means to store and retrieve information throughout the processing life of any report— essentially providing a temporary storage space for valuable information. Examples of information that might be useful to store and retrieve later are previous detail section information, previous group section information, or a one-time calculation that needs to be incorporated into many subsequent report formulas.

Several different types of variables can be declared (for example, String, Number, Date, Time, Boolean, and so on) and three different scopes for each of these variables are as follows:

- **Local**—Accessible only in the same formula within which they are declared.
- **Global**—Accessible from all formulas in the main report, but not accessible from subreports.
- **Shared**—Accessible from all formulas in both the main report and all subreports.

Both the Variable Declaration and Scope operators listings are accessible from the Operators frame in the Formula Editor. To use variables in your report formulas, they must be declared first—and this applies to every formula that accesses any given variable—not just the first processed formula.

> **TIP**
>
> Another important function to remember when using multiple variables in multiple formulas with calculation dependencies is the EvaluateAfter() function. This formula function can force certain formulas (and their variable logic) to be processed after another formula (and its variable logic). This can be very useful when the order of formula calculation is important because of variable and formula dependencies. A good discussion of when things are evaluated in Crystal Report's multi-pass engine is provided at the end of this chapter.

It is worth noting that variables can provide significant power in report creation in their capability to maintain persistent information outside the regular processing path of the report. A practical hands-on use of variables is explored in Chapter 12.

CREATING FORMULAS WITH THE FORMULA EXPERT

The Formula Expert is used to create formulas based on existing custom functions—either from the current report or the Crystal Repository. The expert appears when you click on the Formula Expert/Editor toggle button (the magic wand) in the Formula Workshop. The Formula Expert leverages the power of the custom functions and repository functionality introduced first in version 9. Figure 4.22 displays the Formula Expert dialog.

To use the Formula Expert, follow this simple three-step process:

1. Find the custom function that meets your formula requirements by searching through the Report and Repository Custom Function libraries. The supporting Help description and More Info button can aid in this search.

2. For each parameter of the selected function, select a field from your report data source or enter a constant.

3. Save the new formula using the Save button.

The created formula is now accessible through the Formula Editor and can be enhanced or edited with that tool.

Figure 4.22
The Formula Expert dialog enables rapid creation of formulas through a wizard type interface.

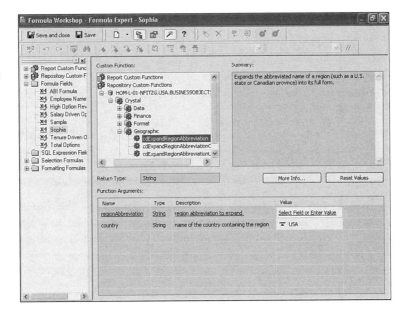

USING THE FORMULA EXTRACTOR TO CREATE CUSTOM FUNCTIONS

The Formula Expert enables you to create formulas from existing custom functions. The Formula Extractor does the exact opposite—it enables you to create custom functions from previously created formulas. This functionality is accessible by creating a new Custom Report Function and selecting the Use Extractor button. Figure 4.23 displays the Extract Custom Function from Formula dialog accessed when creating custom report functions.

Figure 4.23
The Extract Custom Function from Formula dialog enables the creation of a custom function from an existing formula.

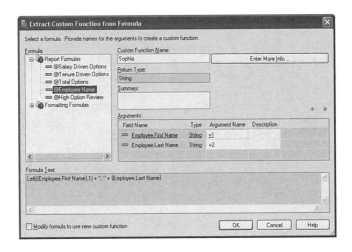

By using the Formula Extractor, it is possible to migrate existing formula logic from a formula field into a custom function. The appropriate part of the migrated formulas can subsequently be replaced with the new custom function and eventually be added to the Crystal Repository.

To create a custom function from an existing formula using the Formula Extractor dialog, follow these steps:

In the Formula Workshop, create a new Custom Report Function. Select the Formula Extractor by clicking on the Use Extractor button after you have ensured that the custom function name you have selected follows your personal or organization's standard naming convention.

Edit the default argument names (v1, v2, and so on) and descriptions that represent the required parameters for the new function. These argument names and descriptions should communicate the expected information to future users of the custom function. The importance of meaningful information here cannot be underestimated with respect to the future usefulness of the newly created custom function.

Add an appropriate summary description to the Summary window so that future report designers using this custom function will understand its proper use.

Click on the Modify Formula to Use New Function check box (in the lower-left area of the Extract Custom Function dialog) to place the new custom function into the formula on which you are basing it. This is not a mandatory step, but it is a nice feature that quickly enables you to take advantage of the reusability of your new custom function.

Click the Enter More Info button to add additional support information for the custom function. Figure 4.24 displays the More Info dialog.

Figure 4.24
The Custom Function Enter More Info dialog enables the specification of supporting information for the newly created custom function.

Enter the custom function author (likely yourself) and custom function category information in their respective text boxes.

NOTE

> When entering a custom function category, it is possible to create it at more than one level of subfolder depth by using forward slashes in the Category text box. For example, by entering **MapleLeafBikes/HR**, the newly created formula will be added to the Custom Function library under the Maple Leaf Bikes category and the HR subfolder. By adding and maintaining your custom functions in a logical hierarchy, future users will find accessing them much easier.

7. Optionally, set default values for your custom functions arguments by clicking on the default value cells and filling in the Default Values dialog.

8. Add Help text describing the custom function by clicking on the Help Text button. Again, it is important to consider future report designers using this custom function when deciding on the detail that you should include in this description.

THE MULTI-PASS REPORTING PROCESS OF THE CRYSTAL REPORTS ENGINE

Despite all the Crystal Reports functionality covered, to this point, it would be understandable if you assumed that the Crystal Reports reporting engine provides all this power with a single pass through the data it retrieves from the database. This would be a faulty assumption—Crystal Reports actually uses a three-pass reporting methodology to generate reports. Understanding the multi-pass nature of the reporting engine can facilitate effective report design and expedite the debugging of potential reporting challenges. Figure 4.25 from the Crystal Reports online Help file provides a good starting point for understanding the different passes through the data that Crystal Reports makes and what is calculated on each pass.

Figure 4.25
Understanding the Crystal Reports Multi-Pass report engine flow can help in creating and debugging Crystal Reports.

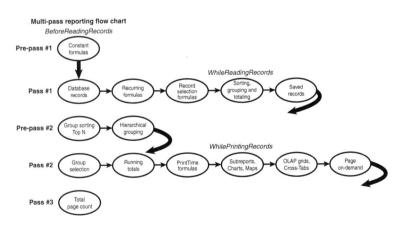

CRYSTAL REPORTS PROCESSING ENGINE—PRE-PASS #1

In the Pre-Pass phase of report creation, only constant formulas are processed. A constant formula example might be 1967*10. These formulas are evaluated at the beginning of the print generation process and are never evaluated again. This process is known as "BeforeReadingRecords."

CRYSTAL REPORTS PROCESSING ENGINE—PASS #1

After the constant formulas have been processed, Crystal Reports begins reading the database records. During the record reading process, known as "WhileReadingRecords," the following occurs:

- **Database connection and Record retrieval**—Record selection and sorting are pushed down to the database in this step if possible.

- **Evaluates recurring formulas**—These formulas are those that contain database fields but do not contain references to subtotals or summary information. This evaluation time is referenced as "WhileReadingRecords" and can be specified within a formula. Formulas that contain references to subtotals or summary information are processed in the second pass.

- **Local Record Selection applied**—If the record selection is too complex to be pushed down to the database, it is applied by Crystal Reports in this step. This is common where the record selection could be not specified in a proper SQL Expression.

- **Sorting, Grouping, and Summarizing**—The data is sorted, separated into groups, and then subtotals and summaries are calculated for each group.

- **Cross-Tab, chart, and map generation**—Only Cross-Tabs, charts, and maps that are based entirely on database fields and recurring formulas are generated in Pass 1.

- **Storage of saved data**—After the totaling process is complete, all the records and totals are stored in memory and to temporary files. Crystal Reports does not read the database again, but instead uses this saved data during all subsequent processing.

CRYSTAL REPORTS PROCESSING ENGINE—PRE-PASS #2

During Pre-Pass #2, groups are ordered in the report for Top/Bottom N and/or Hierarchical Grouping. The reporting engine looks at group instances from Pass 1, and takes the Top N as appropriate, or orders the groups based on the specified Hierarchical Group settings.

CRYSTAL REPORTS PROCESSING ENGINE—PASS #2

Crystal Reports moves through the saved data, if required, to complete any remaining operations and initiates printing of the records in this phase known as "WhilePrintingRecords." During this phase, the following takes place:

- Application of Group selection formula, if applicable.

- Evaluates print-time formulas. These formulas are those that contain any print-time formula functions like `Previous()` or `Next()` or explicitly use the "WhilePrintingRecords" function within the formula.

- Running totals calculations, if applicable.

- Charts, maps, cross-tabs and OLAP grids. Cross-Tabs, charts, and maps that include running totals or PrintTime formulas, and charts that are based on cross-tabs or OLAP grids are generated.
- Subreports. All in-place subreports are calculated during Pass #2. When you're using variables within subreports and expecting certain behavior in the main report based on these shared variables, keep in mind when they are processed relative to everything else in the main report.

CAUTION

> Subtotals, grand totals, and summaries might appear incorrectly if the report has a group selection formula. This occurs because the grand totals and summaries are calculated during Pass 1, but the group selection formula filters the data again in Pass 2. Running total fields or Formula fields with variables can be used instead of summaries to total data successfully with group selection formulas.

CRYSTAL REPORTS PROCESSING ENGINE—PASS #3

In the third and final pass, the total page count is determined. This applies to reports that use the total page count, or Page N of M special fields.

Understanding the multi-pass reporting paths of the Crystal Reports engine helps in the general development and debugging of your production reports. Additional leveraging of the built-in Formula functions discussed previously (`BeforeReadingRecords`, `WhileReadingRecords`, and `WhilePrintingRecords`) in combination with the `EvaluateAfter()` function enable you to design more flexible reports and formulas. These functions also enable you to leverage advanced variable usage and successful sharing among subreports.

TROUBLESHOOTING

ADDING A CUSTOM FUNCTION

I cannot add a custom function directly into the Central Repository.

Custom functions cannot be directly added into the Central Repository. When you add a custom function to the Central Repository for other report developers to use, you must first create it locally as a Report Custom function and only then can it be added to the Central Repository. With version XI (and 10) of the Enterprise Suite of products, you must also be licensed for either BusinessObjects Enterprise or Crystal Reports Server to leverage a Central Repository.

CONVERTING A NUMBER TO A STRING WITH NO DECIMAL PLACES

When trying to convert an existing database numeric field to a string, my resultant strings always get suffixed with two zeros.

When converting an integer to a string field using the CStr() function, the default result will be automatically set to have two decimal places (for instance, 555.00). This can be eliminated through the addition of a second argument in the function that explicitly specifies the number of decimal places to be set to zero. For example, `Cstr({Purchases.Units in Stock},0)` would work.

CRYSTAL REPORTS IN THE REAL WORLD— CUSTOM FUNCTIONS

Some examples of custom functions include handling divide-by-zero errors and handling multi-language text. Both of these examples are described in this section. A common reason for divide-by-zero errors is simply that a field might not be populated. If a given field has not been populated but it is used in the report, Crystal converts it to a default value. Unless modified, the default value for a numeric field that returns NULL is 0. This means that if there is a formula calculating percent of capacity (`Current_Amount/Max_Amount`) but the item is new and therefore no max amount has been set, then the `Max_Amount` field in the database is likely blank. When the preceding formula is applied to the database fields, then the result will be a divide by zero error and the report will fail. `Current_Amount/Max_Amount` would resolve to some real value divided by NULL, the NULL would be converted to the default value of 0, and the result would be some number divided by 0—and a divide-by-0 error is the result.

To avoid this, create a custom function to handle all division. The custom function simply checks for a denominator of 0 and handles it appropriately.

First create the custom function follow these steps:

Open the sample report Chap4Formulas.rpt or the report you have created through this chapter. From the Field Explorer, select Formula Fields and click New. Type in a name for the formula such as **Source Formula** and click Use Editor.

When the Formula Workshop window opens, enter the following formula:

```
If {Employee.Supervisor ID} = 0 Then
    0
Else
    {Employee.Employee ID}/{Employee.Supervisor ID};
```

> Although it seems (and is) odd to build a formula using ID fields in a calculation, what is important is the field types. The fields are used to build the custom function based on their data types rather than actual content. The previous fields are abstracted to simply numeric fields named v1 and v2.

With the Formula Workshop still open, mouse over the New button near the top of the window and click the down arrow. From the list choose Custom Function, enter the name **DivBy0**, and click the User Extractor button.

When the Extract Custom Function from Formula window opens, select the @Source Formula item from the list of formulas. Rename the arguments from v1 and v2 to Denominator and Numerator, respectively (see Figure 4.26).

Figure 4.26
Using the Custom Function Extractor, create a custom function from a formula.

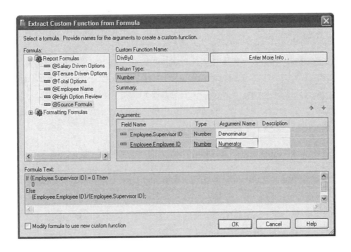

5. Click OK to close the window and the function is now part of the report. If you are using BusinessObjects Enterprise (or Crystal Reports Server), you could now right-click on the function name and choose Add to Repository. When prompted, enter the logon information for your BusinessObjects Enterprise system and the custom function will be added to the Enterprise Repository making it available to all the users who have access to the repository and enabling all report writers to avoid fatal divide by zero errors in their reports.

6. Click Save and Close (see Figure 4.27).

Figure 4.27
The custom function is now part of the repository making it available to users who have appropriate rights.

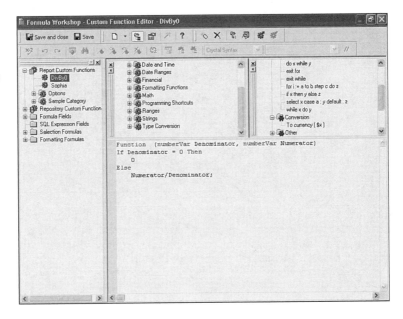

Another example of a custom function might be how to handle some standard text options. For example, it might be useful to have a parameter drive the column header for a field.

Keep the report open. From the Field Explorer, create a new parameter named Language with the potential input values of English, French, or Italian (described in Chapter 5, "Implementing Parameters for Dynamic Reporting"). Also add a new formula named Country Source (described previously). Add the following formula code:

```
If {?Language} = "English" Then
    "Country"
Else If {?Language} = "French" Then
    "Pays"
Else If {?Language} = "Italian" Then
    "Paese";
```

Repeat steps 3, 4, 5, and 6 to create a new custom function called Country extracted from the Country Source formula.

To use the new custom function, create a new formula named Country. From the list of functions, expand the Custom Functions and double-click the Country formula. The function takes one argument, pass in the Language parameter (see Figure 4.28).

Figure 4.28
The custom function accepting the Language parameter. This parameter determines what the function does.

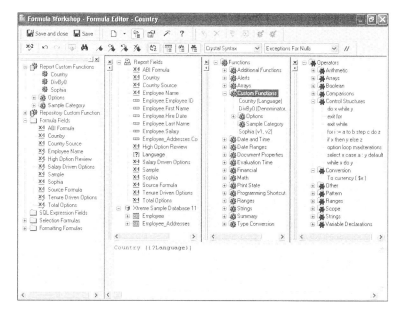

4. Click Save and Close. If prompted, enter the text **English**. Place the new formula in the group header alongside the other column headers and add the country field below it on the detail line.

5. Save the report as Chap4FormulaswithCustom.rpt. Refresh the report passing in "English," "French," and "Italian" to see the effect (see Figure 4.29).

Figure 4.29
The field header changes to display Country in appropriate languages.

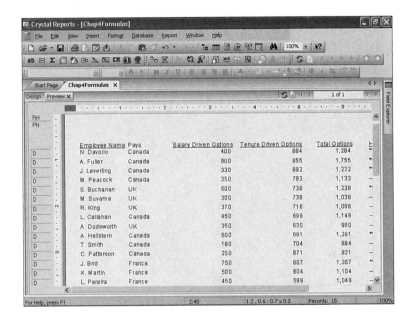

IMPLEMENTING PARAMETERS FOR DYNAMIC REPORTING

In this chapter

INTRODUCTION

A common goal of report design is providing a single report that can service very specific reporting requirements and also accommodate a large audience of business users. Parameter fields enable you to satisfy this requirement and provide three primary benefits:

- **An additional level of interactivity for business users when viewing reports**—A marketing report can prompt a business user for a specific brand or product line she wants to analyze.

- **Ability to segment reports in many different ways to reduce the number of reports necessary to service the demands of the business users**—A sales report can be segmented by district to service the needs of all district-level business users with one report.

- **Greater control over the report query for administrators by filtering the report results to include only the selected parameter value(s)**—A sales report can be filtered to include only data for the appropriate district. This also includes the capability to constrain the report query to avoid including excess or sensitive data.

In this chapter, you take a closer look at using parameters in your reports, as well as how parameter fields can be created and implemented. Like many of the Crystal Reports application features, working with report parameters is very logical but understanding the underlying mechanics facilitates the creation of effective reports.

This chapter covers the following topics:

- Understanding the value of parameters
- Creating and implementing parameter fields
- Creating and implementing dynamic and cascading parameter fields—new to XI
- Using parameters with record selections

UNDERSTANDING THE VALUE OF PARAMETERS

By using parameter fields that enable business users to select from a list of one or more parameter field values (such as district, country, or account type), you can make reports more valuable for business users while limiting the volume of data that the report retrieves. For example, a sales report is likely to be more valuable for a sales professional if it allows him to select his specific territory or district, while the report runs more efficiently because it retrieves only the desired data and not an unnecessarily large data set. Parameter fields can prompt users for a variety of information that can be used in a number of flexible ways within reports—good examples include controlling the sort order, grouping order, record selection (filter), report title and descriptions, report language, alerting thresholds, formula inputs, the N value for a Top/Bottom N sorting/grouping, and so on.

Parameter fields prompt report users to enter information by presenting a question that the user must answer before the report is executed. The information that the user enters determines what appears in the resulting report and also how that report is formatted and presented.

One of the greatest benefits of parameter fields for report designers is the opportunity to have a single report service a large audience while also empowering the users to personalize the information they are viewing within the report. Parameter fields can be used in coordination with record selections so that a single report can be segmented many different ways. Parameter values that business users enter can also be used within record selection formulas to determine what data is retrieved from the database.

TIP

> New to version XI is the ability to set the N value of a Top/Bottom N grouping or sorting through a formula. Combining this new functionality with a user-driven parameter enables end users to drive the value of N in a given report. You do this by creating the parameter and then selecting it as the value of the formula for the selected Top/Bottom N formula.

For example, consider a World Sales Report for a large organization. This report could potentially include a tremendous amount of data. Not only is the report itself large, but also many of the business users are not concerned with the entire worldwide scope of the sales data. Rather than allow each salesperson to generate the report to include worldwide data, you can include a parameter dialog that asks the salesperson to select from a list of available countries, as shown in Figure 5.1. The report would then return the results for only these specific countries. Thus, by using a parameter field to enable the salespeople to select from a list of countries, the report becomes more valuable for the business users while also limiting the scope of the query by using the selected parameter value(s) to filter the report and reduce the volume of data retrieved.

5

Figure 5.1
Prompts enable business users to select values to populate the parameter field.

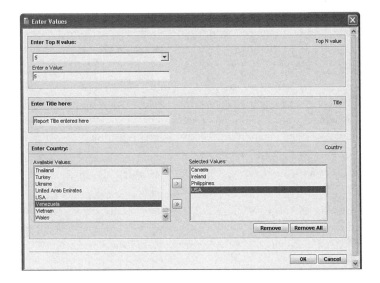

CREATING AND IMPLEMENTING PARAMETERS FIELDS

The process of using parameter fields in reports includes two distinct steps:

1. Creation of the parameter field.
2. Implementation of the parameter field into the report.

The remainder of this chapter uses the example mentioned earlier, the World Sales Report, to create and implement parameter fields into a report. The World Sales Report is one of the many sample reports that are provided by the Crystal Reports installation.

REVIEWING PARAMETER FIELD PROPERTIES

Before you learn how to create and implement parameter fields, it is useful to understand a few common input options and properties associated with creating parameter fields. Each of the following input properties is presented within the Create/Edit Parameter Field dialog, shown in Figure 5.2:

- **Name**—A logical name for the parameter field.
- **Value Type**—A list of available field types that correspond to how you want to use the parameter field within the report, including String (the default option), Boolean, Currency, Date, Date Time, Number, and Time.
- **List of Values Type**—New to XI, you now have the option of sourcing a list of values for the involved parameter from either a static list that does not change over time, or from a dynamic list that is updated regularly or is live. The dynamic list of values can also be cascading and include multiple levels of selection with increasing granularity and filtering as you move through the levels (for instance, selecting a Country leads to a filtered list of states/provinces for end-user selection at the next level and so on).
- **Static List of Values—Value Field**—A drop-down box available when Static is selected as the List of Values type that enables you to specify the list of available parameter values based on a database field. After a desired database field is selected here, you can add the values to the involved parameter through the Action drop-down list and by selecting the Append All Database Values option.
- **Static List of Values—Description Field**—A drop-down box available when Static is selected as the List of Values type that enables you to specify default parameter descriptions based on a database field. This is an optional field that is typically used to facilitate an end user's understanding of the parameter selection.
- **Static List of Values—Action drop-down box**—A list of options that enable the insertion of values from database fields, the clearing of all values, or the import and export of the existing list of values into text files.
- **Static List of Values—Value Table Field**—A table column that is available when Static is selected as the List of Values type that enables you to manually specify an entry for a value in the list of available parameter values.

- **Static List of Values—Description Table Field**—A table column that is available when Static is selected as the List of Values type that enables you to manually specify an entry for a description in the list of available parameter descriptions.

- **Dynamic List of Values—Prompt Group Text**—An optional title that is displayed to end users when they are prompted for the list of dynamic and potentially cascading report parameters. This is typically only used when cascading parameters are used, as it redundant otherwise.

- **Dynamic List of Values—Choose a Data Source**—A user selection enabling either creation of a new set of dynamic parameters or use of an existing list of values. The existing option will only be provided if existing lists of values are present in the report or you are attached to a BusinessObjects Enterprise repository that has them.

- **Dynamic List of Values—Value Table Field**—A table column that is available when Dynamic is selected as the List of Values type that enables you to specify the list of available parameter values based on a database field.

- **Dynamic List of Values—Description Table Field**—A table column that is available when Dynamic is selected as the List of Values type that enables you to specify the list of available parameter descriptions based on a database field.

- **Dynamic List of Values—Parameter Table Field**—A table column that is available when Dynamic is selected as the List of Values type that enables you to create a parameter in the underlying report that is automatically used in the creation of the involved cascading parameter.

- **Prompting Text**—A statement or question presented to the business user within the report prompt dialog for the parameter field.

- **Prompt with Description Only**—A Boolean option that allows the report designer to prompt end users with only a parameter value description (if set to True) or both the parameter value and description (if set to False).

- **Sort Order**—Enables specification of the sort order and the sort field that the parameter values are sorted on.

- **Default Value**—An option that allows the report designer to set a default value for the static list of values.

- **Allow Custom Values**—An option that enables the business user to enter a custom parameter (if set to True). If set to False, end users are only able to select predetermined parameter values.

- **Allow Multiple Values**—Enables the business user to enter more than a single value for the parameter field.

- **Allow Discrete Values**—Enables the business user to enter only a single value for the parameter field.

- **Allow Range Values**—Enables the business user to specify a range, using start and end values, for the parameter field.

- **Length Limit**—The minimum and maximum length limits for the parameter field.

5

- **Edit Mask**—Used to enter an Edit Mask for string data types rather than specifying a range of values. The Edit Mask can be any of a set of *masking characters* used to restrict the values you can enter as parameter values. (The Edit Mask also limits the values you can enter as default prompting values.) Table 5.1 provides a listing of the masking characters and instructions on how to use them.

TABLE 5.1 EDIT MASK CHARACTERS

Mask Character	Mask Description
A	Requires entry of an alphanumeric character for its place in the parameter value.
a	Enables an alphanumeric character but does not require the entry of a character for its place in the parameter value.
0	Requires a digit (0 to 9) for its place in the parameter value.
9	Enables a digit or a space but does not require such an entry for its place in the parameter value.
#	Enables a digit, space, or plus/minus sign, but does not require such an entry for its place in the parameter value.
L	Requires a letter (A to Z) for its place in the parameter value.
?	Enables a letter but does not require such an entry for its place in the parameter value.
&	Requires a character or space for its place in the parameter value.
C	Enables any character or space but does not require such an entry for its place in the parameter value.
. , : ; - / (separator characters)	Inserting separator characters into an Edit Mask is akin to hard-coding the formatting for the parameter field. When the field is placed on the report, the separator character appears in the field object frame, like this: L0L-0L0. This example epicts an edit mask for a Canadian Postal Code (such as M2M-2L5) with a forced display dash.
< or >	Forces subsequent characters in the parameter to be converted to lowercase (<) or uppercase (>).
\	Forces the subsequent character to be displayed as a literal.
Password	Enables the setting of the Edit Mask to "Password," so that subsequent conditional formulas can specify that certain sections of the report become visible only when certain user passwords are entered.

Now that you have been exposed to the primary parameter field properties, you will use these items while creating parameters for a World Sales Report, as referenced earlier in the chapter.

Figure 5.2
The parameter field options and properties are presented within the Create/Edit Parameter Field dialogs.

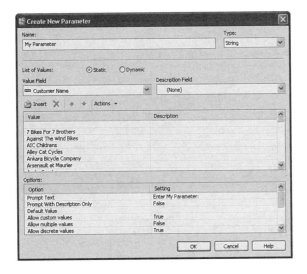

CREATING PARAMETER FIELDS

The first step in using parameters within a report is to create the actual parameter field and define the primary properties associated with it. In the following exercises, you will use the Field Explorer dialog to create three new parameter fields for the World Sales Report:

- A manual text entry field to use as the report's title
- A database field that prompts the business user to select one or more countries and use this selection to filter the data returned for the report
- A Top N parameter field that specifies how many countries are displayed in the edited World Sales report.

To begin your exercise, open the World Sales sample report within the Crystal Reports designer. You can quickly access all the sample reports from the Sample Reports link on the Crystal Reports start page. This sample report should be installed in the following directory, unless you have chosen an alternative location for the sample reports during the Crystal Reports XI installation process:

C:\Program Files\Business Objects\Crystal Reports 11\Samples\en\Reports\General Business

After you have opened this sample report, you can begin the steps necessary to create the parameter field objects in the following way:

1. Remove the existing report title text object. After you have opened the World Sales Report, navigate to the Design tab view, highlight and delete the text object currently used as the report's title that reads World Sales Report, located in the Report Header A section. You will use your parameter field, created below, to populate the report title.

2. Open the Field Explorer dialog by either clicking the appropriate toolbar button or using the View menu.

Open the Create Parameter Field dialog. To do this, right-click on Parameter Fields within the Field Explorer and either select New from the pop-up menu or click on the New button at the top of the Field Explorer.

> In addition to using the right-click menu to create a new parameter field, you can use the Field Explorer's toolbar commands to create, edit, rename, and delete parameter fields. The operations available on this toolbar depend on what you have selected in the Field Explorer dialog. Also new to XI is the ability to sort the parameter's display order to end users through the Parameter Order dialog displayed in Figure 5.3. This option is accessed from the right-click menu on the Parameter sections of the Field Explorer.

Figure 5.3
Use the Parameter Order dialog to control the order that parameters are presented to the end user.

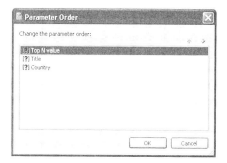

You first create a manual text-entry parameter field to enable the business user to define a title to display on the report. Within the Create Parameter Field, enter `Title` in the Name property, ensure String is the selected Value Type, and provide a meaningful prompting text so that the business user understands how the entered value is used, such as, **Enter a title to be used for this report**.

Ensure that both the Allow Discrete Values and the Allow Custom Values properties under the Options area are set to True and click OK to return to the Field Explorer.

You should now see the `Title` parameter field listed under Parameter Fields in the Field Explorer. Insert this Title field onto the report in the Report Heading using either the right-click menu option or by dragging and dropping the field onto the report. The results are shown in Figure 5.4.

You now create two more parameter fields to use later in the chapter when discussing how to use parameter fields in coordination with record and Top N selections. Once you learn this technique, you can enable your end users to select filters on the involved report data according to their selected parameter values.

Open the Create Parameter Field dialog. To do this, highlight the Parameter Fields item and click the New toolbar button inside the Field Explorer dialog.

Figure 5.4
The Field Explorer is used to access, edit, and create parameter fields.

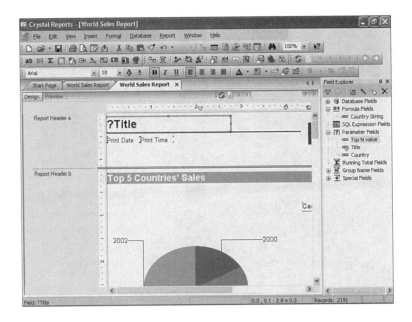

9. Define the key properties for the first parameter object. Within the Create Parameter Field dialog, enter **Top N Value** in the Name property, select Number as the Parameter Type, and provide a meaningful prompting text so the business user understands how the entered value will be used, such as, **Please select the top N selling countries to display on this report**.

10. Ensure that both the Allow Custom Values and Allow Discrete Value(s) properties under the Options area are set to True. The Allow Multiple Values property should be set to False.

11. Create another parameter called Countries. Within the Create Parameter Field dialog, enter **Countries** in the Name property and provide a meaningful prompting text so that the business user understands how the entered value will be used, such as, **Please select one or more countries for this report**.

12. Ensure that both the Allow Multiple Values and Allow Discrete Value(s) properties under the Options area are set to True, as shown in Figure 5.5.

SETTING DEFAULT VALUES FOR PARAMETER FIELDS

You now want to define the Countries parameter field to include all database values within the Country field of the Customer table. This can be accomplished by mapping the parameter field to this database field and quickly importing these values. This enables the business user of the report to select one or more country values from the available list.

5

When setting default parameter values for a static parameter, a list of default values can be read from the database or entered manually to provide the business user with a list of available values from which to choose. With static parameters, the Crystal Reports application enables you to define the default values list when you are designing reports, and no direct database connection exists to populate the prompting parameter field list when the business users run the report. New to XI, Crystal Reports now enables the creation of dynamic parameters that access an underlying database in real-time when a business user is running the report. These will be covered later in this chapter. For now, populate the static Country parameter by following these steps:

Access the Create/Edit Parameter dialog if you have closed it by highlighting the Countries parameter and clicking on the Edit toolbar button. In the Value drop-down list, select the Country field from the Customer table and then select the Append All Database Values action from the Actions drop-down list. All countries listed in that table will be added as parameter options for this report parameter, as shown in Figure 5.6.

Continuing the process started above, now add descriptions to the default values that you have added to the parameter field.

Locate and highlight the USA value in the Default Values list. Click in the Define Description field located just beside the Values field displaying USA.

Add **United States of America** as the description for USA and click OK to close the Edit Parameter dialog. If you want, repeat this step for any additional default values.

Click OK to return to the Field Explorer. You should now see the Countries and Top N Values parameter fields listed under Parameter Fields in the Field Explorer. These parameters are now part of your Crystal Report but will not become functional filters until you attach them to record selection criteria, as described in the next section.

Figure 5.6
The Edit Parameters dialog enables you to define the default selection values for parameter fields.

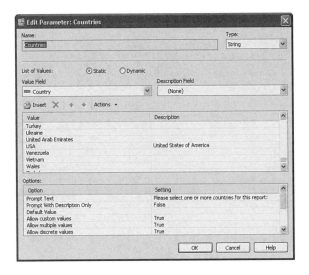

TIP

There are a few considerations to keep in mind when working with parameter fields, such as

- Any parameter field prompting text more than one line in length will automatically word wrap.
- The creation of a pick list enables the business user to select parameter field values from drop-down boxes instead of needing to enter them manually.
- A parameter field does not have to be placed in a report to be used in a record or group selection formula. You can create the parameter field and then enter it in your formula as you would any other field.

IMPLEMENTING PARAMETER FIELDS

You have now completed the first task necessary to use parameter fields within a report—creating the actual parameter field objects. This section, and the exercises included here, discuss how to apply these parameter fields and make use of them to provide the business user of the report with a more dynamic and interactive reporting experience.

First, add the parameter fields created earlier, called Title, Countries, and Top N Value to be displayed on the report. This example demonstrates how different parameter fields can be used to add useful commentary or descriptive information to a report. Continue working with the same report, the World Sales Report and follow these steps:

1. Add and position the Title, Countries, and Top N Value parameter objects onto the report. Open the Field Explorer dialog and expand the Parameter Fields list. Click on the Title parameter field, drag it onto the report, and drop it into the upper-left corner of the Report Header A section, shown in Figure 5.7 in a size 20 Arial font. Place the Countries and Top N Value parameter in the same section with size 10 Arial font.

Drag and drop the parameter fields into the left side of the Report Header A section.

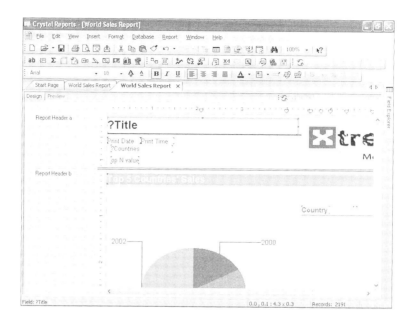

Preview the report. To view how this parameter is now used within the generation of the report, run the report by clicking on the Refresh toolbar button (represented by the two blue arrows indicating a counter-clockwise rotation). As shown in Figure 5.8, the report now prompts the business user to enter a value that will be used as the report's title.

If you have already run the report at least once and then select to refresh the report, you will also see the Refresh Report Data dialog that asks you to select from the following two options:

- Use Current Parameter Values
- Prompt for New Parameter Values

To enter or select new values for any existing parameter fields, you need to select the second option—Prompt for New Parameter Values.

Figure 5.8
Parameter fields offer a means to add additional interactivity for the business users within the report.

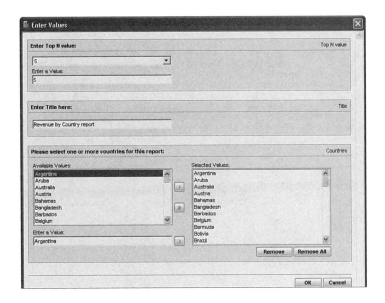

USING PARAMETERS WITH RECORD SELECTIONS

Now that you have completed the task of implementing a parameter field within a report, you learn how a parameter field can also be used to filter the data retrieved by a report. Parameter values that business users enter can be used within record selection formulas to determine what data is retrieved from the database.

In the following exercises, use the same World Sales Report to implement the Countries parameter field (created earlier in the chapter) to filter the report results by including the parameter field within a record selection definition (using the Select Expert dialog). In this case, you enable the business user of the report to select one or more country values to be included in the record selection, thus filtering the report results to include only the desired data. The following steps demonstrate how a single report can be segmented many different ways:

1. Open the Select Expert dialog by clicking the Report menu and choosing Select Expert.

2. Create a new record selection definition. Within the Select Expert dialog, click on the <New> tab to create a new record selection definition. This opens the Choose Field dialog. Choose Customer.Country from the Report Fields list and then click OK to return to the Select Expert dialog.

3. Define the selection formula. Select Is Equal To from the drop-down list on the left, and then choose the {?Countries} option from the drop-down list on the right, as shown in Figure 5.9.

Parameter Field objects are denoted with the question mark, ?, and enclosed in brackets, {}. This convention is used within various application dialogs, including the formula workshop and record selections, to signify that these objects are parameter fields.

Figure 5.9
Parameter fields can be added to record selection formulas quickly via the Select Expert dialog.

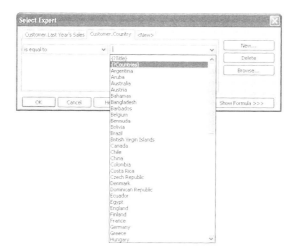

4. Preview the report. To view how this parameter is now used within the generation of the report, run the report by clicking on the Refresh toolbar button. As shown in Figures 5.10 and 5.11, the report now prompts the business user to select from a list of country values that is used to filter the data retrieved by the report and present only the requested values in the report.

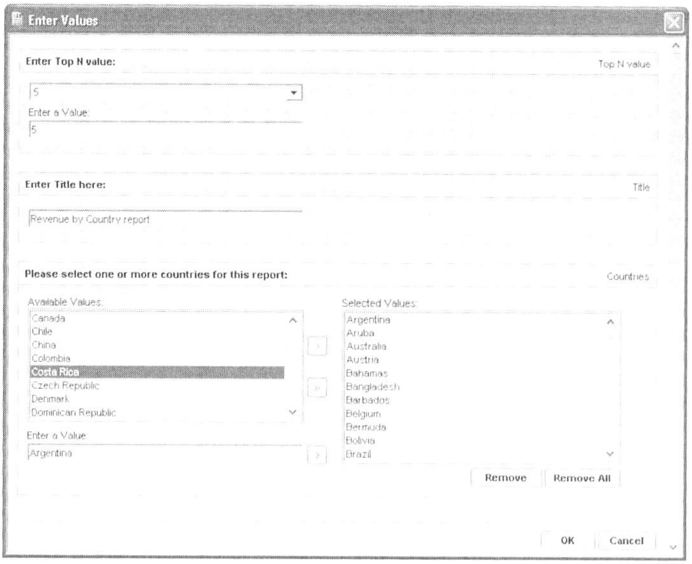

Figure 5.10
Business users can now select one or more countries to be included in the report results.

Figure 5.11
Based on the selected parameter field values, the report results display only the desired data.

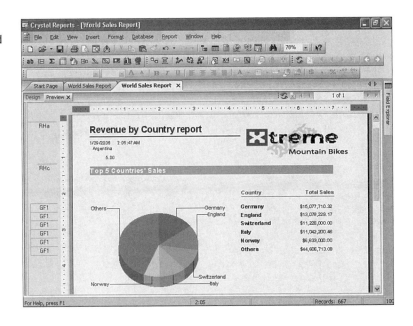

TIP

As Figure 5.11 highlights, when adding a multivalue parameter (Countries in this case) to a report for display, only the first value is displayed. This is because the multiple values of the parameter are stored in an array and the Parameter field only shows the first element of the array by default. To show different values, you can create a formula with the parameter and an index (for instance, {?Countries}[2] to show the second country in the list). To show all the values, you could create a formula like this:

```
Local StringVar CountryString := "";
Local NumberVar i;
For i := 1 To Ubound({?Countries}) Do
(
    CountryString := CountryString + ", " + {?Countries}[i]
);
CountryString
```

USING PARAMETERS WITH TOP/BOTTOM N GROUP SELECTIONS

New to version XI, you can now use a parameter to dynamically affect the value of a top or bottom group selection (for instance, top five countries for sales or top five selling products). You have already completed the task of implementing a parameter field called Top N Value within this chapter's sample report. Now you learn how this parameter field can also be used to filter the data retrieved by a report.

In the following steps, use the same World Sales Report to implement the Top N Values parameter field (created earlier in the chapter) to filter the report results by including the parameter field within a formula definition that specifies the Top (or Bottom) N value (using the Group Sort Expert dialog). In this case, you enable the business user of the report to select a value that will filter the report results to include only the specified number of top-selling countries' data. The following steps demonstrate how this single report can be used to display multiple Top/Bottom N views:

Open the Group Sort Expert dialog displayed in Figure 5.12 by clicking the Report menu and choosing Group Sort Expert. Ensure you are positioned on the Country Group tab.

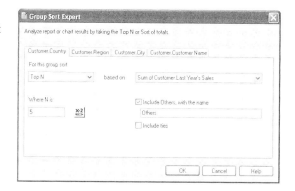

Figure 5.12
The Group Sort Expert enables specification of a dynamic Top/Bottom N value through the x+2 button.

Ensure the Top N sorting order is selected in the first drop-down box and it is based on the Sum of Last Years Sales. Click on the x+2 button beside the Top N value box. This will bring up the Formula Workshop where you add the {?Top N Value} parameter field to the formula. You have now connected the selected number of top-selling countries that will be displayed in the report to the N value specified by the end user through the Top N Value parameter.

Change the value of the various parameters and refresh the report a few times to see the impact of an end user changing just these three parameters.

After the parameters have been created and implemented into a report, no extra effort is required for parameters to also work within the BusinessObjects Enterprise solution. See Part V, "Web Report Distribution–Using BO Enterprise," for more details on BusinessObjects Enterprise.

CREATING AND IMPLEMENTING DYNAMIC AND CASCADING PARAMETERS

New to version XI, Crystal Reports now provides the ability for report parameters to be based on dynamic values derived directly from a database or from the BusinessObjects Enterprise repository (if using BusinessObjects Enterprise). This new functionality enables end users to select from the most recent list of elements dynamically retrieved from the database at run time.

An additional new powerful feature provided in version XI is the ability to link these dynamic parameters together in a cascading manner. These cascading parameters enable end users to select parameter values by entering information at multiple levels, with all levels leading to dynamic filters being applied to all subsequent level parameters. The most common example of this is where a City parameter might be filtered based on the linked Country parameter as described earlier in the chapter. Specifically, if Canada is the only country selected, only cities in Canada are available for selection in the linked City parameter. These dynamic, cascading parameters are set through the same Create Parameter dialog used for static parameters.

The following steps will take you through a practical example of the creation and implementation of a dynamic, cascading set of prompts:

1. Open the sample Chap5 report or the one you have previously created in this chapter, and after removing the Country record selection and the Top N Value formula, delete the existing Countries parameter.

2. Create a new Parameter called Cities with type String and select the Dynamic List of Values type.

3. Ensuring the New radio button is selected, click on the Value field of the parameters table and you are prompted with a drop-down list box where the Country field from the Customer table is selected.

4. Ensure the Allows Multiple Values property is set to True and the Allows Custom Values property is set to False. You have now created Country as the highest level parameter of this group.

5. Now click on the Value field in the next row of the parameters table and you will be prompted with a drop-down list where you select the City field from the Customer table. Ensure the Allows Multiple Values property is set to True and the Allows Custom Values property is set to False. You have now created City as the second and currently lowest-level parameter of this group.

6. To complete the parameter creation process, click on the Parameters fields for each of the Country and City rows in the parameter table. The prompting text of Click to Create a Parameter changes to the specific parameter name consisting of the top level parameter name suffixed by the involved field name. Figure 5.13 highlights what this should look like.

7. Now add a new record selection through the Record Select Expert that filters the report where the City field from the customer table is equal to the newly created parameter `{?Cities - City}`.

8. Finally, refresh the report and you are faced with the parameter selection screen shown in Figure 5.13. Note that as you add countries to the list of countries selected in the Cities parameter group, the list of available cities in the City parameter is dynamically

5

filtered. After testing the filtering process, select USA, Canada, and Ireland as countries with only Las Vegas, Philadelphia, Vancouver, Toronto, and Dublin as selected cities. Click OK and your report resembles something similar to Figure 5.14.

The Create/Edit Parameter dialog enables rapid creation of dynamic and cascading parameters.

The new dynamic and cascading parameter feature enables increased productivity in report design and a better end-user experience.

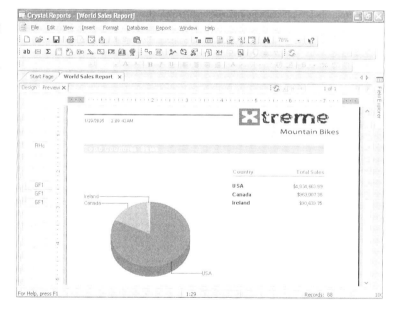

This new powerful cascading parameter feature enables increased end-user productivity through reduced and focused selection sets. When designing reports, careful consideration should be given to use of these dynamic and cascading parameters versus the static parameters. Dynamic parameters are ideally geared for data sets that change frequently. Static parameters might be best used when the involved list of values does not change often because no additional database hits will be required.

TROUBLESHOOTING

PARAMETER REUSE ACROSS REPORTS

Is there a way to store parameters so I can reuse them across multiple reports?

You can store dynamic and cascading parameters' List of Values, and even their associated update schedules, in the repository. However, this is only available for use with the Crystal Reports Server or BusinessObjects Enterprise products.

CRYSTAL REPORTS IN THE REAL WORLD— CUSTOM FILTERING

Sometimes a report needs to return all records for a parameterized field where a record selection filter has been created on this parameter. Although it would certainly be possible to create a parameter and select all valid values for the parameter, there certainly must be a better way—and there is. In this example, a filter is added to a report so that if a user enters a specific value or a list of values, only those values are returned. Alternatively, if the user enters an asterisk (*, or other predefined symbol such as All Values), all values are returned. The following steps highlight this capability:

1. Open the sample report Chap 5.rpt created in the first half of this chapter. Set the Allows Custom Values property to True and Change the Top N sort condition to All in the Group Sorting Expert.

2. From the Report menu choose Selection Formulas, Record. Remove the following line of text.
   ```
   {Customer.Country} = {?Countries}
   ```

3. Replace the text with the following (as shown in Figure 5.15):
   ```
   (If {?Countries} = "*" Then
       True
   Else
       {Customer.Country} = {?Countries};)
   ```

   Click Save and Close.

When prompted for a new parameter value, remove any existing values, enter the * symbol as a manual custom entry, click the Add (>) button to add the symbol to the list of values, and click OK. You should see something like in Figure 5.16.

Figure 5.15
The updated Record Selection Formula Editor enables the end user to select All Values with one easy selection.

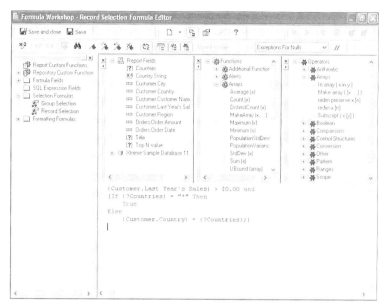

Another way to implement an All Values parameter option for the report consumer is to create a record selection through the Record Selection dialog that uses the `is like` operator instead of the `equals to` operator. Using this operator enables you to use the `*` and `?` wildcards in your filter. By having end users enter `'*'` or providing that as one of the default parameter selection options, the users can specify All Values without needing to add them all independently. One thing to watch for here is that parameters that allow multiple values do not by default allow themselves to be mapped to in the Record Selection dialog with the `is like` operator. A viable workaround, however, is to map the record selection to the parameter using the `equals to` operator and then edit the formula record selection manually and replace the `=` operator with the `like` operator.

Figure 5.16
The report returns all values when * is passed in as a parameter. In this photo, the chart has been edited slightly from the original report but you can clearly see that all countries were returned.

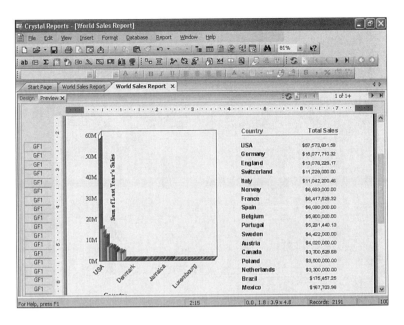

FORMATTING CRYSTAL REPORTS

CHAPTER 6

FUNDAMENTALS OF REPORT FORMATTING

In this chapter

INTRODUCTION

To this point, the majority of material you've seen in this book focused on the various functions of the Crystal Reports design application. Equally important, however, is the form (or format) of the report—especially when a report is used as a corporate or industry-standard document that projects a company's image externally (such as an income statement or balance sheet). This chapter focuses on form over function and discusses a myriad of formatting techniques.

You have already reviewed the Crystal Reports XI development environment and learned about creating a report from a blank canvas, as well as how to select, group, filter, sort, and summarize your report data. Now, you move on to the cosmetic aspects of report design. Working with report formatting and object properties to create professionally designed reports is very straightforward, but does require familiarity with various features of the design-application environment. This chapter reviews the most commonly used object formatting techniques—fonts, borders, page and margin properties, and object layering—and also provides a tutorial to apply these techniques to one of the sample reports created earlier in the book.

This chapter covers the following topics:

- Positioning and sizing report objects
- Modifying object properties for formatting purposes
- Combining and layering report objects
- Configuring report page and margin properties

POSITIONING AND SIZING REPORT OBJECTS

After you have completed your functional report design tasks—connecting to the data source, adding report objects, and structuring the report—the next step in the report design process is to format the various objects on a report. As demonstrated in Chapter 1, "Creating and Designing Basic Reports," objects can be added to a report via a variety of methods—dragging and dropping objects from the design explorers or selecting objects from toolbar and menu commands and placing them in the desired locations—for quick and intuitive report creation. Upon successfully adding objects to your report, each of the respective objects can be positioned, sized, and formatted for display purposes, as demonstrated in the following exercise.

As a visual example of the difference that report formatting efforts can make, compare the presentation value of the report samples shown in Figures 6.1 and 6.2. These two reports accomplish the same functional tasks, but the report in Figure 6.2 is much more visually appealing.

Figure 6.1
A customer contact listing report with little to no formatting applied.

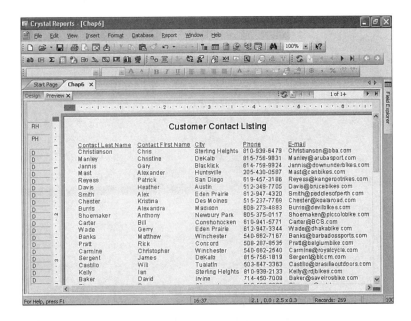

Figure 6.2
A customer contact listing report with a moderate amount of formatting applied.

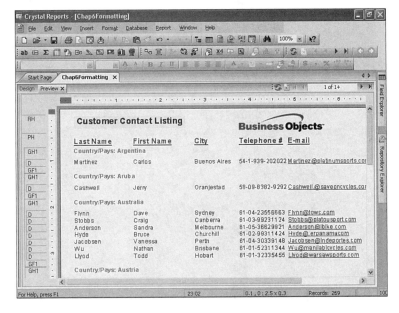

You will spend the remainder of this chapter reproducing many of the visual transformations from Figure 6.1 to Figure 6.2. By completing the following exercises, you create a Customer Contact Listing report using a variety of applied formatting techniques, such as adding a group definition to logically structure customers into their respective countries, and formatting the font styles of the report title, column titles, country description, and e-mail address fields to make for a more precise presentation of the report information. By combining the

Country database field with a text field, you also provide for a bilingual display of the country description.

To begin designing your report, follow these steps to create your own nicely formatted Customer Contact Listing report:

Open the Crystal Reports application and choose to Create a New Report Using the Blank Report Layout from the start page.

From the Database Explorer dialog accessed from the main Database menu, expand the Create a New Connection list, and then expand the ODBC (RDO) node to present the ODBC dialog window that lists the available data sources. Select the Xtreme Sample Database 11 from the list of data sources and click Finish to continue to the Database Expert dialog.

From the Database Expert dialog, use the arrow (>) button to add the Customer table to the Selected Tables list on the right. Click OK to continue.

From the View menu, select the Field Explorer command to open the Field Explorer dialog.

From the Field Explorer, click and drag the Contact Last Name field onto the report's design view and place it to the far left of the Details section area, as shown in Figure 6.3.

Figure 6.3
Add the Contact Last Name field to the Details section of the report.

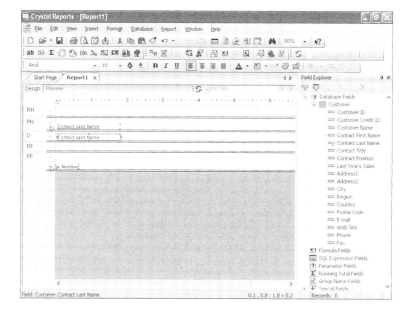

Follow the previous step to add the Contact First Name, City, and E-mail fields to the Details section of the report, as shown in Figure 6.4.

From the Insert menu, select Text Object and drop the object into the middle of the Report Header section and type **Customer Contact Listing** in the text field. Click anywhere outside the text object to remove the cursor focus from the text object and now increase the size of this field by changing the font size through the Formatting toolbar to size 14.

Figure 6.4
The selected fields displayed within the respective sections of the report and a hidden Field Explorer dialog.

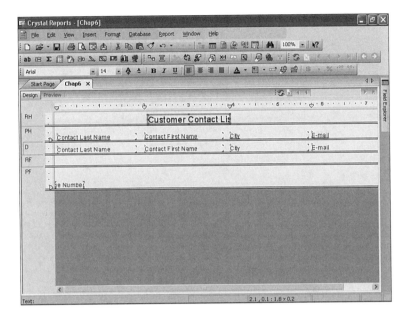

Now that the report includes the field and text objects identified previously, focus on positioning and resizing these fields for display purposes.

8. As Figure 6.4 shows, now you might not be able to see the entire text entered into the report title text object because it is not wide enough to display the text entry by default. To resolve this, click once on the report title text object located in the Report Header section so that it becomes highlighted. Using the dark blue handles that encompass the objects perimeters, float over the handle located on the right side of the text object with the mouse pointer; then click and hold the mouse button while dragging the handle farther to the right to widen the text object's display area. Refer to Figure 6.5 to see the result of this action.

NOTE

Notice that when you float over the perimeter handles of an object with your mouse cursor (or pointer), the cursor icon turns into an alternative shape, such as horizontal or vertical arrows, to illustrate that you can modify the object if you click on the handle.

9. Now that you have widened the display area of your report title object using the concept of object handles, repeat this same step to modify the width of the field objects within the Details report section so that you can insert one additional object into the Details section of your report between the City and E-mail fields. To facilitate this

resizing, you can view the report through the Preview tab and dynamically see the affect of your resizing on the resultant data and the report's appearance.

Using the Field Explorer, insert the Phone database field from the Customer table into the Details section of your report. Based on the previous steps, practice positioning and sizing the objects in the Details section to accommodate for all the database fields, as shown in Figure 6.5.

Although many formatting activities can be exercised on field objects in both the design and preview tabs, some formatting facilities are only available within the Design tab. One useful feature to take note of is the capability to move a highlighted field (or even a set of fields) and its associated column title with the arrow keys on your keypad. This technique is a great help when you're moving report fields around as you did in step 9.

The sample report preview displays five database field objects in the Details section, five database field column header text fields in the Page Header, and one text object in the Report Header section.

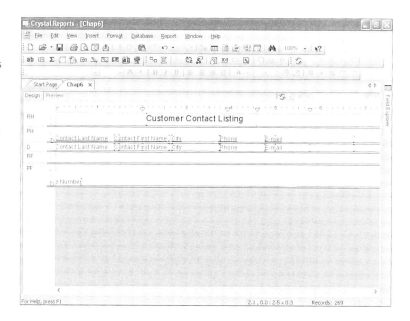

As you might have noticed, the field sizes are often large enough to show the entire field name in the Design view of the report. But from the Preview tab view of the report, you see that fields (such as the E-mail or Phone fields here) are cut off from the display area. This is not unusual, and it might require you to resize the field objects to ensure that they are appropriate for the report display area. It is often useful to use the report's Preview tab as the active window when finalizing the formatting and layout of your reports.

Now click the Preview tab to see a preview display of what the report actually looks like, as shown in Figure 6.6.

NOTE

> If the Preview tab is not displayed in the application, you have not yet run the report against the database. To run the report, click the Refresh toolbar icon to execute the report to run—the Refresh toolbar icon is represented by the two blue arrows indicating a counter-clockwise rotation.

Figure 6.6
To preview your report, either select the Preview tab or click the Refresh button.

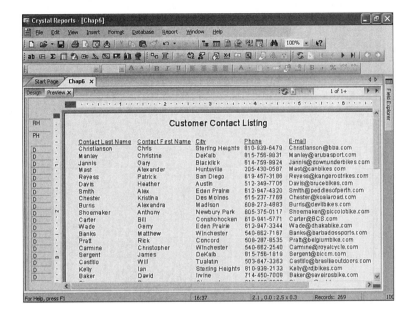

NOTE

> Although it's important to understand the basics of report formatting, you will not necessarily have to go through the often arduous process of formatting reports every time. Report templates can be used to apply predefined and meaningful formatting characteristics in a very quick manner. Additionally, object formatting can be copied from existing objects to other unformatted objects through use of the Format Painter introduced in version 10. The Format Painter is accessed through the right-click menu of any object whose format you wish to copy.

→ For more details on designing and using report templates, **see** "Creating Useful Report Templates," **p. 324**.

MODIFYING OBJECT PROPERTIES FOR FORMATTING PURPOSES

Now that the foundation of our report is complete, it is time to focus on how to improve the form and aesthetic appearance of the report.

By modifying various object properties, the presentation value of the report can be greatly improved. In doing so, you will be using the Format Editor to access a variety of specific properties, such as fonts, borders, colors, and alignment. The Format Editor is a commonly used dialog to quickly and easily modify all report objects, and its contents are reflective of the specific object type being formatted (text, chart, database field, and so on). To explore these formatting capabilities, follow these steps:

1. Continuing with the report from the chapter's earlier exercise, return to the Design tab of your report and right-click on the report title text object (located in the Report Header section) and select the Format Text option from the list, as shown in Figure 6.7. This opens the Format Editor dialog.

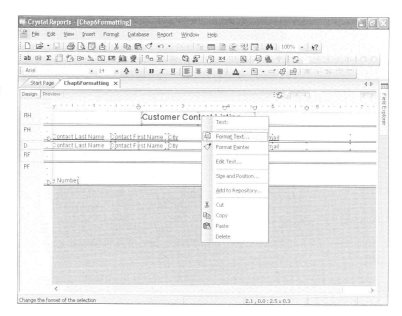

Figure 6.7
The Format Editor dialog is accessed from the right-click pop-up menu on most Crystal Reports's objects.

2. The Format Editor dialog (displayed in Figure 6.8) enables you to set and adjust a variety of properties of the object. For this exercise, navigate to the Font tab of the Format Editor and select the Bold font style, a font size of 14, and a font color of Red. Also, select the Paragraph tab of the Format Editor and choose Centered from the Horizontal Alignment drop-down list.

3. Now select the Border tab from within the Format Editor and then select Single from each of the four border Line Style drop-down lists (left, right, top, and bottom). Under Color, click the Background check box and select Yellow from the drop-down list as the background color. Based on all of your selected properties in the Format Editor, you should now see a representative example of the text object in the Sample area at the bottom of the dialog box. Click OK to save these settings and return to the Design tab on your report.

4. To improve the effectiveness of your report, you can modify the database field column titles to provide more meaningful descriptions for the business users of your report. Working within the Design tab of your report, double-click on the Phone title object in

the Page Header section of the report. When the cursor's focus is on this object, you can delete, append, or update the text as you choose. Modify this text to read **Telephone #** and then click anywhere outside the object to remove the cursor's focus from the object.

Figure 6.8
The Format Editor dialog provides quick and easy access to a variety of report object properties.

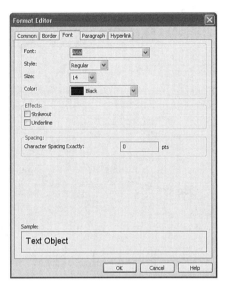

As an alternative to the Format Editor, you can also use the toolbars and menu commands to quickly apply common formatting techniques, such as font and alignment characteristics.

5. From the View menu, select Toolbars to present the Toolbar dialog. Make sure that the Standard, Formatting, and Insert toolbar items are all selected and click OK.

6. Click on the Preview tab to see a preview display of what the report will actually look like. Again, if the Preview tab is not displayed in the application, click the Refresh toolbar button to execute the report. From the Preview mode, hold down either the Shift or Ctrl key on your keyboard and click each of the five column titles so that they are all highlighted with a dashed perimeter. With all five columns title fields highlighted, click the Bold toolbar button, represented with a large bold letter B on the formatting toolbar. Refer to Figure 6.9 to see the results of this action.

7. With the five column title fields still highlighted, click the downward arrow located on the Font Color toolbar button, represented with an underlined letter A on the formatting toolbar. Select the bright blue color from the available list, as shown in Figure 6.9. Lastly, remove the contact prefix for the name fields and increase the size of these column titles to font size 12 with either the font size drop-down box or the A+ increase font size button. The fields might need to be stretched vertically to fit the new font size but can eventually be made to look like Figure 6.9.

6

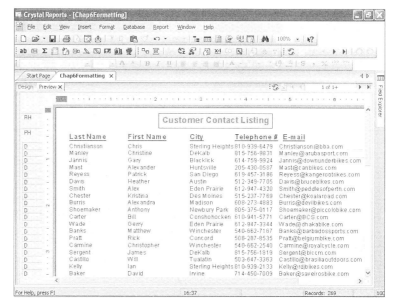

To make the E-mail field appear more meaningful to the business users of the report, let's format the E-mail database field values to resemble and behave like standard hyperlink text.

8. To remove the cursor focus from the five column titles fields, click anywhere outside these field areas or press the Esc (escape) key on your keyboard.

9. In the Preview tab, click any of the actual E-mail field values to highlight the E-mail database field objects and right-click on the same object to present the pop-up menu. From the pop-up menu, shown in Figure 6.10, select the Format Field item.

10. Select the Hyperlink tab after you have opened the Format Editor. From the available Hyperlink Types, select Current E-mail Field Value—this option automatically creates a hyperlink based on the values stored within this field in the data source assuming that these values are formatted as proper e-mail addresses in the data source, such as abc@domain.com.

NOTE

You can use the Hyperlink tab within the Format Editor to create hyperlinks to a website, e-mail address, file, or another Crystal Report. A hyperlink is saved with your report and is available to other users as a way of linking to additional external information from your report. Hyperlink definitions can also be defined by formulas thus enabling context-sensitive, data-driven hyperlinks—a very powerful feature of Crystal Reports.

11. Now let's make the E-mail field appear as a standard hyperlink value, commonly known to have a blue underlined font style. Select the Font tab within the Format Editor dialog to apply the blue font color and select the Underline check box. Click OK to return

to the report Preview, and then press Esc to remove the cursor focus from all report objects.

Figure 6.10
Right-clicking on any field object presents you with a list of commands for that particular object.

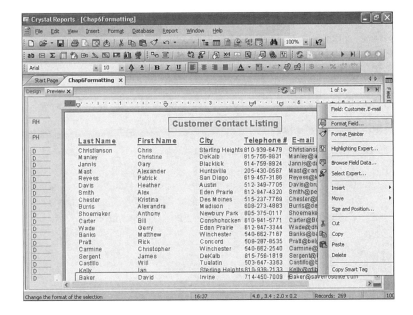

12. Based on the completion of the previous step, your mouse pointer should now change into a hand icon as it floats over any of the E-mail field values on the report. This indicates that upon clicking on any of the E-mail values, you initiate an e-mail message to be sent to that address, as shown in Figure 6.11.

Figure 6.11
By applying an e-mail hyperlink, report end users can initiate a context-sensitive e-mail to any of the respective customer contacts.

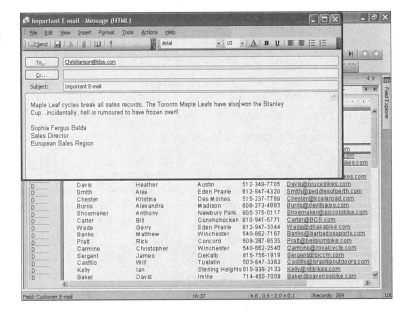

By using the Format Editor, as well as the Toolbar commands, to modify report object properties, you have very quickly and easily enhanced your report's presentation quality. Not only did you enhance this report example visually, but you also easily incorporated hyperlink functionality to add an additional level of interactivity to your report.

For more information on using hyperlink functionality in reports, see Chapter 9, "Custom Formatting Techniques."

EXPLORING THE FORMAT EDITOR DIALOG COMMON OPTIONS

The previous exercises introduced the Format Editor—the dialog where the appearance of report fields and other report objects can be manipulated. Different Crystal Reports objects present different tabs within the Format Editor and each provides specific editing functionality for the underlying object types (such as Date and Time, Boolean, Hyperlink, and so on). The next few sections introduce the most commonly used tabs and underlying formatting options.

THE COMMON TAB OF THE FORMAT EDITOR

The Common tab of the Format Editor provides basic functionality for the majority of Crystal Reports' objects. The most commonly used formatting features accessed through this tab include the following:

- **Object Name**—Assigned by default, this name is referenced primarily for use with Report Part Viewing (that is, when specifying which report parts to view in a report parts viewer).

- **ToolTip Text**—Enables a text bubble to be displayed as the end user hovers over report fields. A common and powerful use of ToolTips is to provide the end users with a database-driven description of the involved field from an associated meta-data table. To see this functionality in Design and Preview tabs, the ToolTips option must be turned on under the Layout tab of the Options dialog, accessed under the File menu.

- **Read Only**—This option makes the selected report object read-only so it can't be formatted. When this option is selected, all other choices in the Format Editor except Repeat on Horizontal Pages and Lock Position and Size become inactive.

- **Lock Position and Size**—This option locks the position of the selected report object so it can't be moved or resized.

- **Suppress**—Enables the suppression of the selected object in the Preview tab and on any report printing. This option is often used with intermediary formula components that the end user is not intended to view or on fields that the user is only meant to view conditionally. The x+2 button is used to suppress (or display) the selected field based on certain data conditions being met (for example, only show "ALERT" text object if Shipping Date is five or more days after Order Date for a specified field) .

- **Suppress if Duplicated**—This option enables the suppression of repeated field names in a report.

- **Can Grow**—Enables for variable length fields to grow vertically in the report and word wrap automatically. A maximum number of lines can be set with this option to control rogue or large data elements.

- **Text Rotation**—Enables the rotated display of the involved object by 90° or 270°. This feature is highlighted in Chapter 9.

- **Horizontal Alignment**—Provides the capability to align the data within an object either left, center, right, or both justified.

- **Display String**—This Custom String functionality enables the conditional formatting and display of field types (for example, number, currency, date, time, date and time, Boolean, string, running total, formulas, parameters, and so on) as a custom string (for example, displaying the number 1,500,000 as the custom string 1.5M). The following sample formula snippet highlights how this would work:

```
Switch (
CurrentFieldValue > 1000000000, ToText(CurrentFieldValue/1000000000, 2) + "B",
CurrentFieldValue > 1000000, ToText(CurrentFieldValue/1000000, 2) + "M",
CurrentFieldValue > 1000, ToText(CurrentFieldValue/1000, 2) + "K",
True, ToText(CurrentFieldValue, 2))
```

- **CSS Class Name**—Provides the capability for Crystal Reports to leverage existing CSS stylesheet classes when deployed in a Web application or with BusinessObjects Enterprise.

- **Repeat on Horizontal Pages**—Introduced in version 10, this option enables the repetition of a report object that does not expand horizontally (such as text objects, field objects, OLE objects, charts, maps, lines, boxes, and so on) for each additional horizontal page that a cross-tab or OLAP grid might create as they expand horizontally.

- **Keep Object Together**—This option keeps an object on a single page. If there is enough room, the program prints the object on the current page. If there is not enough room, the program prints the object on the next page. This is clearly not possible with objects that span over a single page.

- **Close Border on Page Break**—This functionality ensures that borders created on the object close at the bottom of any page and begin again as the object is continued on the next page. This provides for a much slicker-looking border format for your reports.

6

THE BORDER TAB OF THE FORMAT EDITOR

The Border tab of the Format Editor provides border, background, and drop-shadow formatting functionality for Crystal Report objects. The most commonly used formatting features accessed through this tab include the following:

- **Line Style drop-down boxes**—The Left, Right, Top, and Bottom drop-down boxes enable specification of the different types of supported borders (Single, Double, Dashed, or Dotted). For Basic borders, this functionality is more easily accessed through the Borders button on the Formatting toolbar.

- **Tight Horizontal**—This option specifies that a border tightly wraps around the involved object's contents and not the entire field as placed on the report (that is, no spaces are included within the border).

- **Drop Shadow**—This format prints a drop shadow to the right and below the specified object.

- **Border Color**—The color of the border and drop shadow is specified here through the drop-down box.

- **Background Color**—The background check box enables you to specify that a background be displayed for the given field. An additional drop-down box enables you to select the color for the background after the check box has been selected.

THE FONT TAB OF THE FORMAT EDITOR

The Font tab of the Format Editor provides the capability to change the fonts, font size, and font style for text and data fields in your Crystal Reports. The most commonly used formatting features accessed through this tab include the following:

- **Font, Style, Size, and Color**—Enable the designer to specify a variety of available formatting fonts (such as Arial, Courier, Verdana, Times Roman, and so on), styles (such as Bold and Italics), sizes including manually entered 1/2 sizes and colors.

- **Strikeout and Underline**—Enable you to specify the selected formatting on the current report object.

- **Character Spacing Exactly**—Use this option to specify the space that each character in the selected font occupies. The value is defined as the distance in number of points measured from the start of one character to the start of the next. When the character spacing is edited, only the spacing between adjacent characters is changed—not the actual font size of the characters. Using 0 enables the default font character spacing.

THE HYPERLINK TAB OF THE FORMAT EDITOR

The Hyperlink tab is used to create hyperlinks to external websites, e-mail addresses, files, or other reports and report objects from report objects within the current report. These hyperlinks can be data-driven (that is, change on the data coming back from the database) and provide a rather intuitive method for integrating Crystal Reports into a business workflow. The helpful hint section of this tab provides in-place coaching for each type of hyperlink that is to be used. The most commonly used formatting features accessed through this tab include the following:

- **Website on the Internet**—Enables the specification of an external website with or without dynamic context-sensitive components of the URL driven from the database. An example of a context sensitive Web address would be
`http://www.google.com/search?q=` + `{Customer.Customer Name}` where the link would take the end user to a Google search page full of results based on the current value of the customer name.

- **E-mail address**—Enables you to add a link to an e-mail address that would need to be typed into the E-mail address text box or through the associated formula editor x+2 button.

- **File**—Enables the linked upon object to call a specified file and launch its associated application upon end-user activation of this link. Report Designers can specify EXE files with command line parameters through the formula editor accessed by the x+2 button.

- **Current website or E-mail Field Value**—Creates a website or e-mail link to the underlying object on which the hyperlink is being created. The formatting of the data for the involved field must be correct (that is, a proper e-mail address or website URL).

- **Report Part Drilldown**—The Report Part Drilldown option lets you define a hyperlink so that the Report Part Viewer can emulate the drill-down functionality of Crystal Reports. The Report Part Viewer displays only destination objects; therefore, to make drill down work, you need to define a navigation path from a home object to one or more destination objects, all residing in the same report section. Initial Report Part specification for a given Crystal Report is set within the Report Options dialog accessed from the main File menu. The drill-down path is then set for each Report Part in the navigation path through this option. Not all Crystal Reports objects have this option available based on their report section location and their type of object.

- **Another Report Object**—This option enables the definition of a hyperlink to objects in the same or different reports. When defining a hyperlink path to a different report, that report must be managed in a BusinessObjects Enterprise environment. To specify report objects, they must be copied using the right-click Copy command from their source report and then pasted into the current object's Hyperlink tab using the Paste Link button.

OTHER FORMAT EDITOR TABS

The remaining tabs found in the Format Editor are dependent on the type of object selected in the involved Crystal Report. The other tabs that you find and some of the most common formatting options provided in each are as follows:

- **Paragraph tab**—Enables you to specify formatting for string/text fields including spacing, reading order, and horizontal alignment.

- **Numbers tab**—Enables detailed formatting on numbers and currency objects including the handling of zeros, decimal point specification, negative number formatting, rounding, and thousands separator specification. The Customize button enables access to the majority of these formatting features.

- **Date and Time tab**—Provides detailed formatting on dates, times, and `datetime` objects. Many default display options are available with a great deal of granularity provided through the Customize button.

6

- **Boolean tab**—Enables the selection of the format for the return values of Boolean field objects.
- **Box, Line, Rounding, Subreport, and Picture tabs**—Provide for granular level formatting of each of the involved Crystal Reports' objects.

COMBINING AND LAYERING REPORT OBJECTS

The concepts of combining and layering report objects becomes relevant when you need to precisely control the relationship between two or more objects when occupying a common space on the report. For example, assume that rather than having your country field read USA, you would like to combine the Country database field with a text object so that it reads Country/Pays: USA—displaying the textual description for country in both English and French. To accomplish this, you can easily combine a text and a database field into one common report object.

The previous exercises can be enhanced by adding a more descriptive text object to your report as that described above. To complete this, start by adding a group definition to your report. The group definition enables you to logically present each customer within the country in which they are located. To add this grouping, perform the following steps:

From the Insert menu, select Group to present the Insert Group dialog. Select the Country field (located under the Customer table) from the uppermost drop-down list. Leave the sort order as Ascending and click OK to return to the report.

Verify that you are working in the Design view of the report—click on the Design tab if necessary. You should now see two new sections listed in the left column area of the design environment—Group Header #1 and Group Footer #1. From the Insert menu, select Text Object and drop the object to the right of the Group #1 Name field in the Group Header section. Type **Country/Pays:** for the textual content of this new object (including a space after the colon), as shown in Figure 6.12.

Highlight the Group #1 Name field object, click and drag it over the new text object field (you can drag the entire object after the mouse pointer has turned into a four-way cross icon), and drop it onto the text object when the flashing vertical cursor indicates that it falls precisely to the right of the textual description you have entered.

> Dragging and dropping objects to combine them is a very precise maneuver and might require some practice. If you have dropped the Group Name field in the wrong place, click the Undo button (curved arrow pointing backward) and try again until you are comfortable and successful with this technique.

Figure 6.12
The Insert menu enables you to quickly add a group and text object into your report. The resultant group and text object are shown here in the Report Designer.

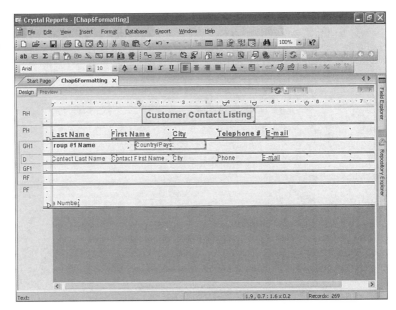

4. After you have successfully combined these objects together, the design application still references the newly combined object as a Text object. You now need to widen the object's display area. Click this object to highlight it and drag the left-side perimeter handle farther to the left until you reach the left margin of the design area, as shown in Figure 6.13.

Figure 6.13
You have now combined a database field object with a text object to form one common report object.

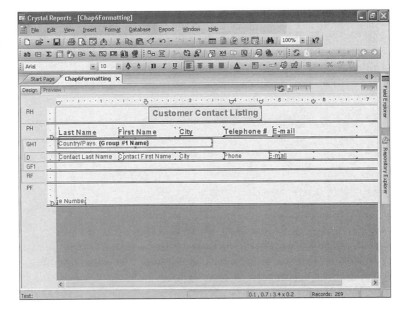

5. With the combined text object highlighted, use the steps identified earlier in this chapter to modify the object's properties to present the field values in a bold red font style, as shown in Figure 6.14. Click the Preview tab to see how the report results are displayed. (Use the Refresh toolbar button if the Preview tab is not visible.)

Figure 6.14
After combining two or more objects, you can specify formatting properties for the newly combined report object.

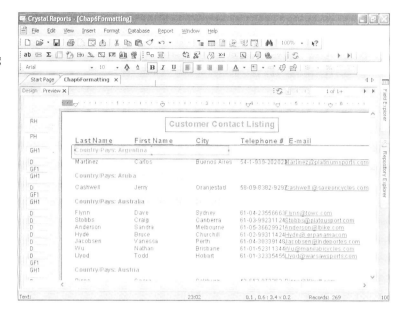

6. Now add a corporate logo to your report and use this to discuss object layering. You need to have a picture file saved in either bitmap, TIFF, JPEG, or PNG format available for use. Use the Business Objects logo downloaded from its website for this example. Select the Picture menu option from the Insert menu. Navigate to and select the Business Objects Logo image and drag it into the Report Header section. Drop the image into the Report Header section so that its left perimeter is aligned directly above the left perimeter of the Telephone Number column, as shown in Figure 6.15.

Notice, as illustrated in Figure 6.15, that you have partially covered the report title object with the new logo image. This could have certainly been avoided by placing the image object farther to the right, but for demonstration purposes, use the Move property of the report title field to once again make it visible.

7. Right-click the report title text object, select Move, and then select To Front from the additional pop-up options. This positions the report title object on top of the logo image, as you can see in the report preview.

8. To resolve the issue of overlapping objects in the Report Header section, adjust the two objects so that the report title is displayed farther to the left of the logo image, as shown in Figure 6.16. Save your report sample if you want.

Figure 6.15
Drag and drop the
Business Objects Logo
image object into
place in the Report
Header section.

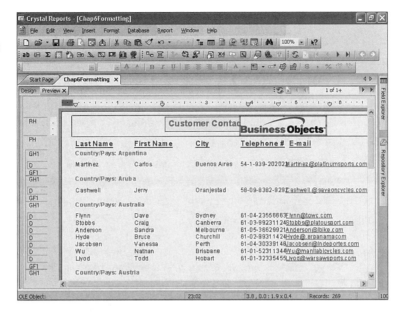

Figure 6.16
By adjusting the
objects located in the
Report Header, you
have resolved the
need to layer these
objects; however,
layering does provide
flexible display
options.

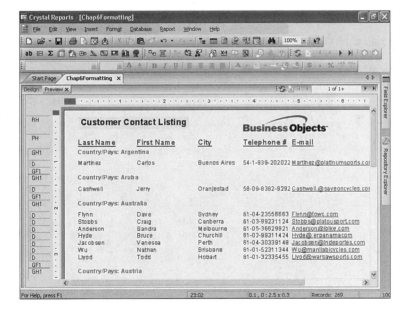

9. As a final step to re-create the report in Figure 6.2, use the Format Expert dialog to modify the report title text so that it appears in a bold, navy blue, underlined, size 20 Verdana font with no displayed borders.

As a result of these exercises, you now have a very useful report that displays each customer contact record distinctively grouped within the country in which they are located. The formatting that has been applied introduces the capabilities that make Crystal Reports the undisputed champion of professionally formatted reports.

CONFIGURING REPORT PAGE AND MARGIN PROPERTIES

With Crystal Reports, page margins can either be set to use specific manually set margin definitions or can be selected to automatically adjust to the report margins. To set your report margins to meet exact specifications, follow these steps:

1. From the File menu, click Page Setup, and the Page Setup dialog appears as shown in Figure 6.17.

2. Modify the default page margins for your exact requirements.

3. Click OK to save your changes.

> Each of the margin settings is calculated from the paper edge. Consequently, a left margin of .25 inches causes the printing of the report page to start exactly one quarter of an inch in from the left edge of the paper.

Figure 6.17
The Page Setup dialog is used to specify report margin settings.

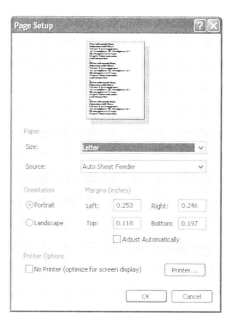

As an alternative to specifying exact report margins, you can select the Adjust Automatically check box if you want Crystal Reports to adjust the report's margins automatically when the paper size changes. This option maintains the ratio of the margins to the printable area of the report by enlarging or reducing the left/right and top/bottom margins by the same factor. For example, this setting could ensure that a report designed for a printer that can only print within .5 inches of the paper's edge would maintain the same overall margin ratio when printed on a printer that could print to within .25 inches of the paper's edge.

The Page Setup dialog also enables you to select a printer for your report or specify no printer at all for optimized web viewing. Based on the printer selection, you are able to set different page sizes and either portrait or landscape orientation. New to XI, a preview of the selected paper size is shown at the top of the Page Setup dialog.

TIP

If you decide to select the Use Default Margins options for your reports, there are two common issues to be aware of when printing reports (also described in the Crystal Reports Help files):

- When printing a report in another environment in which the printer's default margins are greater than the report's setting, the report objects on the right side of the report print off the page.

- When printing a report in another environment in which the printer's default margins are smaller (enabling a larger printing area), the entire report moves to the left side of the page.

As a result, it is recommended that you specify your own report margins. It is encouraged that you do *not* select the Use Default Margins option in the Page Setup dialog to avoid these common problems. It is advisable to set your report margins manually using the Page Setup dialog, even if the margins you want to specify are the same as the default margin settings. This issue becomes especially important when you distribute your reports over the Web and have no idea what type of printer the business user will be using.

TROUBLESHOOTING

FORMATTING PHONE NUMBERS

I need phone numbers that are stored in the underlying database as 5554161010 to display as (555)416-1010. Is this easily accomplished?

Yes. The simplest method to accomplish this is through the Display String functionality accessed under the Common tab of the Format Editor. You can access this dialog by right-clicking on the Telephone_Number field in your report and selecting the Format Field option. Once here, click on the x+2 button beside the Display String title (way down near the bottom of the dialog) and enter something like the following to accomplish your goal:

```
"(" + Left (CurrentFieldValue,3) +
") " + Mid(CurrentFieldValue,4,3) +
"-" + Right(CurrentFieldValue,4)
```

CRYSTAL REPORTS IN THE REAL WORLD—REFERENCING EXTERNAL RESOURCES

A very powerful use of hyperlinks is to be able to take advantage of the many resources on the Internet. Many Internet sites make use of what is called a *QueryString*. By knowing the URL and QueryString that drive a particular site, a report hyperlink can be customized to open a website and perform some functionality. In the next example, the address of the sample customers can be opened in MapQuest.com by using a hyperlink:

Start with opening the report Chap6Formatted.rpt or the report you have created in these last exercises. From the Insert menu, choose Text Object. Add the text **Map** to the report between the customer name and city, as shown in Figure 6.18.

Figure 6.18
A new Map field added to the report provides a dynamic hyperlink directly to maps of the client's locales.

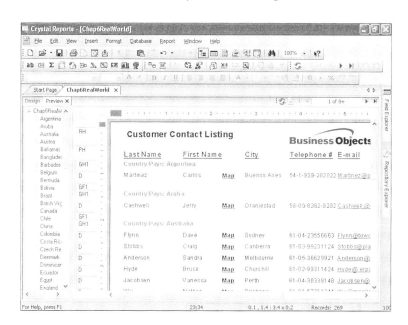

Right-click the newly added text object and choose Format Text. Click the Hyperlink tab, select the Website on the Internet hyperlink option, and click the x+2 button beside the Website Address input box. Figure 6.19 highlights the formula you will enter to provide a dynamic data-driven link to MapQuest maps showing location maps of the client locales. Enter the following code into the formula editor:

```
StringVar URL;

// The prefix of the URL that will not change;
URL := "http://www.mapquest.com/maps/map.adp?";
URL := URL & "searchtype=address&addtohistory=&searchtab=home&address=";
```

```
// Add the country
URL := URL & "&country=" & {Customer.Country};

// Add the state
URL := URL & "&state=" & {Customer.Region};

// Add the city
URL := URL & "&city=" & {Customer.City};

URL
```

Figure 6.19
Code that builds a dynamic data-driven URL that will enable hyperlinks to the MapQuest website from a Crystal Report

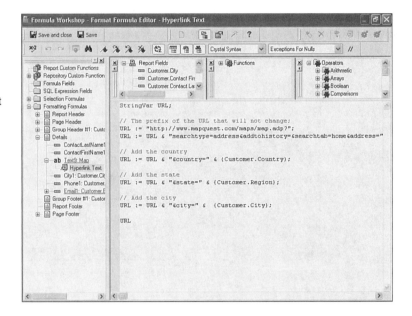

3. Click Save and Close to close the code window. Click OK to close the Format Editor window. Format the hyperlink using the same method used to format the e-mail address to show the user it is an actionable item.

6

NOTE

The sample data does not necessarily use valid addresses but you should find that many of the city, region, and country combinations will in fact be successfully received and processed by MapQuest, as shown in Figure 6.20 for a Toronto-based customer. MapQuest.com might open with only partial information, but the concept remains valid.

Figure 6.20
A MapQuest website that has received a dynamic data-driven request directly from your Crystal Report.

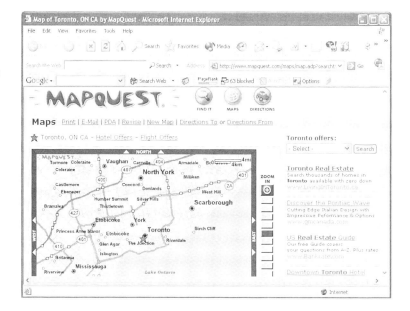

CHAPTER 7

WORKING WITH REPORT SECTIONS

In this chapter

INTRODUCTION

You should now be familiar with some of the most common formatting features within the Crystal Reports XI designer. Building on the concepts and techniques covered in Chapter 6, "Fundamentals of Report Formatting," for report object formatting, this chapter explains how you can format entire sections within your reports. Just as any report object has specific modifiable properties available for formatting, report sections also have unique properties.

→ For more information on report formatting, **see** "Exploring the Format Editor Dialog Common Options," p. 168.

In this chapter, these properties are examined and their use in creating effective professionally styled reports is explored.

This chapter covers the following topics:

- Formatting report sections
- Modifying report section properties
- Using multiple report sections

FORMATTING REPORT SECTIONS

The earlier chapters introduced the concept of report sections such as the detail section and the group header and footer sections. *Report sections* segment reports into logical areas that facilitate logical report design. Report sections are identified by name on the left side of the design environment, and, by default, each report includes a Report Header and Footer, Page Header and Footer, and Details section. If you have inserted any groups into your report, you also have a Group Header and Footer for each defined group item. As reports have been created in the previous chapters, objects such as database fields, text fields, and corporate logo images have been placed into the various report sections and organized based on the report design requirements.

Each section has unique display properties and printing characteristics that can be modified. For example, if a report object, such as an image, is placed in the Report Header section, the image displays and prints only once per report, on the first page. If the same image is placed in the Page Header section, the image then displays and prints once for every single page of the report. The same principals hold true for other custom sections, such as Group Headers and Footers. Finally, the Detail section implies that whatever is placed in this section displays, and prints, once for each and every row retrieved from the data source.

The Crystal Reports design environment is built on a *paper metaphor* with *pages* the driving concept in structuring the presentation of report information. This page metaphor applies when referencing report printing and with respect to various presentation characteristics of report formatting.

Using the report created in Chapter 6, you will take a closer look at how to format report sections. The following exercises demonstrate how to format sections such as the Group Header and Group Footer to improve the overall presentation of a Crystal Report. In addition to modifying display properties, conditional logic is also applied that modifies the behavior of the Page Header section based on the result of the defined condition (format formula). The Section Expert is the central location for working with all report section properties, and it is used to view and modify the properties of each report section throughout the following exercises.

NOTE

> As you might have noticed, long names (descriptive names) of each section are provided to the left of the design environment within the Design tab, whereas only the short names (abbreviated names) of sections are presented while viewing reports from the Preview tab. This maximizes the report viewing space while working in the Preview tab. The long names can, however, be accessed by either hovering the mouse cursor over the section or by right-clicking on the section name (or label).

There are three distinct ways to access the Section Expert; these include

- Right-clicking on the name of the section you want to work with and selecting Section Expert from the pop-up menu.
- Clicking on the Section Expert toolbar button located on the Expert Tools toolbar.
- Selecting the Format menu and choosing Report, Section Expert.

To start the hands-on learning, follow these steps:

1. Open the report you created in Chapter 6. Alternatively, open the report entitled Ch07start.rpt (available for download at www.usingcrystal.com or by searching for the book's ISBN—0-7897-3417-6— at Que Publishing's website, www.quepublishing.com).

2. Open the Section Expert. From either the Design or Preview mode, right-click on the Group Header #1 section and select Section Expert from the pop-up menu. This presents the Section Expert dialog displayed in Figure 7.4.

3. Now apply a background color to your Group Header #1 report section so the report consumers can quickly distinguish between country sections and determine which customer contacts belong to each country. In the Section Expert, select the Group Header #1 item from the Sections list on the left, and then click on the Color tab on the right. Click on the Background Color check box so that it is activated and select Navy from the drop-down list of color options. Click OK to continue.

TIP

> From within the Section Expert, you can easily navigate from modifying the properties of one report section to another without closing this dialog window. Regardless of how you open the Section Expert dialog window, you can quickly toggle to other report sections, providing a central location to access and modify the properties of all report sections.

7

Select the Preview tab to view your report display.

The Red font used for the object in the Group Header #1 does not look good against the Navy background color. To resolve this, highlight the text object—actually a combined object consisting of a text object and a database field object—and change its font color to White, as shown in Figure 7.1.

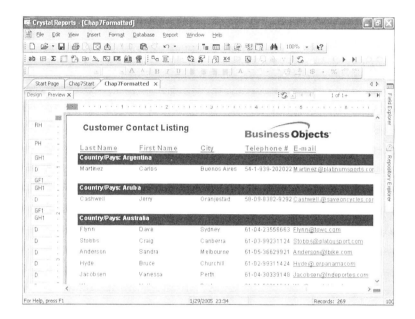

To complement the current report grouping on the Country field, add a summary count of the contacts for each country in the Group Footer #1 section. To do this, select Summary from the Insert menu to present the Insert Summary dialog and select the following items:

- Customer.Contact Last Name field from the Choose the Field to Summarize drop-down list
- Count from the Calculate This Summary drop-down list
- Group #1: Customer.Country from the Summary Location drop-down list

To access the Insert Summary dialog so that you can add a summary field to your report, you can use the Summary command from the main Insert menu, you can use the Insert Summary button located on the Insert toolbar, or you can simply right-click on any report field already in the report and access the Insert Summary menu option from the right-click menu. This last option pre-populates the Choose the Field to Summarize drop-down box and saves you one needless step.

7. After you have made these selections from the Insert Summary dialog, click OK to continue.

8. You should now see the Count Summary field listed in the Group Footer #1 section of your report. To align the field values to the left and make them noticeable, use the Align Left and Font buttons located on the Formatting toolbar to apply the desired alignment and a Red font color.

9. Now add additional report section formatting to the Group Footer #1 section. From the Report menu, select the Section Expert command to present the Section Expert dialog. From the Sections list on the left, select Group Footer #1 and then select the Color tab on the right. Specify a Silver background color for this section and click OK to return to the report preview, shown in Figure 7.2.

10. As a final step, change the font color of the database field column titles. From either the Design or Preview view, right-click on the Page Header section title and choose Select All Section Objects from the pop-up menu. After all the column title objects are highlighted, select Teal from the formatting toolbar Font Color button.

Figure 7.2
Section formatting can be applied specifically to the various sections of your report for a more meaningful report presentation.

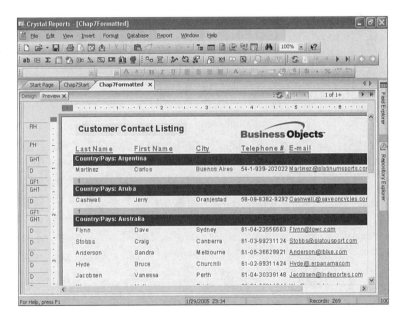

As you have seen, formatting the various sections of your report is very straightforward. Each section has unique and specific properties that can be modified and used collectively to enhance the presentation quality of the entire report.

TIP

To quickly remove blank space within report sections and tighten up the alignment of the objects positioned within the sections, you can use the Fit Section command. The Fit Section command is available from the right-click menu of each report section. This raises the bottom boundary line and reduces unnecessary space within the section.

MODIFYING REPORT SECTION PROPERTIES

In addition to formatting properties, each section has a variety of general properties that can be used to manipulate the behavior of that section within the overall report. For example, if you would like to suppress a particular section from the report display or just hide a detail-oriented section from the initial display but enable business users to navigate to the underlying details, you can use the Section Expert to accomplish this.

Using the report you created in the previous exercise, relocate the Count summary field into the Group Header and hide the Details section to enable the viewer of the report to access this section only if he double-clicks on the Group Header summary values—commonly known as drilling-down on report data. The following steps guide you through formatting several fields and sections, creating a drill-down report:

1. Highlight the Summary field currently located in the Group Footer #1 section (Count of Contact Last Name) and drag it up in the Group Header #1 section so that it is positioned to the right of the Country/Pays field, approximately under the Telephone # column title. The results are shown in Figure 7.3.

2. While the Summary count field is still highlighted, modify the font properties so that it is underlined and in a bold yellow color.

3. Using what you have learned from the previous exercises, remove the background color of the Group Footer #1 section—the background color property can be located on the Color tab of the Section Expert. Figure 7.3 shows what your report should now look like.

Figure 7.3
Report objects can be repositioned into the various report sections to change the presentation of the report.

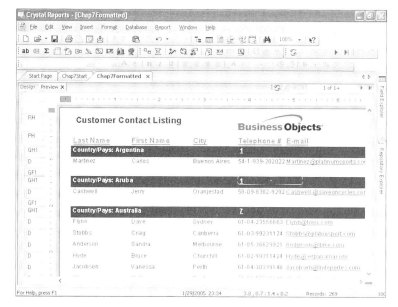

4. To display the listing of customer contacts for each country on a separate and unique page, open the Section Expert and select Group Footer #1 from the section list on the left. As Figure 7.4 shows, the Common tab within the Section Expert provides access to a variety of properties unique to the section that you have selected from the list on the left. In this case, check the box next to the New Page After item and click OK to continue.

Figure 7.4
The Section Expert provides access to a variety of section formatting properties, as well as enabling the specification of what happens before and after each section is printed.

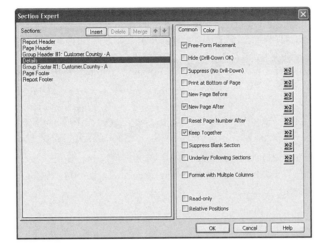

TIP

> Common report section commands—such as Hide, Suppress, Delete, Hide Section Names, and Select All Section Objects—are accessible via the pop-up menu when you right-click on the applicable section's name. Some of these commands are also available within the Section Expert dialog, although unlike the Section Expert, the right-click pop-up menu pertains only to the specific section you have selected.

5. Looking at the preview of your report, you should now see each country's list of contacts on a separate page. Although this might be desirable for those countries with a considerable number of contacts, such as Canada, France, and the United States in this report, it is not necessarily the most visually pleasing presentation for the countries that have only one or two customer contacts. A potential solution here is to conditionally create a New Page After the Group Footer section only when a country has a significant number of contacts. This is accomplished using a formula entered by accessing the x+2 button adjacent to the New Page After title and check box. A simple solution might include adding the following formula:

```
Count ({Customer.Contact Last Name}, {Customer.Country}) > 5
```

This formula is evaluated for every Group Footer (for every country) and will only cause a New Page After the involved Group Footer when the current country has more than five contact names.

7

Exploring the end users behind this hypothetical example a bit more, it is likely that the majority of the business users for this report are primarily interested in the total number of contacts for each country rather than the actual list itself. However, a few of the business users also want to be able to access the complete contact list on occasion. To accommodate both groups of users, you can manipulate the properties of the Details section.

Drill-down functionality is designed to make report viewing easier. You can hide the details of your report and only have the group headers and summaries visible, and, when necessary, the business users of the report can then click on the group header or summary fields to view the report details.

Disable the New Page After property that was set for the Group Footer #1 section. The Section Expert can be used to remove this setting. Click OK to continue.

From either the Design or Preview view of your report, right-click on the Details section title to the far left of the application area and select Hide (Drill-Down OK) from the pop-up menu.

To indicate to the business user of the report that more detailed information is available behind the summary group level, the mouse pointer turns into a magnifying glass icon when it floats over a drillable section (for example, the yellow count field of customer contacts, located in the Group Header #1 section).

As shown in Figure 7.5, a list of each country with the total number of contacts displayed has now been created. Additionally, upon double-clicking the count of contacts (displayed with the underlined, yellow number) the business user of the report is quickly able to drill-down into the Details section and be presented with the actual customer contact specifications.

As you can see in Figure 7.6, after the business user drills down into a particular group's detail listing (France in this example), that group's detailed contact list is displayed in the Crystal Reports application in a separate tab and is cached so that it can be easily accessed for future reference. When a business user of the report selects a refresh on the report, all cached tabs are removed because there is no guarantee that the data being retrieved from the database would be the same as the previously cached page. The end user would have to drill back down into France if he wanted to view the detailed contact listing again.

THE SECTION EXPERT SETTINGS AND FUNCTIONALITY

As discussed to this point in the chapter, the Section Expert provides a great deal of powerful report formatting functionality and flexibility. There are two major areas to the Section

Expert as shown in Figure 7.4—the Sections area and the Formatting tabs (Common, Color, and Layout). This section presents each of these sections and their associated functionality.

Figure 7.5
A manager now is presented with a summary list of customer contacts by country and is also able to access the customer contact details through a drill-down.

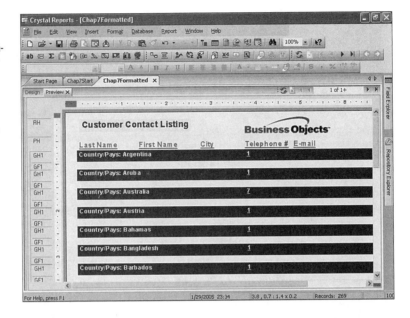

Figure 7.6
The detailed list of customer contacts for England.

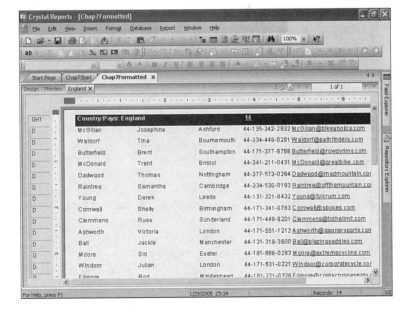

THE SECTIONS AREA

The Sections area is composed of a listing of all the current report's sections and five separate buttons—Insert, Delete, Merge and the up and down arrows. The Sections area takes up the entire left half of the Sections Expert dialog and enables you to create, delete, merge, and reorder entire sections within the involved report. The following list describes each of the Section Expert Sections area components:

- **Sections**—This box provides a list of all the sections in the current report. When a section is highlighted, the program highlights the other Section Expert properties and buttons that you can set, modify, or use for the selected section.

- **Insert button**—This button enables you to add sections below the currently highlighted section. The newly added section is based on the type that is currently selected. (For example, inserting a section while on the Detail section creates another Detail section called Detail b, the original Detail section is called Detail a, and they both exist under a parent node called Detail.) Different formatting and display properties are made available for each child section in addition to the parent section. Creating multiple detail (or other) sections dramatically increases the flexibility in which you can display information as each independent child section can have unique formatting and display properties applied (for example, Only Show Column Titles in Details a Section Every 10th Row).

- **Delete button**—Use this button to delete existing highlighted sections from the current report. Note that only inserted children sections (as described previously) can be deleted—not original primary sections.

- **Merge button**—This button enables you to merge two related children sections (for example, Details a and Details b) into one new section.

- **Up and Down Arrow buttons**—These buttons enable you to reorder children sections within the currently selected report. It is important to note that the original parent sections cannot be reordered in the Section Expert.

THE COMMON TAB

In addition to the Section Expert options that you have already used, the following segment of the chapter provides an overview of the available settings presented on the Common tab of the Section Expert. A subset or all of these options are made available when a section is selected in the Sections area, as described previously. The following options are made available in the Common tab:

- **Free-Form Placement**—When enabled, this option places objects within a section in a free-form manner, ignoring all program alignment grids and guidelines. When this option is not selected, objects are placed at fixed points using an underlying grid (see the Layout tab of the Options menu for more details on grid display). This option is generally used in combination with report graphics (such as boxes) whose default display mechanism is free-form.

- **Hide (Drill-Down OK)**—This option hides the respective section from the report's initial visual display, but still enables report users to access the section's content upon end-user drill-down.

- **Suppress (No Drill-Down)**—Hides the respective section from the report's visual display and disables any drill-down capabilities such that the section's content is *not* available to report users. This is very useful for eliminating the display of sections that contain no data (such as redundant or empty Group Footer sections).

- **Print at Bottom of Page**—Causes the current section to print at the bottom of the page. This setting is most useful for printing invoices and other reports where you want summary values to appear toward the bottom of the page in a fixed position.

- **New Page Before**—Inserts a page break before it prints the section. This option is only applicable to the Group Header, Group Footer, and Details sections.

- **New Page After**—Inserts a page break after it displays and prints the section. For example, you can use this setting in the Group Footer section to print each group on a separate page.

- **Reset Page Number After**—Resets the page number to one (1) for the following page after it prints a group total. When this option is used in conjunction with Print at Bottom of Page, a single group prints on a page, the group value is printed at the bottom of the page, and the page number is reset to 1 for the next page. This option is useful whenever you are printing multiple reports from a single file (such as customer invoices), and you want each report to be numbered beginning with Page 1.

- **Keep Together**—Keeps a particular section together on one page without splitting the section between multiple pages. For example, in a customer list, data on a single customer might extend over several lines. If the standard page break falls within the data for a customer, the data is split—part on one page and the remainder on the next. You can use the Keep Together setting to insert the page break before the record begins so that all the data is printed together on the following page.

- **Suppress Blank Section**—Hides the report section if it is blank, and only prints it if it is not blank. This is a powerful display control to eliminate unnecessary blank space in reports.

- **Underlay Following Sections**—Permits the selected section to underlay the following section(s) when it prints, making the current section transparent. This feature is often used for the printing of Watermarks on a report (such as "Internal Use Only," "Draft," or a company logo). It is also often used to display data in different sections beside each other (for example, a summary pie chart from the Report Header underplayed to show beside the actual details of the pie chart kept in the Group and Detail sections).

- **Format with Multiple Columns**—Only available on the Detail section, this option presents the Layout tab (otherwise hidden from view) within the Section Expert and enables you to use multiple columns in the given report. This powerful feature enables the presentation of row data in the detail section as columns in a report. It is particularly useful when presenting summarized information for comparison or a lengthy list. This is discussed later in this chapter.

- **Reserve Minimum Page Footer (Page Footer section only)**—Reserves space at the bottom of each page for your Page Footer sections (a default setting). This enables you to minimize the space reserved for your Page Footer sections, thus maximizing the space available for other report information on each page. This option only affects a Page Footer area with multiple sections.

- **Read-only**—Locks the formatting and position of all report objects within the section so that they can't be formatted or repositioned. The Read-only setting uses password protection to enable the report designer to return to the report to make future changes.

- **Relative Positions**—Locks the relative position of a report object next to a grid object within a section. For example, if you place a text object one inch to the right of a cross-tab or OLAP grid object, during report generation the program pushes the text object to the right so that the one inch of space is maintained regardless of the width of the cross-tab or OLAP grid object.

The presence of the x+2 buttons to the right of the majority of the options indicates that those options can be set via a formula in addition to setting them via the dialog. When an option is set via formula, this is referred to as *conditional formatting* because the formula typically evaluates a condition.

To implement a conditional option, click on the x+2 button associated with the option and the Formula Editor is presented. Within the Formula Editor, a formula needs to be created that is evaluated for every iteration of the section. If the formula evaluates to a value of True, the involved option is applied; otherwise, it is not. A simple but practical example of conditional section formatting could be a marketing campaign list where the marketing department wants to contact customers in the USA by phone and everywhere else by mail. Two detail sections could be created, one that includes Contact Name and Phone Number, the other with Contact Name and Mailing address. The first section can be conditionally suppressed on the following formula—{Customer.Country} <> "USA" to only show that section for USA-based customers. The second details section would be conditionally suppressed with {Customer.Country} = "USA" to only show non-U.S.-based customers.

THE COLOR TAB

Use the Color tab to set the background color for the entire highlighted section. This can be done absolutely or conditionally. A good example of a conditionally colored background is when presenting a lengthy list of detailed items. To enable easier reading of the report, every second row can be conditionally colored Silver with the following formula:

LISTING 7.1 ALTERNATE ROW COLORING FORMULA

```
IF RecordNumber Mod 2 = 1 THEN
    Silver
Else
    White
```

THE LAYOUT TAB

The Layout tab only appears when you have the details section selected and the Format with Multiple Columns check box has been selected on the Common tab. This tab enables multi-column formatting. As described earlier, this kind of report enables you to present multiple columns of standard row data and have the data flow from column to column. This tab, shown in Figure 7.7, has four distinct settings:

Figure 7.7
The Layout tab is only available for advanced multi-column reports.

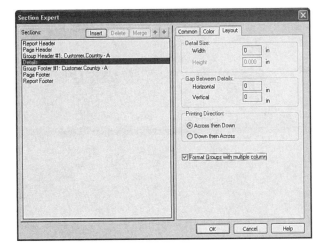

- **Detail Size**—This box enables the specification of the dimensions (height and width) of each detail column.

- **Gap Between Details**—This box enables the specification of the empty area between detail columns and rows. The horizontal gap is the distance between the details going across the page and the vertical gap is the distance between rows going down the page.

- **Printing Direction**—This option enables the specification of the flow path to be followed when printing the detail column and rows on a report page. The Across then Down option prints details across the columns in one row first before moving onto the next row of data. The Down then Across option prints details down an entire column first before moving onto the next column.

- **Format Groups with Multiple Column**—This option formats groups with multiple columns using the Width, Gap Between Details, and Printing Directions specified for the selected Detail section.

> **TIP**
>
> When you format a report to show multiple columns, the Crystal Reports engine reviews the fields in the detail section and sizes the columns in the rest of the report based on the width of those fields. As such, if data labels (text fields) are placed in the detail section for row identification, these increase the width of the report's columns and reduce the number of columns that fit onto a page. To place such fields, consider placing them in a Page or Group header and underlaying them onto the Details section.

7

To begin to truly understand the powerful formatting capabilities of multi-column reporting, it is instructive to edit your current contact list report using this functionality.

Figure 7.8 highlights some appropriate layout settings you can set after you have checked the Format with Multi-Columns check box (remember that it's only available for the Detail section). At this time, do not check the Format Groups with Multiple Columns option but rather simply set the Width and Gap options. You will also need to increase the height of the Details section and stack the current Details columns one on top of the other for the best display effect.

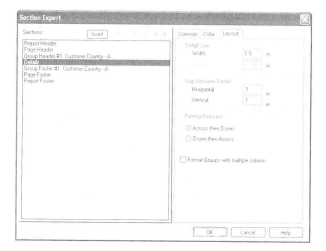

Figure 7.8
The Layout tab is only available for the Details section when the Format with Multi-Columns option is set.

The results of this small report modification are seen in Figure 7.9. You can see that the report now shows the pertinent customer contact information in multiple columns across the page. This flexibility is often effectively used in the creation of financial statements and other reports where a columnar display paradigm is natural or expected.

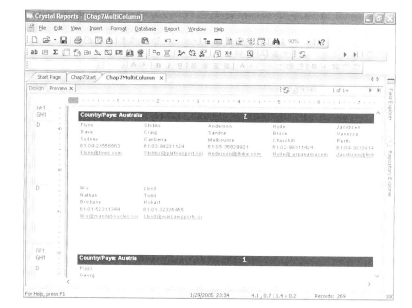

Figure 7.9
A multi-column version of your customer contact report.

USING MULTIPLE REPORT SECTIONS

Including multiple sections within each section area of your report provides for an extremely flexible presentation of your report data. Chances are good that you do not need to create more than one occurrence of any of the existing report sections for basic reporting needs. However, Crystal Reports enables you to define multiple report sections within any given section area and to identify section-specific properties for challenging formatting requirements within more complex reports. Certain reporting tasks are performed most efficiently by creating multiple sections within an area.

For example, multiple report sections would be very useful if you want to create a form letter for your customers and you need to display only one of two possible return addresses on the letter—an American address for customers based in the United States and a Canadian address for the Canadian customers. To accomplish this, you do need to insert two report header sections into your report and use Conditional Formatting to dynamically apply the appropriate return address based on where the customer is located.

To demonstrate how to implement and use multiple report sections, you first need to review the basic operations of resizing, inserting, removing, and merging report sections.

RESIZING REPORT SECTIONS

Report sections might require resizing to accommodate for various sized report objects, such as large database fields, lengthy text objects, or corporate logo images, but they cannot exceed the size of the report page itself. From the Design tab of the report environment, you can drag the bottom boundary of the various sections up and down with the mouse to resize each section. Using the mouse, float the pointer over the horizontal boundary lines of the different sections. When the mouse pointer changes into a double-headed arrow icon, click and hold the left mouse button while dragging the boundary line to the desired position.

INSERTING NEW REPORT SECTIONS

To display only one of two possible return addresses on a form letter based on the country of the customer, you need to insert a second page header onto the report. The following steps walk you through constructing the following report using the Customer table from the Xtreme Sample Database:

1. Create a new Crystal Report using the standard Report Wizard, connecting to the Xtreme Sample database and selecting the Customers table. Do not add any database fields to the report. Click the Finish button at the Fields Selection dialog.

2. Create a Group (by choosing Insert, Group) based on the Customer Name field, but remove the Customer Name field from the Group header section. The Group field should have automatically appeared in the Group Header section when you created the group.

3. Select the New Page After property for the Group Footer #1 section.

7

4. Ensure that the Report Header section is suppressed.

5. Create and insert text objects in the appropriate report sections, as shown in Figure 7.10.

Figure 7.10
This simple form letter report shows the correct return address conditionally.

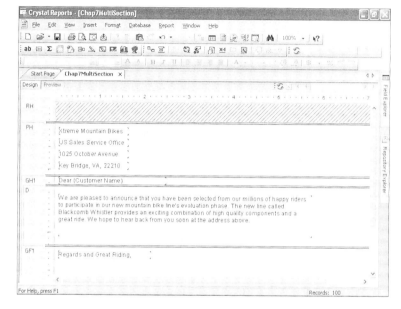

Notice that in this sample form letter report, each report object displayed on the report is just a text object inserted into the appropriate section. There are no database fields included in the report yet.

Next you will insert a new Page Header in which to display an alternate return address for Canadian customers. The following steps will take you through this process:

1. To insert a new Page Header section, locate the existing Page Header section, right-click on the section name (on the left of the design environment), and select Insert Section Below from the pop-up menu.

   The new section is entitled Page Header b and the original section was renamed to Page Header a so that there are now two Report Header sections within your report. The application follows this naming convention whenever multiple report sections are added.

2. After you have inserted a new Page Header section (labeled Page Header b), insert text objects to display a Canadian return address to be used for the non-U.S.-based recipients of the form letter, as shown in Figure 7.11.

Figure 7.11
The form letter report now shows two Page Header sections.

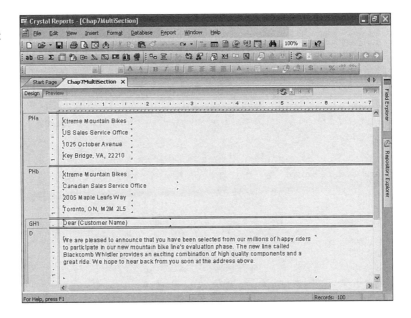

Now that the report has the two different return addresses and report sections created, the logic must be created within the report to implement the appropriate Page Header section based on each customer's location—whether they are based in the United States or Canada. Each customer's mailing address needs to be evaluated—the Country field from the Customer table. For this example, you're only concerned with North American customers, and if this field is equal to USA, use Page Header a to display the return address. If it is equal to Canada, use Page Header b.

3. To isolate your report for only North American (excepting Mexico) customers, choose the Select Expert option from the Report menu. From the list of available fields, select the Country field from the Customer table listing and click OK to continue.

4. You should now see the Select Expert dialog. From the drop-down list on the left, select Is One Of and include Canada and USA in the list box.

5. To add additional personalization to the form letter, use the Field Explorer to insert the Customer Name field into the Text Object—located in the Group Header #1 that reads "Dear Customer,"—so that it appears as Dear {Customer Name} in the Design tab of your report. To do this, you'll need to modify the text portion of this combined object to read "Dear " (the word Dear followed by a space), and then followed by the database field object.

Finally, you need to apply the logic to display the appropriate return address on the form letter. To do this, you apply a conditional formatting statement (format formula) to each of the two Page Header sections.

6. Using the Section Expert for Page Header a, click on the x+2 button (with the pencil symbol) located directly to the right of the Suppress (No Drill-Down) option on the

7

Common tab. After clicking this icon, you should be presented with the Format Formula Editor dialog (see Figure 7.12). Here, you can use the Field, Function, and Operator windows (located in the upper area of the dialog) to insert the necessary format formula within this dialog, or you can just type in the statement in the lower area of the Editor dialog so that it reads `{Customer.Country}` = `"Canada"`. After you have inserted this statement, click Save and Close to return to the Section Expert. Note that the x+2 button has changed color (to red) to signify a conditional formula has been created here.

7. You now need to implement a very similar formatting condition for the Page Header b section. Following the same procedure used for the first section, use the Section Expert to insert a statement that reads `{Customer.Country}` = `"USA"`.

Figure 7.12
The report section is suppressed only if the conditional statement defined in the Format Formula Editor is True.

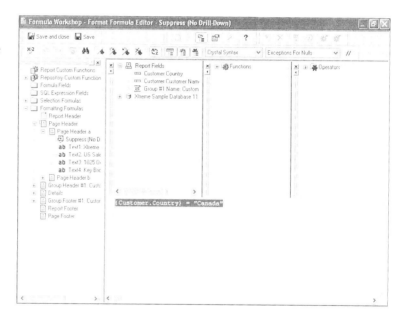

> You do not need to check the Suppress (No Drill-Down) check box in the Section Expert dialog for either report Page Header section. By inserting a format formula, you have effectively applied conditional formatting that suppresses the section if the format formula is found to be true. In this case, one of the two format formulas should always be true because the customers are either located in the United States or Canada.

8. Close the Section Expert dialog by clicking OK. As shown in Figure 7.13, your report should now display only one of the two possible return addresses on the form letter. To verify that the appropriate return address is being populated on the form letter report for each customer, you can easily add the Country field from the Customer table into the Group Header #1 section, also shown in Figure 7.13.

Figure 7.13
A simple form letter report is now dynamically formatted with the appropriate return address based on the customer's location.

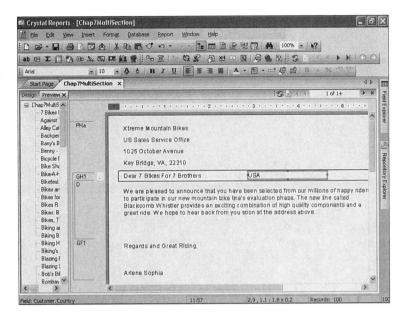

DELETING REPORT SECTIONS

In much the same manner sections were inserted, unused report sections can be removed from reports quickly by right-clicking on the section name and selecting Delete Section from the pop-up menu. Be aware, however, that any report objects positioned within the section are also deleted from the report. If any of the objects within a section that will be removed are required, they will need to be relocated into alternative report sections before deletion.

> **NOTE**
>
> Crystal Reports requires at least one section to be present for certain section types in every report—the Report Header and Footer, Page Header and Footer, and Details sections. These report sections are generated by default when creating new reports. Also, if Group objects exist within a report, you cannot remove the Group Header and Footer sections unless you first remove the Group object itself from the report.

MERGING REPORT SECTIONS

When designing reports, you might periodically want to merge two report sections to simplify the layout of a report. To merge the two Page Header sections from your earlier example, right-click on the Page Header a section title and select Merge Section Below from the

7

pop-up menu. The Merge Section Below command is available from the right-click menu of any report section that meets two criteria:

- There are more than one of the given section type (Page Headers) within the Section Area.

- The section is not last in a series of sections (Page Headers) consisting of the same section types within a common area.

For example, if three Page Header sections are present on a report (as shown in Figure 7.14), the Merge Section Below command would be accessible from the right-click menus of Page Header a and Page Header b, but not from Page Header c.

Figure 7.14
The Merge Section Below command is available from the right-click menu of certain report sections.

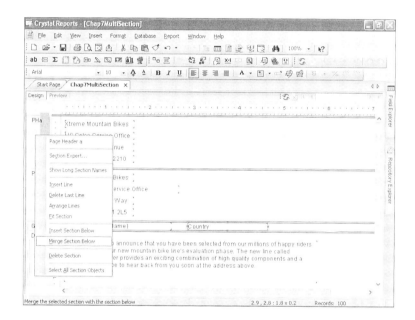

TROUBLESHOOTING

REPORT SECTION FORMATTING

I keep getting blank spaces above and/or below my data fields in my report sections, and I need a quick way of removing them.

To quickly remove blank spaces within report sections and tighten up the alignment of the objects positioned within the sections, use the Fit Section command available from the right-click menu of each report section.

SHOWING GROUP SECTION HEADERS ON DRILL-DOWN

I want the Group headers of each Group Section to be shown as I drill-down into the report's grouping hierarchy. By default, this does not happen and creating conditional suppress functions on each section can be time consuming.

To change the default behavior to always show Group Headers on drilling down, access the Report Options dialog from the File menu and check the Show All Headers on Drill-down option box.

CRYSTAL REPORTS IN THE REAL WORLD— ADVANCED FORMATTING

Often, a report section needs to be more than simply one color or another. A report with many rows might need some color to help guide the reader's eye and make each line distinctly separate from the next. In the following sample, the report created earlier is modified to improve readability:

1. Open the Chap7RealWorld.rpt report or the report you created at the beginning of this chapter.

2. From the Report menu, select Section Expert. When the Section Expert dialog window opens, select the Details section and click the Color tab.

3. As previously described, checking the Background Color box enables you to set all the Detail lines to a single color. The intent here is to highlight the detail lines so they appear distinctly different from the detail line above and below to improve readability. Click the x+2 button and enter the following text into the code window:

```
If Remainder(RecordNumber,2)=1 Then
    crAqua
Else
    DefaultAttribute;
```

4. Finally, go back to the Section Expert. Select Group Footer from the list of sections and check the box labeled New Page After.

5. Now, each group starts on a new page, and long groups have detail lines defined by color. The color improvement can be seen on page 3 of the report, as shown in Figure 7.15.

Figure 7.15
Records are delimited by color for improved readability.

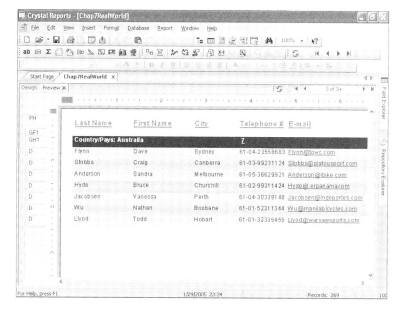

6. Save the report.

8

Visualizing Your Data with Charts and Maps

In this chapter

INTRODUCTION

Chapter 2, "Selecting and Grouping Data," and Chapter 3, "Filtering, Sorting, and Summarizing Data," introduced the importance of grouping and summarizing in report generation. When doing so for business users, it is often effective to present these groups and summarizations using various visualization techniques. The charting and mapping features in Crystal Reports provide a very effective way to communicate relevant information using powerful visualization techniques.

Charts and maps with Crystal Reports provide an extensive array of data visualization options to report designers. In addition to familiar chart types including bar charts, pie charts, scatter charts, line charts, and bubble charts, new chart types in recent versions include the following:

- Histogram charts (v.XI)
- Funnel charts (v.10)
- Gantt charts (v.9)
- Gauges (v.9)
- Numeric Axis charts (v.9)

Geographic Mapping with color-coding and integrated charting options provides another effective method of conveying macro-level information to report consumers.

This chapter introduces various charting and mapping techniques, including

- Enhancing the sample reports from previous chapters with charts and maps
- A review of the Crystal Reports charting expert
- An introduction to the newer chart types—Gantt, Gauge, Numeric Axis, Funnel, and Histogram charts
- A review of the Crystal Reports mapping expert
- Manual chart and map formatting

The Chart Expert is a good place to begin adding visualizations to your reports.

USING THE CHART EXPERT

Reflecting back on the sample reports used in Chapters 2 and 3, you might find that there are opportunities for enhancement through the addition of meaningful charts. As you learned in Chapter 2 with groupings, it is quite easy to summarize the data you collect for a report into meaningful categories or groups. Chapter 2 reviews some examples of grouping based on fields such as country and employee ID. By hiding or suppressing the detail sections of reports, you learned how to bring the meaningful summarizations around these types of groups to the forefront. To further bring this aggregated data to the business user's attention, you can create a chart on this grouped data using the Chart Expert.

To open the Chart Expert, either click on the Chart icon located on the Insert toolbar or select the Insert Chart option under the main Insert menu and then after placing the chart placeholder on your report in the desired section, access the Chart Expert menu option from the chart's right–click menu. Figure 8.1 displays the Chart Expert.

Figure 8.1
The Chart Expert dialog enables the rapid addition of valuable charts to reports.

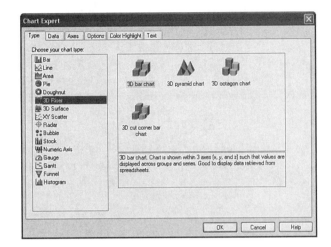

After you access the Chart Expert, several steps are required to actually complete the chart. These are reviewed in the next five sections.

USING THE CHART EXPERT TYPE TAB

The Chart Expert consists of six different tabs. The initial display tab on the Chart Expert is the Type tab, shown in Figure 8.1. On this tab, the type of graphic or chart is selected. In Crystal Reports version XI, there are more than 40 different basic chart types from which to select.

In addition to the classic bar, line, pie, and area charts, new chart types in versions 9,10, and XI are listed in Table 8.1.

TABLE 8.1	NEW CHART TYPES IN CRYSTAL REPORTS VERSIONS 9, 10, AND XI
New Chart Type	**Chart Type Description**
Numeric Axis (v.9)	A Numeric Axis chart is a bar, line, or area chart that uses a numeric field or a date/time field as its On Change Of field. With Numeric Axis charts you can create a true numeric X-axis or a true date/time X-axis.
Gauge(s) (v.9)	A Gauge chart presents data using a speedometer visual and is often used to measure percentage completed against target type metrics.

continues

TABLE 8.1 CONTINUED

New Chart Type	Chart Type Description
Gantt Chart (v.9)	A Gantt chart is a project-focused horizontal bar chart used to provide a graphical illustration of a project schedule. The horizontal axis shows a time span, whereas the vertical axis lists project tasks or events. Horizontal bars on the chart represent event sequences and time spans for each task on the vertical axis.
Funnel Chart (v.10)	Funnel charts are most often used to represent stages in a sales cycle and visually depict proportionality of the different phases in that sales process. A funnel chart is similar to a stacked bar chart in that it represents 100 percent of the summary values for the groups included in the chart.
Histogram Chart (v.XI)	Histograms show the frequency of occurrence of data elements in a data set. The X axis is divided into intervals that denote ranges of data values. Each histogram bar shows the number of data elements whose value falls into that interval.

These charts have been added to expand the visual capabilities of Crystal Reports and enrich your report presentations. Let's create a Sample Customer Order Listing report and add a chart to it that highlights the Company's Top 10 Customers in the following steps:

1. Quickly create the basics of this sample report by selecting the Customer Name, Order ID, and Order Amount fields from the Xtreme Sample Database (Customer and Orders tables). Then Group by Customer Name and Summarize Order Amount by the Customer Name group.

2. To restrict the data to the Top 10 Customers, access the Group Sort Expert from the Report menu option. Select a Top 10 Sort based on the Sum of Order Amount and do *not* include Others or Ties.

3. Insert a Chart onto the report using the Chart toolbar icon or the Chart option from the Insert menu. You will then decide where to place the chart on your report. Drop the Chart object identified by a colored outline in the Report Header section. The location of the report is important in determining the recurrence of the chart. By placing it in the Report Header, the Chart will only appear once. If you had placed it in the Group Header or Footer for Country, a new and separate chart would be created for every group.

4. Right-click on the newly created Chart object and select the Chart Expert option. Select a bar chart as the main chart type in the list box by clicking on it. Then click the Horizontal radio button that is present at the bottom of the dialog.

5. Select the two-dimensional side-by-side bar chart sub-chart type (top left option) by clicking on the associated graphical icon to the right of the Chart Type list box.

Figure 8.2 displays the result of these five steps. You will continue creating this chart in the next four sections.

Figure 8.2
The Type tab on the Chart Expert dialog for the Sample Top 10 Customers report.

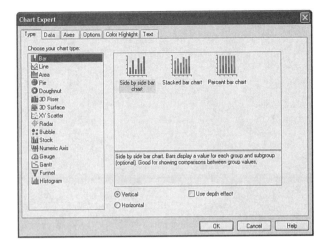

Table 8.2 highlights some common reports, their contained graphics, and the benefits of using them.

TABLE 8.2   COMMON REPORTS WITH CORRESPONDING CHART TYPES

Report	Chart Type	Report and Chart Benefit
Company Sales Report	Pie or Donut Chart	Highlights the regional breakdown of product sales across continents or countries facilitating analysis of revenue contribution.
Product Profitability Report	Horizontal or Vertical Bar Chart	Highlights the profit margin per product that a company sells, facilitating comparative analysis of profitability.
Actual versus Target Report	Gauges	Highlights the progress being made against specified targets through the use of a speedometer visual. When used across projects or divisions, it is relatively easy to compare how they are performing against certain initiatives.

USING THE CHART EXPERT DATA TAB

After a chart type has been selected in the Type tab, click on the Data tab. The Data tab enables the selection of the specific data on which the chart is based and the chart's location on the report. Figure 8.3 displays one view of the second tab of the Chart Expert. This view might vary depending on the different Chart Type options you have selected. The Data tab is composed of two sections: Layout and Data. These sections and corresponding options are discussed next.

Figure 8.3
The Data tab of the Chart Expert enables specification of layout and data options.

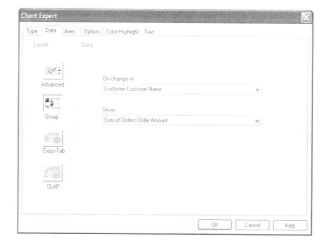

SPECIFYING CHART LAYOUT

The Chart Layout section specifies the data selection options that the selected chart provides to the report designer. The actual data is selected in the Chart Data section. Note that the options presented in that section are dependent on the specific Chart Layout button you have selected. Table 8.3 lists the different layout buttons and their typical uses.

TABLE 8.3   LAYOUT BUTTONS AND TYPICAL USES

Layout Button	Description	Typical Uses
Advanced	This layout button provides complete flexibility in chart creation by providing you with control of all charting options.	Creation of charts based on summaries not already created in the report or charts to be created for every detail record.
Grouping	Although this button is presented second, it is the default layout. This layout limits the Chart Data Selection options (see the following "Chart Data" section) to two drop-down boxes specifying the On Change Of and Show Values and expedites the creation of a chart at the cost of some of the flexibility provided by the Advanced layout button.	Quick creation of charts based on summarized fields already in the report and to be displayed at the Report or existing Group level.
Cross-Tab	This layout button appears as an option only when your current report is a Cross-Tab report.	Creation of a chart based on an existing Cross-Tab in the report.
OLAP	This layout button appears as an option only when your current report is based on an OLAP data source.	Creation of a chart based on an existing OLAP grid in the report.

8

The Cross-Tab and OLAP layout buttons and their related options are explored in Chapters 10, "Using Cross-Tabs for Summarized Reporting," and 16, "Formatting Multidimensional Reporting Against OLAP Data," because they relate to very specific report types. The next section explores the detailed data options that the Advanced and Grouping layout buttons enable.

SPECIFYING CHART DATA

Figure 8.3 displays the Data tab with the Group layout button selected. As previously described, this layout option is designed to facilitate the quick creation of a chart with a minimal amount of effort. To accomplish this rapid chart creation, two pieces of information are requested through two drop-down boxes—On Change Of (grouping item) and Show (field to be shown in the chart) selections. The On Change Of field is used to determine where the selected chart breaks the report data to be displayed. The Show field specifies the summary field to be displayed for each break of the data.

To continue adding a bar chart to the sample report, follow these steps:

1. Ensure that the Group layout button from the Layout section is selected.

2. Select Customer Name in the On Change Of field. This indicates that the chart breaks for each different customer.

3. Select Sum of Orders.Order Amount for the Show field. This indicates that the chart reflects this Sum for each customer. Figure 8.3 should reflect the results of these steps in the Chart Data tab. You will continue creating this chart in the next section.

NOTE

When leveraging the Rapid Chart Creation functionality of the Group layout option, it's worth noting that you are limited to chart creation based on existing summary fields already created in your reports and inserted into existing group sections. For more flexible chart creation, you can use the Advanced layout option described later.

Figure 8.4 displays the Data tab with the Advanced Layout button selected. The additional options presented here give you more flexibility in the charts that you can create.

The On Change Of and Show Values fields should be recognizable in this new window although they are selected in a much more flexible manner (see the right side of the Data section beside the Available Fields listing) described next.

The On Change Of field is now only one selection option (among three) in its own drop-down box. If you need to create a chart based on changing a specific field (as you did with the standard group layout), select the On Change Of charting option and then specify the field or fields to break the chart sections on by selecting any of the fields in the available fields listing. Unlike the drop-down box under the Group layout, you can select any of the available report fields in this interface, dynamically order them with the Order button or restrict their display on the report to a specified Top or Bottom N with the Top N button.

You can also dynamically select multiple fields for the chart to break on, and none of the selected fields need already be on the report or have summary fields previously existing on the report for them.

Figure 8.4
The Data tab with the Advanced Layout button selected.

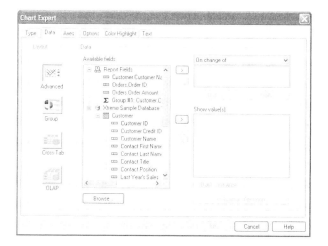

The remaining two options in the On Change Of drop-down box are For Each Record and For All Records. These two options enable charts to be created either against all data in a report or for each detailed record in a report.

> When using the For All Records charting option, you can select the field to be displayed for each break by selecting a field from the Available Fields list in the list box beneath the For All Records drop-down box.

After selecting any of these options, you need to select a Show Value(s) field to enable the chart's creation. This selection specifies the summary field to be displayed for each break of the data and can come from any field (database, report, formula, and so on) that is listed in the available field's list. To select the Show Value fields, highlight the intended field and use the selection arrow buttons adjacent to the Show Values list box.

> You do not need to have an existing summary on your report to use it for a graph in the Advanced Charting layout options. You can add any field to the Show Values list and then dynamically create a summary by clicking on the Set Summary Operation button. These dynamically created summaries are created automatically and used by the chart. This is one of the unique features of Crystal Reports that provides you with more charting flexibility.

8

USING THE CHART EXPERT AXES TAB

The fourth tab in the Chart Expert dialog, the Axes tab, only appears if the Automatically Select Chart Options check box has been deselected on the Type tab. You can then select the Axes tab by clicking it. This tab enables you to customize chart gridlines, data value scales, data value ranges, and data value divisions. Figure 8.6 displays the Axes tab of the Chart Expert dialog for a bar chart.

Figure 8.5
The Axes tab of the Chart Expert allows specification of grid-line display, axis ranges, and divisions.

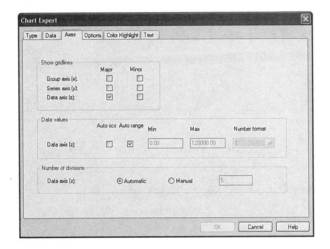

NOTE

This tab only appears when the selected chart type has axes within it (for example, a bar chart or line chart) and does not display for other chart types such as a pie chart.

To continue adding a bar chart to the sample report, try the following step: Select the Major Gridlines check box for the data axis. This facilitates the reading of the bar charts. You will finish creating this bar chart in the following section.

TIP

By manually setting both the Min/Max Data Ranges and the Number of Divisions, you are able to customize your data axis gridline display labels.

USING THE CHART EXPERT OPTIONS TAB

The Options tab in the Chart Expert only appears if the Automatically Select Chart Options check box has been deselected on the Type tab. The Options tab enables you to customize chart coloring, data-point labeling, legend placement, legend format options, and several other chart type–specific formatting options. Figure 8.7 displays the Options tab of the Chart Expert dialog for a bar chart.

Figure 8.6
The Chart Expert Options tab allows specification of data points and legends for the involved chart.

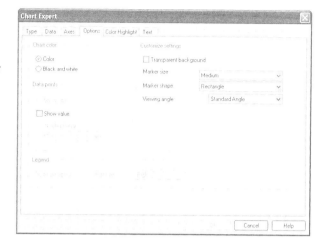

To continue customizing the bar chart you have been adding to your working sample report, follow these steps:

1. Select the Show Value button in the Data Points section.
2. Select the 1K format from the Number Format drop-down box.
3. Click the OK button.

USING THE CHART EXPERT COLOR HIGHLIGHT TAB

New to XI, the Color Highlight tab provides you with an easy method of controlling the color of the different elements (such as bars, pie slices, and so forth) in your created charts. This functionality was hard to find in previous versions of Crystal Reports, yet it was previously available through the Format button under the Chart Expert Options tab.

The color highlighting functionality enables you to create charts with consistent coloring both within and across your reports. In the sample report in this chapter, you could specify the color of any particular customer(s) or you could specify the color of multiple bars based on the sum of the Orders Amount field. An example might be that where the sum of Orders Amount is greater than 75,000, the involved bar should be colored black to highlight the positive impact on Xtreme's bottom line.

USING THE CHART EXPERT TEXT TAB

After a chart type and data have been specified, select the Text tab. This tab on the Chart Expert dialog enables you to specify titles and title formatting that the chart displays when it is placed on the report. Figure 8.7 shows the Text tab of the Chart Expert.

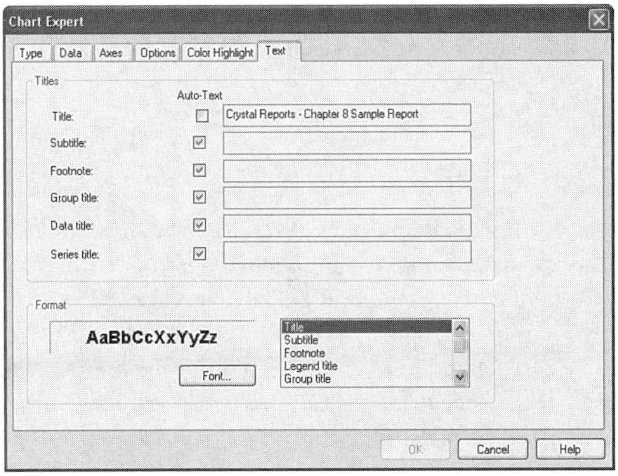

Figure 8.7
The Text tab of the Chart Expert allows specification of text labels for the associated chart.

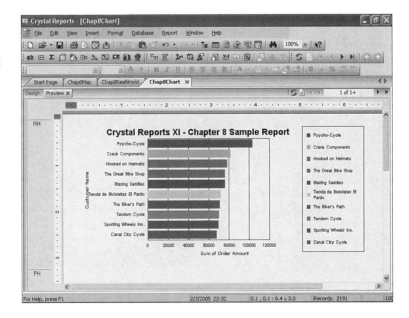

To finish adding the bar chart to the sample report, follow these steps:

1. Deselect the Auto-Text check box beside the Title entry. You should now be able to modify the text box for the title. Change the title to **Crystal Reports—Chapter 8 Sample Chart**.

2. Deselect the Auto-Text check box beside the Data Title entry. Change the Data Title entry to **Order Amounts**. Click OK and you will find a bar chart similar to that in Figure 8.8, providing a snapshot of the Top 10 Customers for this report.

Figure 8.8
A sample Customer Orders report with a bar chart highlighting the visual benefits of charting.

If you find your chart is slightly different in appearance or imperfect, that is okay. You have plenty of powerful fine-tuning tools at your disposal, and they will be explored at the end of this chapter.

USING THE MAP EXPERT

As you explore the charting capabilities of Crystal Reports, you will discover numerous powerful data visualizations that enhance the productivity of your reports and business users. Another valuable form of data presentation available in Crystal Reports is geographic mapping. This enables you to create reports that are logically grouped by geographically related information and that can communicate meaningful information in a familiar mapping model. When working with geographic data, you can quickly create a map or a map/chart combination on this data using the Map Expert.

> The maps and mapping functionality provided within Crystal Reports are bundled from a third-party company—MapInfo. Additional map layers and types can be purchased directly from MapInfo and can be made accessible from Crystal Reports by adding them to the mapping folders under \Program Files\Map Info X. You can order additional mapping information from MapInfo at www.mapinfo.com.

To open the Map Expert, either click on the Map Globe icon located on the Insert toolbar or access the Insert Map option under the Insert menu. Figure 8.9 displays the Map Expert dialog.

Figure 8.9
The Map Expert dialog enables the rapid addition of mapping visuals to a report.

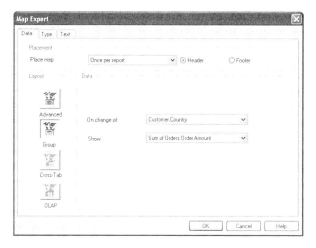

The next three sections introduce you to the functionality of the Map Expert and also escort you through a brief tutorial on the addition of a map to a sample Order Listing report slightly different than the one you just created.

USING THE MAP EXPERT DATA TAB

The Data tab on the Map Expert dialog enables you to select the specific data that the map is based on and where it will be placed on the report. Figure 8.9 displays this tab of the Map Expert. The Data tab is composed of three different sections: Placement, Layout, and Data. These sections, and corresponding options, are discussed next.

SPECIFYING MAP PLACEMENT

The Map Placement section enables the selection of the location of the map on the report and consequently the recurrence of the map throughout the report.

Using the Place Map drop-down box, select the section of the report where the map will be located (for example, Group 1, Group 2, and so on). The options available in this drop-down box are limited to the groups previously created in the report in addition to the option to create the graphic only once for the entire report. Using the radio buttons located beside the drop-down box, choose the header or footer of the selected report section. By making these selections, you have also determined the map's recurrence in the report because the map repeatedly appears in every section you have specified (for example, for each country in the group based on country).

To begin with a walk-through of an example, perform the following steps:

1. Quickly create a new report based on the Xtreme sample data 11 database, include a few columns of data in the detail section, including Order Amount, and group the report by Customer Country and then Customer Name. Finally, add summary fields on Order Amount for each of the Country and Customer Name groups.

2. Open the Map Expert.

3. Select Once Per Report in the Placement drop-down box and select the header as the map's intended location. The following sections contain more steps for this example.

SPECIFYING MAP LAYOUT

The Layout section specifies the data that the map uses. The actual data is selected in the Map Data section (described next), but the options presented in that section are dependent on the Map Layout button you have selected. Table 8.4 lists the different layout buttons and their typical use.

TABLE 8.4   MAP EXPERT LAYOUT BUTTONS AND TYPICAL USE

Layout Button	Description	Typical Use
Advanced	This layout button provides complete flexibility in map creation by giving you control of all mapping options.	Creation of maps based on summaries not already created in the report or maps based on geographic fields not contained in predefined report groups.

continues

TABLE 8.4 CONTINUED

Layout Button	Description	Typical Use
Group	Although this button is presented second, it is the default layout if the involved report has predefined groups and summary fields already created. This layout limits the Map Data Selection options (see next section) to two drop-down boxes specifying the On Change Of and Show Values and expedites the creation of a map at the cost of some of the flexibility provided by the Advanced layout button.	Quick creation of Maps based on summarized fields already in the report and to be displayed at the Report or existing Group level.
Cross-Tab	This layout button appears as an option only when your current report is a Cross-Tab report.	Creation of a map based on an existing Cross-Tab in the report.
OLAP	This layout button appears as an option only when your current report is based on an OLAP data source.	Creation of a map based on an existing OLAP grid in the report.

→ For information on the Cross-Tab and OLAP layout buttons and their related options, **see** Chapter 10, "Using Cross-Tabs for Summarized Reporting," **p. 249**, and Chapter 16, "Formatting Multidimensional Reporting Against OLAP Data," **p. 355**.

The next section explores the detailed data options enabled by the Advanced and Group Layout buttons.

CAUTION

If you attempt to create a geographic map based on a non-geographic field, the Map Expert accepts your request and then displays a blank map when it cannot resolve the selected field values to geographic entities. Make sure you select a valid geographic field in the Geographic Field item of the Advanced layout section or the On Change Of field in the Group layout section.

SPECIFYING MAP DATA

As you saw earlier, Figure 8.9 displays the Map Data section with the Group layout button selected. As described in Table 8.4, this layout option is designed to facilitate the quick creation of a map with a minimal amount of user interaction. To accomplish this rapid map creation, two pieces of information are requested through two drop-down boxes.

The first drop-down box requests you to select the On Change Of field and the second the Show field. The On Change Of field is used to determine where the selected map breaks the report data to be displayed (for example, Country, State, or Province). The Show field specifies the summary field to be displayed for each break of the data.

When using the Rapid Map Creation function of the Group layout option, you are limited to map creation based on existing summary fields already created in your reports and inserted into existing group sections. For more flexible map creation, use the Advanced layout option described later.

Figure 8.10 displays the Map Data tab with the Advanced layout button selected. The additional options presented here provide you with improved flexibility in the maps that you can create.

Figure 8.10
The Data tab with the Advanced layout button selected allows flexible selection of mapping data, layout, and placement.

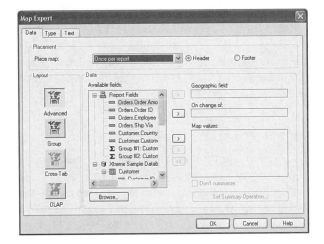

The familiar On Change Of field should be recognizable in this new window although it is selected in a more flexible manner using the selection buttons in the interface. It is selected in exactly the same manner as the Geographic field selection in this interface by selecting any of the fields in the Available Fields listing and clicking on the selection button.

The Geographic and On Change Of fields are often the same, but can be set to be different. These are set to different field values when you want to present pie or bar charts on top of the involved map and for each of the different values in the selected Geographic field. An example of this would be presenting a pie chart for each country that highlights the different order amounts by company—indicated in the On Change Of field.

After selecting your Geographic and On Change Of fields, a Map Values field must be selected to enable the map's creation. This selection specifies the summary field to be displayed for each break of the data and can come from any field (database, report, formula, and so on) that is listed in the available field's list. To select the Show Value fields, highlight the intended field and use the selection arrow buttons adjacent to the Map Values list box.

As mentioned previously, you do not need to have had an existing summary on a report to summarize on it using the Advanced Mapping layout options. You can add any field to the Map Values list and then dynamically create a summary by clicking on the Set Summary Operation button. These dynamically created summaries are automatically created and used by the map.

To continue adding a map to your sample report, follow these steps:

1. Ensure that the Advanced layout button from the Layout section is selected.

2. Select Country for the Geographic field. This indicates that the map breaks for each different country. Leave the On Change Of field as Country when this gets populated automatically.

3. Select Order Amount for the Show field and leave the default Sum as the summary operation. This indicates that the map reflects this Sum of Orders for each country. You will finish creating this map in the next two sections.

USING THE MAP EXPERT TYPE TAB

The Type tab enables you to select from the five different types of maps that are available for presentation. The five map types can be logically broken into two distinct and separate categories—maps that present a summarization based on one variable, and maps that present a summarization based on two variables. The Type tab with these five map types is depicted in Figure 8.11. All five of the map types are also described in Table 8.5.

Figure 8.11
The Map Expert Type tab enables you to select from the different types of maps available for display in your report.

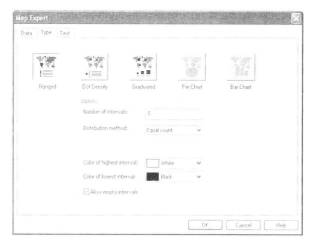

The first three map types shown base their maps on the summary of the selected Show Value field and for each Geographic field—the single fluctuating variable. The last two map types base their maps not only on the changing Geographic field, but also on a second fluctuating variable selected in the On Change Of field. Based on this second variable changing, either bar or pie charts are displayed on top of each of the involved Geographic fields. Table 8.5 describes the different map types, and includes a sample scenario for each.

TABLE 8.5   MAP TYPES WITH CORRESPONDING SAMPLE REPORTING SCENARIO

Map Type	Description	Sample Scenario
Ranged	Breaks data into specified ranges and displays geographic areas on the map in different colors.	A U.S.-based firm looking for a Sales Map that highlights the states that fall into a specified number of sales/ revenue ranges.
Dot Density	Displays a dot for each occurrence of a specified item.	A growing wireless company in Eastern Canada wants to view the density and point location of new customers and map that to ongoing marketing campaigns.
Graduated	Displays data that is linked to points rather than precise geographical areas.	An Irish beverage company wants a report on geographically dispersed distributors, proportionately highlighting the amount of product being distributed.
Pie Chart	Displays a pie chart over each geographic area. Each slice of the pie represents an individual summarization relative to the whole for the given geographic area.	An employee head-count report for the United States with a pie chart over each state that highlights the breakdown of the employees by status including salaried, hourly, or temporary.
Bar Chart	Displays a bar chart over each geographic area. Each bar represents an individual summarization relative to the other summarizations for the given geographic area.	A marketing media report for a U.S.- based company with a bar chart that highlights the amount of advertising and marketing dollars spent in different media in each region: TV, Internet, newspaper, magazine, and so on.

Each Map Type has a small number of associated options that can be set to customize the appearance of that particular map. You are encouraged to explore these options to help you find the maps most useful for your specific design goals.

USING THE MAP EXPERT TEXT TAB

After a map's type and data have been selected, select the Text tab. This tab on the Map Expert dialog enables you to specify titles and legend formatting that the map uses when it is placed on the report.

To finish adding a map to your sample report, follow these steps:

On the Type tab, select the Ranged map type.

Select Yellow and Blue as the respective low and high range colors.

Click on the Text tab and give your map a title such as **Crystal Reports—Chapter 8 Map Sample**.

Click OK, and you will find a geographic map added to your report that should look similar to Figure 8.12.

Figure 8.12
A sample Customer Orders Report with a geographic map.

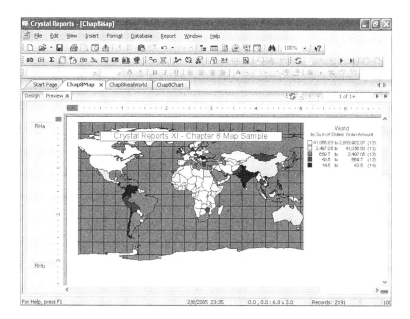

MODIFYING CHART AND MAP PROPERTIES

After you have successfully created a chart or map and placed it on your report, you have a number of post-creation editing options at your disposal within the Crystal Reports Designer. Both charts and maps provide a number of easy-to-use methods to re-visit and edit your charts or maps. Several of the most common editing methods are listed in the following sections.

MODIFYING CHART PROPERTIES

After a chart has been created and placed on your report, you can perform numerous post-creation edits by right-clicking on the chart object while in Preview mode. From the Chart menu that appears, you have both the ability to revisit the Chart Expert and use a number of more finely tuned post-creation editing tools, including the powerful and flexible Chart Option functions.

NOTE

> Versions 9, 10 and XI of Crystal Reports give you greater abilities to perform numerous in-place edits to chart objects. For example, you can grab a chart title (or other object) and move its location or change its font directly in place in these recent versions. Previous to version 9, this functionality was mostly accessible from a separate tab called the Chart Analyzer. This tab is no longer available.

FORMAT CHART OPTIONS

As introduced in Chapter 6, "Fundamentals of Report Formatting," the Format Chart dialog enables you to add common formatting options for the involved chart. Common options set here for charts include borders, ToolTips, and/or general hyperlinks. Review Chapter 6 for a detailed discussion of the different general formatting options you have for the chart.

USING AND CREATING CHART TEMPLATES

The Load Template selection provides direct access to a set of almost 100 custom charts in eight categories, including Basic, Big Data Sets, Corporate, Gradients, Letter Size B&W, Letter Size Color, Surveys, and User Defined. By selecting one of these predefined templates, all of the formatting attributes of the selected template will overwrite those on your existing chart. The Save Template option enables the saving of your own personal charting templates and enables future re-use of those across other reports. Chart templates can be particularly useful if you want to apply standard corporate chart formatting across your organization.

SPECIFYING CHART SIZE AND POSITION

This option enables you to identify very specific x and y coordinates in addition to height and width measurements for the involved chart. Charts can also be dynamically resized and repositioned by grabbing any of the sizing handles that appear on the frame of the chart after it is selected.

MODIFYING CHART OPTIONS

The Chart Options menu choice enables you to fine-tune the look of your charts at a granular level not available in the standard Chart Expert. The following sections explore the variety of chart customizations and formatting options exposed through the Chart Options menu. These are especially useful where the functionality of the standard chart creation expert does not meet your exact requirements. The chart options are made accessible through a rich multi-tabbed interface with a chart preview window. Figure 8.13 highlights the interface, and the following paragraphs describe the details of the respective tabs.

The *Appearance tab* provides general formatting options for each chart type. These settings give you a great deal of flexibility in controlling the details of the involved graphics (such as Pie Chart tilt, rotation, hole size, and exploding pie characteristics, or Bar Chart shape, overlap, width, depth, and so on).

Figure 8.13
The Chart Options dialog provides advanced chart configuration functionality.

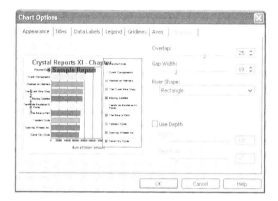

Some common options for pie, bar, and other charts include the following:

- **Overlap**—Use this slider to change how much risers within each category overlap each other.

- **Gap Width**—Use this slider to change the gap between the group of bar risers in each category.

- **Riser Shape**—Use this list box to choose the shape of the chart's bars or risers.

- **Use Depth**—Use this check box to apply a depth effect or to make a completely flat chart.

- **Depth**—When Use Depth is selected, use this slider to specify the amount of depth to be applied to the chart risers and frame.

- **Pie Tilt**—Use this slider to tilt the involved pie chart(s).

- **Pie Rotation**—Use this slider to rotate the involved pie(s).

- **Explode Pie**—Exploding a pie or doughnut chart detaches all slices away from its center. Select the Series option from the right-click menu of a highlighted pie slice if you want to attach or detach an individual slice from a chart.

The *Titles tab* enables you to specify chart titles, subtitles, footnotes, and so on. Many charts also include axis title specifications such as Group Axis title or Data Axis title here.

The *Data Labels tab* provides formatting and display options for data labels. The different options enable you to select the presentation of data labels based on either the underlying value representing the chart graphics, the associated label, or a combination of the two.

The *Legend tab* provides options for changing the appearance of the involved chart. The Color Mode drop-down box enables you to select a color scheme for the involved chart components. This is typically a decision between coloring by group or by series, although other options are provided for surface charts. The visual effects of these modes are only truly seen when more than one Change By field has been set for the involved chart.

The remaining options surround the display of the legend (available on most charts) and its placement relative to the chart.

The *Gridlines tab* provides options for displaying or hiding gridlines for specified chart types. Typical options set here include gridline display for both the group and data axis.

The *Axes tab* provides display options for both the data and group axis. You can also select to use dual Y axes for your chart if you have previously selected two On Change Of fields in the Chart Expert and also decide if you want those dual axes split or shown in the same grid.

The *Multi-Axes tab* provides selection options for the display of your dual Y axes report. By default, when a dual Y axis report is selected, half of your series members will be assigned to each Y axis. You can change that default assignment in this tab. If a split axis has been selected, you can also select some display options about the proportion of the grid taken by each split of the Y axes.

SPECIFYING SERIES OPTIONS

This menu option is used to apply formatting options to an individual series in a chart. The Series Option is only available for selection if a series was previously selected in the chart. This series selection is done in place in Crystal Reports (for example, highlighting a pie slice on a pie chart enables the Series Option functionality for that pie slice's series). Figure 8.14 highlights the Series Option dialog for the chart you created earlier this chapter, and the following paragraphs describe the different tabs available on the Series option dialog and some common usage scenarios.

Figure 8.14
The Series Option dialog provides the capability to specify chart series options such as trendlines, data labels, and number formats.

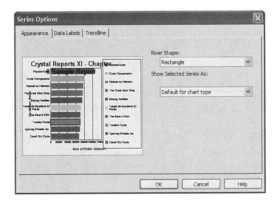

The *Appearance tab* shows general formatting options for a selected series. Common display effects enacted here include altering the visual metaphor for a selected series so it is different than the other series (for example, displaying the U.S. Sales results as an area visual on a bar chart). In certain charts such as 3D Charts, the selection of each series' riser shape is also available.

The *Data Labels tab* shows data label display options for the currently selected series. It enables you to specify series-specific data labels. This functionality is effective for highlighting a series of particular relevance. Unlike the General menu option's Data Labels tab, this series-specific functionality only enables the setting of numeric-based data labels.

The *Trendline tab* provides display and formatting options for a trendline selection. It enables you to represent trends in a data series graphically. You can add trendlines to data series in a number of unstacked charts (such as 2D area, bar, bubble, column, line, and scatter charts). Several different automatic trendline creations are possible including Linear, Logarithmic, Polynomial, or Exponential trendlines, in addition to Moving Averages.

SPECIFYING X AND Y AXIS OPTIONS

These chart options are used to format chart axes, axis numbers, gridlines, and scaling. Unlike versions previous to XI, the axis options are now accessed independently by selecting any axis object and its associated right-click menu, and then the involved Axis Options menu selection. When an axis dialog is selected, the tabs at the top of the dialog reflect the available formatting options for that axis. Figure 8.15 shows the Data (Y) Axis Settings dialog for this chapter's sample report, and the following paragraphs describe the different tabs available on the Axis Option dialogs and some common usage scenarios.

Figure 8.15
The Data (Y) Axis Settings dialog provides granular level control over chart axis display options. A similar dialog is available for the group (X) axis.

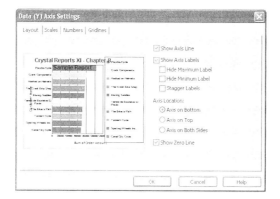

The *Layout tab* shows general formatting options for a selected axis. You can specify the location of the Axis labels here (for example, top, bottom, left, right, both) through the Location of the Label radio buttons. Additional options of interest new to version XI are the abilities to stagger labels automatically and to skip a specified number of labels.

The *Scales tab* provides options around the scale for the involved axis. The most common options set in this tab are the manually set maximum and minimum scale options. These enable increased control over the range presented on the involved axis. Other options include settings around the logarithmic scale and forcing the inclusion of zero in the axis range. New to Version XI, settings for using a descending axis and for selecting a minor gridline interval can be made here.

The *Numbers tab* shows formatting options for data axis numbers. This tab enables you to specify data axis numeric data label formatting. The category drop-down box enables you to select a general format for the numeric component of the data labels. After this is selected, more granular options are exposed for control over the display of each format. If you are looking to format the data label numbers displayed within the chart, you must select them and access the Format Data Label option from their right-click menu.

The *Grid tab* provides access to the Gridline formatting options for the involved data axis. This tab enables you to specify the involved axis' displayed gridlines including Custom Gridlines specified at certain values and different grid formats.

SPECIFYING SELECTED ITEM FORMATTING OPTIONS

This Chart Options menu selection enables you to format line, area, and text objects in a chart. It is only available when a chart object has been selected with the mouse or other pointer. Figure 8.16 highlights the Formatting dialog. Different tabs (Font, Line, or Fill) are highlighted and available based on the underlying selected chart item.

Figure 8.16
The Formatting dialog provides the capability to format user-selected objects within the involved chart.

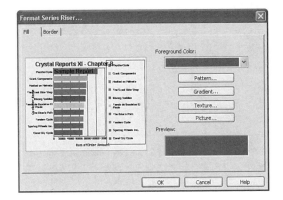

SPECIFYING 3D VIEWING ANGLE OPTIONS

This menu option is only available for 3D charts. It enables you to edit the involved chart's viewing angles, position, wall thickness, and so on. The basic options enable you to select a predefined viewing angle template. The advanced options enable you to create new templates and refine the manipulation of the 3D Chart. Figure 8.17 highlights the Viewing Angles Advanced Option dialog.

Figure 8.17
The Viewing Angles Advanced dialog provides the capability to specify precise viewing angles for 3D charts.

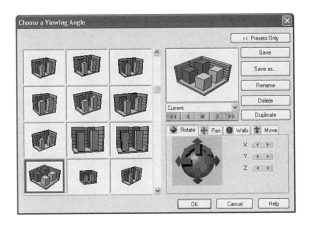

The *Rotate tab* and its X,Y, and Z dimension controls are used to rotate a 3D chart to any angle. There are three different methods or controls to change the rotation of the chart:

- Use the X, Y, and Z left and right control buttons to incrementally rotate the chart in the preview window.
- Use the directional arrows surrounding the globe to affect the rotation.
- Use the preview window itself to click and drag the previewed chart around the different axes.

The *Pan tab* is used to pan and zoom a 3D chart. The same control options exist here as were described for the Rotate tab, with the Zoom option being an additional component.

The *Walls tab* provides a method to increase and decrease the thickness and length of the walls on a 3D chart. The same control options exist for this tab as those mentioned previously for the Rotate tab.

The *Move tab* provides a method to move and set the perspective of the 3D chart. The same control options exist for this tab as those mentioned previously for the Rotate tab.

> You will find separate and advanced charting help instructions for these granular options available through the help button present on all the dialogs accessed from the Chart Options menu. This advanced help is provided by 3D Graphics—the third party responsible for the charting in Crystal Reports.

MODIFYING MAP PROPERTIES

After a map has been created and placed on your report, you can perform numerous post-creation edits by right-clicking on the map object while in the Preview mode. From the menu that appears when you right-click, you have the capability to either re-visit the Map Expert or use a number of more finely tuned post-creation editing tools such as Zooming, Layer Control, Map Navigation, and Data Mismatch Resolution.

FORMAT MAP OPTIONS

As introduced in Chapter 6, the Format Map dialog enables you to add common formatting options for the involved chart. Common options set here for charts include borders, ToolTips, and/or general hyperlinks. Review Chapter 6 for a detailed discussion of the general formatting options available for the chart.

SIZE AND POSITION

This option enables you to specify very specific X and Y coordinates, in addition to height and width measurements for the involved map. Maps can also be dynamically resized and repositioned by grabbing any of the sizing handles that appear on the frame of the map after it is selected.

LAYER CONTROL

By clicking on the Layers menu option, you can specify the different layers that display on your map. Examples of this include World Capital Cities and the Mapping Grid. Crystal Reports version XI is distributed with a number of built-in layers that are accessed through this Layer Control dialog. These layers can be added and removed from Crystal Reports using this dialog and more detail-oriented layers. Additional maps can be purchased separately from MapInfo (a third-party company) and integrated into Crystal Reports.

RESOLVE MISMATCH

The Resolve Mismatch dialog provides two very useful functions for maps. First, the Resolve Mismatch dialog enables you to select a specific map to use for your report. Several maps are provided out of the box with Crystal Reports and others can be purchased separately. Additionally, you can match the field names stored in the Geographic field from which you are basing the map onto the names that the involved map is expecting. This powerful feature enables you to take raw, untransformed data and dynamically match it to a geographical map value that the mapping engine can understand. For example, on a map of Canada, you might have multiple inconsistent data entries in your database for the province of Ontario (for example, ON, Ont, Ontario, and so on). Using this dialog, you can match each of these to the expected value of Ontario, and the mapping engine successfully interprets all of them.

ZOOMING AND PANNING

The Zoom In and Zoom Out options enable you to focus on a particularly relevant part of the involved map. The Panning option enables you to horizontally pan the view of the map to what is most interesting to you and your business users. When any of these options have been selected from the Map menu, you are then placed in an interactive mode with the map and your mouse/touchpad. Clicking zooms you in and out and double-clicking and dragging facilitates panning. When you are finished working in these special design modes, you can change back to the Select Mode for standard map navigation.

TIP

When selecting from the Map menu, the Map Navigator provides a thumbnail of the entire map you are currently working with. As you saw earlier, Figure 8.12 highlights this Map Navigator in your report sample. The Map Navigator also provides a dotted outline of the area that is currently selected for display. You can fine-tune the area that displays by grabbing this dotted line, double-clicking on any of its corners, and subsequently dragging or expanding them out or collapsing them in while holding down your second click.

TROUBLESHOOTING

CHARTING ON A FIELD NOT ALREADY GROUPED IN THE REPORT

I want to create a chart based on changing a specific field but don't know how.

Select the On Change Of charting option under the Advanced layout option and then specify the field or fields to break the chart sections on by selecting any of the fields in the available fields listing. Unlike the drop-down box under the Group layout, you can select any of the available report fields in this interface, dynamically order them with the Order button, or restrict their display on the report to a specified Top or Bottom N with the Top N button.

DISPLAYING A CHART BESIDE RELATED REPORT DATA

I want to add a chart to a report that is displayed alongside or inline with other displayed report data.

This can be accomplished by adding your charts into report sections (for instance, Group or Report Headers) above the data you wish to have them displayed besides. You can then use the Underlay Following Sections option accessed through the Section Expert dialog. With some design forethought, you can create nicely formatted reports that integrate both data and visuals very closely.

CRYSTAL REPORTS IN THE REAL WORLD— COMPLEX CHARTS

Charts can be particularly useful when they display data that is different but complementary. Although it is certainly possible to show data in multiple charts, showing complementary data in the same chart allows direct comparison of information and more efficient use of space. The following steps will walk through a good example of this:

1. Start by opening the report Chap8Chart.rpt. In the chart that will be added, bars represent the individual stores and a line shows the running total across all stores.

2. With the report open, right-click on the field Order Amount and choose Insert, Running Total. When the Create Running Total Field window opens, give the running total a name like Total Order Amount and leave the remaining values as defaults similar to Figure 8.18. Click OK to close the window.

3. From the Insert menu, select Chart and place it on your report above the existing chart (you will need to move the original chart down in the same section). Open the new chart's Chart Expert, go to the Data tab and click the Advanced button. Select the Customer Name field and use the upper arrow (>) button to move the field to the On Change Of window. Finally, select the Order Amount and Total Sales fields and add them to the Show Values window using the lower arrow (>) button. The results of this step should resemble Figure 8.19.

Figure 8.18
Creating this Running Total field will help present a creative use of charts.

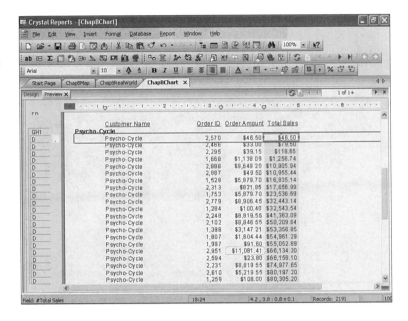

Figure 8.19
Creating an advanced chart with a two summary fields will enable some creative charting.

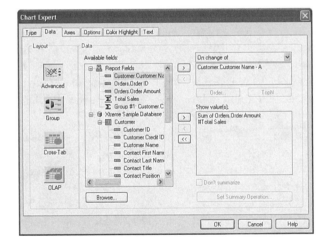

4. Select the Customer Name field in the On Change Of window and click the Top N button. When the Group Sort Expert window opens, select All from the list box and choose Descending. Click OK to close the window.

5. Click the Text tab. Uncheck the Title Auto-Text boxes and type **Comparison Chart** into the Chart Title text box. Click OK to close the window and return to the report.

6. Using the handles on the chart object, stretch the chart to fit the page width. Figure 8.20 provides a good benchmark.

Figure 8.20
Bars representing both Individual Client Sales and Total Cumulative Sales are displayed on the same chart, effectively communicating multiple pieces of information in one chart.

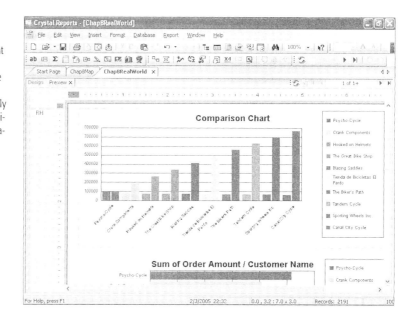

7. Notice that because the Total Sales becomes such a large value, the contrast between individual sales values appears quite small using this scale. To change this, the report will be changed to use a dual Y axis. This enables you to show both sets of values while still highlighting the contrast between individual elements within a set. To change the chart to a dual Y axis, right-click anywhere in the chart and choose Chart Options and then the Axes tab. Click on the Dual Axes box, ensure the Split Dual Axis check box is not checked for this exercise, and then click OK.

8. To enable this chart to better project both sets of information more clearly, you could set a split dual axis back in the Chart Options dialog or you could change the display format of the involved series. To do the latter, first navigate to the Legends tab in the Chart Options menu and change the Color Mode to Color by Series. Next, click any of the individual Total Sales bars to select it, and then right-click the bar and select Chart Options, Series. Change the list box from Default for Chart Type to Line and click OK to close.

9. Save the report.

Figure 8.21
Bars represent
Individual Client Sales
and a line represents
Total Cumulative Sales
with two separate
numeric scales
displayed.

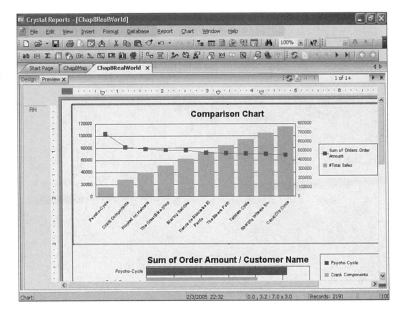

TIP

The preceding example provided a great example of displaying different data sets in the same chart. Another practical use of this functionality is displaying averages (or running total calculations) over time in the line chart to complement the other bar chart sums by some specified time period (such as a month). Essentially, you could create a chart that represents a moving average laid on top of the monthly sums.

CHAPTER 9

CUSTOM FORMATTING TECHNIQUES

In this chapter

INTRODUCTION

This chapter focuses on more complex formatting to make reports look like high-quality information portals rather than simply paper reports. Often a software suite is either powerful or easy to use, but Crystal Reports actually does a great job of being both and can be best described as having layers of complexity. For the beginner, a simple listing report can suffice but the advanced user may extend this listing report with formatting, interactive reports, and powerful charts.

MAKING PRESENTATION-QUALITY REPORTS

Up to this point in the book, the focus of the chapters has been on making sure that the data appears as required. The next step, formatting, keeps users coming back to the reports time and time again. When we talk about formatting, users often assume we're simply making a report "pretty" or "boardroom quality" and this simply isn't the case. With rich formatting, the data should be easier to read, understand, and navigate. Rich formatting should guide the reader's eye to those elements of the report that are most important and in the case of reports that mimic paper documents, your Crystal Report can be made to look identical to the original document—adoption of your new report should be very impressive.

Formatting can take many different forms, from basic font coloring to hyperlinks to conditional formatting (formatting that is based on the data). This chapter examines a cross-section of all these types of formatting to give the report author a good basis for report formatting.

This chapter presents a series of tutorials to enable you to add formatting to a report started in an earlier chapter. Let's assume that you would like to improve the report that was started in Chapter 6, "Fundamentals of Report Formatting."

COMMON FORMATTING FEATURES

The most common formatting feature is changing font color or font face. This can be done by choosing the features directly on the Formatting toolbar, as shown in Figure 9.1.

Chapter 6 introduced the Highlighting Expert, so if more detail is necessary it can be found there.

Figure 9.1
The Crystal Reports Formatting toolbar lets you change object formatting.

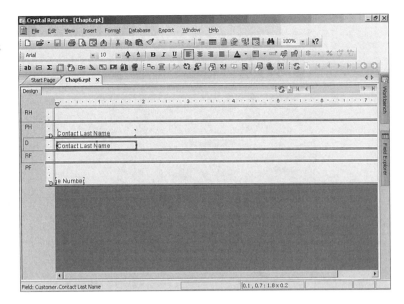

WORKING WITH TOOLTIPS

All report objects can have rollover text or ToolTips available when the report is viewed. For example, if you would like to use descriptive text to explain why a certain formula was created, you could do this with a ToolTip.

In the example created in Chapter 6, you now want to inform the end user about a formula. The text should appear whenever a user mouses over the 'Days Until Shipped' fields on the report. The following steps create a ToolTip:

1. Open Chap6RealWorld.rpt, or the report created earlier in Chapter 6. Select File, Open and browse to find Chap6RealWorld.rpt and open it.

2. Format the e-mail field at the far right. Right-click on it and choose Format Field.

3. Add the ToolTip text. In the Format Editor dialog, select the Common tab. To the right of the ToolTip Text box, click on the formula editor button (see Figure 9.2), and enter the following formula, which makes a custom message for each e-mail address:

```
"Click here to compose an e-mail to " +
{Customer.Contact First Name} + " " +
{Customer.Contact Last Name} + "."
```

4. Test the ToolTip text. Click OK to finish the formatting. In Preview, scroll the mouse over the e-mail field and see that the rollover text now appears as a custom message, which is different when viewed by each e-mail recipient. Before proceeding, save the report as **Chap9_1.rpt** by choosing File, Save As.

Figure 9.2
On the Common tab,
click the ToolTip text
formula button.

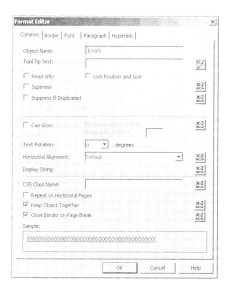

LINES AND BOXES

Adding lines and boxes to a report can make it easier to read as well as visually grouping items for business users.

To add lines under each Detail section as well as a box around each group, follow these steps:

1. View Chap9_1.rpt in Design mode. If the report is not already open, open it using Ctrl+O. Make sure that the report is in Design Mode by choosing Ctrl+D.

2. Insert the line by Choosing Insert, Line. The mouse changes to a pencil. Move the mouse to the bottom-left of the fields in the Details Section. Hold down the left mouse button to begin drawing the line. Scroll the mouse to the right until you reach the end of the Details Section. Once reached, release the mouse button.

3. View the result in Preview mode. Select F5 to refresh the report to see the line with the data as shown in Figure 9.3.

4. Add the box by choosing Insert, Box. The mouse changes to a pencil. Move the mouse to the top-left of the Country/Pays USA data in the Group Header. Hold down the left mouse button to begin drawing the box. Scroll the mouse down to the bottom left of the Summary amount in the Group Footer and then scroll to the right until the end of the Group Footer section. Once reached, release the mouse button. The resulting box should appear similar to Figure 9.4.

5. Choose File, Save As and save the report as **Chap9_2.rpt**.

Figure 9.3
Use the Preview mode view of a report to show a line under each detail record.

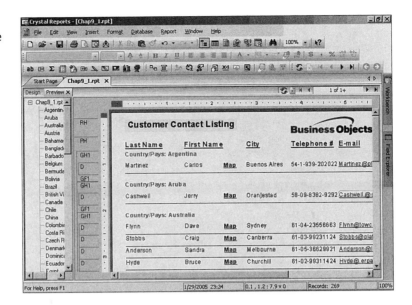

Figure 9.4
Preview a report to show lines and boxes.

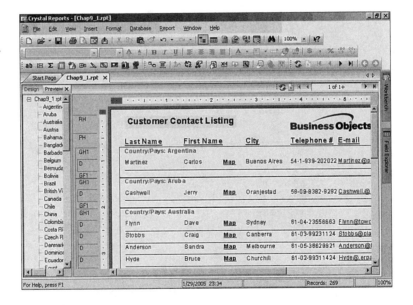

TIP

A feature of boxes is that they can be rounded. To do this right-click on a box, choose Format Box, and select the Rounding tab. The rounding factor can be changed by the slide or the percentage buttons. Figure 9.5 shows how Xtreme's report would look with a rounded box at 30%.

Preview of a report
showing rounded
boxes.

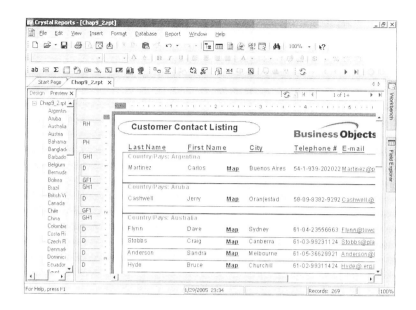

Another visually pleasing feature is the capability to rotate text. This can be very effective when used in conjunction with the Underlay Section property for sections. Follow these steps to make a sample watermark:

Start by using Chap9_2.rpt in Design mode. Choose Insert, Text Object to add a text field in the Report Header. Enter **DRAFT** for the text.

Right-click on the Text field and choose Format Text. Select the Common tab. Change the Text Rotation to 90 degrees and click OK. Go to the Font tab, where you can change the font size to 48pts. Because you want this watermark to be semi-transparent, choose the More item from the Color drop-down, where you can specify a custom color. Choose a light gray (or silver). Increase the Character font spacing by specifying 70 pts in the dialog, then exit the dialog by clicking OK twice.

> This color section, common to all objects within Crystal Reports 10, enables you to specify colors using RGB or Hue, Saturation, and Luminance. By choosing corporate colors and adding them to the custom colors, you can extend corporate branding into report presentation.

Resize the field. Because the field needs to go down the page, it needs to be resized to be narrow and long. Select the field and choose the rightmost square on the field. Resize the object by holding down the left mouse button. Now choose the bottom square on the field and stretch the height to 5". Figure 9.6 shows how this should look.

Figure 9.6
Design tab with text rotation applied to text field.

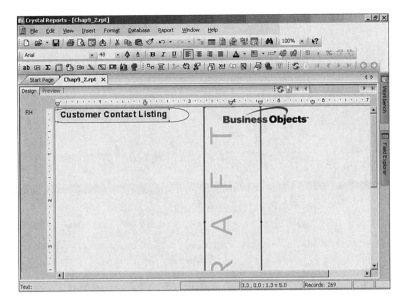

4. Refresh the report to see your progress by pressing F5. It shows the text rotated, although it is not running down beside the records as shown in Figure 9.7

Figure 9.7
Preview of the report with text rotation.

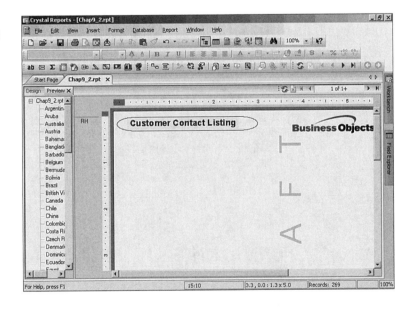

5. Set the Report Header to Underlay. Because the text does not yet flow to the record level, it must be underlayed. This is a section property. Right-click in the Report Header section located on the left side of the report design area, choose Section Expert, and click the Insert button near the top left. Be sure to select Report Header B in the Sections window and put a check in the box to the left of Underlay Following Sections, and click OK. Drag your text box into Report Header B. The desired results should appear similar to Figure 9.8.

Figure 9.8
Preview of the report with rotated text flowing behind the detail records.

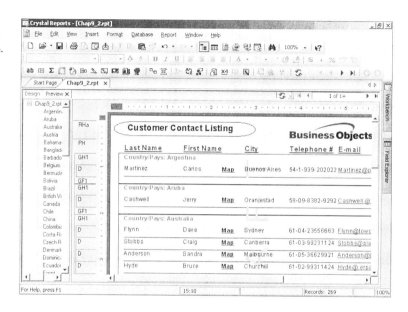

Realize that when rotating text, the justification rules might be opposite of what would normally be expected. In the case of 90 degrees, the text must be right-justified to have the company name appear to be top-justified, as shown in Figure 9.9.

6. Save as **Chap9_3.rpt**.

CONDITIONAL FORMATTING—USING DATA TO DRIVE THE LOOK OF A REPORT

Up to now, the focus has been on static formatting. The next step is to apply formatting based on the data that is being returned from a field or even applying formatting on one field based on the value of another.

Conditional formatting relies on formulas. Because the formula language is extensive, complex statements can be created. This chapter will introduce fairly simple examples to illustrate.

The simplest way to add conditional formatting is to use the Highlighting Expert. This feature enables us to apply font face and font color changes to database fields based on their values.

> **T I P**
>
> Almost every formatting option can be conditional. To determine which ones are conditional, look at the x+2 button next to the option in the Formatting Editor dialogs.
>
> If a formatting option has already been set to a conditional format, the button appears with red text. Otherwise, it appears as blue text.

9

APPLYING FORMATTING FROM ANOTHER FIELD

1. In Design view, right-click the Contact Last Name field, choose Format Field, and then navigate to the Font tab and click the formula button to the right of the Color dropdown. This opens the formula editor, driving your font color choice.

2. Enter the following formula:
   ```
   SELECT {Customer.Last Year's Sales}
   CASE 0 TO 1000: crRed
   CASE 1001 TO 100000: crYellow
   CASE IS > 100001: crGreen;
   ```

> **N O T E**
>
> Here you specified a color as the result of the case expression because the formula controlled color. In cases where the formatting option is Boolean (that is, either you turn the feature on or off) there is an assumed IF statement, and all you have to do is enter the condition (for example, `{table.field} > 100`). Entering a full IF statement in cases like this causes an error.

3. Refresh the report by pressing F5 while you're in the Preview tab. Now you see red, yellow, and green last names depending on the amount of last year's sales for that person (see Figure 9.9).

4. Save the report as **chap9_4.rpt**.

Conditional highlighting based on another field.

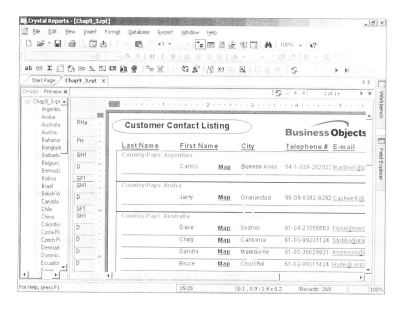

No matter how well designed, no single report can be expected to address all the needs of a business. Even if it could be done, the report would be unhelpful to the users—overwhelming and hard to read. One way of making the information easy to manage is to break it out over several reports but make navigation easy by placing hyperlinks in the report to allow the user to move smoothly from report to report.

In the Chap9_4 report, you'll add a hyperlink that opens a report from BusinessObjects Enterprise. More about Enterprise will be explained in Part V, "Web Report Distribution—Using BO Enterprise," but for now just follow along.

From the menu choose File, Open. In the bottom left of the Open dialog window there is a button labeled Enterprise. Click the button and, if you aren't already connected to Enterprise, you will be prompted to log on. If you don't know the appropriate information to log on, move to the next section.

Browse to the Report Samples folder, then the General Business folder, and finally to the World Sales Report and click open.

With the World Sales Report open, right-click on the chart and choose copy. Using the report tabs displayed right below the toolbars, go back to the Chap9_4 report.

Right-click on the Customer Contact Listing text, choose format text, and click the hyperlink tab.

Select Another Report Object and click the Paste button. You will see much of the window get populated. If the Paste button is not enabled, go back to your World Sales Report, select the chart, right-click the chart, choose copy, and try again. By copying the chart, you're actually trapping significant information about the chart that the designer interprets for you.

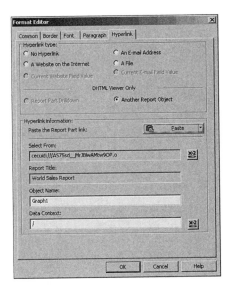

Figure 9.10
Creating a hyperlink to another report.

6. Click OK. From the View menu, choose HTML Preview. When the preview has opened, mouse over the Customer Contact Listing text box and notice that the mouse cursor changes, indicating a hyperlink. Clicking the hyperlink will open the World Sales Report.

7. This powerful feature allows users to flow from one report to another with the potential to drill down from a high level to very low level of detail or to a completely different subject matter altogether.

CRYSTAL REPORTS IN THE REAL WORLD—ADVANCED CHARTING

Nothing enables users to visualize data better than a chart. With a glance, charts enable users to see relative distribution, peaks, and valleys of values. This section describes how to use charting in creative ways. The following creates a report that charts the sum of sales and distribution of customers by country:

1. Open the World Sales Report from C:\Program Files\Business Objects\Crystal Reports 11\Samples\en\Reports\General Business.

   Stretch the chart so it takes the full width of the page. In the left margin, right-click on the text Group Footer 1 (the text might simply say GF1 if you are using short section names), and choose Suppress from the menu.

Right-click on the chart and choose Chart Expert. For Chart Type choose Bar and from the options that refine which type of bar chart, choose the left option listed as Side by Side Bar Chart (see Figure 9.11).

Choosing a chart type.

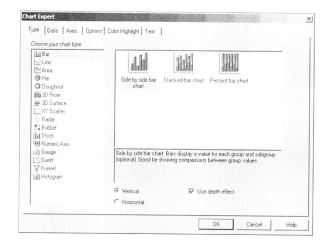

Click on the Data tab and the Advanced button. From the list of available fields select Customer.Country and add it to the window below On Change Of. Again, from the list of available fields choose Customer.Last Year's Sales and Customer.Customer Name and add them to the Show Values (see Figure 9.12).

Selecting data for the chart.

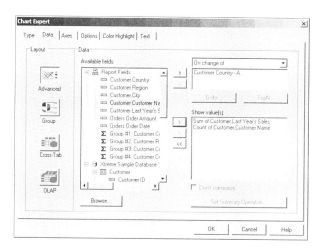

Click the Options tab and uncheck the Show Label option. Click OK to close the window.

5. The bar chart is almost complete. It contains the correct data so it is technically accurate, but because the scale of the values is so different it is unreadable for the user. See Figure 9.13.

Figure 9.13
Technically accurate but not helpful yet….

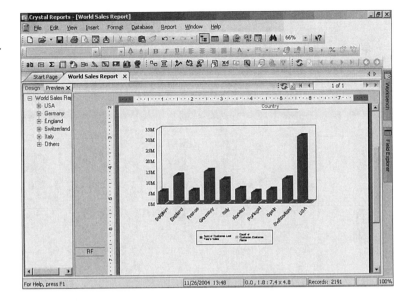

6. Because the scale of the data is significantly different, the chart needs to be broken into two axes. Right-click on the chart and choose Chart Options, Axes tab. Click the Dual Axis check box, and click OK. The resulting chart should look like Figure 9.14.

Figure 9.14
Chart showing two scales of information.

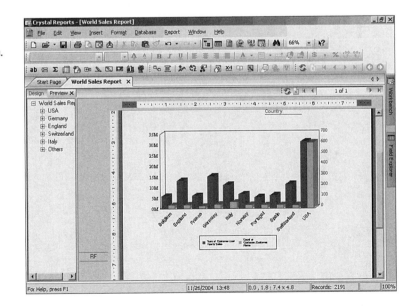

7. Finally, a trend line can be added to the chart to show a trend in the data. Right-click on the customer name bar and choose Series Options. Click the Trendline tab and add a check to the Show Trendlines check box and click OK. The resulting chart should resemble Figure 9.15. Save the report as World Sales Report with Charts.rpt.

Figure 9.15
Chart showing two scales of information and a trend line.

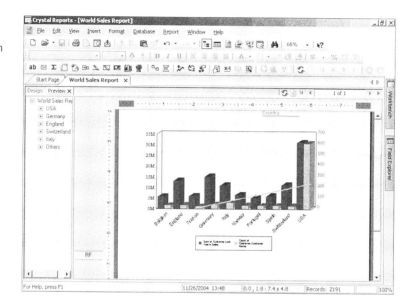

ADVANCED CRYSTAL REPORT DESIGN

CHAPTER 10

USING CROSS-TABS FOR SUMMARIZED REPORTING

In this chapter

INTRODUCTION TO CROSS-TABS

Cross-tabs are highly formatted and densely populated reports that look a lot like a spreadsheet. This chapter gives you an understanding of how and when to use cross-tabs for your reporting needs.

A *cross-tab* is a fully summarized set of cells in a grid format. It summarizes values both across as well as down. It is a compact representation of information that is grouped on two different axes. There can be more than one level of grouping on either axis (row or column).

A *row* goes across the page with the header on the left or right, whereas a column runs down the page with the header at the top or bottom. The intersections between the rows and columns are called cells. Cells are places where a value to be summarized displays. Totals in the cells are summarized for each row and column as well as the break points for the different levels of groupings.

BENEFITS OF CROSS-TABS

Cross-tabs deliver data in a familiar spreadsheet format. They also summarize both vertically and horizontally, have a grid format, and can change size depending on the data.

Several of the most compelling reasons for using cross-tabs are

- Making better use of space
- Leveraging experience with the spreadsheet format
- Horizontal expansion
- Custom formatting

Because cross-tabs are grouped and summarized both vertically *and* horizontally, they are incredibly efficient at saving space as compared to a typical grouping report. They are very good at showing key information if the information required has at least two levels of grouping.

Here's an example: quarterly sales figures for the customers in a sales report. These need to be grouped by customer and quarter. If the report were shown in a standard grouping layout like you've worked with previously, it could be several pages long. Figure 10.1 shows a typical Crystal Report in which nine pages display only the USA customers grouped by customer and quarter.

Cross-tabs replicate the information contained in a sales report while resembling a spreadsheet. Managers get a one-stop view of all the customers and their quarterly sales. Figure 10.2 shows how the information is more efficiently presented when a cross-tab is used to display the same information. Now the manager can view all the sales information at a glance.

Figure 10.1
Standard grouping style used on a typical sales report.

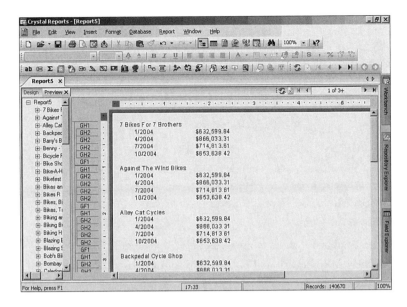

Figure 10.2
Sales shown in a cross-tab.

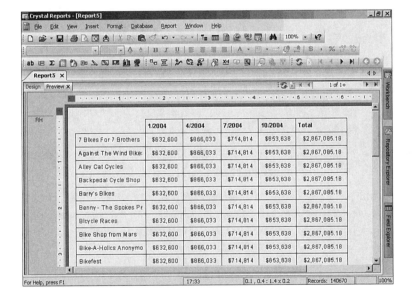

LEVERAGING EXPERIENCE WITH THE SPREADSHEET FORMAT

Another benefit of the cross-tab format is its familiarity to many users of spreadsheet applications. Many people use spreadsheets in their daily routines and are accustomed to their look and feel. Because cross-tabs do appear very much like spreadsheets, Crystal Reports offers a familiar format and reporting style for many users. Again, providing the information in the format most comfortable to the user improves his productivity and your success.

HORIZONTAL EXPANSION

Cross-tabs, like spreadsheets, expand both vertically and horizontally. In Crystal Reports, cross-tabs are one of only two object types that expand across horizontal pages. Crystal Reports handles this expansion automatically. If there is more data to display than the original size of the cross-tab allows for, Crystal Reports doesn't cut off any critical data from the cross-tab area.

CUSTOM FORMATTING

Cross-tab objects are also highly customizable in terms of formatting. Everyone has different needs from their data, so Crystal Reports allows for a great deal of changes to the formatting of these objects. Some of the most highly useful formatting features that are used in cross-tabs are

- Customizable styles (colors, grid lines, and so on)
- Vertical and horizontal placement of summaries
- Formatted grid lines
- Toggle for summary totals (rows/columns)
- Cell margins
- Indented row labels
- Location of totals (beginning or end for both rows/columns)
- Repeatable row labels

USING THE CROSS-TAB WIZARD

Start with an example for the Xtreme Mountain Bike Company—the fictitious company that corresponds to the sample database provided with Crystal Reports.

Xtreme management needs a summary report to provide a quick glance at its shipped orders. The managers want to know how much has been spent by country for every six-month period, but they only want to see the top 10 countries. Follow these steps to create this report:

1. Create a new report by choosing File, New and when the Report Gallery appears, choose As a Blank Report and then click OK.
2. The Database Expert appears. In the Available Data Sources list, expand the following nodes: Create New Connection, ODBC. Select the Extreme Sample database 11, click Next, and then click Finish.
3. Expand Tables, and double-click on Customer and Orders. Click OK.

4. The Database Expert dialog appears again. Click OK again to accept the default linking and click Finish to go to the report.

5. Insert a cross-tab by choosing Cross-Tab from the Insert menu, or click the Insert Cross-Tab button on the Insert toolbar (the fourth item from the left). This will present you with a shadowed box attached to your cursor. Place the box in any Header or Footer of your report (not on a page header or footer) and in this case put it in the upper-left corner of the Report Header. The box will become an empty cross-tab.

6. Set up the initial cross-tab. Right-click on the empty cross-tab and choose Cross-Tab Expert. The rows of the report are the countries, so select Country from the Available Fields and then click the arrow button (>) under Rows. The column grouping is going to be by Order Date, so choose Order Date from Available Fields and then click the arrow button (>) under Columns. Because the Order Date is supposed to be by quarter, click on the Group Options drop-down under Columns and change the third list box from Each Day to For Each Quarter. Finally, choose Order Amount from Available Fields and click the arrow button (>) under Summarized Fields so that the cell's summary is also selected. The final result looks like Figure 10.3.

Figure 10.3
Cross-Tab Expert–
Cross-Tab tab.

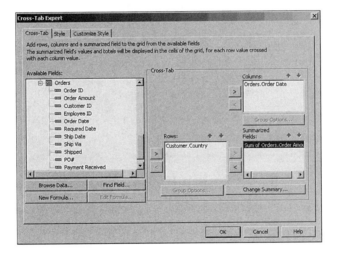

7. Click the OK button to close the Cross-Tab Expert and see the result in the report Preview, as shown in Figure 10.4.

8. Before continuing, save your work. Choose File, Save As. Call this **cross-tab1.rpt** and then click OK.

Cross-tab in Preview.

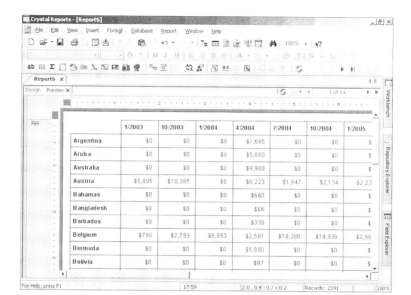

Group sorts can be done on a report level so that the records are sorted and removed as necessary. However, there are times when the records are needed in the overall report but not in a cross-tab.

Right-click in the top-left corner of the cross-tab where there is no data or words and choose Group Sort Expert. Choose Top N for the primary list box and change 5 to 10 in the Where N Is field. In this example, make sure that the Others option is not selected.

Click OK in the Group Sort Expert to view the final result, as shown in Figure 10.5.

Save your work by choosing File, Save As. Call this **cross-tab2.rpt** and then click OK.

What would happen if there was a need to have the option of showing the Top 5, the Top 10, or some other value for N? In previous versions of Crystal Reports, N was hard coded; if this level of flexibility was needed, there would be quite a bit of work involved! New in Crystal Reports XI, however, a formula may be used to set the value of N—and where there is a formula, there can be a parameter. Using the skills you learned in Chapter 5, "Implementing Parameters for Dynamic Reporting," create a parameter.

To create a new parameter, open the Field Explorer, select Parameter Fields, and click the New button. For Name, call this Top N, and set the type to Number. Because you've already learned about parameters, simply click OK to move on.

Figure 10.5
Cross-tab with a Top 10 Group Sort applied.

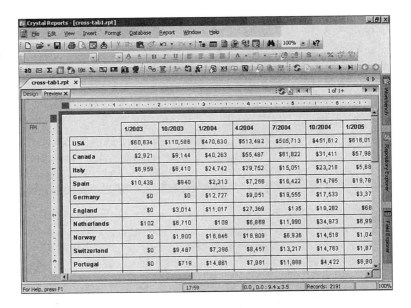

6. Right-click on your cross-tab in the top left where there are no numbers or text, and select Group-Sort Expert. To the right of the number 10, click the Formula button. When the window opens, simply double-click the parameter in the list of fields. Figure 10.6 shows what the formula should look like.

Figure 10.6
Setting the parameter to be the value for N makes this chart much more flexible.

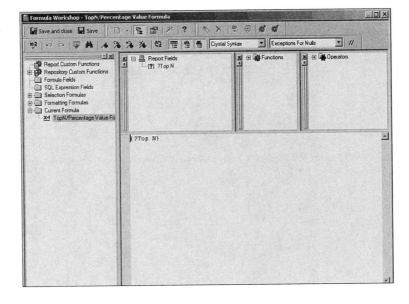

7. Refresh the report several times using different values for N. Save this report as **cross-tab dynamic N.rpt**.

USING ADVANCED CROSS-TAB FEATURES

Crystal Reports version 9 introduced significant cross-tab improvements. The advanced features gave cross-tabs improved flexibility and functionality to satisfy even more reporting requirements.

SETTING RELATIVE POSITION

When it comes to planning the width or length of cross-tabs, remember they expand dynamically. With the addition of new information or data, the number of rows or columns can grow or shrink. This makes putting objects at the end of a cross-tab very difficult because it's unclear when the object will be overwritten if new data appears.

For the same issue at the bottom of a cross-tab an easy solution exists. Place the new object in the next report section—even if it means adding a new section. By default, objects in Crystal Reports do not overwrite a section.

However, you often need to specify an item in the far-right column. In this report you might want a logo to be displayed to the right of the cross-tab. But, in Design, the size of the cross-tab doesn't match what you see in Preview. Follow these steps to set the Relative Position:

Open cross-tab dynamic N.rpt. Start with your last saved document by choosing it from the File list on the File, Open menu.

Insert a text object by opening the Insert menu, and then selecting Text Object. Type something into the text box and color the font red so you can see it easily.

Preview the report. Click F5 to see the result. It's not exactly as you intended (see Figure 10.7).

Design with cross-tab and text field in improper location.

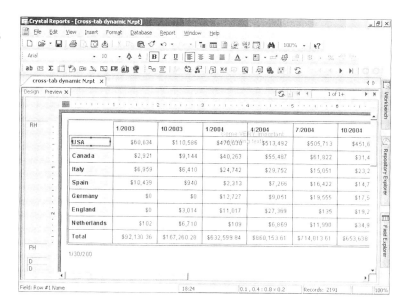

4. Set the Relative Position property. Right-click on the Report Header label (on the left where it says Report Header, or RH, in the gray area). Choose Section Expert. Toggle the Relative Positions check box and click OK. To see the resulting report, refer to Figure 10.8.

Figure 10.8
Preview of the cross-tab and text field as requested.

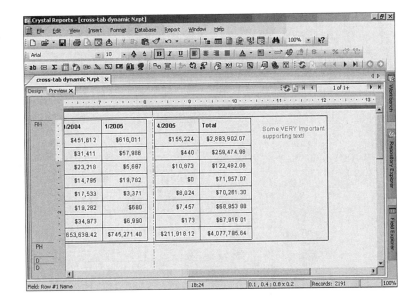

The Relative Position property works on the left, top, and right borders of the cross-tab. Remember that the bottom border of the cross-tab is handled by the end of a section. Relative positions can be used in many situations. For example, showing a chart on the information in the cross-tab can be very useful.

INSERTING A "PERCENTAGE OF" SUMMARY

Cross-tabs are great for compressing a lot of data into a small space, but it can be difficult to find the peaks or valleys in the data when just looking at the raw numbers. In order to highlight these peaks and valleys, summary values can also be displayed as percentages of either the total rows or total columns:

1. Add another summary. Right-click in the top left of the cross-tab where no data appears and choose Cross-Tab Expert. In the Cross-Tab tab, choose to add the Order Amount to the Summarized Fields list box by clicking the arrow (>) button. Notice that it looks like it duplicates the summary above it, so choose the Change Summary button.

2. Change the Summary to a Percentage Summary. In the Edit Summary dialog in the Options box, select Show As Percentage Summary. Notice that it has an option for Row or Column. In this case you want to know by country (row) where the percentage split is, so keep Row selected as shown in Figure 10.9.

Figure 10.9
The Edit Summary
dialog.

Preview the results by clicking OK on both dialog windows. It should look like Figure 10.10.

Figure 10.10
Percentages by
country.

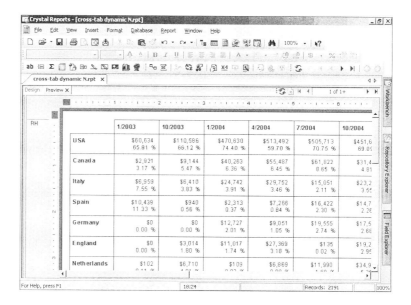

Notice that the USA is consistently the largest percentage of Xtreme's orders. It's very easy to see this when percentages are added to the cross-tab.

HORIZONTAL AND VERTICAL PLACEMENT

Because the percentages add up to 100% down the page, it would be easier to understand if the summaries could be displayed side by side instead of one on top of the other. That way, the numbers down the page could be added up easily.

Crystal Reports allows the toggle between horizontal and vertical placement of summaries:

1. Launch the Cross-Tab Expert. Right-click in the top-left of the cross-tab again and choose Cross-Tab Expert. Select the Customize Style tab. Under Summarized Fields, choose Horizontal; select the Show Labels option.

2. View the report. Click the OK button to see the changes made to the cross-tab (see Figure 10.11).

Figure 10.11
Horizontal placement of summaries.

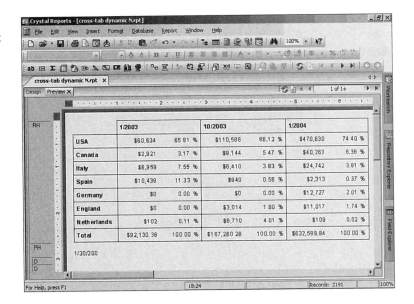

INSERTING SUMMARY LABELS

Notice that on the report in Figure 10.11, the columns don't have a title to identify them. Right-click on the cross-tab as before and choose Cross-Tab Expert, go to the Customize Style tab, and make sure to select the Show Labels option. Both titles for the percentage and the summary are exactly the same (Order Amount). This is because Crystal Reports is showing the field that a summary is acting on. In this case, where the field is being acted on twice, it's not a good choice.

Crystal Reports enables you to edit these labels right on the cross-tab in both Design and Preview modes:

1. Edit the Summary's Title. Right-click on the first Order Amount title in the cross-tab and choose Edit Text. Delete the Order Amount Text and add Sum instead. Then choose the Align Center button on the toolbar while the item is highlighted. Click off the object and see the result.

2. Edit the Percentage Title. Repeat the previous step for the second Order Amount field, but instead of changing the text to sum, change it to %, as shown in Figure 10.12.

Cross-tab with both
labels changed.

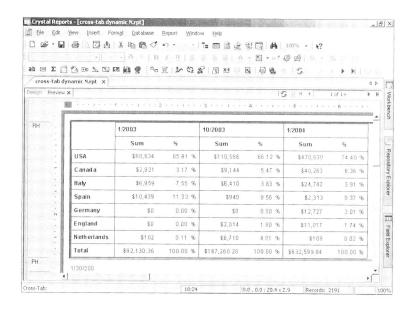

Cross-tabs are based on the need for numbers or currency to be summarized, but there are
times when the numbers don't need to be seen to get the point across. Crystal Reports has a
feature for all fields called Display String. This formatting feature allows a different representation for a field than its underlying value. For example, a manager might want to see
text beside a percentage mark, as shown in Figure 10.13.

Sales report with text
to identify great sales
as display strings.

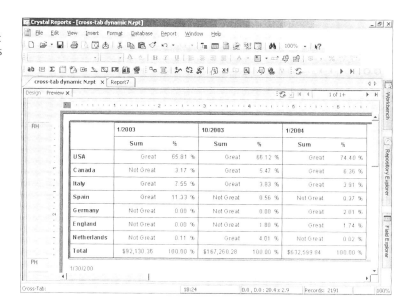

As previously mentioned, cross-tab cells are always an intersection of rows and columns with a summary because the strings are the visual representation of the underlying summary being computed in the cross-tab. You can affect this string using the advanced Cross-Tab features of Crystal Reports.

Crystal Reports can now separate the data value from its display. This is a powerful feature and is *not* limited to cross-tabs, although it plays a major role in cross-tabs because of the requirement of summaries.

To complete this report, ensure that all $0.00 amounts be shown as NONE on the report.

1. Format the Order Amount Summary. Right-click on one of the $0.00 amounts on the report and choose Format Field. Choose the Common tab and then choose the Conditional Formatting (x+2) button to the right of Display String. The Formula Workshop appears.

2. Format Formula for strings. Use an If-Then-Else formula structure to accomplish the task. The final result is If CurrentFieldValue = 0 Then "NONE" Else ToText(CurrentFieldvalue) (see Figure 10.14).

10

Figure 10.14
Display String formatting formula.

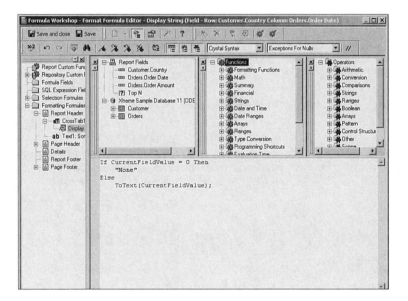

Close the dialog windows. Choose the Save and Close button on the Formula Workshop and then click OK on the Formatting dialog. The result is shown in Figure 10.15.

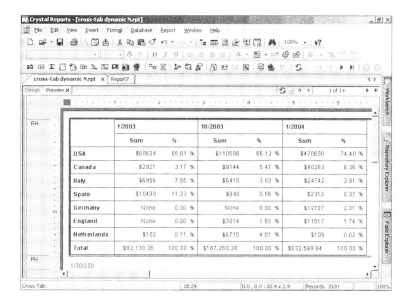

Save the report as **Crosstab3.rpt** by choosing File, Save As.

The same technique that you used to change the display value of the cell can be used on any area, and you can combine the interactivity provided by parameters and other formula functions to drive any section or field in the cross-tab.

CRYSTAL REPORTS IN THE REAL WORLD—ADVANCED CROSS-TABS

Although a single Cross-Tab that covers all the data in a report can be quite useful, with some large datasets it can be quite unreadable. A simple solution to this is to group the report and place the cross-tab in the group header or footer. Cross-tabs are context sensitive and if placed in a group header or footer will show only data for that group.

Using the skills described in earlier chapters, create a new report from the Xtreme Sample Database. Add the Customer table to the report, group the report by country, and remove all fields but the Country field in the group header. See Figure 10.16 to see the report's starting point.

Figure 10.16
Report framework.

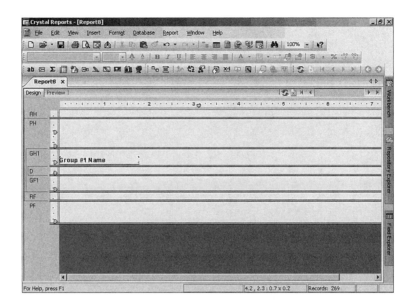

2. From the Insert menu, choose Cross-Tab. Add the Cross-Tab to the Group Header. Right-click on the Cross-Tab and select the Expert. From the list of available fields, select Customer Name and add it to the Rows window of the Cross-Tab. Select the Region and add it to the Columns window. Select Last Year's Sales and add it to the Summarized Fields window. Check your work against Figure 10.17 for accuracy.

Figure 10.17
Building the cross-tab.

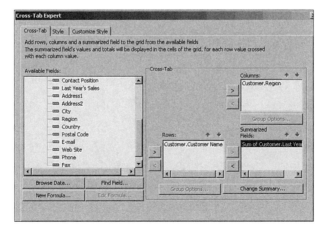

3. Click OK to close the Cross-Tab expert. In Figure 10.18, we see the complete report.
4. Save the report as **GroupedCrossTab.rpt**.

Figure 10.18
Grouped cross-tabs can avoid confusion through improved readability.

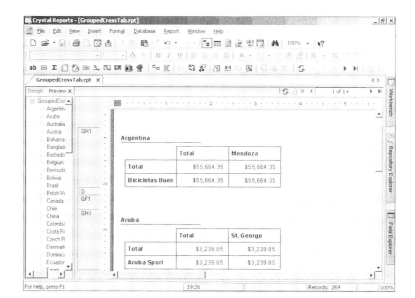

CHAPTER 11

USING RECORD SELECTIONS AND ALERTS FOR INTERACTIVE REPORTING

In this chapter

INTRODUCTION

Not all information is fit for all users, so this chapter discusses how record selection can used to limit the data in a report. Hand-in-hand with limiting the data (reducing the recordset also improves speed and performance) is a review of tuning the report. Even when a report is published to BusinessObjects Enterprise (introduced in many chapters later) and much time is invested in correctly architecting and tuning the servers, the number one performance improvement is often in correct report authoring.

CREATING ADVANCED RECORD SELECTION FORMULAS

Although creating a simple report can be very useful for an end user, highlighting notable information can increase the utility of the report because it saves time spent looking for trends and crucial data. *Outliers*, data that falls above or below the average of a specified threshold, often contain key information.

This chapter focuses on drawing attention to key data by using record selections and introducing SQL expressions, and introduces report alerting.

Although many filters are simple enough to be defined using the Select Expert, most real-world reports require editing the record selection formula itself. Before covering the best practices for creating formulas, review the material on record selections introduced in Chapter 2, "Selecting and Grouping Data."

RECORD SELECTION REVIEW

Record selections, or filters, are defined by a record selection formula built using the Crystal syntax of the Crystal Reports formula language. You can build a record selection formula using the Formula Editor by opening the Report menu and choosing Selection Formulas, Record. A simpler way to build record selections is to use the Select Expert icon accessed via the Experts toolbar.

A record selection formula returns a Boolean value indicating whether a given record should be included in the report. It is evaluated for each record in the database. Any time a database field is used in the formula, it is replaced by the actual field value.

After this quick review, the following sections move on to some of the more important topics in creating record selection filters.

DISPLAYING RECORD SELECTIONS

Although the techniques discussed in this chapter allow powerful filtering, this should not be applied without the end user's knowledge in most cases (certainly there are cases where end users should not know of hidden data, but this more often is handled via filters to secure the data in a Business View). In these cases, you can simply display the current selection filter or other special fields by either dragging the fields onto the report from the Field Explorer, Special Fields area, or by using the same fields in a formula to change the way these fields display as in the previous chapter.

DEALING WITH DATES

Use the select expert, which you access by choosing Report, Select Expert, to manipulate dates with the addition of four specific date-related comparators:

- **Is between**—The selected items fall between these two dates.
- **Is not between**—The selected items do not fall between these two dates.
- **Is in the period**—The selected items fall in the periods selected from the drop-down list.
- **Is not in the period**—The selected items do not fall in the periods selected from the drop-down list.

These date-specific operators appear when you have selected a field of date type, and prompt for the specific values. However, in more complicated situations, you are forced to create a formula in the formula editor rather than using the select expert to create the formula for you.

One of the most common record selection formulas is `{field}` = `value`, where `{field}` is a database field and `value` is a corresponding value of the same data type. An example of this would be

`{Customer.Country} = "Canada"`

This kind of formula is very easy to create, but becomes more complicated when the data types of the values to be compared are not the same. Filtering data based on dates often causes this type of situation; for instance, this formula:

`{Orders.Order Date} > "2/25/2000"`

> **NOTE**
>
> When clicking the Check button to check the formula's syntax, Crystal Reports provides a message saying "`A date-time is required here`" and after closing the message box, "`1/29/1998`" is highlighted. Because the Order Date field has a data type of date-time, the formula attempts to compare a date-time to a string, which is not allowed. Comparisons must always be performed on objects of the same data type. To rectify this, instead of using a string literal to describe a date, the formula could use the `DateTime` function to return a date-time value. Here is an example of the corrected formula:
>
> `{Orders.Order Date} > DateTime(2000, 2, 25, 0, 0, 0)`

Notice that when the `DateTime` function is used, it takes arguments for not only year, month, and day, but also for hour, minute, and second. This is because in order to compare this value to the Order Date field, it needs to be a date-time value. In this case, you might not care about the time part of the date-time value. The best way to solve this would be to first convert the Order Date field into a date from a date-time, and then use the `Date` function instead of `DateTime`. The improved formula follows:

`Date({Orders.Order Date}) > Date(2000, 2, 25)`

To make this even simpler, the Crystal Reports formula language also supports dates specified in the following format:

```
#YYYY/MM/DD HH:MM AM/PM#
```

Using this syntax, the following formula is also valid:

```
{Orders.Order Date} > #2000/2/25 12:00 AM#
```

Another nice feature of this syntax is the capability to omit the time portion. When this is done, a default of 12:00 AM is used.

Various functions are available for converting between strings, dates, and date-times. These can be found in the Function Tree window of the Formula Editor, under the Date and Time folder.

Another issue that comes up often is filtering on a field in the database that contains dates but is defined as a string field. The following fictitious formula, although it will not return any errors when checking the syntax, does not accomplish what you might expect:

```
{Shipments.Ship Date} > "1/1/2001"
```

This will not perform a date comparison because both fields are of type string. To correct this formula, you could use one of the functions provided by the DTS (date time string) user function library called DTSToDate.

> A *user function library* is a library of functions that can be used from the Crystal Reports formula language. Business Objects provides several of these with the product, and others are available from third-party vendors. If you are proficient with Visual Basic or C++, you could even create a user function library yourself. The user function library can be found under the Additional Functions folder in the Function Tree of the Formula Editor.

The DTSToDate function takes a string that is in the proper date format and converts it to a date value. The correct formula is shown here:

```
DTSToDate({Shipments.Ship Date}) > Date(2001, 1, 1)
```

where the Ship Date field contains a date in *DD/MM/YYYY* format.

WORKING WITH STRINGS

As with dates, simple string comparisons are easy to achieve using the record selection expert. Slightly more complex comparisons can easily become tedious unless you are armed with knowledge for effectively dealing with strings. A simple example is a listing of customer data for a set of countries. Creating a record selection formula like the following can become quite tedious:

```
{Customer.Country} = "England" or
{Customer.Country} = "France" or
{Customer.Country} = "Germany" or
{Customer.Country} = "Denmark"
```

Rather than using multiple comparisons, this can be accomplished with a single comparison using a string array.

N O T E

> An array in the context of the Crystal Reports formula language is a collection of values that can be referenced as a single object.

The previous record selection formula can be rewritten to look like this:

```
{Customer.Country} in ["England", "France", "Germany", "Denmark"]
```

Notice that there are several differences. First, instead of using multiple comparisons, only a single comparison is used. This is both simpler to read and easier to maintain. The four country values are combined into a string array. Arrays are indicated by square brackets with values separated by commas. Finally, instead of an = operator, the in operator is used. This operator, as its name implies, is used to determine if the value on its left is present inside the array on its right.

N O T E

> Although string arrays are described here, arrays can be made holding other data types, such as integers and currency values.

11

In this example, the countries are hard-coded into the selection formula. Although this makes it easy to read, the report would need to be modified if the country list were to ever change. A better way to handle this would be to create a multiple value prompt and use it in place of the country list. If you did that, the formula would look like this:

```
{Customer.Country} in {?CountriesParam}
```

During the parameter prompting, the user will be allowed to enter multiple values, and you can even provide a list of default values from which to choose.

PUSHING RECORD SELECTIONS TO THE DATABASE

When dealing with large sets of records, performance becomes important. The record selection used makes a significant difference in report performance. Crystal Reports does have the capability to perform database-like operations on the data such as grouping, filtering, summarizing, and sorting. However, in general, asking the database to perform those operations results in a faster overall transaction. Because of this principle, Crystal Reports attempts to ask the database to perform these operations if possible.

In the context of record selections, when Crystal Reports queries the database it attempts to incorporate as much of the logic of the record selection formula as possible into the query. Ideally, all the logic can be incorporated into the query, which means that the database will perform all the filtering and only return the records that meet the criteria. However, because the SQL language doesn't support all the Crystal Reports formula language, there could be certain situations in which some or all the logic of the record selection formula cannot be converted to SQL. In this case, Crystal Reports needs to pull some or all the records from the database and perform filtering itself.

When working with a desktop database like Access or FoxPro, the performance difference between the database engine or the Crystal Reports engine doing the filtering would be minimal because it really comes down to which filtering algorithm is faster. Because databases are made for just this purpose and are customized for their own data structures, they will generally perform this kind of operation faster. However, when dealing with client/server databases in which the database resides on a back-end server and Crystal Reports resides in your desktop machine, the difference becomes much more apparent. This is partly because of network traffic. There's a big difference between sending 50 records back over the network and sending 100,000. This performance hit becomes even worse when using a slow connection such as a dial-up modem.

To determine whether the logic you've used in the record selection formula or select expert is incorporated into the query sent to the database, it's helpful to have a basic understanding of the SQL language. You need not be an expert at SQL, but being able to recognize if the query is performing a filter on a certain field makes record selection formula tuning much more effective.

Although there are some guidelines for creating record selection formulas that will be fully passed down to the server, often the best approach is to simply check the SQL statement manually and determine whether the record selection logic is present. To view the SQL statement that Crystal Reports has generated, select Show SQL Query from the Database menu. The resulting dialog is shown in Figure 11.1.

Figure 11.1
The Show SQL Query dialog displays the actual SQL code used to retrieve the results from the relational database.

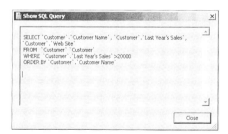

```
SELECT `Customer`.`Customer Name`, `Customer`.`Last Year's Sales`,
`Customer`.`Web Site`
FROM `Customer` `Customer`
WHERE `Customer`.`Last Year's Sales` >20000
ORDER BY `Customer`.`Customer Name`
```

You can infer from the preceding SQL query that this report is based on the Customer table, is using the Customer Name, Web Site, and Last Year's Sales fields, and has a record selection of

```
{Customer.Last Year's Sales} > $20000
```

All the logic of the record selection formula has now been passed down to the database in the SQL query. However, if this report had a formula field that calculated the tax, that formula might consist of the following:

```
{Customer.Last Year's Sales} * 1.07
```

This formula field might be placed on the report to indicate the tax for each customer. A problem occurs when this formula is used in the record selection formula. Although the following formula seems logical, it is inefficient:

```
{@Tax} > $10000
```

If you were to look at the SQL query being generated for this report, you would see that there is no WHERE clause present. In other words, the report is asking the database for all the records and doing the filtering locally, which, depending on the size of the database, could result in poor performance. A better record selection to use—which would produce the same results, but performs the filtering on the database server—would be

```
{Customer.Last Year's Sales} > $142857
```

This works out because at a tax rate of 7%, $142,857 is the minimum a customer would need to sell to have tax of more than $10,000. Using the previous record selection would result in a SQL query with the following WHERE clause:

```
WHERE 'Customer'.'Last Year's Sales' > 142857
```

Although this approach returns the correct data, a slightly less cryptic approach would be to use a SQL Expression.

AN INTRODUCTION TO SQL EXPRESSIONS

Crystal Reports formulas are useful because they enable you to use the full Crystal Reports formula language as well as a suite of built-in functions. However, as you've learned in this chapter, they can be a factor in report processing performance. SQL expressions provide an alternative to this.

A *SQL Expression*, as the name implies, is an expression written in the SQL language. Instead of consisting of a whole formula, a SQL Expression consists of an expression that defines a single field just like a formula field does. The difference between a formula field and a SQL Expression is based on where it is evaluated. Formula fields are evaluated locally by Crystal Reports, whereas SQL Expressions are evaluated by the database server and thus produce better performance when used in a record selection formula.

To better understand this, look at the example discussed in the previous section. The example had a report with a Crystal Reports formula that calculated tax based on the Last Year's Sales field. Although there certainly are situations in which formula fields need to be used, this is not one of them because the logic being used in the formula is simple enough that the database server is able to perform it. Instead of creating a formula field, a SQL Expression could have been created. SQL Expressions are created via the Field Explorer, which was introduced in Chapter 4, "Understanding and Implementing Formulas." Right-clicking on the SQL Expressions item and selecting New will begin the process of creating a SQL Expression. When choosing to create a new SQL Expression, the SQL Expression Editor is launched (see Figure 11.2).

11

Figure 11.2

The SQL Expression
Editor.

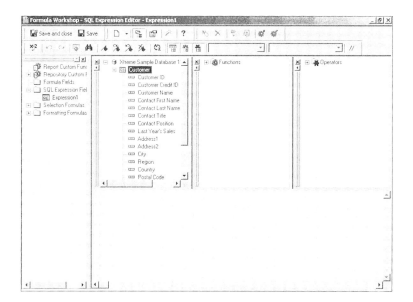

This editor is, in fact, the same editor used to create Crystal Reports formulas, but with a few small changes. First you'll notice that in the field tree, only database fields are present to be used in the expression. Because SQL Expressions are evaluated on the database servers, Crystal Reports constructs, such as prompt fields and formula fields, do not exist and thus cannot be used in the expression.

To create a SQL Expression that calculates the tax, the following expression can be used:

```
'Customer'.'Last Year's Sales' * 0.07
```

Notice that instead of using the {Table.Field} syntax for fields, the 'Table'.'Field' syntax is used. This is because the quoted syntax is how you define fields in the SQL language.

When inserting this SQL Expression into the report and checking the SQL query, you will find Crystal Reports has generated SQL similar to this:

```
SELECT 'Customer'.'Customer Name', ('Customer'.'Last Year's Sales' * 0.07)
FROM 'Customer' 'Customer'
```

The SQL Expression that was defined in the report is inserted into the main SQL statement that Crystal Reports generates. This means that you can use any database-specific syntax or function inside a SQL Expression.

Getting back to the topic of performance, you'll remember that using the tax calculation formula field in the record selection formula resulted in all the records being returned and Crystal Reports having to locally perform the filtering. Fortunately, any SQL Expressions used in the record selection are always passed down to the database server. Therefore, a better record selection for filtering out customers who pay less than $10,000 in tax would be the following:

```
{%Tax} > 10000
```

In this record selection formula, {%Tax} is the SQL Expression discussed previously. This record selection formula would result in Crystal Reports generating the following SQL query:

```
SELECT 'Customer'.'Customer Name', ('Customer'.'Last Year's Sales' * 0.07)
FROM 'Customer' 'Customer'
WHERE ('Customer'.'Last Year's Sales' * 0.07)>10000
```

NOTE

Remember that any formula evaluated after the first pass of the multipass system, for instance grouping criteria or information to prompt a subreport, can cause slow report processing. Again a SQL Expression can retrieve the correct data in the first place, speeding report processing significantly. The next chapter of this book covers the multipass system in detail.

ADDING ALERTING TO YOUR REPORTS

Although calling out outlying values can be accomplished by using conditional formatting, the alerting feature inside Crystal Reports allows for more interactive identification of key data as well as pushing of those alerts to end users via BusinessObjects Enterprise's alerting functionality.

A report *alert* is a custom notification created within Crystal Reports, triggered when a predetermined condition is met. An alert is comprised of three integral parts:

- Name
- Trigger (condition or threshold)
- Message

Alerts serve the dual functions of bringing end-user attention to a certain condition being met and focusing end-user attention on specifically relevant data in a report—thereby increasing user efficiency. Some examples of reports in which alerts could provide a benefit are outlined in Table 11.1.

TABLE 11.1 REPORTS WITH POTENTIALLY USEFUL ALERTS

Report	Alert	Alert Trigger and Result
Product Sales Report	Product Profitability Warning	Trigger: Specific product profitability below 10% Result: A listing of the least successfully selling products
Customer Churn Report	Regional Customer Churn Warnings	Trigger: Specific regions where Customer Churn Rate is higher than 3% in a quarter Result: A listing of regions to increase competitive analysis or to review regional management practice

continues

TABLE 11.1 CONTINUED

Report	Alert	Alert Trigger and Result
Income Statement	Company Divisions with Net Losses	Trigger: Company division with net income < 0 Result: A listing of divisions where deeper business analysis is required

Report alerts are triggered when the report is processed and the associated condition has been met. When this condition is true, the alert message will be displayed. Figure 11.3 displays a triggered alert from within the Crystal Reports Designer.

Figure 11.3
A report alert being triggered.

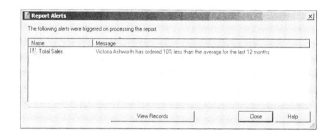

CREATING, EDITING, AND USING ALERTS

To create or edit alerts in Crystal Reports, select the Report, Alerts, Create or Modify Alerts menu items. This dialog (shown in Figure 11.4) enables you to create a new alert, edit existing alerts, and remove existing alerts.

Figure 11.4
Clicking Edit on the Create Alerts dialog opens the Edit Alert dialog.

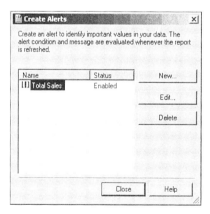

To create the alert, follow these steps:

Give the alert a name. This name should be meaningful and will be displayed to the user when the alert is triggered.

2. Specify a condition for which to trigger the alert. An example of this would be `{Customer.Last Year's Sales} < $10000`. The condition is simply a formula using either Crystal or Basic syntax that evaluates to a true or false result. True means the alert should be triggered; false means that it should not.

NOTE

> You can use other formulas and prompts inside this condition. Using a prompt to determine the threshold on your alert is useful because the report could then be viewed by different audiences with different thresholds, and they could still see the alert triggered for their respective numbers.

3. Give the alert a message to display when it has been triggered. This can be a hard-coded string, or can be a formula such as

```
"Sales are over $" + ToText({Customer.Last Year's Sales})
```

To see your alert in action, refresh the report with data that meets your alert condition, and triggered alerts will be displayed.

Finally, not only are you notified that the alerts have been triggered, you can click the View Records button on the Report Alerts pop-up dialog to filter the report to show only those records that triggered the alert. This is a good way to draw attention to the key outliers in the data.

USING ALERTS IN BUSINESSOBJECTS ENTERPRISE

The Report Alerts dialog displayed in Figure 11.3 is only available from within the Crystal Reports Designer. If you are delivering your reports via another mechanism such as the Web, alerts are handled differently. To have your end users take advantage of Crystal Reports alerting, you will need to either use BusinessObjects Enterprise for report distribution or exploit the built-in alert functions (`IsAlertEnabled()`, `IsAlertTriggered()`, and `AlertMessage()`) within formulas you create in your report.

→ For more information on BusinessObjects Enterprise, **see** Chapter 25, "BusinessObjects Enterprise Architecture," **p. 581**.

Typically, alerts can be shown to end users in a portal, which then links back to the report.

TIP

> End users viewing a report from an alert in BusinessObjects Enterprise do not see the items matching the alert conditions—they see the entire report. This leads to some discontinuity both from the Crystal Reports experience and also from the end users' expectation that they should now see values called out in the alert.
>
> To make this more logical for the end user, create a version of the same report (perhaps use a naming convention like ALERT_*reportname*.rpt) with the alert and also a filtering condition *matching the alert condition*. Thus, when end users click on an alert in BusinessObjects Enterprise, they will see a version of the report containing only the relevant values.

PERFORMANCE MONITORING AND TUNING

As reports grow in data size and complexity, ensuring optimal performance becomes increasingly important. This section serves as both a reminder of some performance tips already covered in the book to this point and as an introduction to some other tools and methods provided by Crystal Reports to optimize report performance in demanding environments.

GROUP BY ON SERVER

This Crystal Reports option enables you to push down the Grouping and Sorting activities to the database server. By performing these functions on the database instead of the Crystal server, less data is passed back to the Crystal Report and report-processing time is decreased. This option can be set locally under the Database main menu when the given report is being edited, or set globally on the Database tab of the Options menu accessed under the File main menu.

Some restrictions apply to the use of this option, including the following:

- The data source must be a standard SQL database.
- The report must have groups within it and the groups must be based on database fields—not formula fields.
- The groups cannot contain specified order sorting.
- The details section of the report must be hidden.
- Running Totals must be based on summary fields (that is, they do not rely on detail records for their calculations).
- The report cannot contain Average or Distinct Count summaries, or use Top N values.

When this option is applicable and used, the involved reports will perform faster. In addition, the detail level on these reports is still accessible through the standard drill-down functionality and will make dynamic connections to the database to bring back any user-requested detailed information.

SQL EXPRESSIONS IN RECORD SELECTIONS

As referenced and discussed previously in the book, SQL expressions are SQL statements that provide access to advanced database aggregations and functions. Using SQL expressions wherever possible in record selections and formula creation (versus using Crystal or Basic syntax) optimizes the amount of work that will get processed by the database server (versus the Crystal server)—and this will increase your report's performance.

Some quick examples of SQL expressions that can be used in place of Crystal formula syntax:

Crystal Formula Syntax	SQL Expression (SQL Server Syntax)
IF/THEN/ELSE	CASE [Database Field]
Or	WHEN Condition THEN Value1
SELECT CASE	ELSE Value2 END
Concatenate (x + y)	CONCAT([Database Field1], [Database Field2])
MONTH(datefield)	MONTH([Database Field])

You should investigate the SQL capabilities of the report's database thoroughly when report performance and optimization becomes a critical business issue. Mature databases like Oracle, DB2, SQL Server, and so on have mature SQL capabilities that can often be leveraged in lieu of the Crystal formula language in field selection and record selection. Using SQL expressions can dramatically increase report performance in many instances.

USE INDEXES ON SERVER FOR SPEED

This is another performance option that is set under the Database tab of the Options dialog accessed from the main File menu. This option ensures that the involved Crystal Report uses any indexes that are present for the selected database and for the given report.

ON-DEMAND OR REDUCED NUMBER OF SUBREPORTS

As discussed in the chapter on subreports, these objects are reports unto themselves and maintain their own database connections and queries. As you can imagine, if too many subreports are added to a main report, this can lead to runaway report-processing times. A typical scenario where this might happen is when you want to include the data inside a subreport for every group within the main report. In a large report with hundreds or even thousands of groups, this can lead to that subreport running thousands of times—a palpable performance hit even when the subreport is small and/or optimized.

To minimize this challenge, it is a good idea to ensure that in-place subreports (as opposed to on-demand subreports) are used judiciously and that they are indeed required in performance-sensitive reports. Often times, only a very small subset of the subreports are ever viewed by a user and an acceptable user experience can be provided with On-Demand subreports instead.

PERFORMANCE MONITOR

After a report has been functionally designed, Crystal Reports provides the Performance Information tool to facilitate performance testing. This tool provides information that helps in optimizing the current report for fastest performance. The Performance Information dialog shown in Figure 11.5 is accessed from the main Report menu.

11

Figure 11.5
The Performance
Information window
provides detailed
report performance
metrics.

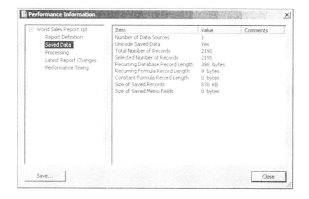

The left side of the Performance window provides a tree structure that facilitates navigation among the different report metrics areas maintained by this tool:

- **Report Definition**—This node provides information about the content of the report: the number of fields, the number of summaries, UFLs (User Function Libraries), Chart objects, and so on. Each of these objects will have some impact on the performance of the report dependent on their quantity and complexity. The Page N of M Used option is relevant because it specifies whether a third pass of the data is needed when processing this report. If not required, this can be eliminated by removing any Page N of M special fields on the report.

- **Saved Data**—This node provides information about the data captured in the involved report: the number of data sources used, the total number of records, recurring database record length, size of saved data, and so on. These metrics are of particular relevance when Group By On Server is properly used but can be generally used to monitor the effects of report changes.

- **Processing**—This node provides information about the processing of the selected report: Grouping on Server?, Sorting on Server? Total Page Count required?, Number of Summary Values, and so on. The metrics provided here have a clear impact on performance and can be used to monitor the effective implementation of the optimization techniques described in this section.

- **Latest Report Changes**—This node provides information about recent changes to the report to facilitate performance monitoring.

- **Performance Timing**—This node provides the timing metrics based on opening the involved report and formatting its pages. These metrics provide the ultimate benchmark to determine the effectiveness of any implemented report optimization techniques.

Additional tree branches and nodes are displayed if the involved report contains subreports—each of these nodes will appear under a new parent node for each subreport facilitating performance analysis at a granular level.

One final note on performance monitoring: to facilitate record-keeping on the progress of any ongoing database or report optimizations, the Performance Information window provides the capability to save the involved report's performance information to a file for future reference and time comparison.

DYNAMIC CASCADING PROMPTS

Probably the most requested feature in years has been the desire to create Dynamic Cascading Prompts—a report prompt that adjusts scope as it's being used, such as selecting Country, Region, and City and having only relevant Regions show for a selected Country and so on. This is now a powerful new feature in Crystal Reports XI. The following steps create a Dynamic Cascading Prompt that will allow the user to filter by Country, Region, and City.

1. Start by opening the sample World Sales Report (the default location is `C:\Program Files\Business Objects\Crystal Reports 11\Samples\en\Reports\General Business`).

2. From the Field Explorer, select Parameter Fields, and click the New button. Figure 11.6 shows the new parameter window.

Figure 11.6
The new parameter window with default properties.

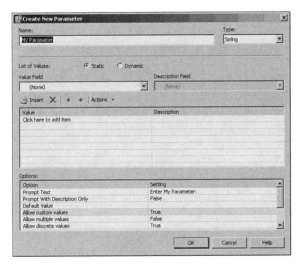

3. Start by giving the Prompt a name such as Dynamic Territory. From the List of Values radio buttons, choose Dynamic, and for the Prompt Group Text enter some helpful text for the report consumer (in this case type in **Select the territory from the list**).

4. When you click the box immediately below the Value header, you are able to select a report field. Choose Country. Click the box below Country and select Region. Click the box below Region and select City. In the three boxes below Parameter (where the text reads Click to Create Parameter), click each box one time to generate the default parameter. When complete, the window should look like Figure 11.7.

Figure 11.7
The new parameter
window with the prop-
erties described in
step 4.

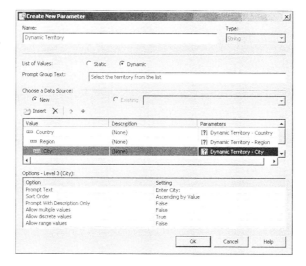

Figure 11.7
The new parameter
window with the prop-
erties described in
step 4.

Now with the prompt created, click OK to save it. Notice in Figure 11.8 that with this one step, three distinct prompts have been created. This will be used in the last step to filter the report.

Figure 11.8
The parameter list
with the three new
parameters.

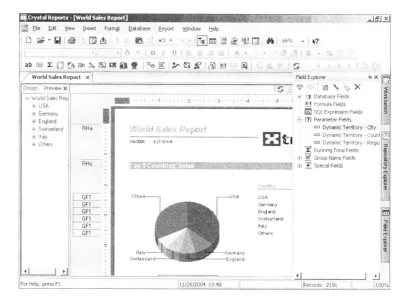

In order to use these new parameters to filter this report, open the Record Selection Formula window (Report, Selection Formulas, Record). Enter the formula you see in Figure 11.9. In order to limit the risk of typing errors, you can simply double-click the fields and prompts from the list of report fields.

Figure 11.9
Using the new prompt to filter the report.

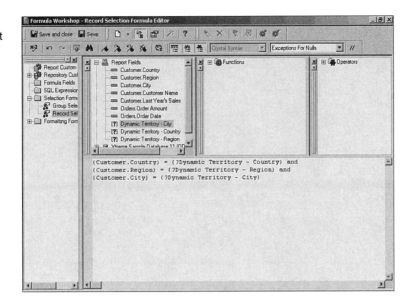

7. After clicking the Save and Close button, you should be prompted immediately to select a Country, Region, and City.

> **NOTE**
>
> Exploring the prompt window, you'll notice several useful features:
> - Only the top-level item is enabled. A user cannot select a Region or City until after they've selected a Country. The user is guided to the correct starting point.
> - As the user selects a Country (such as USA), only those Regions appropriate to that Country are listed (in this case, States). Also, only Region becomes enabled, and City will not become enabled until after a Region is selected.
> - If the user selects a Country, Region, and City but has not yet clicked OK and then goes back and changes the Country, both Region and City will be blanked out and City will again become disabled until the user picks a valid Region from the newly selected Country.
>
> At all points during the process, the user is guided to where they need to go next.

8. Select USA for Country, CA for Region, and San Diego for City. See Figure 11.10 to confirm your selection. Clicking OK runs the report and the report is filtered according to your selection.

11

Figure 11.10
Set values for the
Dynamic Cascading
Parameters.

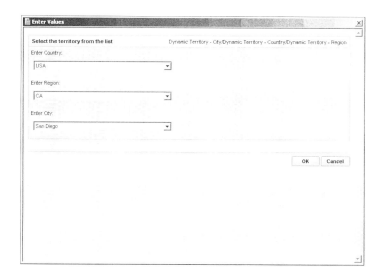

CRYSTAL REPORTS IN THE REAL WORLD—WEB REPORT ALERT VIEWING

This Real World section covers two very practical options. First, good uses of Alerting are discussed and second, learn how put together a complex Record Selection Formula.

There are many creative ways to employ alerting in Crystal Reports to direct the report consumer to information that requires attention. The following scenario helps you understand the use of alerting.

As part of her daily function, a Sales Executive views the World Sales Report multiple times. Although she is familiar with the report, it is easy to overlook an important piece of information if it is hidden in the pages to follow. Simply by looking at the first page of the report, it might not be clear if there is a problem that requires attention. The Sales report that is discussed here is grouped by Country, Region, City, and Customer. The detail section shows the order date and order amount. For the purpose of the example, the problem in the business occurs when a sales order is booked for more than $5,000. An alert will be created that flags this circumstance (see Figure 11.6).

Figure 11.11
Create an alert and
set the properties.

This sample report uses two techniques to draw the viewer's attention to the significant records. The first step highlights the Group Header in red if any record in the group sets the alert. To do this the report will evaluate a built-in function `IsAlertTriggered ('Order Amount Alert')` and set the highlighting appropriately (see Figure 11.12).

Figure 11.12
Set properties for the group header.

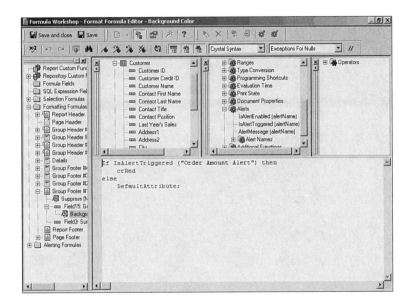

Additionally, to help draw the executive to the order(s) triggering the alert you will highlight the background of the detail record(s) that have triggered the alert. To do this, conditionally set the fill color of the detail section to yellow (see Figure 11.13).

Figure 11.13
Set properties for the detail line.

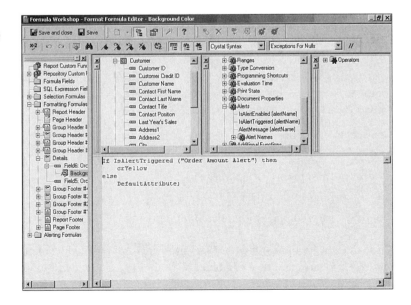

Now, when the executive views the sales report and drills to the detail data, the records highlighted in yellow indicate where the problem occurred.

Conditional formatting techniques described here can be applied to other attributes of report elements such as ToolTips. ToolTips can contain alert messages based on the triggered alerts. You can also conditionally hide or display report sections to highlight (see Figure 11.14).

Figure 11.14
Report highlighting draws attention to critical records.

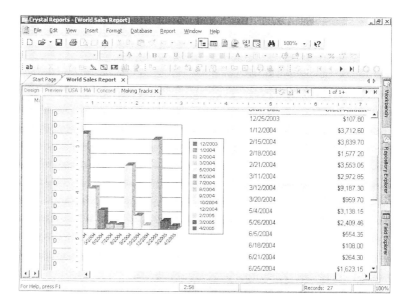

Now consider a complex Record Selection Formula. The goal of a Selection Formula is to determine which records belong in a report. To do this, each record is evaluated against the given Selection Formula and only those records that return True are passed into the report. A number of very simple Record Selection Formula's are listed above. These formulas, so far, have all compared one field to one value, but what happens if there is a need to evaluate several different criteria for the same record? Frequently when this occurs, report authors try to resolve this with a complex nested if-then-else statement. There is a very simple alternative, however.

Consider this situation. What if the World Sales Report (from the samples that ship with Crystal Reports) needed to be filtered on the following three items:

- Only orders from Canada/Mexico/USA
- Only orders greater than $5,000
- Only orders shipped within the last full month

The Selection Formula in Figure 11.15 explicitly shows how the different parts of the formula are evaluated and then combined to resolve to a single Boolean value. There are a number of ways to achieve this goal, and this formula could be written very differently—this example is just intended to show the method step by step.

Figure 11.15
A sample Record Selection Formula that explicitly evaluates each criteria and returns one final evaluation.

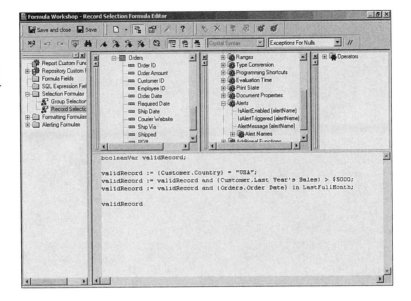

TROUBLESHOOTING

SELECTION FORMULAS

There should be data in the report, but no records are returned.

Start by breaking out the Selection Formula into the component parts. As an example, the Selection Formula from Figure 11.15 is made of three parts. Start by commenting out the existing formula and build it up one part at a time. Test to see when the expected result is different from what is returned. After the specific parts are identified, it should be easier to see what the problem is. Also, remember that the result of the Selection Formula is Boolean (True or False) and only those records that result in True are accepted into the report.

CHAPTER **12**

USING SUBREPORTS FOR ADVANCED REPORTS

In this chapter

INTRODUCTION TO SUBREPORTS

The first 11 chapters of this book introduced you to the design of individual reports using single aggregated datasets. Crystal Reports provides further flexibility and reporting capabilities through the use of additional reports embedded directly within an original main report. These embedded reports, referred to as *Subreports*, provide enhanced value extending your reporting solutions into an expanded domain that will be explored in this chapter.

The next two sections provide you with

- A further introduction to Subreports
- An idea of when you might use them
- A lesson on how to use Subreports

Crystal Reports provides the capability to embed multiple Crystal Reports within a single existing main report to allow for increased flexibility in report creation. Think of these Subreports as entire reports within reports, which can contain their own data sources, formatting, and record selections. The embedded Subreports can be created from existing Crystal Reports files or can be dynamically created at report design time using the insert Subreport functionality. When presenting a report that contains one or more Subreports to business users, the Subreports can be displayed either in-place, providing a seamless integration, or on-demand, minimizing the amount of required up-front report processing.

COMMON SUBREPORT USAGE

A few particular reporting problems are difficult to solve without the use of Subreports. Some of the most common problems and a specific example of each are listed here:

- *The presentation of data from two (or more) completely unrelated data sources on a single report.* Specific Example: On a Manufacturing Plant Efficiency report sourced from your internal Oracle ERP system, you want to display industry average information sourced from a completely different and unrelated industry or trade database.

- *A report that needs to combine data from different tables with only derived (and not direct) database field links.* Specific Example: On a Customer Profile report, you want to combine Order Information from your ERP (for example, SAP, Oracle, Baan) system with call-center information from your call-center application (for example, Remedy) and your CRM system (for example, Siebel, PeopleSoft), but the employee ID field is stored slightly different in each system. The Subreports enable the linking of the different employee IDs by allowing linking on formulas or derived fields.

- *The presentation of the same data in two (or more) different ways in a single report.* Specific Example: On a Sales Summary Report, senior management wants to present a high-level summary of sales by region but also wants to present a separate and personalized summary of sales by product for each salesperson who will be viewing the report.

- *The inclusion of a summary field in the report that is unrelated to the established grouping in the main report.* Specific Example: On an employee HR report, HR managers want to see employee salary information grouped by Business Unit, Division, and Department.

Additionally, they want to view a count of the different departments that this employee worked for in the previous year. The main report groups employees by department (and by division and business unit), whereas the Subreport groups departments by employee to determine a department count.

■ *The inclusion of a reusable component like a standard reporting header or footer in numerous reports across an organization that can be dynamically updated for all reports in a single location.* Specific example: A firm wants to deploy all reports in its organization with a standard header including standard logos and titles. In addition to using the Report Templates and Repository, Subreports can be used within all the reports as a header and provide a single location for updating the header across all the reports.

Data presented in Subreports is often related to the data presented in the associated main report, but it does not have to be. Subreport data can be a twist on the main report's information or sourced from a completely different database.

ADDING SUBREPORTS TO YOUR REPORTS

Adding a Subreport to your main report is as easy as adding any other Crystal Reports object. After selecting the Subreport option from the Insert menu, you are presented with the Insert Subreport dialog (see Figure 12.1).

Figure 12.1
The Insert Subreport dialog enables you to add a Subreport to your main report.

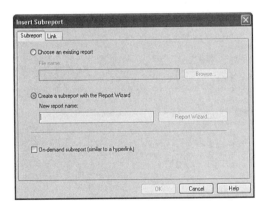

To explore one of the many challenges solved by using Subreports, let's solve the hypothetical reporting problem faced by the Chief Operating Officer (COO) of Maple Leaf Bikes Corporation. This COO wants a single report that highlights the recently acquired company's (Xtreme) top-selling products in one bar chart and additionally highlights the company's top selling sales reps in a corresponding pie chart. The two charts are sourced from the same sales information but have no direct relation or links to each other. To resolve this request, complete the following steps:

1. Create a New Report and point this report at the Xtreme Sample Database 11.

2. Select the Orders, Order Detail, and Product Tables and then select the Product Name and Order Amount Fields to Display on the report.

Group the report by Product Name and Add a Summary to the report that sums Order Amount for each Product Name group. Also limit the report to display only the top five groups based on the Summarized Field. (Reminder: You can use the Group Sort Expert under the Report menu option to accomplish this last task and remember to explicitly not include an Others group by selecting that check box.)

Add a bar chart in the Page Header to represent the top five selling products, and you should have a report similar to that depicted in Figure 12.2.

Figure 12.2
Preliminary sample report to solve COO problem.

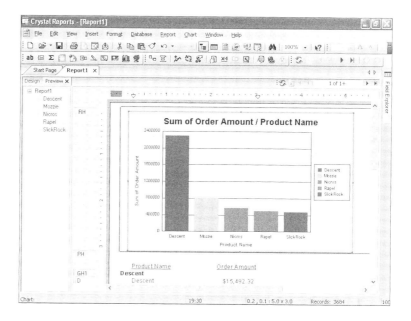

Make room for the COO's requested second visual by resizing the bar chart to only take up half of the page header's width.

Select the Insert Subreport option by either accessing that option from the Insert menu or clicking on the Insert Subreport icon. The Insert Subreport dialog in Figure 12.1 appears.

Select the Create a Subreport with the Report Wizard option by clicking on the associated radio button.

Enter a Name similar to Top Sales Reps and click on the Report Wizard button.

As you step through the familiar Report Wizard to create this Subreport, select the Xtreme Sample Database 11 and the Employee and Orders tables. From the list of available fields, select the First Name and Order Amount.

Group the Subreport on Employee First Name and create a Summary on the Sum of Order Amounts for each Employee Group. Limit the report to display the top five employees based on this sum, add a pie chart to this report, and click the Finish button.

Ensure that the On-Demand Subreport check box is unchecked, and then click OK on the Insert Subreport dialog. Drop the Subreport on the right side of the main report so that it does not overlap the existing bar chart. The details of On-Demand reports are described later in this chapter.

12. To clean up the final presentation of your main report and included Subreport, edit the Subreport by right-clicking on it and then hiding all the sections of the report except the report header a. As a reminder, hiding sections is accomplished by right-clicking on the name of the involved sections in the Design or Preview tab and selecting the Hide option. Lastly, delete the report header b section in the Subreport. Figure 12.3 shows the final result of this quick report. If your final result appears slightly different, review Chapter 8, "Visualizing Your Data with Charts and Maps," and revise the charts accordingly.

NOTE

As mentioned in the previous sections, Subreports *are* Crystal Reports in their own right, and as such they have their own Design tab in the Crystal Reports Designer. To format the details of a Subreport, it is necessary to open the Design tab for that Subreport from within the Designer of the main report. This can be accomplished by right-clicking on a Subreport and selecting the Edit Subreport option. Figure 12.3 displays the tabs for both the sample's main report and the Subreport.

Figure 12.3
Sample report with Subreport to solve COO problem.

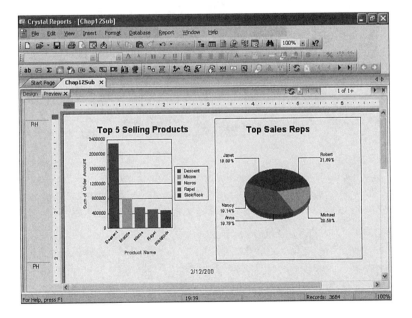

With that introduction to Subreports, you should begin to see some of the flexibility and power that they offer in solving difficult reporting (and even dashboard-related) problems. The next few sections explore this in more detail.

Understanding Linked Versus Unlinked Subreports

The hypothetical COO scenario just explored highlights an example of an unlinked Subreport. In Crystal Reports terminology, this means that the parent, or *main*, report did not have any specific data connections (or links) to its related child report (the Subreport). Unlinked Subreports are completely independent from their main reports and do not rely on the main report for any data. Many reporting problems in which multiple views of the same or different data sources are required in a single presentation can be resolved with unlinked Subreports. If a requirement exists to share data between the parent/main report and its Subreport, linked reports provide the answer.

Contrary to unlinked Subreports, linked Subreports are bound (or linked) to the data in their associated main report. The links are defined in the Link tab of the Insert Subreport dialog shown in Figure 12.4.

Figure 12.4
Link tab of the Insert Subreport dialog.

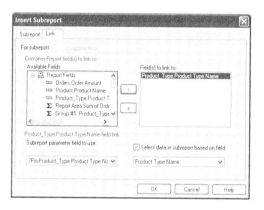

The Link tab enables you to link report, database, or formula fields in the main report to fields in the Subreport and enables you to filter the Subreport based on the data passed in from the main report.

The Available Fields section of the Links dialog enables you to select the field from the main report to be linked on. More than one field can be selected for linking. After at least one field has been selected, a separate Field Links section appears at the bottom of the Links tab. For each linked field, a parameter in the involved Subreport must be selected to receive and hold that information. These parameters can be pre-existing parameters predefined in the Subreport, or they can be a parameter that is automatically created for each field you have selected to link. (These are automatically created in the Subreport with the prefix ?Pm-.)

Finally, for each linked field from the main report, a data filter can be created in the Subreport based on that parameter. This is accomplished by checking the Select Data in Subreport Based on Field check box and selecting the report field, database field, or formula field in the Subreport that you want to have filtered based on the linked parameter from the provided drop-down box. In effect, checking this box creates a selection filter in your Subreport that is based on the selected filter field and the selected parameter field.

Linking Subreports and Reports with Formulas

The capability to link Subreports and main reports with formulas gives you a flexible method of presenting data from different database tables that is not possible otherwise. The Crystal Reports Database Linking Expert only enables joining of fields from different tables and does not permit joining formulas to fields. By using formulas and Subreports, a derived formula can now be linked to another database field in a Subreport.

For example, this would be beneficial if a firm's Order Processing system (SAP, Oracle, Baan, and so on) stored a customer ID as a nine-digit number (999123888), but that same company's Customer Relationship Management (CRM) system (Siebel, Salesforce, Rightnow, and so on) stored the same customer ID as a nine-digit number prefixed with a regional code (ONT999123888). These fields could not be joined in the Crystal Reports Database Linking Expert, but they could be linked using a formula that extracts the nine-digit number from the CRM/Siebel Customer ID and links to the SAP Customer ID in a Subreport.

One last point of interest is that the new Business Views does now enable the linking of formula fields in the creation of Data Foundations. Chapter 18, "Using a Semantic Layer–Business Views and Universes," covers this new functionality.

To explore a reporting solution with linked Subreports, solve the hypothetical reporting problem faced by the same COO of Maple Leaf Bikes Corporation. The COO now wants a single report that highlights the company's top-selling product *types* in one bar chart (similar to the previous example), enables drill-down into the actual products, and produces a list of suppliers for each product type to be available for review—essentially, a Supplier's listing Subreport linked to the main report based on the Product Type Name. To accomplish this, follow these steps:

1. Open the previous sample report from this chapter and delete the previous Subreport containing the Top 5 Sales Rep pie chart. Now add the Product_Type table to this report through the Database Expert under the Database menu option. It is automatically and correctly linked to the Product table. Also, add another Group for Product Type Name on top of the existing Product Name (Hint: You can use the Group Expert under the Report menu.) Then hide the details section of this report.

2. Open the Insert Subreport dialog and create another new Subreport called Supplier Info using the provided Subreport Report Wizard. Connect this new Subreport to the Xtreme sample database, select the Supplier, Product, and Product Type tables (they will correctly smart-link), and add the Supplier Name, City, and Phone Number fields to the report. Finally, click on the Report Wizard Finish button, but do not exit the Insert Subreport dialog.

3. Click on the Link tab in the Insert Subreport dialog. Now, select the Product Type Name field from the Available Fields list as the Field to link on (it can be selected from the Product Type Table). This initiates the Product Type Name ID Link section at the bottom of the dialog. Use the default (and automatically generated) parameter `'?Pm-Product_Type.Product Type Name'` for the link on the Subreport.

Select the Select Data in Subreport Field Based On check box and choose the Product Type Name field from the Product_Type table in the drop-down box. Essentially, you have just specified that this supplier's Subreport be filtered on the Product Type Name that is passed in from the main report every time this Subreport is called. Click OK to add the Subreport and place it in the Product Type Name Group Header on the right side of the report.

To ensure that the desired results are provided and provided in a clean way, edit the Subreport to remove the default provided date and resize its Report Header Subreport section and hide the report footer b in the Subreport. You also need to specify that this Subreport should only return a *distinct* list of suppliers because the COO is not interested in a repetitive list—this can be done through the Report Options selection under the File menu. Click the Select Distinct Records check box.

Lastly, back in the main report, resize the bar chart graphic on the main report and you will have a new sample report for the COO resembling the report depicted in Figure 12.5.

Figure 12.5
Sample report with Linked Suppliers Subreport.

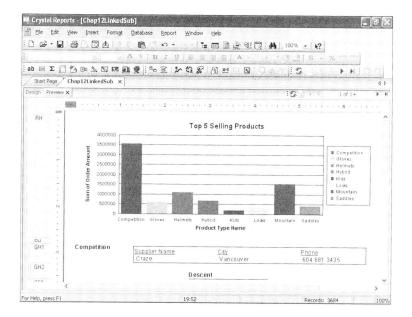

The COO can now make an informed analysis on whether his firm has too much reliance on a small number of suppliers, and you have learned some of the benefits of a linked Subreport.

12

NOTE

> Unlike the initial sample report presented in this chapter where we placed the Top Sales Rep Subreport in the Report Header and it ran once for the entire main report, the Product Suppliers Subreport is run multiple times—in fact, once for every product type. This is the case because the Subreport was placed in the Group Header of the main report, and it therefore is executed for each different group in the main report. This is important to note with respect to performance, specifically when your databases and reports become large.

CONSIDERING SUBREPORT EXECUTION TIME AND PERFORMANCE

There are two types of Subreports—In-Place and On-Demand. Both of the sample reports created previously in this chapter have been In-Place Subreports. An *In-Place* Subreport is virtually indistinguishable from the main report components when viewed because it is run at the same time as the main report. In-Place Subreports are displayed as components of the main report like any other report object and require no special business user interaction to view them. *On-Demand* Subreports, on the contrary, are not executed at the same time as the main report and require user interaction to be viewed.

All In-Place Subreports on a main report are run at the execution time of the main report. In the two examples presented in this chapter, this has clearly not caused any performance problems, but as you might imagine, it could on larger databases and reports. Imagine running the last sample report (with the Product Suppliers Subreport in every Group Header) for a large conglomerate with thousands of products. The Product Suppliers Subreport would need to run thousands of times to complete the presentation of the main report. Moreover, the thousands of supplier Subreports would be unlikely to be used by any given business user and would therefore have run extraneously. An elegant solution to that problem is the use of On-Demand Subreports.

Unlike In-Place Subreports, On-Demand Subreports only execute when a user requests them. They lie dormant until that time. The performance benefits to On-Demand reports are clear; however, it does come at the expense of a less seamless integration than In-Place Subreports and a small delay in viewing because the Subreport executes dynamically after being requested.

Taking the last example, follow these steps to make the Product Suppliers Subreport an On-Demand Subreport:

1. Open the most recent sample report if you have closed it.

2. Right-click on the Product Suppliers Subreport and select the Format Subreport option. Many familiar formatting options are available here (see Figure 12.6), but click on the Subreport tab.

Figure 12.6
The Format Subreport dialog enables specification of many standard formatting options, including whether a Subreport is On-Demand.

3. Click the On-Demand Subreport check box to turn on that option. Notice that the On-Demand Caption section becomes un-grayed.

4. Click on the On-Demand Caption button (x-2) and type '**Supplier List**' (do include the apostrophes) in the Text Editing area. Click on the Save and Close button, and you should now have a main report that resembles Figure 12.7 where the Supplier List link dynamically runs the involved Subreport if and only if a report consumer requests it.

Figure 12.7
Sample report with Linked, On-Demand Suppliers Subreport.

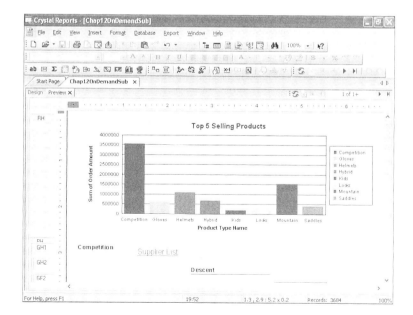

Careful consideration should be given to report design when deciding between In-Place and On-Demand Subreports. There is a trade-off between the seamless integration of In-Place Subreports and the performance benefits of On-Demand Subreports that must be considered in addition, of course, to the specific requirements of the business users' overall experience.

USING VARIABLES TO PASS DATA BETWEEN REPORTS

The examples up to this point in the chapter that involve passing data between a main report and a Subreport have worked exclusively through the Subreport Linking tab or dialog. Although the functionality provided there is certainly powerful, circumstances might require more flexible passing of data between the main report and the Subreport or the passing of data the other way—from a Subreport to a main report.

With the use of variables, it becomes possible to pass data between the main report and any of the Subreports or even among different Subreports in the same main report. By declaring the same shared variable in formulas in both the main report and at least one Subreport, data can be exchanged back and forth fluidly, and each report can leverage information from the other in a very flexible manner.

TIP

Using Subreports and variables to pass data back to a main report from a Subreport is an effective way to capture important summarizations or external information to your main report that is not possible otherwise because of the default groupings of the main report. A simple example in this chapter's last sample report would be the inclusion of a count on the number of suppliers for each product. Using only the default groupings provided in the main report (By Product), this count would be impossible to calculate. By using a Subreport, however, that count can be calculated external to the main report (in a Subreport), shared using variables, and eventually displayed on the main report.

12

To explore the power of shared variables, follow these steps to modify this chapter's last sample report:

1. Open the most recent sample report if you have closed it. Turn the Supplier Subreport back to an In-Place Subreport (versus On-Demand).

NOTE

When passing shared variables from a Subreport to a main report, the involved Subreport cannot be set to On-Demand. The reason, of course, is that Subreports are not run until specifically requested by the business user. Therefore, their associated variables are not set until that time, making them unusable in the main report.

2. Edit the Supplier's Subreport by right-clicking on the Subreport and selecting the Edit Subreport option.

3. Select the Supplier Name field and insert a summary field that counts the distinct supplier names in this report. (Hint: Right-click on the Supplier Name field and access the Summary menu option.) This summary will shortly be assigned to the shared variable that will be created and used to pass the information back to the main report.

4. Insert a formula into the Report Footer of this Subreport and call it **Assign Supplier Count**. In this formula, declare a shared numeric variable called **SupplierCount** and then assign this variable to equal the Supplier Summary created in the last step. (Reminder: You can access the summary created in step 3 for use in your formula by double-clicking on it.) The formula definition should resemble Figure 12.8.

Figure 12.8
Formula with a shared variable declaration in the Subreport.

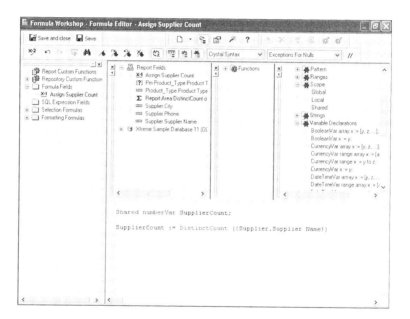

5. Now click on the Preview or Design tab of the Crystal Reports Designer to take you back to the main report, insert a formula into the Product Type Group Footer section, and call it **Place Supplier Count**. In this formula, declare the same shared numeric variable—SupplierCount—and make this variable the output of this formula. Figure 12.9 shows what this formula should look like.

It is important that this Formula is placed in the Group Footer of the Product Type Name Group. This strategic placement ensures that the Supplier List Subreport for the involved Product Type has already completed (as it is in the Group Header) and has set the shared SupplierCount variable appropriately. Careful consideration needs to be given when using variables to ensure they are evaluated at the time and in the order desired.

In addition to the Top to Bottom and Left to Right default evaluation times of Crystal Reports, the `EvaluateAfter()` and a few other functions discussed in the Multi-Pass reporting section in Chapter 4, "Understanding and Implementing Formulas," are useful in ensuring the desired reporting results.

Figure 12.9
Formula with a shared variable declaration and output in the main report.

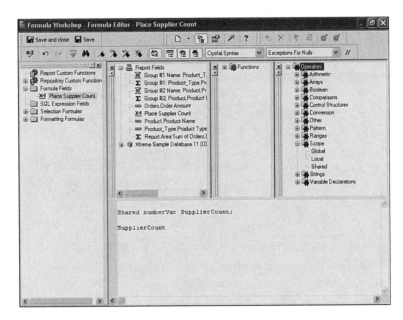

6. Add a text field to the report to complement the Supplier Count field called **Supplier Count**, hide the Details section on the main report and with a little creative formatting and group sorting, the final result should resemble Figure 12.10.

Perhaps not the prettiest report ever designed, this quick example does begin to convey the power and importance of shared variables in report design.

12

NOTE

As you discover the power of variables, you will begin to leverage this programming feature in increasingly complex ways. The Supplier Count example just provided is a relatively simple example that scratches the surface of the power of variables. Another variable-based technique that can be used to circumvent some common reporting challenges is to use variables to manage Running Totals. The flexibility provided within the Formula Editor and with variables enables you to create flexible condition-based running totals.

Figure 12.10
Sample report with
Supplier Count
sourced from a
shared variable in
a Subreport.

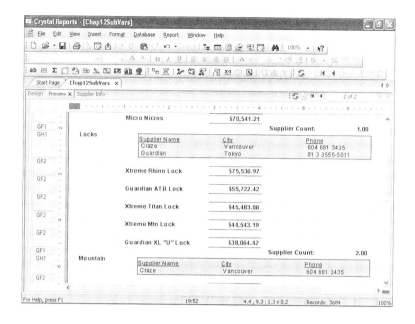

EMULATING NESTED SUBREPORTS

Based on the title of this section, you can deduce that it is not possible to nest Subreports—
why else would you need to emulate that behavior? Crystal Reports does not currently support Subreports within Subreports. Report Hyperlinks and Report Parts do, however,
provide a flexible method in advanced navigation between and within reports. This form of
flexible navigation can be used to emulate nested Subreports and was covered in Chapter 9,
"Custom Formatting Techniques."

TROUBLESHOOTING

FORMATTING THE DETAILS OF A SUBREPORT

I can't figure out how to format the details of a Subreport.

Open the Design tab for that Subreport from within the Designer of the main report. This
can be accomplished by right-clicking on a Subreport and selecting the Edit Subreport
option.

USING SUBREPORTS TO WRITE-BACK TO A SOURCE DATABASE

*I would like to enable report viewers (or end users) to be able to dynamically send updates back to a
source database—can subreports help me accomplish this?*

Using a clever combination of subreports and SQL commands, you can provide this capability to your end users. You can add On-Demand subreports to your main report and have
each of the On-Demand subreports based on a SQL command that includes an INSERT
SQL statement that writes back to a datasource. An example SQL command could be

```
SELECT * FROM   "TestInsertfromCR"."dbo"."TableName";
INSERT INTO "TestInsertfromCR"."dbo"."TableName" VALUES _
    (9999,'test insert',9999,'test','test')
```

Each time a report-viewing end user requests that the on-demand subreport run, this SQL statement will be executed and update the involved datasource. To make this data updating process more dynamic, the preceding example could have the inserted values fields replaced with dynamic data fields from the report (for example, Customer ID or Employee ID).

CRYSTAL REPORTS IN THE REAL WORLD— MULTIPLE SUBREPORTS

As discussed earlier in the chapter, a single report often needs to show data from different and frequently unrelated pieces of information. In the next example, the main report shows both customer and supplier information with two separate Subreports and each of them for a given geographic location using the main report's regional grouping hierarchy as a filter on the underlying Subreports. You will create a main report for the hierarchical geographic structure of Country, Region, and City hierarchy and then add one Subreport to show customer information and another Subreport for supplier information. Because there is no relationship between suppliers and customers, at least one of these pieces of information must come from a Subreport. For this sample, both elements come from a Subreport to highlight the capability to use multiple Subreports in a single main report. Follow these steps to explore this capability:

1. Open the report designer and select Create New Report Using the Report Wizard. Click OK and browse to the datasource Xtreme Samples Database 11 datasource, expand the list of tables, and add the Customer table to the list of report tables by clicking the > button. Click Next.

2. In the Fields window, add the fields Country, Region, and City to the report and click Next. In the Grouping window, add the same fields to the Group By list.

3. Click Finish to complete the report. This builds the hierarchy that is used in the report.

4. Change to Design mode. Move the fields in the group header to the left and indent them slightly at each lower level. Suppress all sections of the report other than the headers and expand each of the header areas below the fields. See Figure 12.11 to view what the framework of the report should look like.

5. With the framework complete, the next step is to create the content. There are different ways to create Subreports; in this instance, you will create the Subreports as separate files and later import them into the main report. Create the report for supplier information by navigating to the Start Page and selecting a new report with the Standard Report Wizard. Select the Xtreme Sample Database 11 connection, browse the list of tables for the Supplier table, and click the > button to move it to the list of selected tables. Click Next. From the Fields window, select Supplier Name and Phone and click the > button to move them to the Fields to Display. Click Finish to close the

wizard. Minimize report content by changing to Design mode, moving the fields to the left edge, suppressing sections with no fields, and minimizing whitespace. Figure 12.12 illustrates a sample suppliers Subreport. Save this report to your local machine.

Figure 12.11
Report hierarchy to act as the framework for Subreport content.

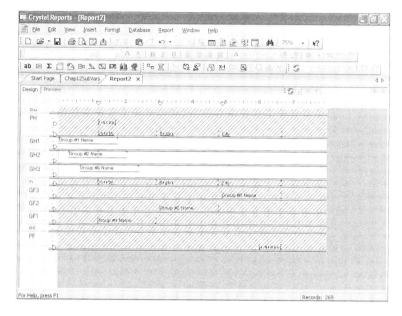

Figure 12.12
Supplier information Subreport, extra whitespace reduced to a minimum.

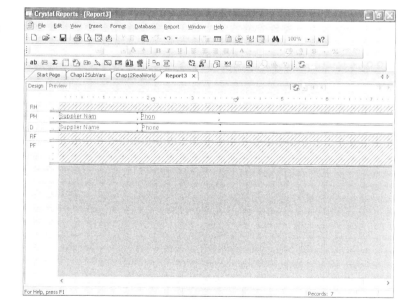

6. Repeat step 5 for the customer table.

7. Add each Subreport to the report three times, once each for Country, Region, and City. Use the Insert Subreport dialog accessed from the main Insert menu and, using the Choose an Existing report option, browse to the location where you have saved the recently created Subreports. Now link the regional fields (Country, Region, and City) to each of the Subreport's associated fields. This can be accomplished by accessing the Change Subreport Links option available on the right-click menu for each Subreport. For the Subreports based in the Country Group Header, you need to link the Country field from the main report to the Country field in the Suppliers table. You will need to link both the Country and the Region fields for the Subreports in the Region Group Header and you will also need to add City for those Subreports in the City Group Header.

8. For each of the Subreports, ensure that the Keep Object Together formatting option is turned off. This is accessed from the Format Subreport dialog on the Common tab. You can use the Format Painter to copy one Subreport's format to the others to save you a few keystrokes.

9. From the Report menu, select Section Expert. In the list of sections, ensure the Keep Together option is not checked for each Group Header. Click OK to close the window. Save the report. The design of the report should look like Figure 12.13 and the final result should resemble Figure 12.14

Figure 12.13
Report with hierarchy and Subreports.

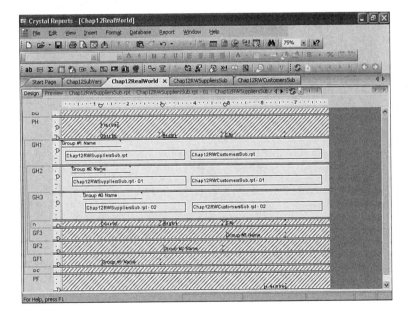

Preview the report and notice on Page 13 (Canada) that there is different and unrelated information for both Suppliers and Customers listed and that the information for both is specific to the location context.

Figure 12.14
Report Preview showing a main-report hierarchy on region and multiple Subreports that are filtering their customer and supplier lists by their placement in the main report.

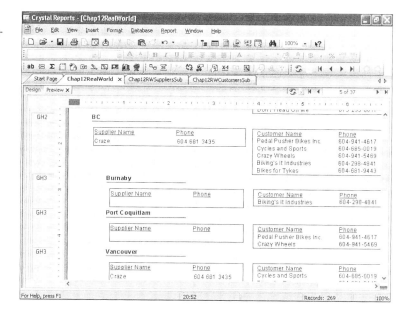

CHAPTER 13

Using Formulas and Custom Functions

In this chapter

INTRODUCTION

This chapter explores the use of advanced formulas and functions to accomplish many mundane and repetitive tasks. Also, you will look at how the formulas and functions can help alleviate redundancy in report design.

Whereas Chapter 4, "Understanding and Implementing Formulas," focused on the basics of formulas, this chapter focuses on some lesser known facts and tricks to make formula work more productive as well as less repetitive.

CHOOSING A FORMULA LANGUAGE: CRYSTAL VERSUS BASIC SYNTAX

In previous chapters, the Crystal syntax was used for all formulas. However, formulas in Crystal Reports can be created, edited, and modified using one of two languages. The Crystal syntax is the most used language, but the Basic syntax is also available.

Both languages are equal in their functionality—meaning that if something was added to Crystal syntax, it was also added to Basic. The reason you're given a choice is for your comfort—you can use whichever language you are more comfortable with using.

UNDERSTANDING SYNTAX DIFFERENCES

The Crystal syntax is most similar to the Pascal or Delphi programming languages. It's not exactly like Pascal, but if you're a Delphi developer or a longtime Crystal Report developer, this syntax is probably your first choice.

The Basic syntax is most similar to Visual Basic as a programming language. If you're a Visual Basic developer, you'll likely find this syntax most beneficial.

Some specific differences between the two languages are described in Table 13.1.

TABLE 13.1   DIFFERENCES BETWEEN CRYSTAL AND BASIC SYNTAX

Description	Crystal	Basic
Variable declarations	`StringVar`	`Dim <name> As <type>`
Statement endings	`;`	None required
Comment characters	`//`	`'`
Variable assignment	`:=`	`=`
Formula statement	None required	Required
Formula returns	None required	`Return statement`
Multiline statement indicators	None required	`_`
If statement ending	`;`	`End If`

WHY BASIC SYNTAX WAS ADDED

Many functions and operators provided by the Basic language increase the productivity of Crystal Reports users. By implementing the whole language, the existing Crystal syntax users could benefit from the new operators and functions and at the same time, newer users who are familiar with the Basic language through other development endeavors could easily make the jump to creating formulas in Crystal Reports.

Some of the functions and operators that were added as a result of the addition of the Basic syntax are

- Date functions such as `DateAdd`, `DateDiff`, and `DateSerial`
- Financial functions such as Present Value (`PV`)
- Control structures such as `Do While`, `Do Until`, and `For Next` statements

SELECTING THE BEST SYNTAX FOR YOU

Whether you choose Basic or Crystal syntax, they are both equally capable of doing the job and there is no performance implication in making this choice. The decision is entirely based on the comfort level and familiarity of each language for report designers.

> **TIP**
>
> Whichever syntax you prefer to use most often, you can set it up as the default for all new formulas by going to File, Options, Reporting, and choosing the desired syntax in the Formula Language list box.

USING BRACKETS IN FORMULAS

Regardless of which syntax is chosen, some fundamental concepts to formula creation are important.

Several variations of brackets are used within the formula language, and it can be confusing to know which one to use at a particular time. To clear up some of the confusion, here is a way to remember them phonetically:

- `{}`French = Fields

  For example, `{Table.Field}` is used to refer to fields, formula fields, or parameter fields in the report definition.

- `[ ]`Square = Selected

  For example, `{Table.Field}[1]` returns only the first character of a string field. Square brackets are used for indexes on array types (for example, strings or array data types).

- `( )`Parenthesis = Parameters

  For example, Function (`{Table.Field}`) passes the field to the function. Parentheses are used to define which parts of a calculation or formula should be performed first (that is, defines order of precedence for mathematical and non-mathematical operations).

13

USING CHARACTERS IN FORMULAS

As with brackets, symbols in the formula language (or in the icons) have specific meaning as well. To shed some light on this, check out the listing of symbols that represent different field types in Crystal Reports:

@ = Formula	{@Formula} is a formula field
? = Parameter	{?Param} is a parameter field
# = Running Total	{#RunTtl} is a running total field
Σ = Summary	ΣfieldName is a summary field on the report
% = SQL Expression	{%SQL} is a SQL expression field

RECENT IMPROVEMENTS TO FORMULAS

Because Crystal Reports has been around for so many years and has released many versions over those years, it's not uncommon to come across users who are still using older versions. To bring those users up to speed this section covers some of the recent additions and improvements to formulas over the past few versions.

MANIPULATING MEMO FIELDS IN FORMULAS

In the past, Crystal Reports developers had not been able to access string fields that were longer than 255 characters within the formula language other than to find out whether they were null. This limitation has been completely removed.

For the purposes here, assume that the Xtreme Mountain Bike Company management needs an HR report that shows only the female employees, but there is no gender field in the Xtreme database. In the Notes field in the Employee table, the word "she" is used for all female employees. However, Xtreme's management has indicated that they might need to search for other words as well, so they want to have a keyword search instead of hard-coding the search values. Follow these steps to create such a report to fulfill this reporting requirement:

1. Open the Employee Profile Report. Press Ctrl+O to open a report. Find the Crystal Reports XI sample report called Employee Profile. Most installations have it in the following folder: C:\Program Files\Business Objects\Crystal Reports 11\Samples\en\Reports\General Business.

2. Create a parameter field by selecting View, Field Explorer. Right-click on the Parameter Field item in the Field Explorer and choose New. In the Create Parameter Field dialog, call the parameter **Search-A-Word**. Prompting Text should be **What word would you like to search for?**. The Value Type should be String.

3. Add "<none>", "she", and "he" to the list of default values. The final result should look like Figure 13.1.

Figure 13.1
The default values and prompt settings for a Search-A-Word prompt.

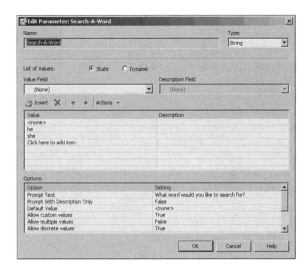

4. Connect the prompt to the Selection Formula. Select the Formula Workshop via Report, Formula Workshop. Then choose Selection Formulas, Record Selection from the Workshop tree. Enter the following selection formula into the editor: **IF {?Search-A-Word} = "<none>" THEN TRUE ELSE ({?Search-a-Word}) IN LowerCase({Employee.Notes})** and click the Save and Close button.

5. Run the report. When prompted, choose she from the Parameter Field prompt and choose to refresh the data. The end result is that only the female employees appear on the report as shown in Figure 13.2. Save the report as **Chap13_1.rpt**.

Figure 13.2
The Employee Profile showing female employees only.

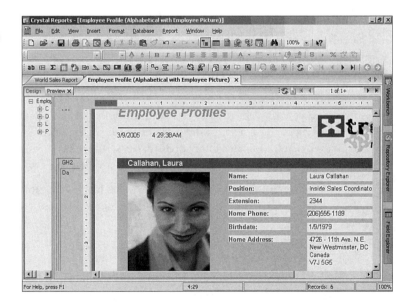

Notice that you only put the `LowerCase()` function call around the `{Employee.Notes}` field and not the parameter. This is because you put the values into the parameter as lowercase by default. However, because you allow the business users to input their own values into the parameter, it might be a good idea to put the `LowerCase()` function on the parameter as well. This allows Crystal to compare apples to apples when evaluating these exact values. Alternatively, both could have been set to `UpperCase()` as well.

A keyword search is just one example of how to use a memo field in a formula. The 255-character limit for formulas that was removed in version 9 of Crystal Reports means that practically all database field types can now be accessed in formulas and manipulated. Remember that memo fields are really just long string fields, so they are treated as strings in the formula language. Wherever a string can be called, now a memo field can be called as well.

Not all databases support the capability to search large string fields, so if this type of keyword search is required, more records than necessary might come across the network. For the preceding example, 15 records were returned from the data source but only the 6 that were female were shown on the report. This is because the data source couldn't be passed this selection criteria to handle on the server side.

It is a powerful new feature, but keep in mind that it might bring back more records than you expect.

WORKING WITH THE ADDITIONAL FINANCIAL FUNCTIONS

In older versions of Crystal Reports, the financial functions capability of the formula language was limited to 13 functions. However, version XI of Crystal Reports provides more than 50 financial functions. With overloads for parameters, these functions count up to about 200 variations.

These functions were implemented to give as much functionality as possible to a highly skilled group of report designers. In the past, they had to hand code the financial functions. By including the standard financial functions that most users have seen in Microsoft Excel, these report developers can now develop their formulas much more quickly.

For more information on the Financial Functions available, refer to the Crystal Reports Help file. In the Index, look up "Financial Functions" for a complete list of what is available.

CREATING CUSTOM FUNCTIONS IN YOUR REPORTS

Custom functions were introduced in Crystal Reports 9 and continue to be a powerful feature of Crystal Reports XI. Although they have been introduced in Chapter 4, this section focuses on some more detailed information on what they are and how they could be used in report development.

Custom functions are packets of business logic that are written in Basic or Crystal syntax. These functions do not have any reference to any database fields at all. Because these functions contain logic that will change values and return a result, the values must be passed in and the results of the logic must be passed out or returned.

Only 10% of a custom function is different from your average formula. As mentioned previously, parameters must be passed in to allow for data manipulation because a custom function is *stateless*. This means that it has no meaning outside the function it has called in. It acts just like all the other formula functions in the formula language. The only difference is that custom functions can be created, edited, and deleted, whereas Crystal formula functions are completely unchangeable.

Here is a custom function that is provided within the sample repository that comes with Crystal Reports:

```
Function cdExpandRegionAbbreviation (regionAbbreviation _
 As String, Optional country As String = "USA")
 Select Case UCase (country)
  Case "CANADA"
   cdExpandRegionAbbreviation _
     = cdExpandRegionAbbreviationCanada (regionAbbreviation)
  Case "USA", "U.S.A.", "US", "U.S.", "UNITED STATES", _
    "UNITED STATES OF AMERICA"
   cdExpandRegionAbbreviation _
     = cdExpandRegionAbbreviationUSA (regionAbbreviation)
    Case Else
        cdExpandRegionAbbreviation = regionAbbreviation
    End Select
End Function
```

Some of the things you will notice about the preceding code are as follows:

- It's in Basic syntax. This is not a requirement of custom functions. They can be in either Basic or Crystal syntax.

- It does not reference database fields directly. Any information that is needed from database must be passed in via the parameters in the first statement (`regionAbbreviation`).

- It has an optional parameter (`Optional country As String = "USA"`). This means that this parameter does not necessarily need to be passed in for the function to work. If this parameter is not supplied by the developer in the formula, the value of `"USA"` is used by default.

- It calls other custom functions. `CdExpandRegionAbbreviationCanada` and `cdExpandRegionAbbreviationUSA` are also custom functions. In fact, they are Crystal syntax custom functions. (This shows that Basic and Crystal syntax can call one another.)

- It has a definite end-point (`End Function`). This allows for the final result (the functions return) to be passed back out to the formula making the call.

13

> **TIP**
>
> The Enter More Info button takes you to another dialog where you can enter much more descriptive text around the custom function. It also contains fields for categorization and authors. From there, you can also add help text via another dialog. For more information on these dialogs, consult the online help.

SHARING CUSTOM FUNCTIONS WITH OTHERS

Two ways in which you can share custom functions are

- **By using them in multiple places in one**—Because custom functions are stateless, different parameters can be passed in to allow for instant function reuse.
- **By sharing them in the Crystal Repository**—Custom functions are one of four report object types that can be shared in the repository.

Custom functions can be used in many ways. Take your existing formulas, convert them, and share their logic with others.

UNDERSTANDING RUNTIME ERRORS

Crystal Reports XI provides the ability to get more information about variables within formulas when a runtime error occurs. In the past, when a runtime error (such as a Divide by Zero) occurred, Crystal would simply take you to the line of the formula giving the error. However, this was not altogether helpful, especially if the error was because the data being passed in from the database could have been at fault. So, since version 9 of Crystal Reports, there is a feature that shows all variables and data field values used in all related formulas when an error occurs. You can think of this as a variable stack.

The runtime error stack only appears when a runtime error occurs (when real-time data forces an error). It appears where the workshop group tree normally would in the Formula Workshop.

The runtime error stack shows all variables and all database field data related to the formula in question. If custom functions are called within the formula, their variables will appear above the formula as well. The last function to be called will appear at the top.

> **TIP**
>
> The idea of a stack (reverse order) is useful in that the last function called most likely will be where the error is. But, of course, that might not always be the case.

This concept is best shown as an example. Assume that Xtreme Mountain Bike Company's management would like to take the World Sales Report and find out how much money is not accounted for by days when not shipped (Calculation = Order Amount / Days until shipped). To see how this works, follow these steps to simulate a formula error:

1. Use the World Sales Report (open it from the same sample location referred to above for the HR report).

2. Create a new formula called Days Until Shipped and use the following calculation: `{Orders.Order Amount} / {@Days until Shipped}`.

3. Use the Formula Workshop. Select Report, Formula Workshop. Right-click on the Formula Field branch in the workshop tree and choose New. Name the formula **Unaccounted Amount/Day** and select Use Editor.

4. Add the required logic. In the Editor, enter the following: "`{Orders.Order Amount} / {@Days until Shipped}`". Click the Save and Close button in the top-left corner. Choose Yes when prompted to save. If the report is not already in Preview mode, press F5 to refresh the report. If you don't see any data, choose Report, Section Expert and make sure that the Details section isn't suppressed. If it is, toggle the option and click OK.

5. Drag the field onto the report. From the Field Explorer (View, Field Explorer), select the newly created formula and drag it onto the detail line of the report. Notice that the Divide by Zero error comes up right away. Click OK.

6. View the Runtime Error Stack shown in Figure 13.3. In this case, the formula is quite straightforward. The problem is occurring because some of the orders are on time (zero days wait). Xtreme's management would like to show 0 if the orders are on time, so change the formula to the following: "`if {@Days until Shipped} = 0 then 0 else {Orders.Order Amount} / {@Days until Shipped}`". Click the Save button.

Figure 13.3
Runtime Error Stack next to the newly updated formula.

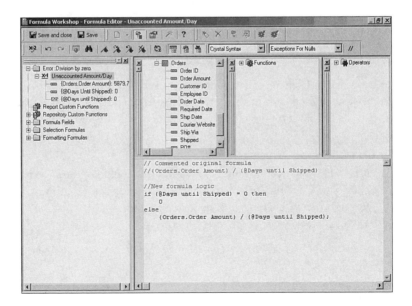

Click F5 to refresh the report. See the values of the resulting formula as shown in Figure 13.4 and then save the report as **Chap13_3.rpt**. In the sample report created here, the new formula was colored red so it can be easily found. You will need to drill to the detail level to see this field.

Figure 13.4
Resulting Report with the latest Xtreme requirements added.

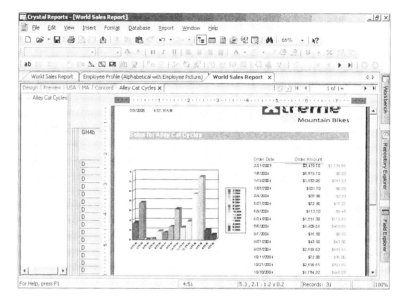

CRYSTAL REPORTS IN THE REAL WORLD—CUSTOM FUNCTIONS

As described in Chapter 4, custom functions can be prepared in advance and can be stateless so they can be used later in a variety of ways. In the next example, a name formula is created in such a way that it builds and formats names in a consistent and reusable manner.

→ For more detailed information on how custom functions can be prepared in advance, see "Navigating the Formula Workshop with the Workshop Tree," p. 99

Open the Employee Profile report. From the Field Explorer, select Formula Fields and click New. Give the formula the name Title and click Use Editor. Enter the following text into the code window of the formula editor:

```
If InStr(LowerCase({Employee.Notes}), " he ")>0 Then
    "Mr."
Else If InStr(LowerCase({Employee.Notes}), " she ")>0 Then
    "Ms."
Else
    "";
```

Click Save and Close. Next, create another new formaula named Suffix and in the code window only type two double-quotes (the string equivalent of NULL); this acts as a placeholder because the table doesn't have a suffix field. Finally, create a formula called Proper Name and add the following text into the code window:

```
Local StringVar strFullName;
strFullName := "";
If {@Title} <> "" Then
    strFullName := {@Title} & " ";
strFullName := strFullName & {Employee.Last Name} & ", " & {Employee.First
Name};
If {@Suffix} <> "" Then
    strFullName := strFullName & " " & {@Suffix};
strFullName
```

3. Click Save and Close. From the Report menu, choose Formula Workshop. Click New and give it the name **ProperName** and click Use Extractor. In the list of formulas, select @Proper Name. Your screen should look like Figure 13.5. By default, the Argument Names are v1, v2, v3, and v4 but this won't help users of your formula so change the names to Title, LastName, FirstName, and Suffix.

Figure 13.5
Custom function properties.

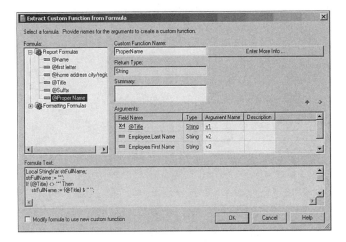

4. Click OK to close the window. Crystal converts the formula from the way it's currently written into a generic custom function for later use. The new custom function is shown in Figure 13.6.

5. Click Save and Close. The custom function is now available for use.

6. Finally, create the formula that will be used in the report. Create a new formula called Custom Name. From the list of functions, double-click the ProperName function and pass in the following values:

```
Title: @Title
LastName: {Employee.Last Name}
FirstName: {Employee.First Name}
Suffix: @Suffix
```

Your completed formula should look like Figure 13.7.

13

Figure 13.6
Custom function
formula.

Figure 13.7
Passing values to a
custom function.

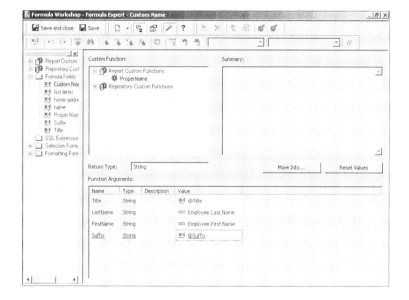

In the sample database there is no Title field, but a formula can be used to generate the Title that will be passed to the custom function. The sample database also doesn't contain a suffix field and because there's no way to determine if the employee name has a suffix, a null string will be passed to the custom function. The custom function can be used later with tables that have both Title and Suffix fields.

7. Add the Custom Name formula to the report and replace the @name formula in the Group Header 2 section. Change the font to Bold and white. Save the report as **CustomName.rpt**. Figure 13.8 shows the completed report.

Figure 13.8
Report using a Name built using a custom function.

CHAPTER 14

DESIGNING EFFECTIVE REPORT TEMPLATES

In this chapter

UNDERSTANDING THE IMPORTANCE OF REUSE IN REPORTING

Up to now, you've been creating feature rich reports that are very functional. Most likely, no two of the resulting reports from the previous chapters have a consistent look and feel.

One of the most demanding and time-consuming parts of Report Design is giving all of your reports a consistent look and feel. In many situations, report designers are asked to conform to a corporate standard like letterheads (all page numbers in the bottom right corner, and so on) or perhaps even something as demanding as GAAP or SEC.

In a perfect world that revolves around report designers, less work would be required if you were allowed to focus your efforts on one report and use it as a guide for all other reports that require visual, presentation-focused (yet time-consuming) features. After one report is completed with the appropriate formatting, why not *apply* its contents and format to other reports? Applying an existing report's layout to other reports is very straightforward with Crystal Reports XI. This is made possible through enhancements to the report template's functionality.

UNDERSTANDING REPORT TEMPLATES

A report template is nothing more than a regular report (.rpt) file. It can be any RPT file. Templates are *applied* to other reports so that their formatting and layout can be used as a basis for the other reports. What is useful about the application of templates to other reports is that formatting is applied to the report as well as the layout. An example of this would be a report that has four fields in a detail section, where all sections are "squished" together before applying a presentation-quality template. After the template is applied, the location of the fields in the template would force the fields in the existing report to span out and possibly even change some font information, depending on the specific template.

USING REPORT TEMPLATES

Think of a template as the form that everyone in a company must comply to. Templates can house many types of objects. These objects can be applied to a report after the data-intensive portion of the report design is completed. Applying an existing template to a report can save hours or potentially days of mundane formatting tasks.

Some types of tasks that can be accomplished by (but are not limited to) applying a template to a report are as follows:

- Corporate logos and other images
- Consistent page numbering formatting
- Font style/color/typeface for data fields
- Field border and background formatting

- Field sizing
- Group headers and footers formatting
- Summary field formatting
- Watermarks
- Tricky formatting
- Lines
- Boxes
- Repository objects
- Report titles
- Web site links
- Formatting based on data-field type

How Are Templates Better Than Styles in Older Versions?

Templates are better than the Styles in older versions of Crystal Reports in so many ways that it's challenging to explain in a short section. However, because not all report designers have used Crystal Reports prior to version 10, they won't know how cumbersome styles used to be. For those of you new to Crystal Reports 10 or XI, feel free to skip this sidebar.

The main problem with the old Report Styles feature in older versions of Crystal Reports (such as 8.5) was that they were not customizable. The styles that one person created when the feature was initially introduced were the only options available. Even if you just didn't like the color red as the group name field and wanted to change it to blue, you were not able to, which was very limiting. This limitation alone made the Styles feature practically useless outside of learning how to create very simple reports.

These styles were also limited to data and group fields. No images or static text objects were included, and again because the styles could not be modified, they could not be updated in this way. The styles were hard-coded into the Crystal Reports designer so that no external .rpt files were used, whereas Templates enable the use of any .rpt file.

USING EXISTING CRYSTAL REPORTS AS TEMPLATES

Now that you've learned the major benefits of Report Templates, apply a template to one of the reports created in Chapter 3, "Filtering, Sorting, and Summarizing Data." The report Chap3Sorts.rpt (shown in Figure 14.1) as it looked was pretty plain because the focus was on making sure that the data requirements were satisfied. There wasn't a lot of time to play with formatting, so now you are going to apply a template that has some nice grayscale formatting and an underlay applied. These steps walk you through that process:

1. Open the report. Choose File, Open to get the Open dialog box, and browse until the report is found. Choose it and click Open to continue.

2. Look at the report prior to applying the template as shown in Figure 14.1. To get a good view of the application of the template, make sure that the Preview tab is selected. If the Preview tab is not selected or available, choose View, Preview.

14

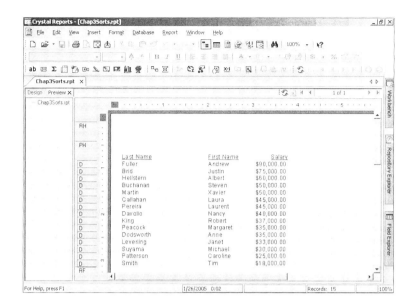

Apply the template. To apply some formatting quickly, Report, Template Expert. In the Template Expert dialog, feel free to choose each file so that you can see the associated thumbnail. For this case, choose Confidential Underlay, as shown in Figure 14.2, and then click OK.

> For more information on thumbnails, review the Preview Pictures sidebar at end of this chapter.

Figure 14.2
The Template Expert
with the Confidential
Underlay template
chosen.

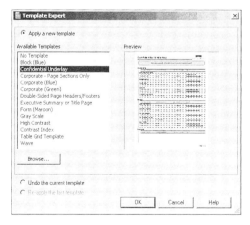

Save the report. The report will then open with the formatting from the applied template as shown in Figure 14.3. You can now save the report as **CHAP14.rpt**.

Figure 14.3
The target report with the Confidential Underlay template applied.

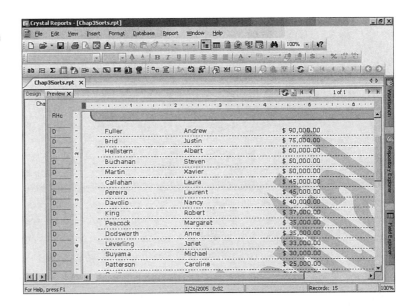

UNDERSTANDING HOW TEMPLATES WORK

A lot of report formatting tasks were accomplished in the two minutes it took to apply the template in the previous exercise, including

- Adding the Business Objects logo to the report (along with its ToolTip and hyperlink) from the Crystal Repository
- Adding an image that says Confidential as an underlay to each page of the report
- Modifying the fonts and positions of all the database fields
- Adding dashed lines between all items in the Details Section
- Adding a rounded box at the top of the page
- Using a rounded box to show where groups start and end

14

TIP

> One of the more advantageous features of templates is that even if more fields are in the target report's Details section than the template has, it duplicates the data field formatting for those extra fields. It puts them into a separate Detail Section (usually titled Details B) so that they will all appear together but they won't overwrite each other. You can then move the fields around without having to worry about applying the same formatting by hand.

CREATING USEFUL REPORT TEMPLATES

If a Crystal Report already exists that has been regularly copied in the past or a report that is viewed as the *perfect report*, consider it to be the beginning of an effective template. Because any report can be the basis for a template, you might just need to refine a few functional or formatting characteristics to make the existing report more robust for use as a formal template.

If you don't have any reports to use for creating templates, you don't need to be concerned. Everything you've learned so far (and in the upcoming chapters) will help with effective template design. By creating a nice presentation-quality report, you have also created a likely candidate that can then be used as a useful report.

Keep in mind a few key things when using an existing report for a template.

As previously mentioned, templates can be used to accomplish formatting tasks at lightning pace after data collection is done. Because any report can be used as a template, a Crystal Reports designer might already have a library full of ideas.

Applying one report layout as a template to another could cause some minor issues if the databases that are connected to each report are completely different in terms of schema, structure, or content. However, with some minor adjustments, the template report can be applied more effectively.

Formulas, for instance, can be problematic when applying a report as a template to another report. Because most formulas require database fields to function, they are closely tied to the actual database and structure of the data that is coming in to the report. Because formulas are used to act on database fields, using them in templates is not very effective because errors might occur when applying a template report to another report that accesses a different database. However, some tools are available that can minimize this effect. Using custom functions instead of prewritten formulas can alleviate some of the data dependencies, as can using the CurrentFieldValue evaluator for formatting formulas.

Also, even relatively small things can make a significant difference. Sometimes just focusing on the page headers or footers can go a long way in effective report template design. By reducing the repetitive nature of general page formatting, you will increase your report design productivity.

USING CUSTOM FUNCTIONS AS REPLACEMENTS FOR DATA-DEPENDENT BUSINESS LOGIC

Because custom functions were introduced in the previous chapter, the focus of this section is how to use custom functions to avoid formula errors when applying templates. For more information on Custom Functions, see Chapter 13, "Using Formulas and Custom Functions."

The reason Custom Functions are more useful in templates than straight formulas is that they are *stateless*, which means that they have no direct dependency on the database fields to get their data. Custom Functions see the data only as parameters that are passed in to the report. Instead of searching through an entire formula to find all uses of a given field, by passing it in to a Custom Function once, Crystal Reports effectively does the search and replace repeatedly on the report designer's behalf.

Another advantage to using Custom Functions in a report template is that within the one report—the template report—it might be possible to use one Custom Function more than once because the logic might be used over and over with the only difference being the data that's used.

If a report that contains many formulas is applied as a template to a report that contains a different table name—for example, template.field and target.field—the formulas would not change over correctly. Therefore, all the formulas will result in compiler errors upon the first run of the report to the preview. Because the report designer would have to go through all the lines of business logic and replace each and every database field occurrence, it could be a very tedious process. If the search-and-replace time could be limited to one line per formula, you would be far more productive.

Of course, current formulas in a pre-existing report are already working and you would not want to break them. The task of manually changing all relevant formulas to custom functions would be a big task. However, the Formula Extractor can automate this process for you.

By using the Formula Extractor, you can actually review the existing formula, break it down, find the data-specific pieces, convert them into parameters, and reformulate the formula to accept those parameters and save it as a Custom Function. It even rebuilds the initial formula that created the Custom Function to apply the new Custom Function so that the report designer doesn't have to go back and perform that step manually.

> **TIP**
>
> In general, to make formulas even easier to work with, use the Formula Workshop as much as possible. This virtual all-in-one workspace for formulas means that navigation between formulas is quick and easy and you don't have to open each one up separately or guess at their names.

14

Even after formulas are converted, you might need to make adjustments for data-specific fields that would need to be passed in as parameters to those functions. However, because most Custom Functions reduce the lines of code, and pass in the data only once, the search-and-replace tasks are greatly reduced.

> If you are concerned about losing old formula logic when converting the formula, just comment out the old formula code and put the Custom Function in. Of course, commenting each line by hand can be cumbersome. By using the Comment/Uncomment (//) button on the toolbar, you can highlight all the contiguous lines of code you want to comment out, and then click this button. It will comment them all out in one quick step.

USING THE CurrentFieldValue FUNCTION

When using formulas to create conditional formatting, they are usually designed to be data dependent—so much so that the database field name is used at every opportunity. However, to make formatting formulas more portable (and reusable), use the CurrentFieldValue formatting function instead of the actual field name that would always change depending on where the formula is located.

CurrentFieldValue is a special signifier in the formula language that tells the formatting formula to look at the value of the field it is associated with, without actually having to know the name of the field. This is advantageous in two ways:

- For general formatting, this allows for copying of formatting formulas and reusing the formatting formulas within a single report or within multiple reports without having to replace data-specific field names.

- For template formatting, this is especially useful because you can't be sure that the database field is going to be of the same name, let alone of the same data type.

By keeping the reuse factor in mind when creating and maintaining formulas from now on, creating effective templates will become much easier over time.

USING TEMPLATE FIELD OBJECTS

During the process of designing a report template, you might need to provide some specific formatting for a field not based on its position in the report, but instead based on the type of field it is. For example, a company might require that all date/time fields be displayed in military time regardless of operating system defaults. For example, "6:02 p.m. on March 31, 2004" would have to look like "3/31/04 18:02". Another requirement could be a space as the thousand separator for all numbers (instead of the usual comma).

These requirements could easily be corporate or industry standard requirements, such as the ISO 9000 standard. At the time the template is created, it's unknown where these fields will be located in the report or how many of them there will be. You would have to find another way of handling special formatting requirements. Template Field Objects help in this endeavor.

When designing a report specifically as a template, Template Field Objects take the place of regular database fields in a report. They can be placed anywhere that a database field would normally be placed.

These fields are a special type of formula field that contain no data but allow formats to be applied to them as if they were of any data type. Template Field Objects have a special dialog associated with them that exposes all the Formatting tabs of the Format Editor regardless of type. This provides a one-stop shop for all of your formatting needs regardless of the data type for a given position of a field in a report.

The best way to explain this is by actually performing it, so start by implementing the examples given previously in this section:

- **Military Time**—"6:02 p.m. on March 31, 2004" to appear as "3/31/04 18:02"
- **Thousand Separator as a space**—1,000 to appear as 1 000

Starting with a new report, follow these steps:

1. Create a new report. After opening Crystal Reports, click the New button. Then within the Crystal Reports Gallery dialog, choose As a Blank Report and click OK.

2. Skip the data source step. Because this report is going to be a template, there is no need to have a data source associated with it. Click the Cancel button in the Database Expert to close this dialog.

3. Insert a Template Field object. To insert the first Template Field object, select Template Field Object from the Insert menu. Place the resulting field into the left-most area of the Details section (see Figure 14.4).

Figure 14.4
The Design tab with the first template object added to the report.

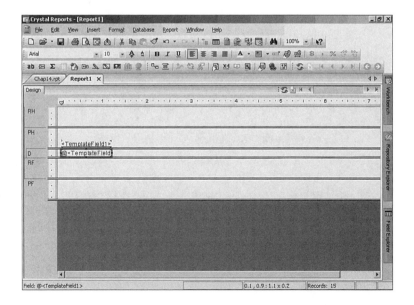

14

Add five more template objects. Repeat the previous step five more times and place each new field to the right of the last one. Once completed, the Design tab will look like Figure 14.5.

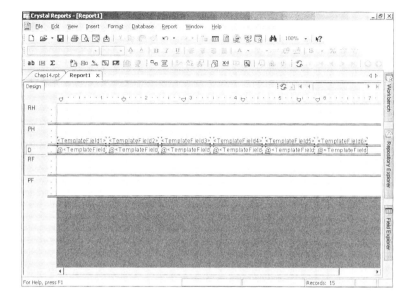

Select all template objects to format. To select all template objects, hold down the Ctrl key while single-clicking on each template object in the Details section. After all six objects are selected, right-click on the last object you chose and select Format Template Fields from the pop-up menu.

Format Date/Time to military time (3/31/04 18:02). After the Format Editor appears, select the Date and Time tab. Choose the third option in the Style list box that represents date/time as 3/1/99 13:23 because this is the option required, as shown in Figure 14.6.

Format Number with a space as the thousand separator (1 000) as shown in Figure 14.7. Now select the Number tab in the Format Editor dialog box. Because this style does not appear in the Style list box, select Customize. In the Custom Style dialog box, change the Symbol from "," to " " (without the quotes). Click OK to return to the Format Editor. Click OK again to return to the Design tab with the changes applied

Give the template a name and a preview picture. When the report appears in the Template Expert, it will have a name associated with it. The name is saved as the Report Title. To change the Report Title, select File, Summary Info. Input the name **Military Time & Thousands** in to the Title property field and select the Save Preview Picture check box as shown in Figure 14.8. Select OK to continue.

Figure 14.6
The Date and Time tab of the Format Editor with Military Date/Time selected.

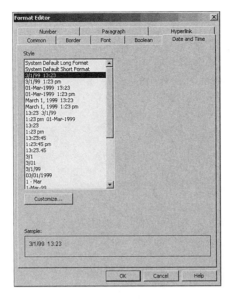

Figure 14.7
The Custom Style dialog box with the space set as the Thousand Separator symbol.

9. Save the report to the template folder. Choose File, Save As to save the report. Call the report **TemplateObjects.RPT** and place it in the Template folder. The Template folder is usually found at `C:\Program Files\Business Objects\Crystal Reports 11\Templates\en`. When it is saved, close the report.

10. Open the report from the previous example (Chap14.rpt) and add the employee birth date field to the report. Notice that all the date fields and numbers are in the standard format as is the birth date field, as shown in Figure 14.9.

14

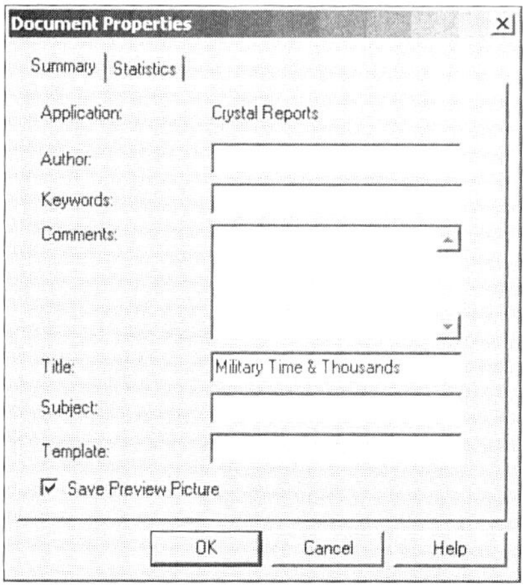

Figure 14.8
The Report Title set to describe the Template report.

Figure 14.9
The Preview tab showing how the report looked when the original report was created.

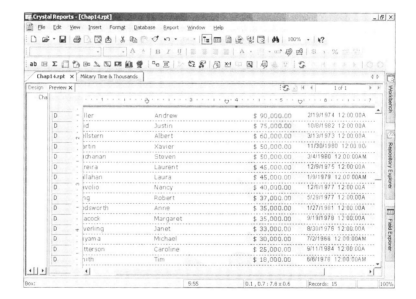

11. Select the template. To select the template that was saved earlier, select Report, Template Expert. Select Military Time & Thousands from the Available Templates list, as shown in Figure 14.10.

12. To apply the template, simply click the OK button. The report will appear as shown in Figure 14.11. You will notice that the report appears to close. Do not be alarmed because this is standard behavior. Crystal Reports saves a temporary file with the old look of the report and then applies the template during the new open command.

Figure 14.10
The Template Expert dialog box with a template selected.

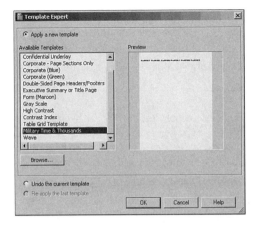

Figure 14.11
The Preview tab showing how the report looked after the template was applied.

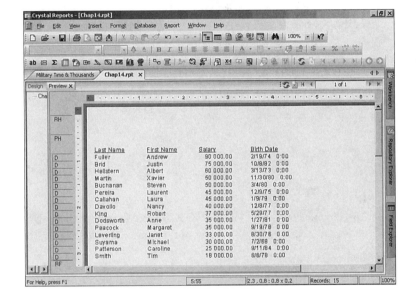

TIP

Undoing a template is always an option. If for some reason you do not like the look that the applied template has given to your report, just return to the Template Expert and choose the Undo command at the bottom of the dialog box. Selecting this option and then clicking OK lets Crystal Reports revert to the original report before the template was applied.

Crystal Reports accomplishes this by opening up the temporary backup .rpt that it saved before applying the template file.

14

13. Save the report. Choose File, Save As, call the report **templateapplied.rpt**, and click OK.

Notice that there was no need to know where the date and numeric fields were located in the report because the Template Field Objects were all formatted to handle the different requirements for the different fields. Using Template Field Objects along with the other template tips mentioned in the chapter will make report design quick and easy.

Preview Pictures

During the previous exercise, you might have noticed that the intended template did not show a preview picture on the right of the dialog window. This can be caused by one of two situations. The Save Preview Picture option in the Document Properties dialog box was not selected. If that option had been checked and the thumbnail still did not appear, it is because the template report was not saved with a Preview.

In the example that you just completed, the template report was not previewed before the report was saved.

Preview Pictures, or *thumbnails* as they are commonly called, are just that–pictures of the Preview of the report. If a report has not been previewed, it will not have the thumbnail to save.

Another key point to notice on Preview Pictures is that if changes are made in the design of the template and then a save is done, the changes will not be reflected in the thumbnail because the Preview tab was not updated with the changes.

Preview Pictures are very useful in the Template Expert because these images provide you with a visualization of what the template does to the existing report. To save them as a default with all reports, select the Save Preview Picture option in File, Options under the Reporting tab.

Preview Pictures are also important to have if the reports will be delivered through Crystal Enterprise because the ePortfolio application uses the thumbnails as a way to show reports in the front-end.

USING REPORT TEMPLATES TO REDUCE REPORT CREATION EFFORT

So far this chapter has focused on new features and functions that can be used to create templates. Templates can accomplish many of the more intense designer-related tasks, including

- Conditional formatting
- Field highlighting
- Page headers and footers
- Charting standards
- Lines, boxes, and borders
- Color standards
- Logos and images
- Web sites, hyperlinks, and e-mail addresses
- Standard custom functions
- Repository objects
- Locking size or position of any object
- Special fields

APPLYING MULTIPLE TEMPLATES

Because any report could be used as a template, it is also conceivable that many reports could be applied to any single report as a template.

This can prove quite useful if the templates are doing different things. For example, one template might be applying the standard page headers and footers to all reports within a company, whereas another template could be used to apply department-based colors to the details section. Because both templates are encapsulated separately, they can be applied separately and will not affect each other. The end result is one report with both the corporate style (headers and footers) as well as the specific department's colors (in the Details section) applied.

TIP

> Templates can be applied repeatedly, even if new fields are added to the report after the initial template was applied.
>
> Simply choose Reapply Template in the Template Expert to have the template address any new fields.

CRYSTAL REPORTS IN THE REAL WORLD— STANDARDIZED TEMPLATES

Arguably the most powerful use of report templates is simply adding consistent headers and footers. As described previously, the job of placing header and footer information in exactly the right place time after time is time-consuming and boring. A very simple template can give you a head start on basic formatting.

To create your template, an image of the company logo will be used. For this example, the Business Objects logo (saved in JPG format) from the corporate Web site is used.

1. Begin by creating a new report without a data source, as described earlier in the chapter. Your starting point should look like Figure 14.12.

2. From the Insert menu, choose Insert, Picture. Browse for the logo (.jpg or .bmp) file and add it to the top left of the report header. In the top right, add a text object and label it **Data as of:** and right justify the text. Add the special field Data Date to the right of the text.

3. Add the special field Report Title to the page header, center justify the text, widen the field so it reaches to both edges of the report, change the font to 14, and add some vertical height so the text fits properly.

4. In the page footer, add the special field Page N of M, centered with the field stretched to both left and right edges of the canvas. The template is now ready to be applied to all reports, effectively standardizing fundamental elements of report look and feel.

14

Figure 14.12
A blank canvas for the
report template.

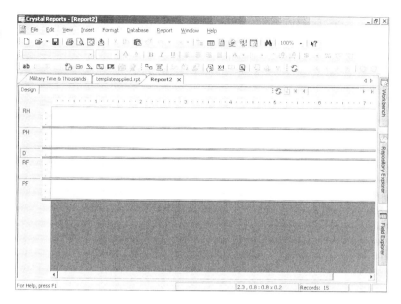

To maximize flexibility, ensure that objects (like the logo) used in the template make full use of the repository. Not only is it important to standardize the look and feel, it should also be easy to update.

Figure 14.13
A sample standard-
ized template.

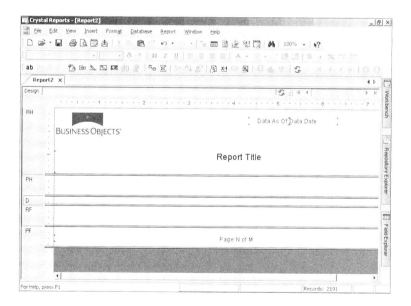

Save the template as **StandardTemplate.rpt**.

TROUBLESHOOTING

TEMPLATES

The template has a chart, but the chart fails to appear when applied to a report. Why is that?

Charts are typically built to show summary values. Make sure to group the data in the report and include one or more summaries. This is the most likely reason the chart failed to show.

Using the sample templates shipped with Crystal Reports works fine for everything except the Title and Report Description fields. These fields are blank and can't be edited. How can Title and Report Description fields be added to the report?

These are special fields accessible from the Field Explorer. In order to populate these fields, go to File, Summary Info. In the dialog box the Title property assigns a value to the Title field and the Comments property assigns a value to the Report Description field.

CHAPTER 15

ADDITIONAL DATA SOURCES FOR CRYSTAL REPORTS

In this chapter

UNDERSTANDING THE ADDITIONAL CRYSTAL REPORTS DATA SOURCES

When thinking about data sources for Crystal Reports, most people tend to think about popular databases such as Microsoft SQL Server, Microsoft Access, Oracle, IBM DB2, and so on. However, the extent of Crystal Reports reaches far beyond these traditional relational databases. You've already learned about how Crystal Reports can use OLAP-based data sources in Chapter 16, "Formatting Multidimensional Reporting Against OLAP Data"; this chapter describes a few more advanced data sources that give you even more flexibility than you already have. The data sources discussed in this chapter are as follows:

- .NET- and COM-based data sources
- Java-based data sources
- XML as a data source
- Solution kits

→ If you would like to review how Crystal Reports can use OLAP-based data sources, **see** "OLAP Concepts and OLAP Reporting," p. 358

CONNECTING TO COM OR .NET DATA SOURCES

Crystal Reports provides *direct access*, or *native*, drivers for some databases. These drivers are written specifically for a particular database and are often the best choice. However, because hundreds of types of databases exist, Business Objects can't possibly write direct access drivers for all of them. So often, users turn to using standard data access layers such as ODBC or OLEDB to connect to their databases. Often, the vendor of a database provides an ODBC driver or OLEDB provider so that other applications can access the vendor's database. Sometimes though, even this is not enough. Customers have data that they would like to report off of that is not accessible by any Crystal Reports data source driver or via ODBC or OLEDB. To accomplish this, customers often turn to the COM Data Source driver, the ADO.NET Data Source driver, or the Java Data Source driver. This section describes the COM version of the driver, but much of the theory applies to the ADO.NET and Java Data Source drivers as well.

The *Component Object Model,* or *COM,* is a Microsoft-based technology for software component development. It's the underlying technology that runs Visual Basic and Active Server Pages. A *COM object* is a piece of code that adheres to the COM specification and is easily used by other components, either inside a single application or between disparate applications. Microsoft has chosen to replace COM as a supported development platform with .NET and as a result ADO.NET will supersede COM. With the volume of COM code that has already been produced, it is expected to be supported for many years to come.

Because COM is a popular technology, Crystal Decisions decided to leverage it to create an extensible data source driver mechanism. This COM Data Source driver doesn't connect to a database—rather it gets data from a COM object written by you. This means that if you are somewhat savvy in the Visual Basic world, you can write your own mini data source driver (called a *COM Data Provider*) that enables access to data that would otherwise be unavailable.

To better understand the concept on writing your own COM Data Provider, look at a few scenarios in which this can be beneficial.

LEVERAGING LEGACY MAINFRAME DATA

Although new technologies are surfacing at an alarming rate, many companies still have data held in legacy mainframe systems. Often, the nature of these systems doesn't allow for any kind of relational data access, and thus lowers the value of the system. However, these systems can often output text-based files, called print files or spool files, that contain the data held in the mainframe system. These text-based files are often more complicated than a set of simple comma-separated values and thus require a bridge between the files and a data access and reporting tool like Crystal Reports. Writing a COM Data Provider can serve just this purpose. The Data Provider would read the text files, parse out the required data, and return it to Crystal Reports for use in numerous reports.

HANDLING COMPLEX QUERIES

Often, companies have a database that is accessible via standard Crystal Reports data access methods. However, the process of connecting to the database and performing a query can be quite complex. Sometimes this is because the database servers are constantly changing, queries are becoming more complex, and other business processes affect the complexity of the query. By writing a COM Data Provider, a clever person can abstract the location and complexity of the database interaction away from the user designing a report. The user simply connects to the Data Provider, and the rest of the logic is done transparently in the background.

RUNTIME MANIPULATION OF DATA

Performing a simple query against a database that returns a set of records is often all that is needed. However, sometimes logic needs to be incorporated into the query that cannot be expressed in the database query language (using SQL). Other times, per-user manipulation of data needs to be performed, such as removing all salaries stored in a database for all other users other than the currently logged in user for confidentiality purposes (often called data-level security). This runtime manipulation can be performed by either a COM Data Provider or a .NET Dataset Provider.

These three scenarios outline just a few of the reasons why you might want to use the COM Data Source driver or .NET Dataset Provider and create your own Data Provider. The following sections describe the technical details of doing this. The example demonstrates creating a COM provider, but the same functionality can be provided from .NET. For the report author, both methods are equal and transparent.

CREATING A COM OR .NET DATA PROVIDER

COM Data Providers can be written in any development language or platform with the capability of creating COM objects. Most commonly, they are created in either Visual Basic or Visual C++. The following example uses Visual Basic, but it can easily be translated to other development languages. To create a simple COM Provider, follow these steps:

Open Visual Basic and create a new project. Instead of choosing the standard project type of Standard EXE, choose ActiveX DLL (see Figure 15.1). ActiveX is another name for COM technology. Choosing this creates a project that contains a COM object (by default called Class1).

Figure 15.1
Creating a new Active DLL project in Visual Basic.

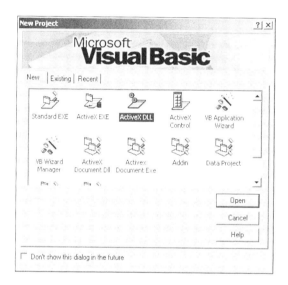

The interface between the COM Data Provider that you create and the Crystal Reports COM Data Source driver is based on *ActiveX Data Objects*, or *ADO*. To use ADO in your project, you must first create a reference to it. From the Project menu inside Visual Basic, select References. From the list on the ensuing dialog, look for Microsoft ActiveX Data Objects. You might have just a single version of this on your machine, or you might have several. It's usually easiest to just select the latest version. Figure 15.2 illustrates this.

After that is done, the only thing left to do is create a function inside your class that returns an ADO recordset. The basic outline for this function is shown here. See the next section for more information on returning an ADO recordset.

```
Public Function GetRecordset() As ADODB.Recordset
    Dim rs As New ADODB.Recordset
    ' Populate the recordset
    Set GetRecordset = rs
End Function
```

Figure 15.2
The Visual Basic Project References dialog is shown here referencing the ADO Library.

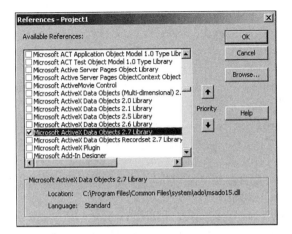

4. By default, the class is named `Class1`. It's best to give this a more meaningful name, such as `DataProvider`. Do this by selecting the Class1.cls file in the Project Explorer and changing the (`Name`) property from the Property Browser.

5. Also, the project name is Project1 by default. It's best to give this a more meaningful name such as the company name or type of data name: for example, Xtreme or Sales. Do this by selecting Project1 Properties from the Project menu and changing the Project Name setting.

6. Build the dll by selecting Make from the File menu; the name is not important.

7. Open the Crystal Reports designer and create a new report. From the data explorer, choose Create New Connection and then expand the More Data Sources item, and then choose COM Connectivity. This presents a dialog asking for you to enter the Program ID. To identify your COM Data Provider, enter the ProjectName.ClassName: for example, Xtreme.DataProvider.

8. You'll receive a table list just like from a traditional database, but the table list is actually a list of methods on your COM object that return ADO recordsets.

RETURNING AN ADO RECORDSET

There are generally two ways to obtain an ADO recordset: performing a database query and constructing it yourself. The following code example illustrates how to perform a database query and obtain a recordset—in this case using a query against the Xtreme sample database.

```
Public Function CustomerOrders() As ADODB.Recordset
    Dim rs As New ADODB.Recordset
    Dim sql as String
    sql = "SELECT * FROM Customer, Orders WHERE Customer.'Customer ID'"
    sql = sql & " = Orders.'Customer ID'", "DSN=Xtreme Sample Database 10"
    rs.Open sql
    Set CustomerOrders = rs
End Function
```

The question you might be asking yourself is how this query could be parameterized. The COM Data Source driver handles this nicely. It maps any arguments you have defined to your method into report parameters. The following code example illustrates a Data Provider function that has a parameter:

```
Public Function Customers(CountryParam As String) As ADODB.Recordset
    Dim rs As New ADODB.Recordset
    rs.Open "SELECT * FROM Customer WHERE Country = '" & CountryParam & "'", _
            "DSN=Xtreme Sample Database 10"
    Set Customers = rs
End Function
```

When a Data Provider with a parameterized method is used from the report designer, the user is prompted for a parameter value.

As was mentioned previously, one way to obtain a recordset is to perform a query. Listing 15.1 illustrates how to construct a recordset on the fly and read data out of a text file.

LISTING 15.1   A COM DATA PROVIDER THAT PARSES DATA FROM A CSV FILE

```
Public Function CSVText(FileName As String) As ADODB.Recordset
    Dim rs As New ADODB.Recordset

    ' Open the text file
    Dim FileSystem As New IWshRuntimeLibrary.FileSystemObject
    Dim fileText As IWshRuntimeLibrary.TextStream
    Set fileText = FileSystem.OpenTextFile(FileName)

    ' Read the first line of text to grab the field names
    Dim buffer As String
    buffer = fileText.ReadLine()
    Dim fields() As String
    fields = Split(buffer, ",")
    Dim i
    For i = LBound(fields) To UBound(fields)
        ' Add a field in the recordset for each field in the csv file
        rs.fields.Append fields(i), adBSTR
    Next

    rs.Open

    ' Read the contents of the file
    While Not fileText.AtEndOfStream
        buffer = fileText.ReadLine()
        rs.AddNew
        For i = LBound(fields) To UBound(fields)
            ' Grab the field values
            fields = Split(buffer, ",")
            rs(i).Value = fields(i)
        Next
        rs.Update
    Wend

    Set CSVText = rs
End Function
```

This code could be used as is or adopted to meet the needs of other kinds of files or data sources. Using the COM Data Source driver gives you complete flexibility and control over the data source.

Connecting to an ADO.NET XML Recordset

Although COM remains an exceedingly popular model for programming, it is no longer supported by Microsoft. The current platform for application development using Microsoft is .NET. As Business Objects continues to remain current on Microsoft technologies, there is a means for reporting off ADO.NET data sources. The following steps describe connecting to ADO.NET data:

1. From the File menu, select New, Blank Report.

2. With the data window open, expand Create New Connection and double-click ADO.NET (XML).

3. When presented with the ADO.NET window, first select the location of the source file. Either manually enter the path to the file or use the Browse button to find the file. When using the Browse button, be sure to select the correct filter (XML File, XML Schema, or .NET Dataset Provider).

4. If a .NET Dataset Provider is selected, the .NET Dataset might expose multiple classes. To identify a specific class from the Provider, check the box beside Use Classes from Project, and select the class from the list of available classes.

5. Multiple Datasets might be exposed from a given class. In order to select a Dataset from a class, check the box beside Use Dataset from Class and select the Dataset from the list of available Datasets.

Connecting to Java-Based Data Sources

The COM Data Source driver is targeted at Visual Basic and Visual C++, and ADO.NET is targeted at .NET developers. Because Crystal Reports XI has a full Java SDK, an equivalent Java Data Source driver provides equivalent functionality of the COM driver for developers using the Java platform.

The process of creating a Java Data Source driver is conceptually similar to that of creating a COM Data Source driver. A Java class needs to be created that has a public function with a return type of `ResultSet` or `CachedRowSet`. A `ResultSet` is the standard object returned from a JDBC-based query, whereas the `CachedRowSet` is a disconnected recordset useful for parsing out things like XML. Listing 15.2 shows a simple Java Data Provider that returns a `ResultSet`.

LISTING 15.2 A JAVA DATA PROVIDER THAT RETURNS DATA FROM THE SAMPLE DATABASE

```
import java.lang.*;
import java.sql.*;

public class XtremeDataProvider
{
    public ResultSet Employee()
    {
    // connect to the database
    Class.forName("sun.jdbc.odbc.JdbcOdbcDriver");
        String url = "jdbc:odbc:Xtreme Sample Database 10";
        Connection con = DriverManager.getConnection(url, "", "");

    // run a SQL query
        Statement stmt = con.createStatement(ResultSet.TYPE_SCROLL_SENSITIVE,
ResultSet.CONCUR_READ_ONLY);
        String query = "SELECT * FROM Employee";
    ResultSet rs = stmt.executeQuery(query);

    // return the results of the query
        return rs;
    }
}
```

To identify a Java class, simply compile the code into the .class file and place that compiled
.class file into the JavaBeans classpath. To define the classpath, edit the following properties in the CRconfig.xml file in the default folder: C:\Program Files\Common Files\Business
Objects\3.0\java\

JAVADIR

This property must refer to a valid Java Runtime Environment (JRE) or J2SE Development
Kit (JDK). If a JRE or JDK was detected during install, this property will already be set. If
not, install JDK 1.4 and set the property manually. A valid setting is the complete path to the
JDK:

```
<JavaDir>c:\Program Files\Java\JRE\bin</JavaDir>
```

JAVABEANSCLASSPATH

If the JavaBeans are unjarred, simply refer to the .class file's path:

```
<JavaBeans>
    <CacheRowSetSize>100</CacheRowSetSize>
    <JavaBeansClassPath>c:\myjavabean</JavaBeansClassPath>
</JavaBeans>
```

and if the JavaBean class files are jarred, refer to the same location with the .jar extension:

```
<JavaBeans>
    <CacheRowSetSize>100</CacheRowSetSize>
    <JavaBeansClassPath>c:\myjavabean.jar</JavaBeansClassPath>
</JavaBeans>
```

During the process of creating a report, Crystal Reports searches through all classes contained in the classpath. It then provides a list of methods with return types of java.sql.ResultSet. The same rules about function arguments apply. Any arguments to the Java method are mapped to report parameter fields. Using Java code, you can control exactly what data comes back.

CONNECTING TO XML DATA SOURCES

Crystal Reports can connect to XML data in three ways. XML can be presented as source data as

- **Local data source**—This is a physical XML file that resides locally or on the network and is identified by passing in the fully qualified path and file name. If a schema (.xsd) file exists, it can also be specified.

- **HTTP(S) data source**—An HTTP(S) data source is XML formatted data accessed from a servlet, an ASP page, or a JSP page. The URL to the source may be HTTP or HTTPS. When using HTTPS, the id and password information passed into Crystal Reports is used for authentication.

- **Web Service data source**—A Web Service data source can be a service on a local machine or network drive that is referenced either via a path and filename or via a servlet/dynamic web page (ASP/JSP). No schema is specified as it is derived through the web services framework. Web Service data sources are accessed using Web Services Description Language (WSDL). After the WSDL is specified, the driver prompts for service, port, and method.

Regardless of the data source, from the File menu choose New, Blank Report. From the Data window, expand Create New Data Connection and double-click XML. From that point, follow one of the following paths.

CONNECT TO A LOCAL XML DATA SOURCE

1. Specify the fully qualified path and filename to the .xml file. If the .xml file does not have embedded schema information, a schema (.xsd) file must be identified. To identify the schema file, ensure there is a check mark beside Specify Schema File.

2. Click Next.

3. If the schema does not need to be specified, click Finish; otherwise, you will be prompted for the location of the schema. The schema may be referenced using a fully qualified path or URL.

4. Click Next and then Finish.

CONNECT TO AN HTTP(S) DATA SOURCE

1. Enter the URL to the .xml file. If the .xml file does not have embedded schema information, a schema (.xsd) file must be identified. To identify the schema file, ensure there is a check mark beside Specify Schema File.

Click Next.

If authentication information is required, enter it here. Click Next.

If the schema does not need to be specified, click Next; otherwise, you will be prompted for the location of the schema. The schema may be referenced using a fully qualified path or URL. Click Next.

As a final step, HTTP parameters may be added/modified/removed in order to modify the set of data returned. Then click Finish.

CONNECT TO A WEB SERVICE DATA SOURCE

Select the Use Web Service Data Source radio button. No schema file is needed so the option will be dimmed immediately on a selection of this data source type. Click Next.

Specify the location of the Web Service. Either a local file or HTTP(S) location may be specified. Click Next.

If prompted for it, enter authentication information and click Next.

Select the service, port, and method from the lists. Click Finish.

After the connection to the data source is complete, the report may be designed as any other. The XM data is presented as a table just like any other Crystal Report data source.

INTRODUCTION TO THE INTEGRATION KITS

The integration kits provide native access and integration to commonly used Enterprise Resource Planning (ERP) applications. They achieve this by providing unique access to the data via the ERP's application layer via the applications published programming interfaces or API. A complete list of supported ERP applications is defined in Table 15.1.

TABLE 15.1   FEATURES BY INTEGRATION KIT

	SAP		Peoplesoft		Baan/SSA	Siebel
Integration Kit	*R3*	*BW*	*Enterprise*	*EPM*		
Software shipped with product	X	X	X			
Integrated security	X	X	X	X	X	X
Sample reports	X	X	X	X	X	X
Portal/UI integration	X	X				X
Crystal Report access	X	X	X		X	X
Web Intelligence access		X		X		
OLAP Intelligence access		X				

This unique approach to data access allows the integration kit to honor the security, access all the data, make sample reports, leverage the metadata of the ERP application, and provide real time access to the data.

HONOR THE SECURITY

Organizations spend a lot of time and effort setting up security in their ERP applications. The integration kits are made so users do not have to recreate this security. This results in organizations only having to change security once in their ERP application and this change is then reflected in the reports.

ACCESS TO ALL THE DATA

Many ERP applications, such as SAP, do not store all their data in the underlying database. Some of the data used in SAP can only be found in programmatic sources, such as cluster tables and other objects unique to SAP. Therefore, if your reporting tool could only connect to the underlying database, you would likely miss some critical pieces of data that might dramatically affect your business decisions. With the BusinessObjects integration kits, you do not have to worry about this problem because the kit connects to the application layer of SAP and can thus leverage SAP functionality and gain access to all forms of data storage that SAP provides.

SAMPLE REPORTS

Sample reports are provided for all the integration kits. These reports can not only provide a basis on which to start; but more importantly provide examples on how to report off hierarchies and use variables, to name just a few.

LEVERAGE THE METADATA OF THE ERP APPLICATION

Changes made to the application might not necessarily be reflected in the database. The native drivers connect to the application's metadata and should see any of the changes. For example, SAP R3 has cluster tables that you will not find in the underlying database, but they are visible in the SAP R3 data dictionary.

CAUTION

In determining whether your ERP application is supported by BusinessObjects integration kits, you should *not* be concerned with the specifics of the underlying database, but instead focus on the specific version or patch level of the application itself.

PROVIDE REAL TIME ACCESS TO DATA

With this approach, data is not extracted from the ERP application in order to report against it. In some cases it might make sense to extract the data to a data mart or data warehouse, and the ERP provider or Business Objects may provide solutions for that. A lot of production reporting requires real time data, however, and ERP's own tools might prove inflexible and difficult to use.

SAP INTEGRATION KIT

The SAP integration includes drivers to allow connectivity to both R3 and Business Warehouse (BW). In addition, it includes a BW toolbar for Crystal Reports, a specific version of InfoView with Role based links, sample iViews for Enterprise Portal, and an SDK in Java, COM, or .NET.

REPORTING OFF R3 DATA

The kit includes two drivers to allow Crystal Reports to connect to the ABAP data dictionary via a remote function call or RFC.

The Open SQL driver allows the user to connect to SAP R3, displaying the field and the short text description of the tables and fields. The developer can then join the tables accordingly, using the database and selecting the relevant fields from which to report. This driver displays not only transparent tables, but includes views, pool tables, cluster tables, ABAP data clusters, and ABAP functions. This driver is suited towards a technical person with functional expertise in joining the tables and then creating the report.

> **NOTE**
>
> In Crystal Reports, you cannot check the SQL generated using the Show SQL Query option from the Database menu. You can check what Open SQL was generated by using SAP transactions.

The InfoSet driver allows the user to connect to an existing InfoSet, as defined by SAP transaction SQ02. Alternatively, you can use an existing ABAP query, as defined by SAP transaction SQ01. The benefit of this driver is that the user does not need to know where the data is stored or how to join the tables. Another advantage is that any prompts defined in the InfoSet become parameters in Crystal Reports.

> **NOTE**
>
> To test the InfoSet query, run the InfoSet using your SAP GUI and ensure it is pulling the required data first before testing it in Crystal Reports.

REPORTING OFF BW DATA

When reporting off of BW data, Crystal Reports has its own toolbar, as shown in Figure 15.3. In other words, to create a new report, the user should use the BW toolbar to create the report. Select the required BW query and this will display a listing of fields available in the query. The user can then create the report using any of those fields. Variables defined in the query will automatically become Crystal Report parameters. After the user has finished building the report, the user saves the report using the BW toolbar. This saves the report to BW and if the user selects the option to do so, automatically publishes the report to Enterprise.

Figure 15.3
Crystal Reports after the SAP integration kit is loaded. Note the SAP menu and BW toolbar.

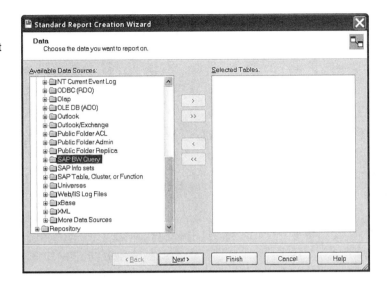

Viewing the Reports

Your SAP reports can be viewed either via the SAP integration kit's InfoView or via SAP Enterprise Portal 6. The integration kit provides a number of sample iViews that can be imported by a portal administrator. These include

- **Folder iView**—The folders a user has access to are displayed, and from here a user can run her reports.
- **Alert iView**—Shows all the alerts that have been triggered by Crystal Reports. The user can then click on the report to view the report. The creation of alerts is defined in Chapter 11, "Using Record Selections and Alerts for Interactive Reporting."
- **Thumbnail iView**—This iView displays the Crystal Report as a thumbnail of the report. The user can then click on the thumbnail to run the report.

NOTE

These are sample iViews. The organization can create its own iViews via the provided SDK.

BusinessObjects InfoView for SAP is a unique version of InfoView designed for integration with SAP BW systems. This integration includes features such as the ability to log on to InfoView using your SAP username and password. Related to authentication is the ability to access your roles and the Crystal Reports saved to these roles. The roles are defined in Enterprise as folders. The user can also schedule reports in the different languages loaded into SAP BW. This creates an instance for each language.

PEOPLESOFT INTEGRATION KIT

Crystal Reports has been embedded in Peoplesoft for many versions. The BusinessObjects integration kit for Peoplesoft extends the usefulness of the embedded reporting functionality by providing all of the features of Business Objects XI to the report consumer.

REPORTING OFF PEOPLESOFT DATA

The native Peoplesoft driver connects to the Peoplesoft query as defined within the Peoplesoft system. Furthermore, because you are required to pass a username to the Peoplesoft system, the driver will honor the parameters and security defined by the Peoplesoft query. To access the Peoplesoft query, select the Peoplesoft driver from the list of drivers available to Crystal Reports. After authenticating, a list of accessible queries becomes available. Select a query, and Crystal Reports treats the query's resulting recordset the same way it treats a table. The developer is presented with a listing of fields that make up the query. These fields can then be dragged onto the report and the report can be developed as described in the first half of this book.

VIEWING THE REPORTS

After the report is complete, the user can publish the report and this report can then be viewed via InfoView. The integration kit allows for Peoplesoft authentication so Peoplesoft users can log onto InfoView using their Peoplesoft credentials. The security integration creates a group in Business Objects XI for each Peoplesoft role that is mapped. A single install of Business Objects XI can be mapped to multiple Peoplesoft domains.

SIEBEL INTEGRATION KIT

The Siebel integration kit provides access to Siebel CRM to allow report developers to create reports off Siebel business objects and have report consumers view this content from within Siebel via the Enterprise web desktop.

REPORTING OFF SIEBEL DATA

The Siebel integration kit provides access to Siebel's data via the Siebel business objects. After a successful logon, Crystal Reports displays a listing of business objects and their respective business components. A user can then select single or multiple business components and then join them the same way tables are joined. In this way, multiple parent-child relationships between business components can be established under a single business object. After this joining is complete, the report designer is left with the multiple fields from the various business components. After the report is complete, it can be published to the respective folder in BusinessObjects Enterprise.

Any join that is created will cause the data to be joined on the Business Objects server and not the Siebel Server.

VIEWING THE REPORTS

Reports can be viewed from InfoView, which is described in further detail in Chapter 24, "Using InfoView." The integration kit also provides an integrated web desktop that users can launch from the Siebel client. This desktop is aware of the current view and can only show the user reports that are linked to that view.

BAAN INTEGRATION KIT

The Baan integration kit allows developers to connect to and report against the Baan ERP and SSA ERP versions.

REPORTING OFF BAAN DATA

Developers can use the native Baan driver to connect to all fields and tables via the application layer. The user can then join up the relevant tables and fields, like they would any other relational database. This driver supports the security defined for company, session, table, and field data.

The Baan integration kit also provides a component called Integrated Baan Reporting (IBR), which allows a user to run an existing Baan report and have the output of this report formatted as a Crystal Report. The user would run the report as he usually would; however, when selecting the Print option, the user should select the Business Objects print device. Business Objects captures the output of the report, formats it according to a Crystal Report template, and then creates a report instance that includes both template and data. This method of reporting is very useful when the print function is one of the steps needed to complete an order.

VIEWING THE REPORTS

The reports are viewed using InfoView. Reports created via the IBR are also located on InfoView. Report instances are found in the Combined Reports folder and then in their respective Baan package and module subfolders. Report layout information can be found in the Baan Report Layout folder and templates are found in the Standard Templates folder.

> **TIP**
>
> The folder structure can become deep and complex. Rather than navigating the folders or moving the reports, create friendly named shortcuts to these reports.

TROUBLESHOOTING

PUBLISHING WITH A COM OR JAVA PROVIDER

I've published a report using a COM (or Java) data provider to BusinessObjects Enterprise, but I am getting errors when the report is run.

Whenever one of these types of reports is published to BusinessObjects Enterprise, you need to make sure you copy the COM or Java component to the machines running the

Page and Job servers. This component needs to be installed and registered properly before the report can invoke it.

I am receiving errors when I try to connect to the Java data provider.

Make sure that you have installed a Java Virtual Machine (JVM, also called the Java Runtime Environment). The JVM is required to connect to Java data providers.

SAP MENU AND TOOLBAR DO NOT APPEAR

After installing the SAP integration kit for BW, I was expecting the SAP menu and toolbar to appear in Crystal Reports, but they are not there.

Before installing the integration kit, ensure you have the SAP GUI installed, including the BW add-ons, and that the GUI is patched to the correct level.

No Tables Appear when I Select the SAP Table, Cluster, or Func pon Driver

When searching for a table using the Open SQL driver, the expected table names do not appear in the list of tables.

Possible causes could be that you do not have SAP access in your profile either to the table or to the required Business Objects transports. Also, you could be filtering the tables using the Data Explorer option in Crystal Reports.

CRYSTAL REPORTS IN THE REAL WORLD—LEVERAGING XML AS A DATA SOURCE

With the emergence of XML as a data interchange format, many customers wanted to create reports on XML documents. So in Crystal Reports 8.5, a new driver was released that allowed just this scenario. This ODBC driver reads certain types of XML documents. Version XI of Crystal Reports provides the capability to read multiple XML files, most commonly a folder of XML files that have the same schema. When using this driver, you specify either a folder name or a file path to an XML file as described in detail earlier in this chapter. Once connected, XML elements at the first level are represented as fields that you can place on a report.

If you require more flexibility around reading XML files, a good approach to take is to write a COM or Java Data Provider to read the XML. This Data Provider can use one of the many readily available XML parsers to read in the XML and choose exactly what fields to return to Crystal Reports. Listing 15.3 is a sample Visual Basic COM Data Provider that reads in a simple XML file. This method is still used by developers who want to exert very strict control over the XML data that is provided to the report.

15

LISTING 15.3   A COM DATA PROVIDER THAT READS XML DATA

```
' Loads an XML document with the following structure:
' <employees>
'   <employee>
'     <name>X</name>
'     <dept>X</dept>
'     <salary>X</salary>
'   </employee>
' </employees>
Public Function SimpleXML(fileName As String) As ADODB.Recordset
    Dim rs As New ADODB.Recordset

    Dim xmlDoc As New MSXML2.DOMDocument
    xmlDoc.Load (fileName)

    rs.fields.Append "Name", adBSTR
    rs.fields.Append "Dept", adBSTR
    rs.fields.Append "Salary", adCurrency
    rs.Open

    ' Loop through each employee element
    Dim employeeNode As MSXML2.IXMLDOMElement
    Dim childNode As MSXML2.IXMLDOMElement

    For Each employeeNode In xmlDoc.documentElement.childNodes
        rs.AddNew
        For Each childNode In employeeNode.childNodes
            rs(childNode.nodeName).Value = childNode.Text
        Next
        rs.Update
    Next

    Set SimpleXML = rs
End Function
```

CHAPTER 16

FORMATTING MULTIDIMENSIONAL REPORTING AGAINST OLAP DATA

In this chapter

INTRODUCTION TO OLAP

Through the first 15 chapters, you have been exposed to a wide variety of the reporting capabilities found in Crystal Reports. Up to this point, however, all the reports you have created were based on relational data sources—often known as *Online Transactional Processing (OLTP)* databases—where most organizations generally keep their operational data.

In many organizations and for many people today, data reporting ends with Crystal Reports pointing at existing relational data sources such as Microsoft SQL Server, Oracle, DB2, Sybase, or even Microsoft Access. All these relational databases have been designed for the efficient storage of information. These databases were not designed optimally, however, for the efficient extraction of data for aggregated analysis across multiple dimensions—that is where OLAP databases excel.

OLAP stands for *Online Analytical Processing* and is designed to enable business users to quickly identify patterns and trends in their data while reporting against multiple dimensions at once. Examples of dimensions for analysis include time, geographic region, product line, financial measure, customer, supplier, salesperson, and so on. Crystal Reports provides powerful OLAP-based formatted reporting capabilities and these will be introduced in this chapter.

This chapter covers the following topics:

- Introduction to OLAP concepts and OLAP reporting
- Recently added OLAP features in Crystal Reports
- Creation of OLAP-based Crystal Reports

OLAP CONCEPTS AND OLAP REPORTING

OLAP is an analysis-oriented technology that enables rapid analysis of large sets of aggregated data. Instead of representing information in the common two-dimensional row and column format of traditional relational databases, OLAP databases store their aggregated data in logical structures called cubes. These OLAP cubes are created around specific business areas or problems and contain an appropriate number of dimensions to satisfy analysis in that particular area of interest or for a specific business issue. OLAP is a technology that facilitates data viewing, analysis, and navigation. More than a particular storage technology, OLAP is a conceptual model for viewing and analyzing data. Table 16.1 highlights some common business areas and typical sets of related dimensions.

TABLE 16.1   BUSINESS AREAS AND COMMONLY ASSOCIATED OLAP DIMENSIONS

Business Area	Associated Business and Common OLAP Dimensions
Sales	Sales Employees, Products, Regions, Sales Channels, Time, Customers, Measures
Finance	Company Divisions, Regions, Products, Time, Measures
Manufacturing	Suppliers, Product Parts, Plants, Products, Time, Measures

OLAP cubes pre-aggregate data at the intersection points of their associated dimension's members. A *member* is a valid field value for a dimension. (For example: Members of a time dimension could be 2000, 2001, Q1, or Q2; and members of a product dimension could be Gadget1, Gizmo2, DooDah1, and so on.) This pre-aggregation facilitates the speed-of-thought analysis associated with OLAP.

Pre-calculating the numbers at the intersection points of all an OLAP cube's associated dimension members enables rapid high-level analysis of large volumes of underlying data that would not be practical with traditional relational databases. Considering the example of analysis on several years of sales data by year, quarter, and month and by region, sales manager, and product, the pre-aggregated nature of OLAP facilitates quick speed-of-thought analysis on this data that otherwise would not be practical working with the phenomenal amount of data and involved calculations required on a traditional relational (OLTP) database system to provide those answers—it would simply take too long.

When a Crystal Report uses an OLAP cube as a data source, it presents the multidimensional data in a two-dimensional OLAP grid that resembles a spreadsheet or cross-tab. The focus of Crystal Reports when reporting against OLAP cubes is to present professionally formatted two-dimensional (or flat) views of the multidimensional data that will be of particular business use for report consuming end users and not necessarily analysts requiring interactivity—the more traditional OLAP end-users.

The concepts of OLAP usually become more understandable after they are actually explored. To that end, later sections in this chapter step you through a Crystal Reports report creation example against an OLAP cube.

RECENTLY ADDED OR CHANGED OLAP FEATURES IN CRYSTAL REPORTS

This section is specifically targeted for users of older versions of Crystal Reports. Table 16.2 lists the new OLAP-oriented features of recent versions and their practical use or benefit. If you are a new user to Crystal Reports or you have not previously used the OLAP reporting features in the product, you might want to skip directly to the next section.

TABLE 16.2 NEW OLAP FEATURES IN CRYSTAL REPORTS 9, 10, AND XI

OLAP Feature	Feature Benefit and Value
Row/Column Dimension Parameter links	Enables the direct linking of report parameters to member selection and filtering in the column and row dimensions of the selected cube. The feature is accessed either through the OLAP Report Creation Wizard or the OLAP Report Settings option under the Report menu.

continues

TABLE 16.2 CONTINUED

OLAP Feature	Feature Benefit and Value
Slice/Page Dimension Parameter links	This Productivity feature enables the direct linking of report parameters to pages and slices in the OLAP grid. This enables the end user to dynamically specify the values of slices and pages in the OLAP grid. The feature is accessed in either the OLAP Report Creation Wizard or the OLAP Report Settings option under the Report menu.
Interactive OLAP Worksheet (Analyzer) in new Cube tab	The New OLAP Analyzer feature (a Cube tab in Crystal Reports Designer) is accessed by right-clicking on an existing OLAP grid object and selecting the Launch Analyzer option. The Cube tab provides a fully functioning drag-and-drop OLAP worksheet that enables rapid selection of the most appropriate OLAP viewpoint for the Crystal Report. All changes made in the Analyzer worksheet are reflected in the associated Crystal Reports OLAP grid, where advanced formatting can be applied.
Interactive drill-down of OLAP grids in Preview tab	The OLAP grid presented in the Crystal Reports Preview tab has now been made more fully functional. In addition to having access to advanced OLAP grid functionality from the right-click button including calculations, exception highlighting, sorting, filtering, and member reordering, the OLAP grid now enables the report designer to expand (drill-down) and contract members directly from within the Preview tab.
New and improved data sources	At the time of writing, Crystal Reports XI provides OLAP access to multiple versions of Hyperion Essbase, DB2 OLAP, SQL Server Analysis Services, Holos, and SAP BW.

The following sections explore the creation of an OLAP report through the OLAP Report Creation Wizard, the added value of the OLAP Expert, and the advanced interactivity features of Crystal Reports.

USING THE OLAP REPORT CREATION WIZARD AND OLAP EXPERT

Crystal Reports provides two easy ways to create reports against OLAP data sources. As introduced in Chapter 1, "Creating and Designing Basic Reports," Crystal provides several report wizards to step you through the creation of some popular types of reports—one of those is OLAP. The OLAP Wizard involves five steps and walks you through the process of creating an OLAP grid and an optional supporting graphic based on an existing data source. The OLAP Wizard is accessible when you are creating a new report.

The second method of creating an OLAP-based report is through the OLAP Expert that is accessed from the Insert OLAP Grid on the Insert menu. This expert provides six tabs that step through the creation of an OLAP grid to be placed anywhere on a report.

The two methods of creation offer very similar degrees of functionality, and their respective dialog screens and tabs are almost identical. The OLAP Report Creation Wizard does provide a built-in Charting screen not found in the OLAP Expert, whereas the OLAP Expert provides Style Customization and Label tabs not found in the OLAP Wizard.

NOTE

> Although Crystal Reports has been designed to report off of numerous multidimensional/OLAP databases including Hyperion Essbase, Microsoft SQL Server Analysis Services, and SAP BW, for the purposes of demonstration in this chapter, examples will be based on the SQL Server sample HR cube—FoodMart. If a different OLAP Database is available, the general principles should be followed against that native OLAP cube.

SPECIFYING AN OLAP DATA SOURCE

The OLAP Data tab (or screen in the OLAP Wizard) requests the OLAP data source on which the report is to be based. This wizard and its associated dialog screens are to multidimensional data sources what the data explorer, introduced in Chapter 1, is to relational data. Figure 16.1 shows the OLAP Data screen from the OLAP Wizard.

Figure 16.1
The OLAP Data dialog from the OLAP Report Creation Wizard.

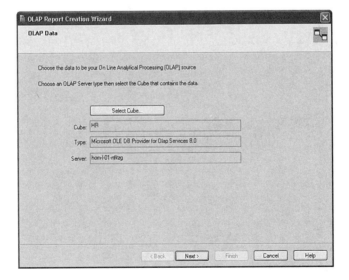

When this screen is first displayed, a cube will need to be selected with the Select Cube button. Clicking on this button opens the OLAP Connection Browser, which is displayed in Figure 16.2. From the tree control presented in this dialog, select the desired cube.

→ For detailed coverage of the OLAP Connection Browser and the functionality it provides, **see** "Accessing OLAP Data with OLAP Intelligence," **p. 422**.

Figure 16.2
The OLAP Connection Browser enables the specification of an OLAP data source for the involved Crystal Report.

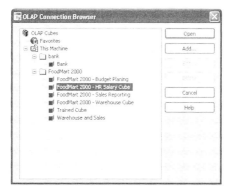

To help you learn about the creation of an OLAP-based Crystal Report, here are the introductory steps to doing exactly that against SQL Server's sample FoodMart HR cube. Other steps will follow these initial steps after subsequent screens have been explained. Start the OLAP Report Creation process with the following steps:

1. Create a New Crystal Report by selecting the OLAP Wizard from the Crystal Reports Start Page.

2. Click the Select Cube button from the OLAP Data dialog.

3. Assuming that the location of the OLAP Server has not already been identified to the OLAP Connection Browser, click the Add Server button and identify the location of your SQL Server Analysis Server and the sample HR cube. Figure 16.3 shows the New Server dialog.

Figure 16.3
The Connection Properties dialog for a new OLAP server is used to create new connections to OLAP data sources.

4. Enter a caption for the OLAP Server you are adding. This caption will appear in the OLAP Connection Browser. Enter the name of the SQL Server Analysis Server for the server name and click OK.

5. Back in the OLAP Connection Browser, navigate into the presented list of servers (there will likely only be the one you just added) and double-click on the sample HR cube.

6. Click the Next button to proceed.

> **NOTE**
>
> A Select CAR File button exists on the Data screen of the OLAP Report Creation Wizard, in addition to the Select Cube button. CAR files are *Crystal Analysis Reports (CAR)* and are created with the sister product to Crystal Reports—OLAP Intelligence (formerly called Crystal Analysis). This product is an OLAP-focused reporting and application tool and will be introduced in Chapter 19, "Creating OLAP Intelligence Reports." These CAR files can be treated as multidimensional data sources because they themselves contain connectivity information to an underlying OLAP data source.

SPECIFYING OLAP ROWS AND COLUMNS

The Rows/Columns dialog screen enables you to select both the dimensions and fields to be presented along the columns and rows of the OLAP grid. All the available dimensions in the selected cube/data source are listed in the Dimensions list box depicted in Figure 16.4.

To select a dimension for placement in the rows section or the columns section of the OLAP grid, highlight the desired dimension and click either the column or row arrow (>) button. It is possible to select multiple dimensions to be displayed and have these nested in the OLAP grid by successively selecting multiple dimensions for either the rows or the columns section. It is also possible to remove dimensions from the existing row or column list boxes; however, the column and row dimension list boxes cannot be left empty.

Figure 16.4
The Rows/Columns dialog of the OLAP Report Creation Wizard.

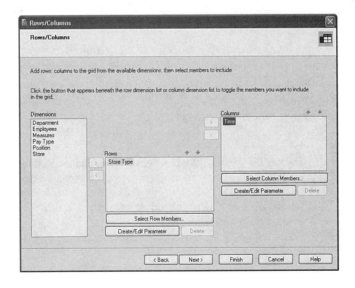

After the desired dimensions are selected, a subset of the fields (also known as *members*) for those dimensions can be selected using the Select Row Members or Select Column Members buttons. Examples of this might be selecting only a certain subset of provinces or states in a region dimension or, alternatively, selecting only a certain year's worth of data in a time dimension. By highlighting a dimension in either of the Rows or Columns list box and then selecting the appropriate Selection button, a subset of the members for the involved dimension can be selected from the Member Selector dialog as shown in Figure 16.5.

Figure 16.5
The Member Selector dialog is used to select default Column and Row Dimension members.

The last and newest feature of the Rows/Column screen is the Create/Edit Parameter functionality provided for each of the Row and Column dimensions. This capability provides the business user or report consumer with the capability to interact with the report and control its content by entering parameters that directly affect the dimension members displayed in the OLAP grid(s) on the report.

Because Chapter 5, "Implementing Parameters for Dynamic Reporting," covered parameters in detail, you are likely familiar with this topic already. Of significance for this wizard screen is that the parameter creation process is directly accessible here, and this facilitates the rapid development of formatted and interactive OLAP reports. If necessary, review Chapter 5 for a refresher on creating and editing parameters.

> The Member Selector dialog provides some powerful shortcuts for the selection of certain logical groups of members. These selection shortcuts are accessed through either the Select drop-down box or by right-clicking on any part of the Member Selection list box. Sample selection shortcuts include the capability to select all base level members or all members at a highlighted level.

Continuing with the creation of the sample report started in the last section, the following steps walk through the Rows/Columns screen part of this report creation example and allow for the refinement of the data to be viewed in the OLAP grid. Follow these steps to add rows and columns to your OLAP-based report:

1. Select the Store Type Dimension from the available dimensions list as the Row Dimension using the Row Dimension arrow button. (Note: It will likely be necessary to remove a default dimension to ensure that this is the only dimension in the Row Dimensions list view.)

2. Using the Select Row Field's button, select all the Store Types (for example, Supermarket, Headquarters, and so on) from the Member Selection dialog, but deselect the aggregated top level All Stores field. This enables the OLAP grid to present all the different store types down the side of the grid as rows.

3. Select the Time Dimension from the available dimensions list as the Column Dimension using the Column Dimension arrow (>) button. (Note: It will likely be necessary to remove a default dimension to ensure that this is the only dimension in the Column Dimensions list view.)

4. Using the Select Column Field's button, select the years 1997 and 1998 from the Member Selection dialog, but ensure that no children members have been selected. This enables the OLAP grid to present a comparison of the two years of data in two side-by-side columns.

5. Click the Next button to proceed.

At this point, you will review the concept of OLAP dimension filters and pages in your OLAP report.

SPECIFYING OLAP DIMENSION SLICES (FILTERS) AND PAGES

The Slice/Page dialog of the OLAP Report Creation Wizard, shown in Figure 16.6, enables you to select values or members for the dimensions that were not selected to be row or column dimensions. In the OLAP world, these dimensions are often called *paged* or *sliced* *dimensions*.

Figure 16.6
The Slice/Page screen of the OLAP Report Creation Wizard allows manipulation of the dimensions not selected for use on either the rows or columns.

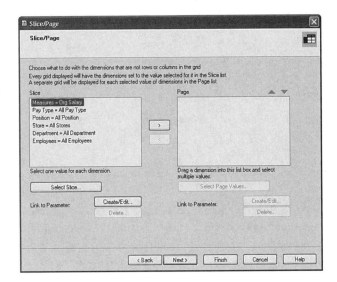

The Slice list box lists all the paged dimensions and their current member settings. The default setting is usually all members for any given dimension. An example is that for the Store Dimension, the default slice setting is All Stores. To change the member selection (slice) for a particular dimension, that dimension must be selected in the Slice list box and the Select Slice button must be used to open the familiar Member Selection dialog (refer to Figure 16.5). This dialog is identical to the Member Selection dialog used previously except that only one member from the selected dimension can be selected. If multiple members from a slice dimension are required in a report, the Page list box should be used and separate pages/grids will be created for each value selected.

The Page list box is initially empty but can contain any dimensions outside the row and column dimensions that require multiple member selection. An example could involve selecting the three countries of North America as store regions. The selection of multiple values for a paged dimension creates completely separate grids (based on the same preselected rows and columns) for each selected member value. To select multiple members for a dimension, the involved dimension needs to be selected in the Slice list box and moved to the Page list box using the transfer arrow buttons between the list boxes. Once moved to the Page list box, the Select Page Values button enables multiple member selection through the Member Selection dialog.

The last, but perhaps most powerful, feature of the Slice/Page screen is the Link to Parameter functionality provided for each of the Filtered and Paged dimensions. This capability provides the business user or report consumer with the capability to interact with the report and control its content by entering parameters that directly affect the information displayed in the OLAP grid(s) on the report.

Of significance for this wizard screen is that the parameter creation process is directly accessible here, and this facilitates the rapid development of formatted and interactive OLAP reports.

→ For more information on creating and editing parameters, see "Creating and Implementing Parameters Fields," p. 136.

Continuing with the creation of the sample report, the following steps walk through the Slice/Page dialog part of this report creation example and will enable you to select the measure that will be displayed in the OLAP grid. Follow these steps to select measures on the page/slice dimensions:

   Select the Measures dimension from the Filter list box.

   Instead of selecting a specific filter using the Select Filter Value button, click the Link to Parameter Create/Edit button to enable the business user to dynamically select this slice every time the report is run. The Create Parameter Field dialog, shown in Figure 16.7, appears.

   In the Prompting Text text box, enter the text that you want your user to be prompted with when this report is run. In this case, it could be something similar to Please select the Measure to be used in your report. Also, ensure that the Discrete Value(s) radio button is selected because a range of entries is not required (or allowed) here.

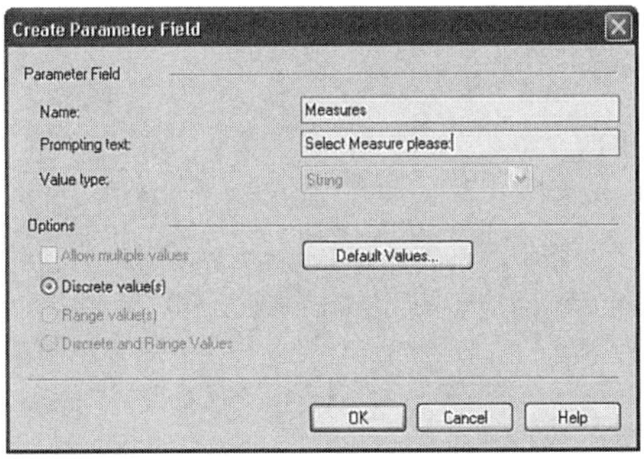

Figure 16.7
The Create Parameter Field dialog called from the Slice/Page screen.

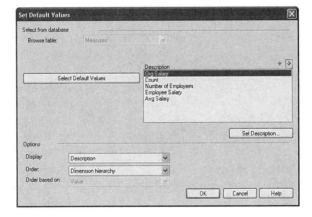

4. To avoid requiring users to type in any text, defaults can be set so that selection from a drop-down box is possible. To do this, click the Select Default button and the dialog in Figure 16.8 appears.

Figure 16.8
The Set Default Values dialog for the OLAP Slice Parameter.

5. The Measures table is pre-selected because the report respects the association with the previously highlighted dimension. Move all the available member values for the Measures dimension to the Description list box by clicking on the Select Default Values button and selecting all the members through the familiar Member Selector dialog.

6. Ensure that the Display drop-down box has Description selected and that the Order drop-down box has no sort selected. Click OK twice to get back to the Slice/Page dialog of the OLAP Report Creation Wizard.

7. Once you return to the Slice/Page dialog, highlight the Pay Type dimension in the Slice list box and click the arrow transfer/select button to move this to the Page list box. The Member Selection dialog will immediately appear with the Pay Type Dimension Hierarchy presented.

8. Select the Hourly and Monthly pay types (children of All Pay Types) and deselect the All Pay Types field. Individual OLAP grids are now created for each of the monthly paid employees and the hourly paid employees. If this isn't clear now, it should make more sense when you are visualizing the report.

9. Click OK and then Next to proceed.

> After Parameters or Multi-Value Paged Dimensions have been set in the OLAP Report Creation Wizard, you can only access them for editing through the OLAP Design Wizard under the main Report menu. These settings are not configurable in the OLAP Expert.

Adding Report Styles in the OLAP Report Wizard

The Style dialog in the OLAP Report Creation Wizard enables you to select any one of a predetermined number of styles for OLAP grids available in Crystal Reports. Figure 16.9 displays the Style dialog. The styles are often considered a good starting point for formatting the OLAP grids on your reports and can be enhanced through both the Customize Style tab of the OLAP Expert (described later in the chapter) and using many of the advanced formatting features you have already learned about.

Figure 16.9
The Style dialog of the OLAP Report Creation Wizard.

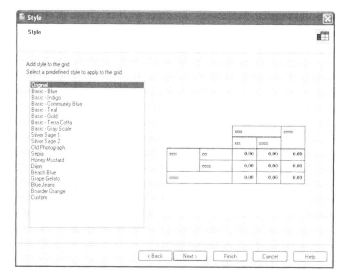

Adding Charts via the OLAP Report Wizard

The Chart dialog provided in the OLAP Report Creation Wizard enables you to add graphics quickly to the OLAP report being created. The graphics available in this wizard, shown in Figure 16.10, are only a subset of the graphics available in Crystal Reports (refer to Chapter 8, "Visualizing Your Data with Charts and Maps," for a refresher), but they do enable the rapid visualization of your OLAP data without the need for using the Chart Expert.

Aside from selecting the type of chart (bar, line, or pie) and specifying a title on this screen, an On Change Of field must be specified with an optional Subdivided By field before this screen is complete. As Chapter 8 discussed, the On Change Of field is the field in your data source that provides the breaking point for the involved graphic. Examples could include country, region, year, store, product, and so on. The Subdivided By field can provide a second variable to base your charts on. An example of a two-variable OLAP Chart using the FoodMart sample cube would be a chart showing salary information by year and then subdivided by store type.

Figure 16.10
The Chart dialog of OLAP Report Creation Wizard enables you to select between different basic chart types.

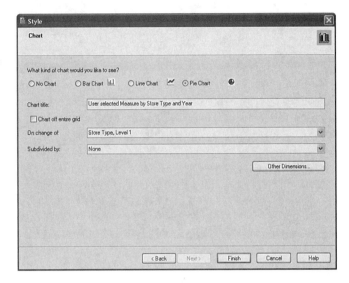

16

Now, to complete the OLAP report creation process, the following steps will take you through the addition of a style, a chart, and the creation of the finished report:

1. On the Style dialog, select any style that suits your preference and click the Next button.

2. On the Chart dialog, select Pie Chart as the Chart Type by selecting the radio button associated with that chart type. This provides a nice way of visualizing comparables across different store types.

3. Provide your chart with a title similar to **Measures by Store Type and Year** by entering this into the Chart Title text box.

4. Select Store Type as the On Change Of field. This facilitates the comparison of the six different store types. Leave the Subdivided By drop-down field empty.

4. Click Finish on the OLAP Report Creation Wizard. You will be prompted to select a parameter for the Measure dimension. After selecting Average Salary (or another field if you prefer), a report is generated that looks similar to Figure 16.11.

The OLAP Report Creation Wizard provides an efficient and effective method to getting value out of OLAP data in a short timeframe. After an OLAP grid or OLAP chart has been placed on your report through the wizard, further formatting and analysis can be performed through a variety of built-in Crystal Reports formatting tools. The next two sections explore further customization options and the three subsequent sections discuss the powerful new interactivity available in Crystal Reports OLAP objects.

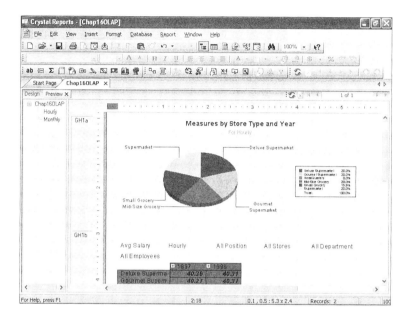

Figure 16.11
The sample OLAP report created using the OLAP Wizard.

CUSTOMIZING STYLES IN THE OLAP GRID

After an OLAP grid has been added to a report, with or without a selected style, Crystal Reports provides the capability to enhance and customize the formatting of that grid through the Customize Style tab accessed on the OLAP Expert. The OLAP Expert dialog is displayed in Figure 16.12 and is accessed by right-clicking on an existing OLAP grid object and accessing the OLAP Grid Expert, or by selecting the Insert OLAP Grid option from the Insert menu.

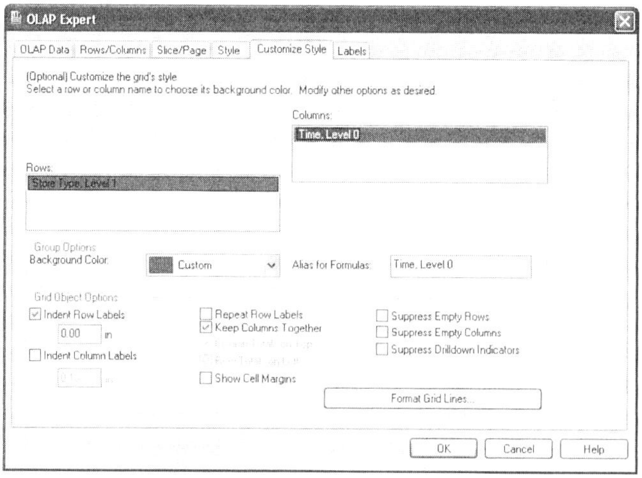

Figure 16.12
The OLAP Expert dialog provides the capability to edit many of the OLAP Grid display properties including the customization of styles.

Four of the tabs in the OLAP Expert have identical functionality as presented in the previous Report Wizard sections. The Customize Style tab shown in Figure 16.12 is unique to the OLAP Expert and provides the capability to fine-tune the formatting of the row and column dimensions selected for the involved OLAP grid. By selecting any of the column or row dimensions from the presented list boxes, custom colors can be selected for the backgrounds of the OLAP grid row and column headings. This tab also provides a number of formatting options for the presentation of the grid including indentation, blank column/row suppression, margins, and labels. Also provided is an option to format grid lines, shown in Figure 16.13. This dialog enables granular level formatting and selection of grid lines for display on the OLAP grid's layout.

Figure 16.13
The Format Grid Lines dialog is accessed from the Customize Style Tab of the OLAP Expert dialog and enables granular level control of the OLAP grid's grid lines.

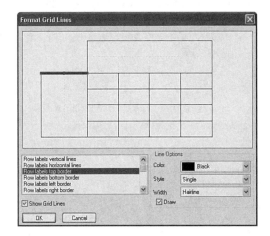

CUSTOMIZING LABELS IN THE OLAP EXPERT

The Labels tab of the OLAP expert, shown in Figure 16.14, provides the capability to customize the display of the paged-dimension (non row/column dimensions) labels on the OLAP grid.

Figure 16.14
The Labels tab of OLAP Expert enables you to specify display properties around the OLAP grid's dimensions.

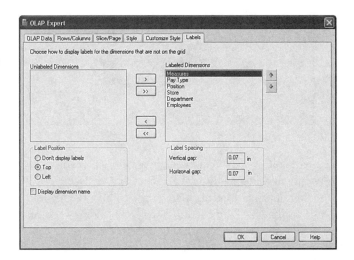

Paged/Sliced Dimension member values for the display grid can be displayed or hidden by simply moving the selected dimension between the unlabeled dimension and labeled dimension list boxes using the transfer arrow (>, >>, <, <<) buttons. Additional labeling options—such as label location, label spacing, and dimension names—can also be selected in this tab.

ADVANCED OLAP REPORTING

Up to this point, the OLAP Expert and OLAP Report Creation Wizard have demonstrated the capability of Crystal Reports to rapidly create OLAP-based reports. More than these capabilities, Business Objects provides advanced analytic capabilities against OLAP data sources through some advanced OLAP-oriented features in Crystal Reports and through a sister product called OLAP Intelligence (formerly called Crystal Analysis). The last four sections of this chapter introduce some of these advanced features for Crystal Reports; OLAP Intelligence is introduced in Chapter 19.

INTERACTING WITH THE OLAP GRID

Crystal Reports provides some powerful interactive OLAP features from directly within the Crystal Reports Preview and Design tabs. Figure 16.15 displays the right-click menu that appears when right-clicking on the year 1998 member in this chapter's sample report.

Figure 16.15
Advanced OLAP features are provided in the right-click menu.

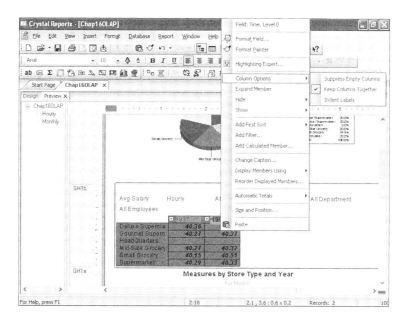

Advanced features made available here include conditional member highlighting, setting column display options, hiding and showing members for asymmetrical reporting, adding calculations, adding filters, reordering members, changing the member caption, expanding members (that is, drilling into the children members), adding sorts, and adding automatic totals to the OLAP grid. Although exploring these features in detail is beyond the scope of this chapter, it is important to note their availability for enhancing your OLAP grid presentations and reports. For detailed information on all these functions, review Chapter 19 where the same functionality for OLAP Intelligence is presented.

One feature of note for now is the active nature of the column and row dimensions in the OLAP grid. By double-clicking on any member in either the row or column headings—and assuming that the selected member has lower level members (children)—the OLAP grid dynamically expands to include that member's children in the grid. In OLAP parlance, this is called *drilling-down*. Figure 16.16 shows the result of drilling-down on the 1998 Header in this chapter's sample report. An alternative means to drilling down is to click on the + icon displayed beside any row or column dimension member.

Figure 16.16
Sample OLAP-based report with 1998 member's children expanded.

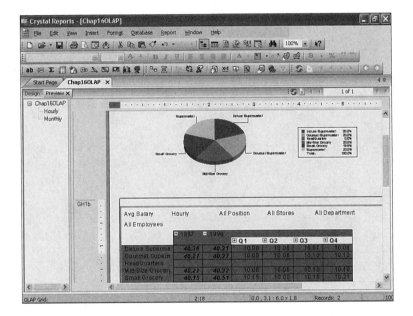

A dimension member can subsequently have its children contracted by double-clicking on the parent member or clicking on the – icon beside the involved parent member. This feature enables you to interactively determine the best static viewpoint to provide to the business user audience for the report.

PIVOTING OLAP GRID

After an OLAP grid has been added to a report, as in this chapter's sample, Crystal Reports provides the capability to easily swap the grid's columns and rows. In OLAP parlance, this is referred to as *pivoting* the OLAP grid. Figure 16.17 highlights this chapter's sample report after being pivoted with this function. To access this function, right-click on the OLAP grid and select the Pivot OLAP Grid option. Pivoting the OLAP grid does not affect any OLAP charts or maps already on the report.

Figure 16.17
A preview of the sample report after pivoting the OLAP grid. Notice how the chart and the grid have changed.

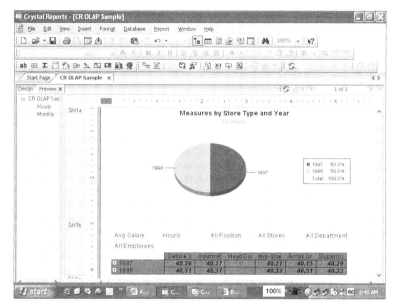

This function is particularly useful when attempting to decide which viewpoint of the involved OLAP grid will be most useful to the business users of the report.

USING THE CUBE VIEW FUNCTIONALITY

The Cube View (previously called the OLAP Analyzer) is a powerful worksheet analysis tool first introduced in version 9 of Crystal Reports. The Cube View is initiated through the View Cube option on the right-click menu of the OLAP grid (make sure that you don't have any specific grid objects selected) and is accessed through a new tab, titled Cube View, in the Crystal Reports Designer (see Figure 16.18). Report designers and analysts familiar with other OLAP interface tools will be instantly comfortable with the Analyzer because it provides access to the OLAP cube through a traditional OLAP worksheet.

Unlike the OLAP grid presented in the Crystal Reports Preview tab, the Cube View tab's worksheet is designed for rapid analysis of the underlying OLAP data through a rich and interactive interface not available in the OLAP grid. Dimensions can be rapidly shifted, swapped, and nested by double-clicking on them and dragging them into any of the row, column, or paged dimension areas. Dimension members can be quickly expanded and contracted by clicking on their associated + or – icons. Additional calculations, sorts, filters, automatic totaling, exception highlighting, data analysis, and custom captions can also be accessed through a right-click menu in the OLAP Analyzer view of the cube.

The Cube View is a powerful new report design tool because it lets Crystal Reports developers create some very powerful flat views of the underlying multidimensional/OLAP data in a very short timeframe and subsequently format the created OLAP grid in the Preview tab.

Figure 16.18
The Cube View tab launched by the OLAP Analyzer provides a powerful analytic tool for report designers and power users.

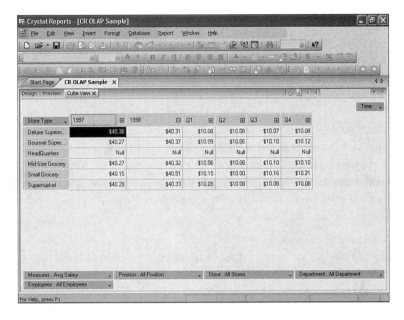

CAUTION

Although both the Cube View tab and the In-Place OLAP Grids within the Crystal Reports Designer offer much of the same functionality, not all the work handled in the Cube View is necessarily translated back into the related OLAP grid on Crystal Reports. Exception Highlighting and Field Formatting are two good examples of functionality that does not cross over. It is generally recommended that the majority of formatting work be done in-place within the Crystal Report's Design or Preview tabs and that cube and dimension orientation be the primary focus of the Cube View tab.

USING CHARTS AND MAPS BASED ON OLAP GRIDS

As described in Chapter 8 and discussed briefly in the "Adding Charts Via the OLAP Report Wizard" section earlier in this chapter, OLAP grid data can be presented through visually appealing charts and maps. To create either a chart or a map based on OLAP data, an OLAP grid must pre-exist on your report as a data source for the chart/map to be based on. Selecting the Insert Chart or Map command from the Insert menu (or the respective icons on the Insert toolbar) enables the creation of an OLAP-based visualization.

The creation process for both charts and maps requires the specification of an On Change Of field. This is the field that the chart or map will break its summaries on (for example, country, state, product, sales rep, and so on). An additional optional Sub-divided On field can be specified as well. The results of specifying an extra variable to divide the data on will have different results for various chart types. Explore these different charts to find those most suitable for your business problem. Using the Sub-divided On field with a map adds either a bar or pie chart to every main region on the selected map. An example of this might be a pie chart depicting the breakdown of sales for each country.

It is imperative that the On Change Of field be a geographic-based field when creating a map. Otherwise, the mapping component returns an empty map.

INTRODUCTION TO OLAP INTELLIGENCE

OLAP Intelligence is a mature reporting tool from Business Objects that enables organizations to deliver action-based OLAP analysis to business users. It enables better insights to help decision makers affect business performance through interactive analysis. OLAP Intelligence takes OLAP reporting to the next level by enabling you to create intuitive and highly interactive reports that offer a guided analysis approach to business issues.

Power users implementing OLAP Intelligence can create analytic reports, based on OLAP data, using a powerful designer (similar in concept to Crystal Reports). OLAP Intelligence Reports can contain many pages, each presenting a different predefined view of the OLAP cube. Data can be presented in tables or visualized through a wide range of charts, exception highlights, data sorts, filters, and analytic transition buttons. Business managers can use the resulting analytical reports to drive the business decisions they need to make every day. Figure 16.19 displays a sample analytic report created in OLAP Intelligence. These reports, in the same manner as Crystal Reports files, can be published to, secured, managed, and distributed by the BusinessObjects Enterprise solution—also available from Business Objects.

Figure 16.19
A Sample OLAP Intelligence report that includes an OLAP grid, chart objects, and several transition buttons for guided analysis.

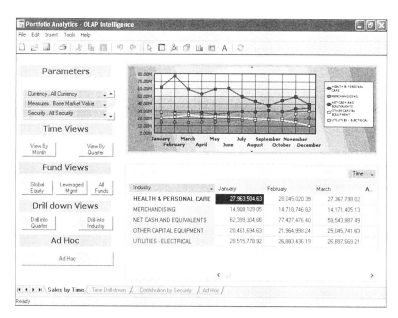

Details of OLAP Intelligence are beyond the scope of this chapter but are covered in detail in Chapter 19.

TROUBLESHOOTING

ADDING AN OLAP GRID TO AN EXISTING REPORT

I want to add an aggregated OLAP grid view to an existing drill-down report.

This can be quickly accomplished by accessing the Insert OLAP Grid functionality from the main Insert menu. An alternative approach that might make sense in certain situations is to insert a subreport that points to the involved OLAP datasource. Using a subreport to host the OLAP grid enables you to dynamically pass in parameters from the main report into the subreport and its associated OLAP grid. These parameters can be used to dynamically filter the columns, rows, and slices of the involved OLAP grid(s).

CRYSTAL REPORTS IN THE REAL WORLD—OLAP SUMMARY REPORT WITH DRILL-DOWN

The scenario discussed here describes the flexibility behind accessing multidimensional and relational data sources in one report. The benefit of this type of functionality is to enable the user to see aggregated information coming from a cube while allowing drill-down on the relational data to provide greater detail. By using parameters in this report you let the user decide which information elements are displayed.

1. Start by creating a simple sales report against the sample Xtreme data source. For the data, select the First Name, Last Name, and Last Year's Sales fields from the Customer table. Group the Report by Region, City, and then Customer. Hide the Details section and the City and Customer groups and enable drill-down on these sections. The report at design time should look like Figure 16.20. Before moving on, also add Summary fields for Last Year's Sales into each of the Group Header fields (Country, Region, and City).

2. Now add an OLAP grid to this report that will go against an offline cube file. Using the steps described earlier in this chapter, point the grid at the sample Holos file xtreme.hdc file located in C:\Program Files\Business Objects\Crystal Reports 11\Samples\en\ Databases\OLAP Data (You will have to add a new Holos server through the OLAP Connection Browser previously discussed in this chapter). Keep the defaults assigned by the grid expert except in the Rows/Columns tab; here, you will change the Customer Rows to only include AZ, CA, and MA to limit the number of rows displaying in the report.

3. Drop the OLAP Grid in the Report Header area. Now insert a pie chart based on the relational source that displays Last Year's Sales on change of values in the Region field and place the chart in the Group Header for Country to enable the user to also visually understand what the contribution of sales is from each of the selected regions. The report in design view should look similar to Figure 16.21. Also, perform the same filtering task in the report select expert so the relational data source is also limited to the same three states (AZ, CA, and MA).

Figure 16.20
Framework for drill-down integrating both relational and OLAP data.

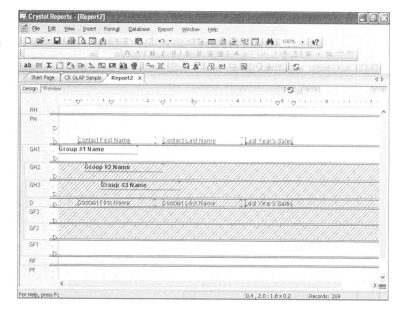

Figure 16.21
A Report using both OLAP and Relational data sources. The pie chart based on the Relational Data enables drill-down into the relational data details.

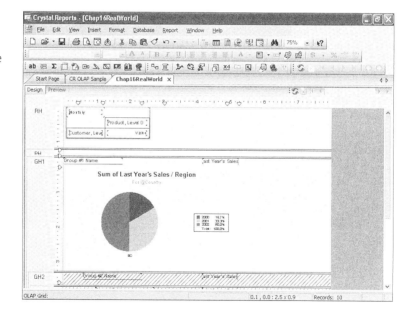

If the user viewed this report he would currently see both the chart and the OLAP grid at the top of the report summarizing the same information but sourced from two different data sources—one, a pre-aggregated Holos data cube, the other a relational database. To enable the end user to turn off the display of the grid, you will create a parameter field that will specify whether to display the grid. This will enable the users to decide if they want to look at the summary information in both a grid and chart format or simply the chart.

5. Create a parameter of Boolean type called Display Grid.

6. Next conditionally suppress sections containing the grid and the chart based on the values supplied to the parameters. To do this, right-click on Report Header and select Section Expert from the Report Explorer. Make sure Suppress is checked and then click next to the suppress option on the formula sign. Inside the formula editor type in

   `{?Display Grid}=false`

   and close the editor. Now if the user runs the report he will be prompted to select whether he wants to see the the summary OLAP grid. Save the report. On Display, it should look similar to Figure 16.22.

Figure 16.22
Report showing both the OLAP grid and charts and enabling drill-down from the high level summary information displayed from the OLAP grid into the relational details.

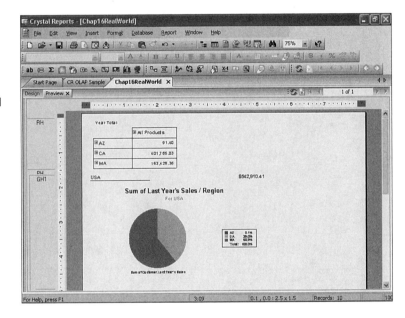

This example illustrates combining relational and multidimensional data in one report to allow for different views based on the same underlying data. This allows drill-down on relational elements and provides aggregate information for views on summary OLAP data.

PART IV

Enterprise Report Design— Analytic, Web-based, and Excel Report Design

CHAPTER 17

INTRODUCTION TO THE BUSINESSOBJECTS XI REPOSITORY

In this chapter

INTRODUCTION

The *BusinessObjects Repository* is a database that stores all of the Enterprise components, such as users, groups, folders, security settings, events, business views, universes, and user and system settings.

It also includes commonly used components that report developers can share between Crystal Reports.

This database is created and populated at install time and is controlled by the *Central Management Server (CMS)*. For this reason, you need to ensure that the database connection or database client software is installed on the server the CMS resides on. However, the physical database itself does not have to reside on the same server as the CMS, and for performance reasons it is recommended that the two are separated.

This repository was separated in the Crystal Decisions version 9 product suite into a repository for Crystal Reports 9 and an Enterprise object repository attached to the Automated Process Scheduler or APS. In Crystal Enterprise version 10, these two repositories were merged and are simply known as the Crystal Repository, which is attached to the CMS.

Administrators often have the misconception that the repository stores the report documents and report instances. These are actually stored on the file system as part of the File Repository Services. Consequently, when backing up the system or creating a fault-tolerant system, these folder structures need to be replicated. Furthermore, the Auditing database is not the same database as the Repository, but rather a separate database requiring a separate install. These concepts are described further in Chapter 25, "BusinessObjects Enterprise Architecture."

> For a listing of supported databases, see the CMS database listing found on the `platforms.txt` on your Enterprise CD.

EXPLORING THE BUSINESSOBJECTS REPOSITORY

Objects stored in the repository are exposed through a SQL-like language that allows the administrator to query the repository. For example, he might wish to know all the objects in the repository that were created by a certain user or after a certain date. Objects in the repository are assigned certain properties when they are saved to the system, logically grouped into components known as *property bags*. It is these properties that are exposed via the SQL expressions.

The Query Builder, as shown in Figure 17.1, is a Web-based application that allows an administrator to query the repository. A link to Query Builder can be found on the

Administator Launchpad page at http://<Server>:<port>/businessobjects/enterprise11/adminlaunch/launchpad.html.

Figure 17.1
The Query Builder displaying all of the object's properties.

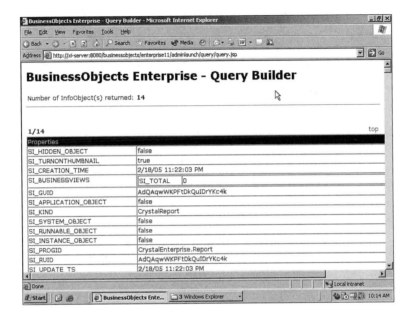

TIP

To get a listing of all exposed properties, an administrator could write a SQL statement such as SELECT * FROM CI_INFOOBJECTS. All objects and all properties would be selected. After the administrator has an understanding of the properties, specific queries can be written, such as SELECT * FROM CI_INFOOBJECTS WHERE SI_KIND = 'CrystalReport' to display a listing of all Crystal Reports published to BusinessObjects XI.

MIGRATION OF THE BUSINESSOBJECTS REPOSITORY

Numerous circumstances exist where an administrator might want to upgrade or migrate the BusinessObjects XI Repository. For example, during an upgrade, she might need to move objects from Development to Test and Production environments, or merge two repositories.

CAUTION

With any migration of data, you should perform any necessary backups. If the repository is not at the correct revision level, the Import Wizard will upgrade it to the correct level.

The Import Wizard, shown in Figure 17.2, is the tool that allows the user to migrate repositories from one version to another. The wizard walks the administrator through a number of steps, enabling her to determine what needs to be moved and which components will remain.

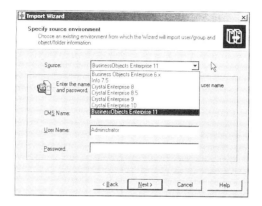

Although the utility is Windows-based, it only requires a client for Windows and can be used to connect to Crystal Enterprise and BusinessObjects systems hosted on Windows, UNIX, or Linux.

UPGRADES FROM EARLIER VERSIONS OF CRYSTAL ENTERPRISE AND CRYSTAL INFO

Prior to version 9, no Report Object repository existed. The Crystal Import Wizard migrates the Crystal Enterprise repository from versions 10.x and below (refer to Figure 17.2). The Import Wizard enables users to import users, groups, report objects and instances, associated permissions, events, and server groups.

UPGRADES FROM CRYSTAL ENTERPRISE 9

In version 9 of Crystal Enterprise and Crystal Reports, the repository was split into two databases. This consisted of the Crystal Reports repository that stored the text, bitmaps, SQL Command objects, and custom functions, and the Crystal Enterprise 9 repository that consisted of objects such as the users, folders, and so on.

To migrate the Crystal Enterprise 9 repository, the Migration Wizard is used as described previously in this chapter.

To migrate a Crystal Reports 9 repository to BusinessObjects XI, use the Repository Migration Wizard. This Windows-based utility is found on the BusinessObjects Enterprise CD and can be installed on the local administrator's workstation. It requires the administrator to create a connection to the Crystal Reports 9 repository. After this connection is established, the administrator connects to the BusinessObjects XI, typically with administrator permissions, and the associated objects are imported.

→ For more information on setting the BusinessObjects Repository permissions, **see** "Setting Security of the Repository," **p. 398**.

CAUTION

With any migration of data, you should back up the repository. The Migration Wizard does not move the data, but rather copies it, leaving the existing database intact.

NOTE

If an object exists with the same name, the Crystal Reports Migration Wizard does not copy over the database, but rather informs the user that there is a duplicate object and the original has not been migrated.

MIGRATIONS FROM BUSINESSOBJECTS 6.X

The Import Wizard allows administrators to migrate BusinessObjects 6.x systems over to BusinessObjects XI systems. Before undertaking this migration, the administrator should be aware what will upgrade and what will not.

WHAT DOES IMPORT?

For a successful import, ensure that your XI system has the same rights and middleware as your 6.x system and that the user performing the upgrade has sufficient operating system rights. For example, if a universe requires the Oracle 9 client to be installed, this needs to be created on the target machine before beginning the upgrade.

The following components are imported into the system:

- **Universes**—You can import all universes and related objects or you can import the universes related to the documents you are importing. The latter approach is best used if you are using this upgrade as an opportunity to clean your XI system of any unwanted universes.

- **Associated users and groups**—Enterprise 6.x profiles map to Enterprise XI groups; for example, the General Supervisor profile maps to the Administrators Group. Any users' personal documents can be added to their favorites folder in Enterprise XI.

- **Permissions**—Supervisor in BusinessObjects 6 has been replaced by the Central Mananagement Console (CMC) in BusinessObjects XI. However, for the users and groups selected, their associated permissions will be migrated in the form of restriction sets.

- **Domains and categories**—Domains are created as folders and all associated categories are created as categories.

CAUTION

User and group permissions might not map directly or might not import; therefore, your target objects can end up being more restrictive than intended. Administrators should check granted permissions at the target location to verify they have been imported as desired.

- **Web intelligence documents**—By selecting their associated domains, the administrator can import the WebI documents. Alternatively, selecting the document will import its associated domain.

- **Third-party documents**—With the ability to host third-party documents, such as Microsoft Office Documents, PDF, and text files, any XI supported document can be imported.

WHAT DOES NOT IMPORT

Before the organization embarks on an upgrade, it needs to be aware of what will not upgrade:

- **Version 5.x and prior versions**—If you are using an earlier version, you need to upgrade to version 6 before you can continue.

- **Any BusinessObjects full-client reports**—These might need to be re-created in Web Intelligence or Crystal Reports, depending on the requirement. If the report cannot be re-created in either of the above tools, you might want to use a parrallel install of XI or contact BusinessObjects as to when this will be available.

- **WebIntelligence OLAP**—A possible solution would be to rewrite these reports in OLAP Intelligence.

- **BCA Scheduler, BCA Publisher, Supervisor, and Auditor components**—These are not included in Enterprise XI. Anything created in these components will have to be re-created in XI using the CMC.

- **Infoview preferences**—The user preferences have changed considerably, so these will need to be reset.

- **Customizations made using the SDK**—If, for example, you have made customizations using the Enterpise SDK, these have to be moved over and retested. Changes made using the WIBean should be rewritten to use the Enterprise Java SDK.

- **Custom Application Foundation components**—Any cutomizations that you might have made to Application Foundation will not migrate.

It is expected that the ability to import and host full client documents (.rep) will be available in a future release of BusinessObjects. Depending on the requirement, it might be acceptable to rewrite the document in either Web Intelligence or Crystal Reports.

SHARING COMPONENTS IN THE REPOSITORY

Imagine the real-life situation where an organization has thousands of Crystal reports, some of which have a copyright notice on the bottom of each page. The legal department decides it wants to change the verbiage on this copyright notice. The administrator faces three problems: which reports have this notice, how to make this change in a timely fashion, and how to effectively make these types of changes in the future.

Without having the ability to check commonly used components into the repository, the administrator would have the unfortunate task of checking each report for the copyright notice and making the change on each report individually.

To solve this problem, Crystal Report developers should store and reuse commonly used components in the repository.

These components include

- **Text objects**—Reusable text, such as company addresses or confidentiality text.
- **Images**—Bitmaps, metafiles, TIFF, JPEG, and PNG image formats.
- **Custom functions**—Business logic that could be reused by passing in new fields as variables.
- **SQL Commands**—Encapsulated SQL Commands enable you to write free-form SQL for data access, including parameters. The results are seen as a table by Crystal Reports.
- **List of values**—Dynamic or scheduled list of available parameter values.

CAUTION

> One component not included in the BusinessObjects Repository is report templates. Although it is possible to secure the template via BusinessObjects Enterprise security, it is not possible to automatically loop through all the reports that reapply a new template. This task is possible but it is a manual process or requires that an administrative script be written.

When publishing the relevant reports back to Enterprise XI, the report developer should check the Update Repository Objects box, as shown in Figure 17.3. This allows the system to check whether any repository components have changed and to make the necessary report changes. If this box is not checked, the report is skipped and nothing in the report is updated, even if the report object has been changed in the repository. The Publishing Wizard and the Central Management Console also provide the ability to set this flag.

Figure 17.3
Select the Enable Repository Refresh box to allow this report to check for modified shared report components.

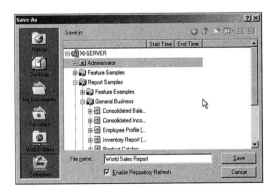

If the organization wants to make changes at a later date to the notice or any other shared objects, the developer would open the report, disconnect the text object, make the change, and resave the object to the repository. All reports that use the text component and have the Repository Refresh flag confirmed will adopt the new component.

ADDING TEXT OBJECTS AND IMAGES

To add text and image objects to your report from the repository, the repository explorer should be open in Crystal Reports. To open the repository explorer, select Repository Explorer from the View menu at the top of your screen. You might need to authenticate with BusinessObjects Enterprise either by logging on as prompted by the logon screen or by clicking on the Logon icon at the top of the Explorer. After this occurs, you can see all the folders and objects available in the repository. To add a text or image field, simply drag the field onto the report. You will notice that the object is read-only. To modify the object, right-click the object and select Disconnect from Repository. You will then be able to modify the object. If the changed object is saved back into the repository with the same name, the original version is replaced and all Crystal Reports that use this object and remain connected are updated the next time they are viewed.

To reconnect a text object or image to the repository, simply drag and drop the object from the Design or Preview tab in Crystal Reports back to its original repository object name in the Repository Explorer. A dialog will appear to confirm that you want to update the original object or add a new one. The user can then set the properties of the object by adding the required information.

→ For information on how to set the security around the object repository, see "Using BusinessObjects Enterprise," p. 397

> The capability to store objects from Web and OLAP Intelligence reports in the repository was not supported at publication time.

SQL COMMANDS

With the introduction of SQL Command objects to Crystal Reports, developers have been able to write custom database SQL to access data. The repository enables the developers to share these objects with others who might not have that skill set or those developers who do not want to reinvent the wheel.

To select a SQL Command from the repository, select the Repository from the Data Explorer or the Data step of the Report Wizard. Once again, BusinessObjects Enterprise will ask you to authenticate to ensure you are a valid user. Select the required SQL Command from the repository. If the command has any parameters associated with it, you will be required to populate the parameters. This enables the SQL statement to run, which will then populate the report with data, providing the report designer with some data to work with.

To add a new SQL Command object to the repository, use the Database Expert, connect to the database desired in the Available Data Sources list box, and choose Add Command from the list of available options. Select Add Command by double-clicking on it. This opens the Add Command to Report dialog. Then follow these steps:

1. Enter the SQL statement you want into the query box. If parameters are required, you can use this dialog to create them as well by clicking the Create button in the Parameter List section. Click OK to close the Add Command to Report dialog.

2. You are brought back to the Data tab of the Database Expert dialog. Before leaving this dialog, right-click the newly created SQL object under the selected tables pane and select the Add to Repository option.

3. Complete the form by giving your SQL command object a name and then selecting a folder where you want to store the object.

If the user wishes to edit the SQL command object, she needs to first disconnect it from the repository, making the edit button accessible.

CUSTOM FUNCTIONS

Custom functions are reusable procedures that enable you to share logic across reports. To allow for this sharing, the function needs to be data- and report-independent and specific guidelines must be adhered to:

- No User Function Libraries (UFL) can be used because these are machine dependent.
- No report or data source fields.
- You cannot associate a particular state with the function, such as Evaluation Time or Print State.
- You cannot use recursion; that is, the function cannot call itself.
- You cannot use variables, either shared or global, because these are report-specific.

CAUTION

> Custom functions are not editable from the Repository Explorer because they are housed inside of Formulas. To view custom functions available in the Repository, go to Report, Formula Workshop. In the group tree, the Crystal Repository branch can be seen and all custom functions can be viewed from there.

Adding a new custom function to the repository needs to be done from within the Crystal Reports designer. The user can select the drop-down list from the new icon in the Formula Workshop. The function is then created and the user can select the Add to Repository icon, which adds the function to the desired location in the repository.

ORGANIZING AND UPDATING THE REPOSITORY

The Repository Explorer represents the repository database as a tree structure made up of folders and objects. It is up to the report designer to decide how he wants to organize it. For example, the sample Repository that ships with BusinessObjects Enterprise XI is sorted by object types. The folders are named to indicate their contents (Images, Text Objects, and Commands). However, the content creator or report designer can use folders to his organizational advantage.

To add new folders to the repository, right-click on the desired folder where the intended subfolder is to be placed. If the folder is intended to be at the root, right-click on the repository name. Choose New Folder from the context menu.

To move objects or folders, drag and drop the object to the desired location. To rename a folder, simply choose the folder to be renamed, right-click on it, and choose Rename from the context menu.

After the shared object has been changed, there is an update process called the Object Repository Helper (found on the Administrator's Launchpad page under the Administrator's Tools section) that will loop through all the reports and update the changed component. An administrator can select all reports, individual reports, or all reports within a folder and its subfolders.

TROUBLESHOOTING

EDITING CUSTOM FUNCTIONS

I can't seem to edit my custom functions from the Repository Explorer.

Custom functions are not editable from the Repository Explorer because they are housed inside of Formulas. To view custom functions available in the Repository, go to Report, Formula Workshop. In the group tree, the Crystal Repository branch can be seen and all custom functions can be viewed from there.

BUSINESS VIEWS ARE GONE

When creating a new report, I see my available Business Views; however, after I open the Repository Explorer in Crystal Reports, the Business Views disappear.

The Repository Explorer in Crystal Reports is context-sensitive and only displays objects that can be used within the report itself.

MIGRATING THE REPOSITORY

In Crystal Reports 9, the sample Repository database was in Microsoft Access format. Can I migrate this to BusinessObjects XI?

In BusinessObjects XI, Microsoft Access is not a supported Repository database. The Access database will need to be migrated to a supported database such as SQL Server. The Crystal Repository Migration Wizard will connect to the Access database and transfer all the data to the SQL Server database for the user. However, for this to be successful, it assumes the user has not modified the Access database.

MIGRATING THE REPOSITORY

Why did the shared components not change on the reports when I updated them in the repository?

The Use Object Repository When Refreshing Report field needs to be checked. This field can be found using the CMC under objects and refresh options.

The Repository Helper process also needs to be run for the objects to be updated.

CHAPTER 18

USING A SEMANTIC LAYER—BUSINESS VIEWS AND UNIVERSES

In this chapter

INTRODUCTION TO SEMANTIC LAYERS

The *semantic layer* is a metadata layer that abstracts the complexities of the data source. The end user only sees a logical grouping of available, well-named fields for use and does not have to concern herself with the intricacies of database design or need any SQL knowledge.

In BusinessObjects XI, two semantic layers are supported—business views and universes. With the merging of Crystal Decisions and Business Objects, a decision was made to keep business views from Crystal Decisions and universes from Business Objects. The author predicts that in future releases there will be only one supported semantic layer that will have the best components of both products. Currently, however, Business Objects has made a commitment to support both business views and universes.

WHY USE A SEMANTIC LAYER

Semantic layers offer tremendous advantages over traditional report design processes by removing the most difficult data-intensive tasks, as described in the following sections, from report design. Furthermore, it allows for reuse of components and promotes the concept of changing a component once and having the change applied to multiple reports.

ABSTRACT THE COMPLEXITIES OF THE DATABASE

With large complex data warehousing projects using many tables and complex joins, the report author might not have the requisite knowledge. If the report author is required to join the tables for the reports, he might not use the most efficient join, resulting in poor performance. Semantic layers allow for a division in labor, whereby the more technical database administrators and developers can create the joins between tables and data sources and the business users can concentrate on designing reports to satisfy their requirements.

PUTTING REPORT DESIGN IN THE HANDS OF BUSINESS PEOPLE

As a result of this division of labor and the reuse of the BusinessObjects repository, business people do not have to be as technically savvy, effectively resulting in less technical skill being required to develop reports.

SUPPORT FOR A WIDE RANGE OF DATA SOURCES

Both metadata layers provide a wide range of database support, including the majority of relational database vendors. Business views also include the ability to connect to some non-relational data sources; for example, a user could abstract the complexity of an XML file by encapsulating the XML with a business view.

REUSE OF METADATA COMPONENTS

One major drawback to specifying the data joins in each report is that this creates a large amount of redundant work. Secondly, should the database change, there is no way to effect this change other than changing each of the individual reports. A semantic layer allows the administrator to create this join once and should this join change, the administrator only needs to change it once.

JOINING DISPARATE DATA SOURCES

Data in corporations typically sits in multiple data sources. A requirement might exist to pull information from multiple data sources and consolidate this information in a single report. A business view allows the administrator to join disparate data sources together or to link two universes together.

DYNAMICALLY SWITCH DATA SOURCES

Organizations typically have two or three environments. Most would have at least a test/development environment and a production environment. In some cases, the test/development environment is split into separate environments. During the development process, reports are developed against the test environment, tested against the test environment, and finally put into production. In prior versions of Crystal Reports, the report had to be opened and the data source mapped to a new data source. Business views can dynamically switch data sources through the use of dynamic data connections. This creates a Crystal Report parameter that prompts the user to select his data source. Alternatively, the report designer can use logic to effect the switching the datasource. For example, an organization may have a production database and periodically archive data to an archive database. The report developer could programmatically swap data sources to the archive database, based upon the date entered for the data that the user wished to view.

Using dynamic data connections, users can easily switch data sources at runtime, yet maintain a single report.

CAUTION

Universes do not support this concept and data sources need to be switched programmatically or manually.

SECURITY

The semantic layer allows the administrator to set up security so data is filtered based upon who the user is. This can be based off of security within an entitlements database, or the Business Objects user model can be used to create the security model. This way rows and columns can be secured by users or groups.

The BusinessObjects repository also secures the semantic layers and only those users with the required permissions can access them. For example, it is generally accepted auditing practice that accounts receivable personnel should not be able to see accounts payable information and vise versa. By using the user group functionality in BusinessObjects Enterprise, the accounts receivable group would be given access to only the accounts receivable semantic layer.

TRANSPORTABILITY

The semantic layers provide the ability to export a business view to an XML file or a universe to an .unv file. These files can then be easily imported into another BusinessObjects Enterprise repository. This simple form of transportability makes semantic layer swapping a simple exercise. It also simplifies the storage of source code, should the organization have a source code storage requirement.

THE SEMANTIC LAYER IS OPTIONAL

This might sound like a strange benefit, but in certain circumstances the costs of building a semantic layer outweigh the benefits. Crystal Reports XI still provides the flexibility to use a semantic layer, or access the data source directly, or a combination of the two. For example, an organization upgrading its reports from earlier versions might be satisfied with the current state of its implementation and hence might never use a semantic layer. Crystal Reports XI even allows for a combination of semantic layer access and direct data source access via subreports.

> **CAUTION**
>
> Joining disparate data sources is limited to business views. With the use of disparate data sources, business views do not allow the Crystal Report option of grouping on the server. In order to concatenate the disparate data sets, most of the processing is performed within BusinessObjects Enterprise and not the database. Keeping disparate data source joins to a minimum for large data sets is recommended to keep performance satisfactory.

INTRODUCTION TO BUSINESS VIEWS

Business views are multitiered semantic layers that sit between report authors and end users and their respective data sources. These layers allow the complexities of the data source to be abstracted into logical groupings of the fields or business views.

The architecture provides multiple tiers with each tier performing a different function. This multitiered system is broken down into three layers: the client, business, and data tiers.

CLIENT TIER

The *client tier* consists of the applications that interact with the business views, in particular, Crystal Reports XI, Live Office, and InfoView.

BUSINESS TIER

The *business tier* consists of the components to create and manage the business views:

- Business View Manager
- Data connections
- Dynamic data connections (optional element)

- Data foundations
- Business elements
- Business views
- Dynamic and cascading prompts and prompt groups

At each component level, different security rights can be applied to the components and security set up. This provides great flexibility as to who controls which component. For example, a database administrator (DBA) can set up the data connections and data foundations but have no rights to view the business element and business view layers.

CAUTION

There is functionality within certain components that might give users access to view the data. For example, when creating a data foundation, the user can browse the data, which will give her a better understanding of the field. If you do not wish for her to be able to do so, you need to explicitly remove her rights.

BUSINESS VIEW MANAGER

The tool used to manage the business views and the repository is the Business View Manager, a Windows-based development tool that can be installed locally on the developer's or administrator's Windows workstation. The Repository Explorer allows the user to manage the BusinessObjects repository. To show the Explorer, click the View menu from within the Business View Manager and then check the Repository Explorer. To reiterate, the objects that can be stored in the Crystal repository are

- Business views
- Command objects
- Custom functions
- Images
- Text objects

It is worth describing some of the functionality of the Repository Explorer because it can become quite large in larger projects, with multiple users adding objects simultaneously. There are certain features that can simplify navigation and security when dealing with many objects.

SORTING ITEMS IN THE REPOSITORY EXPLORER

As a content creator, you need to navigate quickly and effectively through the repository to reduce content development time. Below are some techniques to aid in the organizing of the BusinessObjects repository:

- The view setting icon allows the user to filter objects by item type and then sort the object by name or type.

- The advanced filtering turns on filtering by owner or filters objects by entering text. Only those objects with the associated text in their names will be displayed.

- Users can add or delete objects or folders, depending on their permissions. Creating your own folder structure can be an efficient way of organizing the repository.

- Before deleting and after adding objects, a user can check his dependencies from the standpoints of what might be dependent on that object or what that object might depend on. For example, if the user creates a data foundation, he can check what data connections this is dependent on by clicking the Show Referenced Objects icon, or the user could check what depends on this object by clicking on the Show Dependent Objects icon.

Setting Security of the Repository

The repository security is controlled via the Repository Explorer found in the Business View Manager. It works on an inheritance mechanism, whereby an object inherits the security settings from its parent and is designed so administrators do not have to set the security for every object. For example, you might have an administrators group that has view, edit, and set security rights, another group called Content Creators that only has view and edit rights, and another group called Everyone that only has view rights. Alternatively, objects can inherit security from the folder they are published to. If you set the security of the root folder, any folders created under the root folder will inherit the root folder's security.

Data Connections

The *data connection* component is where the user establishes a connection to the data source. The setting up of the connection component is similar to the setting up of a connection in Crystal Reports and, in a lot of cases, uses the same drivers and dialog boxes. The user can enter in a username and password. This is the username that will authenticate against the data source and the username and password is then stored in the repository.

Dynamic Data Connection

The *dynamic data connection* is an optional component that allows the user to switch data sources dynamically through the use of Crystal Report parameters. If the dynamic data connection component is used, the Crystal Report will automatically have a read only parameter created. The parameter's name consists of the data connection's name concatenated with the dynamic connection parameter and the parameters available selections consist of the various database options.

The dynamic data connections are useful for quickly moving from development to test environments. They can also be used to change languages dynamically; for example, if there are English and French databases, the user can switch between the two. However, bitmaps and text objects do not automatically switch and the report designer needs to have one for each language.

If the database is designed with a column that designates language (hence, there would be a row in the table for each language), a row-level filter is required. This is described in the following "Filters" section.

THE DATA FOUNDATION COMPONENT

The *data foundation* component allows the user to join the various tables exposed by the data connection(s) or dynamic data connection(s). The user would typically have knowledge of the data structures and correct joins. To join a table to another table, simply drag the field from one table to the corresponding field in the other table. The data fields need to be of the same type for the join to be successful. Right-clicking on the join and selecting the link type allows the user to change the join type, as shown in Figure 18.1. The correct joining of the tables, especially when there are multiple disparate data sources involved, is vital from a performance standpoint and for ensuring that the correct data is returned. Related to this is the ability to order the links. The user can set the linking order the business view will use by selecting Order Links from the Linking Diagram menu. In addition, link enforcement can be vital to correct implementation of security filters. For instance, the filter that determines row-level permissions might require information from a particular table. However, if that particular table is not used in the report, you need to force the use of that table to ensure correct filtering. In that case, you can set join enforcement to result in the correct behavior.

Figure 18.1
Double-clicking a join in the Data Foundation will display the join type.

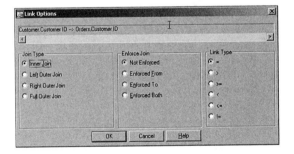

Data warehouses can have hundreds, sometimes thousands, of tables. The data foundation component can become complex to manage. Below are some pointers to aid in the management of the foundation:

- **Only map the tables you require information from**—A common mistake is trying to map all the tables in the data warehouse. This might sound obvious, but you might only require information from certain functional areas of the data warehouse and hence you only need to map those tables.

- **Keep it simple**—It generally requires less effort to go from simple to complex than complex to simple. Bite off as much as you can chew, work out the relationships, test, check performance and expected data results, and then take another bite.

■ **Use indexes**—For performance reasons, try to join indexed fields (indicated by a colored icon to the left of the field) and have the database do the work, as opposed to the business view. Because indexed fields are much faster to find at the database level, the database can return data much faster, especially in large tables, if the fields used for the join are indexed.

> In some cases the index pointer does not appear next to the indexed field. Select the Fetch Table Indexes from the Linking Diagram menu to make these appear.

■ **Keep the number of retrieved records to a minimum**—The data foundation allows the user to create SQL expressions and formulas. SQL expressions are evaluated at the database level, whereas in many cases the formula is evaluated by the BusinessObjects Enterprise server. The number of records retrieved can be reduced significantly by having the database filter the records based on a SQL expression rather than a formula, effectively pushing the filter into the query itself rather than retrieving all the data and then discarding the unnecessary portion.

■ **Use the tools available in the Business View Manager**—A number of tools, described in Table 18.1, are applicable to the data foundation and allow for management of the tables within the business view. All of these can be found under the Link Diagram menu.

TABLE 18.1   AVAILABLE TOOLS FOR MANAGING THE DATA FOUNDATION

Tool	Function
Locate tables	The user can select the table name from a list and be taken to that table in the data foundation. This saves the user from having to search by scrolling.
Rearrange tables	This attempts to arrange the tables, saving the user from having to move tables around.
Select visible tables	Allows the user to hide tables and only show required tables. The other tables are still linked; they just do not show up in the window.
Fetch table indexes	Show what fields are indexed. Related to this is the index legend.
Change linking view	To allow for more tables to be visible, the view can be changed so only the table name is displayed and not all the fields are visible.

SQL EXPRESSIONS   Within the data foundation components, the user can create a SQL expression. A *SQL expression* is a SQL statement that is executed on the database. This are typically used to create data fields that do not exist in the database. A good example of using SQL expressions is to join disparate data sources where one of the data sources is missing a relevant field to join on. For example, you might have a database where you want to join a numeric Vendor Number ID field to a Vendor Number field that is of type string in the other data source. In this case, you can create a SQL expression that converts the Vendor Number to a numeric field so that the field types can be joined.

The administrator has the ability to set security on the SQL expression by right-clicking the SQL expression and selecting Edit Rights. See the previous "Security" section for more detail on setting security.

FORMULAS   In some cases the database SQL might not support the required functionality, or a calculation might be required using fields from disparate data sources. In this case a formula can be used, as opposed to using SQL expressions. For example, you might have a quantity shipped number coming from a Shipping database and a price field from an Orders database. In order to see the total value of orders shipped, these values could be calculated in a formula.

The administrator has the ability to set security on the formula, and any other object, by right-clicking the formula and selecting Edit Rights. See the previous security section for more detail on setting security.

> **TIP**
>
> Customer Functions stored in the repository can be added to the Data Foundation and reused within formulas.

18

PARAMETERS   The user can create parameters at this level to use at the business element level. The parameter can be either static or can make use of list of values or a prompt group. Static parameters are better suited for values that do not exist in the database and are manually entered by the user or the business view designer. Dynamic parameters are better suited for getting the list of values from the database. Implementing parameters at this level ensures reuse and consistency across all your reports.

FILTERS   Business views use filters to select the data based upon a particular logic. In some cases the logic prevents too much data from being returned to the user. For example, the user might only be interested in seeing data from the manufacturing division. Another case might be that the user is not allowed to see the row of data based upon some business security requirement. This is commonly called *row-level security*. To achieve this, the business view creator makes a filter, or multiple filters, and concatenates them together using either AND or OR logic. He must make sure the logic is correct. Users can filter data using fields, SQL expressions, formulas, other filters, parameters, Boolean logic, or a special Crystal Reports field called Current CE User. The user right-clicks the filter and selects either the user or the group the filter needs to apply to. By default, the system creates a Full Data Access Filter and a No Data Access Filter. These are the two extremes—an organization's security will typically fall somewhere in between. For example, the Accounts Payable department or group might have a filter that filters the transaction type to Accounts Payable.

If the organization is not using business views or wants to quickly filter a report without having to set up a business view, `{CurrentCEUserID}` or `{CurrentCEUserName}` can be used with the Record Selection formula of Crystal Reports.

Associated with row-level security is the concept of *column-level security*. In this case, the column's data is displayed or not displayed based upon certain business logic. For example, if you belong to the Human Resources group, you might have permission to see the Identity Number or Social Security column. All other groups would not have access to that column; however, they can see the rest of the report.

In order to enable the column-level security, right-click on the field in the Object Explorer and select Edit Rights. Select the group or user you want to deny or grant access. A user's net rights can be determined using the Rights Test View described in the Business View section below.

BUSINESS ELEMENTS

Business elements provide a layer on top of the data foundation. It is at this level that the developer can further abstract the complexity of the database by aliasing the fields with business terminology and logically grouping these fields around business requirements. It is at this level that the division of labor might occur between technical- and business-oriented focuses. In other words, the business-oriented person might wish to start renaming the fields to business terms.

When creating a new business element, the Business View Manager prompts the user for a data foundation. Select the required one. Insert the required fields for the business element. The business element allows for a logical grouping of the fields. For example, the business elements might be designed based upon a division or department, such as an accounts payable element.

APPLYING CHANGES AT THE BUSINESS ELEMENT LEVEL   Making changes, such as security, at this layer will only effect this layer and will not effect the underlying data foundation layer. However, changes made at the data foundation layer will be added to any changes made at this layer. For example, if you denied a user the right to see the Country field at the data foundation level and now you deny the same user the right to see the Region field, when the user runs the report they will see neither the Region nor Country fields. This illustrates the flexibility in making changes for certain business groups without creating multiple similar data foundations.

BUSINESS VIEWS

Finally, you can collect business elements into business views. A primary consideration is that a business view must contain business elements derived from the same data foundation. Stated differently, a business view can contain data from only one data foundation.

At this stage in the architecture, the appropriate filtering has been performed and the business view is a cumulative view of all the underlying components.

For example, assume the database contains multiple company numbers, each representing a separate organization as part of a large conglomerate. The administrator could set up the data foundation and filter by each company number, assigning only that company the rights to the data foundation. Within that specific company, there might be multiple sales departments. This could be defined in a business element; once again, a filter is applied at this level so only the associated sales department is seen by the relevant personnel. The business view combines the business elements to provide a view of data. This view will be filtered by relevant company and by relevant sales department, which is the cumulative effect of the layers.

To create a new business view, the user can select the New icon, and select a new business view, or from the File menu, select the business view. Select the business elements that are going to be part of the view and save the view.

By right-clicking on the view in the Object Explorer, the user can set the rights to the business view. In this case the rights refer to who has rights to edit, view, and set security on the business view.

The Rights Test view, shown in Figure 18.2, allows the content creator to check each user's net rights for the visible fields. If column-level security is applied, the field has a red cross associated with it and will appear as a NULL value to Crystal Reports. How Crystal Reports is set up to handle the NULL value determines what is displayed. As far as the row-level security is concerned, the cumulative total of all the filters is applied, from both the Element and Foundation level and is shown as the final filter text.

Figure 18.2
Rights Test View showing the final column and row level filters that will be applied for the selected user.

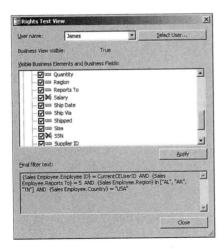

DYNAMIC AND CASCADING PARAMETERS

Crystal Reports XI introduces the concept of dynamic and cascading parameters. The ability to dynamically query a field in the database for a list of values and then filter the list of values for the following parameter based on the prior selected value is now supported within business views. However, business views add one further dimension—the ability to schedule the list of values on a predetermined basis, prepopulating the list of values.

After the user has created the parameters, she can group them logically in the form of *prompt groups*. The user only has to select the prompt group to apply all the parameters within the group.

DATA TIER

The final tier of the architecture is the *data tier*. This consists of all the data sources available to the business view. The available set of data sources changes depending on the platform BusinessObjects Enterprise is installed on.

Please check the documentation, specifically `platforms.txt` (found on the BusinessObjects Enterprise CD), for a list of available data sources for your install.

http://support.businessobjects.com/ provides a searchable knowledge base for related patches (hot fixes), knowledge base articles, and technical papers.

INTRODUCTION TO UNIVERSES

The idea of the *universe* is to capture and encapsulate elements of the database as objects, and that these objects can be selected in any combination by a business user to answer a question (hence, the company name Business Objects). This concept of providing an abstraction of the physical data layer was developed and patented by Business Objects 14 years ago. Since this time, the semantic layer has been continually enhanced and developed in conjunction with the reporting engines to provide a very simple yet powerful user experience for creating ad-hoc reports, interacting with reports, and performing analysis of the data. The overall design paradigm is to provide ease of use for the ultimate consumer who is assumed to be a nontechnical business user.

The universe itself contains no data; it is a file containing the pointers to the data. The universe is utilized by the reporting engine to generate *Structured Query Language (SQL)* queries according to the object definitions and other rules defined within the universe. In BusinessObjects XI, it is used by the Web Intelligence engine to generate all of the SQL for any report requests. The Web Intelligence engine executes the query and creates the report, and will continue to use rules and definitions of object relationships defined in the universe to allow for interactive exploration and analysis of the data (more on this in Chapter 20, "Introduction to Web Intelligence").

Because the semantic layer paradigm is so applicable to any reporting tool, the universe was easily integrated with Crystal Reports 10. As of June 2004 with the release of the Business Objects Crystal Integration Pack, the universe can generate SQL for Crystal Reports. This integration was continued and enhanced in Crystal Reports XI.

UNIVERSE OBJECTS

The universe contains several object types that are represented with different icons. The object types represent different relational concepts and are used by the reporting engines in different ways.

Icon	Object Type	Definition
	Dimension	Parameters for analysis. Dimensions typically relate to a dimension hierarchy such as geography, product, or time.
	Detail	A description of a dimension; usually not used for analysis.
	Measure	Convey numeric information which is used to quantify a dimension object.
	Condition	A predefined condition to limit resultsets.

The universe is accessed by the end user through a query panel. The query panel provides a drag and drop interface where business users can select, in any combination, the objects they wish to see, provide conditions for the query, and then execute the query. The report engines review the objects chosen and, based on the semantic rules defined in the universe, generate appropriate and correct SQL on the fly.

Figure 18.3 shows the Web Intelligence query panel. Note the four object types in the preceding table appear in the left frame. Users see these objects (business objects) and can randomly select any combination by dragging and dropping them in the Result Objects frame on the right. The universe provides the logic for correct, sophisticated SQL generation based on any combination of objects.

The query panel will be discussed in detail in Chapter 20.

CREATING THE UNIVERSE

Universes are created in a separate module known as the Designer. The Designer is a client-server tool installed on the desktop of only those who create the semantic layer. This is generally an IT function. The universe is created with this tool and then exported to the Central Management Server (CMS) database or InfoStore, where it is accessed by the BusinessObjects Enterprise infrastructure and the WebIntelligence or Crystal Reports engines. Other Designers can also access it and enhance it, and re-export it back to the InfoStore. As with business views, there is currently no version control mechanism for universes.

18

Figure 18.3
Web Intelligence
query panel.

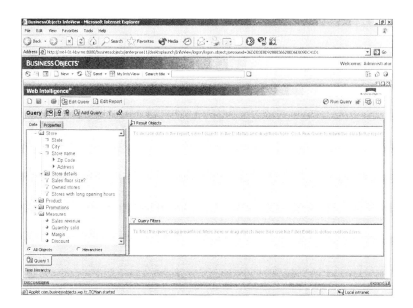

Figure 18.3
Web Intelligence
query panel.

The Designer tool requires authentication via the CMS and the proper rights to access the Designer module. After authenticated, the Designer provides the capabilities necessary to create the universe semantic layer and associated data rules used by the query engines. Figure 18.4 shows a diagram of a universe open in the Designer module.

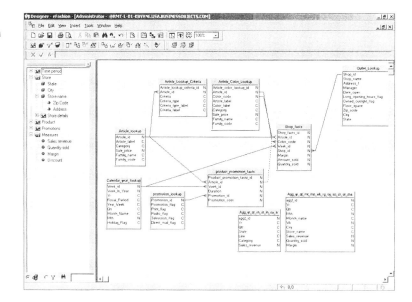

Figure 18.4
The universe is open
in the Designer.

Note that the same objects are showing as in Figure 18.3. The right pane shows the database schema and possible joins defined by the universe creator; the left side shows the objects visible to the end users via the query panel. Users will never see the underlying database structure, only the objects and classes in the left pane.

The window is divided into two main sections. The right side of the window is called the Structure Pane and shows the tables and views of the underlying database, along with any joins defined with the Designer. The left side of the window is called the Universe Pane, and shows all of the objects exposed by the universe. The Universe Pane also shows the object classes (often incorrectly called folders) that are arbitrary groupings of objects to best fit the user requirements. There is no requirement to group objects from the same table in the same object class. Classes can contain subclasses as well as objects, and objects can live at any level of the class/subclass hierarchy, but must be contained within a class/subclass.

> **TIP**
>
> As a best practice, objects are generally separated into classes according to dimensional groupings known as *subject areas*. For example, all of the time objects (Year, Month, Week, Day, Hour, and so forth) are put into a `Time` class; likewise, all customer elements are grouped in a `Customer` class and so forth. Measure objects are also placed in a single `Measures` class that is often the last top-level class in the tree. This is not a required grouping but is the convention used and taught by Business Objects.

In order to create a universe, a preexisting universe connection must be selected from the InfoStore or created via the Designer. The *universe connection* is an object in the InfoStore that defines the connection information to the underlying database. It specifies the RDBMS and version, username, password, and middleware type and version. It is encrypted and stored in the InfoStore and used by the Web Intelligence engine or the Designer module when generating SQL.

The connection can be static or dynamic (based on some parameter such as the logged-in user); there is no differentiation of static or dynamic data connections, as there is in business views.

Unlike business views, the universe has one and only one connection. The WebIntelligence report engine can accommodate multiple resultsets, so reporting can alleviate this somewhat (see the "Microcube" section).

OBJECT DEFINITION

The object itself contains a SQL snippet representing the piece of the database the object reflects. For example, if the database contains a customer table, there might be a dimension object called Customer Name that contains the definition `customer_table.last_name`. If, for example, the business user would prefer the first name and last name, the object definition can be redefined as `customer_table.first_name + " " + customer_table.last_name`.

Object definitions can be defined using any of the native database-specific extensions (such as CASE, CAST, DECODE, DATEPART, and so on). This allows for the development of quite complex objects. The universe supports all native RDBMS-specific SQL extensions, as well as any custom database functions developed in-house.

Dimension objects can be defined to exist in a dimensional hierarchy. A dimensional hierarchy defines natural parent-child relationships within the data. The most common example of a hierarchy is Time, which is often defined in the following hierarchy: Year, Quarter, Month, Week, Day, and so forth. The hierarchy mechanism is used by the Web Intelligence reporting engine to provide drill down capability. With a universe, *drill down* refers to exploring data at some level below the current level of aggregation. In other words, when looking at Sales for the Year, a user can drill down to look at Sales by Quarter, and from there drill down to look at Sales by Month. Users can also *drill up* (move up a level in the dimensional hierarchy) and *drill by* (swap the presentation to other dimensions in a completely different dimensional hierarchy). More discussion on drilling can be found later in the "Microcube" section, and in more complete detail in Chapter 20 in the "Drilling" section.

Measure objects are almost always defined with aggregate SQL functions such as sum, count, max, min, and so on. Although not required, the universe design is such that aggregate functions are preferred in the object definition because this often engages more appropriate SQL optimization on the underlying RDBMS. It also returns smaller resultsets that should aid in a better total request and response time during an ad-hoc request.

In general, database optimization is more important in providing user-expected performance for an ad-hoc application than it is in straight enterprise reporting. Most enterprise reports are generated prior to actual report consumption, such as during off hours in a batch process, so runtime and processing time are less important. Put another way, the computing necessary for report processing does not happen right before report consumption by the user. In an ad-hoc application, you can assume that the query requests happen during the actual report consumption (users are actually generating and executing the SQL requests at the time of report consumption—not in batch). The users expect maximum analytical flexibility and minimal response time—easier said than done, especially because by definition an ad-hoc reporting application does not know what SQL requests will be made (hence ad-hoc). The best practice for developing and deploying successful ad-hoc applications is to gather extensive user requirements to understand *why* the business users are asking for the data and *what they do with it next*, and then build an appropriate model to support those requirements.

Universes are extremely flexible, and many of the universe mechanisms (contexts, aggregate awareness, short-cut joins, aliases, and so forth) can be used to ensure that proper SQL is generated on any model type. Universes do not require underlying star schemas and can be deployed on any underlying supported database regardless of the model type. However, if the goal is to provide maximum analytical flexibility, proper data modeling cannot be avoided. Often times the universe will be used as a cheap and easy way to provide business users access to transactional systems. If ad-hoc data analysis was the goal of the business sponsor, then placing a universe on the transactional system means the reporting application is not designed properly, most likely because proper requirements were not gathered and a model analysis was not completed. This often results in slow performance, or IT re-entering the project to develop reports for the business because the universe is overly complex and not business centric. In other words, if you expect to slap a universe on top of a transactional system without doing a proper requirements gathering and then let your business users try to do data analysis, no one will be happy, especially your DBA. The most important thing IT can do to ensure success of an ad-hoc or analytic application is to gather proper requirements.

SQL GENERATION, CONTEXTS, AND AGGREGATE AWARENESS

Based on the objects selected by the business user via the query panel, the universe determines which tables are necessary and the optimal join paths between these tables, as defined in the Structure Pane. The universe might contain multiple routes, or join paths, between any two tables. This is most evident in a star schema (but would apply in any model type) where multiple fact tables exist. For example, say you have a universe to perform expense analysis, and there is one fact table containing the budgeted amounts along the organizational hierarchy and the time hierarchy (resulting in budget amount by department and by month) and there is a second fact table with the actual daily figures spent by all employees. You might then want to join the time and organization dimensions directly to the budget fact and actual fact. When the business user engages the universe via the query panel, she might want to see the budget amount and actual amount per month for her department. The universe employs a rule called a *context* that is a grouping of tables and joins that dictates proper join paths based on the object selection. In this case, there would be two contexts, one for the budget figures and another for the actual expenses. This tells the SQL engine that two SQL statements need to be generated in order to get proper results—one with time, organization, and budget, and the second with time, organization, and the actual expenses. The results are then rejoined together within the reporting engine (Web Intelligence) to present a single result set.

Another feature of the universe is the use of aggregate awareness. *Aggregate awareness* allows for the inclusion and use of aggregate tables where possible, and use of lower-level tables where appropriate. To further the expense analysis example, suppose that the DBA has aggregated the actual expense data at the month level and by department. This means there is an aggregate of actual expenses, but the atomic-level fact table also exists (which lists each and every expense by employee, expense type, and day.) If the business user chooses department, month, and the expenses amount, the aggregate awareness tells the universe that the query can be handled by the aggregate table and to use it instead of the atomic-level table. This can have a great benefit on query performance. Furthermore, if the business user drills down a hierarchy that leaves the aggregate (say from month down to day), the universe is

18

smart enough to know that a new SQL statement needs to be generated and that now it should execute against the atomic-level table.

THE MICROCUBE ENGINE

The WebIntelligence engine contains tight integration with the universe. One of the main points of integration is the storage of the result set in a multidimensional array commonly called the *microcube* or *microcube engine*. The *cube* part of microcube implies multidimensionality (a cube of data rather than a flat table). The *micro* part of microcube distinguishes it from a macrocube that is a full-fledged multidimensional database (MDDB), such as Essbase, DB/2 OLAP, Oracle OLAP, or MS SQL Server Analysis Services. The microcube is mentioned here in the "Universes and Deployment" section, but is demonstrated in Chapter 20 on the WebIntelligence Reporting engine in the "Drilling" section.

Without understanding the microcube, you cannot fully appreciate how the universe features actually benefit the business user, other than providing a mask for SQL generation. Because the universe knows that the objects are dimensions, details, or measures, these object types can be used to provide for additional methods of post-query processing by the microcube engine. This means the result set that comes back can be processed further simply based on the definition of the result set's originating object type. For example, if a query asks for Year, Quarter, Month, and Actual Expenses, the resultset is returned to the microcube engine, which then further notes that Year, Quarter, and Month are dimensions, and Actual Expenses is a measure. It also notes that Year, Quarter, and Month are part of a dimensional hierarchy that can be drilled, and that the Actual Expenses measure object is defined with a projection that tells it to sum when projected. A *projection* is a behavioral indicator for the measure when placed in the microcube.

When a user displays the data in the report as Year, Quarter, Month, and Actual Expenses columns in a simple table, the user sees a row containing the results just as they were returned from the database. However, if the user removes the Month and Quarter columns from the table, the Actual Expenses value changes dynamically to reflect the value for each year. The measure is "projected at the Year level" because the object definition tells the microcube that it should sum the measure when viewing the measure with any combination of dimensions other than all dimensions returned in the result set.

Additionally, if the user then drills down on Year to the Quarter level, a drill filter is created on Year and the report block displays the quarters and projects the Actual Expenses at the Quarter level. So the drilling capability provides for both proper navigation and projection of dimensions and measures by the microcube.

There are two important things to note here. First, this paradigm is different than Crystal Reports, in which drilling or moving between levels of data requires the creation of sub reports. With the microcube, the table, grid, or chart display of a Web Intelligence report is referred to as a *report block* and there is no concept of bands or banded reporting. What is seen in the report block is the projection of the microcube, which is completely dependent on the objects displayed in the report block. The report often contains more data (additional objects) than are currently projected; generally, the user will use the current projection in the report block as a starting point to navigate through the data. The data dynamically changes as the user interacts with it, drilling up and down or swapping objects into or out of the report block. This might sound terribly confusing but is made clearer in Chapter 20, where more time can be given to this discussion.

Second, the semantic layer does more than query generation—it provides for sophisticated post-query behavioral rules for the reporting engine. It not only tells how to get the data and how to get it with the most optimal SQL, but also how the data should behave after it is presented for analysis to the business user. This is crucial to ensuring that the business user does not manipulate the data in ways which would lead to incorrect results (an overarching theme with the semantic layer).

The microcube also provides for a few additional benefits:

- **Recombining results of multipass SQL**—In certain conditions, such as the one described previously for requesting budget and actual expenses, a question from a business user needs to be broken into multiple queries or multiple passes to the database. The semantic layer automatically generates these multiple SQL statements. When the resultsets are returned, the microcube allows for these multiple passes to be rejoined conceptually into a single resultset that can then be projected for analysis via the microcube. The microcube knows that the dimensions between these two queries are really representations of the same objects and therefore the microcube will synchronize rows with common dimensions, which can then be projected in synchronization. This is done automatically by the Web Intelligence report engine. This also allows for formulas to be built on these measures as if they existed in a single flat table resultset (budget minus actual expenses, for example).

- **Multiple queries**—A Web Intelligence report is the projection of part of the multidimensional array or microcube. The Web Intelligence engine allows for multiple microcubes to exist within a single report file. This means that a report can contain data from multiple universes that could be based on completely different RDBMS platforms.

NOTE

Experienced Business Objects users will note that although Web Intelligence provides for multiple queries to exist within a single report, there is some missing functionality that currently exists in the client-server version of the reporting tool, namely, synchronized resultsets (or synchronized data providers, as a resultset is known as a *data provider* in Business Objects parlance). This capability is extremely powerful and is slotted for the next release of the Web Intelligence engine. This functionality will allow for dimensions from different data providers to be manually linked within the microcube, so that formulas and projection can take place synchronously across these data providers. Note that in the multipass SQL example above, the result set is considered a single data provider by the report engine, even though it is multipass; this is because it originated from a single query panel request. Multiple data providers come from multiple query panel requests (one data provider per request).

UNIVERSES AND DEPLOYMENT

In order for a universe to be utilized by others, it needs to be published as a resource in the CMS. The Designer module will export the universe, meaning it will export the .unv file from the desktop to the CMS, where it is stored in a folder for distribution. From here, other Designers can download the universe or import it to their desktop. Likewise, the BusinessObjects Enterprise infrastructure can access it for use with the Web Intelligence and Crystal Reports reporting engines. The universe is automatically downloaded to the BusinessObjects Enterprise infrastructure when the first user requests usage of the universe. It is cached on the Web Intelligence server to avoid having to retrieve it from the InfoStore for every successive user request.

SEMANTIC LAYER OVERRIDES

After the universe is an InfoObject in the InfoStore, data security overrides can be applied to the semantic layer. The idea behind these overrides is to supply a semantic layer that provides access to the database in general, but can also restrict the access based on user or group profiles. Because the universe is designed for ad-hoc usage, the user should be prevented from asking any questions he should not be able to ask. And because a user's questions cannot be known prior to asking them, the security restrictions need to be applied to the semantic layer for that user. The semantic layer applies these security overrides when appropriate during SQL generation.

The most common semantic layer override is *row restriction*. This is accomplished by forcing WHERE clause usage within the universe. For example, say Joe belongs to the Eastern sales region, and Joe should only be able to see data from his region. Because you cannot predict what queries Joe will ask ahead of time, you want to ensure that any SQL he generates will have a restriction added, limiting him to Eastern region data only. In SQL this might appear as `WHERE Org.Region = 'East'`. With this clause applied, whenever Joe creates an ad-hoc query, he will be limited to only Eastern region data. If you wanted to limit a group of Eastern region users to the same data, you could apply the WHERE clause restriction to a group and place all users within the group, where they would inherit the override.

Other semantic layer overrides are

- **Object hiding**—Restricts users from seeing certain objects (column-level security).
- **Table swapping**—Substitutes one table in the database for one defined within the universe. An example of this would be if a DBA created a restricted view of a fact table (maybe limiting it to only Eastern region data). The DBA wants a certain user, Joe, to use this particular database view in place of the normal fact table as defined in the universe.
- **Connection swapping**—Substitutes a different connection string to a different database. This assumes there are two databases with the exact same table structures as represented in the universe. The different databases exist to segregate data in some way—say, one database contains Eastern region data only.

Note that the same example is used here to illustrate a point. With the exception of object hiding, the other three restrictions perform the same function—limiting the user to a certain set of data. However, DBAs often employ different techniques to achieve this result. Business Objects can handle it one way by applying WHERE clause restrictions. If the DBA decides to use database views to limit the data, table swapping is used to assign the views. If the DBA puts the data in a separate physical database, connection swapping is used. There are additional methods for limiting users to certain records, such as a security lookup table. Security lookup tables, along with other methods, are also accomplished by employing semantic layer overrides. The four mentioned previously are the most common and have been built into the universe for about a decade.

RESTRICTION SETS

Semantic layer overrides are applied via the Designer and are called restriction sets. A *restriction set* contains one or more semantic layer overrides bundled into a single administrative entity. For example, suppose you want to restrict certain objects in a universe, swap a table for a view, add a WHERE clause restriction, and limit the number of rows returned to 50,000. This can all be defined within a single restriction set. The restriction set is then applied to particular users or groups defined via the CMS. In this case, all overrides apply to the users or groups to which they are assigned.

To recap the overrides available for inclusion in a restriction set, see Table 8.2.

TABLE 8.2   OVERRIDES FOR RESTRICTION SETS

Override	Definition
Connection	Changing from the default connectionto an alternate one. A prerequisite here is that both databases contain the tables/views defined in the universe. The assumption is that the data has been segregated in some fashion.
Query controls	There are three controls: number of rows allowed to return, limit of execution time, and limit of long text objects. These do not eliminate the SQL from running; rather, they are designed to protect the report engine from overloading due to bad queries (not to protect the RDBMS from receiving bad SQL).
SQL generation Options	There are five options: allow use of union, minus intersect; multiple SQL statements for each context; multiple SQL statements for each measure; allow selection of multiple contexts; prevent/warn Cartesian products. This control is meant to restrict the generation of poor SQL. It is intended, along with the model design, to protect the database from poor query requests.
Object access	This hides selected objects from the user/group. By default, users can see all objects in a universe unless some restriction is explicitly placed upon the objects.

continues

TABLE 8.2 CONTINUED

Override	Definition
Row access	This limits queries by applying WHERE clauses to the SQL for a particular user/group. This is the most commonly used semantic layer override.
Alternative table access	This replaces a table defined within the universe with a substitute for all queries run by the user/group that use objects calling for this table.

Restriction sets are created by selecting Tools, Edit Security Restrictions and choosing the New button.

Figure 18.5 shows the Edit Restriction Set dialog. The six tabs correspond with the six overrides listed in the preceding table. The Objects tab is highlighted in the figure, showing that the Discount object from the Measures class is restricted and will be hidden from all to whom this restriction set is applied. The restriction set can combine restrictions from all six override types.

Figure 18.5
Designer with Edit Restriction Set dialog open.

After the overrides have been set and the OK button is selected, the restriction set shows up in the list of available restrictions. Clicking OK saves the restriction set.

APPLYING RESTRICTION SETS

To apply the restriction set to a particular user or group, select Tools, Apply Security Restrictions and choose the Select Users/Groups button. This shows the available users/groups as defined via the CMC. The window allows for searches through the InfoStore to aid in managing the list in large deployments.

After the user or group is selected, the user or group is available to apply to a restriction set. This is achieved by clicking on the user or group to highlight it. After it's highlighted, you click on the restriction set drop-down menu, select the restriction set you want to apply, and click on the Apply button.

MULTIPLE RESTRICTION SETS

Because multiple groups can house the same users, it is possible for a user to have more than one restriction set applied to her. If a user belongs to more than one group, the order of restriction sets can be prioritized. Sometimes contrary to expectation, the restriction set with the highest priority number is the dominant one. For example, suppose there are two groups, Sales Management and Sales Field, and both have restrictions limiting row return, with Sales Management limited to 50,000 rows and Sales Field to 20,000 rows. If Sales Management is priority 1 and Sales Field is priority 2, for those users who are in both groups, the priority 2 would apply. (you might think priority 1 would win, but it's the highest number of all restrictions possible). If a user has individual overrides applied through one restriction set and is also a member of a group, the overrides are cumulative. For example, if Joe is limited to the Eastern region only via a WHERE clause restriction and he is in the Sales Field group, he will also be limited to 20,000 rows.

Some restrictions have to be managed by priority because they cannot cumulate, such as connection information (the user must clearly have one and only one connection defined). The other two restrictions that have priority applied are table swapping and query and SQL controls. The other restriction types can accumulate (object access and row access).

CAUTION

It is possible to define a restriction for a user that conflicts with the group. For example, say you define a restriction set for Joe for `Org.Region = 'East'`. You then put Joe in a group called Central, which has a restriction set containing the restriction `Org.region = 'Central'`. In this case, Joe will apply both of these WHERE clauses to the SQL generated. Because there is no row that can be both in the East region and Central region at the same time, Joe will get no results returned. It is best practice to apply overrides at the lowest level possible and to use the Preview Security Restrictions command in the Designer to show the cumulative effect of restrictions on individual users.

18

UNIVERSE CHANGES

Sometimes after a universe is deployed and users begin using it, you might find that an object definition is incorrect and needs to be rectified. Or perhaps you discover the necessity for an aggregate table, create one, and make your universe aggregate aware. Or you find out the DBA made a change to one of your underlying tables and accidentally renamed some of your column names. You corrected the universe, and want all of your users to start using the new version.

However, you have many users who have developed reports (either Web Intelligence or Crystal) off of the universe currently in use. You know the SQL statements they are using are either not optimal or incorrect. How do you get all the existing reports updated with the new semantic definitions?

This capability is built in to the BusinessObjects Enterprise framework. When a new universe is placed in the InfoStore to replace the existing one, the report engines will detect that a newer version of the semantic layer exists, and will fetch it from the InfoStore. It will then be used to dynamically regenerate the SQL statements at execution time. The reports pick up the new object definitions and new SQL, if applicable. It will be done automatically the next time the report is run. So if a user pulls a report out of his Favorites and executes it, the SQL will automatically regenerate with the new universe object definitions. If a user had a report scheduled for refresh every week, the report would generate new SQL at the next scheduled refresh. This holds true for both Crystal and Web Intelligence reports.

In version 10 of Crystal Reports, with the Business Objects Crystal Integration Pack, the universe could be used to generate SQL for Crystal Reports, but it would not dynamically update as the universe changed. However, in BusinessObjects XI, Crystal Reports will regenerate SQL when the universe changes. This is an important change to note.

The reason the SQL should regenerate is simple—security. Users often move from department to department or are promoted to a new job which might have less restrictive data access. After the appropriate semantic layer overrides have been made, all reports used by that user will pick up the new restrictions automatically. It's just part of a Business Intelligence system.

Any instances the user might have run historically will have results based on the old semantic layer overrides. After the SQL is executed, the data retrieved, and the document stored as a report instance, the data is static. Changes to the semantic layer will not rerun historical instances. You can see why this would be impossible given the fact that the underlying data is changing constantly. Therefore, semantic layer changes will modify any SQL generated from the point in time that the new universe is in the CMS—until the next semantic layer change, of course.

DIFFERENCES IN HOW CR/WEBI USE UNIVERSES

Because both Crystal Reports and Web Intelligence can use universes, this discussion of the differences begins by restating what is the same:

- Both report engines utilize the universe to generate SQL.
- Both report engines update their SQL when newer universes are available.
- Both report engines take advantage of semantic layer overrides.
- Both report engines can have multiple resultsets generated from multiple query panel requests.

The main difference between the Crystal and Web Intelligence report engines' use of the universe is the existence of the microcube engine in Web Intelligence. Because Crystal Reports does not have a microcube engine and uses a fundamentally different reporting paradigm, some SQL generated via the universe and accommodated by Web Intelligence will not be accommodated by Crystal Reports. For example, any single query panel request that requires multipass SQL will not be accommodated. This is because there is no microcube to reassemble the multiple resultsets into a single entity (data provider).

TIP

> Again, you cannot overlook the tie between the data model and the expected usage. If you have a complex report with little to no interactivity that needs to be built off of a transactional model, this might be a better use for Crystal Reports without a universe. If you have a fairly decent data model that could possibly be used for analysis (even though reporting requirements don't currently state it), you can use either tool to write the report—either Crystal Reports with or without the universe, or Web Intelligence with the universe. If you want a high level of user interactivity with the report (drilling, sorting, filtering, object swapping, and so forth), use Web Intelligence. If you want ad-hoc reporting with great performance, the ability to ask sophisticated questions, and a high level of interactivity, but do not have an appropriate model, no reporting tool can help you—you must model the data to meet the reporting requirements.

DIFFERENCES WITH BUSINESS VIEWS AND UNIVERSES

The major differences between business views and universes are

- **Multiple data sources versus single data source**—A business view can have multiple data sources defined within it; a universe has one and only one connection. Although a universe connection can be dynamic, the universe itself can point to only one data source at a time.

- **Reuse of business elements**—In business views, the business elements (which are roughly equivalent to the object classes) are reusable within other business views. Although object classes are not reusable, there is a similar functionality with universes in that universes can be linked. This means that a universe can embed another universe within it. The inheriting universe assumes all tables and object definitions, and new joins will need to be drawn to integrate those tables with the existing ones in the inheriting universe. However, the inherited universe and inheriting universe still assume a single connection, meaning all tables exist within a single RDBMS.

- **Report variables as objects**—In business views, you can define an element that will not reflect a SQL snippet, but might be a formula composed of two or more elements that are SQL snippets. For example, there could be a revenue element which points to a column in a database, and a costs element which also points to a column in the database. From these two elements, there could exist a third element called margin, defined as revenue – cost. When the margin element is chosen, the business view understands that the revenue and cost elements must be selected, and the formula executes within the Crystal Reports engine after the data is returned. In a universe, all objects are SQL snippets; you cannot place what is effectively a report variable in the universe.

18

TROUBLESHOOTING

SCHEDULED PARAMETER LIST OF VALUES NOT SHOWING UP

I updated scheduled prompts in my business view but I don't see the list of values in my Crystal Report. I get the old list of values.

In most cases, the user needs to open the report and change the parameters from the static values to the new scheduled list in a business view.

NO REPOSITORY SAMPLES

How do I install the Repository samples?

From the tools menu in the Business View Manager, select Install Repository Samples.

CHAPTER 19

CREATING OLAP INTELLIGENCE REPORTS

In this chapter

INTRODUCTION

The concept of OLAP was introduced in Chapter 16, "Formatting Multidimensional Reporting Against OLAP Data." With OLAP it is relatively easy to create professionally formatted Crystal Reports based on multidimensional data sources. These types of formatted reports are targeted for end users who require only one specific viewpoint into the OLAP Data. OLAP Intelligence provides a more interactive end-user environment with the reports so that speed of thought interactive viewing is available to end users. This chapter introduces OLAP Intelligence and the richness of interactivity it can add to your reporting environment.

One of the key challenges facing organizations today is providing actionable information to business managers, enabling them to make decisions in a timely manner based on concrete data. This chapter shows how OLAP Intelligence can be used to deliver compelling analytical reports to end users.

This chapter covers the following information:

- Introduction to OLAP Intelligence
- Data connectivity options for OLAP Intelligence
- Introduction to the powerful Worksheet object
- Introduction to the Charting object

INTRODUCING OLAP INTELLIGENCE

OLAP Intelligence is another type of reporting tool provided by Business Objects that enables organizations to deliver action-based analysis to end users. More than the flattened views of OLAP and multidimensional data sources that Crystal Reports provides, it offers a rich, interactive interface that facilitates the discovery of business insights and helps decision-makers affect business performance at the speed of thought. The two primary groups of end users for such reports would be Power Users and General Information Consumers.

Power Users can create *analytic reports* (often called applications) based on OLAP data, using the powerful thick-client designer OLAP Intelligence. These reports or applications (which will be called reports from here on) can contain many pages, each representative of a different predefined view of the underlying data source. Data can be presented in tables or through a wide range of charts, as shown in Figure 19.1.

General Information Consumers can also leverage the powerful multidimensional functionality of OLAP Intelligence by taking advantage of the guided analytics provided in the product. These single-click analytic buttons used in combination with the other compelling presentation features (such as exception highlighting, sorting and filtering, and drop-down boxes) enable you to provide multidimensional analysis to less sophisticated users. Business managers can use the resulting analytic reports to inform the daily decisions they need to make with less technical skill required.

Figure 19.1
Design an analytic report with OLAP Intelligence.

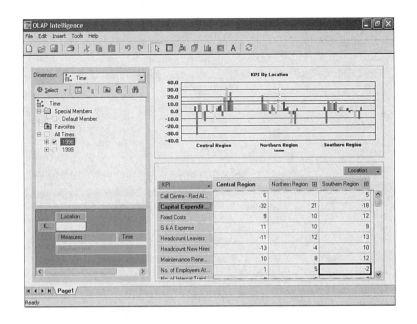

Analytic reports can be delivered to users in two ways: either through distribution of the OLAP Intelligence file (.car extension) to users with the thick-client application installed, or, more popularly, through a Web browser by using BusinessObjects Enterprise. The reports in BusinessObjects Enterprise can be viewed using either Dynamic HTML (DHTML) (see Figure 19.2) or ActiveX. Both viewers are fully functional and provide all the analytic capabilities of the desktop tool in a Web browser.

Figure 19.2
An analytic report viewed using the DHTML Viewer of BusinessObjects Enterprise.

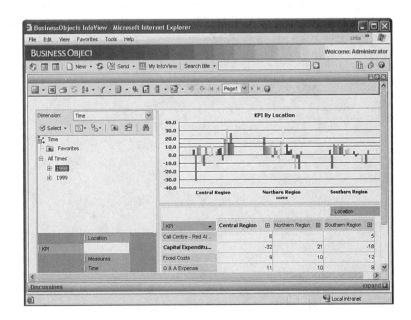

19

OLAP Intelligence is suitable for a wide range of analytic business requirements, including sales and marketing analysis, financial reporting and analysis, key performance indicator reporting, supplier performance and billing analysis, click-stream analysis, and HR analysis. When combined with BusinessObjects Enterprise in providing Web Analytic solutions, OLAP Intelligence is also suitable for delivering analytic reports and applications to both employees inside an organization and to those outside—customers, suppliers, and business partners.

NOTE

> Before using OLAP Intelligence it is necessary to have OLAP cubes created. The OLAP cubes supported include
>
> - Microsoft SQL Server 2000 Analysis Services SP3 and SQL Server OLAP Services 7.0.3
> - DB2 OLAP 8.1 and 7.1
> - Essbase 6.5.4 and 7.0
> - SAP BW 3.1 and 3.5
>
> The most recently supported OLAP servers can be accessed from the `platform.txt` file that come with your Business Objects software.

ACCESSING OLAP DATA WITH OLAP INTELLIGENCE

After starting OLAP Intelligence through the Application Designer option on the Start Programs OLAP Intelligence menu, you can create new Crystal applications by choosing File, New. Similar to Crystal Reports, OLAP Intelligence provides a set of application templates and wizards as potential starting points in addition to the option of starting from a blank application (see Figure 19.3). This chapter focuses on the manual process of creating analytic applications from the ground up but you are encouraged to review the application templates and their associated wizards to determine if a fit exists.

Figure 19.3
You can select a template in the New Application dialog.

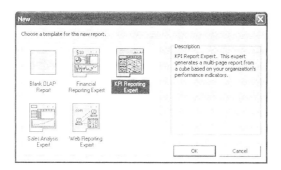

After you select the Blank Application option, OLAP Intelligence prompts you with the OLAP Connection Browser shown in Figure 19.4. This is the equivalent of the Data Explorer in Crystal Reports and enables the user to select an OLAP data source on which to base the report.

Figure 19.4
The OLAP Connection Browser enables data source specification.

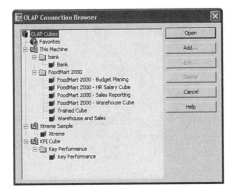

From the OLAP Connection Browser window, you can add new OLAP servers to the tree using the Add Server button. This then displays the New Server dialog shown in Figure 19.5. There are several ways to connect to a cube, all of which can be defined through this dialog.

Figure 19.5
Add an OLAP server connection to the Crystal OLAP Connection Browser.

CREATING AN OLAP SERVER DATA SOURCE

After you select the Add Server button, the New Server dialog appears. The first option in this window is OLAP Server, which defines a regular client/server connection to the OLAP Server and does not change across the different versions of supported cubes. This is the most common type of connection and is compatible with thin-client delivery when BusinessObjects Enterprise and the OLAP Database Server are on the same side of the firewall.

Figure 19.5 shows this type of server being defined in the New Server dialog for a SQL Server Analysis Services cube. Select Microsoft OLE DB driver for OLAP Services as the

Server Type, and then type the server name into the Server Name box and ensure the caption is appropriately filled in. The caption can be changed to give the server a more descriptive name.

ADDING LOCAL CUBE (.cub) FILES AS DATA SOURCES

SQL Server Analysis Services enables a user to create an offline cube file containing a subset of the data held in SQL Server. These cubes can be accessed using OLAP Intelligence when the user is away from the network—for example, when traveling with a laptop. Figure 19.6 shows a .cub file being selected in the New Server dialog. The Browse button (ellipses) enables users to navigate through their directories to locate the .cub file. A caption has been defined to make the entry in the OLAP Connection Browser more readable.

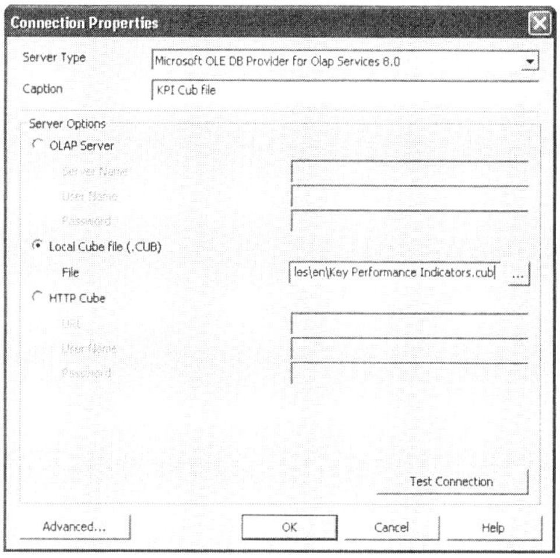

Figure 19.6
Add a .cub file through the OLAP Connection Browser to serve as your data source.

ADDING HTTP CUBES DATA SOURCES

HTTP cubes, which are sometimes called *iCubes*, enable the transport between PTS and Microsoft SQL Server to be tunneled through HTTP, allowing connections through firewalls and proxy servers. Figure 19.7 shows an HTTP connection selected in the New Server dialog. To establish a valid connection to an HTTP Cube server you must specify the full URL, including the http or https prefix. A username and password can optionally be specified. For HTTP cubes, the server checks the authentication of the user who requests the connection. If the password or username is incorrect or blank, the server defines how an anonymous user is logged on.

HTTP cubes were introduced in Microsoft SQL Server 2000 and require Microsoft Internet Information Server (IIS) to be used as the Web server. For more information, see Microsoft's documentation for Analysis Services, which is available either as part of your Microsoft OLAP installation or on the MSDN website at http://msdn.microsoft.com/library/.

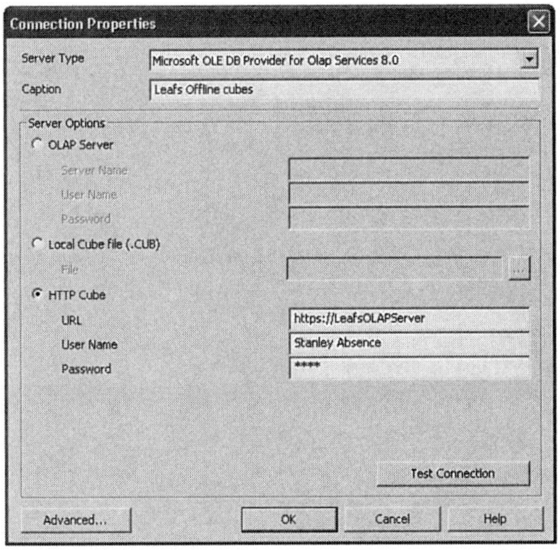

Figure 19.7
Add an HTTP cube server through the OLAP Connection Browser to serve as your data source.

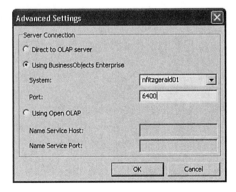

ADVANCED DATA SOURCE CONNECTIVITY

On the New Server dialog, an Advanced Data Source connectivity button is presented that enables you to specify a connection type. Figure 19.8 shows the Advanced Settings dialog, which provides three different options for connectivity to cubes. The Direct to OLAP Server option is almost exclusively used at this time, but the other two forms of connectivity are used currently for connectivity to legacy Holos cubes.

> **NOTE**
> If you need more information on this type of legacy connectivity, please consult your OLAP Intelligence and Holos help files.

19

Figure 19.8
The Advanced Settings are almost exclusively set to Direct to OLAP Server.

FAVORITE CUBES

Favorite cubes are a feature of OLAP Intelligence that enables users to create shortcuts to frequently used cubes. You create shortcuts by simply dragging a cube into the Favorites folder from within the OLAP Connection Browser window (see Figure 19.9). Once defined, a shortcut can be renamed if required.

Figure 19.9
Create a shortcut to a favorite cube.

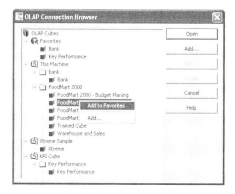

DESIGNING OLAP INTELLIGENCE REPORTS AND APPLICATIONS

This section describes how OLAP Intelligence can create compelling analytic reports that enable users to extract valuable insights from their data. It shows how the Guided Analytic techniques provided by OLAP Intelligence can be used to identify and prioritize problems, and ultimately extract actionable information and value from the underlying OLAP data.

> The examples in this section use OLAP Intelligence version XI and the Key Performance Indicators cube from the provided samples collection. The sample cubes are located in the Samples subdirectory on the OLAP Intelligence CD-ROM: `C:\Program Files\ Business Objects\OLAP Intelligence 11\Samples\en\*.cub`. You might need to look in the appropriate language subdirectory under which you installed the product (for example, *en* for English).

DESIGN ENVIRONMENT OVERVIEW

Think of the OLAP Intelligence Design Environment as a painter's canvas. The Report Designer uses this canvas and a palette of available analytic objects to create an analytic report (often called an analytic application). The point-and-click, free-form designer environment for creating the analytic reports is ultimately flexible and the power of the available analytic objects is impressive. Figure 19.10 shows the major features of the OLAP Intelligence designer.

At the top of the window is a toolbar divided into the following three sections:

- File manipulation tools including New, Open, Save, and Print
- Editing tools including Cut, Copy, Paste, Undo, and Redo

- Object manipulation tools including a Selection tool, Worksheet, Chart, Dimension Explorer, Slice Navigator, Analysis Button, and Text Label

Figure 19.10
The OLAP Intelligence designer components provide unique report creation capabilities.

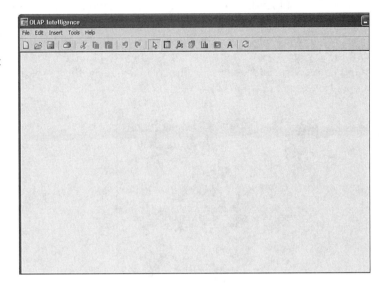

At the bottom of the designer window, there is also a group of controls for managing the pages in the OLAP Intelligence report in much the same way that you would in Excel.

CONNECTING TO AN OLAP CUBE

Whether using an expert or creating a blank report, the first step is to connect to a cube. The cube is selected using the OLAP Connection Browser dialog, shown in Figure 19.11.

Figure 9.11
Select the OLAP server and Key Performance Indicators cube.

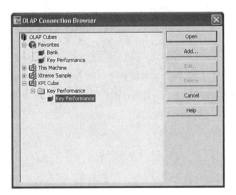

→ For more information on adding cube servers, see the section, **see** "Accessing OLAP Data with OLAP Intelligence," **p. 422**.

19

ADDING PAGES

The design paradigm of OLAP Intelligence is similar to that of an Excel workbook with respect to pages. A OLAP Intelligence report or application can contain multiple pages and each page can provide an entirely unique viewpoint on the same underlying data source. New pages are added to the report by either choosing Insert, Page Menu or right-clicking on any existing Page tab and then accessing the Insert option. A New Page template dialog, shown in Figure 19.12, enables pages to be created quickly. If none of the page templates are suitable, a blank page can be inserted.

Figure 19.12
Use templates to
create pages quickly.

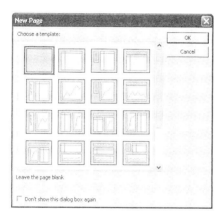

If the New Page template dialog is not displayed when pages are inserted, it can be re-enabled through the Tools, Options menu.

New pages are automatically inserted at the end of the report and named Page 1, Page 2, and so on. A page can be renamed by right-clicking its tab and selecting Rename from the menu. You can change the order of the pages by dragging the tabs to a specific destination or by right-clicking and choosing Move or Copy. Creating analytic reports with multiple pages provides the power of a custom application because it provides varying perspectives of the cube and facilitates guided navigation between them. This guided navigation is explored in the next chapter.

ADDING OLAP INTELLIGENCE OBJECTS TO A REPORT

After a page has been added to the report, individual analytic objects can be added, deleted, and manipulated on those pages to create meaningful report and application content. All the analytic components can be added by using either the Insert menu or any of the toolbar icons previously shown in Figure 19.10. After you select the component, the mouse pointer turns into a cross-hairs pointer. You specify the size and placement of the selected object by locking in one corner of the object with a mouse click and then holding that click while dragging the mouse to the desired opposite diagonal corner. Each of the analytic components, including Worksheets, Charts, Dimension Explorers, Slice Navigators, Transition Buttons, and Text Boxes, is described in detail later in this chapter.

While in Design mode, the currently selected object is indicated by a hatched border and object selection handles, as shown in Figure 19.13.

Figure 19.13
A hatched border shows which object is currently selected.

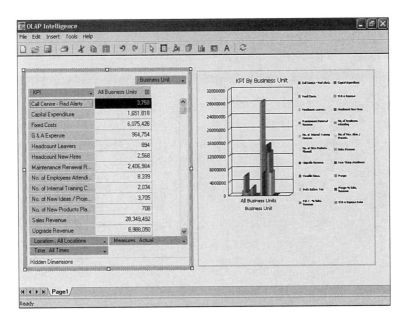

In Design mode, the currently selected object is the only active object and the only object that responds to mouse clicks. To change the active object, simply click a different object until it receives focus as indicated by the hatched border.

NOTE

> The Lock option in the Tools menu prevents users from moving, adding, or deleting report objects. This is useful for finished reports because all the objects become simultaneously active, making the report much more intuitive to use. A locked report can optionally be protected with a password that subsequently must be typed in before the application can be unlocked.

MOVING, RESIZING, AND FORMATTING OBJECTS

After the report objects have been placed on a page, OLAP Intelligence allows a significant amount of freedom in defining the appearance, placement, and formatting of the objects. The appearance and formatting properties belonging to any object can be retrieved and edited by right-clicking on the hatched border of any active object. The formatting details of each object are described in the followed sections. Objects can be moved within a page using the mouse to drag the hatched border. As the mouse is moved over the border the cursor indicates when dragging is possible.

> When dragging objects, the designer snaps the objects to a grid for easier alignment. Using the cursor keys in conjunction with the Ctrl key enables finer adjustments to be made.

Objects can be resized by dragging the select handles on each corner and on each side of its hatched border.

WORKSHEET OBJECTS AND WORKSHEET DIMENSIONS

The most common object and the one that forms the core of most OLAP Intelligence reports is the worksheet. Similar in appearance to a Microsoft Excel worksheet, this analytic object provides two key benefits to OLAP Intelligence users:

- A numeric-based view into the underlying multidimensional/OLAP data for end-user consumption

- A set of dynamic and interactive tools that enable powerful analysis and exploration into the same data

Figure 19.14 highlights the Worksheet object and the key dimension categories. All the row, column, and slice dimensions can be changed, swapped, or nested by simply dragging and dropping them into the different sections of the worksheet or by right-clicking on any of the dimension toolbars and accessing the various swapping and nesting options.

Figure 19.14
Row, column, slice, and hidden dimensions in a worksheet provide a multidimensional paradigm for viewing OLAP data and reports.

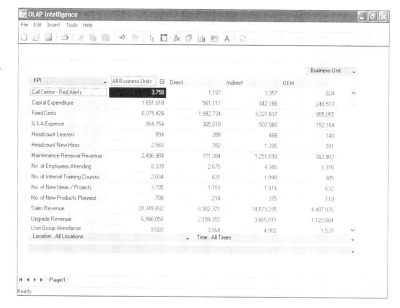

NOTE

> A chart on the same page as a worksheet always reflects the current column, row, and sliced dimension settings and dynamically changes as the worksheet does. Also note that although you can have two or more worksheets on the same page, they always provide the exact same viewpoint and changes in one are always immediately reflected in the others.

As mentioned previously, a worksheet can display several row and column dimensions at once. This technique highlighted in Figure 19.15 is often referred to as the nesting of dimensions and enables multiple dimensions to be displayed in the row or column positions.

Figure 19.15
A page showing two dimensions, Time and Measures, nested in the columns.

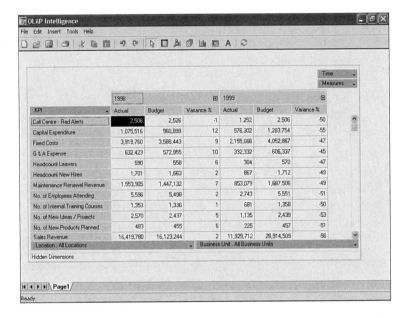

Sliced dimensions can be set to two different states—active and hidden—by accessing their right-click context menu and the Dimension State menu option. When active, the sliced dimension is available for manipulation by the end user. When hidden, the report consumer sees neither the dimension nor its default value. The default value for a hidden dimension is set identically to that of an active dimension—through the use of the member selector. The member selector is introduced later in this chapter.

SETTING WORKSHEET PROPERTIES

The Properties dialog of the worksheet object shown in Figure 19.16 provides the Report Designer with the capability to selectively turn off some of the powerful functionality within the Worksheet for a specific report. The worksheet properties are displayed by right-clicking on the hatched border and choosing Properties from the menu.

For a complete listing of the worksheet properties, see the Worksheet properties table later in this section.

The Worksheet
Properties dialog
enables you to toggle
end-user features of
the worksheet.

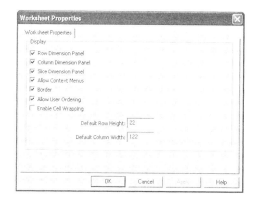

Table 19.1 provides an overview of each of the Worksheet properties and a use case scenario for enabling and disabling the specified property.

TABLE 19.1   WORKSHEET PROPERTIES AND USE CASE SCENARIOS

Worksheet Property	Description	Usage Case Information
Row Dimension Panel	Toggles the Row Dimension title bars and access to their Member Selector dialogs.	This would be turned off if you wanted to provide a fixed list of members in the row dimension and not enable end users to edit those interactively. Turning this off also restricts the end user from swapping the row dimension with any of the other sliced or column dimensions through the drag-and-drop interface—they still might have access to this if the Context menus are toggled on.
Column Dimension Panel	Toggles the Column Dimension title bars and access to their Member Selector dialogs.	This would be turned off if you wanted to provide a fixed list of members in the column dimension and not enable end users to edit those interactively. Turning this off also restricts the end user from swapping the column dimension with any of the other sliced or row dimensions through the drag-and-drop interface; users still might have access to this if the Context menus are toggled on.
Slice Dimension Panel	Toggles the Sliced Dimension title bars and access to their Member Selector dialogs.	This would be turned off if you wanted to provide a fixed set of row and column dimensions and not enable end users to edit those interactively. Turning this off also restricts the end user from swapping the column and row dimensions with any of the

Worksheet Property	Description	Usage Case Information
		other sliced through the drag-and-drop interface, although the end user still might have access to this if the Context menus are toggled on. Also note that individual sliced dimensions can be hidden without turning off the entire Slice Dimension Panel.
Allow Context Menus	Toggles the right-click menu option on the Worksheet for end users. Access to a multitude of dimension-, member-, and cell-related functionality can be accessed through the right-click menus.	This would be turned off if the end user were not intended to access the variety of dimension-, member-, and cell-related functionality. Details of this functionality are covered later in this chapter but include dimension swapping, member selection, filtering, sorting, calculations, and so on. One important note here is that the menus are either on or off; there is unfortunately no means (yet) to restrict access to a subset of the context menu items.
Border	Toggles the display of a border on the worksheet object.	This is left to the report designer's discretion.
Allow User Ordering	Toggles the capability of the report user to swap, nest, and move dimensions.	This would be turned off if you wanted to present a fixed view of the data and do not want the user to be able to interactively edit that. It is important to note that although this sounds similar to the Reorder Dimension Members menu option on the row and column members context menus, it is not related. The Reorder Dimension Members is introduced and discussed later in this chapter.
Enable Cell Wrapping	Toggles cell wrapping in individual cells.	This is left to the report designer's discretion.
Default Row Heights and Column Widths	Sets the global default for column heights and row widths.	Report Designer Preference and the Global settings can be overwritten by dragging and dropping the individual member cell borders.

CHOOSING MEMBERS TO DISPLAY

Worksheet objects enable you to navigate through dimensions by expanding (drilling down) or collapsing (drilling up) through the dimension hierarchies. Any member name with a + displayed next to it can be expanded, whereas those member names with a – displayed can be collapsed. You can enact both traditional drill-down and drill-up functions by clicking on the

+ or – sign. Alternatively, these forms of traditional drill-down in addition to variant forms called Focused Drill-down and Focused Drill-up are available when you right-click any drillable dimension member. Figure 19.17 shows the Drill menu available through the right-click context menu, and Table 19.2 describes four quick examples of the different drilling functions.

Focused Drill-down is different than standard drill-down because it displays only the children of the member drilled on instead of the children and the already displayed members. To access Focused Drill-down, you can simply double-click any drillable dimension member. To drill back up, however, you need to use the right-click context menus.

Figure 19.17
The Drill context menu provides access to the different types of end-user drilling.

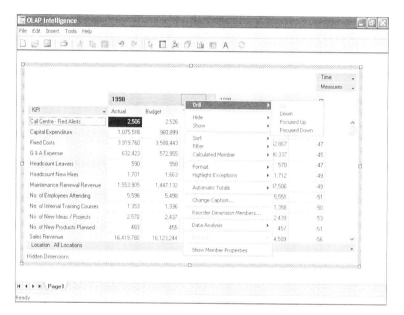

TABLE 19.2   BEFORE AND AFTER DRILLING SCENARIOS

Type of Drill	Sample Time Dimension Before Drill on Quarter 1 Member	Sample Time Dimension After Drill on Quarter 1 Member

Drill down through context menu or clicking on the + icon for the Quarter 1 member	All Times –
	 2003 –
	   Quarter 1 +
	   Quarter 2 +
	   Quarter 3 +
	   Quarter 4 +
	 2004 +
		All Times –
		 2003 –
		   Quarter 1 –
		     January
		     February
		     March
		   Quarter 2 +
		   Quarter 3 +
		   Quarter 4 +
		 2004 +

Type of Drill	Sample Time Dimension Before Drill on Quarter 1 Member	Sample Time Dimension After Drill on Quarter 1 Member
Focused drill down through context menu or double-clicking on the Quarter 1 member name	All Times - 2003 - Quarter 1 + Quarter 2 + Quarter 3 + Quarter 4 + 2004 +	January February March
Drill-up through context menu or through the – icon on the Quarter 1 Parent—2003	All Times - 2003 - Quarter 1 + Quarter 2 + Quarter 3 + Quarter 4 + 2004 +	All Times – 2003 + 2004 +
Focused Drill-up on the Quarter 1 member through the context menu only	All Times - 2003 - Quarter 1 + Quarter 2 + Quarter 3 + Quarter 4 + 2004 +	All Times - 2003 + 2004 +

The member selector is another powerful and flexible means to choose members to display. A member selector can be invoked for any dimension through the downward pointing triangle displayed on the dimension heading, as shown in Figure 19.18. Check boxes are presented next to each member, and selection edits are reflected in real time on the page as members are selected or deselected.

Figure 19.18
The member selector provides the end user with the capability to select members of the involved dimension.

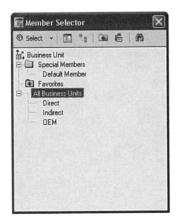

The member selector enables end users to find the data of greatest relevance to them expeditiously. Two of the most useful tools in the Member Selector dialog are the Select menu and the Search tool. Both of these tools (along with a few others) are accessible through icons on the Member Selector toolbar. The Select menu, shown in Figure 19.19, provides a number of shortcuts that facilitate quick and efficient member selection. This shortcut menu is also accessible from each member displayed within the member selector.

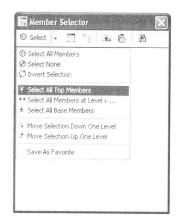

Figure 19.19
The member selector's Select drop-down box provides shortcuts for adding displayed members.

The Search Wizard, shown in Figure 19.20 and accessed through the binoculars icon, provides both standard and advanced filtering mechanisms to enable report users to productively search through a dimension with a large number of members. Because it is not uncommon in industry today to have dimensions (such as Product or Employee) that have thousands or tens of thousands (or many more) of members contained within them, this search mechanism enables you to find sought-after members efficiently. Figure 19.20 depicts a search for KPIs within a KPI dimension that contains the text Sales. After a search has been completed, you can add the entire search result list or a subset of it to the existing member selection or you can completely replace it.

When using the Member Selector Search dialog, you can use the * wildcard to find member names or captions quickly that contain a certain word. For example, typing *Sales* produces all KPIs that contain the word sales, and typing *Coffee* produces all products that contain the word coffee.

If a dimension has multiple hierarchies defined in the underlying data source, the Select Hierarchy button on the Member Selector toolbar is enabled. This enables you to choose the active hierarchy to be displayed.

Figure 19.20
Search the KPI
Dimension for members containing the word Sales.

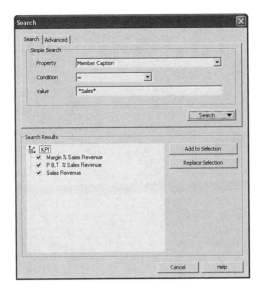

Asymmetrical Member Selection and Display

OLAP Intelligence supplies an out-of-the box method to provide asymmetrical dimension member views. An asymmetrical viewpoint is one where different members of a nested dimension can be displayed for each parent member. By default, when a dimension is nested as shown in Figure 19.21, the nested members are symmetrical in display—that is, whatever members are selected for the nested dimension are displayed for all parent dimension members. Figure 19.22 shows a sample asymmetrical viewpoint that can be created through the right-click context menu Hide and Show commands on the member fields.

19

Figure 19.21
Symmetrical reporting viewpoint–the default display shows all nested members for each parent dimension member.

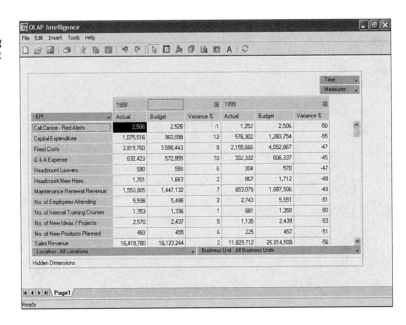

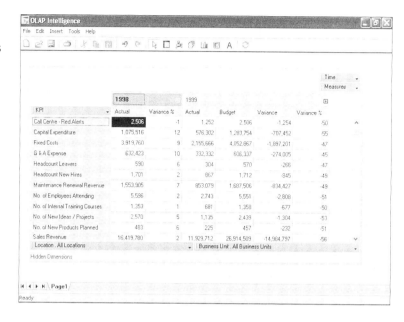

Figure 19.22
Asymmetrical reporting viewpoint enables varied and specific selection of nested members for each parent dimension.

Table 19.3 reviews the commands associated with setting up and removing asymmetrical viewpoints.

TABLE 19.3   ASYMMETRICAL ACTIONS AND DESCRIPTIONS

Right-Click Action	Description
Hide Selected Member	Removes the selected member from the current view. This is different than deselecting a member in the Member Selector—that removes all instances of a member from the view.
Hide All Occurrences	Hides all instances of a member from the current viewpoint. This is identical to clearing a member in the Member Selector.
Show Selected Member	Shows the selected member and hides all other instances of that member.
Show All Occurrences	Shows all instances of a member in the current viewpoint, and hides all other members. This restores symmetry to the view and displays any hidden instances, but also hides all other members on the dimension.

CHANGING THE DISPLAY ORDER OF MEMBERS

By default, members are displayed in a worksheet in the natural dimension order—the order in which they are returned by the OLAP server. Because this might not always be preferred, the shortcut menu for any row or column dimension member contains the option Reorder Dimension Members. Selecting this option displays a dialog where the order of the dimension members can be changed through drag-and-drop operations or using the up and down arrow buttons within the dialog.

NOTE

The chosen order is lost if a drill-down or drill-up operation is performed on the dimension. This feature is best suited to flat dimensions, such as measures, where the display order tends to be more critical.

NUMBER FORMATTING

You can apply number formatting to individual rows and columns by choosing Format, Add from a dimension member's right-click context menu. This displays the Format dialog, shown in Figure 19.23.

Figure 19.23
Change the display format of data for a selected member.

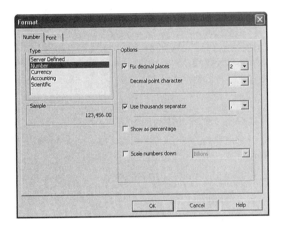

Once added, formats can be edited and removed through the right-click context menu.

CHANGING THE DISPLAYED CAPTION FOR A MEMBER

By default, each member is displayed using the name defined for it on the OLAP server. In some cases a different name might be required. OLAP Intelligence enables you to change the caption by right-clicking on a member and choosing Change Caption from the menu.

AUTOMATIC TOTALS

The worksheet can generate a sum calculation for either the rows, columns, or both directions simultaneously, and automatically update it as the worksheet changes. This is useful when an arbitrary selection of members is made, such as a group of products. Figure 19.24 shows the sum of profit margin for the different store locations and for a number of time periods, with the calculation labeled Total on the worksheet.

19

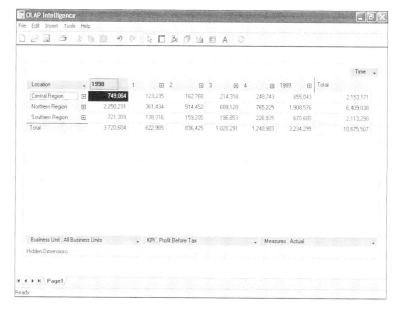

The shortcut menu (right-click menu) of any row or column dimension member in the worksheet controls the display of the automatic totals.

The behavior of the total calculations changes when a filter is added to the column dimension. In Figure 19.25 a Top 3 filter has been added to sales, so the worksheet is now showing just the top three locations. The automatic totals now display the following:

- The sum of the displayed members
- The sum of the members that have been filtered out
- The total of all members considered by the filter

USING CALCULATED MEMBERS AND DATA ANALYSIS

Additional calculations and data analytics not provided in a report's underlying data source can be added to the data presented in the worksheet through the Calculations and Data Analysis menu options accessible through the right-click context menu on any member title. The Calculated Members dialog provides a number of the most common examples and includes shortcuts for contribution, variance, ratio, and growth calculations. Additional shortcuts are provided under the Data Analysis tab on the same Calculated Members dialog and include Linear Regression, Trend Lines, and Moving Averages. To add a calculation or data analytic in OLAP Intelligence, right-click on a member or a dimension name, and then choose the Calculated Member menu item. This opens the Calculated Members dialog shown in Figure 19.26.

Figure 19.25
Automatic totals with a filter applied display numerous pieces of valuable summary information.

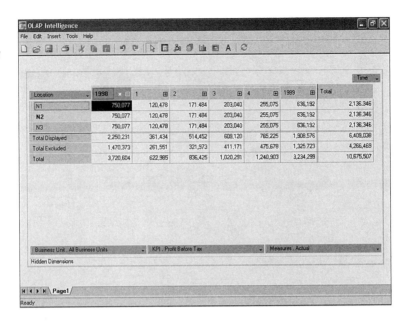

Figure 19.26
The Calculated Members dialog enables creation of advanced members not found in the underlying OLAP data source.

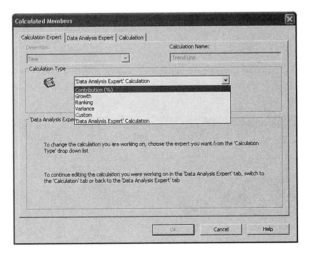

In addition to the Calculation Experts highlighted in Figure 19.26, OLAP Intelligence also enables you to create custom calculations that can leverage a rich set of Multi-Dimensional Expressions (MDX) on SQL Server Analysis Services cubes or Crystal OLAP Syntax on other data sources. The experts and the advanced calculation functionality are covered in more detail later in this chapter.

SORTING AND FILTERING

You can sort and filter reports to isolate important information. These functions help you answer questions such as "What are my top five variances?" and "Which products have the highest sales growth?"

Sorts can be applied to any row or column simply by right-clicking on its heading and using the Sort submenu items, shown in Figure 19.27.

Figure 19.27
The worksheet Sort menu enables the end user to sort the report's data.

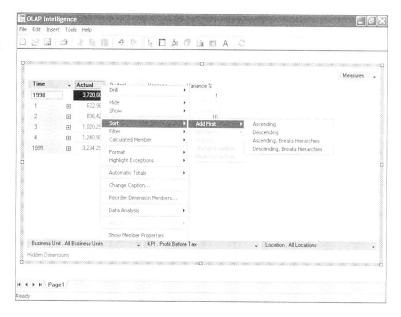

Adding an ascending sort to the variance % column highlights the poorest performing time periods for a given KPI by moving them to the top of the worksheet (see Figure 19.28).

Figure 19.28
You can sort the variances or any member in the worksheet.

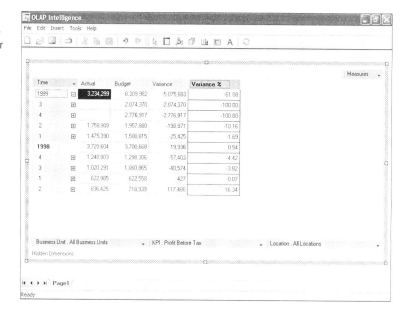

A sort is indicated by an arrow displayed next to a member name. The arrow points up to indicate an ascending sort and down to show a descending sort. Clicking on the arrow changes the direction of the sort.

By default, a sort respects any dimension hierarchies; that is, the members are sorted within their hierarchical groupings. This behavior is changed through the Sort menu and the result of changing the sort to a "breaks hierarchies" sort is shown in Figure 19.29. The hierarchical relationship between All Time and its children has been broken, and it now appears as the second row.

Figure 19.29
Use the Break Hierarchies option to change the order in which the sorted values are displayed.

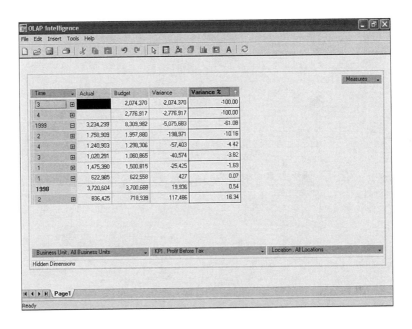

NOTE

Sorts can be nested up to three deep. To add further sorts use the Add Next option in the Sort menu. Nested sorts are indicated by a 1, 2, or 3 displayed next to the sort arrow.

Filters can be applied to any row or column, and also can be applied to the whole worksheet. Filtering the whole worksheet enables null rows and columns to be removed. Access this by right-clicking in the blank area at the top-left corner of the worksheet above the row dimension title and selecting from the resulting menu list, as shown in Figure 19.30. This is a common requirement when using sparsely populated OLAP cubes.

Filtering a specific row or column can be used to pick out the important information in a report. Figure 19.31 shows a filter being added to the variance column, with the aim of isolating time periods with variances less than negative 5.

Figure 19.30

Applying a filter to the
whole worksheet,
removing null rows
and columns.

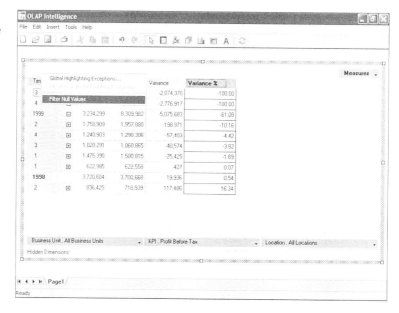

Figure 19.30

Applying a filter to the
whole worksheet,
removing null rows
and columns.

Figure 19.31

Apply a filter to a col-
umn in the worksheet.

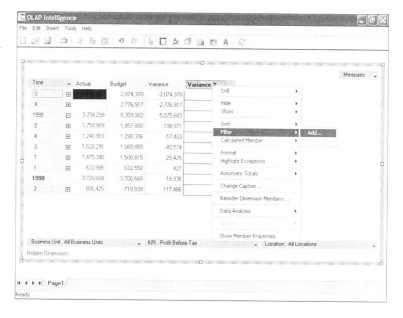

The Define Filter dialog enables the type of filter to be set or changed. In this example the
filter shows variances that are less than zero. These settings appear in Figure 19.32, and the
results are shown in Figure 19.33.

An x displayed in the Variance column heading indicates the presence of a filter. The
filter can be edited by clicking on the x icon.

Figure 19.32
Apply a filter to show only those variances less than 0%.

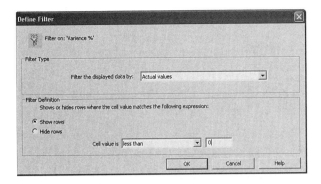

Figure 19.33
A filtered worksheet provides increasingly focused report data for end users.

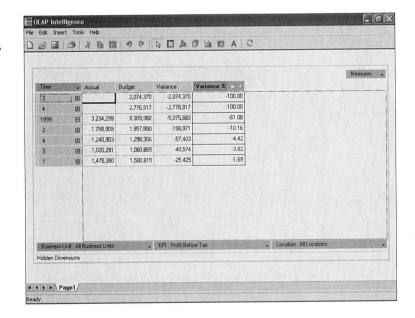

In this example the filter was applied based on the displayed data values. Other types of filters are available from this dialog:

- **Top/Bottom n**—Used to highlight exceptionally good or bad performance; for example, the top or bottom 10 selling products.

- **Top/Bottom n%**—Used to answer questions such as "Which products contribute the top 5% of sales?" and "Which stores contribute the bottom 5% of margin?"

> **TIP**
>
> A filter considers only members that were displayed in the worksheet. To apply a filter that identifies the top five products, first select no members and then select base members in the Member Selector dialog. As a result, the filter considers only the base-level members.

EXCEPTION HIGHLIGHTING

Exception highlighting, also known as conditional formatting or traffic lighting, is a technique using color to draw attention to values that are out of the ordinary. It might be used on the entire worksheet or only for selected rows or columns of the worksheet.

Access exception highlighting for the whole worksheet by right-clicking in the gray area at the top-left corner of the worksheet and selecting the Global Highlighting Exceptions option.

Highlighting exceptions can also be applied to a single row or column simply by clicking on its heading. Doing this displays the Highlight Exceptions dialog (see Figure 19.34). This enables the definition of the upper and lower limits for highlighting and the formatting to be applied. In this example the involved KPI has been changed to No. of New Products Planned and the recently applied filter has been removed. Here, any values less than 0% are highlighted in red, whereas values more than 5% are highlighted in green. Those values between 0% and 5% are highlighted in yellow. The result appears in Figure 19.35.

Figure 19.34
Apply exception highlighting to a column in the worksheet.

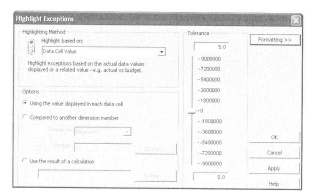

Figure 19.35
Here is an example of exception highlighting, showing adverse variances in red.

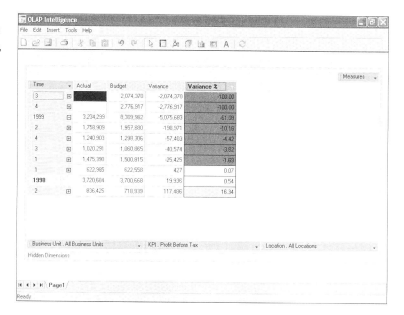

In this example, the exception highlighting is applied based on the displayed data values. This works well where the data value is a percentage but is problematic for absolute values, which change magnitude as the user drills down. To cater to these situations, other types of exception highlighting are available from the Highlight Exceptions dialog:

- **Compared to Another Dimension Member**—Highlights the displayed values according to their relationship to another member on the same dimension. For example, color-coding could be applied to Actual values based on their relationship to Budget. This comparison is valid at all levels of the hierarchy.

- **Based on a Calculation**—Enables more sophisticated situations to be catered to, such as "bubble up" reporting, where the number of exceptions below a parent member is used to highlight members higher up the hierarchy. This method also works well when drilling down. Additional typical uses of this type of exceptional highlighting are to compare current members against recent averages, moving averages, or growth rates. Calculations are covered in more detail in the next chapter.

USING OLAP INTELLIGENCE ACTIONS

Actions are a powerful feature of OLAP Intelligence. They enable you to extend the functionality of your applications in a number of ways through the right-click context menu off the worksheet object. Actions provide impressive flexibility to OLAP Intelligence Reports and Applications through external application launching (such as Crystal Reports), redirection to external URLs or HTML code, sending of e-mail, opening files, and so on. This advanced functionality is covered in detail later in this chapter.

ADDING CHART OBJECTS TO OLAP INTELLIGENCE REPORTS

Similar to the Crystal Reports Report Design environment, OLAP Intelligence provides a visualization capability to facilitate meaningful data analysis on top of the numerically presented data. To the OLAP Intelligence Design Environment, a chart is simply another object that can be added to the report through either the Insert, Chart menu option or the Charting icon. When a chart is added to a report page, the product assumes a number of defaults around the chart's properties that can be edited through the right-click context and properties menus.

19

NOTE

> Unlike the Crystal Reports Design Environment, there is no Charting Expert to step you through the initial chart set-up process. Instead, the chart automatically reflects the current viewpoint of the cube and OLAP Intelligence makes default chart option selections that can be edited using the powerful right-click chart editing options—the same ones available in Crystal Reports after a chart has been created with the Chart Expert.

Because the Charting functionality for OLAP Intelligence is the same as the Chart Options functionality for Crystal Reports, covered in Chapter 8, "Visualizing Your Data with Charts and Maps," please reference that chapter for details on chart editing and manipulation.

As mentioned previously, the Chart on any given page reflects the underlying viewpoint (that is, alignment of dimensions) for that page. To change a viewpoint on a given page that only contains a chart, temporarily add a worksheet object and manipulate the dimensions there until the chart reflects the appropriate view, and then delete the previously inserted worksheet.

Because Charts reflect the current viewpoint of any given page and all of a viewpoint's currently displayed row and column dimension members, it is instructive to pay close attention to the data that is intended to be visualized in a chart. If, for example, a meaningful Visualization on Variance % over different KPIs was required but both the Actual and Budget numbers were still part of the viewpoint, the graphic would appear meaningless because the Magnitude of the Actuals and Budgets would change the scale of the graphic; it would be meaningless for projecting information on Variance %. Figures 19.36 and 19.37 show the differences in visualization. A good workaround here involves setting up a page with only the Variance % viewpoint and chart, and providing navigation buttons (covered later in this chapter) to that page from the other report pages where Actual and Budget are displayed.

Figure 19.36
A Variance % Chart where the Actuals and Budget members overwhelm the scale of the Variance % member.

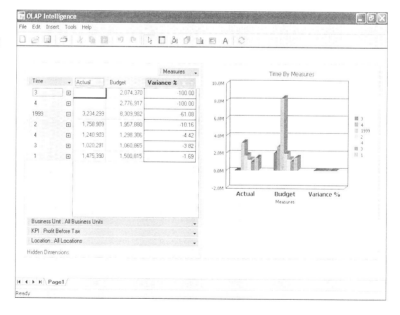

Figure 19.37
A Variance % Chart that does not show Actuals and Budget members.

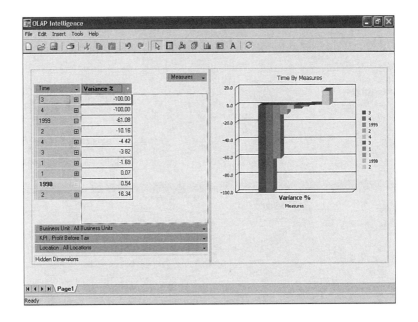

ADVANCED OLAP INTELLIGENCE DESIGNER TOOLS

The chapter up to this point has introduced the most traditional and common multidimensional or OLAP analytic objects with the Worksheet and Charting objects. OLAP Intelligence provides four other analytic objects that can be used to enhance and extend end-user interactivity with the involved reports past the traditional boundaries of other OLAP Client products. The next few sections introduce their powerful capabilities.

USING DIMENSION EXPLORER OBJECTS IN OLAP INTELLIGENCE

The Dimension Explorer gives users direct control of the view of a cube from outside of the worksheet. This object, shown in Figure 19.38 with all options turned on, enables users to dynamically change cube orientation (that is, which dimensions or on what axes) and member selection across one or all dimensions.

Changes that take place within Dimension Explorer directly affect the other analytic objects on the same page (such as a Worksheet or Chart). Table 19.4 highlights the different components of the Dimension Explorer, and their functions and typical uses. Configure these by right-clicking to access the Properties menu of the involved Dimension Explorer.

Figure 19.38
The Dimension
Explorer and its
components enable
end-user manipu-
lation of the report's
data from outside the
worksheet object.

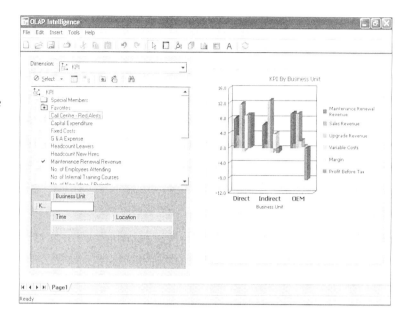

TABLE 19.4   DIMENSION EXPLORER COMPONENTS AND SAMPLE USAGE CASES

Dimension Explorer Component	Function	Sample Usage Case
Favorites	Toggles the display of the Favorite node and the Favorite set-up function on the toolbar.	Favorites provides report end users with the capability to create their own custom favorite groups. These groups are then subsequently available for rapid personalized access. This would likely be only turned off for a novice user group that might become overwhelmed with too much power too quickly.
Dimension bar	Enables users to select the different dimensions in the data source including all non-hidden and hidden row, column, and sliced dimensions.	You can turn this off if you only want the end user to be able to affect a designer-specified dimension. Alternatively, it can be left available to give an end user a single place to select members and member-sets from all dimensions—even hidden dimensions.
Pivot control	Provides a compact area where the end user can reorient the row, column, and slice dimensions.	Generally provided as a compact alternative to the same capability in the worksheet. Open to the report designer's preference.

Dimension Explorer Component	Function	Sample Usage Case
Toolbar	Provides numerous user tools to expedite member-set selection on involved dimensions. These include user shortcuts to member-set selections, display modes, favorite group set-up, and an advanced search utility.	You can turn this off if you do not want to provide end users with the access to the advanced member selection capabilities. It should be left on when the end users will be selecting their own member-sets.
Border	Toggles the display of a border on the Dimension Explorer object.	This is an aesthetic decision made according to the report designer's preference.
Root node	Toggles the display of the dimension's root node.	Can be safely turned off based on report designer preference as long as the dimension bar is displayed to highlight the current dimension.
Allow Context Menus	Toggles the right- click menu option on the Dimension Explorer for end users. Access to a multitude of dimension functions can be accessed through the right-click menus.	This would be turned off if the end user was not intended to access the variety of provided dimension-related functions. This includes dimension swapping, member selection, favorite group creation, and display options. One important note here is that the menus are either on or off; there is unfortunately no means (yet) to restrict access to a subset of the context menu items.

As you might have surmised, the Dimension Explorer does not provide any new functionality over the worksheet introduced in the last chapter but it does provide another method of deploying a good degree of dimension exploration and reorientation functionality to the end user. Figure 19.39 highlights a OLAP Intelligence report presenting a Dimension Explorer based off the sample KPI cube provided by Crystal.

TIP

> The Pivot Control and Member Selection capabilities of the Dimension Explorer can provide a report design option for designers who want to restrict end user's capabilities. By including these within a Dimension Explorer on a report page, end users will be able to manipulate dimensions and member selections in a report but will not be able to access any of the remaining worksheet functionality covered in the previous chapter (such as Calculations, Filtering, Sorting, Exception Highlighting, Formatting, and so on).

19

Figure 19.39
A OLAP Intelligence
report showing a
Dimension Explorer
with three Favorite
groups defined and
one selected to drive
the appearance of the
corresponding Chart
object.

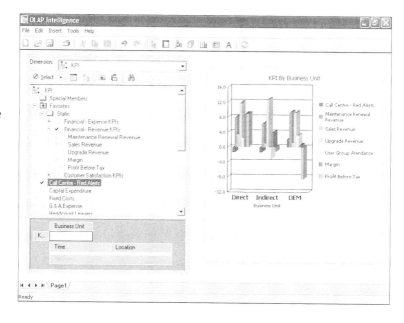

As discussed earlier in this chapter, the chart in Figure 19.38 reflects the viewpoint of the
page on which it is located. With the Dimension Explorer, you relieve the requirement of
needing a worksheet on the same report page as a chart to make it interactive because the
content of the chart can be driven exclusively through the Dimension Explorer. Try to re-
create this report yourself, complete with new Favorite Groups called Customer Satisfaction
and Finance—Revenue Related.

> In addition to enabling end users to create favorite member groupings and selections,
> OLAP Intelligence provides support for Server-side Named Sets created in Microsoft SQL
> Server Analysis Services. The Named Sets, which are themselves server-defined custom
> member groupings (such as Top 10 Selling Products), appear under a new Server node
> found under the Favorites node in the Member Selector.

USING THE SLICE NAVIGATOR OBJECTS

The Slice Navigator object enables users to explore and edit the current viewpoint's slice
dimensions and their associated members. The Slice Navigator, shown in Figure 19.40, is
best thought of as an in-line parameter selection mechanism for the OLAP Intelligence
Report.

Changes that take place within the Slice Navigator directly affect the other analytic objects
on the same page (such as a Worksheet or Chart). Table 19.5 highlights the different components of the Slice Navigator and their functions and typical uses. These are configurable
by right-clicking the Properties menu of the involved Slice Navigator.

Figure 19.40
The Slice Navigator object and its components enables quick parameter or member selection from the paged or slice dimensions.

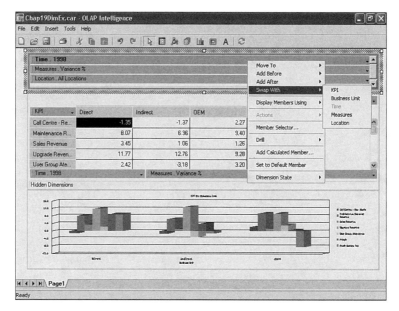

TABLE 19.5   SLICE NAVIGATOR COMPONENTS AND SAMPLE USAGE CASES

Slice Navigator Component	Function	Sample Usage Case
Panel Buttons	Toggles the display and function of the Panel Button drop-down icon. This button provides access to the same member selector dialog covered earlier in this chapter and related to the Worksheet object.	Generally turned off if the Slice Navigator is only being used to display the sliced dimension current members (that is, the non row or column). Often turned on to enable end users to access member selection from this object.
Member Names	Toggles the display of the currently selected member names beside the actual dimension name.	Generally turned off only if the member name was visible elsewhere on the report.
Border	Toggles the display of a border on the slice navigation object.	This is an aesthetic decision made according to the report designer's preference.

continues

19

TABLE 19.5 CONTINUED

Slice Navigator Component	Function	Sample Usage Case
Tile Panels	Toggles the display of the Slice Navigator Dimensions as either horizontally or vertically stacked.	If the Report Page has limited vertical space, use the Tile Panels option to stretch the slice navigator horizontally. If there is limited horizontal space, turn the Tile Panels off to stack the sliced dimensions panels vertically.
Allow Context Menus	Toggles the right-click menu option on the Slice Navigator for end users. Access to a multitude of dimension- and member-related functions is available through the right-click menus.	This would be turned off if you don't intend for the end user to access the dimension- and member-related functions. This includes dimension swapping, member selection, and display options. One important note here is that the menus are either on or off; unfortunately, there is not yet means to restrict access to a subset of the context menu items.

Use the Slice Navigator on OLAP Intelligence Report Pages when you want to present a locked-down worksheet or chart view (that is, no dimension reorientation) yet still want to enable the end user to edit the parameters around the fixed display (that is, edit the sliced dimension members). Figure 19.41 highlights a report page based on the Crystal Sample KPI cube with the slice navigator providing a parameter selection capability that drives the chart and worksheet display.

USING ANALYSIS BUTTON OBJECTS

Analysis Buttons enable end users to rapidly analyze data and move between different analytic viewpoints at the click of a button. The simple user interface that Analysis Buttons provide brings the power of OLAP and multidimensional data sources to the masses.

Analysis Buttons enables single-click provision of any of the following capabilities to end users:

- Changing the current viewpoint of the Worksheet and chart objects on a single report page.
- Moving to another page in the application and controlling the viewpoint of the Worksheet or chart objects on the new report page.
- Flexible Drill-down on user-selected members from the worksheet object.
- Executing actions that can open other OLAP Intelligence or Crystal Report reports, third-party applications, Web pages, e-mail notes, and so on. The Actions section later in this chapter covers these capabilities.

Figure 19.41
Here is an OLAP Intelligence report with the Slice Navigator driving a Viewpoint reflected on the corresponding Chart and Worksheet objects.

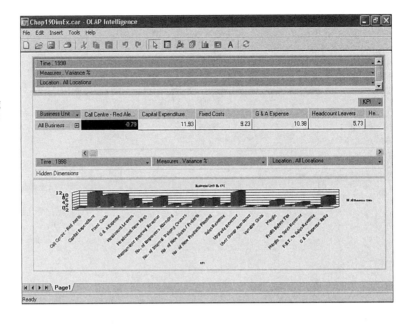

Figure 19.42 shows a familiar sample report that has been enhanced with the provision of three Analysis Buttons—Customer Satisfaction, Finance—Revenue Related, and All KPIs.

Figure 19.42
This is an OLAP Intelligence report with three Analysis Buttons driving the viewpoint reflected on the corresponding Chart and Worksheet objects.

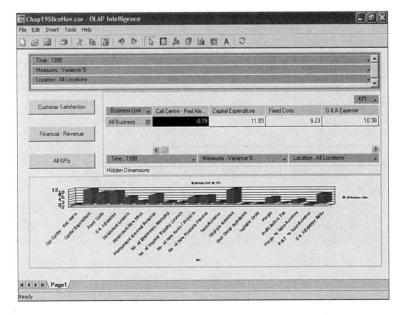

Each of the three Analysis Buttons provides the end user with a single-click method of changing the viewpoint on the associated worksheet and chart objects (after the OLAP Intelligence report has been locked down or published to BusinessObjects Enterprise). The report designer provides this capability by right-clicking on the Analysis button after it has been added to a report page. Figures 19.43 and 19.44 highlight the Analysis Button Properties dialog accessed by right-clicking on an Analysis Button and selecting Properties.

Figure 19.43
The Analysis Button Properties dialog is where you name the Analysis Button and select a transition page or action.

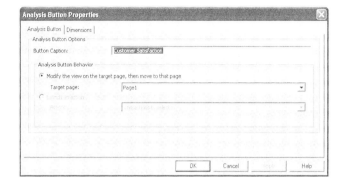

Figure 19.44
On the Dimensions tab of the Analysis Button Properties dialog, you can select a dimension member based on the involved analysis button.

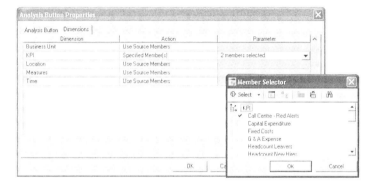

Table 19.6 describes the various properties, functions, and uses that can be set for Analysis buttons.

TABLE 19.6   ANALYSIS BUTTON COMPONENTS AND USAGE CASES

Analysis Button Component	Function	Sample Usage Case
Analysis Button tab— Button Caption	Enables you to specify the label to be displayed on the Analysis button.	To present the end user with a clear button label that indicates the button's purpose.
Analysis Button tab— Modify the View on the Target Page, and Then Move to That Page	Enables you to specify the report page onto which the involved action button takes the user when she clicks it.	By specifying the same report page that the Analysis button resides on, the end user can change the viewpoint of a single report page dynamically and rapidly. By specifying a different page, the end user can navigate

Analysis Button Component	Function	Sample Usage Case
		among the different report pages in a OLAP Intelligence report and pass data context amongst them— and have all that logic wrapped up within the button.
Analysis Button tab— Launch an Action	Enables you to specify the action that is launched when the user presses the involved Analysis button. Actions are covered in detail later in this chapter.	When actions are defined for a report, Analysis buttons can be used to launch them. This power- ful function enables you to link to external applications (such as a product ordering system), email systems, other OLAP Intelligence Reports, or formatted Crystal Reports.
Dimensions tab—Action	The Dimensions tab enables you to specify the members for each of the dimensions in the targeted viewpoint (the new viewpoint after the Analysis button has been clicked).	There are many options for specifying these members: Use these specifications to encapsulate selection logic for the target viewpoint of an Analysis button. These Analysis buttons are then used to provide easy-to-use inter- faces for non-power analyst end users.

- Use Source Members—Copies the member selection from the originating viewpoint. Useful when you intend to keep a dimension's members the same both pre- and post-Analysis button press. This is often the case because it is common to embed the logic to change only one dimension at a time in anAnalysis button.

- Use Target Members—Uses the viewpoint of the targeted report page. Useful when the targeted report page contains a predefined set of members for a dimension that should not be affected.

continues

19

TABLE 19.6   CONTINUED

Analysis Button Component	Function	Sample Usage Case
		■ Drill Down (Single, No Parent)—A focused drill down on a selected member from the worksheet. Useful for encapsulating focused drill down functionality into an Analysis button.
		■ Drill Down (Single, Keep Parent)—Similar to a focused drill down with the exception that the parent member is kept in the viewpoint. Useful for encapsulating the combination of focused drill down functionality with keeping the parent member into an Analysis button.
		■ Drill Down (Multiple, No Parent)—A focused drill down on selected members from the worksheet. Useful for encapsulating focused drill down functionality on multiple members into an Analysis button.
		■ Drill Down (Multiple, Keep Parent)—Similar to a focused drill down on multiple members with the exception that parent members are kept in the viewpoint. Useful for encapsulating the combination of focused drill-down functionality on multiple members with keeping the parent members into an Analysis button.
		■ As Selected (only one accepted)—Displays only the selected member (selected by the end user from the worksheet). Useful for providing users with focused user-driven Analysis buttons.

Analysis Button Component	Function	Sample Usage Case
		■ Selected (multiple accepted)—Displays only the selected members (selected by the end user from the worksheet). Useful for providing users with focused user-driven Analysis buttons. An example might enable the end user to select which products to analyze more deeply.
		■ Specified Member(s)—Displays a predefined (by the report designer) set of members. Useful for providing users with focused Analysis buttons based on predefined views (such as product sets or time periods).
		■ Range Based on Selected Member—Displays a predefined range of members on either side of a user-selected member. Useful for providing users with a navigation mechanism to move through time dimensions in a user-driven focused method (for example, showing three months of data on either side of a selected member).
Dimensions tab—Parameter	The Dimensions Tab Parameter column enables you to specify parameters for both the Specified Member(s) and Range Based on a Selected Member Dimension Column options. Specified members are selected through a traditional Member Selector dialog and ranges are specified by X:Y, where X specifies the number of periods before the selected member and Y afterward.	Both parameter selection options enable you to provide predefined viewpoint navigation logic embedded within an Analysis Button.

19

Unlike the Member Selector dialogs accessed through the Worksheet, Dimension Explorer, and Slice Navigator, the Member Selector dialog box accessed from the Specified Members option does not provide access to Favorites or Named Sets (a Microsoft SQL Server capability described earlier in this chapter). As such, be careful when re-creating these lists through this Member Selector to ensure they reflect the member lists you are targeting.

Often, a report contains multiple Analysis Buttons all providing only slightly different functions to the end user. To facilitate Report Design, make sure to use the Copy and Paste functions accessible from the right-click menu on the Analysis Buttons.

USING TEXT BOX OBJECTS

The Analytic Objects covered to this point have highlighted the powerful function that OLAP Intelligence provides on top of multidimensional (for example, OLAP) data sources. The last object available for use in Report Design is the text box and is exclusively focused on report formatting. Figure 19.45 shows a variation of the sample reports worked on in this chapter with some strategically placed text boxes added for aesthetic affect.

Figure 19.45
Adding text objects to a KPI report can facilitate a clean presentation and end-user comprehension.

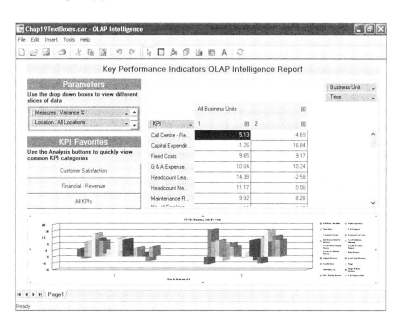

Standard formatting capabilities are provided through the Text Box properties dialog, which you can access by right-clicking on the involved text box.

CREATING PARAMETERS WITH THE PARAMETER MANAGER

Similar to the Crystal Reports parameters discussed in Chapter 5, "Implementing Parameters for Dynamic Reporting," OLAP Intelligence also provides you with a rich parameter capability. These parameters enable you to re-use a single report/application across multiple user groups or users with different filtering requirements. OLAP Intelligence parameters can be set for the following:

- The underlying cube (for example, the report data source)
- The selected member of an active or hidden sliced dimension
- The selected set of members ('member-set') for any of the row or column dimensions
- The opening page of the report

→ For more information on Crystal Reports parameters, **see** "Creating and Implementing Parameters Fields," on **p. 136**.

To add any of these parameters to a report, first use the Parameter Manager shown in Figure 19.46 to define the parameters. You can access this from the Tools menu.

Figure 19.46
The OLAP Intelligence Parameter Manager enables you to add parameters to their OLAP Intelligence reports.

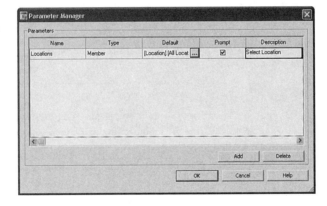

Each parameter is specified through five pieces of information in the Parameter Manager: a parameter name, the chosen parameter type (Cube, Member, Memberset, or Page), the default value for the parameter, a prompting toggle, and prompting text (description). All of these are rather intuitive except for the prompting toggle that is used to specify that end users should be prompted for the report when they view it through BusinessObjects Enterprise. If this is turned off, users will not be prompted for a parameter and the last saved value for that value in the report will be used.

The second step to using parameters in a OLAP Intelligence Report is to configure any dimensions that are to use the incoming parameters (Members or Memberset parameters only) as filters for their associated member selection. You specify this in the Member Selector for the involved dimensions. Figure 19.47 shows this selection for the Location

Dimension on the sample report from this chapter. The parameters that have been created previously are found and selected under the Special Members node.

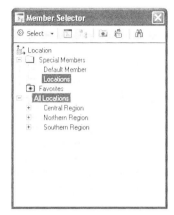

Be careful to test the parameters that you have implemented both in the OLAP Intelligence Design Environment and in the BusinessObjects Enterprise Web Delivery environment. Often, the product behavior can be somewhat surprising when you use prompting.

After a parameter has been configured, you make it active for end users by either locking the report in the designer or publishing to BusinessObjects Enterprise. Figure 19.48 displays a report that has been locked. Note the selection screen that has prompted the user for parameter input that is used for filtering the underlying OLAP Intelligence report.

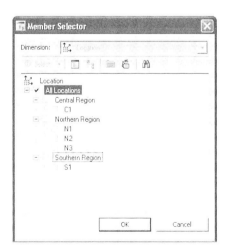

CREATING ACTIONS WITH THE ACTIONS MANAGER

OLAP Intelligence actions are a powerful recent feature addition to OLAP Intelligence. They enable an OLAP Intelligence designer to predefine named operations for report users accessed from four different areas: from dimension headings, from individual members of a dimension, from specific data cells, or from Analysis Buttons. Actions enable end users to kick off other Web pages, link into other applications, initiate e-mail to colleagues, and launch other applications such as Crystal Reports or other OLAP Intelligence reports. These links can be made with flexible context awareness of exactly where on the report they were kicked off from (that is, which product member the cursor was on when the action was kicked off).

NOTE

> In previous versions of OLAP Intelligence, actions defined on a Microsoft SQL Server were supported in much the same way that these new OLAP Intelligence actions are supported. In version 10, both SQL Server actions and the new Custom OLAP Intelligence actions are supported and accessed in the exact same way. More information on SQL Server actions can be found in the documentation for Microsoft SQL Server Analysis Services.

Actions are accessed in OLAP Intelligence by end users by either right-clicking any dimension, dimension member, or data cell, or by clicking an Analysis Button tied to an action, as described earlier in this chapter. If an action is available on the right-clicked report section, the Actions menu option is enabled and access to all defined actions is provided.

A good example of an action could be based on a product dimension and be called Display Detailed Product Information. This might display a detailed Crystal Report based off some relational data from the product master tables and be nicely formatted for printing. An alternative example on the same dimension could be an Order Inventory action based on a product dimension's member. This action would link into the corporate procurement website and dynamically pass in the Product ID or Name.

In both the OLAP Intelligence designer and the ActiveX Rich Client Web Viewer of BusinessObjects Enterprise, each action appears in the Actions submenu. In the Web (DHTML) client the actions are displayed in a dialog. Figure 19.49 shows an action being called in the DHTML Web Viewer, using the KPI dimension of the sample KPI cube.

Actions are created in the OLAP Intelligence Designer using the Action Manager accessible from the Tools menu. The Action Manager shown in Figure 19.50 enables you to Add, Delete, Copy, Edit, and Import Actions from other existing OLAP Intelligence reports. Figure 19.50 shows the New Action dialog and Table 19.7 describes the key components of an action.

Figure 19.49
Invoking an action
from the DHTML
worksheet in
BusinessObjects
Enterprise.

Figure 19.50
Creating a new action
in OLAP Intelligence
with the Action
Manager, which
you access from
the Tools menu.

TABLE 19.7   ACTION COMPONENTS AND DESCRIPTIONS

Action Component	Description
Name	The name of the action that shows up to end users in their Action menus. Clear and active descriptions of actions are recommended.
Applies To	There are five options where actions might apply:
	■ Nothing—These actions might only be launched from a OLAP Intelligence button and cannot include any MDX or Crystal OLAP Syntax
	■ Cube—These actions might also only be launched from a OLAP Intelligence button but can include any MDX or Crystal OLAP Syntax for dynamic context pass-through
	■ Dimension—The action can only be launched from a specified dimension heading
	■ Dimension Members—The action can only be launched from member titles within a specified dimension
	■ Data Cells—The action can only be launched from a Worksheet Data Cell

Action Component	Description
Dimension	Enables you to specify the Dimension where the involved action is available. This option is only available for Dimension and Dimension Member actions.
Type	HTML or URL. URL actions open the specified URL in a Web browser. browser.

Template	The HTML or URL content is the template. The Check Template button on this dialog checks the validity of any involved MDX or Crystal OLAP Syntax in the template. It ignores everything that is kept within double quotes—it does not check URL or HTML syntax. Lastly, the Syntax Editor provides an easy-to-use interface for adding MDX and Crystal OLAP functions and fields into the template. MDX and Crystal OLAP Syntax are introduced later in this chapter. A few examples shown here highlight the use of the context wildcard '*'.
	
	URL with MDX:
	`"http://finance.yahoo.com/q?d=t&s=" + *.Name`
	URL with Crystal OLAP Syntax:
	`"http://finance.yahoo.com/q?d=t&s=" + GetName(*)`
	HTML with Crystal OLAP Syntax:
	`"<HTML><P>KPI = " + GetName(*) + "</P></HTML>"`
	E-mail URL with MDX:
	`"mailto:MakeMeRich@broker.com?subject=Buy Some"`
	`+ [Equity].*.Name`

NOTE

Remember that actions that apply to nothing cannot use any MDX or Crystal OLAP Syntax within their HTML or URL template. This means that these actions cannot take data context with them to their launched application. To pass in data-driven context at a report level, use the Applies to Cube option.

19

As alluded to in the last entry of Table 20.4, you can use an asterisk to make an expression context-aware. The use of the asterisk and context depend on where the action was launched. The most common usage of the context asterisk is on Member and Data Cell actions.

For actions launched from a Member, the context asterisk holds the place of the Member from which the action was launched. For example, with MDX, `*.Name` returns the name of the Member from which the action was launched. With Crystal OLAP Syntax, the expression would look like this: `GetName({*})`.

For actions launched from a data cell, the context asterisk specifies the column or row member to which the data cell belongs to. Each cell belongs to multiple dimensions, so you must specify the dimension you want. For example, with MDX, `[KPI].*.Name` returns the name of the member in the Products dimension that corresponds to the cell from where the action was launched. With Crystal OLAP Syntax, the expression would look like this: `GetName({KPI@*})`.

Finally, the following HTML example shows how to specify the column, row, and sliced dimension members corresponding to a specific data cell:

LISTING 19.1 HTML CODE HIGHLIGHTING CONTEXT PLACEHOLDERS FOR ALL DIMENSIONS

```
"<HTML><P>
KPI   = " + [KPI].*.Name +
"</P><P>
Business Unit = " + [Business Unit].*.Name +
"</P><P>
Time Period = " + [Time].*.Name +
"</P><P>
Measures = " + [Measures].*.Name +
"</P><P>
Location = " + [Location].*.Name +
"</P></HTML>"
```

The calling interface and the results of this action, known as Display Data Cell Context in the samples, are displayed in Figure 19.51.

Although the Edit, Delete, and Copy commands in the Action Manager are quite intuitive, the Import Action option is a little more novel. The Import capability enables you to copy actions from any other OLAP Intelligence report maintained in the BusinessObjects Enterprise system. To complete an import, log on to BusinessObjects Enterprise and navigate to the desired OLAP Intelligence Report. Upon selection of the report, you are prompted to select one or more of the actions that exist in that report to import. The imported actions now become part of the current report.

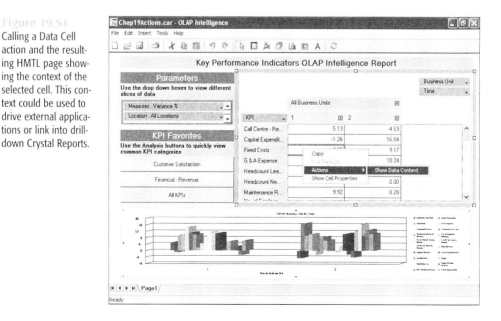

Figure 19.51
Calling a Data Cell action and the resulting HMTL page showing the context of the selected cell. This context could be used to drive external applications or link into drilldown Crystal Reports.

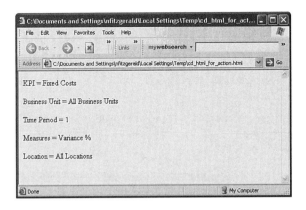

CUSTOM CALCULATIONS AND ADVANCED DATA ANALYSIS

Additional Calculations and Data Analytics not provided in a report's underlying data source can be added to the data presented in the worksheet through the Calculations and Data Analysis menu, which you access by right-clicking on any member header. These are available at Design time and at End-User Delivery time if context menus have been enabled on the involved Worksheet object. A number of the most common calculations are provided in the Calculated Members dialog and include drag-and-drop parameter-based experts. Additional experts are provided under the Data Analysis tab on the same Calculated Members dialog. To add any of these default calculations or to create a completely new calculation, right-click on a member or a dimension name, and then choose the Calculated Member option. This opens the Calculated Members dialog shown in Figure 19.52.

Figure 19.52
The Calculated Members dialog provides the report designer and end user with the capability to create custom calculated members not available in the OLAP data source.

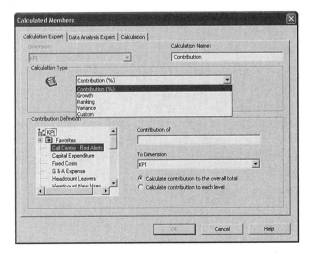

NOTE

OLAP Intelligence automatically chooses a name for any of the predefined calculations. You can change this by typing the preferred name in the Calculation Name edit box.

THE CALCULATION EXPERTS

The Calculation Experts provided by OLAP Intelligence on the Calculation Expert tab are

- **Contribution**—Calculates how much each member of a hierarchical dimension contributes to its parent. For example, how much does each week, period, and quarter contribute to total sales?

- **Growth**—Calculates how much a value has changed from one period to the next. For example, what is the percentage growth in sales week on week, period on period, and quarter on quarter?

- **Ranking**—Calculates the rank of each member in a dimension, usually based on a measure. For example, rank each product based on sales.

- **Variance**—Compares the value of one dimension member with a target value; the resulting variance can be expressed as an absolute value or a percentage variance.

Each of the Calculation Experts requires the specification of a different set of parameters in the Calculated Members dialog. These parameters can be set by either clicking and dragging the appropriate members to the involved parameter field or right-clicking on the chosen member and selecting the appropriate destination from the subsequent pop-up menu.

THE DATA ANALYSIS EXPERTS AND SUMMARIES

The Data Analysis Experts provided by OLAP Intelligence under the Data Analysis Expert Tab are

- **Trend Line**—The Trend Line Expert calculates the straight line that best fits all members of the dimension specified in the Series Dimension list. This is done for the measure specified in the Trend Of box. The least squares method is used: minimizing the sum of the squares of the differences between the actual values specified and the regression line values.

- **Moving Average**—The Moving Average Expert calculates a centered moving average over all the members within each level of a specified dimension. This is done for the measure specified in the Moving Average parameter box.

- **Linear Regression**—The Linear Regression Expert calculates the straight line that best fits all the members within each level of the dimension. The members of this dimension form the columns of the Worksheet (assuming you are adding a calculated member as a row) where the X and Y values of the points are given by the members specified in the X Values box and Y Values box, respectively. The least squares method is used: minimizing the sum of the squares of the differences between the actual Y values specified and the regression line values. The regression line is evaluated at these same X values as specified by the member in the X Values box. Use the Linear Regression Expert when the data values you want to regress are not evenly spaced.

Each of the Data Analysis Experts requires you to specify a different set of parameters in the Calculated Members dialog. For a more thorough discussion on these calculations and how they are derived, please consult the Reference section of the OLAP Intelligence User Manual provided in the docs directory of your install CD.

CAUTION

> It is very important to understand the scope under which the Data Analysis Experts operate. When you select any of these experts, they operate across the entire set of members for the dimension that has been selected regardless of whether they are displayed on the current worksheet or viewpoint. Not taking this into account can lead to suspicious looking data when not all members are displayed. For scenarios where this assumed scope needs to be modified, the underlying MDX or Crystal OLAP Syntax created by the Data Analysis Expert can be modified under the Calculation tab of the Calculated Members dialog. This is introduced later in this chapter.

In addition to the predefined Data Analysis Experts, OLAP Intelligence also provides analytic summaries such as Mean, Variance, Standard Deviation, and Best Fitting Curve. Access these summaries by right-clicking any member header and choosing Data Analysis. You can access common analytic summaries through the Summary Statistics menu option and advanced curve estimations through the Best Fitting Curve menu option. Figure 19.53 shows the Best Fitting Curve window and associated summaries.

Figure 19.53
You access supporting statistics in the Best Fitting Curve dialog box by choosing the Data Analysis menu option.

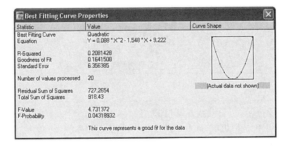

For detailed insights into the statistics behind the Data Analysis summaries, review the `Data Algorithms.pdf` document distributed on the product CD.

CUSTOM CALCULATIONS WITH MDX OR CRYSTAL OLAP SYNTAX

In addition to all the experts introduced in the previous two sections, there are times when additional calculations are required to meet a designer or end user's need. The Calculations tab highlighted in Figure 19.54 enables you to create such calculations—or, as is often the case, modify existing calculations (for example, to change the scope of application for a Moving Average or Other Calculation).

This is the
Calculations tab of
Calculated Members
dialog and the
supporting Functions
Library.

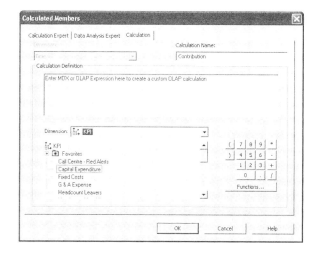

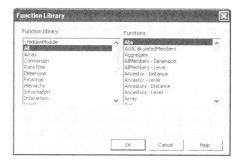

OLAP Intelligence Query Language Syntax and MDX

OLAP Intelligence Query Language (OIQL) syntax and Multi Dimensional Expressions (MDX) are related but different syntaxes that support the definition and manipulation of multidimensional objects and data. They can be conceptually thought of as a parallel to Structured Query Language (SQL), which is used for querying relational data, but for multidimensional data sources. There is, however, no direct relationship between SQL and either MDX or OIQL. OLAP Intelligence uses MDX to access SQL Server cubes and OIQL Syntax for the remaining supported data sources. Thorough descriptions can be found online for MDX at www.msdn.com (search on MDX) and in the OLAP Intelligence Help file (look up OLAP Intelligence Query Language in the Index tab).

Similar to an SQL query, each MDX or OIQP query requires a data request (the SELECT clause), a starting point (the FROM clause), and a filter (the WHERE clause). These and other keywords provide the tools used to extract specific portions of data from a cube for analysis. OLAP Intelligence uses MDX and OIQL queries to capture data from the underlying multidimensional data sources. When using MDX (against SQL Server cubes), these queries can be viewed and edited through the Edit MDX option on the Tools menu. Additionally, both these syntaxes support extension through use of calculated members. This is generally the focal area for the report designer's exposure to MDX or OIQL and there are some practical samples available for download from www.usingcrystal.com.

The Calculations Tab consists of the four major components, shown in Figure 19.54. These components facilitate the creation of OIQL or MDX statements that can be converted into meaningful fields usable by OLAP Intelligence designers and end users:

- **Calculation Definition**—This is the actual MDX (if you're using SQL Server) or OIQL Syntax that is calculated by or through OLAP Intelligence against the underlying data source.

- **Dimension and Member Selectors**—These components facilitate the selection of Dimensions and Dimension Members to be used in creating the custom calculation. When dimensions or members are selected through a double-click, the appropriate syntax for referencing them is transposed into the calculation definition for future editing. It is worth noting that the transposed text might not always reflect the exact user-friendly member syntax displayed in the Member Selector.

- **OLAP Functions Library**—Clicking on the Functions Library button provides a library of MDX or OIQL functions that might be used in the creation of the involved custom calculation. A few of the most common and useful functions are described in the next section.

- **Basic Operations Keypad**—A keypad providing and basic math operations and numerics for use in creating the calculation definition.

Once created, a resultant MDX or OIQL definition created through the Calculations tab appears as just another member in the involved OLAP Intelligence report—which could even be used in future custom calculations.

SETTING REPORT OPTIONS

The one menu option from OLAP Intelligence not covered to this point is the Report Options menu, shown in Figure 19.55.

Figure 19.55
The Options dialog, which you access from the Tools menu provides access to some global OLAP Intelligence settings.

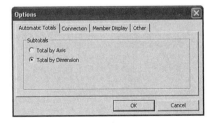

There are four tabs on the Options dialog that control some global behavior on the involved OLAP Intelligence report:

- **Automatic Totals**—The Automatic totaling function accessed by right-clicking on the worksheet can be applied either at the axis or dimension level. This is clearly of relevance in reports with nested dimensions only.

- **Connection Passwords**—This option enables you to specify the degree of database security you want to implement around your OLAP Intelligence report.

- **Member Display**—Enables you to set a global variable on whether a Member's name, caption, or both are displayed in reports.

- **Other**—Two toggles are provided here. One shows the Welcome Screen when OLAP Intelligence starts that enables report file selection, and the other provides a Report Template Selection dialog for every inserted page in a report. Both options are generally worth keeping turned on.

TROUBLESHOOTING

CALCULATED MEMBERS DIALOG

I can't seem to set the parameters in the Calculated Members dialog.

Don't double-click and drag the parameter, but rather click once and drag it. Alternatively, use the right-click context menus created for the different members.

MODIFYING DEFAULT DATA ANALYSIS CALCULATIONS

I want to use some of the default data analysis calculations provided by OLAP Intelligence, but I want to use a variant of the default settings on the calculation. For example, I want a moving average calculation to include two trailing periods and two subsequent periods for every member, instead of the default three.

Use the Calculations tab of the Calculated Members dialog after selecting the default data analysis calculation. Here you can edit the formula syntax for the default calculations to meet your requirements.

CHAPTER 20

INTRODUCTION TO WEB INTELLIGENCE

In this chapter

This chapter is designed to introduce the Crystal Reports writer to the Web Intelligence report engine. The Web Intelligence engine is an extremely sophisticated reporting engine that functions under a different reporting paradigm than Crystal Reports. A single chapter cannot adequately teach you how to use all the capabilities of the Web Intelligence engine. Because this book is primarily devoted to Crystal Reports development, you should not expect to find equally in-depth how-to knowledge on report development using Web Intelligence. However, after reading this chapter you should be familiar with the Web Intelligence reporting paradigm; understand the tools, nomenclature, and workflow of creating Web Intelligence reports; understand some (but not all) of the key differentiating capabilities of the engine; and be able to provide some high-level guidance to the Crystal Report developer about when to use Crystal Reports or the Web Intelligence report engine.

WHAT IS WEB INTELLIGENCE?

Web Intelligence is a report engine. If you are somewhat familiar with Business Objects classic technology, the term Web Intelligence was often incorrectly used interchangeably with several other parts of the product suite. Table 20.1 clarifies this.

TABLE 20.1 COMMON MISUSES OF THE TERM WEB INTELLIGENCE

Item	Common or Business Objects Classic Name	XI Name (Official)
User interface	Web Intelligence, InfoView, Web Intelligence InfoView, Web Intelligence portal	InfoView
Infrastructure backbone	Web Intelligence, Web Intelligence Server	XI Framework
Report engine	Web Intelligence	Web Intelligence

People often refer to Web Intelligence by its nickname, WebI (pronounced *webby*, not *web-eye*). To understand the Web Intelligence reporting engine, you must first understand the WebI reporting paradigm.

HOW IS WEB INTELLIGENCE DIFFERENT FROM CRYSTAL REPORTS?

You might be wondering why Business Objects choose to have two reporting engines in the framework; are they really that different? In some ways they appear similar—both retrieve rows of data and show it in a report. However, Web Intelligence is designed around a completely different user experience of information interaction. What is the reporting paradigm, and why is it different? In Web Intelligence, data is stored in a multidimensional array called a microcube. What does the microcube do and what is its benefit? There are no report bands, but instead there are report blocks and projections. What are these things, and what do they provide the end user? This chapter will help to answer these questions, and a few more.

REPORTING PARADIGM

The focus of Web Intelligence reporting can be summed up in several themes:

- Users who have no database experience should be able to create their own queries and reports.
- Users should be able to perform an analysis on a report, even if they didn't create the report originally.
- The interface should be easy to use and intuitive.
- The interface should be very powerful and provide supporting capabilities for those users who can develop sophisticated analyses and scenarios.

In order to achieve these objectives, Business Objects developed a four-tier approach to reporting, which ties together various functional engines to provide a complete reporting and analysis stack that is called the Web Intelligence report engine. Figure 20.1 depicts the stack of functional engines and the basic workflow for creating an ad-hoc report.

Figure 20.1
This figure shows the four functional engines that make up the Web Intelligence reporting engine. The query is first created via a query panel off of the semantic layer, and when SQL is generated and data retrieved, the microcube and report engines perform post-query calculations and display the results.

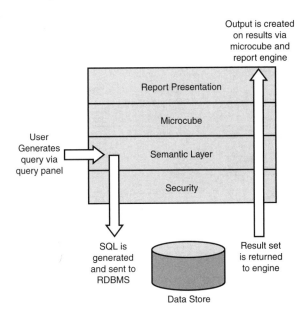

SECURITY LAYER

Fundamental to secure reporting is the ability to provide appropriate access to data. You can think of the access as coarse-grained and fine-grained. *Coarse-grained* refers to accessing reporting resources in the business intelligence environment (meaning objects in the InfoStore) that specifically relate to the WebI engine, such as universes (semantic layers) and preexisting reports. *Fine-grained* security refers to providing access to the resource, but limiting it in some way. For example, managers can see data in an HR database, but cannot see salary information. Coarse-grained access is managed via the Central Management Server, or CMS. Fine-grained access is managed in the universe via the Designer and put into practice by the Web Intelligence engine. The security layer provides access to resources (universes, reports, and application functionality) and user-specific security overrides on these resources. Examples of such overrides are listed in Table 20.2.

TABLE 20.2   COARSE-GRAINED AND FINE-GRAINED SECURITY

Course-grained security (managed via CMC, manifest by CMS)	
Universes	User is granted or denied access to a particular universe
Reports	User is granted or denied access to a particular report
Application functionality (BusinessObjects Enterprise applications)	User is granted or denied access to a particular application, such as Web Intelligence or Designer
Fine-grained security (managed via Designer, manifest by WebI engine)	
Universes	1. User can see a universe but cannot see all objects within the universe; 2. User has SQL restrictions (WHERE clauses) attached to all SQL generated, whether through ad-hoc or through refreshing a previously existing report; 3. User can have specific query governors applied (time- and row-restriction limits); and 4. User can have table substitution overrides and the likes
Fine-grained security (managed by CMC, manifest in WebI engine)	
Reports	User can edit a particular report, but can be denied editing rights on another report
Application functionality	User can have access to an application but be denied a specific right (for instance, user has access to Web Intelligence on-report analysis, but has been denied access to create new reports, or possibly is restricted from the ability to see the underlying SQL)

SEMANTIC LAYER

Tied closely to the security layer is the semantic layer. There are two semantic layers currently available in BusinessObjects XI—business views and universes. The semantic layer used with WebI is the universe (see Chapter 18, "Using a Semantic Layer—Business Views and Universes," for details on universes). The *universe* provides an abstraction layer for the end user that hides the complexities of the database, and presents database elements as business objects that can be selected in any combination by the business user via a GUI drag-and-drop interface called the *query panel*. Behind the scenes, a sophisticated SQL generation engine looks at the objects selected and, based on rules defined in the semantic layer, generates correct SQL for the end user (which they are completely shielded from seeing). Because the semantic layer passes through the security layer, all user-specific security overrides apply to SQL generation at the time it is generated, either initially or at subsequent execution.

MICROCUBE ENGINE

One of the major differences between Web Intelligence and Crystal Reports is the inclusion of the microcube engine. The *microcube engine* stores the resultsets in a multidimensional array providing OLAP-like capabilities on the data. Working closely with the semantic layer that provides instructions to the microcube on how certain objects should behave when rolled up, the microcube can take the resultset data and project it in any dimensional combination based on the objects selected. Again, see Chapter 18 for a more detailed explanation.

The microcube shows *projections*, or slices of the data at a particular level. The microcube also allows for report variables to be calculated based on the underlying objects, and will project these calculations as well. Advanced users can specify levels of aggregation for calculation for a particular report variable, thus creating very sophisticated multilevel report variables.

REPORT ENGINE

The report engine sits on top of the microcube engine and shows the projections in report blocks. A *report block* is a table or chart that shows a particular slice or level of the microcube projection. Unlike Crystal Reports, WebI reports are not banded; there is a report block which shows a particular level of the data, and there are sections that can be placed around the report block (grouping headers and footers). There can be multiple sections or levels in a report. The sections also provide projection of objects at those levels, so calculations specific for each section are not necessary (the microcube takes care of this for the user).

The report engine allows the user to navigate the data and provide analysis via Drill mode. This means that as the user interacts with the report block, the user can select an object and drill down on the object to a lower level. Natural data hierarchies are defined in the semantic layer. Drilling down on a report tells the microcube to move the level of projection down one level in the data hierarchy and recalculate the report block at the next lowest dimensional level. All measures are recalculated to show the proper values at that projection level.

As users move or swap objects in and out of the report block, measure values are constantly being recalculated on the fly and reprojected to the reporting engine. This allows the user to move through the data seamlessly and explore relationships between the different dimensional combinations.

This seems very complicated—and it is. However, as you move through the user experience, you can easily see how intuitive it appears to a business user (or any user for that matter), and that describing this intuitive data manipulation is more difficult than actually using it.

REAL WORLD USAGE

Using the Web Intelligence reporting paradigm, the user generally executes this workflow

1. Select a universe on which to explore the data.
2. Select objects from the universe for the query.
3. Get results back.

20

4. Start manipulating the data.

5. Refine the question; get more data (go to step 2 or step 1 and loop).

6. When the user arrives at a sufficient stopping point, save the report.

7. The user can schedule, publish, or send the report to other users.

This means that data exploration and discovery is part of the reporting paradigm. Many times business users know they need to "look at the numbers" but don't know exactly what it is they are looking for. This often makes it impossible to nail down specific user-reporting requirements. In the Web Intelligence paradigm, the burden for report requirement definition is shifted to the business user, who in turn creates his own report. As he explores the data, he might learn things that take him in a completely new direction, ending up at a much different place than his initial intent. Needless to say, this process of discovery and new insights about the data often provides much more business benefit to the user and the organization as a whole.

As the data is secured through the semantic layer and through the security mechanism, it also allows IT to maintain control over what data is accessed and by whom. Because all connections are masked to the database via the universe, the end user is less likely to know how to circumvent the system. Data can still be exported into Excel or in comma separated values (CSV) format so the user can use the information in ways that are not available via the reporting engine. However, access to the data is secured and all access to the database is controlled via the semantic layer.

Web Intelligence accesses data only via the universe. There is no ability to create a Web Intelligence report off of any other source than a universe. As described in Chapter 18, the universe currently connects to relational data sources and some multidimensional databases. A universe also contains a single database connection, meaning single database access. However, a Web Intelligence report can contain multiple resultsets from different universes, so data can be brought together in the same report from different platforms. There are some limitations on cross-resultset synchronization and calculations in Web Intelligence XI that will be resolved in the next release.

→ For more complete details, see "The Microcube Engine," p. 410.

REPORT ANATOMY

The universe that ships with BusinessObjects XI cannot adequately demonstrate the capabilities outlined in this chapter. Therefore, all examples in this chapter are drawn from two universes that are readily available and shipped with the Web Intelligence 6.5.1. The universes are called eFashion and Island Resorts, and are sourced off of Microsoft

Access databases. These universes, along with instructions for putting them into the XI infrastructure are available on this book's website. Note that because there is no change in universe file format, all existing Business Objects universes are fully functional via Web Intelligence inside the XI framework.

As mentioned in the preceding section, Web Intelligence reports are not banded as they are in Crystal Reports, but they consider the inner-most band or Details section of a Crystal Report to contain a WebI report block. The report block is a projection of the data in the microcube. As such, it does not necessarily represent the atomic level of data in the report resultset. For example, if a query is run that selects Year, Quarter, Month, and Sales Revenue, the report block could be showing only Year and Sales Revenue. Although the data for all four objects is contained within the report, the user sees the projection based only on what objects are in the report block. In this case, the Sales Revenue numbers would be automatically rolled up to the year level, and only one record per year would exist in the report block.

In Web Intelligence, the report designer or user is generally more interested in seeing the data at some level of aggregation (projection) in which her analysis starts, so often times the projection is quite high up in the data hierarchy. This is because a user will interact with the report and drill down into the level necessary when using the report. This also means that the report contains other data elements besides just the values shown, as is evidenced in Figure 20.2.

Figure 20.2
Web Intelligence report with simple table and result set objects in left pane.

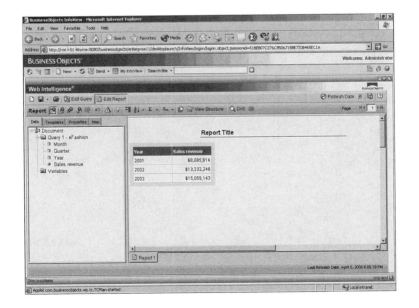

Figure 20.2 shows objects contained in the resultset on the left, and the report block on the right. Clearly, data exists in the report for each month, but when seen in the report block on the right, the data is projected at the year level. When objects are placed into the report block from the left side, the report block automatically recalculates the projection for the proper combination of dimensions.

There are different kinds of block types, which are discussed in the next subheading. All are interactive and allow for drilling into detail.

CREATING REPORTS

In Web Intelligence, a report is created using a report panel. This is often referred to as the query panel, and the terms are interchangeable. There are three report/query panels available:

- **Web Intelligence Java report panel**—This is a java applet that is automatically downloaded from the XI framework onto the client PC and is accessed via the user's browser. The WebI Java report panel provides the most functionality of all three options in terms of query creation and report formatting.

- **Web Intelligence HTML report panel**—This totally thin solution provides a tab-driven approach to creating a Web Intelligence report, as well as some formatting capabilities. The paradigm is not as familiar to the Business Objects user who has used the query panel interface in either Web Intelligence or the Business Objects desktop client because it does not have the same layout.

- **Web Intelligence Query – HTML**—This is a pure query panel, meaning it does not allow for report formatting. Unlike the HTML report panel, it is very similar to the Java report panel query creation paradigm. In BusinessObjects XI, report formatting can be done on the report itself when viewing it in Interactive mode. This means that the Web Intelligence Query – HTML used in conjunction with on-report analysis provides for the query and analysis paradigm in a totally thin zero client solution.

> NOTE
>
> Really, the Java Report Panel and the HTML Report Panel are both query and report panels, as they provide the capability to both generate the query and do report formatting. The Query – HTML is a true query-only panel, as no report formatting is available through this interface. It is intended for use with the On-Report analysis feature to provide for a totally thin query and report formatting solution.

The Web Intelligence HTML report panel was a first generation totally thin reporting solution. It is being supplanted by the Web Intelligence Query – HTML query panel in combination with the on-report analysis features. This paradigm is more akin to the original and highly successful report query and formatting paradigm of the Business Objects desktop product with which the majority of existing customers are already familiar. The Web Intelligence HTML report panel is not discussed in this book.

A report created in one query panel can be opened in another. A report created in the Java report panel could be opened in the HTML report panel. Not all functionality is exposed within each tool, so it might not be feasible to do all functions in each report panel. However, because all solutions are built off of the same underlying object model, the functionality exists even if not exposed through the interface. The query/report panels will be enhanced to bring them to parity in future releases. Prior to the XI release, people often chose to use the Web Intelligence Java report panel. With the XI release, it is anticipated that a significant number of users will use the Web Intelligence Query – HTML and the on-report analysis features instead of the Java report panel.

WEB INTELLIGENCE JAVA REPORT PANEL

The Web Intelligence Java report panel (henceforth referred to as the Java report panel) will open when the user's preferences are set to this option in the Preferences section of InfoView and after a user chooses a universe for building a query. Figure 20.3 shows the Web Intelligence Java report panel with the eFashion universe opened. The Year object was selected from the Time Period class and is in the midst of being dragged and dropped into the result objects pane. Objects can be moved to any of the panes on the right side of the window. Note the help text in the panes telling the user how to use each pane.

Figure 20.3
The WebIntelligence Java Report Panel.

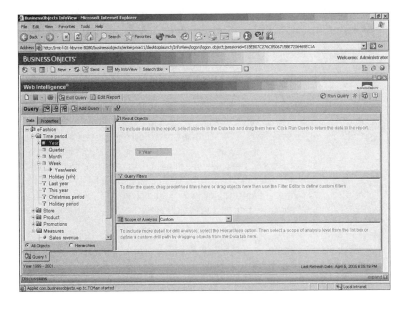

The window is broken into panes. On the left side is the data pane that contains the universe objects. As you can see in Table 20.3, there are four different object types.

TABLE 20.3   OBJECT TYPES

Icon	Object Type	Definition
	Dimension	Parameters for analysis. Dimensions often relate to a dimensional hierarchy such as geography, product, or time.
	Detail	An attribute of a dimension (such as customer phone number); usually not used for analysis.
	Measure	Convey numeric information that is used to quantify a dimension object.
	Condition	A predefined condition to limit resultsets.

Users drag and drop objects from the left pane to the various right panes. Objects put in the result objects pane show up in the report block by default. Objects put in the query filters pane do not show up in the resultset unless a corresponding object is in the result objects pane. Rather, these objects restrict the query (WHERE, HAVING, or subselect clauses), depending on how the filters are constructed. The objects in the scope of analysis pane are included in the query, but are not seen directly in the report block. So this is extra data contained within the report, but not displayed.

> *Scope of analysis* refers to the inclusion of objects in an object hierarchy. For example, a common hierarchy is Time—Year, Quarter, Month, Week, Day, and so forth. If the Year object is chosen as a result object and then the scope of analysis is set to two levels, the next two levels of the time hierarchy are also added to the query (Quarter, Month). Consequently, if Quarter had been chosen in the result objects pane instead of Year and the scope of analysis was set at two levels, the Month and Week objects would be added to the query. The scope of analysis brings in the number of levels specified below the object named in the result object pane. If multiple dimensions belong to hierarchies, all hierarchies are included in the scope of analysis. This will be discussed more in the "Drilling" section later in this chapter.

The interface is fairly simple—pull over the objects you want in the query and press the Run Query button in the top right. The user can use the Condition objects (yellow funnel icons) to place restrictions on the query, or he can build his own filters. If objects are dragged into the query filters pane, the left pane automatically changes to walk the user through the filter creation process. Figure 20.4 shows creation of a filter on the Lines object.

In Figure 20.4, the Lines object has been selected to be filtered, as is indicated in the top left of the Filter Editor dialog. A list of operators is available via a drop-down menu. You can also select an operand type. The operators are common functions, such as Equal To,

`Different From`, `In List`, `Not in List`, `Between`, `Is Null`, and so forth. The operand types tell how the variables should be handled. The report author can enter a constant value, he can choose the values from a pick list, or he can create a prompt so that in subsequent runs of the report, the user can put in different parameters. The right side of the dialog changes context, depending on the operator and operand type chosen.

Figure 20.4
When the Lines object is dropped into the Query Filters pane, the Filter Editor dialog immediately opens to walk the user through the filter creation process.

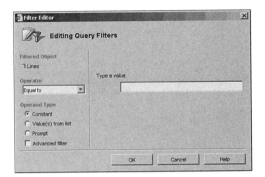

Additionally, the user can choose the Advanced Filter check box. This is the mechanism for putting specific types of subqueries into a query. Discussion of this feature is beyond the scope of this chapter, but the Crystal Report author should note that subquery capability exists within the query panel.

If multiple filters are chosen, the filters can be nested, with and/or operators applied. For example, a query could be restricted on all Customers with an Order level less than 20,000 last year or Customers with an Order level less than 10,000 this year, and, either way, exclude all Customers from Texas.

Keeping in mind that the objects themselves can contain quite sophisticated SQL (such as CASE statements or complex formulas), and understanding how objects can be put together in any combination in the query panel, you can see that sophisticated SQL can be generated by a business user without him knowing any of the underlying database structures or SQL syntax. For those users who might be more familiar with database structures and SQL, there is a Show SQL button that presents the user with the SQL generated from the query panel. As previously mentioned, this application feature is securable via the CMC, so it can be turned off to avoid exposing the database layer to specific users. However, it is a valuable tool for support staff helping to troubleshoot queries when business users run into complications.

Within the Java report panel is an Add Query button. This button enables multiple queries to be generated within a single report. This means that data from multiple and disparate databases can be brought together within a single Web Intelligence report and presented side-by-side.

20

For users familiar with the Business Objects desktop client, multiple queries within a single report are a fairly common occurrence. In the XI version of Web Intelligence, the resultsets (or data providers, in Business Objects parlance) cannot be joined together by the microcube engine as they can in the desktop client. This will be rectified in the next release of Web Intelligence, where multiple data-provider synchronization will be available in the WebI report engine.

WEB INTELLIGENCE QUERY PANEL – HTML

The Web Intelligence Query Panel – HTML (henceforth referred to as Query – HTML) provides the same functionality described in the preceding section but in a truly thin client. The Query – HTML panel is enabled through the preferences in InfoView by choosing Query – HTML from the list of report panels. Figure 20.5 shows how to set the WebIntelligence preferences for a user.

Figure 20.5
Preferences in InfoView, showing Web Intelligence viewing and report panel preferences.

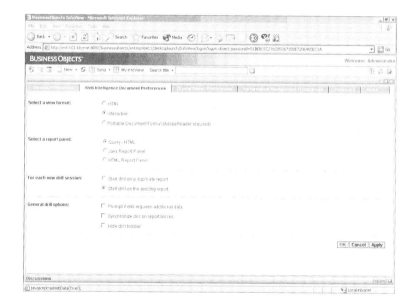

The Query – HTML panel can be seen in Figure 20.6.

Below are some of the HTML panel features:

- The same universe display is available as in the Java report panel (classes and objects in a hierarchical tree structure).
- Objects are moved to the result objects pane or query filters pane (scope of analysis is found in the Query Properties dialog).
- Multiple queries are available via the Add Query button.
- SQL can be viewed.

Figure 20.6
The Query – HTML panel.

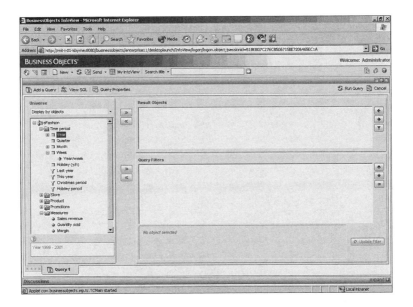

There are fewer features in this panel than the Java report panel because it contains no capabilities for report formatting. However, with the exception of the advanced query filters, the panel provides the same query functionality as the Java report panel. As stated previously, reports created with one report panel can be opened with another. So, for example, if a report was created with the Java report panel and it included an advanced query filter, another user could open that report in the Query - HTML panel and edit it and the report would still maintain the advanced query filter (depicted with a blue funnel to distinguish it from a simple filter). The user would not be able to edit the advanced filter, but could remove it or nest it in conjunction with other query filters. Again, all query panels utilize the same underlying object model, so reports are not query-panel dependent.

After you develop a report with the Query – HTML panel, formatting is the next step. In Web Intelligence, the concept of on-report analysis consists of manipulating the results directly on the HTML by the end user. A key focus of the reporting paradigm is the ability to manipulate a report either newly created via ad-hoc or previously created and published.

ON-REPORT ANALYSIS

Users are expected to use Web Intelligence to explore data, create reports, and then publish those reports for others to see and analyze. Often there are many more users who consume existing reports than users who author reports. However, for this large number of users, there are various report interaction levels that might be desired or allowed by the application administrator. To accommodate different levels of interactivity, Web Intelligence documents can be viewed in three default formats: PDF, which renders them almost totally static; HTML, which provides a little more interactivity; and interactive, which provides the full breadth of analysis and formatting available. Table 20.4 compares the three formats.

20

TABLE 20.4   WEB INTELLIGENCE REPORT VIEWING OPTIONS

Mode	Capabilities
PDF	Virtually static. The report can still be refreshed. If there are prompts in the report, refreshing allows the user to answer the prompts via an HTML dialog. However, report results are returned in PDF format and no on-report interaction is possible.
HTML	A bit more interactive. Users can refresh and answer prompts as in the PDF format, but now drilling is allowed. The navigation map helps the user jump to the report and section desired when browsing long documents. Searching within the document is available, as well as the ability to move to Edit mode (back to the query panel) or to save the output as a PDF, Excel, or CSV file. When in HTML mode, a user can easily move to PDF mode and vice versa.
Interactive	Full analytic and reporting capabilities. The user can perform all report formatting functions, such as adding or removing existing report objects, setting sections, formatting tables and charts, creating report variables, creating breaks, executing sorts and filters, pivoting the data, and so on. Additionally, the user can refresh the report and drill as in HTML mode, as well as save the report in various formats (Excel, PDF, CSV).

The next section focuses on the capabilities of viewing Web Intelligence documents in Interactive mode.

VIEWING A DOCUMENT IN INTERACTIVE MODE

Figure 20.7 is a screenshot of a report created on the eFashion universe as seen in Interactive mode. The query contains the objects seen in the WebI Query – HTML panel example (refer to Figure 20.6) with two levels in the Scope of Analysis. The left pane of InfoView that shows the folders has been hidden to provide more screen space for the report.

Figure 20.7
A Web Intelligence report open in Interactive mode.

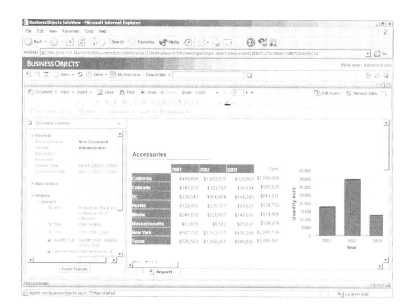

In Figure 20.8, you will first notice that the left side of the screen has a pane with a drop-down list. This pane contains metadata about the report. For example, in the document summary currently seen, a user unfamiliar with the report can learn a great deal about the origin and content of the report. Most notable are the objects selected and their associated descriptions, defined in the semantic layer. You can also see the universes used for each query under the data source section (not expanded), as well as the prompts asked and the values chosen for the report. This report contains data for the years 2001 through 2003, and data for a long list of clothing lines. So if there is ambiguity about the content of the report, a business user can look at the description and see exactly what objects and conditions were used in gathering the data. Also, an important attribute is the last refresh time, letting the user know if the information is fresh.

Figure 20.8
Document summary in WebI left pane.

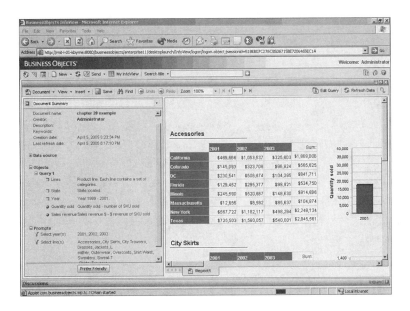

The left pane contains a number of drop-down boxes to help orient the user to the content and layout of the report, as well as to aid in navigating the report via the navigation map. The navigation map provides a navigation tree starting with each report tab, and shows each underlying section and subsection defined within the report. When the user clicks on the section, the screen moves to this section of the report, as depicted in the cross-tab table reflecting the Leather line in Figure 20.9.

A user can also change the prompt values by going to the User Prompt Input drop-down menu and manually editing the dialogs for each prompt, or she could achieve the same result by refreshing the report by clicking on the Refresh Data button in the top-right corner, which brings up the Prompts dialog with the previous refresh values, as seen in Figure 20.10.

20

Figure 20.9
Navigation map with leather selected; report moves to leather section.

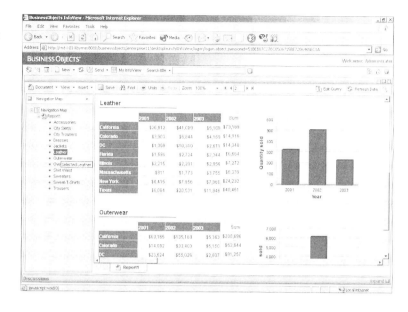

Figure 20.10
A WebI report showing the User Prompt Input in the left pane. The report was refreshed and the Prompt dialog shows the previously selected values.

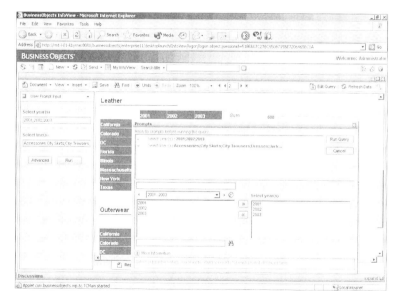

The user can also search for text within the report via the Find drop-down menu. The search does a partial string search unless full word is specified; the case can also be specified, as well as the direction of the search.

TOOLBARS

Notice the toolbars available for report analysis and formatting. These toolbars closely mimic the toolbars available in the Business Objects desktop reporting tool, so they should be familiar to Business Objects users. They provide access to report formatting, report manipulation, and formula creation functions. Also note that the standard Microsoft button icons are used whenever possible for ease of adoption by end users. Some of the capabilities are discussed in the next subheadings.

DATA MANIPULATION

The most common activities users request are sorting and filtering of data on the report. Both are easily achievable by choosing the Sort and Filter buttons. The user can also right-click on the report to bring up a context-sensitive menu that accesses the same function calls. For example, if the user wants to filter the data in the example report to show California, Colorado, and Texas only, she could right-click on the States column on the report and that would bring up the context-sensitive analysis menu, as seen in Figure 20.11.

Figure 20.11
The cross-tab table with State highlighted and the context-sensitive menu open, with Quick Filter highlighted.

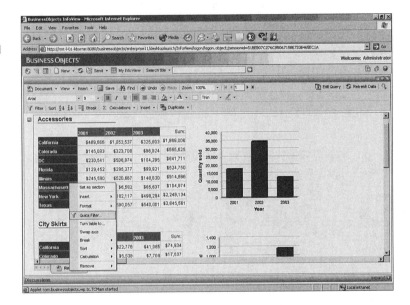

Choosing the Quick Filter option brings up a dialog for the object showing all of the possible values that exist in the report. The user can select the ones she wants and choose OK; the report is instantly filtered with the values. Figure 20.12 shows the Quick Filter dialog with some states selected.

Figure 20.13 shows the result of applying the filter on State. The filter was applied to the cross-tab table and not the chart, so the values were filtered by report block. This underscores that the report block is showing a particular intersection of the microcube beneath it, and each report block can function independently of the other, or can be synchronized to reflect common filtering during drill-down analysis (more on this later). Although this is a complicated technical concept, to a business user this makes intuitive sense; the chart is a different presentation than the cross-tab and therefore follows different filtering rules, unless it is explicitly told to follow the same rules. Note that this shows considerable difference from the banded report writing approach seen in Crystal Reports.

Figure 20.12
The Quick Filter dialog with some states selected.

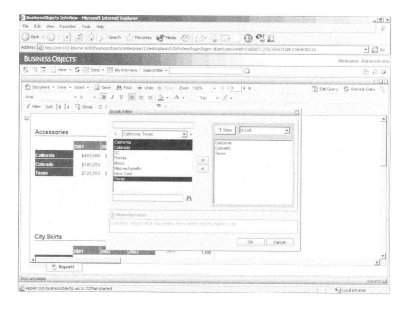

Figure 20.13
The report with the filter applied; only the selected values appear in the report. The data dynamically recalculates to accommodate the filter.

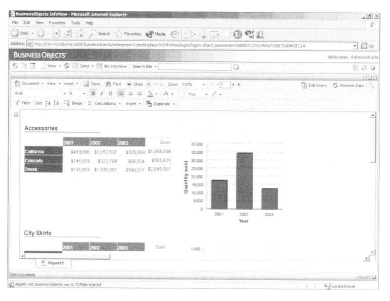

Suppose the user wants to sort these rows descending alphabetically. The user can simply click on the values (click directly in one of the cells) and then just click on the Descending Sort button on the toolbar, and the results are instantly sorted. More than one column can be sorted and sorts occur in the order applied.

The left pane in Figure 20.14 now shows the Document Structures and Filters view. This shows that at the report level, the Year and Line filters apply to the entire document. It also shows that the cross-tab has a filter on State and the values of that filter. It shows that there are no filters applied to the bar chart—again, all this metadata is useful for the business user when determining exactly what makes up the results in the report.

Figure 20.14
The Document Structure and Filters view is in the left pane. Notice that the query filters are applied globally, but the State filter is applied to the cross-tab block only and not to the bar chart.

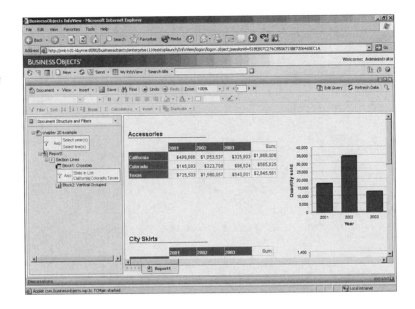

Pivoting and Swapping Objects

Imagine that the user would like to swap the axes within the cross-tab, showing states across the top and years down the side. The easiest way is to just drag and drop the row or column names directly on the report. Another way that shows a bit more of the internals of the reporting engine is achieved by right-clicking on the report to bring up the context-sensitive menu and by then choosing Format/Table. The following dialog appears as shown in Figure 20.15, the last tab of which is labeled Pivot.

The dialog displays the objects in the cross-tab configuration. The objects can then be dragged from the Row area to the Column area and vice versa, thus swapping the columns and rows. Note too that all other objects in the report are available on the left side, so completely different objects could be put into the cross-tab, or all of the objects completely replaced with a new selection. Likewise, report variables could be used as well (more on how to create report variables in the next subheading). So the reports can be completely redesigned by the end user, all through the Interactive mode, with no trip back to the query panel. This allows report designers to give the users maximum analytic flexibility while further shielding them from the database. Because reports can function as containers of predefined finite resultsets, the users can pick the reports and manipulate and analyze them in myriad ways without going back to IT for report refinement. Figure 20.16 shows the result of the pivot.

20

Figure 20.15
The Format Table dialog with the Pivot tab highlighted. Objects can be moved to change the values of the cross-tab. Objects can be chosen from any in the Available Objects pane or can be swapped from within the rows and columns boxes by dragging and dropping.

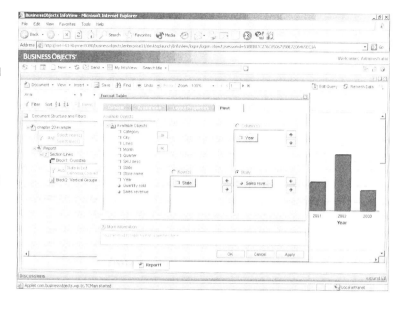

Figure 20.16
The axes are swapped, along with sums.

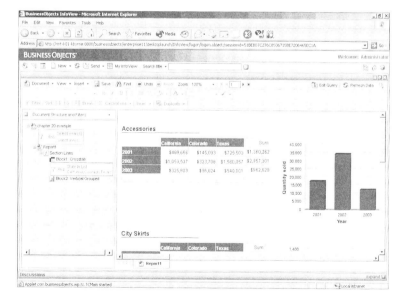

You could have more easily chosen Swap Axis from the context-sensitive menu, but then you would not have been able to see the ability to move objects in and out of the cross-tab. In Web Intelligence there are often several ways to accomplish the same thing. Just as in Microsoft Word, where a user can select text to copy and press Ctrl-C, click on the Copy button, or choose Copy from the Edit menu, so, too, in Web Intelligence users can choose one of several ways to manipulate the interface that is more compatible with their computing style.

REPORT VARIABLES AND FORMULAS

What if, in this report, you wanted to know the sales per unit? You could go back to the universe and see if there is a Sales per Unit measure object. In this case there is not, but because you have Sales Revenue and Quantity Sold objects, you can calculate the sales per unit within the report itself. Web Intelligence has a formula language just like Crystal Reports, with dozens of available functions.

The formula language can be used in two ways. First, a user could just type a formula into a cell and have the formula applied to the report block directly. As such, it resides only within that one cell for that one report block. The formula can also be within an object defined within the report. This is called a *report variable*. As an object, it is available for projection and reuse just like a measure object, meaning it can be swapped in and out easily or reused in multiple charts or tables.

NOTE

> Although both report formulas and variables can be created in the WebI Java report panel and in the Interactive Viewing mode, the XI release provides a bit more support in the user interface when using the Java report panel. The examples in this section use the Java report panel for ease of understanding.

TIP

> When developing a report and using formulas, it is best practice to encapsulate the formula in a Report Variable object so other users can interact with the object when doing analyses.

In the Java report panel, there is an icon with three little objects on it and a down arrow (indicating it will drop down into the report space). This is the Show/Hide Variable Editor button. Clicking this reveals the variable editor, as seen in Figure 20.17.

The Variable Editor contains an area to write the name of the variable, a text box to type in the formula (Formula Definition box), and helper boxes where objects, functions, and operators can be double-clicked and included in the Formula Definition box.

The Available Functions box groups the functions into folders so they can be easily found, or the user can choose the All folder to see all available functions. The major function categories are

- **Aggregate**—These are aggregate functions: sum, count, max, and so on. These aggregate functions also dictate how the variable behaves as it is projected within the microcube. These functions apply to report variables that are also measures.

- **Character**—Typical string manipulation functions: Ltrim, Substr, Length, Formatdate, replace, and so forth.

- **Date & time**—Typical date and time functions: CurrentDate, CurrentTime, DayNumberofWeek, DaysBetween, RelativeDate, and the like.

- **Document**—Functions detailing document specific parameters: `DocumentAuthor`, `DocumentDate`, `DocumentName`, `DocumentPartiallyRefreshed`, `DocumentTime`, and `DrillFilters`.

- **Data provider**—Functions that describe the individual data providers (resultsets) within the report: `DataProvider`, `LastExecutionDate`, `LastExecutionTime`, and `UserResponse`.

- **Misc**—Miscellaneous functions.

- **Logical**—Typical logical functions: `IsDate`, `IsError`, `IsNull`, `IsNumber`, `IsString`, and `IsTime`.

- **Numeric**—Typical numeric functions: `Abs`, `Sqrt`, `Floor`, `Exp`, `Log`, `Truncate`, `Round`, and so forth.

Figure 20.17
The Java report panel with the variable editor showing. This dialog can be toggled with the Show/Hide Variable Editor button.

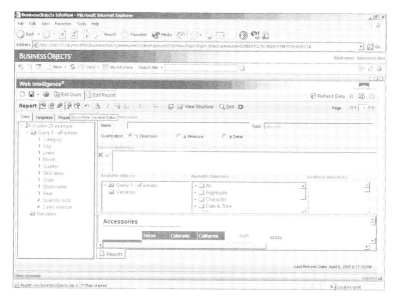

Readers that are more familiar with the Business Objects full client will note that the function library available in Web Intelligence is not as extensive as the one available in the desktop version. The function capabilities are continuously expanded and there will be many additional functions supported in the next release, with continual expansion for all subsequent releases.

The Crystal Reports function library is more extensive than the Web Intelligence function library. This is due mainly to two reasons. First, Crystal Reports can provide highly sophisticated formatting, so it requires a function language that enables this. Web Intelligence functions are focused on report object creation for on-report analysis. Second, the Web Intelligence function library is relatively new compared to the Crystal Reports function library, so expect it to expand significantly in future releases.

This example creates a Sales per Unit report variable. First, type in the report variable name in the Variable Definition box, and choose Measure as the Variable Qualification (this tells it what type of object it is). Then create the variable formula. In this case, you want to divide Sales Revenue by Quantity Sold to get the Sales per Unit. Find the Sales Revenue object in the Available Objects box and double-click it; it appears in the Formula Definition box. Select the solidus (division bar) from the Available Operators box, and then go back to the Available Objects box to double-click on the Quantity Sold object. You can check the variable formula before saving it by clicking on the green check mark just to the left of the Formula Definition box, and, if it passes, save the formula by pressing the Save button. Figure 20.18 shows the outcome of the actions described above.

Figure 20.18
The Variable Editor dialog with a completed formula. Note the Report Variable object in the left pane; the object has been saved and is now available for use in the report. Report variables are kept in a separate folder from universe objects.

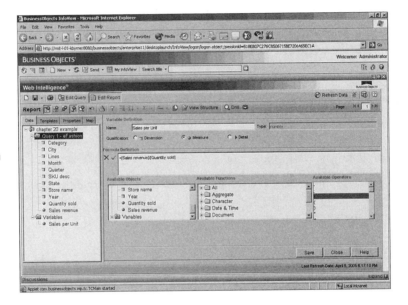

Notice the Web Intelligence syntax—all formulas start with an equal sign and universe objects are noted with square brackets [ ] around the object name. The formula shows the Sales Revenue object divided by the Quantity Sold object.

Because these values change at all dimensional intersections in the microcube, this formula changes its results in the report block. So, unlike Excel where the formula is dependent on a particular row/column combination, the Web Intelligence formula is not, and recalculates as the projection in the report block changes. Simply put, you can use it like any other object—swap it in and out of the table, place different dimensions next to it, drill on it—and it recalculates the proper values for each appropriate level.

Again, the capability to create report variables also exists using on-report analysis, but the dialog does not provide the same level of interactivity with the functions, objects, and operators as is available in the Java report panel. Figure 20.19 shows this same variable defined in Interactive mode.

20

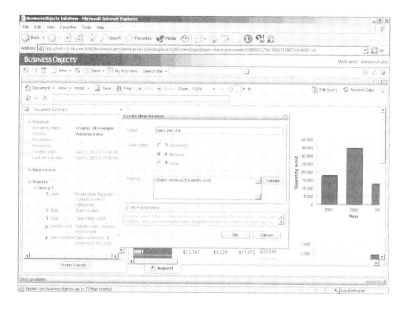

Figure 20.19
Creating a report variable in Interactive Viewing mode.

Notice that the formula needs to be typed in by hand. You can expect this dialog to be significantly enhanced in the next release.

An in-depth discussion on creating report variables is beyond the scope of this chapter. If you would like more information, refer to the Web Intelligence User Guide that has a more thorough discussion of all functions and uses.

DRILLING

Drilling shows the power of the various engines in the reporting stack seen in Figure 20.1 working in tandem. The report engine provides the display of the microcube and interactivity; the microcube creates the calculations, and the semantic layer provides behavioral rules for the engine when the data is being manipulated, calculated, and projected. In drilling, this becomes even more apparent as the semantic layer defines the data hierarchies through which the data can be navigated. Likewise, the semantic layer also provides the means for the user to drill "beyond the cube" seamlessly and return to the database when his analysis goes beyond the content contained within the report. Thus, SQL is autogenerated on the fly, and the data is returned to provide the next step for the business user. The next sub-headings cover this in detail.

HIERARCHIES

Hierarchies are natural data relationships that exist in the data. The term *hierarchy* refers to the aggregate relationship between entities. For example, time is often thought of as a hierarchy of entities—Year, Quarter, Month, Week, Day, and so on. The nature of the entities is such that they can be thought of as parent-child relationships—all of the days comprise a

Week, a certain number of weeks comprise a Month, three months comprise a Quarter, and so forth.

When navigating data, *drilling* refers to moving up and down the data hierarchy. If the user is looking at Year and wants to explore the data at the Quarter level, this is referred to as *drilling down* because it moves from the parent to the child (year to quarter). Drilling down therefore refers to moving downward through the hierarchy, from parent to child. *Drilling up* refers to moving upward through the hierarchy, from child to parent.

Business Objects uses a third term, *drill by*. Drill by refers to moving more than one level up or down, or moving from one dimensional hierarchy to another—say, from Time to Geography. So, if the user drilled down from Year to Quarter, but then wanted to see the data by Region, this would be drilling by (Region).

The microcube not only takes the resultset from the query, but it understands the hierarchies defined in the semantic layer and allows for navigation down, up, and by these hierarchies. As mentioned previously, the microcube recalculates as the dimensions change, so measures are recast as the drilling takes place.

DRILLING ON THE WEB INTELLIGENCE REPORT

In order to activate Drill mode, click the small magnifying glass button in the top-right of the report window. When clicked, the report redraws itself with hyperlinks under the dimensions and measures. Drilling can take place on any of the report blocks or sections, and can take place on dimensions as well as measures. Detail objects, depicted by the small green tetrahedron, are not drillable. Figure 20.20 shows the document in Drill mode.

Figure 20.20
The document in Drill mode. Note that the rows, columns, and values are all underlined, indicating they are drillable.

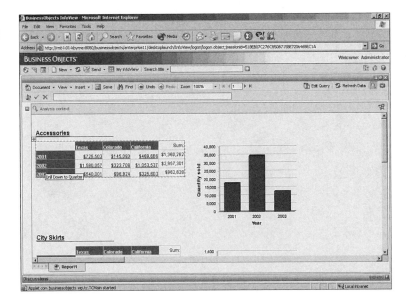

The ToolTip in Figure 20.20 tells the user what the next dimension is in the hierarchy. The option here is to drill down because year is at the top of the hierarchy—there is nowhere to go up from here. Note that California is also drillable, as are the measures in the cross-tab. Likewise, the chart to the right is also drillable. Drill down on 2001; the result is seen in Figure 20.21.

Figure 20.21
When the report is drilled down by Year, Quarter is replaced in the row of the cross-tab block and Year appears on the Analysis context in the Year drop down.

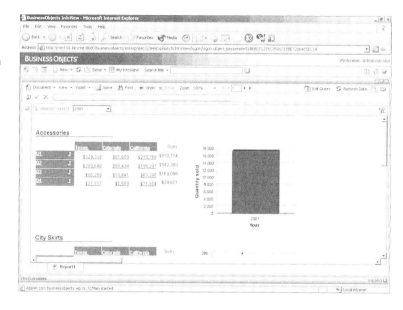

Notice in Figure 20.21 that the Year object is replaced with the Quarter object in the rows. Also note the up arrow that allows the user to drill up the hierarchy. The hyperlink on the Quarter values implies drilling down. Also note that the chart shows only 2001 data. Unlike report filters, drill filters apply universally to the report tab.

At the top of the pane is the Analysis Context drop-down menu containing 2001. This box allows the user to change the values of the Year variable and change the report display automatically.

Now drill up to Year, and then drill down on California.

In Figure 20.22, note that the columns in the cross-tab changed to Los Angeles and San Francisco. The drop-down list on State shows all of the possible values contained within the report. By choosing another state, the report will show the projections for those states.

Now drill up to the original state, and then drill down on the measure intersection for California and 2001.

Figure 20.23 shows drilling on the measure moved both dimensional hierarchies down, from Year to Quarter and from State to City. There are now two drop-down lists in the Analysis Context bar.

Figure 20.22
When the report is drilled down by State, City replaces State in the column of the cross-tab block and State appears on the Analysis context bar in the State drop down.

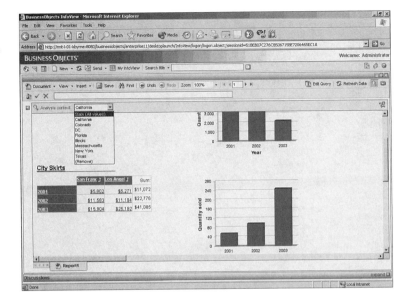

Figure 20.23
The report is drilled down by the measure object, and Quarter and City replace Year and State in the row and column of the cross-tab block, and Year and State appear in drop downs on the Analysis Context bar.

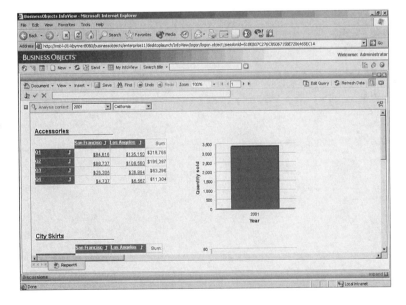

Now right-click on Quarter and choose Drill By, as seen in Figure 20.24.

When drilling by, all dimensional hierarchies present in the report can be seen. By choosing one hierarchy, you see the elements in the hierarchy starting at the top of the hierarchy and moving down, as is demonstrated by Lines, Category, and SKU Desc in the Product hierarchy. By choosing Category, you swap the Quarter object with the Category object, and the cross-tab is redrawn, as shown in Figure 20.25.

Figure 20.24
The context-sensitive menu is visible and Drill By is selected. All hierarchies represented in the report are available, so drilling by will swap the row with any dimension from any hierarchy.

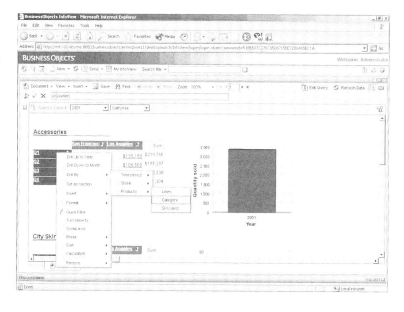

Figure 20.25
This is the report after drill by, with Category replacing Quarter. The Quarter object is now in the Analysis Context bar with the State and Year drop-down menus.

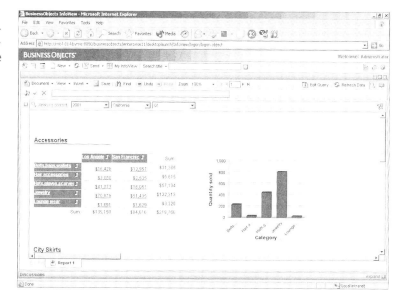

Do you see a difference in the accompanying bar chart? It now reflects the categories in the cross-tab. Another feature of drilling is synchronizing the dimensional drills of report blocks when they are being displayed. To synchronize the cross-tab and chart, go to the InfoView Preferences and change the drill behavior to Synchronize Drill on Report Blocks. As previously mentioned, the table and chart do not need to be in sync, but they can be. Regardless of whether the dimensions change in the chart, the chart data is filtered by the values in the

Analysis Context drop-downs. The only difference is changing the dimensional display in the chart to match the cross-tab display. Without the synchronization option, the x-axis on the chart would show the Year object (filtered for 2001).

DRILLING BEYOND THE CUBE

The report contains a small resultset, but presumably the database contains much more data. Some of this data might be defined within the data hierarchies in the semantic layer, but the objects were not chosen at report runtime. When drilling, the user can drill beyond the data in the report. He would then be faced with some options that are explored next.

NOTE

> It is possible via the CMC to disable the user from drilling beyond the cube and into the database. If the administrator turns this feature off, the user will not be able to explore data outside of the resultset contained within the report itself.

Go back to the original drill showing Quarter and City (Figure 20.23), and drill down to month. Click on the Month drill-down hyperlink, which presents the following dialog in Figure 20.26.

Figure 20.26
The Extend the Scope of Analysis dialog. The hierarchy selected shows the same values in the Analysis Context drop-downs.

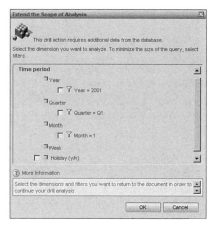

The Drill dialog asks to extend the scope of analysis on the Time dimension by including Week, which is the next object in the hierarchy. It also shows another object, Holiday, which is the fifth and final object in the hierarchy, with a check box to include it in the results if desired. The filters under each dimension reflect the current state of the drill filters displayed in the report. When fetching more detail data, the results can be quite large. Therefore, the user is presented with the option of filtering the results at any level, based on the current drill filters, to help ease the resultset size.

20

> On very large databases, this can be a significant performance enhancement. Runaway queries are managed by the semantic layer and security layer, when row restrictions and query run time governors are in place. This means that multimillion row resultsets can be avoided through proper security administration.

Choose the Week option from the dialog. Figure 20.27 shows the result.

Figure 20.27
The report after Week was chosen. The SQL was dynamically generated and executed, the microcube was dynamically updated, and the crosstab row reflects the Week object. Month now appears in the Analysis Context bar with the other dimensional drop-downs.

CONCLUSION

You should understand that this is in no way a full description of the reporting capabilities of Web Intelligence. However, the goal of this chapter was to introduce the Web Intelligence reporting paradigm and to show some of the main features that differentiate Web Intelligence from Crystal Reports. Having both of these engines available within a single framework is an extremely powerful set of report authoring and analysis capabilities. If you are interested in learning more about the intricacies of the Web Intelligence reporting engine, refer to the extensive product documentation that accompanies the product because it is quite detailed and will lead you through the full breadth of WebI capabilities. There are extensive features on report formatting and placement for printing, linking of reports, complete description of the formula language, in-depth discussion of the advanced query filters, and how multipass SQL is handled by the microcube for starters. It sounds like it could be another Que book in the making…

CHAPTER **21**

USING REPORTS EXPLORER FOR AD HOC WEB REPORTING AND MICROSOFT INTEGRATION

In this chapter

INTRODUCING AD HOC REPORTING CONCEPTUALLY

With many Ad Hoc reporting definitions, it is worth introducing the different types quickly. This chapter doesn't address the holistic question of defining Ad Hoc, but rather seeks to place the Crystal Reports Explorer and the LiveOffice tool into their proper contexts as Ad Hoc reporting tools. Simply put, Ad Hoc reporting or queries are impromptu questions you put to the data to extract answers. Although many permutations exist, from systems that enable the end user to directly query source data in raw form to accessing OLAP cubes, from tools for very SQL-savvy users to point-and-click tools, from preformatted or unformatted query tools to tools that enable pixel-level formatting, many tools and definitions exist in the marketplace.

Crystal Reports Explorer most facilitates end-user Crystal Reports development and modification through a Web browser. Whether the data source is a database or Business View, or another Crystal Report, the result is always a Crystal Report. Although OLAP Intelligence provides end users great interactivity, its exclusive connectivity to an OLAP data source helps you categorize it as an Analytic rather than Ad Hoc tool.

Most organizations debate the amount and type of deployment of various types of Business Intelligence, from reporting to ad hoc reporting, to query and analysis, to analytic workbooks, to purpose-built applications. Briefly, a typical organization, after reaching a mature stage of Business Intelligence deployment, finds that roughly 80%–90% of information distribution takes place with preformatted reports. Roughly 10%–15% might be ad hoc queries and another 5% analytics. Every organization varies, but a balance between the time and training necessary for end users to interact with data and the value they derive in the process should be fundamental.

Many organizations actually adopt ad hoc reporting as a method to reduce IT workload/spending and to provide increased end-user access to data. The Ad Hoc tool facilitates this approach by enabling end users to develop a Crystal Report themselves. This Crystal Report can then be saved into the BusinessObjects Enterprise system and viewed at any time, or even passed to IT for special features to be added. This concept that end users can do more themselves provides significant cost-savings, but recognition that IT will always play a role in Business Intelligence marks a mature approach to the problem at large.

The remainder of this chapter focuses on how to use the Crystal Reports Explorer application as well as the LiveOffice add-in for Microsoft Office.

> **NOTE**
>
> In previous versions, the Crystal Reports Explorer was known as the Crystal Enterprise Ad-Hoc tool.

INTRODUCING THE CRYSTAL REPORTS EXPLORER APPLICATION

The Crystal Reports Explorer application uses the capabilities of BusinessObjects Enterprise to present report modification and creation capabilities via a Web browser.

HTML and CSP/ASP or JSP pages make up the application itself in the .NET or Java environment, respectively. These pages interact with the appropriate SDK and interact heavily with the Report Application Server (RAS), which provides the server-side report modification capabilities. Through heavy use of JavaScript in the browser, Crystal Reports Explorer interacts with the end user more in the fashion of an application rather than a static Web page.

Because of the heavy level of interaction expected with usage of the Ad Hoc application, administrators should carefully project and monitor usage at the Web server, BusinessObjects Enterprise, and database levels.

Crystal Reports Explorer consumes Business Views, Crystal Reports, or ODBC data sources, so database credentials, BusinessObjects Enterprise credentials, and a data access policy should be in place to maximize effective use of the application. For organizations that have determined to use Business Views for all data access, appropriate Business Views should be in place to enable end users to create reports Crystal Reports Explorer application, and appropriate permissions on those Business Views granted. For organizations that choose to enable direct access to the databases, again permissions should be granted.

INSTALLING CRYSTAL REPORTS EXPLORER

Installation of BusinessObjects Enterprise, along with either the XI Premium bundle or BusinessObjects Enterprise Professional with the appropriate "report modification and creation" key-code, are required before installing Crystal Reports Explorer.

Note that Crystal Reports Explorer supports the same platforms as BusinessObjects Enterprise XI with the exception of Netscape/Mozilla browser support—the heavy use of JavaScript precluded the compatibility between Internet Explorer and Netscape/Mozilla.

Two versions of Crystal Reports Explorer exist and require different installation methods: a CSP/ASP version and a JSP version, and a variant of the CSP/ASP installation where a Unix Web server works with a Windows BusinessObjects Enterprise server. Depending on your environment and preferences, the proper version should be selected. The install.pdf file on your distribution of Crystal Reports Explorer contains detailed instructions on the various installations.

CONFIGURATION OF CRYSTAL REPORTS EXPLORER

Several areas must be configured before deploying Crystal Reports Explorer. Because the application heavily uses the RAS service/daemon, the settings for the RAS server should be specified for optimal performance. Also, because Crystal Reports Explorer enables you to create and modify reports and save them back to the BusinessObjects Enterprise system, you must modify or write appropriate rights to grant to the user or group on the particular folders affected.

→ For more information on optimizing the RAS server performance, **see** "Report Application Server," **p. 607**, and "Servers and Processing Options," **p. 669**.

Further settings inside the Central Management Console, under Home, BusinessObjects Enterprise Applications, Crystal Reports Explorer determine which folders should be used

21

for the default report templates and data sources. The actual contents of those folders display on the right side. In the displayed tree on the left, which shows BusinessObjects Enterprise's folder structure, right-clicking a particular folder opens a menu to manage the folders (see Figure 21.1). At the bottom of the context menu the two options particular to Crystal Reports Explorer let you designate the default folders to be used in the application for Data Sources (which displays the folder icon in red) and Templates (in blue). These folders, respectively, contain reports whose data definition provides a starting point for ad hoc reporting and which you can use to reformat reports by using the template functionality. Often, for simplicity's sake, administrators create a root folder labeled Ad Hoc and subfolders labeled DataSources and Templates, and then designate them accordingly using the right-click functionality.

Figure 21.1
The Central Management Console's Crystal Reports Explorer application management display.

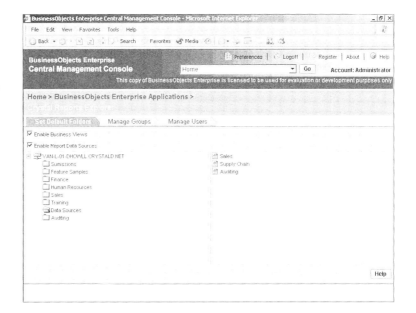

Checking the boxes to enable/disable Business Views or Reports as data sources determines what types of data sources the end users have access to. Business Views provide an easy way to define data in business terms, enabling end users to create reports in Crystal Reports Explorer and provide self-service end-user scenarios.

The Manage Groups and Users tabs are identical and manage permissions for Crystal Reports Explorer at the group and user level, respectively (see Figure 21.2). Using the group-level permissions enables more efficient management as fewer groups exist than users. You can then set individual user permissions by changing group permissions. If current groups do not map cleanly to the rights appropriate for this particular application, new groups can be created that map existing users or user groups to groups specifically created to manage Ad Hoc application permissions. The permissions on the right part of the management screen manage which capabilities the end user can see in the toolbar that appears in the end-user application at the left side, the control buttons along the application's top right, and the tabs in the center of the application. Each of these capabilities is considered in the following sections.

Figure 21.2
The Manage Groups/Manage Users area for Crystal Reports Explorer in the Central Management Console.

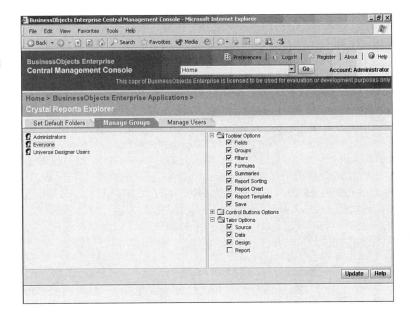

REPORT SOURCE SETUP

The Crystal Reports Explorer application enables an end user to create a report from either a Business View or a Crystal Report. Business View creators create and store the Business Views in the BusinessObjects Enterprise system (refer to Chapter 18, "Using a Semantic Layer—Business Views and Universes"). Creating an Ad Hoc report from an existing Crystal Report requires a Crystal Report be in the Data-Sources folder as defined previously. You can either design this report in Crystal Reports and save it into the appropriate folder in BusinessObjects Enterprise, move an existing report into that folder, or create it in an administrative area of the application itself. Exercise caution when moving an old report into the report definition folders because groupings and table names might confuse end users creating new reports from that definition. Testing in this situation is mandatory to ensure end user success.

To set up this report definition, start the Crystal Reports Explorer interface. This interface is automatically integrated with the .NET InfoView interface during the installation of Crystal Reports Explorer. The installation guide also covers the steps for integrating Crystal Reports Explorer in the Java version of InfoView. In either case, Crystal Reports Explorer has two modes: an Administrator's mode and an end user's mode. Access the application by the application URL (by default, http::// <Machinename>/businessobjects/ enterprise11/adhoc/). Logging on to this page with Administrator's credentials provides two options: to Define Report Datasource or to Create Ad Hoc Report. The Create option

21

refers to the end-user capability covered in the next section. The Define capability refers to the capability to create a report definition that can be used as a data source for an end user creating an Ad Hoc report at a later time.

Set the report data source definition by choosing to either select an ODBC connection via the Select DB Data Source drop-down on the left under the toolbar, or by clicking on the Load Definition option immediately below it. The Load Definition accesses Crystal Reports stored in the Default Datasources folder designated earlier. Choosing a report here enables you to modify the way that this report's data definition is displayed to an end user creating an Ad Hoc report. The drop-down list displays the data sources you can connect to if you want to create a Crystal Report from scratch. Typically it contains only the ODBC option. Choosing that option opens a dialog box asking you to select an ODBC connection existing on the server machine that hosts the Report Application Server service/daemon of the BusinessObjects Enterprise system. By choosing the ODBC connection name (DSN), and then supplying the database credentials (username and password), and optionally any connection strings for the ODBC connection, you establish a connection to the database. Keep in mind that because this is a Web application, the dialog to choose the ODBC connection often has an approximately five-second lag, so wait for default values to show in the top line before clicking.

> NOTE
>
> After a data definition loads, commence moving down the rest of the toolbar—the application design concept has the user start at the top of the toolbar and proceed down by first choosing the definition, selecting tables, linking them, choosing fields, determining filters and then formulas, and then saving this definition. Each of these items on the left is first single-clicked initially, displaying either a dialog box or a simple modification section immediately below it.

Because the dialogs and modification sections in Crystal Reports Explorer behave very consistently, a short detour to discuss how you interact with them helps you move through the rest of the material smoothly—especially because this Web application interacts with the end user so much and differs from many Windows conventions and Internet conventions for clicking and maneuvering. Note that the mere inclusion in this book of the following descriptions should trigger the thought that end users require training to successfully use this application. Although quite simple, the application does require some training even if this is only 15 minutes of introduction for the savvy user.

Each item in the toolbar on the left should be clicked *once* only to open it or its dialog box, and then clicked again to hide details that have displayed beneath it. Many users double-click on the toolbar items and wonder why they see nothing! Close dialog boxes by clicking OK or Cancel once. Most dialogs have a list on one side and another list on the other side (see Figure 21.3). In these cases, a single-click selects an item, Ctrl+click adds each clicked item to the current selection, and Shift+click selects everything between the item first selected and the item Shift+clicked. Moving items can be accomplished by double-clicking them, dragging a selection from one area to another, or by clicking the single chevron (>)

to move a selection in that direction. Clicking the double-chevron (>>) moves all items in that direction, effectively clearing one area. Remember that response is always slower in a Web application and that clicking multiple times usually results in strange behavior because the application catches up with the user. Counsel end users to wait until they see the desired reaction visibly before going on to the next click or action so that they do not inadvertently cause strange behavior.

Figure 21.3
The Data Source Table dialog.

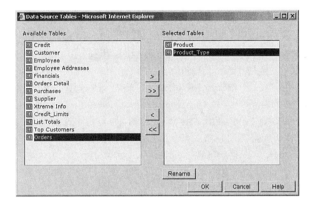

This cannot be stressed enough as a crucial part of the education process because end users also often click on an item to open a dialog box, and then click again somewhere else in the same window before the dialog box has opened, causing the dialog box to open *behind* the main window, effectively freezing the application. In cases like this, a savvy user simply minimizes the foreground window and finds the dialog waiting there. However, many times a frustrated user compounds the situation by clicking away in the vain hope that something will happen because he is clicking more, and eventually calls tech support with a frozen application. End users must be carefully instructed that although this application seems like a Windows application, it is still a series of Web pages, and that Web technology has these limitations. You gain by extending the capability to modify and create reports with nothing installed on the machine—you also must live with the resultant limitations.

Users might notice a similarity between the items in the toolbar and the Report Creation Wizard in Crystal Reports itself. This similarity is purposeful and makes migration to the concepts in Crystal Reports Explorer simple for the user familiar with Crystal Reports. In addition, the underlying functionality of Crystal Reports Explorer mirrors that of Crystal Reports, now presented more simply and over the Internet. Thus in an effort not to repeat information here about actual feature behavior, the reader can refer to the appropriate chapter on Crystal Reports for a more detailed understanding of the underlying concepts such as table linking, filter and formula creation, and the like.

The toolbar itself, incidentally, can be moved by clicking and dragging the Toolbar label on the top left, and restored by clicking on the × on the right of the toolbar. The original position of the toolbar on the left side, described as docked, also enables the end user to close it by clicking on the ×, and then restore it by clicking on the triangle icon at the top left.

21

Returning to the flow of designing a report source, you click once on the Select Tables item to open the select tables dialog box (refer to Figure 21.3). Moving tables to the right includes them in the definition. After you've moved them to the right, you can rename tables by selecting them and clicking once on the Rename button. When you're finished choosing tables to include, choose OK. Again there is a pause after clicking OK as the page redraws after a round-trip to the server. End users have to be instructed not to click before the page loads again.

After selecting tables, you link them by clicking Link Tables in the toolbar, which opens the Table Linking dialog box (see Figure 21.4). To link tables, select a table on the left, another table on the right, and then the columns in the tables that will make up the link underneath the tables, respectively. Select the desired type of join from the drop-down list, and finally click the Link button once to create the link you have selected. This link now shows up in the Links area of the dialog box. Selecting a join and then clicking the Delete button deletes that join, and clicking the Smart Link button replaces *all* the current joins with joins that the server believes are the best based on column names and index and key positions in the database, if that information is available. Best practice recommends that if you want to use Smart Link functionality, attempt that first, and then examine the results. This way you save work if the joins are correct and can simply delete the incorrect links. When finished, click OK and move to the next item: field selection.

Figure 21.4
The Table Linking Dialog Box.

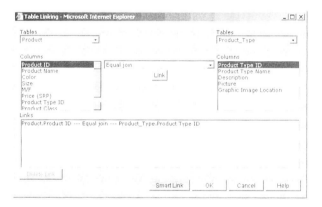

Clicking once on the Fields item in the toolbar opens a mini-dialog box underneath the Fields item. Clicking again on the Fields item hides the mini-dialog. Each time you click on a field in the mini-dialog, an asterisk appears next to that field, and it appears to the right in the Fields area of the Source tab (see Figure 21.5).

Clicking on the Advanced label underneath the Fields mini-dialog opens an advanced Field dialog box. This dialog enables you to bulk move items and arrange them left-to-right on the report by moving them up or down (up means to the left, and down to the right) in the Fields to Display area by selecting a field and then clicking the up or down arrows at the far right of the dialog box. This advanced dialog arranges available fields by table, but enables you to search for fields by clicking on the Find Fields button, as well as rename fields by selecting the field in the Fields to Display area, and then clicking on the Rename button (see Figure 21.6). Again click the OK button to finish this area and return to the main window.

Figure 21.5
The Field Selection
mini-dialog.

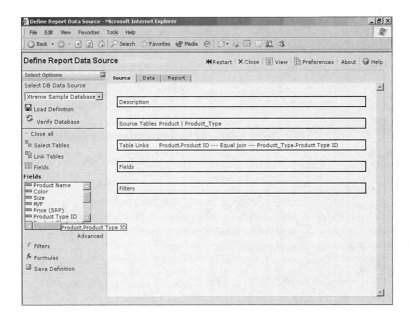

Figure 21.6
The Advanced Field
Selection dialog.

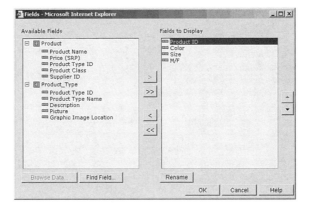

Clicking on the Filters item opens the Filter mini-dialog, which can be hidden by single-clicking on the Filters item in the toolbar. The process of adding a filter mirrors that in Crystal Reports. Choose the field to filter on in the top drop-down list and choose the operator in the next drop-down list. Then enter the value, or click the Browse button (this is represented by an ellipses […] on the button), which retrieves values from the database for that field, enabling you to select a particular value from the database if you do not remember the correct value. The Browse button might disappear if the field data type changes to a field type with limited values. For instance, a Boolean field type with only True and False values simply shows True and False in the Value drop-down list, and no

21

longer includes a Browse button. Once you have specified the filter criteria click Add and confirm the filter has been added in the Filters section of the Source tab.

The Advanced option in this mini-dialog, launches the Filters dialog (shown in Figure 21.7), which provides the opportunity to create complex filter specifications using AND, OR and parenthetic expressions. Elements that appear in the top area of the dialog can me moved by clicking and dragging them within the text window.

When in the Advanced Filter dialog, remember to click the Add button on the right to add the filter to the top area of the dialog before clicking OK. Clicking OK before adding the filter is like clicking Cancel and results in no filter being applied. Once added, a filter can be modified or removed via the Advanced filter dialog by highlighting the filter specification and then clicking on the proper button at the bottom left of the dialog box.

NOTE

> The one case where the user is required to double click instead of single click in when adding an AND, OR or parenthesis to the filter specification. You must double click these to add them to the top area of the dialog.

Figure 21.7
The Filter dialog box.

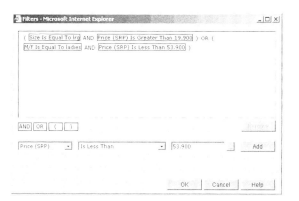

After creating the appropriate filters, you can add a formula. The formulas appear to end users as fields, and they will not know that these are calculated items. Thus if a database or Business View does not contain a necessary field for a query, but the field can be created in a formula from existing data source values, the formula here can present the desired value. Clicking on the Formulas button opens a dialog (see Figure 21.8). After it opens, initiate the process by clicking on the New button on the bottom left, which enters a default formula name above at the top right which you can overwrite with the chosen field name for the formula you are about to create. By typing in a valid Crystal Reports formula in the Formula Text box, you create the desired expression. Double-clicking on either a field name or a Function name in the Fields or Functions boxes enters that value into the Formula Text dialog at the point where the cursor was last positioned in that box. For a more detailed discussion of formula syntax, refer to Chapter 4, "Understanding and Implementing Formulas," because the formulas here are exactly the same as formulas in Crystal Reports. In fact, should the report definition require very complicated formulas, the designer should either use Crystal Reports to create the report definition and save it into the correct data sources folder in BusinessObjects Enterprise, or use the Business Views tool to create the formula in a Business View, as both Crystal Reports and Business Views feature a full formula editor. At the bottom of the left side of the dialog box are buttons to check the formula syntax and give a status on whether the formula is valid, and a Remove button, which deletes the formulas highlighted above on the left-hand side. When you've finished entering the desired formulas, choose OK.

Figure 21.8
The Formula
dialog box.

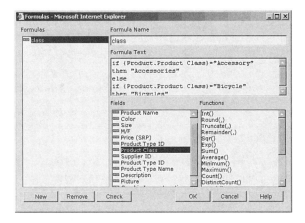

Next save the definition you have created into the BusinessObjects Enterprise system. The name you choose for the definition will be presented to end users who want to create reports based on that definition.

Although there are Query, Data, and Report tabs along the top of the screen, they are not important at this stage and are detailed in the next area. Additionally, at the top right, you have buttons to (from the left to right):

- Restart the process and clear any work you have just done
- Close the application window altogether
- View the report on which you are working
- Change preferences
- Give version information (About)
- Show the application help

The preferences enable you to do the following:

- Select default colors
- Determine which tab opens first
- Determine how the toolbar behaves in terms of whether it is docked at the left, floats in the window, or does not show up at all

- Choose whether to display mini-dialogs or the advanced dialogs initially
- Choose whether to display field names, descriptions or both
- Reset to default preferences
- Choose whether to use a report template to format the reports by default
- Choose how many rows to show initially in the data grid
- Choose which areas to show in the Design tab
- Choose whether to show and/or snap to grid on the Design tab

Alternatively, creating a Business View provides much of the same capability, and should be the first method used to create data definitions for Crystal Reports Explorer report design. However, in cases where the database administrator cannot access the Business Views tool, or where a Crystal Report has already been created and there is a need to quickly modify it into a data definition for Ad Hoc report creation, the Report Definition process can be extremely useful.

REPORT CREATION AND MODIFICATION

With the data definition or Business View in place, end users create reports by logging directly into the Crystal Reports Explorer application or by selecting Crystal Report from the New menu within InfoView. In both cases, the user is presented with the Choose Data Source dialog where they can select from the available data sources. (see Figure 21.9). An examination of the application screen shows that the top-right area is identical to the section detailed previously, and behaves in exactly the same way. Again, most of the items on the left are also exactly the same as the section just covered, except that they do not include the same starting point. The assumption that the end user does not have database skills or desire to optimize the database query precludes those items from this end-user oriented section.

Figure 21.9
Choosing a Business View as a data source.

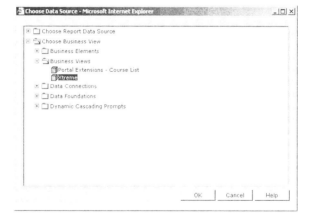

After choosing a Data Source, you choose Fields in exactly the same way that you chose them above. You then create groups by clicking on the Groups item on the toolbar, which behaves exactly as the Fields chooser, except the order of the groups might be more important because groups nest inside one another. Moving items up or down within the Advanced Groups dialog enables you to change the grouping order.

Again, the Filters and Formulas items mirror the previous section.

The Summaries area enables you to create summaries of values for each group and behaves exactly as the Filters dialog, except that the result is the summation of fields rather than filtering them (see Figure 21.10). You choose the field to be summarized, the type of summary desired (note that the options displayed depend on the field-type so string fields have different options than numeric and the like), and the level of the report (for example, the group name) at which the summary is desired. Again, make certain to click the Add button before clicking OK to add the summary to the report.

Figure 21.10
The Summaries
dialog box.

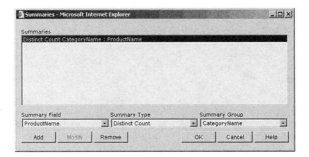

The Report Sorting item on the toolbar defines sort orders for the report details or groups. You can enter a simple definition by selecting the field to sort on and the order (for example, ascending) in the mini-dialog. The advanced item opens a dialog box allowing more advanced sorting on groups or summaries in addition to sorting on fields. Note that multiple sorts can be created here (see Figure 21.11).

→ For more information on sorting options, including Top N and the like, **see** "Using Group Selection and Sorting," **p. 89**.

If you want a chart, click on the Report Chart item in the toolbar to open the Report Chart dialog box, which enables you to choose a chart type (Bar, Line, or Pie), provide a title for that chart, place it either in the report header or footer section, and if there are multiple groups or summary values, choose the appropriate values for the chart.

The Report Template item in the toolbar opens the door to one of the most advanced features in Crystal Reports—the capability to format a report in one step. The report template dialog asks you to choose a template from several default templates, which will format the report accordingly. As you select any item in the template list in the dialog, a preview thumbnail image appears on the right giving you an indication of what the report might look like. Even more powerful is the capability to create your own templates, store them in

21

your designated Report Templates folder (see the beginning of this chapter for more information), and then by clicking on the Templates button at the bottom left of the dialog (see Figure 21.12) apply the formatting in that report to the report you are designing, including fonts and other field formatting, headers and footers, and chart formatting.

→ For a more complete discussion on templates, **see** "Understanding Report Templates," **p. 320**.

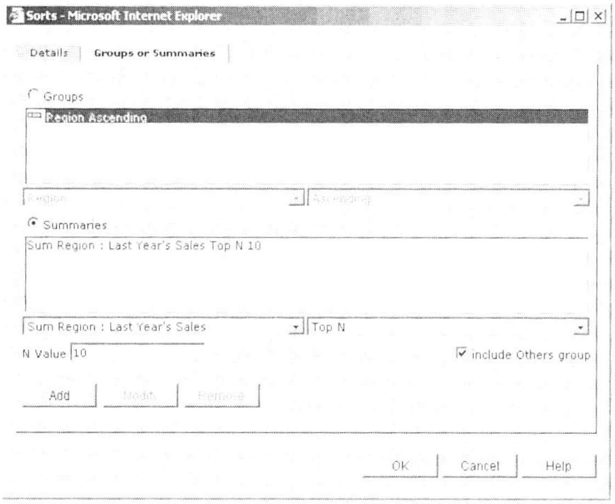

Figure 21.11
The Advanced Sort
dialog box.

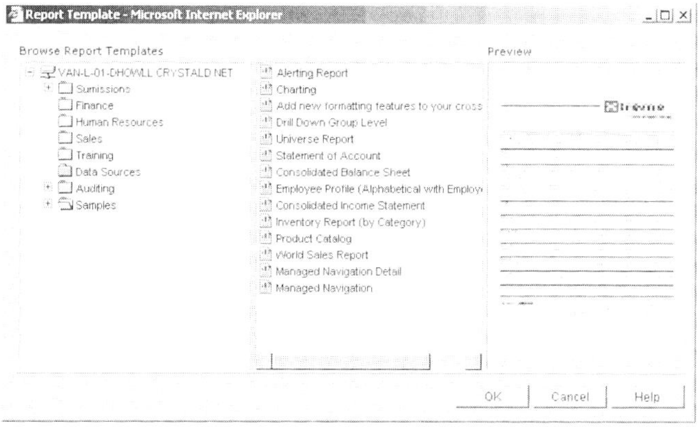

Figure 21.12
Choosing a template
to apply to the report.

Again, as per the previous section, end users can save this report into the folder of their choice, assuming that they have write permissions on that folder. Often end users save into their Favorites folders.

At any stage in the process end users can move to a different tab than the Query tab that you have used so far to work through different views of the material. Now this chapter takes a closer look at the Data, Design, and Report tabs.

THE DATA TAB

The Data tab shows you a data grid of the values selected in the report. Note that you can use this, or any other tab, while creating the report and see things develop as you add fields, filters, and the like to the report. When a report includes groups, a group tree shows on the left side of the view. This can be toggled on and off by clicking the group-tree icon at the top left of the report viewer toolbar (see Figure 21.13). Clicking on an item in the tree shows the values for that group in the display grid. The rest of the report viewer toolbar is a standard Crystal Reports toolbar with export and navigation capabilities, with two exceptions. Because the view includes row numbers, the white page with the red arrow icon (near the right side of the toolbar) enables you to navigate to a particular row number, and the Flat View icon (the second from the left) toggles between a grouped view, which enables drill-down by clicking blue-underlined values and a flat view, which has no grouping applied.

Figure 21.13
The Data tab of the Crystal Reports Explorer application showing a group tree with several countries.

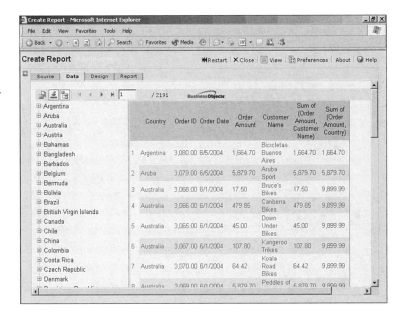

TIP

In previous versions, you can select information right from the grid and copy and paste it into Excel and it falls into the right row-and-column structure, which saves time for simple data transfer. In the XI release of Crystal Reports Explorer, you must first select the export function, and choose Excel format. The Data tab view will change from a text format to a grid object which supports the above mentioned functionality.

21

THE DESIGN TAB

Much like in Crystal Reports, Crystal Reports Explorer offers a Design tab for formatting the report in a detailed fashion. Many of the basic formatting options are available here. To move a field, click and drag it to the desired location. To select a field, click on it. You will know you have selected it when you see small gray blocks appear at the visible corners of the field. You can then move your mouse over the blocks and resize the field, or right-click on the field to access a menu that gives you formatting and alignment options. The formatting options are a subset of those in Crystal Reports and behave in exactly the same way (see Figure 21.14).

→ For more information on the options in the format dialog or the right-click menu, **see** "Exploring the Format Editor Dialog Common Options," **p. 168**, and "Modifying Object Properties for Formatting Purposes," **p. 163**

Figure 21.14
The Format dialog in the Design tab.

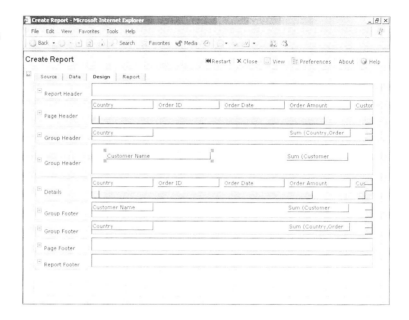

Right-clicking in a white space not occupied by a field, but still in the report sections, enables you to enter a text field or open the section expert. Like the section expert in Crystal Reports, you can determine here how sections should behave, and for instance, create a drill-down report section on the Web (see Figure 21.15). For a complete discussion of sections and section behavior, refer to Chapter 7, "Working with Report Sections."

AD HOC REPORT DESIGN SUMMARY

Crystal Reports Explorer provides powerful report creation and modification over the Web, with many of the core features of Crystal Reports exposed to an end user without any desktop installation. Coupled with the power of Business Views to simplify database interaction, most users can create or modify reports quite easily. Although out of scope in this chapter, Crystal Reports Explorer can easily be modified to open existing reports for modification as well as the report creation capability detailed previously. The end users of this application can then share the newly created value with their colleagues by publishing their newly created or modified reports back into BusinessObjects Enterprise directly from Crystal Reports Explorer.

Figure 21.15
The Section Expert dialog in the Design tab.

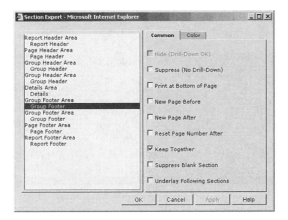

With the overview of Crystal Reports Explorer completed, you now move to the second major Ad Hoc tool in BusinessObjects Enterprise, the BusinessObjects LiveOffice Add-in for Microsoft Office.

BUSINESSOBJECTS LIVEOFFICE ADD-IN

Because so many information workers today use the Microsoft Office suite and, in particular, Microsoft Excel extensively for worksheet applications and data manipulation, it follows that enterprise report data should also be accessible in Microsoft Excel and other Microsoft Office applications. With the release of XI, the Crystal Reports plug-in for Excel has merged with the former Office add-in to become BusinessObjects LiveOffice.

LiveOffice provides a bridge between enterprise report data and the applications that are part of an information worker's everyday tasks. Whether the data is needed in a simple table in PowerPoint, or extensive data manipulation is needed in Excel, LiveOffice provides the link back to a centralized Business Intelligence repository. In this section, we will cover the LiveOffice add-in in the Microsoft Excel, PowerPoint and Word applications.

ARCHITECTURE AND DEPLOYMENT SCENARIOS

The LiveOffice plug-in requires installation on the local machine, and so requires administrative rights on the local machine.

The connection between the LiveOffice plug-in and BusinessObjects Enterprise uses TCP/IP over the local area network. Because of the direct connectivity between Microsoft Office and BusinessObjects Enterprise, an Internet connection does not easily support the plug-in; usually a LAN connection to the BusinessObjects Enterprise server is required.

ADMINISTRATION AND SETUP

The installation commences by executing the setup executable on the client machine. Because the plug-in opens Crystal Reports, the BusinessObjects Enterprise server should be

21

configured to grant View, Edit, Refresh, and View instances permissions to the end users who would use this application.

The LiveOffice connector on the BusinessObjects Enterprise system is enabled with a LiveOffice keycode or a Premium keycode.

CONNECTING TO A REPORT

The following steps connect to a report:

From Excel, highlight a cell where you would like to display the report values, and then choose the Business Objects menu, and the New View item.

Expand the BusinessObjects Enterprise folder in the Data Source dialog. If you have not already logged on to the system provide credentials to log on to BusinessObjects Enterprise, and see the BusinessObjects Enterprise folders, from which you can choose a report as a starting point for your query.

In the Data Selection dialog box, specify whether to use fields from the report or report part(s) of the report.

This in turn opens the Report View Expert, which starts with the Select Fields item. Like the Crystal Reports Explorer application and the Crystal Reports Wizard, you simply move items to the right to include them in the view. Note the origin button at the bottom left: This enables you to choose to report off of the underlying data source of that Crystal Report, saved data in a historical instance previously scheduled in BusinessObjects Enterprise, or saved data in the latest instance of the Report (see Figure 21.16). This dialog also enables you to specify or change report parameters if required for the report.

Figure 21.16
The Select Fields dialog of BusinessObjects LiveOffice Add-in.

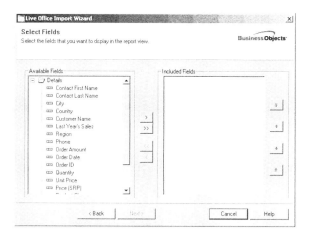

This is particularly valuable for creating time-series analysis, as many different Crystal Report views can be created within one Excel worksheet, not to mention across many tabs. Of course, any Excel calculation can be applied to these values as well, facilitating the creation of summarized and formatted dashboard views that might refer to many worksheet tabs in a workbook.

5. By clicking the Next button you navigate to the Filters dialog. If you had no need to filter the content, you could simply click Finish to populate the data into Excel starting from where the cursor was placed before you chose the menu item. The Filters dialog asks you to choose a field on the left, and then working from the top on the right, choose an operator (for example, is one of, equals) and appropriate values beneath to filter the returned data (see Figure 21.17).

6. Once finished adding appropriate filters, you choose Finish and populate the data into Excel.

Figure 21.17
The Filter the Data dialog of the BusinessObjects LiveOffice Add-in.

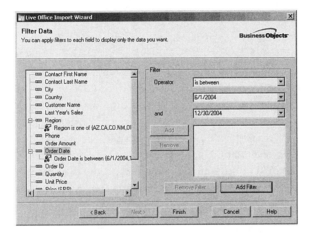

MODIFYING THE REPORT VIEW

The data then displays in Excel. Should you then want to modify the report display, both right-click menus and the Business Objects menu enable you to manipulate the data view in real time. To activate the right-click menu, you have to right-click a cell that contains data populated by the Crystal Reports view (typically cells with a light yellow background).

The right-click menu has several choices. The Insert choice enables you to insert a blank row or column in the display. The Filter submenu enables you to only see data where the value includes the value you clicked on (the Focus On Value), everything other than the value you have right-clicked on (the Exclude Value option), and the Add/Modify option, which opens the Filters dialog. This enables you to simply right-click a value like USA for country, choose Filters and then Focus On, and see only values for the USA. Choosing the right-click option for Remove does exactly as advertised and clears any filters on the selected column.

NOTE

When inserting or deleting rows and columns, notice that a full row or column is inserted within the report view only. Cells outside of the report view do not change.

21

The Field choice on the right-click menu enables you to remove the selected field or open the original Select Fields dialog box where the full list of available and selected fields are listed.

The View choice exposes the options available on that report view. The View Report Source choice opens the report in the report viewer where the user can select parts of a report and add them to the current view. The Refresh choice connects to the database and refreshed the data from the database at that moment. The Remove option removes the entire report view from the worksheet; a confirmation dialog is provided when this choice is selected.

The Properties opens a dialog with details on the report view like the Report Title, the BusinessObjects Enterprise system supplying the view, the connection ID (useful for troubleshooting), the view ID, the field name, the current value and the field data type. The Data Source choice displays the type of data source connected to (such as Data source versus Report instance), whether the particular instance is the latest and when it was run, and if this data comes from an instance at all. The user can change the selected data source in this view, similar to the Set Origin choice from the Crystal Reports Excel Add-in in version 10. The Options choice allows the user to specify the Appearance, Instance and Formatting options. When Conceal data when saving option is selected, the data is concealed to prevent unauthorized access to the information. The Instance option provides a choice to use always the latest instance or the latest instance for a specified user. The formatting choices provide the option to preserve any end-user formatting when refreshing the report or whether or not to inherit formatting defined in the source report. Finally, the Parameters choice from the View menu opens a dialog to change the parameter values in the report.

Lastly, the BusinessObjects LiveOffice menu offers one option not available from the right-click menu: the Options dialog. This dialog exposes many of the default behaviors of the plug-in. The View tab enables you to specify default data values through the Data Defaults button, and also specify whether you want to conceal the data retrieved when saving the workbook. Additionally, specifying inherit report part or field formatting sets format inheritance on all data views in the workbook. This inheritance option can be over-ridden on an individual data view as explained above. The View tab also provides a choice to display filters and sorts as comments, and whether to display a field by name, description or both. Should you want to change the right-click behavior or how cell widths or cell protection occurs, you accomplish this from the General tab. The Enterprise tab enables you to set a default login for convenience. The Analysis tab is new in version XI and specific to the OLAP Intelligence component of the LiveOffice Add-in. This tab allows you to specify drill-down options and dimension member display options when connecting to an OLAP data source.

The Excel plug-in, although simple in terms of usage, results in powerful interactivity. Users value this particular method of accessing report data very highly, as they are accustomed to doing data manipulation in Excel, and the value of having enterprise data from a variety of sources available in this format increases knowledge worker efficiency greatly.

USING LIVEOFFICE WITH DIRECT OLAP CONNECTIONS

In previous releases, the Crystal Analysis Add-in for Excel provided users with the capability to connect to OLAP data sources. The Crystal Analysis Add-in functionality is now available within the single BusinessObjects LiveOffice Add-in. Instead of connecting to a report or report instance, the Direct OLAP Connection option in the Data Source dialog exposes the list of OLAP Connections defined in the BusinessObjects Enterprise XI system. In this way, users can combine data from both Crystal Reports as well as OLAP data sources in a single worksheet. The Business Objects menu now lists Direct OLAP Connections along side of reports, Universes, and Business Views.

Establishing a Direct OLAP Connection differs from the predecessor, the Crystal Analysis Add-in for Excel, in that it does not report directly from existing OLAP Intelligence workbooks stored in BusinessObjects Enterprise—instead it connects to a cube and works from there. The BusinessObjects Enterprise ActiveX viewer for OLAP Intelligence reports and the thick client OLAP Intelligence designer also enable exported OLAP Intelligence views to the LiveOffice Add-in and enable continued analysis from within Excel.

End users find that the Direct OLAP Connection offers very much the same interface that they are accustomed to within the OLAP Intelligence worksheet, and offers the capability to massage a view, or several views, at a time, and then tie them together using standard Excel formulas and functionality. This flexibility facilitates much more self-service. The user interface, although powerful, uses simple concepts that enable data manipulation that most users prefer to Excel's own pivot tables, which require quite a bit of training to properly use.

SETTING UP AND ADMINISTERING DIRECT OLAP CONNECTIONS

Note from the previous paragraph that the add-in connects directly to the data source. The direct connection from Excel to the data cube uses either the appropriate drivers or Microsoft's Pivot Table Services when connecting to a Microsoft SQL Server Analysis Services cube. Similar to using the OLAP Intelligence Rich Client, these drivers sit on the client machine and connect directly to the data source, compared to using the HTML viewer that directly connects to BusinessObjects Enterprise, which in turn connects to the data source. So direct connectivity to the data source—usually in the form of a LAN connection—must be available for Direct OLAP Connections to function properly.

The installation requires that an actual set of files install on the local machine, which again requires local administrative rights during the install process.

CONNECTING TO A WORKBOOK

This section pre-supposes that you have already read Chapter 19, "Creating OLAP Intelligence Reports," that covers OLAP Intelligence in depth. You should also be familiar with the concepts in OLAP and in OLAP Intelligence. Thus the following discussion of Direct OLAP Connections via the LiveOffice Add-in focuses on how these are implemented, not on the actual functionality.

21

To begin with, the user either exports a view from the OLAP Intelligence viewer, rich client, or designer, or starts a new connection from within Excel through the Business Objects menu. Then you open a new Cube View, connect to a cube using a dialog identical to the one in OLAP Intelligence, and then orient the view in a dialog screen identical to the Worksheet tool in OLAP Intelligence (see Figure 21.18).

Figure 21.18
Orienting a cube view using LiveOffice.

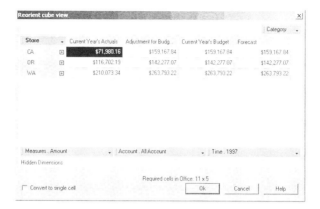

After orienting this view, you choose OK to return to the worksheet with your new view. Here you also have the option to save or open a viewpoint file (an XML file ending in *.cvp), which describes a particular orientation. This creates a cube view in Excel where your cursor was last positioned (see Figure 21.19).

Figure 21.19
The Direct OLAP Connection cube view within Excel.

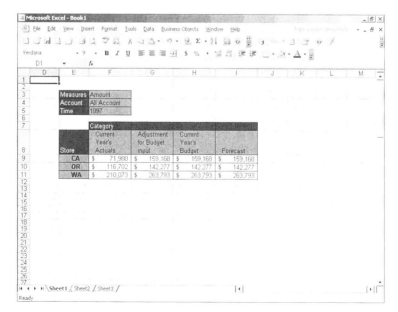

MODIFYING THE WORKBOOK VIEW

After the view has been established within Excel, you can manipulate it just as you did in OLAP Intelligence either by using the Business Objects menu commands or by right-clicking on a cell in the cube view as illustrated in Figure 21.20.

Figure 21.20
Right-clicking on a cell will display the LiveOffice menu.

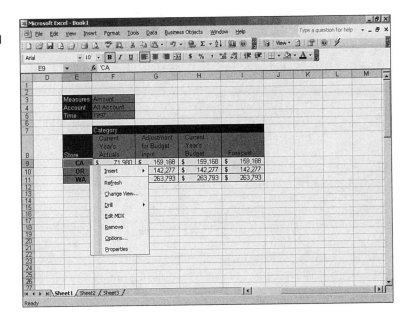

The LiveOffice right-click menu appears slightly different when positioned on a Direct OLAP connection. The menu for each item is discussed next.

The Insert item allows a user to insert rows or columns within the context of the view. Inserting a row or column in a view does not affect the cells outside the view.

The Refresh option refreshes the current view only. It does not refresh other views. If you want to refresh all views, the Business Objects menu provides the option to do this. If a connection to BusinessObjects Enterprise or the OLAP data source has not yet been established, a logon dialog will appear to confirm you have access to the data source.

The Change View option is very similar to the interface provided in InfoView or the OLAP Intelligence designer. In the Reorient Cube View dialog, the user can specify the cube orientation and which dimensions are hidden. The number of required cells are calculated and displayed in the dialog.

The Edit MDX menu option is valuable to those skilled in MDX. This syntax, known as Multidimensional Query language, is used for sending requests to Microsoft Analysis Services. A library of functions are exposed through the MDX query panel, as shown in Figure 21.21.

21

The MDX Editor invoked by the Edit MDX option.

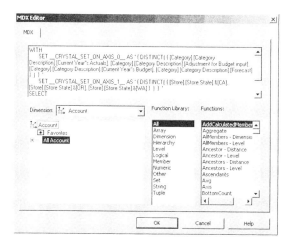

The Remove option on the menu removes the view entirely from the workbook.

The Options menu item provides the user with a dialog for specifying View Layout and Formatting options. View Layout relates to displaying or concealing items in the view, such as slice panel and column and row dimension headings. The View Layout is also where Conceal Data When Saving is specified. This is an important feature to keep in mind when dealing with sensitive information. The formatting options are the same as when connecting to a report, Business View, or Universe, and relate to retaining custom formatting applied to views.

The Properties option displays the Properties dialog. Depending on whether a data cell or dimension member cell is selected, the dialog will either display cell information or dimension information respectively (see Figure 21.22).

The Properties Data tab.

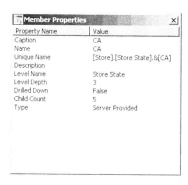

Also unique to this OLAP view in Excel is the capability to drill up and down by double-clicking on the cells with a [+] or [-] cell. Double-clicking on a dimension label (which is blue by default) opens the Member Selector as well. Clicking and dragging an item, however, does not have the effect of swapping or pivoting dimensions within Excel—instead you will find an area of the worksheet selected. Use the right-click menus to choose Re-orient

Cube, which opens the worksheet dialog that supports the click-and-drag operations you are accustomed to within OLAP Intelligence.

USING BUSINESSOBJECTS LIVEOFFICE IN MICROSOFT POWERPOINT

The use of enterprise report data in Excel is of great value to the information worker who needs extended analysis capabilities in a spreadsheet environment. However, the value of centrally located enterprise data does not stop at the analyst's desk. Consider the PowerPoint presentations that are created based on the data contained in spreadsheets. Most often, the data in those presentations was placed there using classic cut and paste tactics. This is an enormously resource-intensive process that can be prone to error and is repeatable only at the same cost of resources.

BusinessObjects LiveOffice Add-in addresses many of these issues by enabling the PowerPoint user to embed data directly from BusinessObjects Enterprise into a presentation and in a single action refresh all the data based on the individual view settings. In a single presentation, multiple reports, report instances, Business Views, and OLAP data sources might be used as a basis for a single slide deck (see Figure 21.23). After the presentation has been established, it can be refreshed without repeating the process of rebuilding the entire presentation.

Figure 21.23
LiveOffice in
PowerPoint connect-
ing to multiple reports
and OLAP data.

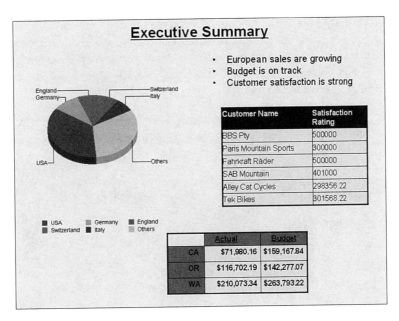

The process for placing data into a PowerPoint presentation uses the exact same menu and right-click functions used in Excel. Refer to the beginning of this section for details on the Insert, Filter, Field, View, Refresh, and Drill functions.

Keep in mind that there is a distinction between LiveOffice in Excel and LiveOffice in PowerPoint. This distinction reflects the nature of the two different applications as opposed to LiveOffice itself. It is more likely that higher-level information, report parts, and charts will have a more appropriate use in PowerPoint, the same way long lists of values are appropriate for Excel.

USING BUSINESSOBJECTS LIVEOFFICE IN MICROSOFT WORD

In the same way LiveOffice in PowerPoint uses the same menu and right-click functionality as Excel, LiveOffice in Microsoft Word also uses this standard menu. The use of BusinessObjects LiveOffice in Microsoft Word can provide enormous value as a productivity tool, but in a slightly different way than an Excel or PowerPoint user might leverage information from a BusinessObjects Enterprise system. Documents that combine highly formatted text, such as an annual report, require a top-of-the-line word processing tool. However, those documents often require a number of charts, tables, and other substantive information housed in an enterprise reporting system. Whether it is a financial document or a form letter, the BusinessObjects LiveOffice Add-in simplifies repetitive tasks and provides extreme accuracy when generating documents.

The ability to place views into a Word document as illustrated in Figure 21.24 might seem to be a trivial value at first glance. In some cases, however, this could be the difference between meeting a deadline or not. Consider a smaller company with limited staff and no marketing department, per se. Each month the company needs to create and print out a hundred or so special flyers to be including in the monthly mailing to top customers. The flyers advertise special promotions for the upcoming month. Other than the promotions, the flyer stays relatively unchanged each month. Creating a Word document with LiveOffice views now changes a rather time-consuming task into a matter of opening a document and printing it. Over the course of one year, the time saved on this one monthly task could be as much as one full work week.

Figure 21.24
LiveOffice in Microsoft Word connecting to a report, a Business View, and a Universe.

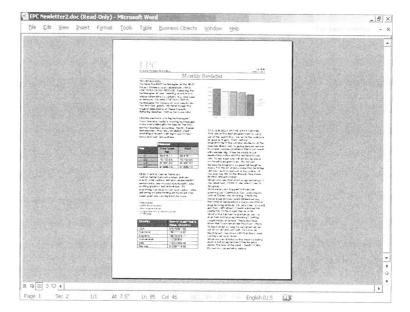

SUMMARY

Business Intelligence systems are both centralized pillars of corporate information and a multitude of access methods to that information. In some cases, a browser displaying a report is sufficient. Other times, the user needs to alter or create their own reports, but remain within a browser-based environment. And yet other times, that information needs to be taken on the road and shown at a conference, mailed to a partner, or analyzed in a powerful spreadsheet environment. With the combination of BusinessObjects Enterprise XI as a centralized source and Crystal Reports Explorer and BusinessObjects LiveOffice as interfaces to this common repository, a corporation can find countless ways to expand the scope of the usefulness of corporate information.

21

Web Report Distribution—Using BusinessObjects Enterprise and Crystal Reports Server

CHAPTER 22

INTRODUCTION TO CRYSTAL REPORTS SERVER

In this chapter

WHAT IS CRYSTAL REPORTS SERVER?

Crystal Reports Server is new to the Crystal Reports product suite. It allows companies to create, manage, and deliver Crystal Reports over the Web or embedded in Enterprise applications. It includes a complete set of reporting services to address all steps in the reporting process, from data access and report design to report delivery and management to portal and application integration to report maintenance. Designed for use on a single server, Crystal Reports Server is ideal for departmental reporting requirements.

On the surface, the Crystal Reports Server looks like BusinessObjects Enterprise. Indeed, Crystal Reports Server provides a rich set of Enterprise-level reporting functions including

- Accessing any data source
- Designing any report
- Delivering and managing reports over the Web
- Integrating reporting with applications and portals
- Maintaining reports with minimal IT overhead

In fact, Crystal Reports Server is built from the same object model as BusinessObjects Enterprise. The following core components are included in the product:

- Report Designer (all drivers and access methods)
- Business Views
- Report publisher
- InfoView web portal interface
- Portal integration kits
- Viewers (including offline viewer)
- Scheduler
- Security (BOE, Active Directory, LDAP, and NT authentication)
- Software development kits (SDKs)
- Management console

The main differences between Crystal Reports Server and BusinessObjects Enterprise lie in the enterprise-level functionality. BusinessObjects Enterprise is a multiserver Business Intelligence (BI) platform designed to address large-scale reporting and BI requirements. Fault-tolerance, load balancing, scalability, and reliability are provided by the multiserver capability of the environment. BusinessObjects Enterprise also provides enterprise-level features such as auditing, Crystal Reports Explorer, and the new Encyclopedia and Process Tracker.

Crystal Reports Server is a single-server enterprise reporting solution that delivers Crystal Reports over the Web. Web Intelligence, OLAP Intelligence, or other BI content are not supported.

Compared to BO Enterprise, Crystal Reports Server is targeted more towards addressing the reporting infrastructure needs of small- to middle-sized companies. It has the following limitations over BO Enterprise:

- **Concurrent Access License (CAL) limitation**—Crystal Reports Server is limited to a maximum of 20 concurrent users. An error message will be displayed when the administrator attempts to enter key codes that exceed 20 CAL licenses.
- **Scalability limitations**—Crystal Reports Server can only run on a single server and there is a license limiting the installation to a maximum four-processor server.
- **Platform limitation**—Crystal Reports Server only runs on Windows, while BO Enterprise runs on other operating systems, such as AIX and Solaris.
- **Content limitation**—Crystal Reports Server only runs Crystal Reports; it does not run Web Intelligence reports.

CRYSTAL REPORTS SERVER ARCHITECTURE

Crystal Reports Server is a multi-tier system. Although the components are responsible for different tasks, they can be logically grouped based on the type of work they perform.

Crystal Reports Server has five tiers: the client tier, the application tier, the intelligence tier, the processing tier, and the data tier. Figure 22.1 illustrates how each of the components fits within the multi-tier system.

The servers run as services on Windows machines. On Unix, the servers run as daemons. These services can run in multiple instances on a single machine.

CLIENT TIER

The client tier is the part of the BusinessObjects Enterprise system that administrators and end users interact with directly. This tier is made up of the applications that enable people to administer, publish, and view Web content (Crystal Reports, Microsoft Office files, and so forth).

The client tier includes the Central Configuration Manager (CCM), Central Management Console (CMC), Publishing Wizard, Import Wizard, and InfoView.

APPLICATION TIER

The application tier hosts the server-side components that process requests from the client tier as well as the components that communicate these requests to the appropriate server in the intelligence tier. The application tier includes support for report viewing and logic to understand and direct Web requests to the appropriate BusinessObjects Enterprise server in the intelligence tier.

The application tier includes application tier components, Web development platforms, and Web application environments.

Figure 22.1
The relationships
between the
BusinessObjects
Enterprise tiers.

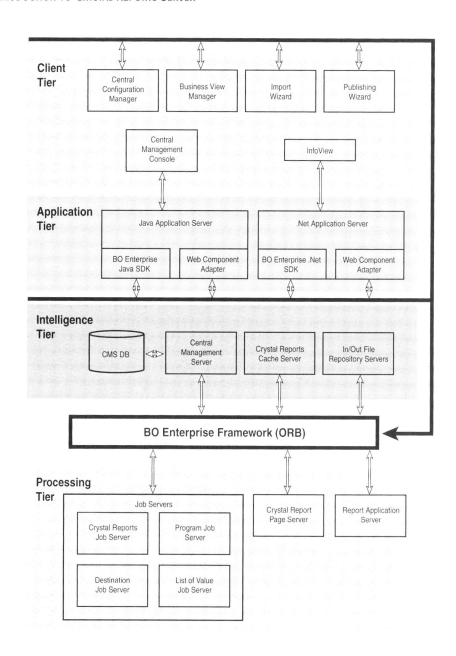

For both the Java and .NET platforms, the application tier includes the Application Server, BusinessObjects Enterprise SDK, and Web Component Adapter (WCA). In BusinessObjects Enterprise XI, the web server communicates directly with the Application Server.

BusinessObjects Enterprise systems that use the Java SDK or the .NET SDK run on a third-party application server.

The Application Server acts as the gateway between the web server and the rest of the components in BusinessObjects Enterprise. The Application Server is responsible for processing requests from the user's browser and hosts InfoView and other Business Objects applications. The SDK is a software development kit that exposes the functionality of BusinessObjects Enterprise to developers.

The WCA runs within the Application Server and provides all services that are not directly supported by the SDK. The web server passes requests directly to the Application Server, which then forwards the requests on to the WCA. It processes ASP.NET (.aspx) and Java Server Pages (.jsp) files and it also supports Business Objects applications, such as the Central Management Console (CMC) and Crystal Report viewers that are implemented through viewrpt.cwr requests.

INTELLIGENCE TIER

The intelligence tier manages the BusinessObjects Enterprise system. It maintains all of the security information, sends requests to the appropriate servers, manages audit information, and stores report instances. The intelligence tier includes the Central Management Server, Cache Server, File Repository Server, and Event Server.

The Central Management Server (CMS) is responsible for maintaining a database of information about the system. The data stored by the CMS includes information about users and groups, security, folders and report objects, and servers. The CMS also maintains the repository and a separate audit database of information about user actions.

The Cache Server is responsible for handling all report viewing requests. The Cache Server checks whether it can fulfill the request with a cached report page. If the Cache Server finds a cached page that displays exactly the required data (with data that has been refreshed from the database), the Cache Server returns that cached report page to the user. If the Cache Server cannot fulfill the request with a cached report page, it passes the request along to the Page Server. The Page Server runs the report and returns the results to the Cache Server. The Cache Server then caches the report page for future use and serves the page to the viewer. By storing report pages in a cache, BusinessObjects Enterprise avoids accessing the database each and every time a report is requested. If multiple Page Servers are running for a single Cache Server, the Cache Server automatically balances the processing load across Page Servers.

There is an Input and an Output File Repository Server in every BO Enterprise implementation. The Input File Repository Server manages all of the report objects and program objects that have been published to the system by administrators or end users (using the Publishing Wizard, the Central Management Console, the Import Wizard, or a Business Objects designer component, such as Crystal Reports or the Web Intelligence Java or HTML Report Panels). The Output File Repository Server manages all of the report instances generated by the Report Job Server. The File Repository Servers are responsible for listing files on the server, querying for the size of a file, querying for the size of the entire file repository, adding files to the repository, and removing files from the repository.

The Event Server manages file events. When the appropriate file appears in the monitored directory, the Event Server triggers the file event and notifies the CMS that the file event has occurred. The CMS then starts any jobs that are dependent upon the file event. After notifying the CMS of the event, the Event Server resets itself and again monitors the directory for the appropriate file.

The processing tier accesses the data and generates the reports. It is the only tier that interacts directly with the databases that contain the report data. The processing tier includes the Report Job Server, Program Job Server, Web Intelligence Job Server, Web Intelligence Report Server, Report Application Server (RAS), Destination Job Server, List of Values Job Server, and Page Server.

A Job Server processes scheduled actions on objects at the request of the CMS. A Job Server can be configured to process either report objects or program objects. If a Job Server is configured to process report objects, it becomes a Report Job Server. The Report Job Server processes scheduled reports, as requested by the CMS, and generates report instances (*instances* are versions of a report object that contain saved data). To generate a report instance, the Report Job Server obtains the report object from the Input File Repository, opens the report, executes the SQL for the report, and when all the data has been returned to the report, both the report object and the data are saved to the Output File Repository.

The RAS processes reports that users view with the Advanced DHTML viewer. The RAS service also provides the ad hoc reporting capabilities that allow users to create and modify Crystal Reports over the Web. The RAS service is very similar to the Page Server: It, too, is primarily responsible for responding to page requests by processing reports and generating cache pages. However, the RAS service uses an internal caching mechanism that involves no interaction with the Cache Server. As with the Page Server, the RAS service supports COM, ASP.NET, and Java viewer SDKs. The Report Application Server also includes an SDK for report creation and modification, providing you with tools for building custom report interaction interfaces.

The Page Server is primarily responsible for responding to page requests by processing reports and generating Encapsulated Page Format (EPF) pages. Each EPF page contains formatting information that defines the layout of a single report page. The Page Server retrieves data for the report from an instance or directly from the database. When retrieving data from the database, the Page Server automatically disconnects from the database after it fulfills its initial request and reconnects to retrieve additional data if necessary. The Cache Server and Page Server work closely together. Specifically, the Page Server responds to page requests made by the Cache Server. The Page Server and Cache Server also interact to ensure cached EPF pages are reused as frequently as possible and new pages are generated as soon as they are required. BusinessObjects Enterprise takes advantage of this behavior by ensuring that the majority of report-viewing requests are made to the Cache Server and Page Server. (However, if a user's default viewer is the Advanced DHTML viewer, the Report Application Server processes the report.)

DATA TIER

The data tier is made up of the databases that contain the data used in the reports. BusinessObjects Enterprise supports a wide range of corporate databases.

CRYSTAL REPORTS SERVER APPLICATIONS

Crystal Reports Server provides several client tier applications that enable people to administer the system as well as to publish, view, and manage Web content.

CENTRAL CONFIGURATION MANAGER

The Central Configuration Manager (CCM) is a server-management tool that allows you to configure each of the Crystals Reports Server components. This tool allows an administrator to start, stop, enable, and disable servers, and it allows an administrator to view and configure advanced server settings. The CCM also allows an administrator to add or remove servers from the Crystal Reports Server system.

To launch the CCM, go to the Start button, and click Programs, BusinessObjects 11, Crystal Reports Server, Central Configuration Manager. The CCM is shown in Figure 22.2.

Figure 22.2
The Central Configuration Manager for the Crystal Reports Server.

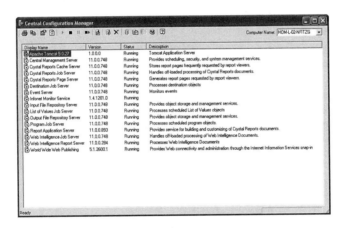

The pull-down menu by the computer name on the top-right corner of the CCM displays the Central Management Server to which the CCM is connected.

The servers in the intelligence and processing tiers of the Crystal Reports Server are displayed in the CCM. To start, stop, enable, and disable servers, click on the corresponding buttons on the toolbar. To view and change the configurations of a certain server, right-click on the display name of the server and left-click on the Properties menu item on the pop-up menu (see Figure 22.3). To add or remove servers, click on the Add Server and Delete Server button on the toolbar.

Figure 22.3
View server properties
by using the CCM.

USE THE CENTRAL MANAGEMENT CONSOLE

The Central Management Console can be launched via a different menu path, depending on which application tier is used. For .NET, go to Microsoft Start, Programs, BusinessObjects 11, Crystal Reports Server, .Net Administration Launchpad. For Tomcat, go to Microsoft Start, Programs, BusinessObjects 11, Crystal Reports Server, Java Administration Launchpad.

After logging on, the administrator is shown the CMC home page (see Figure 22.4).

Figure 22.4
The Crystal Reports
Server Central
Management Console
home page.

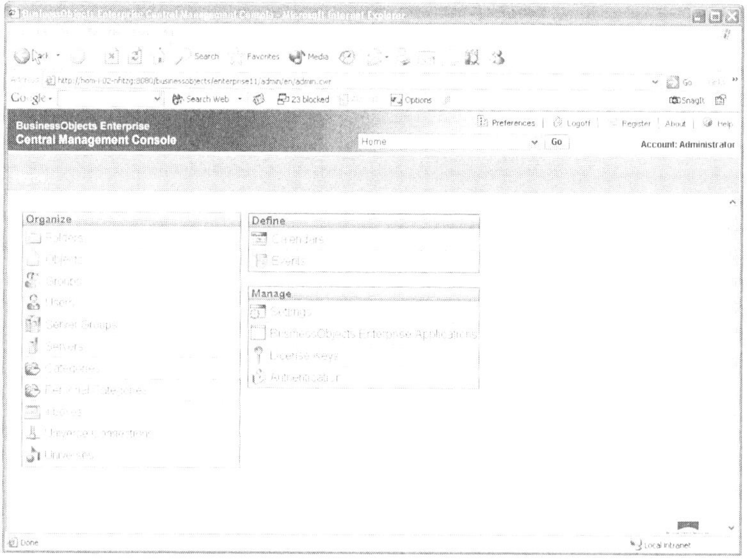

From the CMC home page, the administrator can enter various areas to conduct administrative tasks, such as creating, organizing, and removing folders; creating, organizing, and removing users and user groups; and publishing reports and other content into the Crystal Reports Server.

To create a new folder, click on the Folders link in the Organize area. Then, in the subsequent folder-listing page, click on the New Folder button. In the New Folder page (see Figure 22.5), specify Folder Name and other properties of the folders and click OK.

Figure 22.5
Create a new folder in Crystal Reports Server.

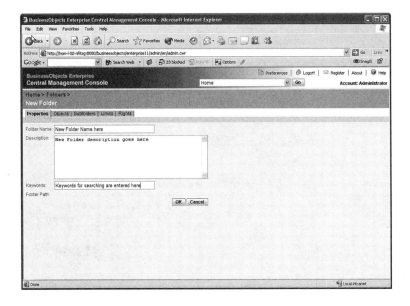

To publish a report to a specified folder in Crystal Reports Server, navigate to that folder in CMC and click the Objects tab. In the object-listing page, click the New Object button, and the New Object page will display (see Figure 22.6).

Highlight Report on the left navigation menu. In the Content area, specify the Crystal Report file to be published using the file browser, select a destination folder in which to save the report, and click OK.

To view a report on-demand, navigate to the folder in which the report is located and click on the report title of the report you want to run. In the Properties tab of the report object's page, click Preview. If the report has no parameters, the report viewer is launched to display the resulting report (see Figure 22.7). In the case that the report has report parameters, the report viewer is launched to display the report parameter page for the user to fill in (see Figure 22.8). After the user has specified the input parameters and clicked OK, the report viewer displays the resulting report.

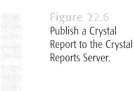

Figure 22.6
Publish a Crystal
Report to the Crystal
Reports Server.

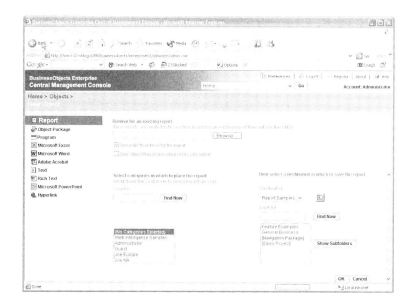

Figure 22.7
The Crystal Reports
viewer.

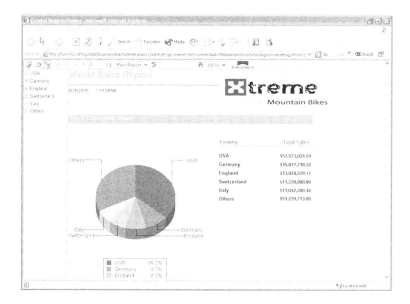

LAUNCH INFOVIEW

InfoView is a Web-based portal interface for end users to view and schedule reports, and manage their content. To launch InfoView, go to Microsoft Start, Programs, BusinessObjects 11, Crystal Reports Server, Java InfoView (or .NET InfoView, depending on whether the .NET or Java environment has been configured). The InfoView portal is shown in Figure 22.9.

Figure 22.8
The report parameter page.

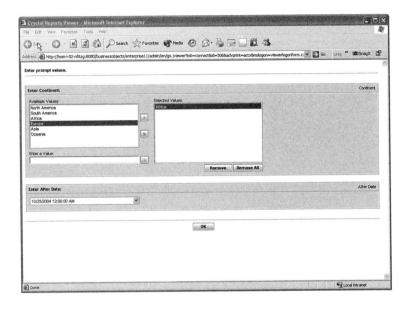

Figure 22.9
InfoView for the Crystal Reports Server.

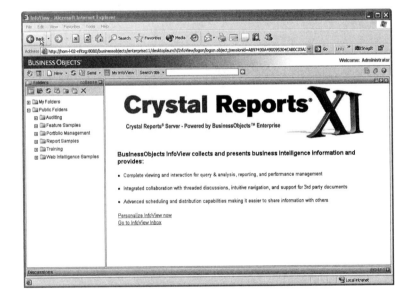

Infoview and the BusinessObjects Enterprise Infrastructure that underlays both Crystal Reports Server and BusinessObjects Enterprise are covered in great detail in the upcoming chapters in this part of the book, including Chapters 23 through 27.

CHAPTER 23

INTRODUCTION TO BUSINESSOBJECTS ENTERPRISE

In this chapter

WHAT IS BUSINESSOBJECTS ENTERPRISE?

With the explosion of databases and ERP/CRM/SCM functionality in the eighties and nineties, organizations have been increasingly been creating and storing data about their business. One of the major complaints about these implementations is that although a substantial effort was made to capture the data, in a lot of cases, the reporting and analysis of this data was often overlooked.

This infrastructure provides the underlying foundation to the reporting, query and analysis and performance management tools, as show in Figure 23.1.

Figure 23.1
The Business Objects product stack. (Used with permission from Business Objects.)

The stack consists of the following five components:

- **Data Integrator**—An extraction, transformation, and load (ETL) tool that can populate your data warehouse or data mart with the required data. Online transactional databases usually do not provide the optimal reporting schema. Data Integrator provides the ability to extract data from these transactional systems; cleanse, consolidate and transform the data into the required format; and then load this data into a data warehouse or data mart. The result is easily accessible data your users can trust.

- **Performance Management**—Provides the ability for users to define goals based on a corporate strategy. Users then compare actual performance against these goals, identifying trends, tracking their progress, and taking corrective action. These metrics and their associated performance are presented to the users in the form of a scorecard or dashboard. The performance management applications are a set of predefined but modifiable reports, analytics, dashboards, and scorecards built on industry best practices. These provide an excellent starting point for a performance management deployment.

- **Reporting**—Refers to the ability to create production reports and is the functionality provided by Crystal Reports. In addition to just creating reports, developers might want to embed reports inside applications or users might want to embed report components in their Office documents.

- **Query and Analysis**—The Query and Analysis tools allow the users to answer their business questions without the need for a developer to create a predefined report. Aided by the semantic layers, users can select their required fields and sort, group, and sum these fields to answer their questions. The product is designed in such a way that after one question has been answered, the query result should drive another question. For example, if sales were down, the user could query and sort by geography to determine which geography was performing poorly. After the user determined this, they might want to drill on this geography to see what products are usually sold there but have not been.

- **BI Platform**—The underpinning of all these products is the Business Intelligence (BI) platform.

BusinessObjects Enterprise provides a prefabricated, extensible infrastructure for creating, managing, and distributing information to a wide variety of information consumers.

The distribution of information is not limited to reports but can be anything from XML files to Excel spreadsheets. Furthermore, the device on which the information is distributed is not limited to the PC. It can be a cell phone, printer, or PDA. In some cases, the information from BusinessObjects Enterprise might not be viewed by a human at all, but uploaded into another computer system.

The last statement brings up the topic of what is an information consumer. For the most part, an information consumer is a human who is reading (consuming) the information. However, the information consumer could be another computer system that requests that a file be transferred to it, or it could request the information via a Web service. For example, a nightly scheduled job could transfer a file to another system and this file is then uploaded (consumed) by that system.

The key word in all of the above is information. The value that BusinessObjects Enterprise and its content creation tools bring is that they provide the tools to transform data into information. This transformation enables users to ask questions about how much inventory they have or what their share trades were for the day. This easy and efficient transformation of data to information is the real value of BusinessObjects Enterprise.

WHY IMPLEMENT A BUSINESSOBJECTS ENTERPRISE SOLUTION?

Having defined what BusinessObjects Enterprise is, the following sections describe some of the reasons why an organization would want to deploy a BusinessObjects Enterprise infrastructure.

Standardize on one Business Intelligence vendor. Many organizations, especially larger ones, tended to have many business intelligence tools. This was a direct result of these tools focusing on the different reporting requirements. For example, some vendors focused on production reporting while others believed in query and analysis or an OLAP solution. BusinessObjects Enterprise provides the organization with solutions to handle all of the above situations, thereby consolidating support and development activities.

Leverage existing infrastructure. BusinessObjects Enterprise is built on open standards, supports a variety of operating systems, and is extensible via industry-standard programming languages. Further, it supports authentication against popular LDAP stores, integration into common portals, and integration with common ERP packages, such as SAP and Peoplesoft. This open nature results in Enterprise fitting seamlessly into the organization's existing infrastructure.

> Please see http://support.businessobjects.com/ for a listing of supported platforms. An alternative source of supported platforms is Platforms.txt, which can be found in the Platforms folder on the BusinessObjects Enterprise CD.

Self service. Through the use of the semantic layers, Enterprise reduces the reliance on the Information Systems department by giving users the ability to write and modify their own reports. These documents can then be saved back to Enterprise to share with other users. Furthermore, Encyclopedia allows the report creator to store pertinent information such as keywords and a definition of the business problem this report is solving. This facilitates easier searching and ensures that the user is using the appropriate reports to answer their questions.

Increased user adoption. By providing business intelligence components in familiar environments such as Microsoft Office or delivering the content through a portal familiar to the user, users are far more likely to adopt the technology.

Leverage existing skill sets. At the time of this writing, there are more than 14 million registered copies of Crystal Reports. Furthermore, the organization stated that the Business Objects technology is embedded in more than 650 third-party software products. Business Objects has a wide installed base and if an organization does not already have Business Objects skills, they can be readily attained or existing staff members trained. In addition to this, Business Objects Live Office allows the end user to populate Microsoft Office documents with information via BusinessObjects Enterprise XI. The user never has to leave the familiar Office environment to populate and interact with their data, increasing adoption of the tool.

Leverage your existing Business Objects investment. BusinessObjects Enterprise allows for an easy and efficient way to consolidate all your existing Web Intelligence and Crystal Reports into one manageable infrastructure. The Import Wizard enables users to easily point to multiple Business Objects 6 systems or Crystal Enterprise systems and import the relevant objects.

Integrated into your development environment. If your organization develops its own web applications, creating reports within these applications is often ignored, untimely, and are not easily maintained. Business Objects has integrated its reporting engine and development API's into the leading Integrated Development Environment (IDE) packages, such as Borland's JBuilder and C# Builder, BEA's Weblogic Studio, IBM's Websphere Studio, and Microsoft's Visual Studio. Without leaving the IDE, the developer can embed reports within the application, while using the scalability and security of the Enterprise system.

One tool—many data sources. Crystal Reports is well known for its capability to connect to a wide variety of data sources. This includes not only standard relational databases such as Oracle or SQL Server, but also ERP applications such as SAP or even data objects, such as JavaBeans or ADO.NET.

This great range of connectivity results in organizations only requiring one tool to access their information, versus possibly multiple software tools that require multiple skill sets.

Simplified content creation. BusinessObjects Enterprise XI incorporates metadata layers that abstract the complexity of the data source. Databases typically have complex joins between tables, technical field naming conventions, and complex security requirements. The combination of these factors makes report design challenging without detailed knowledge of the data source. A metadata layer allows, for example, a database administrator to join, filter, and secure different data sources, providing the content creator a listing of user-friendly field names, formulas, and parameters that she can make use of in her content. The creator does not need to concern herself with the complexities of the data source, rather with meeting the business requirement.

This division of labor speeds report development as the content creators can focus on their task of report development. Furthermore, this reduced dependency on database knowledge enables more business-oriented people to become content creators.

Reuse of components. The capability to change a component and have this change cascade through all content makes reuse a valuable proposition. For example, the organization wishes to change how it calculates a formula—say "Days Sales Outstanding." In this example, the designer could simply make one change to the formula in the repository and have this change cascade through all reports that use this formula. If the user just had a bunch of reports on a shared drive somewhere, he would need to sort through these reports and determine which reports had this formula and then make changes to all the affected reports.

The Crystal Reports repository that was available in versions 9 and 10 of the product has been migrated to BusinessObjects Enterprise XI. This repository allows sharing of commonly used content such as formulas, text, image files, and custom SQL statements. One of these objects can now be updated and any content using the object will be updated, saving a large amount of maintenance work.

Another example of reuse is the capability to have multiple reports using a single Business View or Universe as its data source. If the Business View or Universe is changed, for example, its data connection is pointed at another data source; all reports that use this data source are updated.

> One of the main components missing from this reuse and update functionality is the capability to do version control. In other words, it is difficult to go back to the old version after an update has taken place.

→ For more detailed information on Business Views and the Repository, **see** Chapter 17, "Introduction to Business Objects XI Repository," **p. 381**, and Chapter 18, "Using a Semantic Layer–Business Views and Universes," **p. 393**.

Change Management. Related to the reuse of components is the concept of change management. When your business requirements are going to change, it is critical to know where a report is used or what its data source is. For example, a database administrator wants to move one database over to another; however, he is uncertain what reports are using this database. BusinessObjects Enterprise can provide him a listing of reports that would be affected. Furthermore, should the administrator use the Business Objects Data Integrator product for this migration, he would then have full visibility from the final report to the originating data source.

Information flow. Information flow refers to the flow of information from the bottom of an organization to the top. With the increased focus on corporate accountability, it is vital that senior management know what is actually happening at lower levels. BusinessObjects Enterprise, through its process tracker, allows for effective passing of information from one employee to another based on a defined business process.

Corporate accountability also places a large emphasis on security, ensuring users should only see what they are allowed to see and preventing outsiders from accessing the data. The metadata layers secure the underlying data, the Enterprise security model defines who can access the objects, and the auditing options record who accessed the data. Outsiders are prevented from accessing the system via flexible firewall options and support for third-party security systems such as Computer Associate's SiteMinder or Kerberos's authentication protocol.

Scalability and reliability. Reliable and timely access to information is not something that should be taken lightly. Performance and downtime are difficult to predict in real world situations. BusinessObjects Enterprise provides an infrastructure that is designed to scale and enables fault tolerance. To achieve this, BusinessObjects Enterprise takes the process required to create and deliver the data and breaks it down into various services (daemons on Unix). Auditing tools enable you to determine over/under usage and you can then take the appropriate action. For example, when scheduling a job, there is a service (or daemon on Unix) called the Job Server that performs this task. If the jobs are taking too long to run, another Job Service can be registered with the framework. This new service could run on the same server as the initial service or another server on the network. By adding this service on the second server, a level of fault tolerance is achieved and should the initial server fail, the Job Service on the second server will take over.

→ For a more detailed discussion on BusinessObjects Enterprise Architecture, **see** "BusinessObjects Enterprise Architecture Overview, " **p. 582**.

VERSIONS OF BUSINESSOBJECTS ENTERPRISE

BusinessObjects Enterprise comes in multiple versions, each with its own set of functionality and scalability as show in Figure 23.2. In general, the versions build upon one another; for example, the Premium Edition includes all the functionality of the Professional Edition, but includes added functionality that is not included in the Professional Edition.

Figure 23.2
The BusinessObjects Enterprise editions (including Crystal Reports Server.

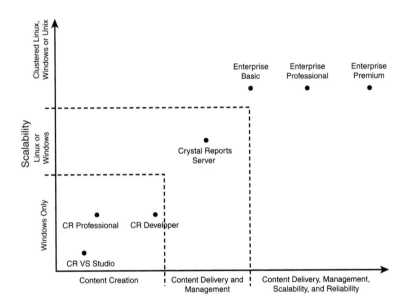

ENTERPRISE BASIC

Enterprise Basic is a new offering providing the ability to create, manage, and distribute Crystal Reports. It is ideally suited to smaller organizations or as a departmental solution.

This edition is not generally available for resale but is designed for those customers who want to upgrade from BusinessObjects Enterprise 5 and 6, where the customer did not require scheduling functionality. In general, this version is not really applicable to long-time Crystal Report users.

Enterprise Basic does not provide any modification capabilities or scalability over multiple machines, but it does allow for report and user management and on-demand and scheduled Business Objects Reports. It is available only on the Windows and Linux platforms.

ENTERPRISE PROFESSIONAL

Business Objects Enterprise Professional is a true enterprise platform designed to provide scalable, centralized management of information delivery. This version includes all the functionality of Crystal Report Server but adds scalability and clustering, enabling the user to distribute the infrastructure over multiple servers and platforms, including Unix, Linux, and Windows.

For report and application development, reports can be embedded in an application, processed on Enterprise, and then sent back to the application. Alternatively, the framework, via the software development kits, can be used to develop the application. Portal Integration Kits provide prebuilt integration into the common portals, such as Microsoft's Sharepoint.

However, the version limits the consumer to viewing only one content type—Crystal Reports or Web Intelligence or OLAP Intelligence. Should the organization require additional content types, they should consider the Premium version. Therefore, this edition is ideally suited as a point solution where the organization is looking for a robust analytical solution or a reporting solution.

THE PREMIUM EDITION

This edition includes all functionality of the previous version described, but adds the ability to view Crystal Reports, Web Intelligence Reports, and OLAP Intelligence Reports. It also includes Live Office, Encyclopedia, Process Tracker, Auditing, Crystal Reports Explorer, and Universe design and deployment.

This version, with its wide variety of functionality, is ideally suited for organizations looking to standardize on one product suite for all of their business intelligence needs.

> The packaging of Business Objects Enterprise editions are subject to change. See http://support.businessobjects.com for exactly what is included in each package.

DETERMINING WHICH VERSION BEST SUITS YOUR REQUIREMENTS

When trying to determine which version is best suited to your requirements, the following factors should be considered:

- **Standardization**—Is the organization looking to deploy one enterprise product to meet all of its users' needs? Some users require the ability to write their own reports, others might only wish to view reports, while others require complex drilling and analysis. For these different requirements, Business Objects has different reporting types, all of which are provided by the premium version.

- **Data sources**—Different data sources are available for different report types; for example, OLAP cubes are only accessible by Crystal Reports or OLAP Intelligence. Check the `Platforms.txt` file or the Product Advisory Report or PAR found at the support website to determine what report types access which data sources. The solution kits are optionally available for the Professional and Premium Editions only.

- **Functionality**—Although Crystal Reports Explorer, Auditing, and Live Office can be purchased as an add-on to the Basic and Professional versions, it might make more economic sense to consider the Premium version rather than purchasing the individual components. Remember the basic version does not include scheduling and the Process Tracker and Encyclopedia are only available on the Premium versions.

- Are Universes only available for the Premium Editions?

UNDERSTANDING THE CORE FUNCTIONS OF BUSINESSOBJECTS ENTERPRISE

In the previous chapters, some of the BusinessObjects Enterprise functionality has been exposed; however, it is the three core functions of content creation, content management, and content distribution.

CREATING CONTENT

Content creation is developed by

- Report developers typically using Crystal Reports and OLAP Intelligence clients and then publishing this content to the Enterprise system for the users to run. The Crystal Reports client can either be a stand-alone client or one embedded into an IDE.

- End users using Enterprise's self-service web capabilities to build or modify their own reports using Web Intelligence, OLAP Intelligence, or the Crystal Reports Explorer.

- With the introduction of Live Office, the end user can embed content, such as a chart, inside a Microsoft Office document. These office documents fall under the definition of content because they can be saved back to and hence managed by the Enterprise system.

- Application developers can use the application program interface (API) to programmatically create content. For example, an XML schema could be programmatically interrogated to determine its definition and a corresponding report programmatically created.

CONTENT MANAGEMENT

The capability to take reports, Excel spreadsheets, and other business intelligence content and centrally control and manage these pieces of information is one of the key functions of the BusinessObjects Enterprise infrastructure. Consider all the reports, Adobe PDF files, or Microsoft Office Documents that are saved locally on an employee's workstations. Now consider what the organization stands to lose should a virus destroy this or what happens when an employee leaves and his hard disk is reformatted to make way for a new employee.

The process of getting content into BusinessObjects Enterprise is commonly referred to as publishing content. The publishing of a report results in the report being copied to the BusinessObjects Enterprise infrastructure. An object ID and description, among other fields, are populated and the content is then referenced either using the object ID or the description.

Content management can occur in one of three places—the Central Management Console, InfoView, or the BusinessObjects Enterprise SDK.

CONTENT MANAGEMENT USING THE CENTRAL MANAGEMENT CONSOLE

The Central Management Console, or CMC, is a Web-based application that gives administrators further control over published content. It also provides the interface to manage the infrastructure, the users, and their related security. Like InfoView, this application is based on the BusinessObjects Enterprise SDK and can be extended within this object model.

The CMC is described in Chapter 27, "Administering and Configuring BusinessObjects Enterprise."

CONTENT MANAGEMENT USING INFOVIEW

Chapter 24, "Using InfoView," references InfoView, a Web-based application that enables the end user to manage and view her content stored in BusinessObjects Enterprise. Users can copy, move, and create folders and content within the Enterprise framework.

This application provides personalization features permitting users and administrators to change the look and functionality of InfoView. If further personalization is required, it is based upon the BusinessObjects Enterprise SDK and can be programmatically extended to add new features.

CONTENT MANAGEMENT USING THE BUSINESSOBJECTS ENTERPRISE SDK

The BusinessObjects Enterprise infrastructure provides a Java, COM, or .NET SDK for managing content within the infrastructure. For example, the types of functionality that are exposed are tasks such as scheduling, exporting, and viewing of reports. Additional tasks could include the management of users, folders, objects, and their related security. For example, a common request is to schedule Crystal reports via a third-party scheduler and this could be accomplished using this SDK.

This topic is discussed in further detail in Chapters 30, "Using the BusinessObjects Enterprise APIs."

CONTENT DELIVERY

The third component of the Business Objects Enterprise infrastructure is that of content delivery. This is the process of delivering the content in the requested format to the requested destination.

This process consists of running the reports, checking associated security to determine what data the requestor is allowed to see, transforming the data to the requested format, and lastly, sending the information to the requested destination.

Content delivery can take two forms—the data pull method and the data push method.

THE DATA PULL METHOD

The *data pull method* consists of viewing reports on demand. In this case the user requests that the report be run against a data source and the data is "pulled" from the data source. A data source or data provider could consist of a traditional database or, alternatively, the report might have already been run, creating a report instance, and the user is viewing the data from within that report instance. After the data is pulled into the report, the user can then interact with the data.

THE DATA PUSH METHOD

BusinessObjects Enterprise gives administrators and users the capability to push information to specific users and locations, in specific formats and, if required, as a result of specific data changing.

For example, an administrator could set up a Crystal Report to run on the last day of the month and email the user the link to his information. As another example of exception type reporting, a user could create an alert within a Crystal Report whereby if sales fall below $200,000 for a particular product, she wants the report in PDF format in her email inbox. In this case, the information is only pushed to her if an exception exists.

In both of these cases, BusinessObjects Enterprise is pushing the information to the information consumer, based upon some event, scheduled to some destination, and in a required format.

As you will learn in the following chapter, users can push information to other users by easily sending reports to users' inbox or email.

USING INFOVIEW

In this chapter

Chapter 23 provided an introduction to the BusinessObjects Enterprise infrastructure and building on that, this chapter describes InfoView, a user Web-based application for interacting with content published to BusinessObjects Enterprise.

From an architectural standpoint, InfoView is based upon a published application programming interface (API) as described in Part VII of the book, "Customized Report Distribution—Using BusinessObjects Enterprise." This effectively means that the InfoView application is customizable and in fact, the source code for the applications ships with them.

> **NOTE**
>
> Prior versions of Crystal Enterprise included an application called Web Desktop or ePortfolio. Prior versions of BusinessObjects included a Web-based application called InfoView. This is the successor to those versions and includes functionality from both Crystal Enterprise 10 Web Desktop and BusinessObjects 6 InfoView.

INSTALLING INFOVIEW

InfoView is developed to run in a multitiered architecture on both the Java and .NET frameworks. The multitiered architecture results in the processing load being spread over the Web Server, Application Server, Reporting Server, and Database Server. These two editions are, for the most part, identical in functionality, and both can be run simultaneously on a server that supports both the .NET and J2EE frameworks. This becomes useful when dealing with heterogeneous environments when an organization might have both Java and .NET environments.

INSTALLING THE JAVA EDITION

Desktop.war is the application that needs to be deployed on the Java Application Server. For a listing of supported application servers, see `Platforms.txt` on the BusinessObjects XI CD. The supported Java Virtual Machine (JVM) is the same JVM the appropriate Application Server supports. See the associated Application Servers documentation on how to deploy a WAR file. Likewise, the supported Web Server is whatever the associated Application Server supports.

This Web Archive or WAR file can typically be found after installation under `/Business Objects Enterprise 11/java/applications/desktop.war`. InfoView requires components of the Java API to run; however, this WAR file includes all of the Java API JAR files required, hence this is self-contained and has all you need to deploy and run InfoView on a Java Application Server.

INSTALLING THE .NET EDITION

The .NET InfoView version is an ASP.NET application that runs on Microsoft's Internet Information Services (IIS) versions 5 and 6. If this is selected at installation time, the install will search for IIS on the server and attempt to install InfoView. This is an ASPx application, so IIS needs to be set up accordingly to allow ASPX pages to be run. Consult your product (IIS) documentation for the appropriate configuration.

Like its Java version, the .NET version of InfoView is based upon the BusinessObjects .NET Software Development Kit (SDK) and hence this is also required on the server, or at least access to the assemblies needs to be granted. It requires the .NET framework on the IIS server and if one is not found, it will install version 1.1. If a different version or configuration is required, it is generally recommended that the framework be installed ahead of time.

A default install will create a virtual mapping on IIS called businessobjects and this will map to a local path of `c:\Program Files\Business Objects\BusinessObjects Enterprise 11\Web Content\`. Under this virtual directory of BusinessObjects, you will find a subfolder of Enterprise11 and below that you will find an InfoView folder that stores all the required files for the InfoView application. Hence, the default URL for accessing the .NET version of InfoView is http://<Server>/businessobjects/enterprise11/InfoView/.

By default, this URL usually runs `logon.aspx`, which is different from previous versions of Crystal Enterprise.

USING BUSINESSOBJECTS INFOVIEW

InfoView is accessed via a URL in a supported web browser. A typical URL would look something like this:

http://<WebServer>:<port number>/businessobjects/enterprise11/InfoView/

The user specifies the name of the web server, his username, and password. He also needs to specify what form of authentication he wants to use, such as Enterprise, Active Directory, LDAP, or one of the ERP integration kits (for example, SAP). See Chapter 27, "Administering and Configuring BusinessObjects Enterprise," regarding authentication configuration, and see Chapter 15, "Advanced Data Sources in Crystal Reports," regarding ERP authentication.

CAUTION

> The SAP integration kit has its own version of InfoView.

Upon successful logon, a session is created on the Enterprise server and the user is taken by default to a welcome page. The starting page for InfoView can be changed by the user and this is explained in the Customizing InfoView section of this chapter.

The starting page is broken down into four sections, as shown in Figure 24.1.

Each of the sections permits the hiding or showing of each section as deemed appropriate by the user. For example, when viewing a report, the user might want to hide the folder section to maximize the report viewing area. This is accomplished by clicking on the Expand or Collapse button.

Figure 24.1
The InfoView XI
welcome page.

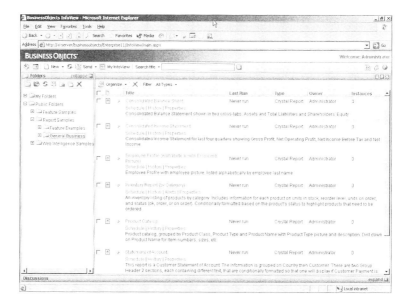

THE TOOLBAR SECTION

This section is found along the top of the browser viewing window and allows for the following functions:

- Takes the user back to her initial view. The user can customize her initial view.

- Collapses the Navigation section, described in the next section. This is used to increase the viewable area when looking at documents.

- Allows the user to create a new document. The content of the new document list is determined by what the system is licensed for. To upload documents from the local disk or a networked drive, select the Document from Local Computer option. Business Objects XI can then become a document repository for all the supported document types displayed.

- Refreshes the screen to reflect any changes, such as new documents that have been published. Users often wonder why they are not seeing all of their documents and sometimes all they need to do is refresh their screens.

- Permits the forwarding of documents to destinations such as e-mail, disk, inboxes, and FTP locations. Each specific destination needs to be enabled by a system administrator before users can successfully send documents to that location. See Chapter 27 regarding the setting up of these destinations. The default values referred to here are the defaults specified by the administrator when setting up these destinations. The available options change depending on the destination selected; for example, when forwarding to a person's inbox, a user can choose to forward either the document or a shortcut to the document. This option is not available when forwarding to an FTP site because FTP is usually used to forward the complete document.

■ My InfoView is a web page the user can customize to display documents or parts of documents that might be of interest to the user. For example, a shipping manager might want to periodically check the status of shipments. To do this, he uses multiple reports. Instead of having these reports linked together, he might want to display them all on one page to get a complete view of his shipping operations. See the "Customizing InfoView" section for more detail on customizing My InfoView.

 ■ You can search using different object properties and locations.

TIP

At the start of an implementation when the Enterprise system hosts relatively few objects, users and administrators often leave the object properties blank. As the number of objects grows, these property fields allow for effective searching, so establishing guidelines for populating these fields at an early stage might serve you well at a later stage.

24

CAUTION

Wildcard characters such as * or ? are not supported.

 ■ A user can set the preferences to tailor InfoView for his individual requirements. A detailed description of what these preferences are is defined later on in this chapter under the "Customizing InfoView" section. Whether this icon is displayed for the user is defined in the Central Management Console (CMC) under the Applications section. See Chapter 27 for more information.

THE NAVIGATION SECTION

The Navigation section of InfoView is found along the left side of the browser viewing area and allows the user to move between her various folders or categories to locate and manage objects. Folders provide physical locations for reports. A company division might have established a folder structure. A category would define the type of report, such as finance or Sarbanes Oxley reports. Somebody in the finance department might be interested in all finance reports across all divisions and use the Category view, whereas a divisional manager might only want to see the reports associated with her division, so the folder view would be more appropriate.

Every user created by Enterprise XI is assigned a Favorites folder, a Personal category, and an inbox. By default, only that user and the group administrators have rights to these three objects.

NOTE

The user will only see the folders or categories to which she has appropriate security rights. For more details on creating folders and categories and their applicable security settings, see Chapter 27 for more information.

THE WORKSPACE SECTION

This section is the largest section and is found to the right of the folders and below the Toolbar sections. It displays the objects residing in the folders or categories. The available actions are shown for each object after the folder is selected. These actions are a combination of the user's rights and the permitted actions for the object type. See Table 24.1 for a listing of what actions are permitted for each object type.

TABLE 24.1   PERMITTED ACTIONS BY OBJECT TYPE

	View	Schedule	History	Modify	Saved Views	Alerts	Properties
Crystal Report	x	x	x	x		x	x
WebI Report	x	x	x	x			x
OlapI Report	x				x		x
Microsoft Office Document	x						x
PDF	x						x
Text	x						x
Object Package	x	x	x				x
Program Object		x	x				x
Hyperlink	x						x

You can then click on the appropriate action to execute that function.

VIEW FUNCTION

The object is rendered in its chosen viewer. For example, Web Intelligence or WebI reports are rendered in the WebI viewers and a PDF document is rendered in its viewer.

> Related to the View function is the Saved View function and View Latest Instance function. The Saved View function applies to OLAP Intelligence reports only. A specific view of the data can be saved, allowing the user to return to those specifically aligned dimensions and dimension members. The View Latest Instance action allows the user to view the most recently scheduled instance. This is useful if a user wants to view the most recent version of the scheduled report. This action is often provided to the majority of end users, with the ability to View (On-Demand against the database) provided to only an elite segment of users.

Crystal Reports, Web, and OLAP Intelligence can have multiple viewers. The viewer is determined by the user preferences described in the "Customizing InfoView" section.

Before continuing, it is worth investigating these report viewers in a little more detail.

The Crystal Reports viewers take the data from the Business Objects XI platform and format the data into a report so it can be viewed.

Table 24.2 provides a listing of the base functionality all the Crystal Report Viewers provide.

TABLE 24.2   CRYSTAL REPORT VIEWER FUNCTIONS

Function	Description
Export	This allows the user to export the report to another format. The report is not re-run against the data provider; rather, the data already in the report is exported.
Print	Depending on how the DHTML viewer printing parameter is set, the DHTML viewer will either use a small ActiveX print control to print the document or export the report to Adobe PDF before using the Adobe client to print it.
Group tree	The Group Tree icon allows the user to either display or hide the group tree, if one exists in the report. By default, this is set to dis play the group tree.
First page navigation	User is taken to the first page of the report.
Previous page	Pages up the report.
Next page	Pages down the report.
Last page	User is taken to the last page of the report.
Go to page	User can go to a specific page.
Drill down viewer name	If the report allows for drill down, the current section is displayed.
Refresh	The report can be refreshed against the data source. This effectively means that it will be re-run against the data source.
Find	User can search for any text inside of the report and Find highlights any associated match. It is not case sensitive. If the text is located in a hidden drill down, Find might not work.
Zoom	Scale the report by setting the percent.

The look and feel of the Crystal Reports viewers is consistent with the Crystal Reports Designer, and the output displayed in the Crystal Reports HTML preview should be consistent with InfoView. The drill down function, as described in Chapter 2, "Selecting and Grouping Data," is honored by the viewers, and users can drill down on charts, group sections, and the group tree.

24

The Crystal Reports viewers delivered as part of InfoView are either client-side or server-side viewers. The server-based viewers can be cosmetically changed or functionally modified via a Java, COM, or .NET object model. This is further described in Chapter 33, "Customizing the Crystal Reports Viewers."

SERVER-SIDE VIEWERS   The server-side viewers run within the application server framework. For example, the Java DHTML viewer consists of Java classes that run within the Java Application Server.

Upon receiving a report request, the Enterprise XI framework sends the data in Encapsulated Page Format (EPF) to the Application Server. A viewer object is instantiated and the Application Server processes the EPF pages. DHTML consisting of both the data and the viewer controls is then sent through to the web server.

DHTML VIEWER   The DHTML Viewer provides a rich functional interface for viewing and navigating Crystal Reports in a zero client interface. This zero client viewer is implemented via viewreport.aspx, or in the Java environment via viewreport.jsp.

ADVANCED DHTML VIEWER   The advanced DHTML includes all of the functionality of the DHTML viewer but also includes an Advanced Search Wizard that has the capabilities to search for data in the data source by setting conditions and to return the data in table form.

Use the Advanced Search Wizard icon to toggle the report to display the Advanced DHTML Viewer options, as described in Table 24.3.

TABLE 24.3   ADVANCED DHTML VIEWER OPTIONS

Tab	Description
Fields	This tab shows all the fields that were available in the original report, including any formulas and summaries. Select the fields required and sort them, by changing the sort order, and the field at the top of the list will appear first on the report.
Conditions	Apply any filtering to the report as deemed necessary by selecting the fields and setting the conditions that apply, remembering that Strings are case sensitive. Add as many conditions as required, separating them using an AND or OR condition. The Free Form button allows you to write free-form conditions or to check your condition statement.
Results	The Results tab provides the search results (if any) associated with the fields selected in the Fields tab and after application of the filters set in the Conditions tab. These results are provided with active hyperlinks to their respective position in the associated report. Additionally, some quick export functionality is provided to Excel, Word, and/or HTML. Of further interest is that the active hyperlinks back into the main Crystal Report are maintained through the export and can be used within the newly exported environment.

NOTE

> The Advanced DTHML viewer requires the Report Application Server to be installed and running.

WEB INTELLIGENCE HTML QUERY   With the correct setting, a user can create and perform on-report analysis and view reports using pure DHTML, as shown in Figure 24.2. At the time of publication, this was only available in the Java version of InfoView. For more information on Web Intelligence, see Chapter 20, "Introduction to Web Intelligence."

Figure 24.2
The HTML Query panel shown in InfoView.

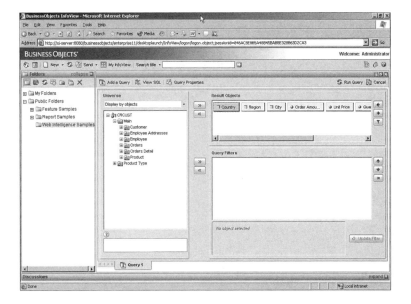

WEB INTELLIGENCE HTML REPORT PANEL   The HTML report panel provides basic reporting creation capabilities. At the time of publication this was only available in the Java version of InfoView.

MOBILE VIEWER   The mobile viewer allows the user to simulate viewing reports over a WAP-enabled mobile phone or Web-enabled PDA. The design paradigm is simple, with only a certain number of characters fitting across the page into the device display area. Additionally, these devices typically have limited bandwidth, so transferring large reports with thousands of rows is not an acceptable end user experience. The mobile viewer requires that the involved report contain a report part that allows the user to see the critical piece of the report.

CLIENT-SIDE VIEWERS   The client-side viewers require some components to be downloaded and executed on the client (browser). The client-side viewers do offer some enhanced printing and functionality enhancements. Additionally, as a result of the initial download to the client, some of the report processing is performed on the client.

ACTIVEX VIEWER   This viewer is available using Microsoft Internet Explorer supporting ActiveX controls. Over and above the standard viewer functionality previously described, this viewer allows users to freeze the panes; in other words, the users can scroll across or down the report and "frozen" sections will remain part of the viewable area, as shown in Figure 24.3. This is achieved by right-clicking on a field where you want the panes to the left and above to be frozen. This allows the user to scroll while the heading and other sections remain frozen.

The user can also copy a cell value from a report by right-clicking the cell and selecting Copy from the drop-down menu.

Figure 24.3
The ActiveX viewer allows sections of the viewer to be frozen, illustrated by the lines on the viewer.

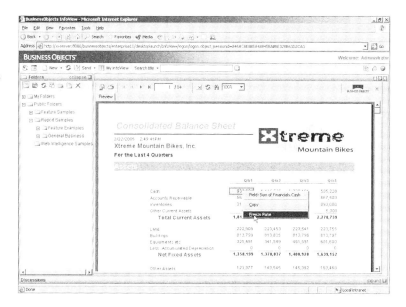

JAVA VIEWER   The Java Viewer is a client-side viewer that is downloaded. It requires a suitable Java Virtual Machine (JVM) be running on the client. If one is not available, the user is prompted to install one.

WEB INTELLIGENCE JAVA REPORT PANEL   The Web Intelligence Java report panel requires a Java applet to be downloaded but then adds the flexibility of drag-and-drop formula creation. This option is available for both the .NET (see Figure 24.4) and Java version of InfoView.

SCHEDULE FUNCTION

With the required permissions, the user has the ability to schedule an object, specifying the following input to ensure the report runs appropriately. Each object allows for different options depending on the object type. For example, when scheduling a Crystal Report, you can specify a database logon. This option is not available when scheduling a program object. Table 24.4 describes all the available options, although some options might not be available depending on the object type.

Figure 24.4
InfoView displaying
the Java report panel.

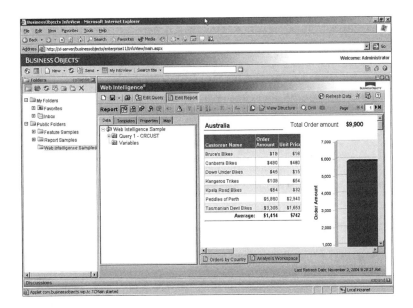

TABLE 24.4   SCHEDULING OPTIONS

Selection	Options
When	Now, Once, Hourly, Daily, Weekly, Monthly. All of the above are fairly self-descriptive except ■ Calendar—This option, as shown in Figure 24.5, enables the selection of a calendar of dates. Created by the Enterprise XI administrator, calendars are customized lists of schedule dates. A report instance can then be scheduled to run each day specified in the calendar.
Database logon	The database user that is used to authenticate against the database.
Filters	Users can create their own filters; however, this assumes they understand the correct syntax. This option can be hidden from the user using the InfoView preferences.
Destination	■ Default Enterprise location—The instance is stored in the Enterprise XI infrastructure, namely the File Repository Server. ■ Inbox—Select the user's inbox where you want this object to appear. ■ File location—Specify the file destination on the network where you want the object to appear. ■ FTP Server—Specify the host and port and a user for authentication, if required. ■ Email recipients—Specify the From and To and whether you want the file as an attachment or just a link to it. The URL is better suited for internal personnel because this method does not clog the internal network if the attachments are large. If the recipient is outside of the firewall, a link might not be the best approach because the recipient might not be able to pass through the firewall to get to the Enterprise XI infrastructure.

continues

TABLE 24.4   CONTINUED

Selection	Options
Format	Some users never want to see the report but only want to see a PDF or Excel spreadsheet. If you specify the format here, the user only gets the object in the specified format. The page layout for Crystal Reports will determine the margins for the report itself. Unique Crystal Reports features, such as drill down and the group tree, are lost when the report is converted to another format. These formats work typically on a "what you see is what you get" paradigm. In other words, if the report is using multiple groupings and the latter groups are hidden in the report, when it comes time for exporting, the user only gets the first group and the hidden sections are not exported. The user gets a similar result with on-demand subreports and with conditionally suppressed sections in a report.
Print settings	If the report needs to be sent to a printer, the user can specify the printer here.
Server group	Specify the default servers to use when running this report. By default it will use the first available server and Enterprise XI will handle the load balancing. For very important reports, you could have a specific server group dedicated to this task.
Parameters	If a specified report contains parameters, a parameters option will appear in the scheduling dialog and the user is expected to enter the required parameters. If a report does not contain parameters, this option is not available.

Figure 24.5
Scheduling based
upon a custom
calendar.

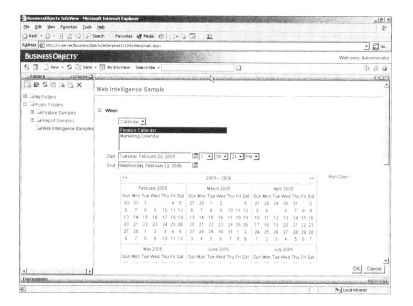

NOTE

> The defaults described here are established by the administrator when enabling the Destinations in the CMC under the Destination Job Server.

TIP

> If a business requirement is such that the users are going to do a lot of exporting, determine the format and how the user wants to view the exported format before designing the report because the export will have an effect on the design of the report.
>
> Check http://support.businessobjects.com for technical papers on preferred formatting and export limitations when the report is intended to be exported to another format.

CAUTION

> The ability to e-mail users based on the triggering of an alert must be set up in the CMC. Alerts will still be triggered but a message will not be sent unless you enable the alert notification.

24

HISTORY FUNCTION

The history shows the user a listing of all attempts to schedule the report and the status of those attempts, whether they succeeded or failed. The user can click on the status to view reasons for failing or succeeding. If the report succeeded, the user can click on the date-time stamp of the instance to view the report instance. If the report failed, the user can reschedule the report by selecting the report instance and clicking the Reschedule button.

This ability to return to a previous instance makes comparing data from previous dates easy. For example, if the user wants to know what last month's inventory value was, he could just click last month's instance, without having to rerun the report with different date parameters.

The function also provides a good audit trail of what report was run, who ran the report, and the data generated.

TIP

> Instances can be removed from the system using the CMC. The company should set a policy; for example, keeping the last 30 instances or moving a year's worth of data for that particular report.

MODIFY FUNCTION

If Enterprise XI has been installed with the Report Explorer application or Web Intelligence reports, the user will have the ability to modify Crystal Reports or Web Intelligence reports. In the case of Crystal Reports, clicking the Modify button launches the Report Explorer, and with Web Intelligence objects, the report will be opened with edit capabilities.

ALERT FUNCTION

Should the report have an alert that has been triggered, the report will appear in the alerts page. The user can go directly to the alerts page and see if there are any reports that have triggered an alert.

OBJECT PROPERTIES

The properties action allows the user to set the properties of the objects. The Title, Description, and Keywords sections are useful for searching. Some of the date properties are exposed and, finally, the user can assign the report to a specified category.

The Workspace section also includes the ability to organize objects into different folders and is described in Table 24.5. To add or change the appropriate category for an object, click on the properties action. Check or uncheck the category to add or remove the object.

TABLE 24.5 FUNCTIONS AVAILABLE IN THE WORKSPACE SECTION

Function	Description
Organize	By selecting the appropriate object and with the correct authority, the user can move and/or copy objects to existing or new folders and categories. Creating shortcuts, in certain circumstances, is an effective approach because if you modify the original object, all the shortcuts will reflect the change. The user can also copy the object to her Favorites folder.
Delete	With the correct authority, a user can delete an object.
Filter	With large numbers of reports on a page, a user can filter by object type. Whether this icon is displayed is set by the administrator (see the "Global InfoView Settings" section).

Under the Administrators Tools Console (not the Central Management Console), there is an application called Shortcut Manager. This application removes any orphaned shortcuts from a specified folder and all of its subfolders.

THE DISCUSSIONS SECTION

The Discussions Viewer found along the bottom of the browser's viewing window (collapsed in Figure 24.1) allows the user to make notes or annotations associated with the object. For example, the sales manager might want to post a note specifying that sales were below what he had expected. Sales representatives could then post their responses to the relevant sections of the report. Users can add notes as an update to an existing note, creating what is called a discussion thread, or they can create a new note, starting a new thread. The available functionality is described in Table 24.6.

TABLE 24.6   FUNCTIONS AVAILABLE IN THE DISCUSSIONS SECTION

Function	Description
New message	The user creates a new message by selecting this and completing the message and subject fields.
Reply to group	All users that have access to this discussion thread will see this note.
Reply to sender	Only the sender will see the note.
Delete	Deletes the highlighted message.
High importance	Adds a red exclamation mark to the message.
Low importance	Adds a blue arrow to the message.

In many organizations, this discussion thread usually takes place in the form of e-mail. The Discussion section now incorporates this into the Business Intelligence platform, storing references to reports with the report object.

CUSTOMIZING INFOVIEW

There are three ways you can change the look and functionality of the InfoView Application. Administrators can globally change the behavior of InfoView for all users. The users, if permitted, can set their preferences by selecting the Preferences icon. Finally, because this application is based on a published API, the application can be modified by changing the underlying code.

NOTE

Crystal Server Pages (CSP) has been deprecated for both the Unix and Windows platforms. Although CSP on the Windows platform might still work, it is recommended that any custom ePortfolio CSP pages be migrated to JSP pages for the Unix platform or ASPX pages for the Windows platform.

GLOBAL INFOVIEW SETTINGS

During the implementation of the InfoView, an organization might want to globally change the InfoView application to tailor the application to suit its needs. This might include cosmetic changes such as adding its logo or security changes that remove certain functionality from the users.

The changes made to InfoView will change the application in its entirety and will affect all users. This differs from the user preferences discussed later in the User Preferences section because those preferences are saved on a user-by-user basis and not for the InfoView application as a whole.

To access the InfoView administration page, the administrator or somebody with administrator rights can, via the CMC, click the BusinessObjects Enterprise Applications and then select InfoView. This should open the page seen in Figure 24.6.

Figure 24.6
The properties page of InfoView.

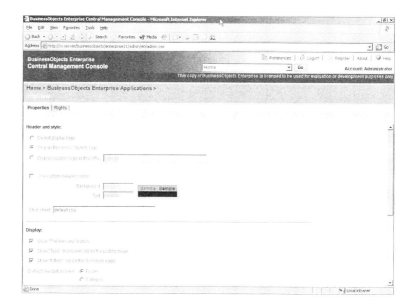

HEADER AND STYLE

The properties page is broken down into multiple sections as described in Table 24.7.

TABLE 24.7 INFOVIEW COSMETIC CHANGE OPTIONS

Option	Description
Do not display logo	No logo is displayed and the colors selected for the header are displayed.
Display Business Objects logo	This is the default setting and the image can be located at `/BusinessObjects Enterprise 11/Web Content/ Enterprise11/InfoView/images/ banner_logo.gif`.
Display custom logo	Specify the URL where the custom logo is located. Ensure that this URL is mapped to the web server.
Use custom header colors	Change the default colors on the header.
Style sheet	Found at `/BusinessObjects Enterprise 11/Web Content/ Enterprise11/InfoView/default.css`, this style sheet can be replaced with your own or the default can be modified. The style sheet can be used to change such items as font, color, and size. Each entry in the style sheet is documented; however, make a backup copy of the default before making changes.

DISPLAY

This section hides or displays certain features, as described in Table 24.8.

TABLE 24.8 GLOBAL DISPLAY FEATURES OF INFOVIEW

Option	Description
Show Preferences button	If checked, this displays the Preferences icon. If this is not displayed, users will have no control over setting their preferences.
Show Type drop-down list	Removes the ability to filter the page by object type and all objects are displayed.
Show Filters tab on the Schedule tab	Administrators might not want users applying filters to reports. The filters section gives the user the ability to rewrite the filter or SQL WHERE clause, and this is recommended only for advanced users.
Default navigation view	Administrator can select either Category or Folder as an initial view of the navigation section.
Maximum number of pages of objects to show	Pages of objects are created by the number of objects the user chooses to display on a page. If more objects are available than are displayed on the page, additional page numbers are shown.

OBJECTS LISTING

If a user has view rights, he can click the objects title to view the object. The administrator can select between either running the object against its data provider or against its latest successful scheduled instance.

VIEWERS

If checked, this option allows the users to use the Advanced DHTML Viewer. The Advanced DHTML Viewer enables report modification and this requires that the Report Application Server be running. See Chapter 27 for more information on the Report Application Server.

The Default Viewer sets the default viewer for InfoView when viewing Crystal Reports.

THE USER PREFERENCES

A user can set or change her individual InfoView interface and interactions with user preferences.

GENERAL PREFERENCES

The General Preferences tab of the Preferences screen provides access to a number of customizable user display settings for InfoView XI. These are described in Table 24.9.

24

TABLE 24.9   GENERAL PREFERENCE SETTINGS FOR INFOVIEW

Option	Description
Initial view	Upon log on, this is the first page that will be displayed for that user. If My InfoView is selected and running on-demand reports, the user has to wait until those reports are complete before the page is rendered. If this is the case, a scheduled instance might be a better option.
On my desktop	Sets the number of objects per page. Should the number of objects exceed this number, the additional pages are displayed as a link in the Workspace section.
For each object, show me	User can select what he finds applicable for display purposes for description, owner, date, instance count, and available actions.
View my documents	The InfoView portal will, by default, display the report in the Workspace section. If the reports require more screen real estate, the other options can be used. In a single full-screen browser, this option creates another browser session and displays the report and any other reports using this new session. The final option will create a new session for each report viewed.
Current locale	This is the locale that is sent to the browser.
Time zone	This is important for users that are going to schedule reports at a particular date and time. The default time entered to start the scheduling process is local to the web server (not the CMS). For example, if the user schedules the report and his time zone is PST and the web server is running in EST, the report will run three hours sooner than expected. This issue is further emphasized when the system has anonymous or guest access enabled because the guest user account can only have one time zone associated with it but it may be used by many users around the world. If this is the case, establishing an account for each of the scheduling users is recommended.

WEB INTELLIGENCE DOCUMENT PREFERENCES

The preferences for Web Intelligence documents will differ by the platform on which Business Objects is installed. The differences are explained in Table 24.10.

TABLE 24.10   WEB INTELLIGENCE PREFERENCES

Option	Description
Select a view format	This determines the format of the Web Intelligence document when viewing. The HTML or PDF options are available for all platforms. The Interactive option enables the DHTML interactive viewer (currently Java-based only).

Option	Description
Select a report panel	This Java-only option changes the query panel used to create or modify a query. The Java Report panel requires a download of a Java applet, so it might not be suitable for extranet environments. The HTML Report and Query panels do not require any download.
For each new drill session	If drilling on the report is enabled, the user can specify whether he wants to drill on a duplicate report or the existing report.
General drill options	If drilling on a document requires a further query to be run, the user can choose whether he wants to run the query. The Synchronizing Drill on the Report Block option results in all report blocks showing the same data, as opposed to only the report block where the drill was initiated showing the new data. The Hide Drill Toolbar option enables the user to show the drill path on the report.

OLAP Intelligence Preferences

If Enterprise XI is licensed for Crystal Analysis, the user can select between running the ActiveX (sometimes called the rich client) or the DHTML versions of the viewer.

Crystal Reports Preferences

This page allows the user to set preferences specifically around the Crystal Reports viewers. Table 24.11 highlights the different options available.

TABLE 24.11   CRYSTAL REPORTS PREFERENCES

Options	Description
View my reports using	Allows the user to specify the type of viewer. A comparison of the viewers is described previously in the chapter. The ActiveX and Java viewers require an initial download.
DHTML viewer printing uses	If the user has selected the DHTML viewer, the user has two options when printing—either export the report to PDF and use the Acrobat Reader printing control, or download an ActiveX printing control.
Preferred measuring units	Determines the preferred unit of measure for defining the reporting page layout.
Rendering resolution	If the DHTML viewer is used, the user can select an appropriate resolution.

The final two tabs are the Password tab where the user can change his password and the About tab that describes the version.

CUSTOMIZING MY INFOVIEW

My InfoView is a page that allows a user to add the most important report or report parts onto a single page. Each frame within the template can contain one reference. The reference can point to a supported object type, such as Crystal Reports, a Crystal Reports part, an instance or an instance filtered by username, a Web Intelligence report, an OLAP Intelligence report, any Microsoft Office document, a PDF, or a hyperlink. After the page is complete, it can be saved by clicking the Save link, which will save the page to the user's Favorites folder. Multiple versions of My InfoView can be saved by using the Save As link. The My InfoView button launches the object called My InfoView from the user's Favorites folder. If this page is deleted, clicking the My InfoView button brings up a blank page and the user can re-create the page.

To create this page, click the My InfoView icon and select a template from the list. If the user is unsure of what the template looks like or which one will be best suited to her needs, she can select the template (see Figure 24.7) and preview it. If all the templates are unsuitable, the user can select the Split Screen button to split the screen horizontally, vertically, or a combination of the two.

Figure 24.7
Select a suitable template for your InfoView.

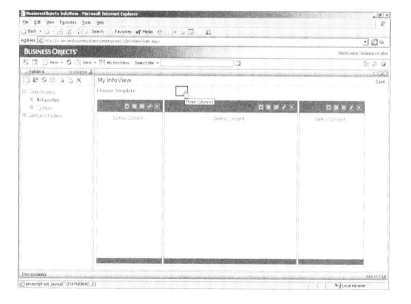

After the user is satisfied with the page splits, the user selects the Define Content link for each section of My InfoView to define the object that will populate that section. This brings up the form where the user selects the object she wants to display in that pane. The selections on the right are context sensitive to the object selected. For example, if the user selects a Crystal Report, she gets to select whether she wants a report part or the whole page, as shown in Figure 24.8. If the user selects a Web or OLAP Intelligence report, this option does not appear because report parts are not supported with this object type.

Figure 24.8
The Crystal Report Specific Options area has options for defining the content of a pane within My InfoView.

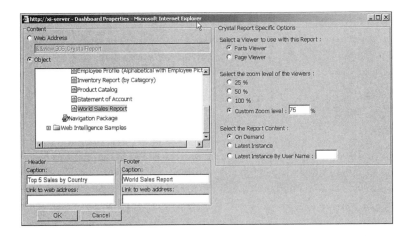

NOTE

The Object list only displays what the user has the rights to see. Also, if the view time security has been defined by either a Business View or Universe, the data displayed is limited to only what the user is allowed to see. See Chapter 18, "Using a Semantic Layer–Business Views and Universes," for more information.

After the user is satisfied, she can return to My InfoView to see the result. If the object is too large for the pane, a scroll bar will be automatically added (see Figure 24.9). The user can repeat the process until all the panes on the page are populated.

Figure 24.9
A report part added to My InfoView.

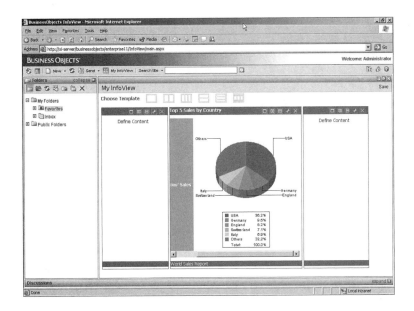

As mentioned earlier, InfoView is based off of a published API. The use of this API is described in Chapter 30, "Using the BusinessObjects Enterprise APIs." Some configuration files require further explanation.

Web.xml in the Java version and web.config in the .NET version of InfoView contain certain settings where an administrator can functionally and cosmetically change the way InfoView works.

In the Java edition, the web.xml file (usually located under the WEB.INF directory) contains some of the settings that might be of use to an administrator (see Table 24.12). This XML file is well-documented and an administrator should be able to determine what each tag describes.

TABLE 24.12   SOME USEFUL INFOVIEW SETTINGS FROM Web.xml

Setting	Description
path.dhtmlviewer	The path that describes the location of the DHTML Viewer. Check this if your report viewers are missing icons or do not display.
cms.default	The CMS default name for the logon page.
authentication.default	Sets the default authentication for logging on to InfoView. You can also hide this field or not allow a user to change it.
session-timeout	Sets the default amount of time a session will remain open.
homepage.default	Can specify the home page for the InfoView application.

TROUBLESHOOTING

LOOKING DIFFERENT

After making changes to modify the look of InfoView, such as updating the logo, I don't see the changes.

In a lot of cases, the browser will cache the page or logo. Delete the cache and restart the browser.

CRYSTAL ERROR

In My InfoView I select a Crystal Report as an object I want to display, but when I execute My InfoView, I get the error "Sorry, you do not have the right to execute this action. If you require this right, please see your system administrator."

This error is caused by selecting the latest instance option (the default) for a Crystal Report when there is no instance created. This is solved by either creating an instance or requesting that the report run on demand.

LOOPING LOGON ERROR

I am unable to schedule or view a report and InfoView continuously prompts me for a database logon.

The database logon is the user that is required to access the database. In other words, if the report accesses an Oracle database, the user entered here would be the user that Oracle authenticates against. However, should the Oracle database reside on a different physical server and network authentication is required to access the Oracle server, a user account that has access to this server needs to be established. This account should then be used to start the Job Server and Page Server.

CHAPTER 25

BUSINESSOBJECTS ENTERPRISE ARCHITECTURE

In this chapter

INTRODUCTION

This chapter introduces the BusinessObjects Enterprise Framework and the components that make up its architecture. It describes how each of the services or daemons that are part of the BusinessObjects Enterprise Framework operate and what role they have in an information infrastructure. The chapter also discusses the benefits of having a distributed architecture: vertical scalability, horizontal scalability, innate load balancing, failover, high availability, and tune-ability—the capability to tailor the system to a particular environment and type of load.

This chapter uses a progressive approach: considering the highest level first, and then approaching each part of that whole in more detail.

BUSINESSOBJECTS ENTERPRISE ARCHITECTURE OVERVIEW

At the highest level, BusinessObjects Enterprise has four main tiers: the client tier, application tier, BusinessObjects Enterprise Server tier, and database tier (see Figure 25.1):

Figure 25.1
The client, application, server, and data tiers compose an enterprise business intelligence infrastructure.

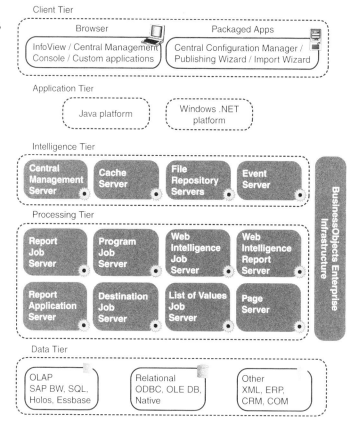

- The *client tier* consists of Web-based and installed applications. You can alternatively categorize these applications into end-user applications such as the Web-based InfoView, which enables end users to access data, management applications such as the Web-based Central Management Console, and content creation applications such as Crystal Reports or OLAP Intelligence. In the majority of cases, the client tier for a BusinessObjects Enterprise user is a Web browser.

- The *application tier* consists of application processing—typically on an application server, using the BusinessObjects Enterprise Software Development Kit (BOE SDK). The BOE SDK provides a programmatic interface to the BusinessObjects Enterprise server tier. These server-based programs are processed on an application server, such as BEA WebLogic, IBM's WebSphere, a Servlet container like Apache Tomcat or Microsoft .Net server. This application tier could provide an application centered on BusinessObjects Enterprise functionality, like InfoView, or an application that uses BusinessObjects Enterprise functionality as part of a greater application (for example, an online banking application that provides full-service banking for customers, and provides detailed statements via BusinessObjects Enterprise).

- The *server tier* consists of services (in Windows) or daemons (in Unix) registered with the BusinessObjects Enterprise Framework. (They are generically referred to as either services or daemons as these terms are interchangeable.) Although this chapter uses the term "service" or "daemon" for technical accuracy, you might see references to these services as "servers" as well, for instance the Central Management Server. The server tier is usually subdivided into the intelligence and processing tiers.

- The *data tier* is comprised of two parts. First is all data sources from which an organization can pull data. This data can be in a database, an application, a programmatic data source, XML, a Web service, or a variety of other sources. The second part is that which is offered as part of the BusinessObjects Enterprise solution, specifically, Meta Data services via Business Views and Universes and data connectivity via ODBC and native drivers.

With a high-level understanding of the role of the client, application, server, and database tiers, you now consider each one in depth.

THE CLIENT TIER

The client tier is the "face" that you associate with BusinessObjects Enterprise. A particular end user might think of the ePortfolio application page that shows up in her Web browser as BusinessObjects Enterprise. However, BusinessObjects Enterprise has many faces, each distinct and useful. By adopting a flexible approach toward potential client applications, BusinessObjects Enterprise offers a system architect diverse means of sharing information with diverse audiences: an executive receives a text message on his cellular phone with the latest profitability statistics; a shipping clerk receives an order on the workgroup printer; a supplier company receives an XML file with detailed order specifications. These are but a few faces of BusinessObjects Enterprise.

To begin categorizing the client tier, define three groups of audiences that will use client applications: the end user, content creator, and administrator. Although these groups are not mutually exclusive (a particular person can have all three roles), this distinction helps to explore important dimensions of each.

The most common end-user client for BusinessObjects Enterprise is a Web browser. Many of the client applications that are included with BusinessObjects Enterprise, such as InfoView, use a Web browser as their client. Additionally, most custom application development targets the Web browser.

With the proliferation, adoption, and maturation of the Internet as a communications medium, additional client tools offer diverse venues for end-user experiences. Internet-connected phones and mobile devices already grace the belts and briefcases of the more tech-savvy.

With each client targeted for an end-user community, specific considerations take the fore. For instance, most Internet-connected phones have small screens—they can only display a few lines of text at a time. Because BusinessObjects Enterprise is so widely experienced within the Web browser, several browser-related considerations merit your attention. Web browsers such as Internet Explorer and Netscape or Mozilla are page-oriented: They display one page at a time. Users expect these pages quickly and become frustrated at what they consider long waiting times for pages to display. The benchmark hovers at between 5 to 10 seconds for the patience of a typical Web user.

The Web experience also is by and large a simple one. You see a blue-underlined word, and know that you can click on it to go somewhere. Originally, Web browsers were simple text display programs. The capability of today's browsers to render complex graphics and reflect exact positioning represents a tremendous maturation of the technology, but you must remember that a Web browser was not initially designed for this, and even today limitations, most notably around printing, reflect these origins. For content such as Crystal Reports, where pixel-level formatting is vital, and for content such as OLAP Intelligence reports, where interactivity is vital, BusinessObjects Enterprise provides special facility for overcoming the limitations of the Web browser.

The BusinessObjects Enterprise report viewers were presented in Chapters 23, "Introduction to BusinessObjects Enterprise," and 24, "Using InfoView." For each type of object managed in BusinessObjects Enterprise, there are specific viewers made available. These viewers appear in the browser and include buttons for exporting, printing, navigating, searching, and so on. These viewers provide pixel-level positioning, tremendous interactivity, and graphical capability. Crystal Enterprise 9 implemented a new viewing architecture which has been expanded on over the subsequent two releases. The viewer object in the SDK renders reports and provides a simple interface for the Web developer to embed a Crystal Report or OLAP Intelligence document. The developer sets the properties of the viewer to determine the capabilities an end user has. For instance, the report export capability might be inappropriate for a certain end-user population, and so can be turned off by setting the `HasExportButton` property to 0.

The Web browser receives only DHTML and images, with the exception of the optional print control. Should a user choose to print a report, either an ActiveX print control or an Adobe Acrobat file is used to print while maintaining pixel-level formatting and fidelity.

In earlier versions of BusinessObjects Enterprise, reports were rendered via a URL request to the viewrpt.cwr page, which was processed by the Web Component Service provided by BusinessObjects Enterprise. The new control enables a developer to embed a viewer control wherever they want in a Web page, to be platform independent, and to fully secure and control the report viewing experience.

BusinessObjects Enterprise supports the following browsers:

- IE 6
- Netscape 6.2
- Netscape 7.0
- Safari 1.2 on OSx (not including Japanese)

CONTENT CREATION APPLICATIONS

Applications, such as Crystal Reports or OLAP Intelligence, install on the report developer's machine and create and publish content to the BusinessObjects Enterprise Framework. These were introduced and covered extensively in Parts I through IV.

ADMINISTRATIVE CLIENT APPLICATIONS

Applications such as the Central Management Console (CMC) allow administrative users to manage the BusinessObjects Enterprise system. Administrators might also use the Central Configuration Manager (CCM) for server-level management. The CMC is a Web-based application, but the CCM is an installed application. Coverage of these administration tools is provided in Chapter 27, "Administering and Configuring BusinessObjects Enterprise."

THE APPLICATION TIER

Various applications dynamically create end-user pages, most typically in HTML. These applications are processed on an application server. In the past few years, the Enterprise application server market has consolidated dramatically, with two main camps now extant: the Microsoft .Net technologies and the Java technologies.

BusinessObjects Enterprise provides a Software Development Kit in three formats for each of the three most popular development environments: COM, Java, and .Net. These allow an organization maximum flexibility in integrating BusinessObjects Enterprise into its applications.

The COM SDK includes a set of COM objects that interact with BusinessObjects Enterprise via the BusinessObjects Enterprise Framework.

In prior versions of the product, the typical use and installation used the COM SDK as the primary conduit into the system. This architecture included a Web Connector on each of the web server machines and a Web Component Server (WCS) within the framework. The WCS provided application services for server side processing of Crystal Server Pages (CSP). CSP is a technology analogous to the Microsoft Active Server Pages (ASP) technology, with the key distinction that the processing occurs within the Enterprise framework in the CSP scenario. In the XI release, the default installation options include both a Java and .NET version of the packaged interfaces. The Web Component Server is removed from the framework. Support for CSP pages is provided through the Web Component Adapter running on the application server.

The BusinessObjects Java SDK includes a set of Java classes that communicate with the BusinessObjects Enterprise Framework. In a Java application server environment, no Web Connector (WC) or Web Component Service (WCS) is required. Instead the Java SDK is processed on the Web application server, which communicates via the Java SDK directly with the BusinessObjects Enterprise Framework. In addition, the BusinessObjects Enterprise Web Component Adapter (WCA) installs on the Web application server and provides the capabilities that you expect from the WCS: CSP processing and specific application support.

Microsoft produces the .Net Framework. Applications written within the .Net Framework are supported by BusinessObjects Enterprise via the .Net BOE SDK. This SDK includes primary interop assemblies and visual development controls for visual application development in Microsoft Visual Studio .Net. In a .Net application, there is no WCS, WCA, or WC required, as the native .Net assemblies are loaded into the .Net framework and communicate with BusinessObjects Enterprise via the COM SDK.

The current state of support for the SDK is both a reflection of the marketplace and a reflection of the historical progression of BusinessObjects Enterprise in response to the maturation of the Web server market. Because the previous versions of BusinessObjects Enterprise were introduced before the Web application market had matured, the product included its own application server: the WCS. Now that the Web server and Web application server markets have consolidated and matured, the WCS has been replaced by the capabilities of those application servers. Generally, all custom applications should be developed using the technology that is most appropriate: the Java or .Net SDKs. Although COM technology is supported in BusinessObjects Enterprise XI, with Microsoft's migration to .Net from COM, it is recommended that development take place in .Net over COM where possible.

THE SERVER TIER: INTRODUCING THE BUSINESSOBJECTS ENTERPRISE FRAMEWORK

The BusinessObjects Enterprise Framework, the backbone of BusinessObjects Enterprise, provides a distributed mechanism that manages the interaction and communication of the

BusinessObjects Enterprise services that make up the server tier, as well as communication between this server tier and the BOE SDK. Each BusinessObjects Enterprise service uses the framework to describe the capabilities it offers and to discover other services that are registered with the framework. The framework treats each of the registered services as equals, which enables one service to use the capability of another BusinessObjects Enterprise server directly, thus enhancing scalability.

The Framework's foundation is a communication bus that handles dialogue between the various services and facilitates automatic load-balancing and fault tolerance. This communication bus registers each service, categorizes the type of service, and maintains a tally of the status of each service. For scalability reasons, much of this service interaction is distributed and decentralized. This is one of the reasons BusinessObjects Enterprise leads the industry in scalability.

The BusinessObjects Enterprise Framework uses programmatic components, known as plug-ins, to represent each object type within BusinessObjects Enterprise. Plug-ins contain the appropriate properties and methods needed to handle a particular object within BusinessObjects Enterprise, and determine how BusinessObjects Enterprise should treat it. For instance, a service might require information about a Crystal Report, and will use the properties of the Crystal Report plug-in to retrieve the information. The Crystal Report plug-in properties include things like the report title, the database login information for that report, and the report thumbnail image. In contrast, a user plug-in might have the username, the type of login, and the group membership as its properties.

Although plug-ins become much more important as you start to explore application development using the BusinessObjects Enterprise SDK, they are a great way to start to explore the capabilities of BusinessObjects Enterprise. Figure 25.2 shows how a plug-in is used. They help you to categorize the types of objects you find in BusinessObjects Enterprise, and understand what you can do with each of them.

Figure 25.2
A plug-in is the way BusinessObjects Enterprise exposes the services of a server on the framework.

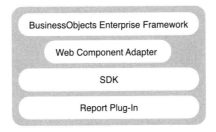

The object types that are part of the BusinessObjects Enterprise Framework are classified in the following groups:

- Administration
- Authentication
- Content
- Distribution

Administration Plug-ins

Administration plug-ins provide a way to manage the BusinessObjects Enterprise servers. Each plug-in exposes the control and configuration properties of a server within the BusinessObjects Enterprise system so that you can configure the behavior of each BusinessObjects Enterprise server. These plug-ins also provide activity metrics for each server.

Authentication Plug-ins

Authentication plug-ins provide a mechanism for BusinessObjects Enterprise to interact with external security systems and treat these systems as native authentication sources. The authentication plug-ins provided with BusinessObjects Enterprise are

- BusinessObjects Enterprise
- Windows NT
- LDAP
- Windows Active Directory

→ These authentication types are discussed in more detail in "The Server Tier: Overview of the BusinessObjects Enterprise Services," **p. 589**.

Content Plug-ins

Content plug-ins describe the types of objects that end users (report viewers) would typically interact with, such as, but not limited to, a Crystal Report. The content types that are provided as part of BusinessObjects Enterprise are

- Folder
- User folder
- Shortcuts
- Crystal Reports
- OLAP Intelligence
- Microsoft Word
- Microsoft Excel
- Microsoft PowerPoint
- Rich Text Format
- Adobe Acrobat
- Text
- Users
- User groups
- Servers
- Server groups
- Events

- Connections
- Licenses
- Calendars
- Object packages
- Program objects
- Web Intelligence documents
- Universes
- Universe Connections

DISTRIBUTION PLUG-INS

A *distribution plug-in* allows anyone who is scheduling an object such as a Crystal Report to be able to send that report outside the BusinessObjects Enterprise environment. This facility enables the application to schedule reports to destinations such as e-mail. Distribution plug-ins that are provided with BusinessObjects Enterprise are

- Disk location
- FTP server
- E-mail (SMTP)

NOTE

> BusinessObjects Enterprise also provides the capability for a Crystal Report to be scheduled to a printer. The printer object is not exposed as a distribution object, but rather as a function of the Crystal Report content plug-in.

These plug-ins play a fundamental role in the BusinessObjects Enterprise Framework by encapsulating and exposing the knowledge of the object type that they represent. The remainder of this chapter discusses how these plug-ins are used by the BusinessObjects Enterprise servers within the BusinessObjects Enterprise Framework.

THE SERVER TIER: OVERVIEW OF THE BUSINESSOBJECTS ENTERPRISE SERVICES

Now that it's clear that the functionality of individual BusinessObjects Enterprise servers is exposed through plug-ins, it's important to understand exactly what that functionality is. The BusinessObjects Enterprise servers are designed to register themselves with the BusinessObjects Enterprise Framework and provide one or more services that can be consumed by other servers or by the plug-ins described in the last section. The services offered by each of the servers is dependent on the type of task that the server is expected to perform.

The following list shows the servers that are delivered with BusinessObjects Enterprise. These servers can be thought of as *core servers*:

- Central Management Server
- Cache Server
- Page Server
- Report Application Server
- Report Job Server
- Program Job Server
- Destination Job Server
- List of Values Job Server
- Event Server
- File Repository Server
- Web Intelligence Job Server
- Web Intelligence Report Server
- Web Component Adapter

These servers can be seen in the architecture diagram in Figure 25.3.

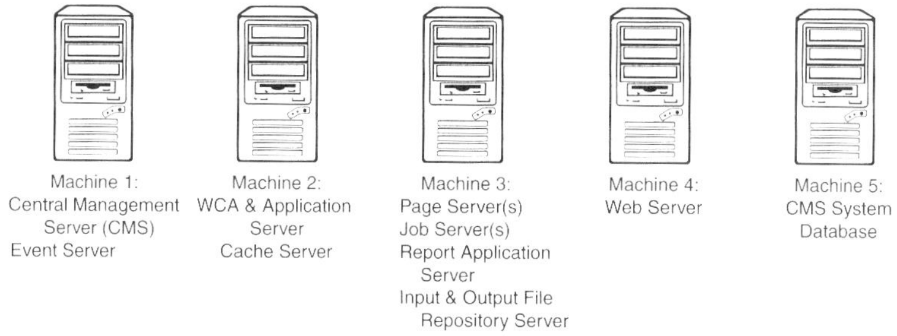

Figure 25.3
The core server architecture for BusinessObjects Enterprise.

Machine 1:
Central Management
Server (CMS)
Event Server

Machine 2:
WCA & Application
Server
Cache Server

Machine 3:
Page Server(s)
Job Server(s)
Report Application
Server
Input & Output File
Repository Server

Machine 4:
Web Server

Machine 5:
CMS System
Database

With these servers in place, BusinessObjects Enterprise manages reporting and business intelligence content (such as Crystal Reports, OLAP Intelligence reports, Web Intelligence documents, Excel, Word, PDF, and PowerPoint documents) and offers rich customization services allowing organizations to deeply embed and integrate BusinessObjects Enterprise into their already established applications or Web services.

It's important to note that multiple instances of the same server operating in the BusinessObjects Enterprise Framework at the same time are fully supported. This provides a scalable, reliable, and fault-tolerant system.

CENTRAL MANAGEMENT SERVER

The Central Management Server (CMS) provides a number of the core services that the BusinessObjects Enterprise Framework uses. These services include allowing other servers to register with the framework, allowing users to be authenticated with the system, and providing a storage mechanism for maintaining the metadata about each object. The services provided by the CMS fit into four main categories:

- Controlling access to content
- Managing objects and scheduling
- Managing servers
- Managing system auditing

The CMS provides for the following:

- System security
- Object metadata storage
- Object management
- Object scheduling
- Event handling
- Name-server capabilities
- Server clustering
- License management
- Auditing

SYSTEM SECURITY

The security service breaks security down into three main elements:

- Authentication
- Authorization
- Aggregation

AUTHENTICATION   BusinessObjects Enterprise provides mechanisms to allow for third-party authentication services to be used as the basis of user and group/role definition. The CMS interacts with these third-party authentication mechanisms by using the following authentication plug-ins, described earlier in the chapter:

- BusinessObjects Enterprise security plug-in
- Windows NT security plug-in
- LDAP security plug-in
- Windows Active Directory plug-in
- Application authentication such as PeopleSoft or SAP

The Enterprise security plug-in enables organizations to define users and groups directly within BusinessObjects Enterprise and restrict use of an external source for those users. This is useful if an organization has chosen not to use an external security source or has not yet defined one. All authentication information is stored in BusinessObjects Enterprise and does not rely on an outside source to determine whether a user is valid.

The NT and Active Directory security plug-ins enable a customer to map any number of users and groups into BusinessObjects Enterprise. Although these two are separate plug-ins, they function in similar manner and so are discussed here together.

An administrator is required to go into the Central Management Console (see Chapter 27) or use an application written using the SDK and define the default NT or Active Directory (AD) domain as well as any user groups that might need to be mapped into BusinessObjects Enterprise. After this initial mapping is complete, BusinessObjects Enterprise will dynamically query for users within that group and establish those users as BusinessObjects Enterprise users. When a user logs on for the first time, the security service using the NT or AD security plug-in asks the NT or AD security database if this is a valid NT or AD user and whether the user belongs in any of the mapped groups. If the user is indeed a valid user, he will be granted access to BusinessObjects Enterprise. If at any time in the future that user is removed from that NT group, he will not be granted access to BusinessObjects Enterprise (and, hence, reports within the system) because the security service would be told that this user is no longer a valid NT user. There's no requirement for the administrator to manually inform BusinessObjects Enterprise that the user is no longer a valid NT user.

The LDAP security plug-in operates in a similar manner to the NT security plug-in; however, instead of talking to the operating system for a list of valid users or groups, this security plug-in communicates with a directory server using the LDAP protocol. BusinessObjects Enterprise does not require the LDAP schema in the directory server to be modified in any way for use with BusinessObjects Enterprise. This security plug-in provides default mappings for several directory servers, including

- iPlanet Directory Server versions 5.1 and 5.2
- Lotus Domino versions 5.0.12 and 6.0.2
- IBM Secureway 5.1
- Novell Directory Services eDirectory 8.7
- Custom

When the BusinessObjects Enterprise solutions kits for PeopleSoft and SAP are installed, they provide additional authentication plug-ins for each system, respectively.

Users and groups are queried by leveraging attributes within the LDAP schema, such as InetOrgPerson, which is an attribute used by iPlanet Directory Server. If the directory server that is to be used with BusinessObjects Enterprise is not in the preceding list, it's also possible to create a custom mapping of LDAP attributes. The attributes that are used to define a group or user must be mapped to the LDAP security plug-in for these attributes to be used when querying for a user or a group.

Application-specific authentication plug-ins enable BusinessObjects Enterprise to validate a user's credentials against an ERP system such as SAP or PeopleSoft. Installing a BusinessObjects Enterprise Solution Kit installs the respective plug-in, which then appears next to the default authentication tabs in the Central Management Console. Each of these application-specific plug-ins requires configuration to enable BusinessObjects Enterprise to interact with the application, and require information on group mapping.

AUTHORIZATION   After configuring BusinessObjects Enterprise with external users and groups, it's necessary to determine which objects within the system an end user has the authority to view. This central mechanism of controlled access to certain reports is a key component of the system. Setting up authorization rules or access control is straightforward after users and reports have been added to the system. Chapter 27 reviews how to apply access control on objects in the system.

NOTE

> Authorization within BusinessObjects Enterprise is enforced through a strong inheritance model throughout the system. This enables you to set desired access levels at a root folder for a large group and have that setting be respected, regardless of how many new subfolders are created or objects are added to those folders (as well as any new users added to groups or subgroups).

AGGREGATION   BusinessObjects Enterprise can aggregate or group users in two ways, as Chapter 27 reviews in some detail. A group can be created directly in BusinessObjects Enterprise or it can be mapped from one of the external authentication sources. The grouping within BusinessObjects Enterprise is quite powerful because native and mapped groups can be used at the same time. If this method of user aggregation is implemented, a native group would contain a mapped group. The use of mapped groups simplifies administration: As users are added or removed from groups in the external systems, this will be automatically reflected in BusinessObjects Enterprise. It's also possible to create a hierarchy of groups to better organize the end users of the system.

OBJECT METADATA STORAGE

Among other tasks, the CMS stores a repository of information about each object in the BusinessObjects Enterprise system. After this information is stored, it becomes available to other objects or servers within the system. This persistent data describes an object (such as a Crystal Report) and makes it possible to dynamically query the system and discover the properties of that object. This repository expanded in version 10 of Crystal Enterprise to include storage of objects used to design Crystal Reports as well as Business Views Objects (see Chapter 18, "Using a Semantic Layer—Business Views and Universes").

This information is stored in a repository to enable scaling; to do otherwise would require dependence on the information being stored in memory on a physical server—not scalable. The CMS stores this information by writing it to a relational database. As the product matured through version 10 and now, XI, database querying capabilities were more fully leveraged than in previous versions, resulting in even faster request processing and

25

enhanced scalability. However this changed functionality also requires that more attention be paid to database optimization.

The CMS service is able to access these databases by using ODBC or by a direct, also known as native, interface to the database. Because the CMS also provides auditing capability, the database compatibility is the same for the auditing database (you will consider the auditing capability later in this chapter). Although the BusinessObjects Enterprise system database and the audit database can be on the same or separate database servers, the actual databases are separate.

The following list shows databases supported by the CMS and how they are accessed by BusinessObjects Enterprise XI when the CMS is operating on Windows NT:

- Direct IBM DB2 8.1 and 8.2.
- Direct Oracle 9.2 and 10.1
- Direct Sybase System 12.5
- ODBC-MSDE
- ODBC-MS SQL Server 2000
- ODBC-MS SQL Server 7

The databases that the CMS can access on Unix are a subset of what is available on Windows. If the CMS is operating on Unix, it's able to use the following databases:

- IBM DB2 8.1
- IBM UDB DB2 8.2
- Oracle 9.2
- Oracle 10.1
- Sybase ASE 12.5

All database connections for the CMS repository are done by a direct interface.

The default Windows-platform database that the CMS will use if one is not provided is the MSDE, a simple implementation of Microsoft's SQL Server. Because performance of the CMS database can dramatically affect system performance, MSDE is used to provide an organization a useful out-of-the-box experience. The repository is set up and configured without the need for interaction with a database administrator. If BusinessObjects Enterprise is initially configured to use the default repository database and the need arises to move the repository to a different database server, BusinessObjects Enterprise provides tools (the Central Configuration Manager) to easily migrate the data from one server to another.

NAMESERVER CAPABILITIES

The CMS allows all other BusinessObjects Enterprise servers to register with the BusinessObjects Enterprise Framework. After each service has registered through the CMS, it is able to discover the other servers active within the framework and use any services it needs from those servers.

New BusinessObjects Enterprise services can be added to the system from either the Central Management Console or the Central Configuration Manager. The addition of these new services provides additional scalability and higher availability.

OBJECT MANAGEMENT

One of the key benefits of BusinessObjects Enterprise is how it manages objects. After an object (such as a Crystal Report) is published to BusinessObjects Enterprise, the properties of that object are read and added to the repository. The object is then represented by metadata in the repository, which makes it possible for other services to interact with the object, and the object is formally considered a "managed object" by the system.

Managed objects facilitate simplified administration of an Enterprise Business Intelligence system and represent a principal benefit of BusinessObjects Enterprise. After an object is managed by the system, all of that object's properties become managed from a single access point. For instance, if a server needs access to an object, it asks the CMS for an ID to the object. Additionally, if you want to maintain a certain number of reports in the system, or only keep objects more recent than a certain date, this can be automated within the system. If you want to schedule a report, or organize similar reports into folders, or control access rights, or link reports, or change database properties of multiple reports—all of this and other similar actions are possible when you manage the objects within BusinessObjects Enterprise.

By having objects managed, a Web application developer can use BusinessObjects Enterprise to manage and provide access to all objects. Rather than requiring knowledge of object filenames or network share locations, or even which objects or reports are available at all, developers can simply query BusinessObjects Enterprise for the desired objects—perhaps those kept in a certain folder or of a certain type. Each time a user accesses the Web application, the content might be different, depending on the actual reports (objects) published by or scheduled into BusinessObjects Enterprise. Web developers are not required to make changes such as adding and maintaining reports. This can be done by a report developer or system administrator through delegated administration and provides a logical separation of tasks.

Managed objects can be categorized into folders, which themselves are managed objects. This categorization adds to the manageability of BusinessObjects Enterprise because content can be easily organized into something that is meaningful to end users. In addition to residing in a folder, BusinessObjects Enterprise XI introduced the concept of categories. Objects can be associated with one or more categories to further organize a collection of related objects that span multiple folders.

BusinessObjects Enterprise XI adds several new types of objects to the system, such as program objects and third-party objects such as Microsoft Word objects (please see "The Server Tier: Introduction to the BusinessObjects Enterprise Framework" earlier in this chapter for a complete list). The system database also includes a report component repository that simplifies access to corporate objects such as logos, images, disclaimers, and so on, and a rich semantic layer called Business Views.

25

If are not familiar with the database changes which occurred in Crystal Enterprise 10 and you were to look at the database directly, you would see that these additional capabilities have altered the database tables from previous versions of BusinessObjects Enterprise, and you now see four tables in the system database instead of the previous two. The two additional tables represent the report component repository. No additional tables were added between Crystal Enterprise 10 and BusinessObjects Enterprise XI.

For performance and security reasons, the vast majority of the information about objects is stored in a binary format in the database, making it unreadable to direct database access. Instead, the CMS provides access to database objects via the BOE SDK via a SQL-like query language. This system ensures authenticated and authorized access only; the application provides access to objects based on their authenticated identity only.

Schedules

The scheduling service of the CMS makes it possible for objects such as Crystal Reports to be processed at a particular time or on a recurring basis. This service determines when a report object gets processed using the Report Job Server, or a program object gets processed using the Program Job Server. When a scheduled event occurs, the two main servers that interact with the object are the relevant Job Server and the Event Server. Additionally, an object package combines objects such as reports or programs for simplified scheduling.

When scheduling a job, the scheduling service gathers information from various objects before running. It needs information from the report object regarding how to connect to the database, the desired format to output the report to, where it might be delivered (such as an e-mail address), and which server is going to process it (if there are multiple Job Servers). An object can be scheduled to run at a particular date or time, on a recurring basis, or perhaps according to a custom calendar. This information is then stored in the system as a scheduled instance of the object. This is known as a ProcessingInfo object.

The ProcessingInfo object contains all the properties set on the report object when it was scheduled. It knows when the job will run as well as all the data-connection information and all the formatting and distribution settings.

A scheduled object can be made to be dependent on an event occurring within or outside the BusinessObjects Enterprise system before it will run. By using events with schedules, it's possible to provide meaningful control around when a schedule should actually run. If an object is due to run every day but the databases that it queries are updated sporadically, an event can be used to initiate the running of the scheduled job and eliminate unnecessary scheduled jobs or reports.

A notification capability is built in to provide the capability to send e-mail upon a scheduled job completion, either in the case of success or failure. Common use cases include an administrator receiving notification of a report processing failure, or an end-user group being notified of the latest quarterly results.

In some instances, batch scheduling can take place via a custom program. In these cases, report instances might be distributed to many users. The scheduling service makes this possible by allowing a job to be scheduled on behalf of another user. This is useful when an organization wants to configure its system to only show instances of objects to a user if she "owns" that instance. This is exposed in the BOE SDK in the `ScheduleOnBehalfOf` property of the `SchedulingInfo` object.

EVENT HANDLING

Events make it possible for users to ensure that scheduled jobs are processing only when external systems, like a database, are ready to be accessed. All events interface with the CMS Event service.

BusinessObjects Enterprise supports three types of events. The first event type is a *scheduled event*. The scheduled event allows an organization to create dependency chains when scheduling reports. This enables the user to determine the schedule of a report based on a preceding report successfully completing or failing. Users can easily configure scheduled event conditions such that if report 1 is successful, run report 2. If report 1 is not successful, run program object 3. This can continue so that a process flow is established.

> **N O T E**
>
> With the inclusion of Program Objects in version 10 of BusinessObjects Enterprise, it should become apparent that these scheduling daisy chains could now include workflow that reaches outside of the BusinessObjects Enterprise environment and could affect external systems or applications.

25

The next event type is a custom event. The *custom event* is sometimes also called a *generic event* in the predecessor to BusinessObjects Enterprise, known as Seagate Info. This event requires application developer interaction to trigger the event by using the `Trigger()` method via the BusinessObjects Enterprise SDK. This event type gives an organization a great deal of flexibility. Having an event that can be triggered by code makes it possible to have an external system determine when the event is triggered and the scheduled jobs that are dependent on it will run. A good example of this would be a database update trigger user event for BusinessObjects Enterprise.

The third type is a *file-based event*. These events are managed by the Event Server and are discussed later in the chapter.

SERVER CLUSTERING

As a BusinessObjects Enterprise system grows and access to information that it contains becomes increasingly mission critical, it's important that the system be fault tolerant, ensuring that end users are always able to access their information.

The CMS can be clustered to provide load balancing and fault tolerance for the services that it provides. When two or more CMSs are clustered, they perform as an active-active collection of servers. By being active-active, they are sharing the workload and this translates into increased scalability and performance.

AUDITING

The auditing capability introduced in Crystal Enterprise 10, simplifies gathering statistics on system performance and enables administrators to profile the usage of reports or system resources. Because the auditing database is separate from the CMS/system database, you must create the "blank" database and any necessary ODBC DSN first. From within the Central Configuration Manager (CCM) you then stop the CMS, click on the Specify Auditing Source icon (the fourth icon from the right in the toolbar), specify the database or DSN you want to use, and then restart the CMS, whereupon the CMS creates the auditing database structure and connection. On Unix platforms you take the same approach, except that you stop and start the CMS with the ccm.sh script and use the cmsdbsetup.sh script with the selectaudit option to specify the audit database, including the connection port (which is 6400 by default).

After the CMS starts and connects to the audit database, you can specify which items you want to audit. The administrator enables auditing of each of the following items by entering the Central Management Console (CMC), navigating to the Servers, choosing the particular server you want to affect, and then checking the appropriate boxes in the Auditing tab. Table 25.1 shows each server's auditing features. Note that the table does not include the Page Server; the Page Server's auditing occurs through the Cache Server, which takes reports from the Page Server and passes them to the appropriate viewer. Note also that although the Job Servers are treated as one, they must be specified on each server. Additionally, you must specify auditing on each instance of a server if multiple instances exist.

TABLE 25.1   DETAILED AUDITING CAPABILITIES BY SERVER

Server	Audit feature
CMS	Folder creation, deletion, modification User logon (concurrent and named) User password change, logon failure, logoff Report or Program Job communication lost (that is, timeout on Program/Report JobServer)
Cache Server	Report view success/failure
RAS	Report open success/failure and which viewer was used Report creation success/failure, and which viewer/application was used Report save success/failure and which viewer/application was used
Event Server	Event registered, updated, or unregistered Event triggered
Job Servers	Job success/failure, failure-retry state

Note that the CMS periodically broadcasts a request to all system services requesting audit information to be returned for writing to the database. The default is every five minutes. Your BusinessObjects Enterprise documentation describes several command-line flags to specify this and other audit-specific CMS parameters. You must specify the same command lines on all CMSs if clustered.

WEB COMPONENT SERVER

The Web Component Server (WCS) which existed in previous versions of the product has been removed from the framework. However, it warrants a brief mention here. The WCS in Crystal Enterprise served as an *application server* to provide seamless integration of Enterprise content into any Web application. This integration was be hosted on a variety of Web servers and provided a robust scripting interface known as Crystal Server Pages that enables the creation of rich server-side Web applications.

At the time the product was introduced to the market many organizations already had licensed and installed Web servers, but did not possess an application server. Crystal Decisions found it necessary to provide this application server so that applications could be written against the SDK on any operating system platform. With the maturation and con-solidation of the Web server market many of the functions that the WCS provided are now supplanted by the combination Web and application servers common in the marketplace, rendering the WCS application-serving capabilities unnecessary for most organizations.

However, the WCS did provide some capabilities in addition to CSP processing, and these functions, if desired in an installation, are now provided by the Web Component Adapter. In summary, the WCS capabilities include the following:

- Processing of CSP
- Report parameter prompting at report view time
- Report database logon requests at report view time
- Central Management Console server processing
- Rendering of OLAP Intelligence reports

To provide these capabilities, should they be required by the use case, BusinessObjects Enterprise includes the Web Component Adapter (WCA) that provides all the above, except the processing of CSP pages.

BusinessObjects Enterprise XI no longer uses the WCS. This server has been deprecated, although the functionality of the service continues to be available via the .NET or Java SDK or via a Web Component Adapter as an intermediary to on of the BOE SDK.

A typical Unix installation, for example, uses a client application such as InfoView written in Java Server Pages (JSP), rather than in Crystal Server Pages (CSP). Therefore, it does not require the WCS to process CSP pages. Instead, it uses a Java application server to process the JSP against the Java version of the BusinessObjects Enterprise SDK. In such a scenario, should you require the functions listed above, a WCA installed on the application server will provide that application server functionality.

Using the .Net BOE SDK in a Microsoft .NET environment, application-processing func-tions are carried out by Microsoft Internet Information Services (IIS) Web server and the

25

.Net Framework application serving capability, as well as the BusinessObjects Enterprise Primary Interop Assemblies.

Although CSP is not specifically deprecated in BusinessObjects Enterprise XI, it has indicated in the help files that CSP is to be fully deprecated in a future release. CSP in BusinessObjects Enterprise XI is supported via the WCA for backward compatibility.

CRYSTAL WEB REQUEST(CWR)

A type of request that is not mentioned in the above paragraphs is a Crystal Web Request, or CWR. A CWR is a server-side request that is executed by the WCA working in tandem with the services BusinessObjects Enterprise to provide access to managed objects contained within the BusinessObjects Enterprise repository.

In the prior version of the product, support for URL-based requests to directly view an object such as a report was deprecated because the report viewing model changed to a Crystal Report viewing control within the Application tier. Certain legacy applications might still use .cwr requests, but this method is not recommended for new installations to ensure forward-compatibility.

WEB COMPONENT ADAPTER

In the default configurations in either a Java or ASP.NET environment, the Web Component Adapter serves the purpose of providing the following functionality.

- Processes CSP pages
- Services Central Management Console requests
- Handles viewrpt.cwr requests (legacy support)

The Web Component Adapter supports the following Java application servers:

- BEA WebLogic 7.0(SP5), 8.1(SP2)
- IBM WebSphere 5.0 (Fix-pack 2)
- IBM WebSphere 5.1 (Fix-pack 4)
- Tomcat 5.0.27

JOB SERVERS (REPORT AND PROGRAM)

The Job Servers process scheduled jobs. Job Servers are informed about the content that they process by loading a Job Server plug-in. This plug-in, like all other BusinessObjects Enterprise plug-ins, describes what capabilities it exposes to the service using it. In BusinessObjects Enterprise XI, there are four different Job Server plug-ins: one for Crystal Reports, one for Programs, another is for Web Intelligence documents and the fourth is for List of Values job server. When the system administrator adds a new Job Server to the BusinessObjects Enterprise system, he must choose which type of plug-in, and thus which type of Job Server it will be.

REPORT JOB SERVER

The Report Job Server allows scheduled objects to access the necessary data source required, provides row-level data security services, and distributes the content to a location chosen by the user.

Essentially, the Job Server provides three main services to BusinessObjects Enterprise:

- Database access
- Distribution of objects
- E-mail

DATABASE ACCESS

When a scheduled job is about to be processed by the Job Server, it gathers the appropriate information from the `ProcessingInfo` object mentioned earlier. This information includes database connection information and any filters or parameters required that determine what the final query is. After it has this, it opens the object and queries the database for the appropriate information. The data is retrieved, compressed, and stored back into the system as a report instance.

DISTRIBUTION OF OBJECTS

It's the Job Server's responsibility to distribute the object to the destination set by the user scheduling the job. To do this, the distribution service interacts with the distribution plug-ins mentioned earlier and receives the information appropriate to each plug-in type. For example, if a user scheduled a job to be delivered by e-mail, the distribution service would get the To:, Cc:, subject, and body properties as well as the SMTP server that is configured for use with BusinessObjects Enterprise. Chapter 26, "Planning Considerations when Deploying BusinessObjects Enterprise," shows how to configure the distribution service.

This service enables a user to send a report outside the BusinessObjects Enterprise environment and deliver it to one of four destinations using the distribution plug-ins mentioned earlier.

INBOX AS A DESTINATION

New in BusinessObjects Enterprise XI is the ability to send objects to an user's Inbox within the BusinessObjects Enterprise system. When a job is scheduled and it is to be sent to a user's Inbox, the Job Server uses the appropriate methods to direct a copy or shortcut to the appropriate destination.

E-MAIL AS A DESTINATION

Crystal Enterprise supports SMTP as its e-mail distribution protocol. Virtually all Internet mail servers support SMTP, so it's easy for an organization to integrate BusinessObjects Enterprise into its mail system, regardless of platform. By supporting standards such as SMTP, organizations are not restricted in the e-mail server types that can be used with BusinessObjects Enterprise.

25

FTP SERVER AS A DESTINATION

Organizations send objects directly to an FTP server location so that it's available for other users or applications. This is useful for getting information that can be used offline by customers, partners, or suppliers. A report can also be scheduled to update information at an FTP location on a regular basis to drive another application or business process. For example, a report could be designed to provide a product pricing list, including dynamic calculations of discounts that vary by customer, and then deliver it automatically to an FTP folder on a customer's Web server. Another example might be a scheduled Crystal Report output to an XML document sent via FTP to an external server for a business partner's application to pick up.

UNMANAGED DISK AS A DESTINATION

The unmanaged disk distribution service is used in the same fashion as the FTP server except that this service distributes the scheduled report to a disk location that is available on an organization's internal network. Building on the preceding example, an organization could have BusinessObjects Enterprise distribute a general pricing list to a location on disk and have this information populated on a purchase form or as a way of populating values into a Web service.

PRINTER AS A DESTINATION

Distributing reports to a printer available on the network is as simple as deciding which printer is to be used when the report is processed. Printing reports often is necessary when the information on the report needs to be shared with people who don't have access to a computer during analysis of that information. Situations such as team or board meetings often require that each member have a printed copy of the information to be covered.

INTERACTING WITH EXTERNAL SYSTEMS

Sometimes, it's necessary for a job to be intercepted before being run. Typically, organizations choose to do this so that information from an external entitlement database can be queried, and they can determine what data the user is allowed to view and modify the filter to reflect their restrictions. Prior to the introduction of Business Views, this primary technique for handling this requirement was achieved using a component called a *processing extension*. The processing extension is loaded by the Report Job Server during a schedule or by the Page Server or Report Application Server if being viewed. This extension allows for row-level security. Row-level security makes it possible for organizations to have content, such as a Crystal Report, shared by many users but the actual data that they see is targeted to them. It's also important to note that defining row-level security does not affect the content template but rather filters the view that the user sees based on the data that user has the right to see. There is no need to go into Crystal Reports and modify the report to affect which pages a user can see.

NOTE

> With the inclusion of Business Views in Crystal Enterprise 10, it became possible to directly include external entitlement databases into Business Views and easily provide both column- and row-level security through that mechanism. This has become the preferred method for achieving row and column level security.

Processing extensions are just that, an extension of BusinessObjects Enterprise. Some examples of processing extensions are available for BusinessObjects Enterprise with the product.

PROGRAM JOB SERVER

Much in the same way that the Report Job Server processes Crystal Reports, the Program Job Server processes programs. These programs consist of three types:

- Executable
- Java
- Script

These objects are published to the BusinessObjects Enterprise Framework, scheduled to be run by the Program Job Server, and executed. The goals of the programs differ as organizations can write programs according to their needs. Although processing a report results in a report instance, processing a program results in only a record that the program was run. The results of the program will depend on the program itself. Some programs might do maintenance on the BusinessObjects Enterprise system and some programs might have functions totally unrelated to BusinessObjects Enterprise—a powerful new capability to integrate BusinessObjects Enterprise functionality into an organization's workflow.

DESTINATION JOB SERVER

The Destination Job Server introduced with the XI version of BusinessObjects Enterprise is a slightly different type of Job Server. In contrast to the Report Job Server that can both process and send an object, the Destination Job Server does not process or execute the object. Instead, the Destination Job Server uses objects already in the system, such as a report instance, and delivers that object to a destination. The default, enabled destination on a Destination Job Server is BusinessObjects Enterprise Inbox. Additional destinations such as SMTP, FTP, or file can also be enabled.

LIST OF VALUES JOB SERVER

Also new with BusinessObjects Enterprise XI is the List of Values Job Server that handles the processing of lists which are exposed as parameter pick-lists. The List of Values Job Server is very similar in nature to the Report Job Server, but the purpose of the service is distinctly used for generating and displaying Lists of Values.

25

WEB INTELLIGENCE JOB SERVER

The Web Intelligence Job Server also introduced with the XI release is much like the Destination Job Server in that it does not execute requests itself. Instead, the Web Intelligence Job Server receives the scheduled request from the CMS and then passes the request to the Web Intelligence Report Server, which runs the report.

PAGE SERVER

The Page Server is responsible for delivering three key functions to the framework. The primary function is to generate pages for viewing reports. This capability is relevant for performance and the scalability of viewing reports because it only ever sends a single page of a report to the viewers. It does this by using a function known as Page on Demand. Other functions performed by the Page Server are refreshing a report's data using a feature known as on-demand viewing as well as the capability to export a report to another format for end-user download.

PAGE ON DEMAND

The Page on Demand function of the Page Server receives a request to view a certain page of a report and then generates just enough information to have the report viewers display that page. As described previously, it's much more efficient in a multi-user or low bandwidth environment to have pages of a report rather than the entire report sent to the viewer. This feature not only ensures a positive user experience by getting them the view of the report they're after quickly, it also is important to administrators.

Page on Demand minimizes demand on network bandwidth. Each page of the report generated by the Page Server is approximately 2KB in size. A report is usually much larger than this, especially if it's many thousands of pages containing thousands, if not millions, of rows of data. It should now be apparent why Page on Demand is a useful feature. This service goes one step further by ensuring a positive user experience through a technology known as *report streaming*.

Report streaming builds on Page on Demand by determining which objects in the page might take longer to calculate than others and then delivering them to the viewer slightly behind objects that can be generated quickly. For example, the report might contain summaries or charts that require additional calculations to be performed before rendering for the end user who is viewing the report. Report streaming will ensure that the rest of the information, such as the details making up the chart or summaries, is sent to the user right away. The remaining portions of a report are sent as soon as they are calculated on the server. Report streaming is similar to the placeholder technologies that browsers use when loading images.

ON-DEMAND VIEWING

The Page Server allows a user to refresh the view of the report dynamically instead of scheduling the report. To take advantage of this service, users first must be granted the proper access level for the object that needs to be updated.

If a user has this access level, he has the capability to force the report to connect to the database upon his request. When the user refreshes the report, he will be prompted to enter any relevant information the report requires, such as database connection information or parameter values. Before enabling on-demand viewing for all users, the use of the system and size of reports must be taken into consideration. If many users are querying the database at the same time, are they asking for similar information? If so, the report could be run once and then shared among many users. What amount of data is expected to be returned or how long is the report expected to run? Often, a report might be too complex to enable all users in an organization to run it themselves. Based on the amount of time spent in the database, on the network, and in the report engine, a report can take several seconds, or even minutes, to complete. If this situation occurs, it makes sense to schedule any complex reports that spend a lot of time processing and allow that report to be shared among the users.

Exporting to Other Formats

The Page Server makes it possible for users to request to have the report presented to them in a format other than Crystal Reports. These formats are Crystal Reports, Microsoft Word, Microsoft Excel with formatting, Microsoft Excel data only, Adobe Acrobat, Rich Text Format, Editable Rich Text, text, or Comma Separated Value (CSV) format. The user can request these formats typically by selecting the Export button in the report viewers.

Row-Level Security

In the same manner as the Job Server, the Page Server is able to restrict information presented to users based on a row restriction set by a processing extension. The main difference here is the Page Server is providing this capability at view time rather than at schedule time. Each method has its benefits. If a report has a row restriction applied to it during scheduling, the amount of data being returned to the report is filtered during the query. This means that the report instance only contains data that is relevant to the user who scheduled it. Another method is to apply the row restriction at view time.

If restrictions are applied at view time, the report instance contains the data necessary for the report, regardless of who is viewing it. When a user requests the report, the Page Server communicates with the processing extension to determine the row restriction to be applied for the user viewing the report. The data is then dynamically filtered so that the user is seeing only the data that he is able to see.

Cache Server

The Cache Server is an integral component to the overall scalability of BusinessObjects Enterprise. It establishes a cache of report pages generated by the Page Server, which are called *encapsulated page format* (EPF) files, and promotes the sharing of this information. This is an important facet of the BusinessObjects Enterprise Framework because, instead of having the report page regenerated for each user who requests it, the Cache Server determines whether the page can be shared among users. If it can, it will return the cached page. The Cache Server receives these requests from the report viewer and when the request is received, it checks to see whether the page requested is available in cache. If it is, the page is

25

returned to the report viewer to complete the request. If it is not, the request is sent to the Page Server to have it generated.

In the case that the Report Application Server serves the view request, caching occurs inside the Report Application Server itself, and the Cache Server does not interact with it. The Report Application Server would service view requests requiring interaction; for instance, when using the Interactive Viewer, the Report Application Service renders reports, as it has the additional capabilities that the Interactive Viewer requires.

CACHE MANAGEMENT

The Cache Server is responsible for maintaining a cache of report pages generated by the Page Server on disk. When a request for a page is received, the Cache Server checks to see whether the page is available in its cache and whether it can be shared. If it is a sharable page, the server returns the page to the user. If the page cannot be shared, the request is sent to the Page Server to generate a new page.

CONSTRAINTS

Sometimes, pages are not sharable. The Cache Server determines that a report page is not sharable if it meets one of these conditions:

- **Row-level security is being enforced**—If row-level security is being used, the page of information is valid only for the user who requested it; therefore, the Cache Server is unable to pass this page onto another user.

- **The query within the report has changed**—The query for the report can change if a user chooses to view a report and change the filter already previously defined or change a parameter value. When this occurs, the cached page is invalidated and must be regenerated.

EVENT SERVER

The Event Server provides a way for BusinessObjects Enterprise to monitor and use events that are occurring outside of its environment. It enables an organization to trigger the running of BusinessObjects Enterprise scheduled jobs dependent on external events.

The Event Server monitors the operating system for the existence or modification of a file. Using a file to trigger an event is a useful way of determining when an event is triggered because the generation of a file is a simple thing to achieve. For example, an organization might perform a nightly data warehouse update, and have the same program that does the database load create a file after finishing the load. Upon file creation or update, the event server then reports to the CMS that the required trigger is present, allowing the scheduled job to be processed.

FILE REPOSITORY SERVERS

The File Repository Server provides the BusinessObjects Enterprise Framework with two core services. The first is the capability to provide a centralized content storage facility, and the second is the capability to abstract the location of these objects from other services within the framework.

CENTRALIZED STORAGE OF CONTENT

BusinessObjects Enterprise provides two File Repository Servers (FRS). An input FRS is used to store any content that has been published to BusinessObjects Enterprise by the Publishing Wizard or from the content creation tools. When content is published to BusinessObjects Enterprise, the object is copied from the client to a location in the FRS. This location is set by the installation of BusinessObjects Enterprise but can be controlled by the administrator through modification of the FRS root directory. The objects are placed into unique folders on the server and are given unique names to ensure that there will not be any conflicts with other objects.

An output FRS is used to store the content generated by a scheduled job. The output server operates in the same manner as the input server by generating a unique name and location for each object.

ABSTRACTION OF CONTENT LOCATION

Now that the content is centrally stored and managed, the FRS abstracts the actual location of the objects from the other framework services. By using Uniform Resource Identifiers, or URIs, the framework sees a virtual "location" for the content. This makes it easy for services to request an object from the FRS without the need to ensure that it has access to the actual physical disk location. From a deployment and administration perspective, the job is much easier if objects are referred by URI. There is no need for complex network configurations, such as setting each service to run as a user account so they can access network shares.

However, this means that the system administrator must ensure that the account privileges of the FRS daemon or service include access to the disk location(s). This concept, of appropriate privileges for services, echoes throughout the entire system. The various services or daemons all interact with the operating system in different ways, and each requires the appropriate rights to function.

REPORT APPLICATION SERVER

The Report Application Server is a powerful add-on server to the BusinessObjects Enterprise Framework. It enables organizations to take their Web reporting a step or two further than the simple viewing of report content over the Web. The Report Application Server provides three new components for the framework: an alternative processing component for the report, a full object model for creating and modifying a Crystal Report, and a dedicated server for handling the creation and modification requests.

Although BusinessObjects Enterprise includes the Report Application Server, appropriate licensing must be purchased to use the report modification and creation capabilities within the BusinessObjects Enterprise Framework. This license can be purchased in addition to BusinessObjects Enterprise licenses, or as part of a BusinessObjects Enterprise Premium bundle.

CRYSTAL REPORT MODIFICATION AND CREATION CONCEPTS

One of the main benefits of adding the Report Application Server to the BusinessObjects Enterprise Framework is that organizations can quickly and easily add Crystal Report creation and modification capabilities to their Web applications. The Report Application Server makes it possible to connect to a server-side data source, query for information, and then display that information, all within a zero-client Web viewer. By using any of the built-in clients that are delivered with the Report Application Server or using the object model to create a custom user interface, it's possible to provide ad hoc Crystal Report creation and modification to the system end users—and essentially provide self-service reporting.

WEB REPORT DESIGN

The Report Application Server can take the data returned as part of the previously mentioned ad hoc report query issued by an application user and allow her to begin to format the report. The user is able to modify the query in many ways to format it into a quality report. Many people, after seeing these capabilities within a Web browser, remark that the experience is similar to a Web-based version of Crystal Reports. The Report Application server enables the making of database connections, selecting and joining tables, choosing fields, grouping and summing, creating formulas and charts, and formatting fields and sections.

INTERACTIVE REPORT VIEWING

In addition to the capabilities of the BusinessObjects Enterprise report viewer connected to the Page Server, a benefit of connecting to the Report Application Server from a report viewer is that it provides an object model that enables the report to be manipulated on the server. You can modify the viewer to provide a flexible viewing experience.

The viewer supports an event model that provides you with the information selected by the user in the viewer. This makes it easy for organizations using the Report Application Server to make closed loop systems.

This means that when the event model is used, a report can become much more interactive and drive more business value. For example, a retail organization uses BusinessObjects Enterprise to present its product catalog to its users. The reports are very useful and allow users to browse the catalog or drill in for more details on items. If the user wants to order something, he needs to navigate to another form to enter his order and he has to keep looking back to the catalog report to remember the part number he wants to order.

Using the event model of the Report Application Server this organization can, without changing its catalog report, enable the user to click on the item he wants right within the view of the catalog. This event captures the data that the user clicked on and enables the Web developer to populate the order screen with this information with no user interaction. If the report also displayed inventory counts, the report could be updated as soon as the user finished his transaction.

RICH OBJECT MODEL

The Report Application Server provides a powerful object model (covered in detail in Chapters 33, "Customizing the Crystal Reports Viewers," and 34, "Crystal Report Modification and Creation APIs") that allows an organization to control any aspect of how a user performs an ad hoc query or formats it. In typical ad hoc tools the users are given the same tool and the organization deploying the tool has no say in how the user is able to perform her tasks.

> **TIP**
>
> The Report Application Server provides a significant level of report modification and interactive report viewing. However, using a combination of Report Application Server features and Web Intelligence functionality should be considered in order to provide the suitable end result.

25

THE DATA TIER

Every organization has data in a wide variety of sources: databases, applications, XML files, Excel spreadsheets, EJBs, and so on. BusinessObjects Enterprise provides unparalleled access to data in a wide variety of formats. Although data access was covered in Chapter 1, "Creating and Designing Basic Reports," several architectural concepts around this topic merit our attention. First, BusinessObjects Enterprise XI includes Business Views, which provide a level of abstraction above data sources, greatly simplifying report writing and data security. Second, you will explore some of the most common sources of data.

BUSINESS VIEWS

Rather than connect directly to data sources, an organization can use Business Views to simplify data access. Using the Business Views (BV) Semantic layer speeds report development because the report developer bypasses several typical steps of report development: connecting to the data source, choosing tables, joining tables, and adding calculations. Instead, by choosing the BV, the report developer sees a complete set of fields logically organized around business problems and areas.

During development of a BV, a database administrator or subject matter expert with database skills chose the appropriate data sources and tables or other constructs, joined them together, selected the necessary fields, created any formulas or functions, and applied security at row and column levels against BusinessObjects Enterprise User groups.

Architecturally, this can be seen as a separate layer between the processing services in the server tier and the data sources. BVs are not required to access data because direct connections to data sources remain. BVs are covered in greater detail in Chapter 18.

UNIVERSES—SEMANTIC LAYER

Another alternative to mapping complex data sources, is the use of Universes as a Semantic layer providing similar efficiencies to Business Views. A comprehensive coverage of Universes is out of scope in this book, however it is recognized that Universes are a powerful device for managing complex data models.

DATA SOURCE TYPES

Although available data sources were discussed in Chapter 1, a brief summary helps to understand some key architectural concepts when connecting to different types of data sources. The following few sections cover some of the most popular data sources in the enterprise computing environment.

DATABASE SYSTEMS

Databases are the prototypical data source. There are several ways that the Server tier connects to databases. An ODBC connection uses an ODBC driver to communicate with the Database Management system (RDBMS), which returns the relevant data. Every machine hosting report processing services from the BusinessObjects Enterprise Framework, namely Page Servers, Report Job Servers, and Report Application Servers, must have the requisite ODBC Data Source Names (DSN) configured. ODBC connections require special support on Unix-based machines, often in the form of an ODBC driver that must be purchased in addition to the operating system.

Using a direct connection to a database most often requires a database client application installed on any machines. Most RDBMSs that support native connections ship with their respective database client applications, which then must be installed on machines hosting BusinessObjects Enterprise report processing services.

APPLICATION DATA SOURCES

BusinessObjects Enterprise offers a variety of Solution Kits that include application-specific integrations to provide data access to those applications. For instance, the SAP Solution Kit facilitates access to SAP's R/3 and Business Warehouse.

These Solution Kits represent a high level of integration, usually providing single-sign on so end users can use their application credentials to log on to BusinessObjects Enterprise. They are also notable in that data access does not proceed directly from the BusinessObjects Enterprise processing services or daemons to the application databases, but rather connects to the applications themselves, which subsequently manage queries and security and often data transformation to simplify data access. So application data sources present an additional level of abstraction from the underlying data source. These are covered in detail in Chapter 15, "Advanced Data Sources for Crystal Reports."

PROGRAMMATIC DATA SOURCES

A data source might not be accessible in the correct format, or might require some transformative or conditional logic. In these cases a software developer can write a program using the appropriate logic, and then expose the resulting data to BusinessObjects Enterprise. BusinessObjects Enterprise supports connectivity to these programmatic, or `Active`, data sources. Typical programs would expose a JavaBean, ADO (COM), or ADO.NET data provider, which would be consumed by BusinessObjects Enterprise.

→ For more information on this, **see** "Understanding the Additional Crystal Reports Data Sources," **p. 338**.

THE BUSINESSOBJECTS ENTERPRISE ARCHITECTURE IN ACTION

This section takes a look at how all the BusinessObjects Enterprise services come together and which of the services are used when a user requests objects. Each scenario is based on the following situation: Over a corporate intranet site, a user is browsing a Web page that connects him to a BusinessObjects Enterprise system. The user has provided proper login credentials and is logged into BusinessObjects Enterprise. He has been presented with a list of report objects that he has rights to access.

For this scenario to occur, a browser has connected to a Web Server with a request for BusinessObjects Enterprise. The request, assuming it does not require WCA processing, is passed from the Application server to BusinessObjects Enterprise Framework via the BOE SDK. For example, if the page is written in JSP, the Java application server passes a request to the BusinessObjects Enterprise Framework via the BOE SDK classes loaded on that application server. The continued interaction between the user and BusinessObjects Enterprise Framework occurs through the facility of the BOE SDK on the application server.

If you are using the CSP pages provided in a COM environment, the request is passed to the WCA for processing. The .csp is processed and in this scenario, the page asks the user for logon credentials and is returned to the user to complete. The credentials are submitted and passed to the WCA. The WCA now takes this information and relays it to the CMS via the BOE SDK. After the user is logged on to BusinessObjects Enterprise, the CMS is queried to present a list of folders and reports to the user. (The query is generated within the CSP page as well.) This scenario diagram can be seen in Figure 25.4.

If you are connecting to the BusinessObjects Enterprise via the Web Component Adapter or directly through the SDK, the general process flow remains the same. For simplicity, the following examples will use the .Net and Java environments without pointing out when the Web Component Adapter is invoked.

25

Figure 25.4
The login process for a user validated by BusinessObjects Enterprise.

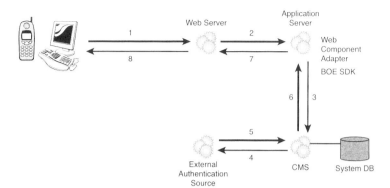

> The numbered flow in Figures 25.4, 25.5, 25.6, and 25.7 represents the flow of information and requests to get a report processed and delivered to the end user. Dashed lines in the figures represent optional steps.

REQUESTING A CRYSTAL REPORT

The user in the preceding scenario has two methods of viewing a report.

The first method is to view an instance of a previously scheduled job. If an instance is chosen, the report contains cached data from when the job was run. When the request to view the report is received, the Cache Server is interrogated to see if the first page of this report is available in cache. If the first page is available, the Cache Server returns the page to the Application Server so it can be delivered to the report viewer. The report viewer then displays the report for the user. If the page is not in the cache, the request is forwarded onto the Page Server to generate the page.

As Figure 25.5 shows, when the Page Server receives the request, it loads the report from the output File Repository Server. After the Page Server loads the report, it generates the page that has been requested and then passes it back to the Cache Server. The Cache Server sends the page onto the Application Server to be given to the report viewer.

Figure 25.5
The report-loading process in BusinessObjects Enterprise.

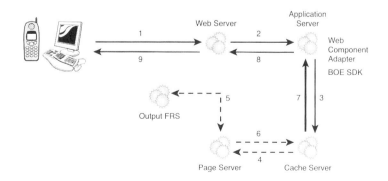

The second method for viewing a report is to view the report itself, which is also known as on-demand viewing. If a user selects the report itself, she must first have the "view on demand" access level. When the report is requested it goes through the same process as shown in Figure 25.5; however, because the report does not have any cached data within the report like the instance has, the Cache Server passes the request directly onto the Page Server.

Figure 25.6 shows the extra steps required for on-demand viewing. The Page Server queries the input FRS for the report and loads it. After the report loads, the user will be asked to enter the database logon information and any parameters for the report to run. The Page Server then passes this information to the Crystal Reports engine through the report plug-in. The Crystal Reports engine connects to the database and queries for the necessary data. After the data has been returned to the report engine, the report is recalculated and page information is determined. The Page Server now generates the first page of this report and sends it to the Cache Server, which in turn passes it to the Application Server and then to the report viewers.

Figure 25.6
The report loading process for on-demand viewing.

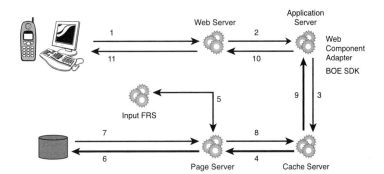

In both scenarios of viewing a Crystal Report, if a processing extension is being used with this report, the cache is then not sharable. The Cache Server will pass the request directly to the Page Server. The Page Server will load the report from the FRS. During the time that the report is being loaded, the processing extension is engaged to determine the proper row-level restrictions that need to be applied to the cached data within the report. The cached data is then filtered and the page is generated with information that is viewable by that user only.

SCHEDULING A CRYSTAL REPORT

When a report is scheduled, BusinessObjects Enterprise requires the appropriate informa-tion so that the scheduling service knows what tasks are to be performed. Figure 25.7 depicts a typical scenario where an end user schedules a report with the appropriate criteria set. This information is passed to the Application Server, which in turn forwards the infor-mation to be stored in the CMS. The schedule is set to run at a particular point in the future. When the schedule time occurs, the CMS loads the information from the repository and submits the request to a Job Server. The Job Server asks the input FRS for the report and then loads it into the report Job Server plug-in.

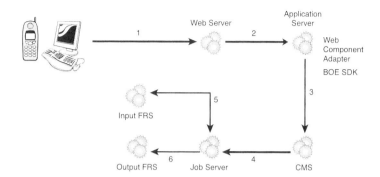

Figure 25.7
The process for scheduling reports.

With the report loaded, the Job Server applies any of the parameters set when the user scheduled the report earlier. These parameters might be filters that affect the overall data query. If a processing extension is in use, the report would be further manipulated. After the processing extension is finished with the report, the Job Server connects to the database and completes the processing of the report.

When the job has completed, the Job Server checks two remaining pieces of information the user would have set when scheduling the report; the format in which the report is to be delivered and where it will be delivered. At this stage, the Job Server would output the report into a supported BusinessObjects Enterprise format, including Crystal Reports, Microsoft Word, Excel, Adobe Acrobat, Rich Text Format, Editable Rich Text format, or text.

Next, the Job Server needs to distribute the report to the desired location. As previously mentioned, these locations can be a location on disk, an FTP server, or an e-mail address, or remain in the managed BusinessObjects Enterprise environment by distributing it to the output FRS as a general report instance object or inbox instance object. Regardless of where the user decides to distribute the object, a copy is always stored in the output File Repository Server so that it can be further shared between users.

REQUESTING A OLAP INTELLIGENCE REPORT

If an organization is using OLAP Intelligence, it's important to note that report viewing is handled differently from a Crystal Report. Requesting an OLAP Intelligence report starts by the user clicking on a link to the report in a Web browser.

The request is delivered to the Application Server, and it asks the CMS for the object that was asked for. The object is returned to the Application Server and then is loaded by the OLAP Intelligence engine. The reports created in OLAP Intelligence are dynamic queries to a multidimensional cube of data—the OLAP Intelligence engine must connect to the cube referenced in the report.

After a connection to the cube is made, data is retrieved and populated into the .car file, which is an XML document. This XML document is transformed through a style sheet into DHTML and delivered as the first view of the report. This information is sent from the Application Server to the Web browser along with the OLAP Intelligence DHTML viewer. The viewer makes additional requests for data from the cube via the Application Server as it is needed to populate the view of the report.

Taking Advantage of the BusinessObjects Enterprise Distributed Architecture

This section of the chapter discusses how the BusinessObjects Enterprise Framework and all the services that it provides are most effectively deployed. As mentioned earlier, BusinessObjects Enterprise is designed as an n-tier distributed system for information delivery. This distributed nature gives an organization a great deal of flexibility in how it might want to deploy BusinessObjects Enterprise in its environments. How BusinessObjects Enterprise is deployed will depend on the way in which the system is expected to be used, how many users are expected to be active in the system at any given time, and how many objects are expected to be processed at any given time.

Scaling Up

The term *scaling up* implies that a software product is able to take full advantage of the physical hardware resources it has access to and ultimately increase its performance as the hardware increases. BusinessObjects Enterprise was designed from its inception to effectively scale up.

All the BusinessObjects Enterprise servers are multithreaded components that are able to scale to take advantage of available physical hardware resources. They have been designed to operate on multiprocessor machines efficiently.

When a system is under high load, even being multithreaded isn't enough. If the load on the servers is high enough, I/O might start to become the limiting factor. BusinessObjects Enterprise deals with this by allowing an organization to configure multiple instances of a server on the same physical piece of hardware. This makes it possible for additional servers to share in the load and remove any I/O bottlenecks. A benefit in doing this is that automatic load balancing kicks in, making the system that much more efficient.

Scaling Out

Building on the scalability in BusinessObjects Enterprise for scaling up, the capability to distribute report processing loads to multiple physical machines is also available. This is beneficial in many ways.

As an example, an organization can scale its systems to very large levels by adding physical servers to the environment when needed. If an organization chooses to license BusinessObjects Enterprise using named or concurrent access licenses, additional hardware resources can be added to the environment as needed without purchasing additional BusinessObjects Enterprise user licenses. If processor licenses are initially purchased, new processor licenses must be purchased when the additional hardware is added. This is why it's important to understand the expected usage of the system as well as project the future growth of the system so that the appropriate license model is chosen.

The second benefit is the capability to assign tasks to certain computers. For example, the Job Server, Page Server, and File Repository Server could be grouped together on the same physical computer. The Page Server and Job Server both connect to databases and both communicate with the File Repository Server. Locating them on the same computer makes sense in many situations.

The next benefit of scaling out with BusinessObjects Enterprise is fault tolerance. BusinessObjects Enterprise provides the capability not only to have multiple instances of the same service running on the same computer, but also allows for those servers to be spread across multiple machines. BusinessObjects Enterprise has automatic fail-over support in each of its servers to complement the automatic load-balancing capabilities. This means that if a server goes offline for any reason, other servers registered to the BusinessObjects Enterprise Framework will automatically pick up the workload without user interruption.

SCALING ACROSS PLATFORM BOUNDARIES

Some deployments of BusinessObjects Enterprise might require a distributed system on different operating systems. BusinessObjects Enterprise makes it possible for an organization to deploy BusinessObjects Enterprise across any of its supported operating system platforms. This provides a way for organizations to decide what deployment scenario best fits their needs, given the hardware available to them. A key benefit to being able to do this is that organizations might want to seamlessly mix functionality available from different operating systems. For example, an organization might require that reports process on Unix but still want the users authenticated using Windows NT accounts.

There might be situations in which it's necessary to have certain servers running on one operating system and the rest of the system running on another. For example, an organization might have the majority of BusinessObjects Enterprise operating on Unix, but want to seamlessly integrate the SQL Server Analysis cubes being used in the OLAP Intelligence reports created by the finance department. These reports can easily be added to the BusinessObjects Enterprise system running on Unix, as long as a WCS is running on Windows so that the OLAP Intelligence reports have access to SQL Server Analysis Services.

Although a mixed-platform deployment can solve problems, do not put clustered CMSs on different platforms. Because they both work together connected to a single database, and because drivers on platforms differ, database corruption can occur on some platform combinations.

EXTENDING BUSINESSOBJECTS ENTERPRISE

An important aspect of information delivery is how the information is presented to the user community. BusinessObjects Enterprise enables organizations to easily customize how information is presented to end users by providing a rich object model for Web application developers to tightly integrate BusinessObjects Enterprise into their Web applications. Developers can present content to end users, as well as provide Web-based administration applications to their organization, using the BusinessObjects Enterprise SDK. The upcoming sections detail the flexibility of the entire Business Objects suite of products and how they can be easily integrated into any environment.

25

CHAPTER 26

PLANNING CONSIDERATIONS WHEN DEPLOYING BUSINESSOBJECTS ENTERPRISE

In this chapter

ENSURING A SUCCESSFUL BUSINESSOBJECTS ENTERPRISE IMPLEMENTATION

The time spent planning a deployment of BusinessObjects Enterprise directly relates to the success of that deployment. In other words, failing to plan is planning to fail. This year in North America, 77% of IT software deployment projects will fail due in part to inaccurate requirement gathering, inexperienced project team members, and insufficient executive interest and sponsorship.

All too often, the average scenario when deploying BusinessObjects Enterprise consists of placing the BusinessObjects Enterprise installation CD into the CD drive, double-clicking setup.exe, crossing fingers, and hoping for the best. Whether the person in charge of deploying BusinessObjects Enterprise is an experienced system administrator or a novice at deploying applications to a small or large group of users, certain steps can be taken to increase the deployment success and adoption of BusinessObjects Enterprise.

With its flexible system architecture and SDK, BusinessObjects Enterprise provides organizations with the capability to build uniquely customized information delivery environments scaling from a single-user or workgroup to enterprisewide deployments with tens of thousands of users. Because of this broad scope of functionality, project teams will find themselves planning to deploy an enterprise reporting environment as well as providing application development support to customize the user interface. This is, of course, assuming an organization chooses not to use one of the out-of-the-box BusinessObjects Enterprise end-user interfaces.

The first part of this chapter defines a project management *planning* approach that will enable a BusinessObjects Enterprise system administrator or deployment manager to form a framework around which a BusinessObjects Enterprise deployment project can be successfully built and delivered, thus increasing the rate of success.

The second portion of the chapter focuses on the specific topics related to actually *deploying* BusinessObjects Enterprise, from organizational reporting requirements to server sizing and architecture.

APPROACHING THE PROJECT

Many organizations have standard application development practices and methodologies that are followed with every project that involves system deployment efforts and some level of programmatic customization. These methodologies can trace their ancestry to a simplistic methodology that was used with the invention of the wheel.

The "invention of the wheel" approach goes something like this: Ug is bored of carrying his mammoth tusks on his back all day (business pain); he needs something that will help reduce his effort and allow him to carry more, increasing his efficiency and keeping his boss happy (requirements). After he finds and refines the solution (development) and tests it (pilot), Ug can show his colleagues and find out what they think (user acceptance testing). After this is completed, he can manufacture it and allow his colleagues to carry their tusks more efficiently (deployment). After his colleagues have their tusk carriers, Ug will monitor what they think of it and make changes where necessary (support and maintenance). Needless to say, Ug used this process to develop a cart with wheels, and the rest is history.

Things have changed somewhat since then, but the concept remains the same. This process can help any person responsible for a BusinessObjects Enterprise software project, or any project for that matter:

- Identify business pain
- Establish project requirements
- Develop the application
- Complete user acceptance testing
- Deploy the technology
- Support and maintain the application

IDENTIFYING BUSINESS PAIN

Necessity is the mother of invention. Most organizations implement new policies, systems, processes, and applications for good reasons: to improve efficiency; save money, time, and effort; and to improve work environments, for example.

Companies have their own processes for discovering business pain. Regardless of how it's discovered, business pain drives the success of the project. In the case of enterprise reporting, existing user interface and application restrictions or data source connectivity requirements and limitations help define the business pain. BusinessObjects Enterprise can be customized to suit most Web delivery GUI requirements and connect to virtually any data source—hence, the reason BusinessObjects Enterprise and its associated report design tools (Crystal Reports) are looked to when solving these types of problems.

Business pains should be documented, concrete, specific, describe the business issue rather than any technical analysis, and taken directly from as many key stakeholders as possible. That way any project success can be evaluated against the initial pain. Key stakeholders feel themselves more involved in the project and therefore more interested in its success when they are directly interviewed regarding their needs. Business Intelligence pains are particularly sensitive to end-user pains, as one of the key benefits of the system is increased decision-maker efficiency, which is very dependent on how end users perceive data.

The project administrator should be thorough in exploring the root of the business pain: business pains are typically confused with project requirements or generalized statements of need, leading to inappropriate solutions. For example, "We need a reporting solution" exemplifies a solution looking for a problem, rather than a business pain. A business pain might be: "It takes all 10 people in the finance group three hours each Monday to calculate and distribute the latest budget versus actuals variances." Note that the business pain naturally leads into a Return on Investment (ROI) analysis: a great foundation for any project.

26

ESTABLISHING PROJECT REQUIREMENTS

Without question, the number one reason for a software project's downfall is the failure to gather adequate requirements, and gather them correctly. Anyone undertaking a project to deploy BusinessObjects Enterprise must take the time to discover exactly what the tool is required to accomplish. This need is initially defined by the business problem. Remember, the business problem should be considered the starting point for a BusinessObjects Enterprise solution, allowing the enterprise reporting technology to be embraced and extended to an entire organization.

Don't get caught stating technical solutions as requirements rather than the true requirements. For example you might state a requirement that: "I want to produce .pdf files from a report." This is actually a solution statement! If you examine why you made this statement, you might see that you thought an Adobe Acrobat (.pdf) file would enable you to share information over the Web. In that case, your requirement should state: "End users can all see the information on Internet Explorer and Netscape browsers on the corporate network." The technical solution to this problem arrives in the next phase, and stating technical solutions instead of actual requirements is a typical and costly mistake.

With these points in mind, some of the key questions that need to be considered when defining the requirements for a deployment of BusinessObjects Enterprise involve four concepts: users, user interfaces, reports, and environments. The following lists show the important questions that should be considered:

Users

- How many users will you have?
- What are the skill sets of these users: business/end users; power users; administrators; developers?
- How many concurrent users will you have?
- Where will your users be located?
- How many users will be viewing reports only?
- How many users will design reports?
- How many users will modify/create reports online?
- How many users will schedule reports?
- Will customers be using this application?
- What are the training requirements for administrators? Report designers? Users?

User Interface

- What look and feel is required for the user interface?
- Is this look and feel supposed to inherit the company's intranet appearance and functionality?
- Will users need to input data or will data extraction and delivery be sufficient?

  These questions will help determine whether an out-of-the-box BusinessObjects Enterprise interface, such as InfoView, will meet end-user requirements, or if customization to InfoView will be necessary. Some organizations develop a completely custom front-end to BusinessObjects Enterprise based on end-user feedback to the previous questions. In the case of the latter scenario, some organizations integrate BusinessObjects Enterprise information delivery as a portion of a larger application, which can involve data entry as well.

- Do users need alert notification via e-mail? What merits e-mail attention?

  The alerting capabilities of BusinessObjects Enterprise call out values that merit special attention and can e-mail end users regarding that value.

- Do end users need to discuss reports or record reactions to reports?

Reports

- Are legacy reports in use? If so, in which application environments were they created?

  Identifying any requirements for support of legacy reports will help identify the extent of the BusinessObjects Enterprise solution. Use of the BusinessObjects Enterprise SDK might be required to link new reports to legacy reports.

- What type of database(s) will be used with reports in BusinessObjects Enterprise?
- What is the planned or preferred method of data connectivity, ODBC, OLE-DB, native, Business Views, or something else?
- Are any existing Crystal Reports connected to the target data sources?

  It's also important to consider the data source connectivity methods provided with BusinessObjects Enterprise. They might or might not match up with organizational requirements. Native drivers provide for many data sources, but some data sources can be connected to only through ODBC.

- Is a DBA available that is familiar with the required data sources?
- Do any reports cross data sources? Are complex row- or column-level security filters required? Is the report developed on one database, and then run in production on another? Does the data source contain complexity that should be hidden from the end user or even report developer?

  All the questions in this bullet point indicate that Business Views should be developed to ease issues around accessing data.

- How many reports are required?
- Are enough human resources available with the skill set to develop all the initial reports required by end users?

When setting out to develop reports, consider whether sufficient human resources are available to develop the reports to meet end-user requirements. If not, a third-party consulting organization might be leveraged here to complete report design. One of the biggest challenges organizations have when deploying BusinessObjects Enterprise has nothing to do with BusinessObjects Enterprise itself. It's with the data source. Understanding the database schema and *where* the actual data is can be the most complex portion of the deployment. This area is one where a semantic layer, such as Business Views or Universes, can dramatically improve report writing efficiency because a skilled DBA works with the database, allowing less skilled resources to develop reports. This both lowers costs and speeds development.

- How frequently will reports be scheduled?

- How many total report instances will be maintained in the BusinessObjects Enterprise system?

- What is an acceptable length of time for reports to process, from initial user request to completion?

Also consider how many report objects BusinessObjects Enterprise will store and manage. A report object in BusinessObjects Enterprise doesn't hold any data. The report instances, reports that have been scheduled, actually contain the data. Chapter 27, "Administering and Configuring BusinessObjects Enterprise," discusses this in more detail. Consider that each report instance occupies space in the File Repository Server. If an organization has 1,000 unique reports and allows 25 scheduled historical instances to be held in BusinessObjects Enterprise for each report, that's 25,000 instances! If each instance held a large amount of data, the File Repository Server would clearly need an ample amount of disk space to manage those instances.

Determining the target length of time for a report to run might not necessarily be achievable, but should be established nonetheless. If a report is based off a database stored procedure that takes 12 hours to run in the database, it's unrealistic to blame BusinessObjects Enterprise for the report taking a long time when, in fact, BusinessObjects Enterprise has nothing to do with the long report runtime.

Bear in mind that ODBC and native drivers affect report runtime; sometimes ODBC is faster and vice versa.

Environment

- What are the current software and hardware configurations on client workstations?

Although BusinessObjects Enterprise delivers information through a Web browser, there are many mechanisms by which this can be accomplished. For example, choosing to deploy the ActiveX viewer with BusinessObjects Enterprise rather than the DHTML viewer can exclude Netscape viewers from using reports. Perhaps the client workstation is actually a mobile device or phone.

- Where will the database servers be physically located?

  The specialized roles of BusinessObjects Enterprise servers, such as the Page and Job Servers, can be maximized through effective placement of physical servers. The Page and Job Servers should be placed close to the actual database servers to which reports connect. *Close* is a subjective word, in that it implies a substantial amount of bandwidth and low latency available between the services and database if reports contain a large amount of data. This reduces the impact to an organization's WAN traffic by isolating communication between the database and report processing services.

- Will OLAP data sources be required?

- If so, which OLAP server types are required?

  OLAP servers imply that another type of report object, OLAP Intelligence reports, will be stored in BusinessObjects Enterprise. Although Crystal Reports connects to OLAP data sources, it does not provide the same robust interactivity in OLAP report and application creation as OLAP Intelligence. Using OLAP Intelligence reports with BusinessObjects Enterprise also implies that the Web Application Server hosting the WCA will require OLAP server connectivity because this is the hosting point for the OLAP Intelligence server-side services.

  If, for example, an organization were using Microsoft's OLAP server, SQL Server Analysis Services, to stage data in OLAP cubes, OLAP Intelligence would be required, and the Web Component Adapter service would require some level of network access to the SQL Server.

- What type of physical network is in place?

  Although most organizations use standard networking components and protocols, such as 10/100 Ethernet and TCP/IP, the speed of a physical network can affect where BusinessObjects Enterprise server components are placed on the geographic network topology.

- What is the projected growth of the BusinessObjects Enterprise system?

- What, if any, dedicated hardware resources are available for BusinessObjects Enterprise?

- Will additional hardware be required?

  Planning considerations must be made not only for an imminent BusinessObjects Enterprise deployment, but also for how the system might look one year from now. Most deployments of BusinessObjects Enterprise grow quickly because end users like to share the new source of information they have accessed.

- What are the security requirements for the reporting environment?

  Determining a strategy for security can be a daunting one because many options are associated with BusinessObjects Enterprise. BusinessObjects Enterprise provides a native security model where users, groups, and objects can be created and managed without the need for any third-party security components. BusinessObjects Enterprise also supports Windows NT or Active Directory security integration, as well as support for a host of major directory servers through LDAP. As a final option, an organization could use the BusinessObjects Enterprise SDK to link in or create a homegrown security model for BusinessObjects Enterprise.

26

BusinessObjects Enterprise also allows the creation of custom administration modules using the administrative portion of the SDK, which allows for certain users to be restricted to various portions of the product for system administration.

■ What BusinessObjects Enterprise licensing model is the best fit?

Several licensing models are available for BusinessObjects Enterprise, so understanding the current licensing program for BusinessObjects Enterprise can save your organization some money when it comes time to purchase.

■ On what operating system will BusinessObjects Enterprise be deployed (Windows, Solaris, or both)?

Although BusinessObjects Enterprise XI is available on the Windows, Solaris, Linux and HP platforms, some organizations will deploy a "mixed mode" environment, meaning some BusinessObjects Enterprise services or daemons will be installed on different platforms. The Unix versions have a few minor variations from the Windows version.

■ What bandwidth and latency exist between LAN/WAN sites that will participate in the BusinessObjects Enterprise deployment?

As mentioned earlier, different server components of BusinessObjects Enterprise benefit through close physical proximity to database servers. It's important to understand the various functions of the individual BusinessObjects Enterprise servers and what data traffic is passed between them. Chapter 25, "BusinessObjects Enterprise Architecture," covers this in some detail. Understanding this will help the BusinessObjects Enterprise system planner or administrator effectively place server components within a corporate LAN/WAN environment to maximize system performance.

■ Will a firewall be incorporated in the solution?

BusinessObjects Enterprise was designed with a "DMZ" or firewall deployment in mind. This means that BusinessObjects Enterprise can be effectively deployed in a multiple-firewall network environment with minimal impact to security because all information and reports delivered by BusinessObjects Enterprise can be DHTML.

■ Will users require dial-up to access the BusinessObjects Enterprise system?

This might seem like a trivial consideration because BusinessObjects Enterprise delivers reports that essentially amount to Web pages to an end user through a browser. If, for example, an organization chooses to deliver all reports from BusinessObjects Enterprise as .pdf files rather than Crystal Reports as Web pages through the DHTML viewer, a significant feature is sacrificed: page on demand. *Page on demand* means that only one page of a report is delivered to an end user at a time. If a report contains 3MB worth of data, the user won't notice this because the server opens the report and delivers the requested page of the report to the viewer. This provides a responsive environment for end users, even in a dial-up session at less than 56Kbps.

■ What is the current load and performance of existing Web servers that BusinessObjects Enterprise will use?

BusinessObjects Enterprise is not a Web server. It works with most major Web servers or application servers. Although BusinessObjects Enterprise doesn't place a significant load on a Web server, there is some load nonetheless, especially if an organization decides to install BusinessObjects Enterprise on the physical Web server itself. It's always preferable to have a dedicated server for BusinessObjects Enterprise and offload processing onto a dedicated set of servers for BusinessObjects Enterprise.

■ What is the current skill set of system or network administrators that might support BusinessObjects Enterprise?

BusinessObjects Enterprise is a complex enterprise reporting and information delivery product that involves many systems, from databases to operating systems and development platforms. Troubleshooting issues with BusinessObjects Enterprise might not have anything to do with BusinessObjects Enterprise at all. More often than not, issues with reports often lie with database access, operating system permissions, and the like. It's of paramount importance that system administrators understand the spectrum of these issues.

The previous list of questions is by no means complete. It is meant to be a solid foundation from which to formulate an implementation plan. Ideally, the temptation to install any software until after this stage is complete can be resisted.

Each answer should lead a BusinessObjects Enterprise deployment manager to create an action item for delivery before, during, and after the project. For example, the answer to the question "What is the projected growth of the BusinessObjects Enterprise system?" might be "Company A currently derives about $100M in annual revenue and has 200 employees. During the next two years we hope to double in size." This can lead to the deduction that, although current hardware availability will allow for an initial implementation of the project without further hardware and software purchase or budgeting, scalability planning should be performed or at least considered for future growth.

It might be useful to build these questions into a questionnaire format, breaking the organization down into management, users, and IT department members. Submitting a questionnaire or having interviews with the end-user community are exceptional ways to get buy-in from all project stakeholders.

DEVELOPING THE APPLICATION (CUSTOMIZING BUSINESSOBJECTS ENTERPRISE)

Although BusinessObjects Enterprise comes with several out-of-the-box client applications such as InfoView, this doesn't exclude the customization of one of those applications or development of a completely custom solution from the ground up. The good news is if an organization is deploying InfoView without any customizations, this section can be skipped entirely.

The development of a BusinessObjects Enterprise application can be very personal. Whatever the approach, it should follow these guidelines:

■ *Pick the proper project manager.* Someone must be in command. This is not necessarily going to be a promotion for someone into the lofty ranks of a management position; instead, the person in this role must have the authority, knowledge, and character to implement command and control. The size of the project determines how many members compose the team, but their actions should be managed and they must have someone to refer to for information and direction. If possible, the project manager should be able to focus on the application without having to double hat on other jobs.

- *Plan, plan, plan.* There are many project planning tools on the market. A company will probably have its own standard. Whether planning is done on a piece of paper, on a spreadsheet, or in an application, it is another cornerstone of a successful project. No plan survives the first shot of battle, so it is important to keep in mind that this is a work in progress. Without a plan, coordination is impossible, chaos prevails, and the project stands a good chance of going off track. A project plan should involve the following:
  - Tasks
  - Delivery timelines
  - Specification as to who is responsible for delivering those tasks
  - A definition of task weightings

- *Build the project team.* The project team's skill set must be put together very carefully. If internal team members cannot be found, outsourcing should be considered as a very cost-effective way to improve chances for success. In most cases, consultants with proven track records using the technologies surrounding BusinessObjects Enterprise increase the chance of the project's success.

- *Keep an eye on the prize.* Begin with the end in mind. After the project has started, the project manager and team members must be sure that they understand what the end goal is.

- *Control change.* Change is inevitable, and the longer a project goes on and the more complex it becomes, the more likely change will occur. Change is a good thing. Without change you would be back where Ug started his tusk movement improvement project. The important thing to remember is that change must be controlled. Team members need to be encouraged to share their ideas and think outside the box.

However, a process must be in place to manage this and be sure that any new changes are implemented with the support and knowledge of the project team, management, and end users. Another result of ignoring change management is the bane of any project, *scope creep*. Scope creep occurs when a project's deliverables, functionality, or look and feel extend past the project plan and definition. Scope creep can blow budgets away, extend project timelines dramatically, and can lead to bad morale on the project team.

One good example might be a specification to customize the look and feel of the DHTML viewer. A corporate logo is to be applied to the background of the viewer. After the addition of the logo, the end users ask whether each individual icon image in the viewer can be changed to match other images the company has, such as product images. Although this might seem trivial and seems to add little value to the overall solution, it could set the deployment timeline back at least half a day.

Table 26.1 is an example of a change control matrix.

TABLE 26.1   CHANGE CONTROL MATRIX

Change Number	Description	Requestor	Assigned to:	Completed on:	To Test (date)	Tested by:	Released to and Date:
1	Provide top 10 customers parameter	Dawn Gugoi	Paul Kooker	4/24/04	4/26/04	Tess Tor	5/5/04

■ *Control risk.* Risk mitigation is another cornerstone of success. The key to this mitigation is the ability to spot risk before it happens and plan ahead to be sure it does not happen. A useful way of doing this is to use the simple matrix shown in Table 26.2.

TABLE 26.2   RISK CONTROL MATRIX

Top Ten	Risk	Chances of It Happening (1–5)	Damage to Project If It Does Happen (1–5)	Risk Multiple	What to Do About it
1	Server hardware takes four weeks from order	4	5	20	Be sure server sizing is completed by week 2 and pass to procurement by week 3

■ *Get end user buy off ASAP.* User acceptance is the make-or-break point of a project. If users do not like what they are given to use on a daily basis, the project will not succeed. It will be relegated to the recycle bin very quickly. Involve users whenever possible from requirements gathering and development and training. Also give users the capability to provide feedback after the application is deployed.

■ *Set up environments.* Development of your application will be iterative and should go through a process to ensure that users get what they asked for. The standard formats for application development environments are

- **Sandbox (sometimes used)**—Initial proof of concept testing and development.
- **Development**—Phased development and testing. Strictly controlled, versioned environment.
- **Test**—Beta testing only. No development should occur here. Any faults and bugs should be referred back to the development team and tested again in development.
- **Production**—Application in everyday use.

■ *Documentation.* The application development process must be documented at all stages to ensure that if it needs improvement, if key project members leave, or if bugs need to be identified, people are not hunting around for the answers, wasting time unnecessarily. This documentation should be controlled by the project manager, and can also be used by training departments for the education of users and administrators.

26

COMPLETING USER ACCEPTANCE TESTING AND DEPLOYMENT

This phase should deliver the 99.9% finished application to a defined user base. End users should take the BusinessObjects Enterprise application front end and follow a testing script that is given to them at the beginning of the phase. Users then should document and return their findings to the project team, and any last-minute changes will be made to the code.

This process could go through as many iterations required for the users to finally put a check in the box that says, "We are satisfied." As mentioned previously, user acceptance ensures a successful project.

When the users are happy, the application can be deployed in a production environment.

MOVING TO THE SUPPORT AND MAINTENANCE PHASE

After the application enters production, users should know who to call for support. This can be achieved through access to defined members of the project team, an organization's internal support desk, or an outsourced tech support organization. The BusinessObjects Enterprise application manager should keep a log of issues, bugs, and any user feedback so that, where relevant, this information can be implemented in the current application and any future releases.

UNDERSTANDING ORGANIZATIONAL REPORTING REQUIREMENTS

Designing reports is one of the initial steps in designing a BusinessObjects Enterprise system, and easily is the most obvious consideration. An equally important consideration, and one that is most often left until much later in the implementation process, is how and when the reports will be run. Answering some of the questions asked earlier in the chapter will pay off when reports are actually published to BusinessObjects Enterprise. Additional related questions include the following:

- Will reports be run on-demand or scheduled?
- Will reports be batch scheduled by an administrator while end users can only view these scheduled instances?
- Will end users be allowed to freely schedule their own reports?
- Will developers or subject matter expert end users develop reports?
- Will report developers get access only to BusinessObjects Enterprise, which will broker access to the various databases via Business Views, or have direct access to databases?

Such questions are examples of key planning considerations that must be considered in conjunction with a report's design. Primarily, this needs to be analyzed from a business perspective. For example, perhaps end users need to run reports with impunity because the data is constantly changing and they always need an up-to-date view of the data. However, this perspective then must be tempered by a technological "sanity check" to determine whether such requirements are technologically feasible. For example, does it really make sense to run a

3,000-page report dynamically? Can parameters be added to the report so that less data is brought back to reduce the resultset of the database query?

The benefits of different reporting approaches will be explored through the next few sections of the chapter.

DEPLOYING BUSINESS VIEWS OR UNIVERSES

Although the use of Business Views or Universes might at first seem a technical decision which most affects development time, business requirements drive the utilization of Business Views or Universes more than any other requirement. First, you must understand end-user requirements with regard to how end users view data: If data is organized to the end user in one way, but captured in the database in another, Business Views or Universes bridge the gap and show end users data as they see it. For instance, you might want to see revenue per headcount, which requires the headcount value from an HR system and the revenue total from a finance application. A Business View or Universe can connect to both databases and present a unified logical view of revenue per headcount.

The two most significant impacts of business views, however, have everything to do with end users:

- Extending report authoring to a wider audience
- Using BusinessObjects Enterprise to broker database access

Through the development of browser-based report modification and creation capabilities, BusinessObjects Enterprise now offers end users greater possibilities in interacting with data. By encapsulating the database connection and query aspects of the reporting process, end users can now be shielded from the more technical aspects of report creation and instead focus on what to show and how to show it.

The development of Business Views and Universes allows organizations to extend this model to develop a more efficient business intelligence model. Most organizations use developers to build the vast majority of reports, referred to as the developer-centric model. End users can now develop more reports themselves instead of a developer-centric model of report development, usually resulting in trivial work for developers, long wait time for end users, poor communication of end-user requirements, and a high opportunity cost. In the end-user centric model, developers and DBAs handle database connectivity, database and table joins, filtering and security, parameterization, formulas, and the like. Report creators then start designing by placing fields on the report and formatting the data. This separation of tasks into distinct roles of DBA versus end user facilitates more efficient report creation and a lower total cost of ownership. It places those who know the business uses of the data closer to report creation, yet allows for tight organizational control over data sources.

Using BusinessObjects Enterprise to control access to data via Business Views or Universes tightens and secures access to databases, even for report creation, by asking users to connect to BusinessObjects Enterprise, which provides access to Business Views or Universes according to a particular user's permissions. Because Business Views or Universes can secure the row- and column-level access to data sources, very fine control over data access can be attained.

Although this model might not be practical for all organizations, it yields cost savings and speeds time-to-market when implemented. In addition, because total security can be attained while still allowing appropriate access to data, confidentiality requirements can be met across organizations.

USE CASES FOR SCHEDULED REPORTING

As alluded to previously, BusinessObjects Enterprise allows two modes of report execution: on-demand and scheduled. In the scheduled reporting case, a report template is scheduled to run either right now or at a future point in time or possibly on a recurring basis. When it is time for the report to run, the Crystal Report Job Server accesses the report template, the report is processed against the reporting database, and then the report is saved with data under a different file. This report with saved data is commonly referred to as a *report instance*. This instance is a snapshot of the data in a moment of time. End users can then view an instance to see the report's data from when it was run.

The advantages of scheduling reports and creating instances are numerous. The most important advantage of report instances is that when a user views an instance, the report loads almost instantaneously in the report viewer because the report does not need to execute the database query. In addition, because instances are a snapshot of data in time, you can leverage them as historical reports. For example, when reporting against a transactional information system, the database often contains volatile data. Consequently, running the report with the exact same parameters on different days might return different data because the database contains fewer records because of deletion and so on.

DETERMINING SCHEDULING PERMISSIONS AND REPORT RUNTIMES

If scheduled reports are the preferred method of reporting in BusinessObjects Enterprise, you must determine who will be allowed to schedule reports and when those reports can actually be scheduled. In a tightly controlled environment, a system administrator individually schedules reports either singly or on a recurring basis (for example, weekly, monthly). End users are not allowed to run reports; they can only view instances. Thus, by having a central scheduling authority, you can govern what and when database queries will be executed from your reporting application.

Additionally in this scenario, if scheduling is completed with regards to end-user viewing use, hardware use can be minimized. For example, if end users view reports only during the day, reports could be batch scheduled to run only at night or on the weekend. This means that report execution and report viewing are mutually exclusive, which they are. Report execution is processor-intensive and primarily the responsibility of the BusinessObjects Enterprise Job Server component. Report viewing can be processor-intensive and a major responsibility of the BusinessObjects Enterprise Page Server component.

In this scenario, common hardware can be shared between the Job and Page Servers because their functions will be used mutually exclusively. Otherwise, if report execution and report viewing occur at the same time, and the Job and Page Servers are on the same shared hardware, they might contend with one another for CPU or operating system resources. Because the Page Server plays a key part in report viewing, report viewing responsiveness might be negatively affected during this period.

Although administrator-controlled scheduling makes for a tightly regulated system, it can be constrained by its potential inflexibility. For example, if the report has parameters, these parameters must be determined by the administrator. Thus, report instances might contain too much data or too little data for end users. In addition, if the database is updated and a user wants to see the latest data, he will have to wait until the next scheduled runtime because he cannot run the report manually. As a result, timely access to data can be an issue.

If these issues of data scope and timeliness can be acceptable or managed, controlled scheduling is an excellent solution for organizations with tight server access or hardware restrictions. For example, some data warehouses are updated at fixed intervals (weekly, for example), so the administrator can schedule the reports to run after the update process is complete. Thus, in this case, if data scope is also not an issue, it doesn't make much sense to allow end users to run reports because the data is unchanged between database update periods.

> **NOTE**
>
> *Data scope* is the specific range or breadth of the data. For example, some reports are useful only if the user provides parameters. If you're checking frequent flyer points you're only interested in data related to you. Thus, a prescheduled report with all data for all customers in this case would not be relevant to you because you're only concerned with your personal data.

On the other end of the spectrum is the scenario where end users are allowed to schedule reports on their own, whenever they want. This allows for maximum flexibility for the end users because they can run reports at their leisure with the parameters they choose. However, if the parameters are unchecked, poor parameter selection (because of user inexperience) can cause rogue database queries that tie up the DBMS if they become unnecessarily large or complex. This can lead to the scheduling queue backing up as other jobs waiting to execute are idling for a free spot on the Job Servers. If the Job Servers are configured to run too many concurrent jobs, this can overrun the DBMS with too many simultaneous queries. Thus, the Job Servers should be scaled back so that the number of concurrent jobs allowed is small enough that DBMS access is appropriately managed. If the Page Server and Job Server are on the same shared hardware, the issue might arise where these processes contend for server resources (CPU time, memory, file system, network bandwidth, and so on).

ON-DEMAND REPORTING

The second mode with which reports can be executed is called *on-demand* reporting. When used correctly and in the right situation this can be a very powerful function in a BusinessObjects Enterprise deployment. To determine which situations should use on-demand reporting, apply the eight-second rule as a guideline: "Users have eight seconds worth of patience while waiting for a Web page to load." To use this measurement, run the report on a test system or in the Crystal Reports designer and determine how long the report takes to execute. If it takes fewer than eight seconds, that report may be a good candidate for on-demand reporting in BusinessObjects Enterprise.

Another consideration with on-demand reporting is whether the database driver and database client are *thread safe* (meaning that multiple threads can access the driver at the same time without unwanted interaction). If these components are not thread safe, database queries from the Page Servers will be serialized. Using the ODBC database drivers that ship with BusinessObjects Enterprise will ensure this concurrency because they are thread safe and thoroughly tested.

COMPARING SCHEDULED VERSUS ON-DEMAND REPORTING

Even if reports are ideal candidates for on-demand reporting, scheduling reports still might offer additional benefits. For example, scheduled reporting helps set the right expectations and context for a report. When end users schedule a report, even if it is scheduled to run right now, they will expect the report to take some time to process. Thus, they can better tolerate delays. Users who are utilizing on-demand reporting typically don't understand that doing so actually requires the database query to execute. They expect the report to come up in the viewer instantly and are less tolerant of delays and might become frustrated when the only feedback they get is the spinning Web browser logo.

DETERMINING DATA ACCESS CONTROL METHODS

If the BusinessObjects Enterprise reporting system is designed so that users can schedule reports or run reports on demand, you must decide how to control access to the database. That is, what database user account is used to access the reporting database? With some implementations, individual users are given distinct database accounts that they would provide before running the report. In other implementations, a generic data reader account is used as the default database login for all reports. Having individual users with separate database accounts allows for better auditing if auditing is done at the DBMS level. You can easily track who is running what type of queries against your database. However, this comes with some costs.

First, more database administration is required because these user accounts must be managed. Second, users will potentially have to remember an additional set of usernames and passwords. Additionally, by providing individual users with database credentials, they do not necessarily need to use BusinessObjects Enterprise to access the database. They could freely use any database access tool to communicate directly with the DBMS.

By using a generic database reader account, the shortcomings of individual accounts are eliminated. Database administration is simpler because only one account must be managed. The password for this account is abstracted from the end user, so she won't be able to use any other database tool to access the DBMS directly.

However, this data access model might not be able to leverage databases that have data-level security invoked for users. For example, some databases have data-level security in that different users see different data from the same query based on who they are. This security often is based on which credentials were used to access the database. If an organization were using a generic database account for BusinessObjects Enterprise, such a security model would not integrate well. As part of designing the BusinessObjects Enterprise system, this determination of data access authentication should be agreed upon by all project stakeholders.

NOTE

> The deciding factor for using a generic database user account or individual user accounts typically is the data access level to be enforced.

Using Business Views can alleviate much of this complexity because Business Views can secure the data at the column and row level, and even apply at report development time. The use of Business Views can also alter the development process because the BusinessObjects Enterprise logon becomes the paramount logon, giving access to the databases, via Business Views, as well as the BusinessObjects Enterprise objects, even during the design process.

PLANNING A BUSINESSOBJECTS ENTERPRISE ARCHITECTURE

BusinessObjects Enterprise is a system that can scale up on a single server by adding processors, memory and storage. In addition, adding servers can scale BusinessObjects Enterprise out. Scaling BusinessObjects Enterprise provides benefits such as greater performance, high availability, fault tolerance, and redundancy. However, determining how to scale a system can be a bit of a challenge. A few best practices and guidelines can be followed to guide you. Ultimately, scaling will be determined by usage profile and behavior of the BusinessObjects Enterprise system. One key point is for system administrators to not be fearful of experimenting and trying different configurations to achieve better performance. Different architectures each have benefits and considerations. The idea is to choose those that have the best fit for the given requirements.

DETERMINING PROCESSING REQUIREMENTS

The four key BusinessObjects Enterprise server components that require some considerable thought in sizing are the Cache Server, Page Servers, Report Application Server, and Job Server. Additionally, because most BusinessObjects Enterprise actions query the CMS, optimizing the CMS database can greatly speed overall system response.

TIP

> Crystal Enterprise 10, and subsequently BusinessObjects Enterprise XI, relies more heavily on the database for key data retrieval functions than in previous versions of the Enterprise product. Paying attention to tuning the system database and DBMS will result in faster system response.

26

This section focuses on how many instances of the services, processors, and physical servers are required and what the settings for these system services should be. The first step in sizing a BusinessObjects Enterprise environment is to answer a few important questions:

- How often will there be on-demand report and report instances viewing?
- When will scheduled reports be processed?
- Is there a report processing time window?
- Is redundancy required?

One key metric also needs to be determined: What is the number of concurrent users of BusinessObjects Enterprise? Even if you have an overall Web application into which BusinessObjects Enterprise will integrate, it is important to remain concerned only with the number of concurrent BusinessObjects Enterprise users when sizing BusinessObjects Enterprise. A concurrent user of BusinessObjects Enterprise can be described as someone who is interacting with BusinessObjects Enterprise. This includes logging into BusinessObjects Enterprise, processing CSP or other pages that utilize the SDK, scheduling reports, querying the system, or viewing reports. If the number of concurrent users is unknown but the size of your total user base is known, a general guide to estimate what the number of concurrent users might be is about 10% to 20% of the total application user base. For example, if your application has 1,000 total users, you can estimate the number of concurrent users for BusinessObjects Enterprise to be between 100 and 200. Often you can use Web logs of previous applications to determine utilization as well.

When reports are processed on-demand or report instances are viewed, a complex chain of processes takes place involving the Web browser, Web server, Application Server, Web Component Adapter, Cache Server, and Page Server or Report Application Server. When sizing the system for on-demand reporting and viewing, the last two components in the process are the most critical for consideration.

SIZING THE CACHE SERVER   The Cache Server is responsible for storing and forwarding epf cache pages created by the Page Servers. The Page Servers are primarily responsible for generating epf cache pages either from reports that are opened from report instances or opened and processed from report templates.

Consider one individual viewing request or on-demand reporting request to be equivalent to one thread being used by the Cache Server and one thread being used by the Page Server. This is an oversimplification of the viewing process but is a good starting point when making considerations and conservative considerations for sizing. Thus, if 200 concurrent users will be running on-demand reports or viewing report instances, then ideally 200 Cache Server threads and 200 Page Server threads should be available. Typically, 100 cache server threads per processor are recommended with up to a maximum of 400 threads per physical cache server service. Thus, on a quad processor server, a single cache server service could be set to 400 threads whereas with an eight-way server two cache server services would need to be installed, each set to 400 threads for a total thread count of 800 threads.

It is important to note that BusinessObjects Enterprise allows a physical server to host multiple copies of the same logical server service for the same or different BusinessObjects Enterprise system environments. This further increases the scalability of BusinessObjects Enterprise. In the preceding example with the eight-way server, two cache server services were configured.

SIZING THE PAGE SERVER   Whether viewing reports or running reports on-demand, Page Servers can optimally manage up to 75 threads per processor. In previous versions such as Crystal Enterprise 10 and earlier, it was common practice to run a Page Server for each processor—this is no longer done. With the new re-architecting of the Page Server, it is only necessary to install one Page Server service and it will detect the number of physical processors and self-tune. If the Page Server is sharing the processors with other processes, it will be necessary to reduce the maximum 'Simultaneous Report Jobs'. Also, keep the total number of cache server threads exactly equal to the total number of Page Server threads in the entire system for optimal performance.

Consider the following example.

A particular environment has a requirement for 300 concurrent users all running on-demand reports with some redundancy also built into the architecture. Because this is more than a single cache server can optimally handle, two cache server services will be needed. A good choice would be to have two cache server services set to 150 threads each. Because this requires two processors per service, at least a server with four processors will be needed. However, because a level of fault tolerance was required, the cache server services will be split over two dual processor servers. Therefore, the final architecture for the cache servers would have two dual processor servers each with a cache server service set to 150 threads each.

For the Page Servers, 300 concurrent users will consume 300 threads with a split over 2 servers for high availability (150 threads per processor) so 2 dual processor servers will be required. Therefore, the final architecture for the Page Servers would be two dual processor servers with one Page Server service each set to 150 threads per service.

SIZING THE REPORT APPLICATION SERVER   The Report Application Server (RAS), much like the Page server, handles 75 threads. However, some important additional configurations affect RAS performance due to its high level of interaction with the reporting database. You can set these values by going to the Central Management Console and locating the Servers section, in the Report Application Server area, within the Database tab.

Setting the Maximum Number of Records to read prevents end users from inadvertently creating runaway queries. Specifying a Batch Size determines the number of records to be retrieved from the database at a time; for instance a batch size of 100 means that to retrieve 1,000 records 10 batches will need to be run. Setting this value very high will allow large amounts of data to be processed quickly, but might slow retrieval of smaller data sets. Because report creation and modification can often call for browsing data, for instance when choosing a data value to filter results, you set the browse data size to determine the number of sample values brought back from the database. Although setting a smaller number can

26

speed retrieval, this will also constrain the possible values returned, which might affect some end-user scenarios.

Because the RAS caches report data itself instead of using the Cache Server, setting the Data Refresh value determines the oldest data that should be returned to an end user. Setting a value of 20 minutes means that no query will return data more than 20 minutes old. Higher values speed performance but might show old data, whereas low values show very recent data, but at the cost of report performance.

Setting the Report Job Database Connection determines when to close the connection to the database. Keeping the connection open, by selecting the When the Job is Closed option, saves the time required to reconnect to the database for subsequent queries, but uses additional database connections, which might require additional database licenses with some database licensing methods.

Additionally, RAS processes should be monitored for usage patterns. A typical report modification session might retrieve and format many records from the database and have high processor utilization. For instance, a user can group, filter, and re-format results, causing another full retrieval of records from the database and high processing load on the RAS machine. Additionally, certain types of viewers—such as the Interactive Viewer—also use the RAS. Thus you cannot simply equate RAS use with Page Server use, but must instead monitor the RAS from time to time to ensure that your projections are correct.

SIZING THE JOB SERVER   If scheduled reporting is part of the BusinessObjects Enterprise deployment, it will be necessary to determine how many Job Servers will be required to support the total BusinessObjects Enterprise end-user base.

Optimally, a Job Server service can process roughly five concurrent jobs per CPU. Given a quad processor server, no more than four Job Server services should be installed on a single server. Having too many Job Servers in the BusinessObjects Enterprise system can overwhelm the DBMS because too many jobs try to process concurrently. Alternatively, having too few Job Servers could mean that users have to wait a long time as their job gets queued up waiting for other jobs to complete processing. If the BusinessObjects Enterprise environment has a fixed reporting time window in which all reports can only be processed, the following formulas can be used as a rough guide to determine how many servers to dedicate as Job Servers:

> Total Processing Time required = Average Process Time (per job) * number of jobs
>
> Total Time to Process (per processor) = Total Processing Time required / Number of Concurrent Jobs (per Job Server service)
>
> Number of Job Servers required = Total Time to Process / Time Window for Processing.

A company needs to run 58 reports where each report takes on average 20 minutes to run. Because they will be reporting off a production database, they will be given a time window of only one hour nightly. How many Job Servers and processors will they need?

Total Processing Time required = 20 minutes/report * 58 reports = 1,160 minutes

Total Time to Process (per processor) = 1,160 minutes/5 concurrent jobs/Job Server service = 232 minutes

Number of Job Servers required = 230 minutes/60 minutes = 3.87 Job Server services

Therefore, for BusinessObjects Enterprise to process 58 20-minute reports in one hour, four Job Server services set to process five concurrent jobs each on four processors would be required.

Given the fact that four processors are required for the Job Server services, a single quad processor server, two dual processor servers, or four single processor servers could be used with the BusinessObjects Enterprise system.

The option to use a single server does not provide any logical Job Server redundancy; that is, if a report processing job fails on one server it isn't picked up by another. Only physical hardware "high availability" is achieved. The four-server implementation also requires added administration and maintenance. In this situation, it would be advisable to use two dual processor servers because it provides a good balance between a level of physical fault tolerance, less resource contention/conflicts, and ease of maintainability. As mentioned before, if report processing of scheduled reports happens during office hours, it is advantageous if the Job Server services reside on dedicated physical servers. If report processing of scheduled reports occurs off-hours, the Job Server services can potentially reside on the same physical servers as the Page Server services, given that the number of processors required is also satisfied.

MONITORING THE BUSINESSOBJECTS ENTERPRISE SYSTEM: AUDITING

The Auditing features of BusinessObjects Enterprise can provide feedback on the current configuration of the system. With the results of the auditing captured in an auditing database, system performance can be examined to determine if services are operating outside of requirements and also to determine how resources are being used. For instance, if you see that a particular report is being viewed many times by many different users, you might elect to schedule that report so that users will not be causing high load on the reporting database.

In addition to the auditing capabilities of BusinessObjects Enterprise, the operating system's native monitoring can help you determine how a system is performing. For instance, in Windows environments, perfmon (the Windows Performance Monitor) can trace the amount of processor time a particular server uses and thus whether a particular server is over- or underutilized.

The use of Auditing in BusinessObjects Enterprise creates a nominal increased load on the overall BusinessObjects Enterprise system. Small sets of data are written to a separate auditing database on a set frequency. The overhead involved is barely noticeable in both small and large deployments.

SAMPLE BUSINESSOBJECTS ENTERPRISE DEPLOYMENT SCENARIOS

This section describes several different classes of BusinessObjects Enterprise configurations. The first is a centralized BusinessObjects Enterprise architecture followed by a distributed architecture and then a fault-tolerant architecture.

A CENTRALIZED, SINGLE-SERVER DEPLOYMENT

A centralized architecture (see Figure 26.1) has all BusinessObjects Enterprise system components installed on the same server. This is the simplest configuration and the easiest to manage because the entire system is self-contained.

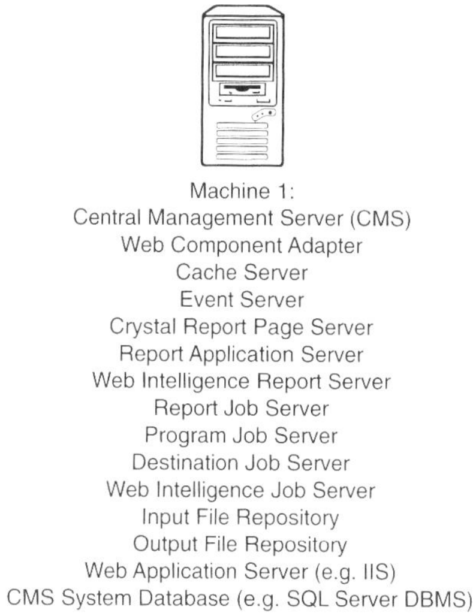

Figure 26.1
Centralized architecture: single-server configuration.

Machine 1:
Central Management Server (CMS)
Web Component Adapter
Cache Server
Event Server
Crystal Report Page Server
Report Application Server
Web Intelligence Report Server
Report Job Server
Program Job Server
Destination Job Server
Web Intelligence Job Server
Input File Repository
Output File Repository
Web Application Server (e.g. IIS)
CMS System Database (e.g. SQL Server DBMS)

This also is the easiest configuration to maintain; for example, it takes the guesswork out of performing backups because Web pages, report templates, and the system database all reside on this server. This is advantageous for smaller implementations and yet it still allows for outward scalability by adding more servers when and if they are required. This setup is perfect for workgroup applications, small projects, or Web applications that have modest and light report processing and viewing needs. Such a configuration can be very CPU-intensive because all the BusinessObjects Enterprise components, as well as the DBMS and Web server, are running concurrently.

A system administrator must be proactive in identifying potential system bottlenecks and thus scale those components out onto other separate servers accordingly. Also, this configuration offers little in terms of fault tolerance because all components are centralized.

DISTRIBUTED COMPUTING: THREE-SERVER IMPLEMENTATION

The benefits of distributing components over multiple servers are numerous. By separating BusinessObjects Enterprise components onto separate physical servers, contention for resources that would normally have to be shared in a single server configuration is reduced. For example, components on the same server usually contend with CPU time, context switching, memory substructure, and the disk subsystem sharing.

Admittedly, there are considerations involved with such a configuration. Although separate physical servers help resolve resource conflicts, components now must inter-communicate across the local area network. This adds network traffic and introduces network latency to the whole equation. Although this probably is a negligible issue when compared to the benefits, it is worthwhile to point out that there is always a trade-off. Additionally, adding more servers to the BusinessObjects Enterprise architecture increases server operation and maintenance costs.

This three-server configuration (see Figure 26.2) is the most commonly used deployment by most organizations. The main feature of this configuration is the separation of the intelligence components from the report-processing tier. By separating these processes, user interaction processes have the highest priority and are not affected by CPU contention issues. Server 1 is responsible for Web server interaction, such as processing of Web scripts and presentation of Web pages, as well as caching of repetitive requests. Server 2 handles system database inquiries. Server 3 processes reports and stores processed results.

Figure 26.2
Distributed computing: three-server configuration.

Machine 1:
Web Component Adapter
Cache Server
Web Application Server (e.g. IIS)

Machine 2:
Central Management
Server (CMS)
Event Server

Machine 3:
Crystal Report Page Server
Web Intelligence Report Server
Report Application Server
Report Job Server
Program Job Server
Destination Job Server
Web Intelligence Job Server
Input File Repository
Output File Repository

Server 3 is tasked mainly with report-processing duties. Report processing is a highly CPU-intensive activity. It's advisable to assign the best performing hardware for this server. As an example, most companies use a dual-processor server for Server 1 and 2 and have a quad-processor server for Server 3.

In this simple example, Server 3 is processing on-demand reports, generating epf cache pages, and processing scheduled reports. Processing on-demand reports and cache page generation are also response time–sensitive tasks and should have high CPU-processor precedence. Thus, if these tasks are not mutually exclusive with the processing of scheduled jobs, it is advisable to separate Page Servers from Job Servers onto separate servers.

Notice that with this configuration, Server 1 houses only the Web server and the CMS is on a separate server. Often companies already have a Web server and DBMS in place that they would like to leverage. In these cases, these BusinessObjects Enterprise components can be offloaded from Server 1 and 2 (see Figure 26.3).

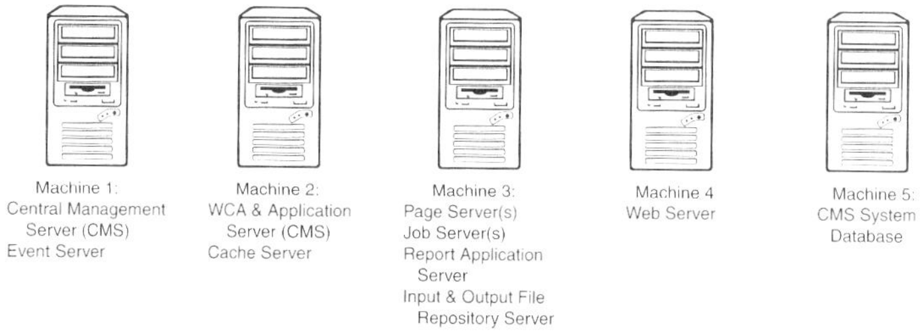

Figure 26.3
Three-server configuration with offloaded system database and Web server.

Machine 1:
Central Management
Server (CMS)
Event Server

Machine 2:
WCA & Application
Server (CMS)
Cache Server

Machine 3:
Page Server(s)
Job Server(s)
Report Application
Server
Input & Output File
Repository Server

Machine 4:
Web Server

Machine 5:
CMS System
Database

Depending on hardware availability, this can have either a positive or negative effect on system performance (that is, network traffic, shared Web, and DBMS services). The CMS database must be highly available to the CMS. Thus, it is advisable not to put the CMS database on the same DBMS as reporting databases (the databases that report access for end-user data). For those reasons it's also advisable not to place the CMS database on the same server that houses either the Page or Job Servers because of their CPU-intensive activities. The BusinessObjects Enterprise system administrator must examine issues such as leveraging of existing services, performance, and maintainability to determine which route to go.

A BUSINESSOBJECTS ENTERPRISE DISTRIBUTED ARCHITECTURE: MULTIPLE REPORT PROCESSING SERVERS

Future growth commonly comes from more concurrent users and thus more report processing and viewing. In most BusinessObjects Enterprise environments the report processing servers are the first to be "extended" (see Figure 26.4). If this is the case, additional Page, RAS, or Job Servers can be added to the architecture without impact or major change to the rest of the system.

Figure 26.4
Configuration with multiple report processing servers.

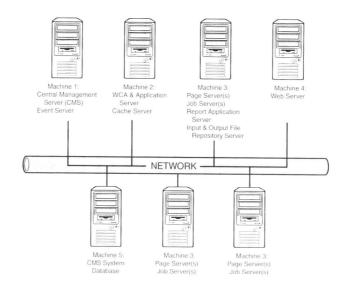

Machine 1:
Central Management
Server (CMS)
Event Server

Machine 2:
WCA & Application
Server
Cache Server

Machine 3:
Page Server(s)
Job Server(s)
Report Application
Server
Input & Output File
Repository Server

Machine 4:
Web Server

NETWORK

Machine 5:
CMS System
Database

Machine 3:
Page Server(s)
Job Server(s)

Machine 3:
Page Server(s)
Job Server(s)

NOTE

> Page and Job Servers must access the Input File Repository to find the report template to process. The Job Server must access the Output File Repository to write out the completed processed reports.

When duplicating BusinessObjects Enterprise components onto different physical servers, it is ideal if those servers have reasonable server affinity. That is, it is suggested that the servers with duplicated components should have similar hardware and run the same applications and services as their other counterparts. In addition, duplicated BusinessObjects Enterprise components should all have the same configuration settings (number of threads, timeouts, and so on) to better use the BusinessObjects Enterprise load-balancing algorithms.

The fault-tolerant configuration (see Figure 26.5) is for organizations that are looking for a highly available, reliable, and robust system architecture. This configuration can tolerate a higher level of server failures than previous configurations, thus eliminating single points of failure.

Figure 26.5
BusinessObjects Enterprise in a fault-tolerant configuration.

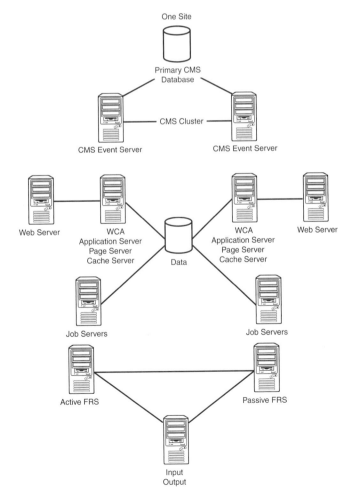

26

The key design feature of a fault-tolerant BusinessObjects Enterprise architecture is each BusinessObjects Enterprise service or daemon has a minimum of two separate instances running on physically separate servers. With the distribution of each component over two or more servers rather than just a single server, fault tolerance is gained. If one server becomes unavailable but the other is still functioning, your entire system is effectively functioning. In this configuration, additional fault tolerance is gained by using a separate fault-tolerant RDBMS for the CMS database, and a SAN (Storage Area Network) or other fault-tolerant file system for the File Server storage location. However, the price paid for this redundancy is the increase in number of servers and maintenance of those servers.

For the File Repository Servers, all the services should be clustered and pointed to the same file locations for Input and Output respectively. The File Repository Servers would also be installed onto this second server; however, they are running but dormant by default. These File Repository Servers will become "active" only if the primary server fails.

Note that this implementation also has redundancy at the Web server level; however, some method of redirecting Web requests to either Web server is required. This can be accomplished through the use of any Web farm load-balancing mechanism (such as Hardware load balancer, DNS round robin, or Microsoft Network Load Balancing [NLB]).

> Although using Microsoft's Network Load Balancing (NLB) on a Web server works very well, using NLB on any machine that has any BusinessObjects Enterprise services running on it will damage the BusinessObjects Enterprise Installation. NLB acts by changing effective IP addresses on several machines, which allows external requests to one IP to contact several machines. BusinessObjects Enterprise, however, expects that a particular service on a particular machine will *always* have the same IP address. Using NLB results in system corruption such that the system must be totally uninstalled and reinstalled, losing all system data. Remember that BusinessObjects Enterprise automatically load balances, so an external load balancer is unnecessary and indeed can make the system unstable.

TROUBLESHOOTING

As with any form of troubleshooting, the main goals are first to be able to replicate the problem and second to be able to isolate the issue. Sometimes this sounds easier than it really is. However, keeping this philosophy in mind when troubleshooting will be very helpful. This troubleshooting section discusses solid troubleshooting techniques with regard to BusinessObjects Enterprise rather than specific troubleshooting issues.

BusinessObjects Enterprise systems in a production environment can be quite complex. System components might be duplicated and spread across various servers, and these servers also can span firewalls and DMZs. Throw into the mix a custom-developed BusinessObjects Enterprise Web application and it becomes obvious that the domain of the problem can initially appear quite large. By removing this "noise" from a BusinessObjects Enterprise implementation, most issues can be distilled into one key issue. Many companies have separate development, QA, or test environments. If the problem also exhibits itself in these environments it makes troubleshooting much easier than having to tinker with a production system.

Often the most crucial information regarding problem replication seems too trivial to be verified or checked. Additionally, factors that are taken for granted, or assumed, can raise their heads as essential to solving the problem. So documenting, if possible, *all* the factors contributing to the environment improve greatly the chances for success. This includes documenting the operating system, patch levels, virus checking systems, disk quota control systems, backup programs, any logs or error reports, and the like.

After documenting and reproducing the problem, preferably in a test environment, you move on to problem isolation where the goal is to simplify the issue. For example, if issues arise when viewing a report instance through a Web application, try to remove the Web application from the equation by verifying that the report instance can be viewed in InfoView or through the Central Management Console (CMC). Another tip in simplifying a problem is to remove duplicate services from BusinessObjects Enterprise. For example, ensure that during troubleshooting only one CMS, WCA, Cache, Page, and Job Server service are running. Isolation of the problem usually consists of reproducing it given one set of circumstances and not experiencing it in another. For instance in this scenario, seeing a problem when viewing a report with the Web application but not with InfoView indicates an issue with the Web application.

When you troubleshoot BusinessObjects Enterprise, having Crystal Reports Designer installed onto the servers where the Page and Job Servers reside provides tremendous value. Often, when a scheduled report fails in BusinessObjects Enterprise, the properties of the instance display the infamous statement: Cannot open SQL Server. This is a very generic statement that can mean a multitude of error conditions.

With Crystal Reports installed on the Page and Job Servers, the report can be run interactively in Crystal Reports so a more meaningful error message can be viewed. If a report doesn't run correctly in Crystal Reports on the physical Job Server, there is certainly no chance of successfully scheduling the report in BusinessObjects Enterprise. Should a report not run in BusinessObjects Enterprise, you should run the report on the BusinessObjects Enterprise server machine within Crystal Reports as your first step. If the report runs, you can look elsewhere for issues.

CHAPTER 27

ADMINISTERING AND CONFIGURING BUSINESSOBJECTS ENTERPRISE

In this chapter

INTRODUCTION

This chapter reviews the administration tools for BusinessObjects Enterprise, including best practices and other important information related to the management of the BusinessObjects Enterprise system. Also covered are common system administration tasks such as adding new users, groups, folders, documents, and reports, as well as configuring various BusinessObjects Enterprise server components. The primary application for managing the BusinessObjects Enterprise objects and components is the *Central Management Console*. A supplement to the Central Management Console is the *Central Configuration Manager*, a Windows-based application for managing certain server functions. The reason for a separate Central Configuration Manager is because the CMC is a Web-based management application. If the primary Web server to which BusinessObjects Enterprise is tied were to become unavailable, the Central Configuration Manager provides backup server management capabilities.

> **NOTE**
>
> Although this chapter deals with the out-of-the-box BusinessObjects Enterprise administrative functions, the BusinessObjects Enterprise Software Development Kit provides programmatic access to the capabilities provided through the CMC.

USING THE CENTRAL MANAGEMENT CONSOLE

Holding true to the zero-client model of BusinessObjects Enterprise for end-user applications, the Central Management Console (CMC) is a DHTML-based tool for managing and configuring the BusinessObjects Enterprise system. The CMC provides BusinessObjects Enterprise administrators with an intuitive way to manage any type of system object, including users, groups, reports, documents, servers, and folders.

You can start the CMC by clicking the Central Management Console link in the BusinessObjects Enterprise Launchpad. Initialize the BusinessObjects Enterprise Launchpad by clicking Start, Programs, BusinessObjects 11, BusinessObjects Enterprise, BusinessObjects .NET Administration Launchpad or the BusinessObjects Enterprise, BusinessObjects Java Administration Launchpad. The Launchpad provides a link to the CMC. Visiting the URL directly can also start the CMC. The URL for the Central Management Console looks similar to http://*yourservername*/businessobjects/enterprise11/admin/en/admin.cwr, shown in Figure 27.1. The URL for the Java Central Management Console looks similar to http://*yourservername*:8080/businessobjects/enterprise11/admin/en/admin.cwr.

> **NOTE**
>
> If this is the first login to BusinessObjects Enterprise, the Administrator password is set to blank. You should change this as soon as possible.

Figure 27.1
Only those with some administration rights can log on to the CMC.

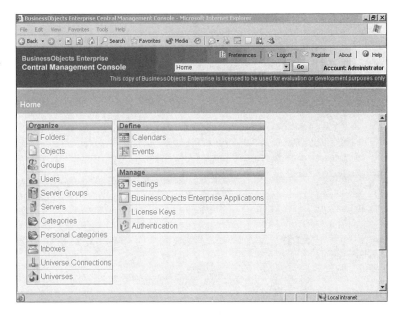

After logging into the CMC, the BusinessObjects Enterprise administrator is presented with a desktop-style screen from which all CMC functions can be accessed. Icons linking to frequently accessed CMC functions are prominently displayed in three general groupings of Organize, Define and Manage. They include

In the Organize grouping

- Folders
- Objects
- Groups
- Users
- Server Groups
- Servers
- Categories
- Personal Categories
- Inboxes
- Universe Connections
- Universes

In the Define grouping

- Calendars
- Events

In the Manage grouping

- Settings
- BusinessObjects Enterprise Applications
- License Keys
- Authentication

These common procedures, in addition to several others, can also be accessed by clicking the CMC drop-down menu in the top banner area of the screen. The BusinessObjects Enterprise administrator can return to the main CMC screen at any time by clicking the Home link at the top of every page as well as any parent area indicated in the breadcrumb trail at the top of the page (see Figure 27.2).

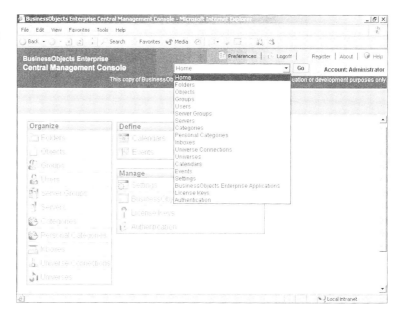

Figure 27.2
All CMC functions can be accessed from the main screen.

This chapter groups the previously listed common system functions into broader groups because tasks such as managing groups and users are intertwined. This first group of sections focuses squarely on the CMC because a bulk of administration time takes place there.

The first section, "Managing Accounts," includes sections on managing users and groups. The second section, "Managing Content," covers objects and folders. The third section, "Introducing Servers," reviews individual server configuration for all the BusinessObjects Enterprise servers and server groups. The last section on the CMC, "Managing BusinessObjects Enterprise System Settings," covers management of system settings and authorization.

A subsequent section to these shifts gears to focus on the CMC.

MANAGING ACCOUNTS

The most common use of the CMC is to manage user accounts. Although this chapter provides a review of managing user accounts, this should always be combined with an effective user-management strategy appropriate for your organization. For example, managing users is best accomplished through an effective group inheritance model, where object restrictions are never assigned to individual users, but rather to groups. When users are placed as members within those groups, they inherit the restrictions of the group. Often a single *system of record*, such as an LDAP or Active Directory system, establishes one set of users and groups that the entire organization and all software can use, greatly speeding user administration.

> **NOTE**
>
> Rights are not assigned to users or groups, but to the objects within BusinessObjects Enterprise themselves (Reports, Documents, Connections, Universes and Folders). This is explained later in the chapter.

This section reviews all the various components that factor into account management, which includes users and groups.

MANAGING USERS

To access BusinessObjects Enterprise resources, a physical end user must possess a username. Upon initial installation, by default, BusinessObjects Enterprise creates the Administrator user and the Guest user only.

The Guest account is a generic account meant for use in a scenario where certain global reports contain public information that could be accessed by anyone using BusinessObjects Enterprise. Without an assigned username, a user can log on only as an administrator (if they know the password) or a guest (provided the Guest account remains enabled).

> **NOTE**
>
> The Administrator and Guest accounts are required for proper system functionality. The Guest account can be disabled by the system administrator; however, it should not be deleted.

All BusinessObjects Enterprise permissions ultimately originate from, or apply to, individual user accounts/usernames. In light of this, one of the most important aspects of system administration is the creation of new user accounts or mapping accounts from the system of record. Whether adding one user or several hundred, the Central Management Console makes this process fast and intuitive. To begin adding new users, click the New User icon displayed on the main CMC screen (see Figure 27.3).

27

Figure 27.3
The initial CMC page
for adding a new user.

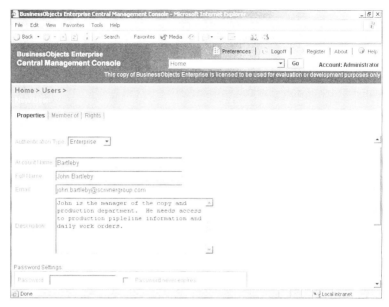

In the Account Name field, enter a unique name that the user enters to log on to BusinessObjects Enterprise. Generally, usernames are entered as a single word in lowercase (for example, Ed for Ed Conyers). If the BusinessObjects Enterprise administrator prefers, the username can contain mixed-case letters as well as spaces. BusinessObjects Enterprise is not case sensitive to usernames.

Next, enter the user's proper name in the Full Name field. The full name can contain mixed-case letters and spaces. A freeform text description can be included.

The administrator can provide the user's e-mail address that is used when a report or document object is directed to the user's e-mail account. More details on this function are covered in Chapter 24, "Using InfoView."

The BusinessObjects Enterprise administrator can also specify a password in the Password Settings dialog; however, it's not necessary because users can be forced to change their passwords the first time they log on. Checking Password Never Expires exempts the username from the BusinessObjects Enterprise global password expiration rules (discussed later in this chapter). Selecting User Cannot Change Password prevents end users from changing their passwords in the future.

The Connection Type radio buttons enable the BusinessObjects Enterprise administrator to indicate whether the username will capture a concurrent user license or a named user license when logged in to BusinessObjects Enterprise. A concurrent user license is not absorbed unless the user is logged in to BusinessObjects Enterprise.

After the user's session ends, a default of 20 minutes, the concurrent license is released. This means that another user within BusinessObjects Enterprise can log in to BusinessObjects

Enterprise and use the concurrent license. A named license is relinquished only when the username is deleted or changed to use a concurrent license. An in-depth discussion of license keys is covered later in this chapter in the Authorization section of the CMC.

After the required information for creating a new user is provided, click the OK button at the bottom of the screen. The new user is created. The screen will refresh and the view will enable the Membership and Rights tabs, as well as expose alias information.

After the User Properties screen has been reloaded, two new options appear at the bottom of the page. The Authentication setting enables you to specify whether the user's password validation will be processed by BusinessObjects Enterprise, LDAP, Windows NT, Active Directory, or even perhaps a system such as SAP via the BusinessObjects Enterprise Solution Kit for SAP. By default, BusinessObjects Enterprise handles authentication internally. The Account Is Disabled option disables an account without deleting it. Although the account can always be enabled again in the future, this is useful for employees who might take a leave of absence from the company.

In addition to the Properties of a user, two additional pages provide Membership and Rights settings for the user. These pages are accessible by clicking on the respective tabs at the top of the User screen.

The Membership settings, accessed by clicking on the Member Of tab, allow administrators to add users to existing groups that have been established in the BusinessObjects security model. These groups might have been set up manually within the system or imported from an external system such as a LDAP server. Although this is an effective way of granting users group membership, this is a less common use of users and groups in an Enterprise system.

In the primary Membership screen, the groups membership currently assigned to the user are listed with a description of the group itself. To assign membership to a group, click on the Member Of button in the upper-right corner of the User Membership screen. The screen will now display two lists. The list on the left contains all available groups of which the user is not a member. The list on the right contains all groups of which the user is currently a member. The administrator can move any group from one list to the other.

After the membership lists are set, clicking OK returns the view to the primary Membership screen. Regardless of what changes were made in the lists, clicking Cancel discards any changes and returns to the primary Membership screen.

The Rights tab at the top of the User screen can confuse a new administrator into thinking that he can grant the user whose profile he is viewing certain system rights. Actually the opposite is true! The Rights tab, which appears on *almost every object in BusinessObjects Enterprise*, supports the Delegated Administration paradigm, which enables different users to administer different portions of one BusinessObjects Enterprise system. Use the tab to specify which users or groups have access to this object; in this case to the particular user you are viewing. If you only enable access to this user's profile for the Administrators group, a user who is not a member of the Administrators group logging onto the CMC will not see the user at all. In this way you can have administrators in different departments or functional areas do their own system maintenance without seeing the information of other groups or departments.

A list of all the users in the system, including the BusinessObjects Enterprise administrator, can be accessed by selecting Users from the CMC drop-down menu (see Figure 27.4).

Figure 27.4
All user-management functions are accessible from the Users screen.

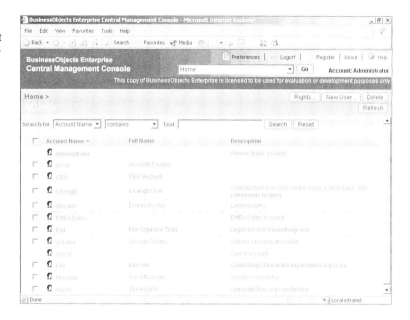

From the Users screen, you can search the list of account names or account descriptions for exact values or partial values, either inclusive or exclusive. Additionally, you can edit an existing username, add a new user, or delete an existing user. To delete a username, place a check mark in the corresponding box on the right side of the screen. You can select more than one username. After a minimum of one username has been selected in this manner, click the Delete button at the top of the screen. The Central Management Console then prompts to confirm deletion of the user account. The built-in Administrator and Guest accounts can not be selected to prevent inadvertent deletion. There is a Rights icon as well; again, this is to specify which user/group has the rights to see this portion of the administrative console.

MANAGING GROUPS

A user *group* is a collection of BusinessObjects Enterprise users with one or more logical characteristics in common. For example, the users in the Marketing department should be grouped together based on the fact that they all belong to the same business division. Because these users work together, they are more likely to share the same reports. Creating groups such as marketing enables the system administrator to globally assign permissions to a broader audience.

Groups are useful for classifying users according to their job function and report needs. In most cases, it's advisable to create a series of logical user groups to reduce the complexity of managing permissions in BusinessObjects Enterprise.

> **TIP**
>
> Globally managing permissions for user groups is significantly less complex than trying to manage permissions for each individual user. However, there might be situations in which it's desirable to make an exception to a group's security policy for a minimum number of users within that group. BusinessObjects Enterprise has the flexibility to make object restriction exceptions on a user-by-user basis.

BusinessObjects Enterprise contains two default user groups:

- Administrators
- Everyone

The Administrators Group

The Administrators group is for system administrators only. Users who belong to this group have full, unrestricted access to BusinessObjects Enterprise, including the capability to manage servers using the CMC. Administrators can run any report and access any report folder. *Use discretion when adding users to this group.*

The Everyone Group

The Everyone group contains all users by default. When new users are created, they are automatically enrolled in the Everyone group. The Everyone group is useful for globally setting permissions for all BusinessObjects Enterprise users.

> **NOTE**
>
> In previous versions of the product, there was a third default group called New Sign-up Accounts. This functionality is still available, but has been disabled by default.

27

Creating New User Groups

To create a new user group, click the Groups icon on the home CMC page and then click the New Group button in the upper-right corner of the primary groups page (see Figure 27.5).

In the Group Name field, enter the group name exactly as it should appear in BusinessObjects Enterprise. The group name field accepts upper- and lowercase, spaces, and punctuation. A freeform text description is optional and limited to 256 characters. After the required information has been provided, click OK to create the group.

Figure 27.5
Creating new user groups is a fundamental system administration task. It's often helpful to seek input from business users when formulating user group names and hierarchies.

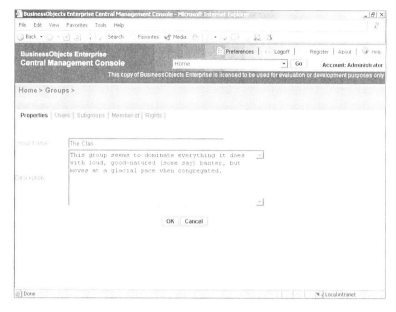

Figure 27.5
Creating new user groups is a fundamental system administration task. It's often helpful to seek input from business users when formulating user group names and hierarchies.

After clicking OK, the group creation screen should momentarily reload. The OK and Cancel buttons are replaced with the Update and Reset buttons. This indicates that the group was created successfully. The BusinessObjects Enterprise administrator now has access to three new tabs at the top of the screen: Users, Subgroups, and Member Of, as shown in Figure 27.6.

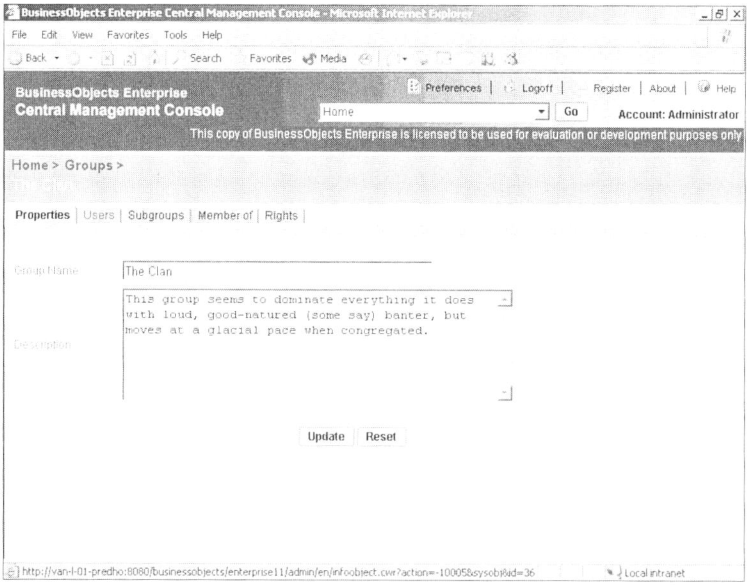

Figure 27.6
After the group has been created, additional options are available via the tabs at the top of the screen.

ADDING USERS TO A GROUP

Creating a group name is the first step in configuring a new group. By default, the new group does not contain any users. You must click the Users tab to add users to the group (see Figure 27.7).

Figure 27.7
Initially, the Users tab is empty. New users can be added to the group by clicking on the Add/Remove Users button.

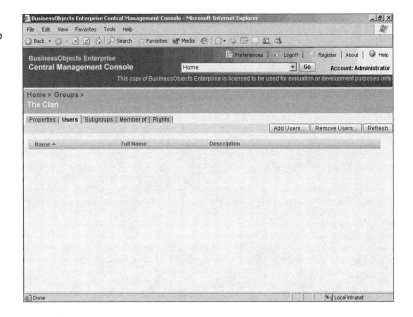

The Users tab does not contain any users initially. To add users to the new group, click the Add Users button at the top of the screen. A list of all BusinessObjects Enterprise users appears on the left side of the screen, as shown in Figure 27.8. Highlight the users to add to the group. You can select several, noncontiguous names by holding down the Ctrl key when clicking. After the desired usernames are highlighted, click the Add button (">") to verify the selection. Highlighted users are moved from the Available list to the Users list. When satisfied with the selections, click OK to commit, as shown in Figure 27.8.

To select a range of users, click the topmost username in the desired range. Then, while holding down the Shift key, click the bottom username in the range. All users between the top and bottom names are selected.

To add all available users or to remove all users from the currently selected group, use the >> and << buttons respectively.

The Look For feature allows the administrator to reduce the list of available users to a subset of all users in the system. This is particularly helpful when the system contains a large number of users. The search function will find any occurrences that match the search string in part or entirely.

27

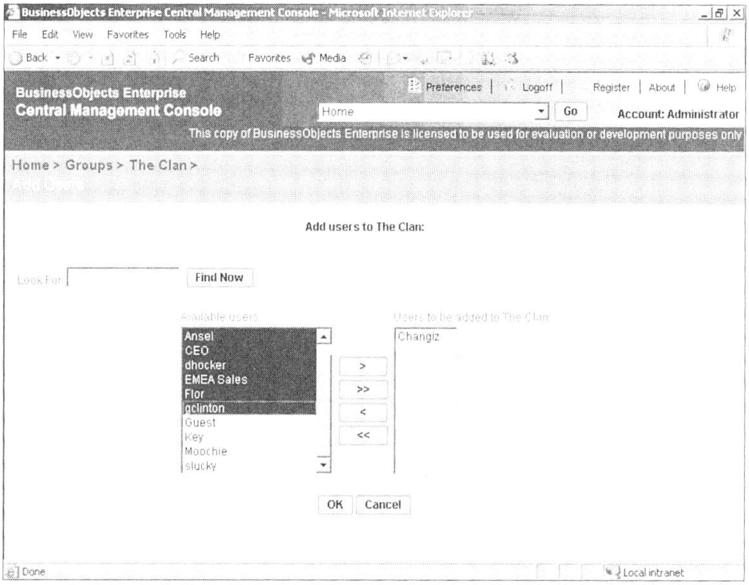

Figure 27.8
All BusinessObjects Enterprise users appear in the list box on the left.

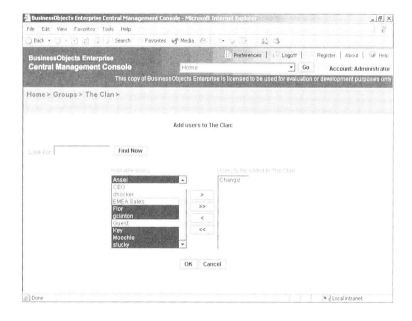

Figure 27.9
Any changes to the group membership are not committed until the BusinessObjects Enterprise administrator clicks OK.

The CMC returns to the Users tab after the changes have been committed. The Users tab immediately reflects the membership of the group, as shown in Figure 27.10. Keep in mind that BusinessObjects Enterprise enables a single user to be a member of multiple groups, so it's possible for users to belong to other groups, such as the Everyone group.

Figure 27.10
The new group now
contains several users.

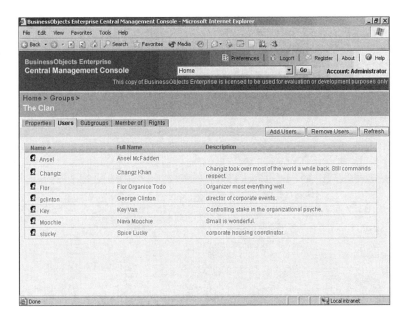

CREATING SUBGROUPS

In addition to adding individual users to a group, the administrator can add subgroups to a group. As the name implies, a *subgroup* is a child of the parent group. Subgroups can be used to further define user roles and permissions at a more detailed level. A top-level group can contain several subgroups, and those subgroups can also contain subgroups, as Figure 27.11 shows. The benefit is that permissions need not be applied at a user level, even though they can be. Even if an individual user's needs might seem unique, there is always the distinct possibility that someone else could come along with similar requirements. Creating subgroups minimizes individual user permission/restriction management.

Click the Subgroups tab to add new subgroups.

Click the Add/Remove Subgroups button to designate a new subgroup. The Add/Remove Subgroups page works just like the Add or Remove Users screen with the exception that there is no Look for functionality. All available groups are listed in the list box on the left.

To be clear, a subgroup is not a special kind of group, but rather an ordinary group that has a hierarchical relationship established with another group. Like parent or top-level groups, subgroups are created by using the New Group option on the main CMC screen.

If a subgroup needs to be created (that is, it doesn't exist yet), you need to create the new subgroup in the same manner as other groups would be created, from the New Groups screen. Figure 27.12 shows a list of groups where the intended subgroup has already been defined.

27

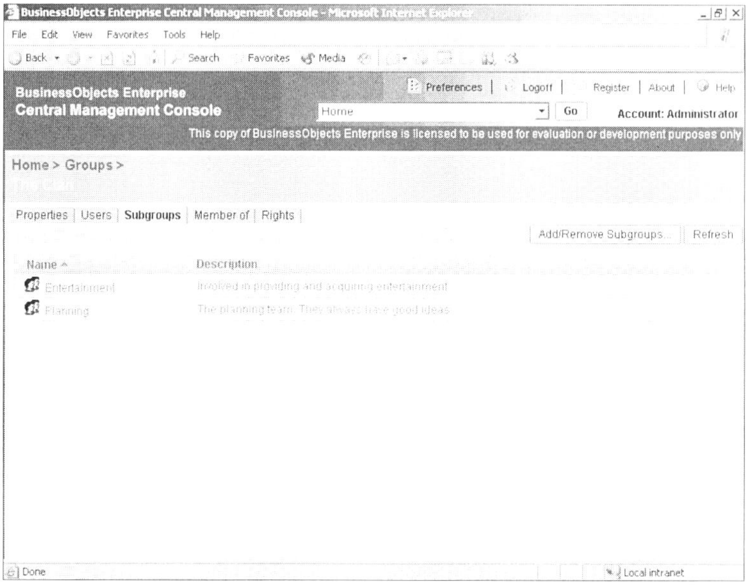

Figure 27.11
The Subgroups tab
identifies any child
groups that belong to
the current parent
group.

Figure 27.11
The Subgroups tab
identifies any child
groups that belong to
the current parent
group.

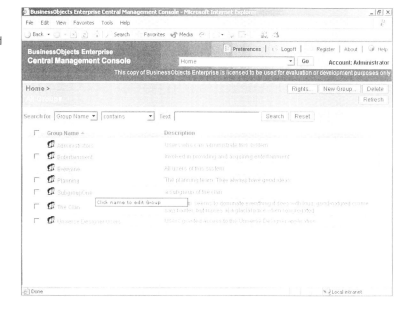

Figure 27.12
SubGroupOne has
already been created
and you can move
this into a parent
group. (The name
can be anything—
"SubgroupOne" is
used to clarify the
relationship in this
text.)

Any group can also be a subgroup. This can get a bit messy with respect to restrictions because overlapping inherited security can be confusing. Try to keep things streamlined by using naming conventions and inherited permissions. This lowers administrative cost and Total Cost of Ownership.

Add the subgroups to the parent group and click OK to commit the change to the system database (see Figure 27.13). The CMC returns to the subgroup listing screen, which now reflects the new subgroups.

Figure 27.13
The subgroup SubgroupOne is added to two existing subgroups.

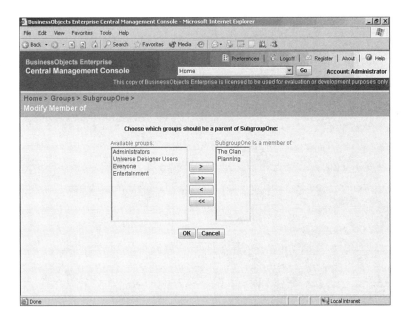

This particular subgroup tree is only one level deep. It's possible to create subgroups of subgroups for more granular management of users. For example, a few regional subgroups (East, Central, and West) could be added to the North America Sales subgroup. To do this, you only need to click the name of the subgroup, and then repeat the preceding steps to add another subgroup.

MANAGING CONTENT

Managing content means managing all the various objects, for instance Crystal Reports, Web Intelligence Documents, Excel and Word files, programs, packages, and OLAP Intelligence reports that are published to BusinessObjects Enterprise. As discussed in earlier chapters, all of these are referred to as *content*.

The management of content implies a host of tasks, from organizing items into various container folders to applying restrictions (or *rights*) to the actual objects. If not planned correctly, content management can be one of the most time-consuming tasks for a BusinessObjects Enterprise administrator. Again, with delegated administration, this task can be distributed to various subject matter experts around the organization, saving the IT department this type of work, which often involves knowledge of a particular department's requirements in detail.

27

The flexible BusinessObjects Enterprise architecture accommodates almost any content-management scheme. However, there are some general guidelines to follow when determining the best approach to content management. A content management scheme consists of a folder/subfolder tree that can be defined within BusinessObjects Enterprise and the associated permissions on those folders. Categories, which are new in BusinessObjects Enterprise XI, allow for a secondary grouping of objects that may traverse the folder/subfolder hierarchy.

An effective content-management scheme should have the following characteristics:

- Both descriptive and easy to understand folder and report names
- A standard report naming convention consistently applied throughout the system
- Strictly controlled object access that adheres to the organization's business rules
- A folder hierarchy that facilitates rapid end-user navigation to every report object
- Reliable reports with accurate database logon information

MANAGING OBJECTS

Objects in BusinessObjects Enterprise are published into the object store. Objects, when published into BusinessObjects Enterprise, are managed through the CMC. This chapter uses the terms *report* and *object* interchangeably because most objects are, in fact, reports.

This book has already provided some object publishing and management review. The Publishing Wizard, a Windows-based application for publishing reports to BusinessObjects Enterprise, primarily publishes most content through the Save As functionality of Crystal Reports or OLAP Intelligence. This chapter reviews object publishing and management from the CMC perspective.

It's also important to note that the object type determines the options and properties available to the BusinessObjects Enterprise system administrator. For instance, because OLAP Intelligence reports cannot be scheduled like Crystal Reports, no scheduling options are displayed when administering an OLAP Intelligence report.

Because Crystal Reports are the most widely used report type, this chapter focuses primarily on that object type. Special attention is also paid to Web Intelligence because it is new in the XI release.

PUBLISHING OBJECTS FROM THE CMC

To add a new report to BusinessObjects Enterprise, start the CMC and, from the home page, select Objects, and then the New Object button, as shown in Figure 27.14.

→ For more information on objects in BusinessObjects Enterprise, **see** "Content Plug-ins," **p. 588**

Figure 27.14
The New Object function enables you to add a new object to BusinessObjects Enterprise.

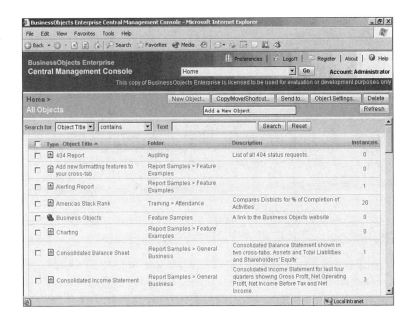

After selecting New Object, the New Object dialog launches, shown in Figure 27.15. On the left is a list of all supported objects which can added to the system. This list is restricted by the added keycodes. In BusinessObjects Enterprise XI Premium edition, all the possible supported objects are listed.

To add a report, choose to add a report type of object on the left, and then type the path and filename of the report in the File Name box, or click the Browse button to locate the report file.

Figure 27.15
The New Report dialog enables you to add objects to BusinessObjects Enterprise from an external directory location. Supported objects are listed on the left.

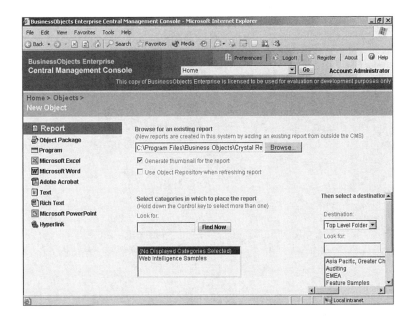

After selecting the report filename, indicate whether a thumbnail image of the report should be generated and displayed. A report *thumbnail* is an image snapshot of page one of the report. This feature is currently available for Crystal Reports only. A thumbnail is merely a property of the report object, something that can be called programmatically or displayed only as an option. BusinessObjects InfoView, the default end-user interface for BusinessObjects Enterprise, is a good example of an application that uses the report thumbnail.

The Generate Thumbnail for the Report option is useful for visually identifying reports, and it's recommended that the BusinessObjects Enterprise administrator leave the setting enabled.

In order to take advantage of the Generate Thumbnail for the Crystal Reports object, the report designer must save the report with the Save Preview Picture option at design time. This achieved in the Crystal Reports Designer application by clicking File, Summary Info.

While enabling this option in Crystal Reports, it's highly recommended that the Title, Author, and Comments fields be filled in because this information is available to users in BusinessObjects Enterprise applications for report identification and searching. All these properties are stored in the BusinessObjects Enterprise system database and can be leveraged for more specific report discovery.

The Summary Info dialog must be completed during report creation for the thumbnail (or report description details) to be available inside BusinessObjects Enterprise.

Checking the Use Object Repository when refreshing report option, refreshes the repository objects added to the report with the most current objects in the Object Repository. The Object Repository is a feature in BusinessObjects Enterprise where standard report components are centrally stored for use several reports. For instance, if the report designer had placed a corporate logo image file stored in the Object Repository onto the report and the check box was enabled, BusinessObjects Enterprise would check to see that the copyright text was the latest version stored in the repository and update it if a more current copy is available.

As mentioned earlier, a new feature in BusinessObjects Enterprise XI is Categories. When publishing a report the administrator can select any number of the existing categories that exist in the system. These can be from the list of Corporate Categories, Personal Categories or both. By enabling the All Selected Categories check box, the list will be only those categories that have been selected. By unchecking the check box, the list of categories will return to all available categories in the system.

The final step to adding a new report to BusinessObjects Enterprise is to select the desired enterprise folder that contains the report. This is done using the Destination option at the bottom of the New Report screen. Simply highlight the folder that should house the new report and click OK. The BusinessObjects Enterprise administrator can also navigate to subfolders by highlighting the parent folder and clicking the Show Subfolders button.

Web Intelligence documents are an exception to the report publishing described above. Web Intelligence documents are created interactively against available universes then saved into the BusinessObjects Enterprise system.

CONFIGURING REPORT PROPERTIES

The CMC now displays a report Properties tab, shown in Figure 27.16. The Report Title is indicated at the top of the screen. This is the actual name that BusinessObjects Enterprise displays when users browse for the report. The report name is actually taken from the report's Title field, which can be edited in the Summary Info dialog screen in Crystal Reports. The BusinessObjects Enterprise administrator can override the default title by manually typing a different title. Report titles can contain upper- and lowercase characters, as well as spaces.

Use a consistent naming convention for all reports, and make the report titles reasonably descriptive. This reduces object management issues when dealing with hundreds or thousands of distinct reports.

Figure 27.16
The Properties screen displays the report title, description, and other pertinent details.

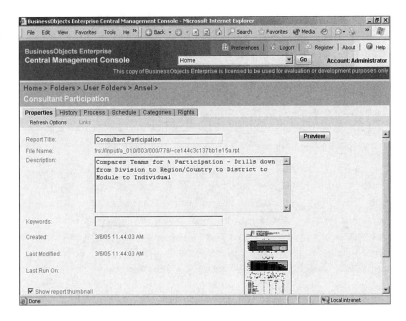

The File Name field indicates the true path and location of the actual file as it is managed by the File Repository Server (FRS). This information is controlled by BusinessObjects Enterprise and *cannot* be edited. It's displayed as a reference for troubleshooting purposes.

The Description field can be used to add a detailed paragraph to note any special information about the report. The Description field is displayed in the Web Desktop, and it also will be parsed by the Web Desktop report keyword search feature.

Developers sometimes use the Description field as a catchall for keywords about the report that can be searched by a BusinessObjects Enterprise application. Although this might be effective for a small number of reports, it can adversely affect system performance when you're dealing with large numbers of reports and is not recommended.

The Folder Path at the top of the screen immediately above the title of the report, shows the folder structure that contains this report. Each word can be clicked to navigate to that folder. To move this object, you would first go to the containing folder, and then choose the Copy/Move/Shortcut button.

The upper-right corner of the report Properties tab contains a Preview button. The Preview button runs the report immediately on the first available Page Server. This option is useful for verifying database connectivity for the report without opening the Web Desktop.

The bottom of the report Properties tab, shown in Figure 27.17, allows the BusinessObjects Enterprise administrator to enable the report thumbnail image using the Show Thumbnail check box. Be aware that the report must be designed with the Save Preview Picture option enabled for this setting to take effect, in addition to the settings required in Crystal Reports discussed earlier.

If any changes are made to the report Properties tab, you need to click the Update button at the bottom of the screen to commit the modifications to the system. After clicking Update, the Properties tab refreshes; this indicates that the changes were successfully committed to the system database.

On the Properties tab, just below the word Properties, links to navigate to the Refresh Options and Links appear. Clicking on Refresh Options navigates to an area where you can designate which properties of the report you want to refresh from the Object Repository or the report stored in the BusinessObjects Enterprise system. If the report is linked to other reports in the system, the Links option is enabled. Clicking on Links brings you to a display of the managed links in this report object so that you can verify that the links are valid. The actual links should be managed within Crystal Reports.

In the case of Web Intelligence documents, on the Properties tab, just below the word Properties, links to navigate to the Universe properties appear. The Universe properties include the Universe name and DSN connection name. Refresh Options and Links are not applicable to Web Intelligence documents.

Figure 27.17
Additional options in
the report Properties
tab–the links sub-
section.

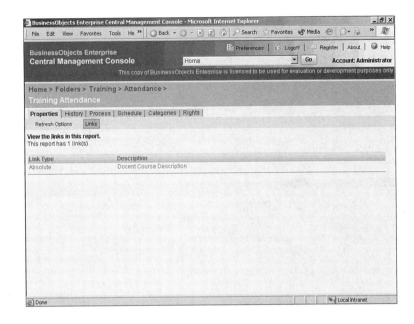

REVIEWING REPORT HISTORY

In addition to the Properties tab, several other tabs pertain to the report or document. The
first is the History tab. The History tab, shown in Figure 27.18, displays all instances of the
report, including completed instances—successful or otherwise—pending (queued)
instances, recurring instances, currently running instances, and paused instances. The
BusinessObjects Enterprise administrator can use this screen to manage all instances of this
report.

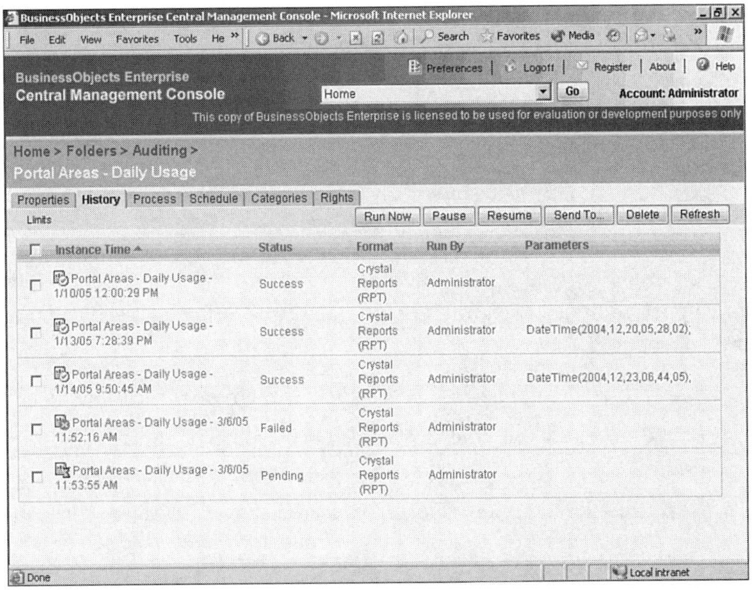

Figure 27.18
The History tab lists
all instances and
recurring schedules of
the report.

27

Recall that a report instance is a version of the parent report that has been scheduled and run at a specific point in time. The instance might have certain parameters that were specified at the time of scheduling, so very few assumptions about the report instance can be made without verifying this information. Fortunately, BusinessObjects Enterprise stores the schedule time, scheduling user, start time, end time, and so on, as properties of the instance.

> Although the number of report objects and instances stored and managed within BusinessObjects Enterprise is, in theory, unlimited, the hardware dedicated to the CMS, CMS Database, and File Repository Server plays a major role in determining true system scalability.

To see the details of instances (shown in Figure 27.19), including error messages for failed instances, look at the instance status message on the History tab. To view the instance of the report, click the instance date/time stamp.

Figure 27.19
The instance's properties can be reviewed in the CMC.

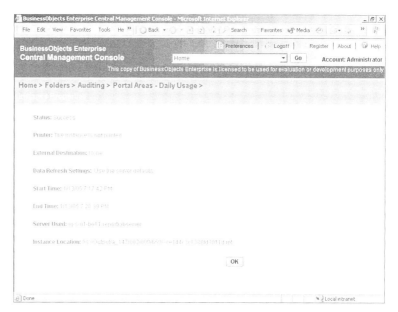

The upper-right corner of the History tab displays a row of action buttons. These include the following:

- **Run Now**—Schedules a new instance of the report for immediate processing.
- **Pause**—Pauses, but does not cancel, processing of any selected pending or running instances.
- **Resume**—Releases any selected paused instances so the report can continue processing.

- **Send To…**—Sends the selected instance of the report to one of the supported destinations.

- **Delete**—Permanently removes selected instances from BusinessObjects Enterprise.

- **Refresh**—Refreshes the current view of available instances.

A large BusinessObjects Enterprise deployment might generate thousands of report instances every day. Over time, the accumulation of old report instances unnecessarily consumes system resources. BusinessObjects Enterprise has instance-limit controls for automatically managing the expiration (deletion) of old report instances. There is a global instance expiration setting in the Settings section of the CMC (discussed later in this chapter). The global expiration limits apply to all report instances in BusinessObjects Enterprise, unless the system administrator defines exceptions on a report-by-report basis.

If a report is scheduled and a format other than Crystal Reports is specified, it's still stored in the BusinessObjects Enterprise system as a report instance. This means that report instances could be Microsoft Excel spreadsheets, Word documents, and so on. BusinessObjects Enterprise provides a series of server plug-ins that enable objects to be stored in the system in any of the supported file formats.

MANAGING OBJECT LIMITS

Exceptions to the global instance expiration limits are defined on the Limits tab for each report. The Limits tab, shown in Figure 27.20, enables the BusinessObjects Enterprise administrator to override the global or folder instance expiration limits for the current report only. This expiration limit can be based on the number of instances, the number of instances per individual user or group or by the age of instance.

In the upper-left corner of the Limits tab is a checkbox option to Delete Excess Instances When There Are More Than N Instances of an Object. You can use this option to trigger old report instances to be deleted when the specified threshold has been exceeded.

This setting applies to all users and user groups unless an exception is made in the Delete Excess Instances for the Following Users/Groups section of the Limits tab. The BusinessObjects Enterprise administrator can click the Add/Remove button in this tab to add overriding expiration limits for specific users or user groups. The user/group expiration limits take precedence over any global or folder expiration limits.

THE PROCESS TAB

Several subtabs exist within the Process tab. These subtabs allow you to set the options for how reports are processed.

SERVERS AND PROCESSING OPTIONS   Clicking on the Process tab navigates to the processing servers page. The Default Servers to Use for Scheduling area controls which server group executes the report.

27

Figure 27.20
The Limits tab can be used to configure report instance expiration rules for the current report object. Object-level expiration limits take precedence over folder and global limits.

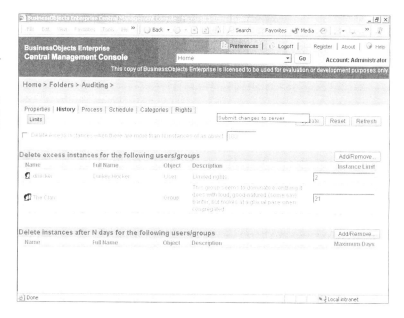

Server groups are useful for categorizing servers by geographic region, function, processor speed or a combination of all these properties. The server group options are useful for ensuring that reports are executed on a BusinessObjects Enterprise Job Server that is in close physical proximity to the database server. For example, reports scheduled in Paris against the Paris sales database should be executed by a Job Server that is on the same network segment as the Paris database to maintain maximum report performance.

Server groups can also be used to direct high-priority reports to servers with the most processing power. For example, this option could be used to force the CFO's weekly financial reports to execute on the fastest server in the company. (A detailed discussion of server groups appears later in this chapter.)

The Use the First Available Server option is enabled by default and should remain enabled in most cases since it leverages the built in load balancing capabilities of the system. However, the administrator can direct BusinessObjects Enterprise to give preference a specific server group when possible by enabling the Give Preference to Servers Belonging to the Selected Group option. If this option is enabled, BusinessObjects Enterprise forces the report to execute on the first available Job Server in the group. If no Job Server is available, the report is executed by the first available Job Server outside the specified server group.

The option to Only Use Servers Belonging to the Selected Group causes the report to execute only on Job Servers within the specified group. BusinessObjects Enterprise queues the scheduled instances of the report for the first available Job Server in the specified group. If no server is available, the report remains in the queue until one becomes available.

NOTE

Be aware that the option to Only Use Servers Belonging to the Selected Group restricts BusinessObjects Enterprise's capability to intelligently designate a Job Server for the report, and might cause scheduled instances of the report to remain in the job queue longer than normal. Properly planning your particular needs is an important factor when enabling this feature.

In similar fashion, viewing and modification servers designate preferences for real-time viewing and report modification. Finally, default values on the PageServer and Report Application Server (RAS) regarding how often to refresh data versus caching can be overridden for any object, enabling you to tailor settings for more and less time-sensitive reports, for instance.

DATABASE SETTINGS   The Database subsection of the Process tab contains database logon information for the report, shown in Figure 27.21. Although the database information, such as server name, is stored in BusinessObjects Enterprise by default, database logon information is not stored and can only be added on this tab by the system administrator.

When a user attempts to run a report that does not already have database logon information provided, BusinessObjects Enterprise prompts the user to enter the database username and password. Note, however, if the BusinessObjects Enterprise administrator has already configured database logon information for the report, the user is not required to enter any additional passwords. This is the preferred method for running reports that do not rely on database-level security.

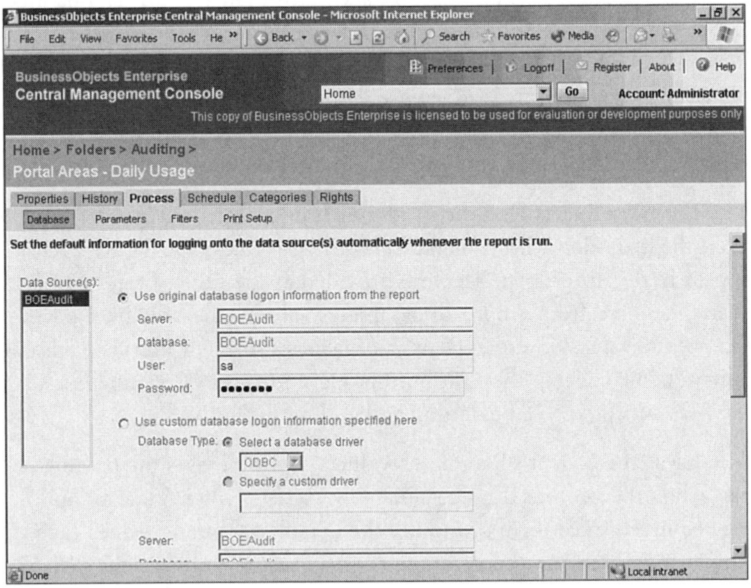

Figure 27.21
The Database subsection enables you to manage database logon information for the report object. Storing the logon information along with the report enables users to run the report without knowing a database username and password.

To configure database login information, click the Database link and highlight the report data source to configure first. All report data sources appear in the Data Source(s) list box. Most reports only have one data source; however, reports that contain subreports or multiple databases might have more than one data source. Note that each data source must be configured independently.

To store database logon credentials with the report, highlight a data source and fill out the database, logon name, and password for the data source. Remember to click the Update button to confirm the changes. If the report has multiple data sources, you are required to highlight each data source and provide the proper logon information. Database logon information is encrypted in the BusinessObjects Enterprise system database, and it cannot be accessed by end users, even by querying the system database directly.

Enabling the Prompt the User for New Value(s) When Viewing option causes BusinessObjects Enterprise to confirm the default database logon information each time the report is viewed.

If a database has changed, the Use Custom Database Logon Information Specified Here option should be checked, and the relevant information added. This feature enables flexibility in changing databases even after an object enters the BusinessObjects Enterprise system. Should batch maintenance of database connections be required, a script file can change these settings via the SDK. Please see Part VII, "Customized Report Distribution—Using BusinessObjects Enterprise," for more information.

MANAGING OBJECT PARAMETERS

The Parameters subsection options, shown in Figure 27.22, can be used to provide default values for parameters in the report. If no parameters exist in the report, the link to the Parameters subsection is disabled. Specifying default parameter values can reduce the number of steps required for a user to schedule a report. Of course, users can always override the default values if they want. To specify a default value for a parameter, click the parameter value listed in the Value column. Unspecified values are indicated as [EMPTY].

The BusinessObjects Enterprise administrator might select a default value for a parameter from the drop-down list of default parameter values (see Figure 27.23). The values that appear in the drop-down list were provided at the time of report creation in Crystal Reports or are gathered from the list of parameter values generated by the List of Values server. If the desired values do not appear, the BusinessObjects Enterprise administrator can type a new value by clicking the Edit button. Certain types of parameters, such as range parameters, can accept both a beginning and ending default value.

The Clear the Current Parameter Value(s) option erases the parameter's current default values, while the Prompt the User for New Value(s) when Viewing option ensures that users are reminded to confirm or modify the default parameter values each time the report is run. Any changes made to the Parameters area must be confirmed by clicking the Update button.

Figure 27.22
The Parameter subsection can be used to store default values for report parameters. Users have the capability to override the default values with their own values.

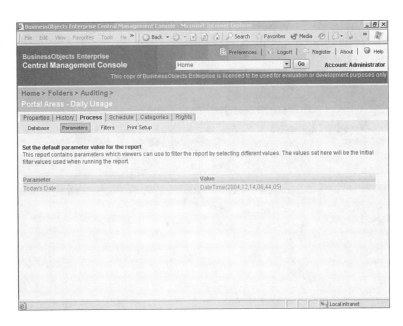

Figure 27.23
A default value for a parameter can be specified. Range parameters can have default values for both beginning and ending values.

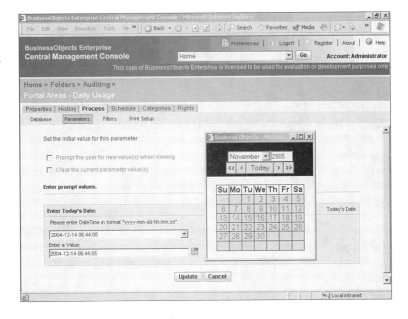

The benefit of using parameters with reports in BusinessObjects Enterprise is that the user is prompted for value entry if the report is run or scheduled. No special programming is required, regardless of the report viewer in use.

FILTERS The Filters subsection enables you to set the default record selection expression for the report, shown in Figure 27.24. The default record selection is normally adopted from the original report file. In most cases, the default selection expression should be left intact, but it can be useful to override this feature for specific purposes. With a proper understanding of Crystal syntax, you can modify the Record Selection Formula or Group Selection Formula manually.

Figure 27.24
The Filters subsection can be used to override the report's preconstructed record selection expression. You need a solid understanding of Crystal Reports record selection expression syntax to modify the default filter.

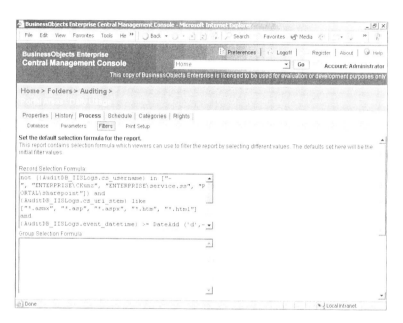

At the bottom of the Filters tab is a section for indicating which Processing Extensions the report uses. A *Processing Extension*, discussed in Chapter 25, "BusinessObjects Enterprise Architecture," is an optional programmatic library for controlling the display of report data. Processing Extensions were new to Crystal Enterprise 8.5 but are now largely superseded by Business Views in BusinessObjects Enterprise XI. (Refer to Chapter 18, "Using a Semantic Layer—Business Views and Universes," for a complete discussion of Business Views.)

PRINT SETUP   Print settings for a report are managed through the Print Setup subsection of Process tab. BusinessObjects Enterprise XI enables you to print the scheduled report by checking the Print in Crystal Reports Format option and specifying the details on the printer. Note that the printing occurs from the Job Server, so any network and other permissions must be configured on the appropriate Job Server(s). Note that this modality allows the job to be scheduled to the printer and a destination in the same run, thereby letting you schedule to an archiving system, for instance, which has a printer driver as its front-end image acquisition method.

In versions prior to Crystal Enterprise 10, the print settings were managed in the Destinations area.

The bottom of this section enables you to set whether you want to use the print options stored in the report itself during report creation, the default printer options, or set custom options for that object.

A new feature in this release is the ability to specify the report's page layout from within the BusinessObjects Enterprise environment instead of exclusively through the Crystal Reports designer and SDKs. The printer settings can be determined from the report definition, or the administrator can override the report definition and use specified settings from a particular printer or custom printer settings. The available custom settings include the ability to change orientation, paper size, and page width and height. This allows for greater control on the printed output of the scheduled report.

NOTE

> For Web Intelligence documents, the Process tab provides the capability to define the default server properties and the capability to administer any associated prompts for the Web Intelligence document. Database, Parameters, and Filters are inherent in the Universe and document definitions therefore are configurable via the CMC.

MANAGING OBJECT PROCESSING SCHEDULES

The Schedule tab enables you to schedule the report to run at selected times (see Figure 27.25). The CMC provides this feature as a matter of convenience so the administrator doesn't have to refer to InfoView for scheduling. When scheduling a report, the number of retries allowed (and the retry interval in seconds) can be specified before the report instance is marked as failed.

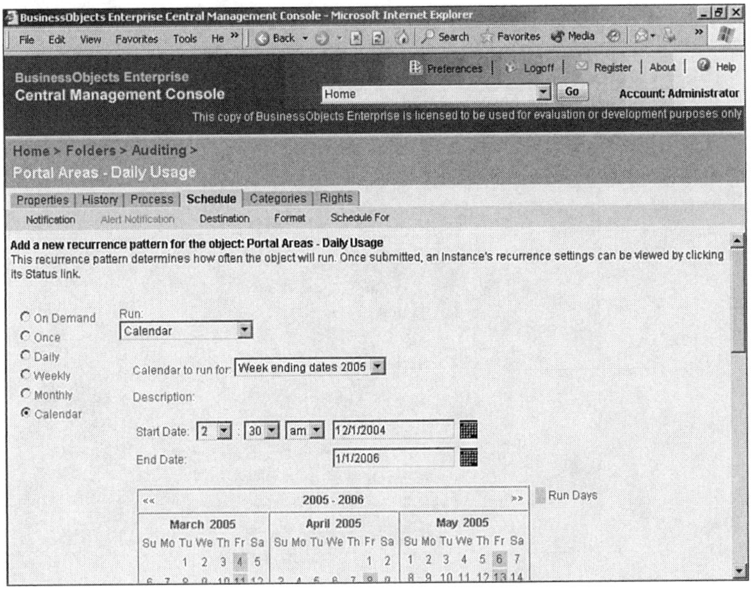

Figure 27.25
The Schedule tab provides the same report scheduling functionality as the Web Desktop.

The calendar option sets the recurrence of the schedule based on calendars stored in the system. A fuller discussion of calendars follows later in this chapter.

NOTIFICATION   BusinessObjects Enterprise XI offers two methods of notification around specific jobs, in addition to the general audit logging options available in the system. The notification can audit on successful and failed jobs, and e-mail notification can also be sent, perhaps to an administrator's pager to call attention to a particular failure or success.

ALERT NOTIFICATION   Many organizations today work to streamline management practices and manage against goals. Thus management by exception increases daily in popularity. To fulfill the potential of this method, BusinessObjects Enterprise sends e-mails when alerts have been triggered on reports, enabling users to receive notification when measured values are out of bounds and trigger a report alert, making it simple to manage actual results in real-time. Note that a link back to the triggering report can be composed at the bottom of the screen.

→ For a description of how to create alerts in reports, **see** "Adding Alerting to Your Reports" **p. 273**.

DESTINATIONS   BusinessObjects Enterprise XI supports scheduling to destinations. You can specify a default destination, shown in Figure 27.26, for the report output on the Destination sub area. The default destination is the BusinessObjects Enterprise FRS. This is generally the preferred destination for all report instances because the report maintains its status as a managed object within BusinessObjects Enterprise. New in this release is an additional destination known as an Inbox. This also retains the instance with BusinessObjects Enterprise FRS, but is directed to individual users or groups on the system, either as a copy or a shortcut.

Figure 27.26
Destinations enable you to specify a default output location for all new scheduled instances of the report. Supported destinations include network shares, FTP, and SMTP e-mail and Inbox.

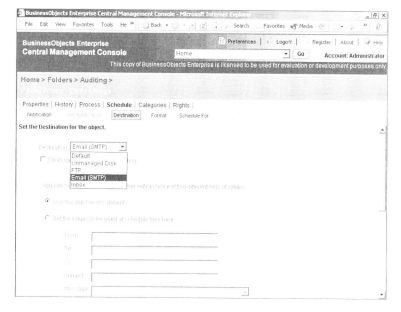

The administrator can configure BusinessObjects Enterprise to output the report's instances to a network folder using the Unmanaged Disk option, for example. BusinessObjects Enterprise also supports FTP (File Transfer Protocol), which is useful for transmitting the report instances to a remote destination, such as an archiving system. Another option, Email (SMTP) is a popular solution for distributing reports as an e-mail attachment. New in BusinessObjects Enterprise XI is the ability to schedule to Inboxes. Inboxes are managed by BusinessObjects Enterprise and are associated to an individual user's ID. A good example of this feature in action is scheduling the Monthly Profit and Loss Summary report to be sent to the Inbox of a finance officer.

NOTE

> The BusinessObjects Enterprise Job Server must have a destination enabled for destination scheduling features to work. Job Server destinations are configured from the Servers section of the CMC. Configuring Servers is discussed later in this chapter in the "Managing BusinessObject Enterprise Servers" section.

DETERMINING REPORT FILE FORMATS

Not to be confused with the format or look and feel of a report, report formats imply a file format. The Format subsection, shown in Figure 27.27, enables you to specify a default output format for the report. Keep in mind that certain cosmetic report formatting features might not be supported by every export format. Also, proprietary Crystal Report features, such as drill-down and on-demand subreports, are supported only in the native Crystal Report format. These special features are ignored when exporting a report to a non-Crystal format.

Figure 27.27
Use the Format subsection to specify the default output format for the report. Popular output formats include but are not limited to Excel, Adobe Acrobat PDF, Word, and CSV (Character-Separated Values).

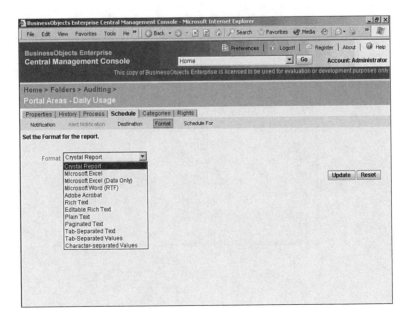

SCHEDULING FOR PARTICULAR USERS OR GROUPS

New in BusinessObject Enterprise XI is the ability to schedule a report for particular users or groups. The default setting is to schedule the instance only for the user scheduling the report. Alternatively, the user can schedule the report for specified users and/or groups.

ASSIGNING OBJECTS TO CATEGORIES

The Categories tab allows administrators to assign a report to categories or to remove a report from a category. Categories are a new feature in BusinessObjects XI. In contrast to the folder hierarchy model where the parent-child relationship is absolute, a report can be assigned to multiple categories. This allows the end user to view a collection of objects in a single view even if they exist in multiple folders, thus providing an endless number of combinations of objects.

The Categories tab has two subareas—Corporate and Personal. In the upper-right of the Categories tab is an Assign Categories button. When assigning an object to Corporate Categories, a list of all corporate categories is displayed. Moving an available category from the Available Categories list to the Assigned Categories list and clicking OK adds an object to the selected categories. When assigning an object to Personal Categories, the process is similar, except that the administrator is presented with a list of all users, as shown in Figure 27.28. When a particular user is selected from the Users list, the user's personal categories appear in the available or assigned categories list.

Figure 27.28
Reports can be assigned to both Corporate and Personal categories.

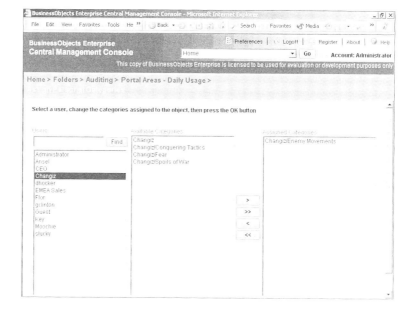

The administrator can leverage the view of personal categories for a specific report to determine if additional corporate categories might help to serve the user community in a more effective way. By using a heuristic approach to defining categories, the overall effectiveness of the BI system is improved.

OBJECT RIGHTS

The Rights tab, shown in Figure 27.29, is used to grant report access/restrictions to different users and user groups. By default, report objects inherit the same rights as their parent folder.

Figure 27.29
Report privileges are assigned on the Rights tab. The BusinessObjects Enterprise administrator can use rights to define permissible actions for each user and user group.

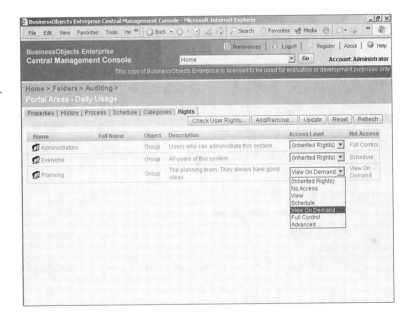

TIP

Much like managing groups is more effective than managing individual users, it's much easier to set restrictions for those groups by folder rather than by report objects themselves.

27

The Rights tab lists all the users and groups with permissions explicitly defined for the current report object. Note that if a group is not listed, permissions have not been defined for the group.

The Everyone group and the Administrators group are automatically attached to all new objects and folders in the system, and cannot be removed. Note that the rights build on each other: A lower bullet in this list includes the rights above it.

Each user or group can be assigned one of the following rights:

- **Inherited rights**—The user or group inherits the parent folder's rights. This is the default setting for all new objects.

- **No access**—The user or group is not aware of the object's existence. Note that this setting also would hide this object from any delegated administrators based on the new delegated administration feature.

- **View**—This setting enables the user or group to view instances scheduled by other users. On-demand viewing and scheduling is not available.

- **Schedule**—Allows the scheduling of the object as well as the previously listed rights.

- **View on demand**—The user or group has View rights in addition to the capability to run the report on demand.

- **Full control**—The user or group is granted all privileges except the capability to delete, hold, and release their own instances.

- **Advanced**—This option enables you to set detailed, specific permissions for the user or group, and is generally reserved for only the most complex security models.

In most organizational security models, the Everyone group is assigned the No Access privilege, or the parent folder's permissions are set to No Access for the Everyone group. Doing so prevents users from accessing an object unless access is specifically granted through another user group.

Permissions in BusinessObjects Enterprise are cumulative. In other words, the net rights of a user are equal to the sum of the permissions granted to the user. To further clarify this point, consider the permissions scenario in Table 27.1.

TABLE 27.1   DERIVING NET SALES FOLDER PERMISSIONS FROM GROUP MEMBERSHIP

Group	Folder	Assigned Rights
Everyone	Sales	No Access
Sales	Sales	Run
Management	Sales	Full Control

Because permissions are cumulative, the net rights of each user are equal to the sum of the rights assigned to each group to which the user belongs (see Table 27.2).

A user's net permissions are determined by combining the rights they inherit from their group memberships. By combining permissions derived from group memberships, BusinessObjects Enterprise enables a user to have access to the Sales folder as long as at least one of their group memberships permits it. Table 27.2 illustrates why the user Navar is allowed Full Control of the Sales folder, even though the Everyone group is denied access as defined in Table 27.1.

TABLE 27.2   GROUP MEMBERSHIPS AND THEIR NET PERMISSIONS FOR THE SALES FOLDER

User	Everyone	Sales	Management	Net Permissions
Navar	X	X	X	Full Control
Garbo	X			No Access
Kevvan	X	X		Run
Arsel	X		X	Full Control

Deciphering a user's net permissions can be tricky. In the XI release, the Check User Rights action button has been added to the object's Rights tab. This allows an administrator to select a user or group from a list and display the inherited, explicit, and net permissions for each object.

DIFFERENT OBJECT TYPES

BusinessObjects Enterprise XI includes support for several object types (refer to Figure 27.15 for a complete list). Note that each of these objects has more or fewer configuration areas depending on the inherent type of object. For instance, a program object can be scheduled, while a Word document cannot.

MANAGING FOLDERS

Without exception, each report object in BusinessObjects Enterprise must reside inside a folder. A folder in BusinessObjects Enterprise is analogous to a folder on a Windows-based workstation or server. Many objects can populate a single folder, and folders can be nested inside other folders.

In general, the BusinessObjects Enterprise folder hierarchy and report management behaves just like a standard network file system. The difference between the folder hierarchy in BusinessObjects Enterprise and a standard network folder hierarchy is that any information about the folders is stored in the BusinessObjects Enterprise system database, which can be queried to retrieve object information.

You can access folder management tasks by selecting Folders from the CMC's drop-down menu and clicking Go. The Folders screen in Figure 27.30 appears with a listing of all top-level folders in the folder hierarchy tree. You can click a folder name to see a list of all the reports the folder contains.

27

NOTE

The Users folder contains a private subfolder for each BusinessObjects Enterprise user. These personal folders store users' favorite reports, if an application such as InfoView allows for it.

Figure 27.30
The Folders screen displays all top-level BusinessObjects Enterprise folders. You can navigate to the entire folder hierarchy from here or search for particular folders.

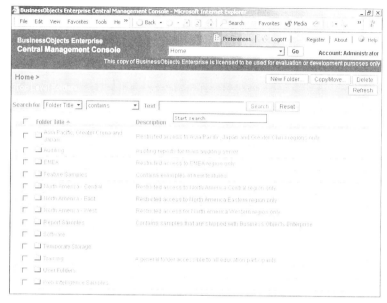

To add a new top-level folder, click the New Folder button. On the Properties tab, shown in Figure 27.31, type the folder name. The folder name can include spaces and should be descriptive for end users because they often navigate folders themselves. The BusinessObjects Enterprise administrator can also type a freeform description. Keywords can be associated with a folder to facilitate finding groups of reports based via the search mechanism. After entering a new folder name and any description or keywords, click the OK button to commit the change to the system database. Four additional tabs for configuring the folder are now available.

ADDING OBJECTS TO FOLDERS

Use the Objects tab, shown in Figure 27.32, to add new objects to the folder or copy, move, shortcut, and delete objects. Administrators often also use folders to navigate to objects via this route.

> **NOTE**
>
> The Copy function duplicates an object and assigns the duplicate object a slightly different filename on the FRS; the Shortcut function creates a duplicate report listing that points to the same filename on the FRS (similar to Windows file shortcuts). The Move function relocates the report to another folder.

Figure 27.31
From the New Folder screen you can create a new folder, add reports and subfolders, specify instance expiration limits, and set folder rights.

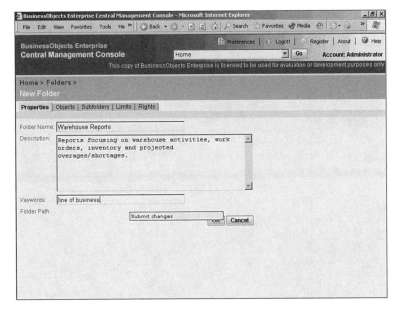

Figure 27.32
The Objects tab is used to add new reports to a folder. You can also manage existing objects from this screen.

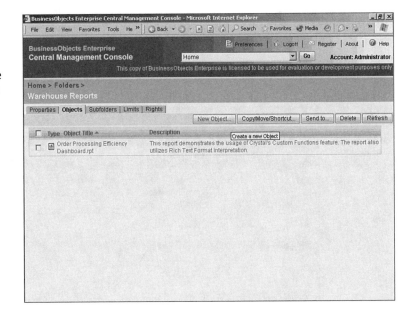

The Subfolders tab in Figure 27.33 enables you to create and manage subfolders of the current top-level folder. Subfolders are useful for subcategorizing reports. Each subfolder can also have one or more child folders. Like a file system, the nesting of folders can traverse as many levels as necessary to convey the hierarchy of an organization.

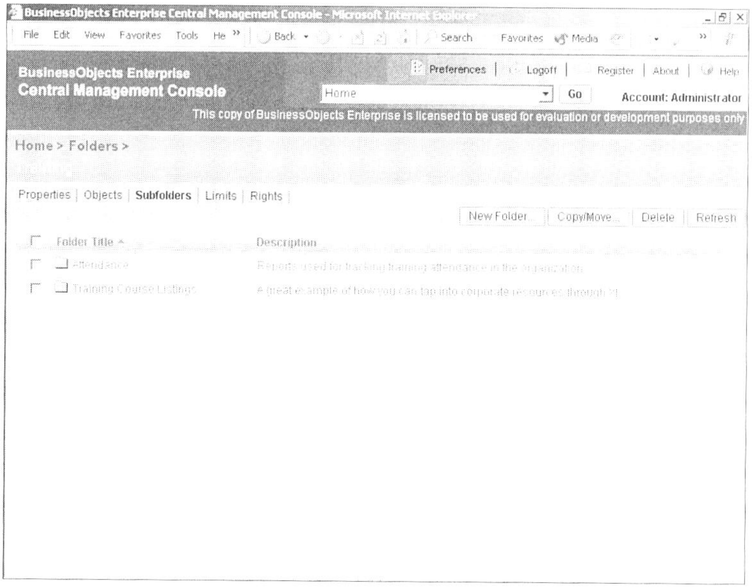

Figure 27.33
You can use the Subfolders tab to add one or more subfolders to a top-level folder. In turn, each subfolder can have one or more subfolders (nested subfolders).

FOLDER LIMITS

The Limits tab, shown in Figure 27.34, controls instance expiration limits for reports contained within the folder. Note that report object limits (if specified) take precedence over folder limits. Folder limits only take precedence over global limits.

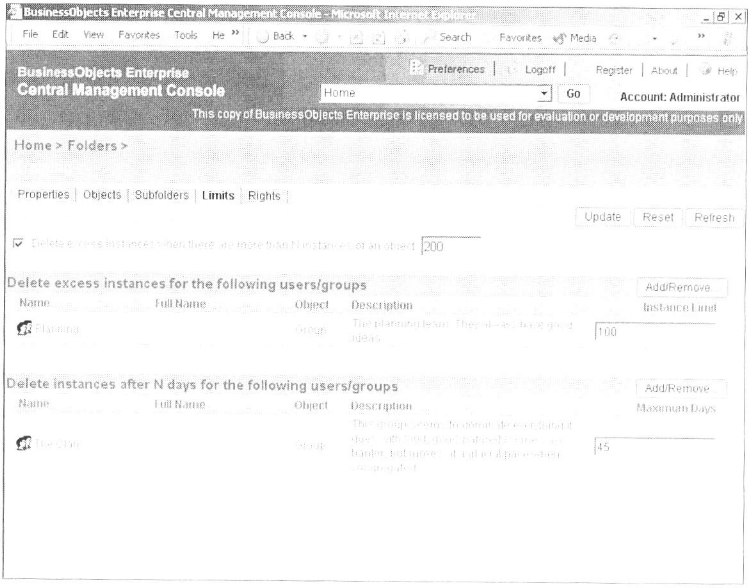

Figure 27.34
Like report objects, folders can be configured to override the global instance expiration limits.

NOTE

Report object limits take precedence over folder limits, and folder limits take precedence over global limits.

The Rights tab, shown in Figure 27.35, is used to control access to objects. The rights provided at the folder level are the same as those provided on the object level. (Refer to object rights for a definition of each option.) Instead of trying to manage rights for each individual report object, it's usually easier to secure reports by specifying rights at the folder level only. Report objects always inherit the rights of their parent folder, unless exceptions are configured at the object level shown in Figure 27.34.

Figure 27.35
Any rights specified on the Rights tab are inherited by new objects. Unless an object has object-level rights specifically configured, it inherits the rights of its parent folder.

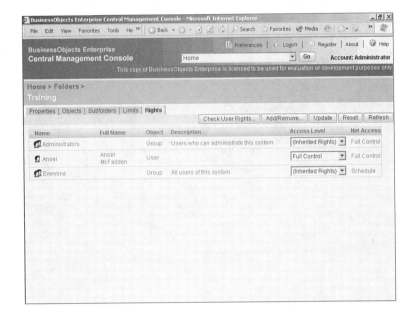

Note that with the addition of Delegated Administration, the CMC hides folders depending on folder rights. For instance, if an HR analyst logs on to the CMC, he does not see the Sales folder if the Sales folder Rights are set to disallow the HR analyst view rights. If a user doesn't have folder rights, he doesn't see any Folder information at all.

MANAGING BUSINESSOBJECTS ENTERPRISE SERVERS

BusinessObjects Enterprise is built on the BusinessObjects Enterprise Framework. At a high level, the Framework provides a communications bus between the various services or daemons that make up BusinessObjects Enterprise.

Services or daemons, in the Windows or Unix environments respectively, are compartmentalized processes that perform a specific task. The use of individual services affords fault-tolerance (service redundancy), load-balancing, scalability, and greater system reliability.

BusinessObjects Enterprise uses the generic term "server" to refer to these services or daemons; for instance "Job Server." For simplicity, this book uses the product nomenclature: that is, server. The reader should realize that servers in this case are not physical machines. Please see Chapter 25 for additional discussion on this topic.

CONFIGURING SERVERS

Managing BusinessObjects Enterprise servers is straightforward with the CMC. You can use the CMC to stop, start, restart, and manage various services from almost any location on the network.

To manage servers, select Servers from the CMC drop-down menu. Figure 27.36 shows a standard list of BusinessObjects Enterprise servers in the CMC. Buttons in the upper-right corner enable you to start, stop, restart, delete, disable, or enable any server on the framework. Additionally, the BusinessObjects Enterprise administrator can specify the order of the servers list by clicking on the column heading to specify a sort order.

Figure 27.36
All configured servers (services) in BusinessObjects Enterprise can be managed from the CMC.

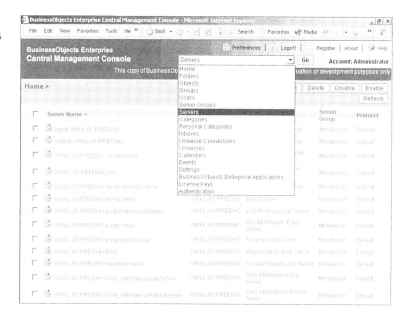

A disabled server cannot be started until it is enabled, even if the machine is rebooted. Disabling a server can be useful for, among other things, temporarily interrupting the server's availability while maintenance tasks or hardware repairs are performed.

Clicking on each server navigates to the server settings area. The Properties tab provides server-specific management controls. The metrics tab shows a wide range of information about the performance of the server and the physical machine on which it resides (see Figure 27.37). The Rights tab again provides a way for delegated administration to take place because the system administrator can allow area administrators to have access to certain servers but not others. Finally the Auditing tab, when available, determines which features on each server are audited (see Chapter 25 for a complete discussion of auditing capabilities).

Figure 27.37
Performance and server resource data is displayed on the Metrics tab for each BusinessObjects Enterprise service. This information can be used to monitor the activity of each service.

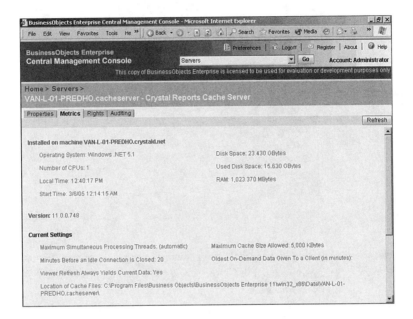

MANAGING THE CACHE SERVER

To adjust the settings for the Cache Server, click the Cache Server name from the main Servers screen. The Properties tab shown in Figure 27.38 appears for the Cache Server. The Location of Cache Files field contains the path to the actual cached report files. This path is local to the Cache Server machine. The Maximum Cache Size Allowed field specifies the maximum size of the cache directory. When the threshold has been exceeded, BusinessObjects Enterprise deletes the oldest, least-used cache files first. Preserving old cache files is not critical because missing cache files can be rebuilt on-the-fly, transparent to the user.

The Maximum Simultaneous option restricts the number of application threads that can be spawned concurrently by the cache server. A processing thread is responsible for converting .rpt pages into cache pages. In most cases, it's not necessary to adjust the automatic setting.

The Minutes Before an Idle Connection option causes the cache server to release a stale cache page from RAM to make room for other cache pages. The cache page is still physically stored on the disk, but it's no longer kept in RAM. By default, cached pages that have not been requested for 20 minutes are released from RAM and will have to be reloaded from the disk if they are requested again.

27

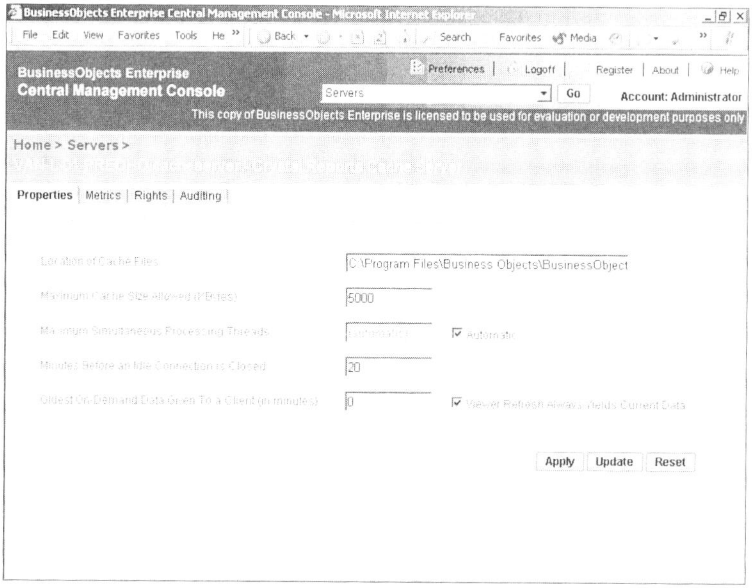

Figure 27.38
The Cache Server's Properties tab enables you to control the cache performance.

Oldest On-Demand Data controls the persistence of cached pages for on-demand reports. For example, assume that John requests an on-demand copy of the World Sales Report at 3:00 p.m. A few minutes later, at 3:04 p.m., Jane requests an on-demand copy of the World Sales Report with exactly the same parameters and record selection formula as John specified—an identical report in every way. In this case BusinessObjects Enterprise serves Jane the same cached pages that John loaded only moments before. This has the benefit of giving Jane the fastest possible response time while relieving the database and Page Server of additional processing work. By default, on-demand cached pages expire after 20 minutes.

Keep in mind that users have the option to hit the database and rerun the report by clicking the Refresh button within the report viewer. The Viewer Refresh Always Yields option causes the report to be rerun against the database, not the cached data, if the user clicks the Refresh button within the report viewer. Normally, this option should remain enabled to give users the flexibility to "freshen" the report data at their convenience.

MANAGING THE EVENT SERVER

The Event Server, as explained in Chapter 25, is designed to allow BusinessObjects Enterprise to interact with events external to the system. Events are conditions that trigger report processing to occur. The Crystal Event Server polls the system at set intervals to determine whether any configured events have been triggered. This is shown in Figure 27.39.

The File Polling Interval in Seconds option enables you to control the frequency of the Event Server's polling process. A lower value results in faster recognition of triggered events, but it also expends CPU cycles that might otherwise be devoted to more important tasks. A value of 10–60 seconds between system polls is generally acceptable.

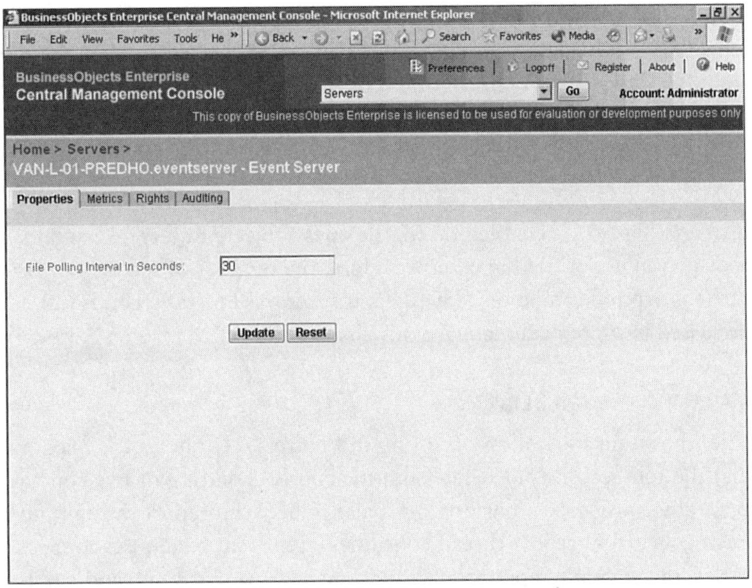

Figure 27.39
The Event Server periodically polls the system to check for triggered events. Setting an unnecessarily short poll interval value could negatively affect system performance.

MANAGING THE PAGE SERVER

The Page Server handles on-demand report requests. The Properties tab of the Page Server has several options for controlling Page Server performance, as shown in Figure 27.40. The Maximum Simultaneous Processing Threads setting controls the maximum number of concurrent application threads allowed. On-demand reports consume a minimum of one processing thread; if all available threads are busy, BusinessObjects Enterprise queues any excess threads for processing on a first-come, first-served basis.

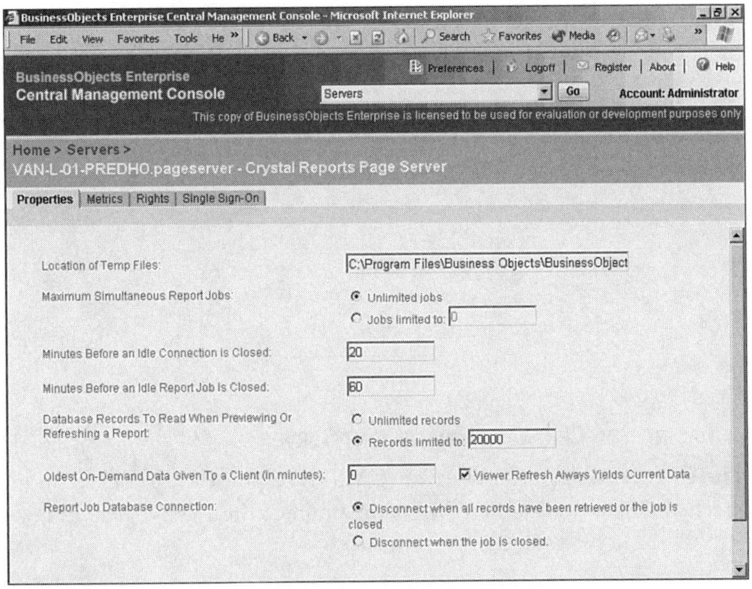

Figure 27.40
The Crystal Page Server is responsible for processing on-demand report requests.

27

The Minutes Before an Idle Connection Is Closed option affects the persistence of open Page Server jobs. For example, if a user starts to view an on-demand report and walks away from her desk without closing the report viewer, the job is left open until the specified period of inactivity has passed. If the user does not request any new pages within the default 20-minute window, the job is closed. New page or drill-down requests reset the 20-minute job expiration timer.

If Single Sign-on is enabled on the BusinessObjects Enterprise system, a Single Sign-on tab is displayed under the Page Server. Here, the number of seconds before the contents of the cache is expired can be set. The default setting is 86,400 seconds (60 days). Single sign-on is discussed in more detail later in this chapter in the "Managing Authentication" section.

MANAGING THE JOB SERVERS

The Maximum Jobs Allowed setting in Figure 27.41 affects the maximum number of reports that the Job Server can execute simultaneously. A setting of five concurrent report jobs is generally considered a harmonious balance between report throughput and server resources. Each concurrent report thread consumes significant system resources, not only in CPU cycles, but also in temporary disk space use, RAM overhead, and database resources. A robust multiprocessor machine with 2GB of RAM can comfortably process 10 jobs simultaneously. However, most servers run best with five or fewer concurrent jobs.

Figure 27.41
The Job Server processes scheduled jobs only. You can specify the number of jobs the Job Server can simultaneously process.

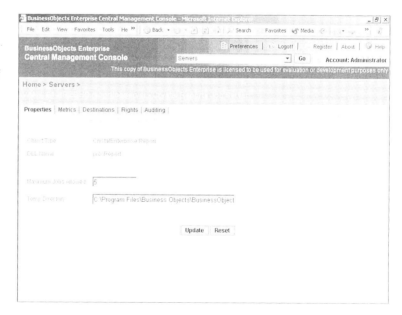

MANAGING THE CENTRAL MANAGEMENT SERVER

The Central Management Server (CMS) is responsible for object and user security as well as scheduling of jobs. The CMS is the brain of BusinessObjects Enterprise.

In addition to its role in enforcing object permissions, the CMS monitors and records the processing status of every scheduled job. The Properties tab of the CMS displays a listing of all currently connected users, as well as the number of sessions opened by each user ID (see Figure 27.42). Note that most of the time, a user ID has only one session open. However, it's possible for two people to log in with the same user ID from different computers, in which case the user ID would reflect two concurrent sessions. Each session consumes a license until the user logs off, or the session is released after 20 minutes of inactivity.

Figure 27.42
The CMS handles object and user security, as well as management of report instances.

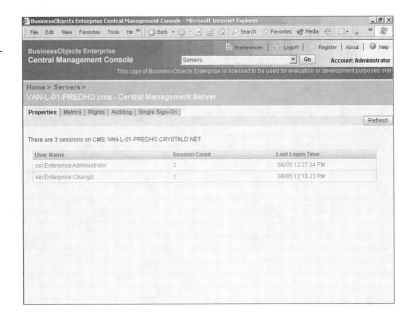

Possibly the most critical feature of the CMS is clustering. BusinessObjects Enterprise includes out-of-the-box clustering capability for the CMS. This means that without any special hardware, two physical CMS servers can be clustered together. If one becomes unavailable, the other CMS supports authentication requests and scheduling tasks. CMS clustering is reviewed in the "Managing BusinessObjects Enterprise System Settings" section of this chapter.

MANAGING THE INPUT/OUTPUT FILE REPOSITORY SERVERS

File Repository Servers (FRS) are services that manage the storage and retrieval of report files from the file system. BusinessObjects Enterprise has an Input FRS and an Output FRS. Both FRS systems store report files using a proprietary naming convention. For example, the report template for the World Sales Report might be named 73422e16f293d0.rpt by the Input FRS. Any instances of the World Sales Report would be assigned a similarly cryptic name by the Output FRS. Both FRS servers store name translation information in the CMS system database, enabling users to see the true English name of a report instead of the cryptic file system name.

27

The Properties tab in Figure 27.43 for the Input and Output FRS has two configuration options. The Root Directory field stores the path of the physical file repository on the server's file system. This path is local to the FRS server. The Input FRS stores .rpt templates in one folder, whereas the Output FRS stores .rpt instances in another folder. Both servers also have a Maximum Idle Time option that controls the amount of time that an idle .rpt file remains cached in the FRS memory. When the idle time expires, the .rpt files are dropped from the memory cache and must be loaded from disk if required again.

Figure 27.43
The Input and Output File Repository Servers have the same Properties tab settings. Note that a special tab called Active Files displays any .rpt files currently in the memory cache.

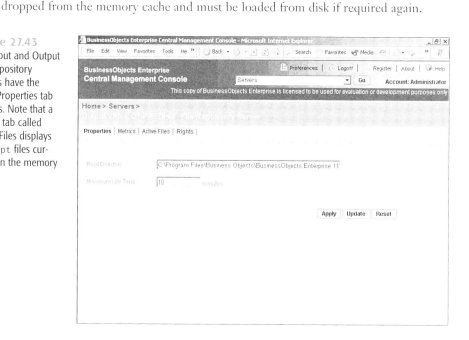

MANAGING SERVER GROUPS

A large BusinessObjects Enterprise deployment can have several physical Page and Job Servers spread over a wide area network. Some of the servers might have more processing power than others, and some might be located in specific regions such as San Francisco and New York. In multiple-server environments, it's often advantageous to categorize servers into specific groups. Server groups are helpful for managing processing just as user groups help manage permissions.

After a server group has been created, the BusinessObjects Enterprise administrator can configure reports to process on specific server groups. For example, the CEO's personal reports could be configured to execute on a server group that contains one or more high-powered Job/Page Servers. This would ensure that the CEO's reports always process on the most powerful servers available, and thereby finish running as quickly as possible. Without server groups, the CEO's reports might get routed to a slower Job/Page Server, and the CEO would end up spending more time than necessary waiting for critical information. Server groups are also useful for forcing reports to execute on a Job/Page Server that is in close proximity to the report's database server.

To create a server group, select Server Groups from the drop-down menu in the CMC. Click New Server Group, and then type the name of the server group in the Server Group Name field. An optional Description for the server group can also be entered. Click the OK button to add the new server group to BusinessObjects Enterprise. Figure 27.44 shows a server group.

Figure 27.44
Server groups are configured like user groups. You can create groups and add servers to them. A server can reside in more than one group, and a group can also have several sub-groups.

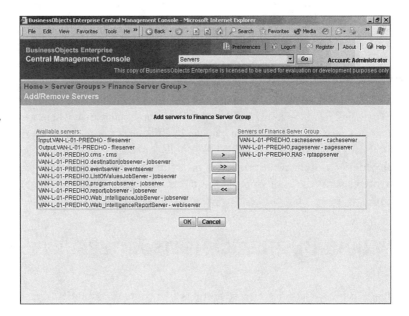

Managing Calendars

The predecessor to BusinessObjects Enterprise included a very popular feature for scheduled processing: business calendars. Simply put, this feature allows processing to take place based on specific calendars. Calendars can be configured by administrators and then selected by users for scheduling purposes.

Click on the *Calendars* icon from the home page of the CMC to enter the Calendars area.

> **NOTE**
>
> The Calendars area has a rights button at the upper right to set delegated administration privileges. Setting permissions here controls access to this area in the CMC.

You can add new calendars or manage current calendars here. Like most objects in BusinessObjects Enterprise, you see a simple *Properties* tab and *Rights* tab, which operate like the other tabs of those titles. The *Dates* tab, however, provides the heart of the functionality by allowing the administrator to configure a calendar. By clicking on months to enter that month, then clicking on days to select/de-select a day, the administrator sets days on which processing should occur. By simply clicking on a day you change the current setting, clicking on a row or column header selects that area. The drop-down at the top also exposes other calendar configuration types to allow tailoring to another calendaring option—for instance, a quarterly fiscal calendar with a set alternating number of weeks in a "fiscal month" that does not align with calendar months. That way you could configure a financial report to run on the first day of every quarter or fiscal month, for instance.

After calendars are configured, the administrator or end users would schedule reports using the Calendar option from the scheduling page.

MANAGING EVENTS

Administrators must first set up events before objects can be scheduled against them. The Events link from the home page navigates to the Events area, where new events can be added. There are three types of events. The File event polls for a certain file in a certain location to appear. The Schedule event polls for success or failure of another scheduled object. The custom event provides a programmatic hook that can be triggered by a program written against the SDK to provide a programmatic interface into the scheduling system. Once created, events can be used for scheduling as per the previous section.

MANAGING BUSINESSOBJECTS ENTERPRISE SYSTEM SETTINGS

The BusinessObjects Enterprise Settings area contains a number of system wide settings that aren't specific to a particular server. Information on system properties, metrics, clustering, instance limits, and user rights are available in this section. To configure system settings, select Settings from the Crystal drop-down menu in the CMC.

MANAGING AUTHENTICATION

There are two key components to managing BusinessObjects Enterprise authentication:

- Licensing
- Authentication

The first one is a less technical topic but still important to understand. The second is discussed in subsequent sections.

MANAGING LICENSING

The License Keys tab displays important information about each license key (see Figure 27.45). Highlight a license key to display specific information about the key. BusinessObjects Enterprise supports three types of licensing: named licenses, concurrent licenses, and processor licenses.

Figure 27.45
The License Keys tab provides information about each of the BusinessObjects Enterprise license keys.

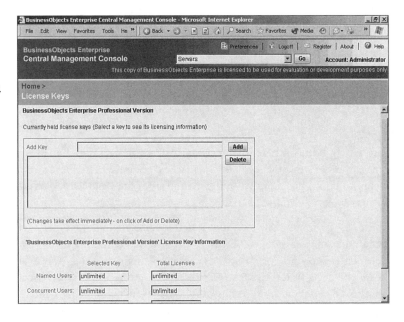

> **NOTE**
>
> The license certificate keys determine the number and type of licenses available (name user or concurrent access). During the initial install of BusinessObjects Enterprise, a license key was entered. Additional licenses can be added to BusinessObjects Enterprise from the License Keys tab on the Authentication section of the CMC.

BusinessObjects Enterprise gives you the flexibility to mix and match named and concurrent license types. *Named licenses* are assigned to specific users. Any number of named licenses can be simultaneously logged in to the system.

Concurrent licenses permit an unlimited number of named users to be added to the BusinessObjects Enterprise, but only a certain number of those users can access the system simultaneously.

Processor licenses enable an unlimited number of both named and concurrent users for a specific processor. Processor licenses are most efficient in high-powered server environments where the server CPU is robust enough to support a large number of concurrent users.

It's best to contact Business Objects and discuss the optimum licensing strategy for your organization.

MANAGING AUTHENTICATION

The different types of authentication that can be leveraged with BusinessObjects Enterprise are also found under the Authorization portion of the CMC.

BusinessObjects Enterprise provides several authentication models for providing secure report access, including Native BusinessObjects Enterprise authentication, Windows NT

Authentication, Active Directory authentication, and LDAP authentication. BusinessObjects Enterprise supports single sign-on for both the Windows NT and Active Directory methods, so users won't have to constantly enter credentials after exiting and reentering the system.

The reason BusinessObjects Enterprise supports more security models than its own is simple: If an IT organization has already implemented an existing security model, it is more efficient to leverage existing entities such as user accounts and passwords.

Fortunately, none of these options is mutually exclusive; they can all be used simultaneously. This can cause some management headaches, so proceed with caution. Every topic in this chapter up until this point, with the exception of the Page Server, has used native BusinessObjects Enterprise security as an example.

This does not imply that if Windows Active Directory authentication is used, for example, that administration is done exclusively from Active Directory. It simply implies that objects such as user accounts and passwords can be maintained within Active Directory, yet BusinessObjects Enterprise feeds off those existing accounts when users try to retrieve reports. The configuration of BusinessObjects Enterprise groups and objects, as well as relevant restrictions to those objects, are still created and configured from the CMC, in the same way that this chapter has shown. This is reviewed in greater detail later.

To configure system authentication settings, select Authentication from the drop-down menu in the CMC.

BUSINESSOBJECTS ENTERPRISE AUTHENTICATION   BusinessObjects Enterprise provides its own native security model. This means that BusinessObjects Enterprise is not dependent on a foreign, third-party security database to configure and restrict access to any system function, object, or entity. The BusinessObjects Enterprise authentication model is the default model. To leverage another security database, select the appropriate tab.

Selecting the Enterprise tab, shown in Figure 27.46, enables you to enforce password rules when using BusinessObjects Enterprise authentication. You can use this tab to control the frequency that users are forced to change their passwords, as well as the length of the passwords and whether or not the password must contain mixed-case letters.

In general, the password options offered are similar to those provided by the Windows NT and Solaris operating systems.

DIRECTORY SERVER AUTHENTICATION THROUGH LDAP   Selecting the LDAP tab enables a system administrator to configure LDAP connectivity to a directory server, as shown in Figure 27.47. LDAP (Lightweight Directory Access Protocol) enables a network administrator to maintain a central directory server for managing user access to a variety of applications and operating systems. BusinessObjects Enterprise can be configured to work with a variety of directory servers via LDAP. BusinessObjects Enterprise support for LDAP was designed and tested to the LDAP version 3 specification.

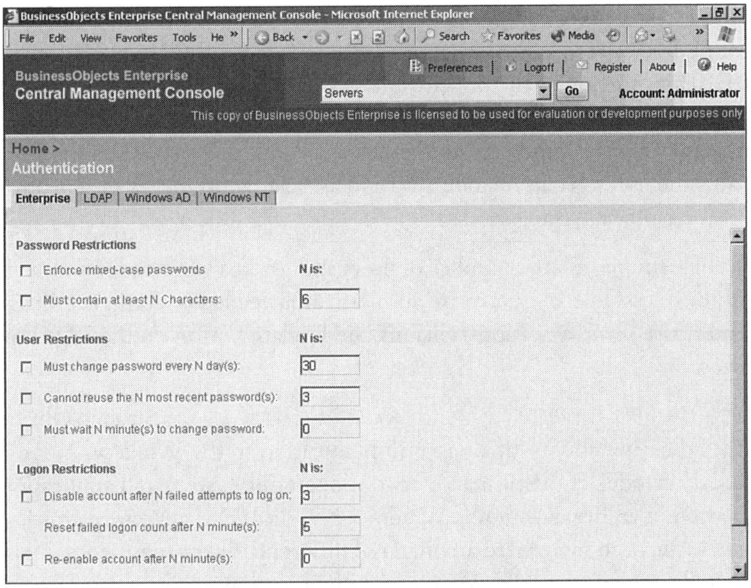

Figure 27.46
You can set BusinessObjects Enterprise password expiration rules on the Enterprise tab. This tab only applies to the BusinessObjects Enterprise native authentication method, not LDAP or Windows NT.

Figure 27.47
Configuring LDAP enables Business-Objects Enterprise to connect to a Directory server, such as Netscape iPlanet, and leverage existing usernames and pass-words.

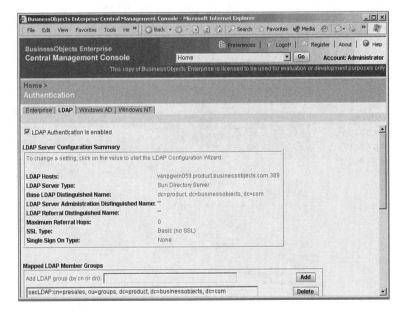

BusinessObjects Enterprise can tie into an LDAP server for User and Group information. Folder and Object permissions (that is, authorization) are still defined within BusinessObjects Enterprise. When BusinessObjects Enterprise is tied to an LDAP server, equivalent BusinessObjects Enterprise accounts are either created, if they don't already exist, or aliased if they do exist. The BusinessObjects Enterprise system must have references to users and groups inside the system such that report object restrictions can be configured. User passwords are not stored in BusinessObjects Enterprise. When using LDAP, it's the job of the directory server to verify passwords. Any time a user attempts to access BusinessObjects Enterprise resources, a password confirmation request is sent to the directory server. If the user authenticates properly, BusinessObjects Enterprise then compares the user's group membership and associated privileges assigned to those groups in BusinessObjects Enterprise.

If, for example, a large number of users and groups were added to the directory server and the BusinessObjects Enterprise administrator needed to configure BusinessObjects Enterprise security settings, clicking the Update button on the LDAP page forces synchronization.

WINDOWS NT OR ACTIVE DIRECTORY AUTHENTICATION   BusinessObjects Enterprise provides the capability to tie in user authentication to the Windows NT or Active Directory security model. If the primary network operating system and application authentication method in an organization is Windows NT or Active Directory, this feature can be a useful timesaver. Although there are material differences between the methods, they are similar enough to be discussed as Windows authentication.

Windows authentication can be configured from the Windows AD or NT tabs, as shown in Figure 27.48. To enable Windows authentication, select the Is Enabled option. Enter the name of the Default Domain. The default domain should be the same domain that contains the majority of the Windows users that will also be BusinessObjects Enterprise end users.

Figure 27.48
Selecting the Windows AD tab enables you to configure BusinessObjects Enterprise to support Active Directory authentication.

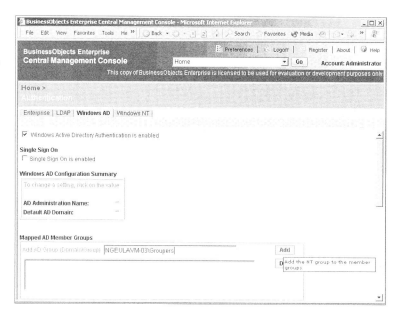

Users who do not have accounts in the specified default domain need to specify their domain name each time they log in to BusinessObjects Enterprise.

The Mapped Member Groups section enables specification of which Windows user groups are permitted to access BusinessObjects Enterprise. Any Windows users who belong to mapped Windows member groups are able to log in to BusinessObjects Enterprise using single sign on.

Users who are not a member of at least one mapped Windows group will not be able to access BusinessObjects Enterprise unless the administrator has specifically created a BusinessObjects Enterprise user ID for them in the CMC. To import a new Windows group to BusinessObjects Enterprise, type in the name of the Windows group (preceded by the group's domain or machine name) and click the Add button. Remember to click the Update button when you're finished adding or removing Windows groups.

The bottom of the Windows tab has two additional options for configuring NT integration. Assign Each Added Windows Alias to an Account with the Same Name forces BusinessObjects Enterprise to match imported Windows usernames with existing BusinessObjects Enterprise usernames. If BusinessObjects Enterprise already has a username with the same name as an incoming Windows username, the two usernames are mapped to each other so that a duplicate account name is not created. In other words, an alias is created.

On the other hand, the Create a New Account for Every Added Windows Alias option causes BusinessObjects Enterprise to add a new BusinessObjects Enterprise username for each incoming Windows username. If a duplicate username exists in BusinessObjects Enterprise, an alias is not created; instead, a new username is created with a slightly different name. When the group is added, navigate to the Manage Groups section of the CMC. Note that \\NGEULAVM-03\RUHI is now listed as a group within BusinessObjects Enterprise. Selecting this user group allows access to the same options as a native BusinessObjects Enterprise group.

Managing Crystal Applications

BusinessObjects Enterprise allows for the configuration of applications via a central location which simplifies system administration. For instance, setting default colors or preferences (even setting a custom logo for InfoView!) can be accomplished from this location. As more applications, such as the Ad-Hoc application, are installed, these applications also add to this section.

By default, the InfoView area appears to allow configuration of the InfoView's preferences (see Chapter 23, "Introduction to BusinessObjects Enterprise," for more information on the Web Desktop, and Chapter 21, "Using Reports Explorer for Ad Hoc Web Reporting and Microsoft Integration," for more information on the ad hoc application). These settings become global for this installation.

Using the Central Configuration Manager

The Central Configuration Manager (CCM) is a Windows-based tool installed on the BusinessObjects Enterprise server by default (see Figure 27.49). A CCM script (ccm.sh) is also available for the Unix version of BusinessObjects Enterprise. Although the "interface" discussion that follows does not apply to the ccm.sh, all the capabilities are present and can be accessed. Please refer to your BusinessObjects Enterprise documentation for specific command-line options.

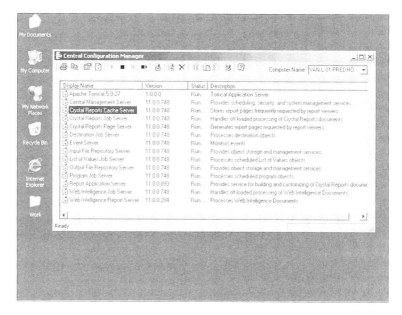

Figure 27.49
The CCM enables you to restart and configure BusinessObjects services.

The BusinessObjects Enterprise administrator can use the Central Configuration Manager to start and stop BusinessObjects Services on the local machine or remote machines, as well as configure the CMS database and Audit database, and add and register new servers to the Framework.

You can use the CCM to administer several BusinessObjects Enterprise servers remotely by changing the computer name.

To start the CCM, click Start, Programs, BusinessObjects XI, BusinessObjects Enterprise, and Central Configuration Manager. When the CCM loads, it displays a list of all BusinessObjects Enterprise services running on the current machine, as well as the World Wide Web Publishing Service and associated services if the machine runs Microsoft IIS. The name of the current machine is indicated in the upper-right corner of the CCM. To administer another BusinessObjects Enterprise server, type in a new server name and press Enter. The drop-down box of server names maintains a list of each server visited. A BusinessObjects Enterprise administrator can also click the Browse for Computer icon to select a different machine.

To start, stop, pause, or restart Crystal services, highlight a service name, and then click the appropriate icon at the top of the screen. Note that you can also select several Crystal services at once by using the Shift or Ctrl select methods. One interesting fact about the CCM is the use of command-line options to start various BusinessObjects Enterprise servers. To view the command line used to start up a given server, such as the Web Component Server, right-click the service name and choose Properties. Notice that the dialog title Command Line shows the server startup command as well as potential parameters supplied to the server service.

Starting up servers from a command line can be a useful approach to solving or trouble-shooting problems that might arise. More will be discussed on server startup command lines later.

To view the properties of a service, right-click on the service and select Properties from the drop-down menu. Note that the BusinessObjects Enterprise administrator must stop the service first to make changes to the service's properties. From the Properties dialog, the BusinessObjects Enterprise administrator can change the NT account used to run the service, and also view the service's dependencies. Depending on the service, the administrator might also be able to specify a communication port, although the default port is normally acceptable.

TIP

> In order for a BusinessObjects service to utilize network resources, such as a network printer, the service must be running under a valid network account with rights to utilize that resource.

The BusinessObjects Enterprise administrator can also use the CCM to add or remove instances of a service. To remove a service, highlight the service name, and then click the delete icon at the top of the screen. To add a new instance of a service, click the Add Server icon. A wizard walks you through the steps of adding the new service.

CONFIGURING CMS CLUSTERING FROM THE CONFIGURATION MANAGER

The CCM is also the location where the BusinessObjects Enterprise CMS can be clustered. Clustering in BusinessObjects Enterprise does not require any special hardware; it's software based. The CMS is the only server for which clustering is required because other servers, such as the Job Server, are managed from the CMS.

BusinessObjects Enterprise could have two or more physical Job Servers and the CMS will actively load balance report processing tasks between those servers. If a Job Server fails, that CMS no longer sends report processing requests to that physical server.

As for CMS clustering, a few things are required for it to work:

- The CMS System database must be in a supported format such as Microsoft SQL Server. MSDE is not sufficient.

27

- Multiple CMS servers must be available.

- All CMS servers must connect to the same CMS database, and the connectivity options to the database must be identical.

- Multihomed CMS servers are supported, but special consideration is required. Refer to the BusinessObjects Enterprise admin guide for more information on multihomed server support.

Figure 27.50
After a service has been stopped, the administrator can modify the service properties, such as CMS cluster member-ship.

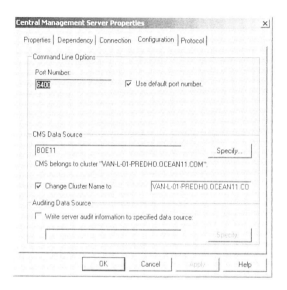

After ensuring the system is properly configured and a backup of the CMS system database is complete, open the CCM, right-click on the CMS service, and choose Properties. Select the Configuration tab and check the Enable CMS Clustering box. The Clustering Wizard walks through the steps required to complete the CMS cluster. Afterward, the cluster name can be changed.

NOTE

> BusinessObjects Enterprise refers to CMS clusters with the server name of the first server in the cluster preceded by the @ symbol. For example, @Era0441863 would be a CMS cluster name.

Command-line options can be specified by right-clicking the services, and then changing the command line. Note that the server must be stopped first.

NOTE

> Refer to the Crystal Enterprise Admin guide for a complete listing of all the various server command-line arguments that can be leveraged at server startup.

PART VI

CUSTOMIZED REPORT DISTRIBUTION— USING CRYSTAL REPORTS' COMPONENTS

CHAPTER **28**

JAVA REPORTING COMPONENTS

In this chapter

OVERVIEW OF THE CRYSTAL REPORTS JAVA REPORTING COMPONENT

Business Objects has had a commitment to Java developers for quite some time. Crystal Reports version 9 included a Java edition of the Report Application Server Software Development Kit (SDK), and Crystal Enterprise version 8.5 had a Java edition of the Crystal Enterprise SDK. Both of these solutions consisted of a processing tier of non–Java-based services and then an application tier of Java-based objects that acted as the entry point to those services. The theme here was around multi-tier, large-scale, enterprise applications. This might sound quite natural to some Java developers, who would argue that's what Java is for.

In the version 11 suite of products, the Report Application Server and corresponding Java SDK have been moved out of the Crystal Reports product line and into the BusinessObjects Enterprise product line. This makes it clear that all servers are part of the BusinessObjects Enterprise offering. However, without any other changes this would leave the Crystal Reports product without any Java-based developer components. Because developers have always been important to Business Objects—especially Java developers—the Business Objects folks have spent a significant amount of time building a new offering in version 11 for Java developers: the Crystal Reports Java Reporting Component.

The key word in the name of the Java Reporting Component is "component". There is a clear distinction between the Crystal Reports–based developer solutions and the Crystal Enterprise–based developer solutions. This is based around the distinction between components and servers. Crystal Reports provides reporting components and BusinessObjects Enterprise provides reporting servers. The following sections describe some of the key differences between components and servers.

COMPONENTS RUN ON THE WEB APPLICATION SERVER

Components are self-contained and reside on the Web application tier. They are single tier in that there is no separation between the programmatic interface and the report processing. Although they can be run on multiple machines in a Web application server farm, they themselves are individual components and have no built-in mechanism to load balance or share state.

Although this kind of deployment architecture is initially attractive to many Java developers, many eventually find that the report processing degrades the performance of the Web application server to an unsatisfactory level. Keep in mind the size of your user audience before deciding to do all report processing on the Web tier.

COMPONENTS ARE GENERALLY LESS SCALABLE

Although the actual report processing of a single report is generally done just as fast with a component as it is done with a server, the capability to scale the components differs. Although a farm can be created, components running on different machines are not aware of each other and thus don't have the smarts to figure out which component is least busy or has some information that is needed by another server. In general, the servers provide a more scalable, extensible solution for high-volume reporting. Obviously, cost can be a factor because the server solutions have higher licensing costs, so do your research about the product capabilities before you start development.

COMPONENTS ARE 100% PURE JAVA

Besides product line differentiation, the other reason Business Objects created the Java Reporting Component was so it would have a 100% pure Java reporting engine. Although the server solutions have a pure Java SDK, the Java Reporting Component consists entirely of native Java code. This is attractive to both Java purists and also partners who embed Crystal Reports technology inside Java-based applications, and finally for customers wanting to deploy a reporting component on a Unix platform. Providing a 100% pure Java reporting engine means Business Objects rewrote a portion of the Crystal Reports engine into Java. Because this was not a total port of the functionality, some reporting features are not available. However, in practical terms, most reports off standard relational data will run just fine.

UNDERSTANDING THE JAVA REPORTING COMPONENTS ARCHITECTURE

Now that you know why Business Objects created the Java Reporting Component and how it differs from some of the server solutions, you will move on to learning more about the components. The Java Reporting Component has three main pieces to it, as shown here:

- A report engine
- Report viewer controls
- Helper tag libraries

The report engine is the component that processes the reports. Its job is to load the report template (.rpt file), run the query to the data source, process the report's pages, and communicate with the report viewer controls to provide the information they need to render the reports. The main report viewer is an HTML viewer control that is used to display the report's output in JSP pages or servlets. The other viewer control is used to view the reports in other formats such as Rich Text Format (RTF) or PDF. Finally, there are helper tag libraries that make the process of using the report viewers easier by wrapping up their logic into a simple tag that can be inserted into JSP pages. Also of note is that the Java Reporting Component has integration with both Borland JBuilder and BEA WebLogic; more will be discussed on what this integration provides later in this chapter.

From an architecture point of view, all these components reside on the Java application server. The officially supported application servers are

- BEA WebLogic 7 (SP1)
- BEA WebLogic 8.1

28

- IBM WebSphere 5.0 (Fix-pack 2)
- Tomcat 4.1.27

> If the exact application server or version of application server you are targeting is not listed here, it does not necessarily mean that the Java Reporting Component will not work there. It just means that it was not one of the configurations explicitly tested by Business Objects, and although not "officially supported," chances are you will be able to use it. If you are unsure, contact Business Objects to see if they are aware of any issues with that particular application server. There are customers using other application servers such as JBoss in production today.

Although the Java Reporting Component comes with some JSP and servlet samples, the actual API is simply raw Java classes. These classes can be used inside of JSPs, servlets, EJBs, or other Web-based technologies. The advantage here is that there is no dependency on any particular version of the J2EE specifications such as servlets or struts. You might have noticed that desktop applications have not been mentioned thus far. This is because there is not currently a desktop viewer control (that is, based on the AWT or Swing frameworks). Because the viewer controls that exist are dependent on a Web framework being in place—they require servlet-based objects in order to work—there is currently no way to view reports in desktop applications. At the time of this writing, Business Objects has expressed interest in producing a desktop report viewer for the Java world at some point in the future. Check back with the company if you're interested. In the meantime, a good solution for delivering reports inside desktop applications is to host a Web browser applet inside of a Java form.

DIFFERENCES WITH THE JAVA REPORTING ENGINE

Although there are clear advantages to having a 100% pure Java reporting engine, the developers at Business Objects had to rewrite it from scratch. Anytime a large software component such as the Crystal Reports engine is rewritten, there are bound to be some differences, at least in the first version. Some of those differences are conscious decisions made by Business Objects to limit the scope of the development to meet the target release date. Other differences surface because of development platform differences: Java versus native Windows. The result is that some features are not currently supported by the report processing engine included with the Java Reporting Component. The following sections address some of these issues.

SUPPORTED FILE FORMATS

The first and most important limitation is that only version 9, 10, and 11 report files are supported. This doesn't mean that reports designed in version 8.5 or earlier are useless, but it does mean they have to be converted to version 9. To make this process easier, you can download a Report Conversion Utility from the Business Objects website. It can open up reports in batch, make any necessary changes, and save them into a version 9/10/XI file format. New reports can be created using the standard Crystal Reports XI designer.

TIP

> The file format has not had any major changes between version 9, 10, and XI of Crystal Reports. If you have report files created in version 11, you can generally use them in version 9 applications.

SUPPORT FOR USER FUNCTION LIBRARIES IN VERSION XI OF THE JAVA REPORTING COMPONENTS

Historically, the ability to define your own functions that extend the power of the Crystal Report's formula language has been available through the ability to write your own COM libraries that can be utilized within the report's formula designer. Such functionality could be implemented by writing your own dll in any COM development environment, such as C++ and Visual Basic.

As of version 11 of the report designer component, this functionality can now be built and leveraged inside the Java report engine api. This is accomplished by implementing a class that exposes methods consumed by the Crystal Report.

NOTE

> Keep in mind that inside one report there can only be one flavor of the UFL implementation, meaning you can not utilize both COM and Java user function libraries.

Example creating a user defined function:

```
public class UserFunction1 implements FormulaFunction
import com.crystaldecisions.reports.formulas.*;
import com.crystaldecisions.reports.common.value.*;
public FormulaValue evaluate (FormulaValueReference[] arguments) throws
FormulaFunctionCallException
{
    String strArg0 = ((StringValue)arguments[0].getFormulaValue()).getString();
    String string1 = "Input entered: " + strArg0;
    FormulaValue formulaVal = StringValue.fromString(string1);
    return formulaVal;
}
}
```

In the preceding example, the function simply returns a string value supplied as an argument to the calling function inside the formula workshop. All user defined functions appear under additional function tree items inside the formula editor.

THE JAVA REPORTING ENGINE USES JDBC

Another difference related to the Java platform is the way queries are run against the database. Although the Windows world has many different data access technologies, Java has

28

just one: Java Data Base Connectivity (JDBC). Previously, Crystal Reports did not support JDBC, but a new JDBC driver is available for version 11 as a website download.

> At the time of this writing, the version 11 JDBC driver was not yet available but should be available for download shortly from the Business Objects Download Center found at http://www.businessobjects.com/products/downloadcenter/. Check the website for a status update.

For any new reports that you develop, choosing JDBC is generally the best approach. You will save yourself time and effort this way. The Crystal Reports JDBC driver shows up as "JDBC (JNDI)" in the Crystal Reports data explorer when creating a new report. It has two ways to connect to a data source: through a JDBC URL or a JNDI reference. This can be problematic at times because there are several steps involved in setting up your environment for JDBC access. Make sure you take your time going through the steps and double-check the changes you are making.

When connecting via a JDBC URL, you need to specify two items:

- **Connection URL**—a standard JDBC URL that specifies a data source
- **Database classname**—the fully qualified classname of the JDBC driver

The best way to figure out what these two values should be is to consult the documentation for the JDBC driver you'd like to use. The following bullets provide sample connection information for connecting to SQL Server using the SQL Server JDBC Driver. Figure 28.1 shows this information being used from the Crystal Reports designer.

- **Connection URL**—jdbc:microsoft:sqlserver://abc:1433 (where *abc* is the name of the server running on port 1433)
- **Database classname**—com.microsoft.jdbc.sqlserver.SQLServerDriver

Figure 28.1
Connect to a JDBC data source through the Crystal Reports designer.

Before you try to connect, you need to modify a configuration file. This file, `CRDB_JavaServer.ini`, can be found at the following location:

```
\Program Files\Common Files\Crystal Decisions\2.5\bin\
```

You should make the following changes:

- Set `PATH` to where your Java Runtime Environment (JRE) is, for example, `C:\jdk1.4\bin`.

- Set `CLASSPATH` to the location of the JDBC driver you want to use, and also include `C:\Program Files\Common Files\Crystal Decisions\2.5\bin\CRDBJavaServer.jar`.

- Set `IORFileLocation` to a location where the driver can write temporary files; make sure this location exists.

The other method of connecting to JDBC is through a JNDI reference. *JNDI (Java Naming and Directory Interface)* is a Java standard around resolving names and locations to resources in complex environments. In the case of the Crystal Reports JDBC driver, it is used to store JDBC connection strings. Connecting via JNDI has a few key benefits. First, the person creating the reports doesn't need to know the exact server name; he only needs to know an "alias" given to it in JNDI such as "FinanceData". Second, if that connection information were to change, no report change would be needed, only a change in the JNDI directory. Lastly, JNDI supports connection pooling which the Crystal Reports JDBC driver can take advantage of. As a recommendation, if you have an available JNDI server, use it to define all your database connections; this will save you time and effort later on.

Any existing reports you deliver through the Java Reporting Component will be converted on-the-fly to JDBC. This conversion is configurable using JNDI. To set up a configuration mapping, register a JDBC connection in a JNDI directory under the same name as the existing report's data source. For example, an existing report is connecting via ODBC to Oracle. With the same name as the ODBC DSN name, create a JNDI entry for a JDBC connection to the same Oracle server. When the report is run, it looks to JNDI and resolves the connection to the Oracle server.

CONFIGURING THE APPLICATION SERVER

Although building Web applications in Java is meant to be independent of application servers, the J2EE standard tends to be interpreted differently for each vendor's application server. Because of this, each application server has a different way of performing Web application configuration. The general rule is that there is a folder structure like this:

```
\webApplicationFolder
    \WEB-INF
        web.xml
        \lib
        \classes
```

28

When setting up the Java Reporting Component for a given Web application, the following steps are required:

- Copy all the Java Reporting Component .jar files from `C:\Program Files\Common Files\Crystal Decisions\2.5\java\lib` into the lib folder.

- Copy all the third-party .jar files from `C:\Program Files\Common Files\Crystal Decisions\2.5\java\lib\external` into the lib folder.

- Copy CrystalReportEngine-config.xml from `C:\Program Files\Common Files\Crystal Decisions\2.5\java` to the classes folder.

- Copy the crystalreportviewer11 folder from `C:\Program Files\Common Files\Crystal Decisions\2.5` to the Web application folder (webApplicationFolder in the previous example).

- Add the following entry to the web.xml file:

```
<context-param>
    <param-name>crystal_image_uri</param-name>
    <param-value>crystalreportviewers11</param-value>
</context-param>
```

There are two additional steps required if you intend to use the Crystal tag libraries:

- Copy crystal-tags-reportviewer.tld from `C:\Program Files\Common Files\Crystal Decisions\2.5\java\lib\taglib` to the WEB-INF folder.

- Add the following entry to the web.xml file:

```
<taglib>
    <taglib-uri>
        /crystal-tags-reportviewer.tld
</taglib-uri>
    <taglib-location>
        /WEB-INF/crystal-tags-reportviewer.tld
    </taglib-location>
</taglib>
```

DELIVERING REPORTS IN WEB APPLICATIONS

Report viewing is done primarily through the HTML report viewer included with the Crystal Reports Java Reporting Component. This report viewer is a control that runs inside a JSP or servlet. Its job is to get the information the report engine produces for a given page of a report and render that data to HTML format into the page's response stream.

The programmatic entry point to the report viewer is a class called `CrystalReportViewer`. This class is found in the `com.crystaldecisions.report.web.viewer` package. It can be instantiated as follows:

```
CrystalReportViewer viewer = new CrystalReportsViewer();
```

Make sure you add the class's package name in the import attribute of the page clause like this:

```
<%@ page import="com.crystaldecisions.report.web.viewer.*" %>
```

This is the main class you use to render reports to HTML. Its two main methods used to view reports are `setReportSource` and `processHttpRequest`. These methods are outlined in the following sections.

THE setReportSource METHOD

This `CrystalReportViewer` object's `setReportSource` method is used to indicate to the viewer which report it should display. Specifically, it accepts an object that implements the IReportSource interface. The Java Reporting Component's engine supplies this object. There are generally three steps involved in setting the report source.

The first step is to create a `JPEReportSourceFactory` object found in the `com.crystaldecisions.reports.reportengineinterface` package. As the name implies, this object's job is to create report source objects. This object has one relevant method: `createReportSource`. Its definition is as follows:

```
IReportSource createReportSource(object reportPath, Locale userLocale)
```

The `reportPath` argument should be a string consisting of the filename of the report file (`.rpt`). With the Java Reporting Component, the path from where the report file should be loaded is configured in the CrystalReportEngine-config.xml file. This XML configuration file has a <reportlocation> element that indicates the location of the report files relative to the location of the config file. The default value for the reportlocation is `..\..`, which (if the config file was in the classes folder as outlined in the previous section) would point to the webApplicationFolder folder. It's a good idea to create a reports folder inside the Web application's folder and store all your reports there. Then change the report location setting to `..\..\reports`. Then when reports are referenced in the call to `createReportSource`, you only need to pass the name of the report, not the folder location.

The second argument to `createReportSource` is a Locale object. Generally, you should pass in `request.getLocale()`. This means that whatever the user's locale is, it is passed down to the report engine so any locale-specific formatting can be applied.

THE processHttpRequest METHOD

After the viewer is told which report it needs to view, the only other method left to call is the `processHttpRequest` method. This method kicks off the actual report processing and renders the report to HTML. Its definition is as follows:

```
void processHttpRequest(HttpServletRequest request,
                        HttpServletResponse response,
                        ServletContext context,
                        Writer out)
```

The first argument passed in is the current servlet's request object. The report viewer uses this to access the HTTP request's form data where the viewer holds its state information such as what page it was showing, what level of drill-down, and so on. Also stored in the form data is the piece of data that indicates what action is to be performed. For example, the user might have clicked the Next Page button, or might have also drilled down. You simply pass in the servlet's request object.

28

The second argument is the response object. The report viewer uses this object to access the page's response stream so it can write the HTML output of the report. Here, you simply pass the servlet's response object.

The third argument is the servletContext, which is used to access the servlets container. Generally, you pass getServletConfig().getServletContext() for this argument. The final argument is a Writer. You generally pass null here unless you want to provide your own Writer.

Listing 28.1 shows these concepts all brought together in a JSP page that displays a report.

LISTING 28.1   VIEWING A REPORT IN HTML

```
<%@ page contentType="text/html;charset=UTF-8"
    import="com.crystaldecisions.reports.reportengineinterface.*,
            com.crystaldecisions.report.web.viewer.*"   %>

<%
// name of report file
String reportFile = "Income_Statement.rpt";

// create the JPEReportSourceFactory
JPEReportSourceFactory rptSrcFactory = new JPEReportSourceFactory();

// call the createReportSource method
Object reportSource = rptSrcFactory.createReportSource(reportFile,
                                                request.getLocale());

// create the report viewer
CrystalReportViewer viewer = new CrystalReportViewer();

// set the report source
viewer.setReportSource(reportSource);

// tell the viewer to display the report
viewer.processHttpRequest(request,
                          response,
                          getServletConfig().getServletContext(),
                          null);

%>
```

The output of this page is shown in Figure 28.2. All content for the report consists of HTML elements, keeping all formatting and layout preserved. Every once in a while you will find a discrepancy in the report output between the designer and the HTML viewer, but the advantages of the HTML viewer generally outweigh the disadvantages. Besides drilling down or hyperlinking from the report's main content, a toolbar along the top provides a way for the end user to interact with the report. Buttons for page navigation as well as printing and exporting are present. When a command is performed by the user such as navigating to the next page or drilling down, the report viewer using a JavaScript function causes a form post to occur back to the same page. Both the current state and the new command are sent as part of the form's post data. The JSP or servlet reruns and the new state of the report is again rendered back to HTML.

Figure 28.2
This is the HTML
report viewer in
action.

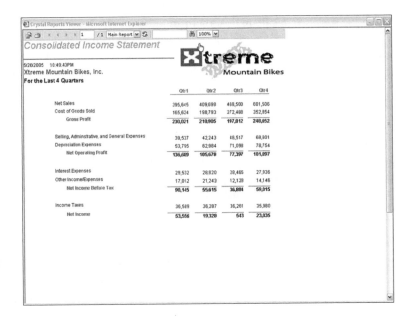

There is a collection of methods that the `CrystalReportViewer` object exposes that can be used to customize how the viewer looks and behaves. For the full list of methods, consult the API documentation; however, the following sections cover some of the more useful types of customizations.

CUSTOMIZING THE TOOLBAR

Each button or set of buttons on the report viewer toolbar can be individually turned off and on. These are done by a set of simple methods that accept a Boolean argument. They are listed here:

- `setHasToggleGroupTreeButton(boolean)`
- `setHasExportButton(boolean)`
- `setHasPrintButton(boolean)`
- `setHasViewList(boolean)`
- `setHasRefreshButton(boolean)`
- `setHasPageNavigationButtons(boolean)`
- `setHasGotoPageButton(boolean)`
- `setHasSearchButton(boolean)`
- `setHasZoomFactorList(boolean)`
- `setHasLogo(boolean)`

Finally, the entire toolbar can be turned off by calling `setDisplayToolbar(boolean)`. If the toolbar is turned off, the user does not have a way to interact with the report such as

28

navigating pages. To facilitate this, there are other methods on the `CrystalReportViewer` object that can be called to drive the page navigation, including `showFirstPage`, `showPreviousPage`, `showNextPage`, `showLastPage`, and `showNthPage`. Similar methods exist to re-create the functionality of most of the other buttons as well. In general, the methods related to toolbar customization are almost self-explanatory.

CUSTOMIZING THE GROUP TREE

The group tree's width can be set via the `setGroupTreeWidth` method. To change the formatting of the group tree's text, change the CSS styles defined in the default.css file found in crystalreportviewers11/css. Alternatively, the entire group tree can be hidden by passing false to the `setDisplayGroupTree` function.

USING THE CRYSTAL TAG LIBRARIES

Now that you understand how the report viewer works, it's beneficial to understand some of the ways that it can be used in a more productive manner. Java tag libraries are a great way to accomplish this. A *tag library (taglib)* is an HTML-like tag that can be embedded inside a JSP page; it has some compiled code logic behind it that knows how to render itself to HTML. The beauty of a tag library is that you don't need to clog up your JSP page with a bunch of code; you simply need to insert the tag. When Business Objects created the HTML report viewer, they were wise enough to create some Java tag libraries alongside it. This is not to say you could not create your own tag libraries to suit your own needs, but the ones provided with the product will probably meet most requirements.

Refer to the Application Server Configuration section in this chapter for steps to configure the Crystal tag libraries. After you've finished the setup, you can start adding the tags to your page. The first step in using the tag is to add the taglib directive to the top of your JSP page. This directive looks like this:

```
<%@ taglib uri="/crystal-tags-reportviewer.tld" prefix="crviewer" %>
```

This indicates to the JSP page that any time it finds a tag prefixed with crviewer, it should look in the crystal-tags-reportviewer.tlb file to find out how to work with that tag.

There are two tags that must be added to the JSP page: viewer and report. Listing 28.2 shows a simple page using the viewer and report tags.

LISTING 28.2 USING THE TAG LIBRARIES

```
<%@ taglib uri="/crystal-tags-reportviewer.tld" prefix="crviewer" %>
<crviewer:viewer viewerName="" reportSourceType="reportingComponent">
  <crviewer:report reportName="Income_Statement.rpt"/>
</crviewer:viewer>
```

The `viewerName` and `reportSourceType` attributes of the viewer tag are required. The `viewerName` can be set to blank unless there are multiple viewer tags on the same page, in which case you'll need to name them uniquely. There is only one report source type supported in the Java Reporting Component, which is "reportingComponent." Inside the viewer tag, you'll see a report tag. For the reportName attribute, pass in the name of the report you want to display. The output of this page would be exactly the same as the output of the previous code example using inline Java code. The advantage of this page is that it is cleaner and simpler. To customize the viewer, rather than writing code, simply add attributes to the viewer tag. For example, adding the following attribute to the viewer tag hides the group tree:

```
displayGroupTree="false"
```

There are many other attributes supported. Consult the documentation for a full list but the general rule is that most methods on the CrystalReportViewer object have a corresponding tag library attribute.

EXPORTING REPORTS TO OTHER FILE FORMATS

You've learned so far how the CrystalReportViewer object can be used either in code or as a tag library to view reports in HTML format. This is useful for having a quick look at a report online, but users often require the capability to save the report to their own machine either for their own reference or so they can send the report elsewhere. Exporting is a perfect solution to this. The Java Reporting Component supports exporting reports to both Adobe PDF and RTF. There are two ways exporting can be done: via the export button on the toolbar and via code.

EXPORTING VIA THE TOOLBAR BUTTON

By default, the export button on the report viewer's toolbar is hidden. To enable it, either set the displayToolbarExportButton attribute to true if you are using the tag library or call the setHasExportButton method if you are using the viewer directly.

NOTE   Even though you instruct the viewer to show the export button, you might find that it is still now showing up. This is most likely because you have not told the viewer that it owns the whole page. This is done via the setOwnPage method or isOwnPage attribute for the viewer or tag library, respectively.

When the Export button is clicked, a pop-up window appears asking the user which document format she would like to export the report to and which pages she would like to export to. This is shown in Figure 28.3.

When the user clicks OK, the browser sends back the report in the requested format. Figure 28.4 shows the Income Statement report from the previous examples, exported to PDF.

28

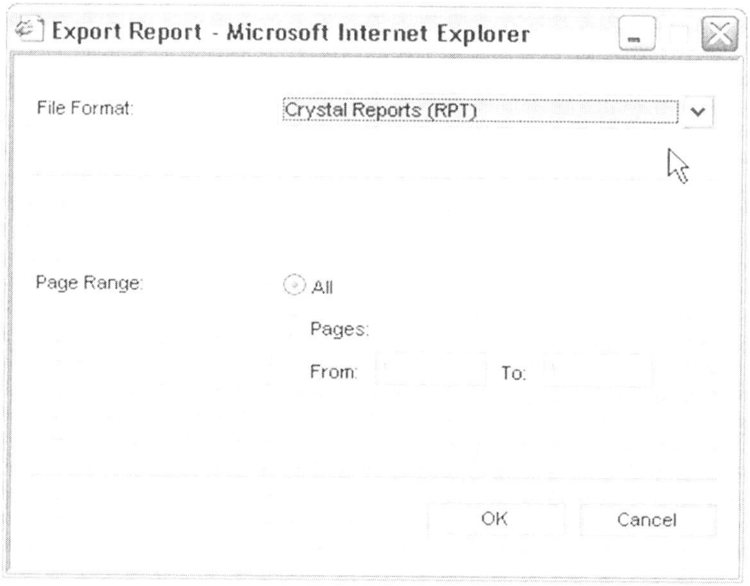

Figure 28.3
Export a report
through the report
viewer.

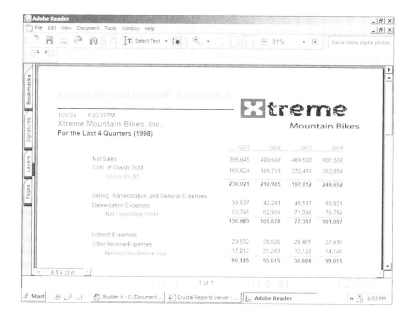

Figure 28.4
Here is a report
exported to the PDF
format.

EXPORTING VIA CODE

There are a few reasons why you might want to export via code. Perhaps you always want to deliver reports in PDF or RTF format instead of using the report viewer at all. Or perhaps you want to control the user interface for exporting. In any case, this section describes how to export using the ReportExportControl.

NOTE

> Although some developers find it attractive to bypass the Crystal Report HTML viewer, and instead use either PDF or RTF as the primary way to deliver reports, this is often not the best way to go. Exporting is one of most processor-intensive operations and thus should be used sparingly if possible. In addition, when you export reports you lose all the interactive functionality like drill-down and group tree navigation. Use exporting where appropriate.

The `ReportExportControl` is the Java object used to render reports to both PDF and RTF. Because it is derived from the same class as the `CrystalReportViewer` object, it has many of the same properties and methods. The two main methods used in the report viewer—`setReportSource` and `processHttpRequest`—are used in exactly the same way in the `ReportExportControl`. Also, when exporting there is an additional method that is required: `setExportOptions`. This method is used to tell the `ReportExportControl` which export format should be used, and optionally, which pages should be exported.

The argument that is passed into the `setExportOptions` method is an object of type `ExportOptions`. This is found in `com.crystaldecisions.sdk.occa.report.exportoptions` package. With it, you call the `setExportFormatType` method passing in one of the following values:

- `ReportExportFormat.PDF` (for PDF)
- `ReportExportFormat.RTF` (for RTF)

NOTE

> Although the `ReportExportFormat` object has additional export formats not mentioned here such as MSExcel and Text, these are not currently available with the Java Reporting Component. These show up because the `ExportOptions` object is a shared object between other Crystal products that do support those export format types.

Listing 28.3 pulls this all together and shows a JSP page that exports a report to PDF format.

LISTING 28.3 EXPORTING VIA THE REPORTEXPORTCONTROL

```
<%@ page contentType="text/html;charset=UTF-8"
import="com.crystaldecisions.reports.reportengineinterface.*,
        com.crystaldecisions.report.web.viewer.*,
om.crystaldecisions.sdk.occa.report.exportoptions.*"  %>
<%

// name of report file
String reportFile = "Income_Statement.rpt";

// create the JPEReportSourceFactory
JPEReportSourceFactory rptSrcFactory = new JPEReportSourceFactory();
```

28

continues

LISTING 28.3   CONTINUED

```
// call the createReportSource method
Object reportSource = rptSrcFactory.createReportSource(reportFile,
                                                       request.getLocale());

// create the report viewer
ReportExportControl exporter = new ReportExportControl();

// set the report source
exporter.setReportSource(reportSource);

ExportOptions exportOptions = new ExportOptions();
exportOptions.setExportFormatType(ReportExportFormat.PDF);
exporter.setExportOptions(exportOptions);

// tell the viewer to display the report
exporter.processHttpRequest(request,
                            response,
                            getServletConfig().getServletContext(),
                            null);

%>
```

There are a few additional options that you might find useful. The first is the capability to specify which page numbers should be exported. This enables you to export just a small number of pages from a very large report. This is accomplished by creating either the `RTFWordExportFormatOptions` or `PDFExportFormatOptions` objects and calling their `setStartPageNumber` and `setEndPageNumber` methods. The resulting object is passed into the `setFormatOptions` method of the `ExportOptions` object. The code snippet shown in Listing 28.4 illustrates this.

LISTING 28.4   SPECIFYING PAGE NUMBERS WHEN EXPORTING

```
ExportOptions exportOptions = new ExportOptions();
exportOptions.setExportFormatType(ReportExportFormat.PDF) ;

RTFWordExportFormatOptions rtfOptions = new PDFExportFormatOptions();
rtfOptions.setStartPageNumber(1);
rtfOptions.setEndPageNumber(3);
exportOptions.setFormatOptions(rtfOptions);

exporter.setExportOptions(exportOptions);
```

The other option related to exporting is whether the resulting exported report should be sent back to the browser as an attachment or inline. When sent as an attachment, the browser pops up a dialog asking the user if he would like to save or open the file. This is useful if you think most of your users will want to save the file to their machines. The default behavior is for the report to open inside the browser window in either the Adobe or Microsoft Word embedded viewer. This is controlled via the `setExportAsAttachment` method of the `CrystalReportViewer`. This method simply takes a Boolean value, which determines whether the file should be an attachment.

PRINTING REPORTS FROM THE BROWSER

Viewing reports in electronic form is very valuable but as much as the "paperless office" is talked about, people still need to print reports to printers. The Java Reporting Component has the capability to print reports via the print button on the viewer's toolbar. Like the Export button, for the Print button to show, the viewer must be set to own the page via the `isOwnPage` attribute or `setOwnPage` method of the `CrystalReportViewer` object. When this button is clicked, a window opens asking the user which pages they want to print. This dialog is shown in Figure 28.5.

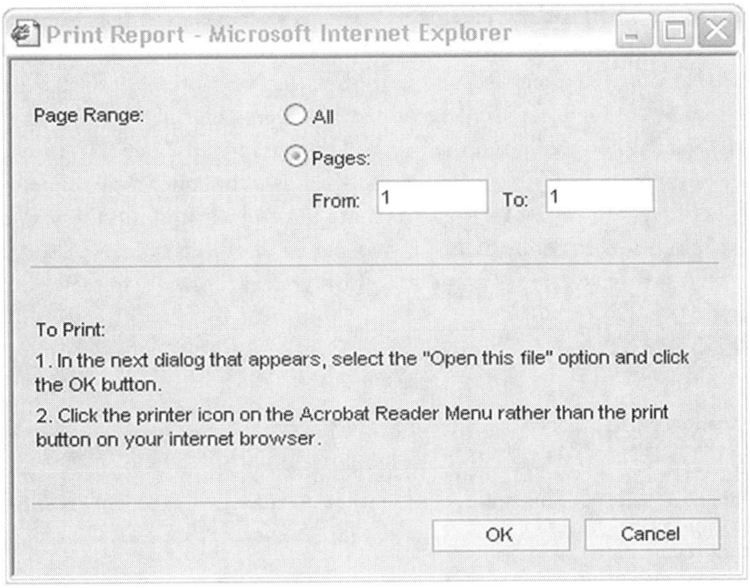

Figure 28.5
Print a report using the report viewer.

When the user clicks the Print button, the report opens in the Adobe PDF viewer, from which the user can then click Adobe's Print button. This prints the report to the user's printer.

COMMON PROGRAMMING TASKS

The different delivery mechanisms for the report viewer have been discussed. Now let's look at some of the common programming tasks that go along with delivering reports. This includes passing parameters to the report viewer and setting or changing the data source. The following sections will discuss these topics.

PASSING PARAMETERS

One of the most common programming tasks with any Crystal Reports product is to pass parameters to the report viewer. This really isn't a hard task but developers often find this difficult because of a lack of proper examples in the product documentation. This chapter

28

will attempt to provide concrete examples. Typically, reports are designed to be dynamic and so have multiple parameters that drive how the report functions. There are two ways to handle parameters: either have the report viewer prompt the user for the parameters automatically or pass the parameter values via code. Which method you choose is determined largely by whether you want the users to pick their own parameter values themselves.

Using the automatic parameter prompting requires no extra code or configuration. Simply view a report using either the viewer class or tag library and a default parameter prompting screen is displayed. Alternatively, you can pass the parameter values by code. This involves creating a series of objects as outlined below.

The first step in passing parameter values is to create an instance of the Fields class. This is a container class for parameter fields. This and the other objects are found in the com.crystaldecisions.sdk.occa.report.data package. Next, create an instance of the ParameterField object. To determine which parameter you are setting values for, call the setName method passing in the name of the parameter. Then to set the parameter values, create an instance of the Values class, which is a container for parameter value objects. Finally, create a ParameterFieldDiscreteValue object and call the setValue method to pass in the actual parameter value. This collection of objects is then passed to the report viewer via the setParameterFields method. Listing 28.4 shows a parameter being passed.

LISTING 28.4   PASSING A SIMPLE PARAMETER

```
Fields fields = new Fields();
ParameterField param = new ParameterField();
param.setName("Country");
Values vals = new Values();
ParameterFieldDiscreteValue val = new ParameterFieldDiscreteValue();
val.setValue("Canada");
vals.add(val);
param.setCurrentValues(vals);
fields.add(param);
viewer.setParameterFields(fields);
```

Because there tends to be a bunch of objects you need to create, a nice way to handle this is to wrap up the parameter logic into a function. Listing 28.5 provides a sample function like this.

LISTING 28.5   A SAMPLE PARAMETER-HANDLING FUNCTION

```
public ParameterField createParam(string name, object value) {
   ParameterField param = new ParameterField();
   param.setName(name);
   Values vals = new Values();
   ParameterFieldDiscreteValue val = new ParameterFieldDiscreteValue();
   val.setValue(value);
```

```
        vals.add(val);
        param.setCurrentValues(vals);
        return param;
}
```

After you have a function like this in place, passing parameters looks as simple as in Listing 28.6.

LISTING 28.6   CALLING THE SAMPLE PARAMETER-HANDLING FUNCTION

```
Fields fields = new Fields();

field.add( createParam("Country", "Canada") );
field.add( createParam("Product Line", "Widgets") );

viewer.setParameterFields(fields) ;
```

SETTING DATA SOURCE INFORMATION

Setting data source information works very similar to the way setting parameters works. There is a collection of objects that you create, which then gets passed to the report viewer. In this case, the method used is setDatabaseLogonInfos. This method takes a ConnectionInfos object, which is found in the com.crystaldecisions.sdk.occa.report.data package. The ConnectionInfos class is a container class for any data source information for a given report. Each connection's information is held in an object called ConnectionInfo. This object has setUserName and setPassword methods for passing credentials. Also, each ConnectionInfo has a collection of properties associated with it called a *property bag*. The property bag contains information such as server name, database name, connection type, and so on. The property bag stores information in a name/value pair structure. There are variations as to what items are held in the ConnectionInfo, but the best way to figure it out is to look in the Set DataSource Location dialog from the Crystal Reports designer. There you can see which items are associated with a connection. Listing 28.7 shows how to pass logon information for a report.

LISTING 28.7   PASSING DATA SOURCE CREDENTIALS

```
ConnectionInfos connections = new ConnectionInfos();

ConnectionInfo connection as new ConnectionInfo();
connection.setUserName("Ryan");
connection.setPassword("123BAC");

connections.add(connection);
viewer.setDatabaseLogonInfos(connections) ;
```

In version 11 of the Java Reporting component the following methods have been deprecated:

```
com.crystaldecisions.report.web.viewer.ReportServerControl.
➥getEnterpriseLogon()
com.crystaldecisions.report.web.viewer.CrystalReportViewer.
➥getPageToTreeRatio()
com.crystaldecisions.report.web.viewer.ReportServerControl.
➥getReportSourceClassFactoryName()
com.crystaldecisions.report.web.viewer.ReportServerControl.
➥setEnterpriseLogon(Object)
com.crystaldecisions.report.web.viewer.CrystalReportViewer.
➥setPageToTreeRatio(double)
com.crystaldecisions.report.web.viewer.ReportServerControl.
➥setReportSourceClassFactoryName(String)
```

DEVELOPING WITH A VISUAL DEVELOPMENT ENVIRONMENT

Not only has Business Objects delivered a full Java reporting offering with the Crystal
Reports Java Reporting Component, but it also provides integration with some of the major
Integrated Development Environments (IDEs) in the market to drive developers to build
applications with the Java Reporting Component more quickly. The vendors Business
Objects is currently working with on IDE integration are BEA and Borland. The integration
consists of the following:

- **An integrated project item for reports.** This enables developers to add a report to
  their projects easily. It launches the Crystal Reports designer to edit the report automatically.

- **A report viewer wizard.** This is a visual wizard that walks users through the process of
  adding the report viewer tag to their JSP page.

Figure 28.6 shows the integration info BEA WebLogic Workshop and Figure 28.7 shows the
integration into Borland JBuilder X. There are various other plug-ins to the IDEs as well
that can be explored, such as automatically importing the Crystal libraries and configuring
the web.xml.

For more information on IDE integration into these and other developer tools, visit the
Business Objects website.

Figure 28.6
The Java Reporting Component integrated into BEA WebLogic Workshop.

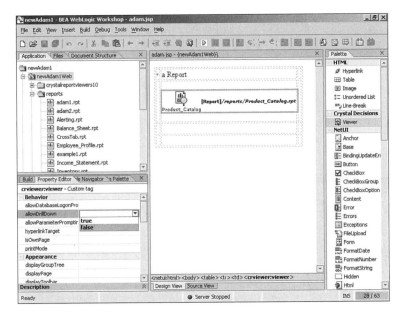

Figure 28.7
The Java Reporting Component integrated into Borland JBuilder X.

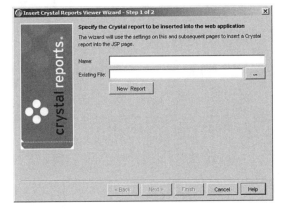

TROUBLESHOOTING

VERSION 11 JDBC DRIVER

I can't seem to find the version 11 JDBC driver.

This is not yet available at the time of this writing but should be available soon. You can check for status updates on this by visiting the Business Objects Download Center at http://www.businessobjects.com/products/downloadcenter/.

CHAPTER 29

CRYSTAL REPORTS .NET COMPONENTS

In this chapter

UNDERSTANDING MICROSOFT'S .NET PLATFORM

Business Objects has a long partnership history with Microsoft. This has continued with Microsoft's .NET platform. This chapter provides an overview of the various .NET reporting technologies that are available both within Visual Studio .NET and with Crystal Reports XI.

Microsoft .NET is a next-generation platform that enables developers to create programs that transcend device boundaries and harness the connectivity of the Internet. .NET and the tools and languages that compose it are the foundation for building Windows-based components and applications, creating scripts, developing websites and applications, and managing source code.

Many of the terms used in this chapter are specific to the Microsoft .NET solution or the Visual Studio .NET development environment. Before you learn the Crystal components, review some of the key .NET technologies that are relevant to Crystal Reports developers:

- **XML web services**—A *web service* is a unit of application logic providing data and services to other applications. Applications access web services via ubiquitous Web protocols and data formats such as HTTP and XML, with no need to worry about how each web service is implemented. Web services combine the best aspects of component-based development and the Web, and are a cornerstone of the Microsoft .NET programming model.

- **ASP.NET**—*ASP.NET* is a set of technologies in the Microsoft .NET Framework for building Web applications and XML web services. ASP.NET pages execute on the server and generate markup such as HTML, WML, or XML that is sent to a desktop or mobile browser. ASP.NET pages and ASP.NET XML web services files contain server-side logic (as opposed to client-side logic) written in Visual Basic .NET, C# .NET, or any .NET-compatible language.

- **ADO.NET**—*ADO.NET* is an evolutionary improvement to Microsoft *ActiveX Data Objects (ADO)* that provides platform interoperability and scalable data access. Using *Extensible Markup Language (XML)*, ADO.NET can ensure the efficient transfer of data to any application on any platform.

- **SOAP**—*SOAP (Simple Object Access Protocol)* is a lightweight and simple XML-based protocol that is designed to exchange structured and typed information on the Web. The purpose of SOAP is to enable rich and automated web services based on a shared and open Web infrastructure.

For more detailed information on the Microsoft .NET solution, refer to Microsoft's website at http://msdn.microsoft.com/library/default.asp.

UNDERSTANDING THE DIFFERENT CRYSTAL .NET COMPONENTS

There have been multiple releases of both Visual Studio .NET and the Crystal Reports .NET Components. This has created some confusion in the marketplace. In an attempt to clear this up, the following section describes the history of the various Crystal .NET products. Way back in 1993—a long time ago in the computing industry—Business Objects (then called Crystal Decisions) signed an agreement with Microsoft to include Crystal Reports version 2 with Visual Basic 3.0. This relationship continued over the years as the Microsoft developer community embraced Crystal Reports technology. Late in the year of 2000, when Microsoft began to create the next generation of its development platform, it again looked to Business Objects to provide the reporting solution. The Crystal folks ran full speed ahead with this project and embraced all the new technologies composing the .NET development platform.

In March of 2002, Visual Studio .NET shipped with a new product as part of the install: Crystal Reports for Visual Studio .NET. This was a special edition of Crystal Reports targeted at the .NET developer. It was seamlessly integrated with both the Visual Studio .NET integrated development environment (IDE) and the .NET Framework. It provided report viewer controls for both the Windows Forms and Web Forms application frameworks, a managed report engine object model, and a report designer integrated into the Visual Studio .NET IDE.

Another variant of the Crystal Reports .NET product came about when Microsoft released Visual Studio .NET 2003 (code named Everest). This was a point release of Visual Studio .NET and again included an updated edition of Crystal Reports for Visual Studio .NET. There were no new features per se, but the latest patches and updates were included. Many developers today have one of these Crystal Reports editions and believe that they have the most recent and complete Crystal Reports release. This is not true.

Subsequent to that release, Business Objects updated its .NET offering by adding new features such as additional report viewer controls, more functionality through its API, and support for more data sources. This functionality was bundled with the Crystal Reports 9 release. Therefore, Crystal Reports 9 Advanced Edition served as an upgrade to Crystal Reports for Visual Studio .NET. Finally, version 10 and XI again include upgrades to the .NET components that shipped with version 9. The rest of this chapter covers the functionality of the .NET components included with Crystal Reports XI.

AN OVERVIEW OF THE CRYSTAL REPORTS XI .NET COMPONENTS

Crystal Reports XI provides developers working within Visual Studio .NET with a fast, productive way to create and integrate presentation-quality, interactive reports to meet the demands of their application's end users. Crystal Reports XI enhances the .NET platform by allowing you to

- Create reports from virtually any data source.
- Deliver interactive, graphical report content in rich-client (Windows Forms), zero-client environments (Web Forms), or any device through an XML web services model
- Save time and write less code by leveraging existing Crystal Reports and report creation knowledge within .NET projects

To accomplish this, Crystal Reports XI provides a broad offering of .NET technologies for delivering reports inside .NET applications. The following sections cover each component at a high level. They are

- The Report Designer
- The Report Engine Object Model
- The Windows Forms Viewer
- The Web Forms Viewers

THE REPORT DESIGNER

Like the original Crystal Reports for Visual Studio .NET product, Crystal Reports XI provides an integrated report designer inside of the Visual Studio .NET development environment. This edition of the report designer enables you to create and edit reports from within the comfort of Visual Studio .NET. Figure 29.1 shows the report designer in action.

Figure 29.1
This is a report being designed in the Visual Studio .NET Report Designer.

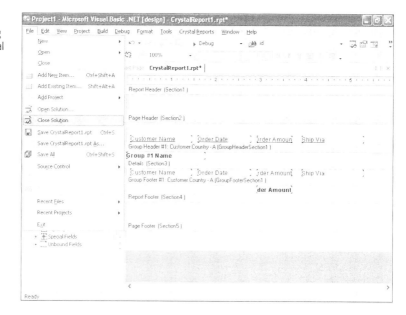

To add a new report to a project, select Add New Item from the Project menu. Select Crystal Reports from the Add New Item dialog. The filename you use here maps to the name of the report file as well as the name of the class created behind the scenes for the report (called the code-behind class).

> **NOTE**
>
> Many of you may be familiar with the Visual Basic report designer that was part of the Report Designer Component package made for Visual Basic 6.0. This new Visual Studio .NET report designer is the evolution of that component and works in a very similar manner.

After selecting Crystal Reports from the Add New Item dialog, the Report Wizard will be displayed. Select Using the Report Wizard or As a Blank Report to create a new report from scratch. The From an Existing Report option provides the capability to import any existing Crystal Report file (.rpt) and use the Visual Studio .NET report designer to make further modifications. This is a great way to leverage any existing work an organization has put into Crystal Reports. A report that is added or imported into a Visual Studio .NET project is just a standard RPT file. This means the standalone report designer can also be used to edit the report. The Visual Studio .NET Report Designer supports almost all the features of the standalone report designer and can be used to create everything from simple tabular reports to highly formatted professional reports. Although the feature set of these two editions of the designer are almost exactly the same, there are a few things for which the standalone designer is good, namely being able to preview the report without having to run the application.

> **TIP**
>
> A quick way to launch the standalone designer from within Visual Studio .NET is to right-click on a report in the Solution Explorer and select Open With. In the dialog that opens, select crw32.exe. This is the executable for the standalone report designer. This usually proves to be a better method to build reports anyway because you have a built-in and active preview screen available for dynamic viewing, editing, and testing.

Even though the capabilities of the two editions of the designers are similar, there are some differences in the way the designer works. This is not meant to be inconsistent, but rather to adapt some of the standalone report designer tasks to tasks that Visual Studio .NET developers would be familiar with. Ideally, the experience of designing a report with the Visual Studio .NET report designer should be like designing a Windows Form. The following sections cover these differences.

UNDERSTANDING THE REPORT DESIGNER'S USER INTERFACE CONVENTIONS

Several user interface components work differently in the Visual Studio .NET report designer. One of the first things you'll notice is that the section names are shown above each section on a section band as opposed to being on the left side of the window. However, the same options are available when right-clicking on the section band. This actually takes up less real estate and tends to be preferred by developers.

The Field Explorer resides to the left of the report page by default but can be docked anywhere as per most Visual Studio .NET tool windows. The Field Explorer can be easily shown or hidden by clicking the Toggle Field View button on the designer toolbar. Other explorer windows found in the standalone designer such as the Report Explorer and Repository Explorer are not available in the Visual Studio .NET report designer.

NOTE

Reports that contain objects linked to the Crystal Repository are fully supported; however, no new repository objects can be added to the report without using the standalone designer.

The menus that you would normally find in the standalone report designer can be found by right-clicking on an empty spot on the designer surface. The pop-up menu provides the same functionality.

THE PROPERTY BROWSER

To change the formatting and settings for report objects in the standalone designer, users are familiar with right-clicking on a report object and selecting Format Field from the pop-up menu. This would open the Format Editor, which would give you access to changing font, color, styles, and other formatting options. In the Visual Studio .NET report designer, this scenario is still available; however, there is an additional way to apply most of these formatting options—via the Property Browser.

The Property Browser is a window that lives inside the Visual Studio .NET development environment. It should be very familiar to developers as a way to change the appearance and behavior of a selected object on a form or design surface. In the context of the report designer, the property browser is another way to change the settings (properties) for report objects. In general, any setting that is available in the Format Editor dialog is available from the property browser when that object is selected. This generally proves to be a faster and better way to set properties than using the Format Editor. To see which properties are available for a given object, click to highlight the object, and then check out the Property Browser window shown in Figure 29.2.

The property names are listed on the left and the current values are listed on the right. To click a value simply click on the current value and either type or select from the drop-down list.

One property to pay attention to is the Name property. This becomes relevant in the next section when you learn how to use the Report Engine Object Model to manipulate the report on the fly at runtime. This is the way to reference that object in code.

Figure 29.2
Using the Property
Browser window to
modify a report
object's settings.

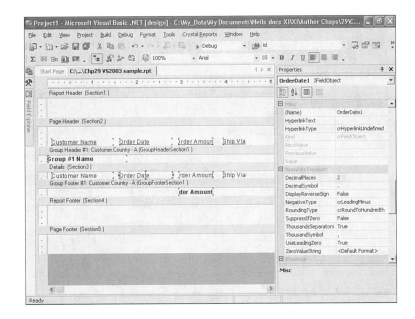

THE REPORT ENGINE OBJECT MODEL

The Report Engine Object Model is the .NET programmatic entry point to the Crystal Reports engine. It provides a collection of objects, methods, and properties that enable you to process, save, export, and print reports. While doing that, you are able to manipulate the report by modifying parameter values, database credentials, sorting, and grouping. The Report Engine Object Model (hereafter referred to as the object model) consists of a standard .NET assembly called CrystalDecisions.CrystalReports.Engine.dll. As the name of the dll implies, the namespace for all the objects contained in this dll is CrystalDecisions.CrystalReports.Engine. Because this is a standard .NET assembly, the object model contained within it can be used from any .NET programming language or tool. All sample code within this chapter uses the Visual Basic .NET language, but any .NET-compliant language could, of course, be used. Keep in mind that although the object model is pure managed code, the underlying report engine is not. This means you can't perform a pure xcopy deployment that Microsoft likes to advertise that all .NET applications can do.

There are many objects, and thus capabilities, in the object model. This chapter does not explain all of them but rather covers the most common scenarios. For a complete reference of all objects, properties, and methods, consult the Crystal Reports XI documentation that is installed to the MSDN Help Collection. Some of you may be skeptical about the product documentation because in the past it was very sparse. However, there is much more information in the documentation in version XI than ever before; have a look through it and you will be impressed.

OPENING REPORTS

The main object you use when working with the object model is the `ReportDocument` object. It is the root object in the object model hierarchy and forms the entry point to opening reports. The first step in opening reports is to create a new instance of the `ReportDocument` class. Then to open a report file, call the Load method. This method takes a single parameter, which is a string that points to the RPT file. An example of this is as follows:

```
Dim Report As New ReportDocument
Report.Load("C:\My Reports\Sales.rpt")
```

> One common way to handle file paths is to use Application.StartupPath to determine the current location of the Windows Forms executable and reference report files relative to there.

The other way to load a report is to use a strongly typed report object. A *strongly typed report object* is an object automatically generated when a report is added to the Visual Studio .NET project. This object (sometimes called *code-behind*) is specific to the report file both in its class name and properties. For example, a report added to the project called InvoiceReport.rpt would in turn have a class called `InvoiceReport`. Instead of calling the Load method, a developer only needs to create an instance of the `InvoiceReport` class. This class knows how to locate the report. In the case of strongly typed reports, instead of having an external RPT file, the report file is compiled into the application executable. The report is loaded out of the application's resources from there. Whether you use a `ReportDocument` (untyped report) or a strongly typed report, the rest of the object model is the same.

EXPORTING REPORTS

One of the most common uses of the object model is to run a report and export it to another file format. In past versions, exporting required a good-sized chunk of code. Fortunately exporting in version XI is very easy with the updated object model. First, a `ReportDocument` object needs to be created and a report loaded into it. After that is done, several exporting methods are available to you:

- **ExportToDisk**—This is the simplest way to export a report; it accepts an argument to indicate the export format type to use and a filename to export to. This method is useful when you just need to export a file to the disk.

- **ExportToStream**—This method only accepts a single argument—the export format type. The return value of this method is a `System.IO.Stream` object. This is actually a `MemoryStream` object so you can cast it to a `MemoryStream` if need be. This method is useful when you intend to send the exported report elsewhere as a stream without having to write to an intermediate disk file. It's best to call the steam's `Close` method when finished with the stream to release memory.

- **ExportToHttpResponse**—This method is similar to the ExportToStream method in that it is intended to be used when the resulting report is streamed back to the user. However, this method accepts as an argument the ASP.NET HttpResponse object and automatically streams the exported report back to the Web browser handling the mime type and response stream for you.

- **Export**—This method is the master Export method. It accepts an object called ExportOptions as an argument that describes the export format type and destination type. You can think of this as the long-hand way of exporting but it does allow for a few additional options such as e-mail and Exchange destinations and page range options.

A common argument to all these exporting methods is the export format type. This is specified using the ExportFormatType enumeration found in the CrystalDecisions.Shared namespace. It's generally a good idea to add a reference to CrystalDecisions.Shared.dll because you will find many common objects used in the object model located in this assembly. The following list describes the members of the ExportFormatType enumeration:

- **Excel**—Microsoft Excel format
- **ExcelRecord**—A variation of the Microsoft Excel format that just exports the data, not the formatting
- **HTML32**—HTML for Netscape Navigator or other non-common browsers
- **HTML40**—HTML for Microsoft Internet Explorer
- **PortableDocFormat**—Adobe PDF
- **RichText**—Microsoft's Rich Text Format (RTF)
- **WordForWindows**—Microsoft Word format
- **Text**—Plain text format
- **CrystalReport**—Standard Crystal Reports (RPT) format

TIP

> When exporting to Crystal Reports format, a standard RPT file is created; however, the report has saved data. This is quite useful because you can run a report once, export to Crystal Reports format, and then have many people view that report using the saved data. In this scenario, only one hit is made to the database even though many people are viewing the report. This is similar to creating a report instance in the BusinessObjects Enterprise environment. This feature can be used to affect a greater scalability by introducing a report instance delivery model.

A common scenario for exporting would be processing many reports in a batch job. This is a great use of the object model. Here are a few tips to help you do this effectively. First, you need to clean up to make sure memory is released, and second, use multiple threads to maximize the time available for processing reports. The report engine object model is thread safe. Listing 29.1 illustrates a multithreaded report processing class. Listing 29.2 shows how this class could be called.

LISTING 29.1 MULTITHREADED BATCH PROCESSING CLASS

```
Imports System.Threading
Imports CrystalDecisions.Shared
Imports CrystalDecisions.CrystalReports.Engine

Public Class BatchProcessor
    Private ReportList As New ArrayList
    Private OutputFolder As String
    Private BatchCounter As Integer

    ' Call this method to add a report to the list of reports
    ' to be processed by the batch processor
    Public Sub AddReportJob(ByVal ReportPath As String)
        ReportList.Add(ReportPath)
    End Sub

    ' This runs an individual report job
    Private Sub ProcessNextReportJob(ByVal Index As Object)
        Dim report As New ReportDocument
        Dim outputFileName As String

    ' Load the report based on index
        report.Load(ReportList(Index))
    ' Construct an output filename
        outputFileName = "Report" & Index & ".pdf"
    ' Call the ExportToDisk method
        report.ExportToDisk(ExportFormatType.PortableDocFormat, _
                            OutputFolder & "\" & outputFileName)
    ' Make sure to clean up the report object
        report.Close()

    ' Decrement a counter of remaining jobs
        BatchCounter = BatchCounter - 1
    End Sub

    Public Sub ExecuteBatch(ByVal OutputFolder As String)
        Me.OutputFolder = OutputFolder

        BatchCounter = ReportList.Count

        ' Grab the current time
        Dim startTime As DateTime = DateTime.Now

        ' Start the batch job
        Dim i As Integer
        For i = 1 To ReportList.Count
        ' Use the .NET ThreadPool class to handle the multiple requests
            Dim wc As New WaitCallback(AddressOf ProcessNextReportJob)
            ThreadPool.QueueUserWorkItem(wc, i - 1)
        Next

        While BatchCounter > 0
            Thread.Sleep(250)
        End While
```

```
                Dim elapsedTime As TimeSpan = DateTime.Now.Subtract(startTime)
                MessageBox.Show("Batch completed in " + _
                                elapsedTime.Seconds.ToString() & " seconds")
        End Sub

End Class
```

LISTING 29.2   CALLING THE BATCH PROCESSOR

```
Dim bp As New BatchProcessor

bp.AddReportJob("C:\Temp\Reports\Report1.rpt")
bp.AddReportJob("C:\Temp\Reports\Report2.rpt")
bp.AddReportJob("C:\Temp\Reports\Report3.rpt")
bp.AddReportJob("C:\Temp\Reports\Report4.rpt")
bp.AddReportJob("C:\Temp\Reports\Report5.rpt")
bp.AddReportJob("C:\Temp\Reports\Report6.rpt")
bp.AddReportJob("C:\Temp\Reports\Report7.rpt")
bp.AddReportJob("C:\Temp\Reports\Report8.rpt")
bp.AddReportJob("C:\Temp\Reports\Report9.rpt")
bp.AddReportJob("C:\Temp\Reports\ReportXI.rpt")

bp.ExecuteBatch("C:\Temp\Output")
```

PRINTING REPORTS

Although the fantasy of a paperless office floats around our heads, the reality today is that no matter how much technology for viewing reports is produced, people will always want to print them. Along these lines, the object model supports printing reports to printers. This is accomplished by calling the ReportDocument's `PrintToPrinter` method. It takes the following arguments, which determine basic print settings:

- **nCopies**—An integer representing the number of copies to print
- **collated**—A Boolean value indicating whether the printed pages should be collated
- **startPageN**—An integer representing the page number on which to start printing
- **endPageN**—An integer representing the page number on which to end printing

In addition to these printing options, there is another set of more advanced options. These options are in the form of properties and are contained in the ReportDocument's `PrintOptions` object:

- **PaperSize**—An enumeration of standard paper sizes, such as Letter or A4
- **PaperOrientation**—An enumeration to indicate the orientation of the paper, such as Portrait or Landscape
- **PageMargins**—A PageMargins object containing integer-based margin widths
- **PageContentHeight/PageContentWidth**—Integer-based width and height for the main page area

- **PaperSource**—An enumeration containing standard paper tray sources such as upper and lower

- **PrinterDuplex**—An enumeration containing duplexing options for the printer

- **PrinterName**—A string representing the name of the printer device or print queue

> NOTE
>
> Keep in mind that whatever account the report engine object model is running under needs access to the printer when the `PrintToPrinter` method is invoked. Sometimes when the object model is used in ASP.NET, it is running under a Guest-level account, which does not have access to the machine's printers. If this is the case, you need to install and grant access to the printers for that account.

DELIVERING REPORTS WITH THE WINDOWS FORMS VIEWER

After reports are imported into or referenced from a Visual Studio .NET project, the next obvious step is to have a way to view those reports. This section covers report viewing in Windows Forms applications.

Windows Forms is the new .NET technology for building rich-client applications. It is the evolution of the COM and ActiveX platform that Crystal Reports was so popular in. When it came to .NET, Business Objects decided to write a native .NET control based on the Windows Forms technology. This control is simply called the Windows Forms Viewer. Its corresponding class name is CrystalDecisions.Windows.Forms.CrystalReportViewer.

Like other Windows Forms controls, this control ultimately inherits from the System.Windows.Forms.Control class. It has many public methods and properties that enable you to drive the appearance and behavior. In addition to these runtime capabilities, the Windows Forms Viewer has design-time support to increase the efficiency and ease of using the control. The control can be found in the toolbox on the Windows Forms tab. You can see what the control looks like after being dropped onto a form in Figure 29.3.

THE ReportSource PROPERTY

Although there are many properties and methods, the ReportSource property is key. It is this property that is used to indicate to the viewer which report it should display. Because the ReportSource property's data type is object, it can accept multiple types of values, the most common of which are listed here:

- **Filename**—The full path to an RPT file as a String object.

- **Report object**—An instance of a CrystalDecisions.CrystalReports.Engine.ReportDocument class. This report should already have been loaded by calling the ReportDocument's Load method.

- **Strongly typed report object**—An instance of a strongly typed report object derived from ReportClass.

Figure 29.3
A Crystal Report displayed in the Windows Forms Viewer control.

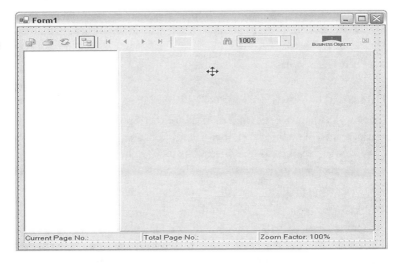

The following code shows VB.NET examples of setting these types of report source objects:

```
' #1 - A filename as a string
Viewer.ReportSource = "C:\Program Files\My Application\Reports\Sales.rpt"

' #2 - a ReportDocument object
Dim Report = As New ReportDocument()
Report.Load("C:\Program Files\My Application\Reports\Sales.rpt")
Viewer.ReportSource = Report

' #3 - A strongly-typed report object
Dim Report As New SalesReport()
Viewer.ReportSource = Report
```

If the viewer is visible when the ReportSource property is set, it displays the report immediately. If the viewer is not visible yet, that is, the form has not been shown yet, the viewer waits until it is shown onscreen to display the report. After a report source is provided to the viewer, it maintains that report until the viewer is destroyed or another report source is passed into it.

Because the viewer can generically accept report filenames and report objects, a single viewer can be reused for viewing multiple reports. One of the ways you could handle this is to create a form dedicated to report viewing. This form would contain the Windows Forms viewer. To easily invoke this form and pass in a report source, make the viewer a public variable and then create a shared method to accept a report source as an argument. An example of this function is shown here:

```
Public Shared Sub Display(ByVal ReportSource As Object)
    Dim newForm As New ReportViewerForm()
    newForm.Viewer.ReportSource = ReportSource
    newForm.ShowDialog()
End Sub
```

After this is in place, to invoke the report viewer from anywhere in the application, use the following code:

```
strReportPath = ...
ReportViewerForm.Display(strReportPath)
```

CUSTOMIZING THE WINDOWS FORMS VIEWER

There are many properties and methods of the report viewer that can be used to customize its appearance. The first level of customization is to show or hide the individual components of the viewer. The group tree on the left side can be shown or hidden via the `DisplayGroupTree` Boolean property. The toolbar works the same way via the `DisplayToolbar` property.

In addition to hiding the entire toolbar, each button or button group on the toolbar has corresponding properties that allow them to be individually hidden or shown. These properties can be found in the property browser or accessed via code. They all start with `Show`, such as `ShowExportButton`, `ShowPrintButton`, and so on. The names should be self-explanatory.

There is a status bar at the bottom of the viewer that does not have a corresponding show/hide property. It tends to not add a lot of value and ends up more of an annoyance than anything. A trick to hide this status bar is to drop a panel control onto the form and drop the viewer onto the panel. Set the viewer's `Dock` property to `Fill` so that the viewer always sizes itself to the size of the surrounding panel. Then set the `DockPadding.Bottom` property of the viewer to –20. This sizes the height of the viewer to 20 pixels more than the panel, effectively hiding the status bar below the extents of the panel. Keep in mind that any methods and properties that need to be accessed from the report viewer after you've done this need to be accessed via the panel object's controls collection. Figure 29.4 shows the report viewer with no group tree, no toolbar, and the status bar hidden.

Figure 29.4
The Report Viewer is shown here with its status bar hidden.

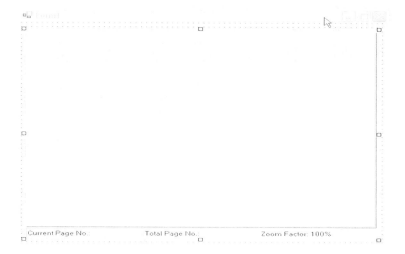

29

Another property that can be used to change the behavior of the report viewer is the `EnableDrillDown` property. Setting this Boolean property to false disables the user from performing any drill-down operations. Finally, the `SelectionFormula` and `ViewTimeSelectionFormula` properties can be used to create and append filters to the report. Keep in mind that the filtering is actually done by the report engine, but the report viewer simply exposes the property and then sends the information down to the report engine. The `SelectionFormula` property should be used when creating or overwriting a selection formula. To append to an existing formula, use the `ViewTimeSelectionFormula` property, which automatically appends using an AND operator.

DELIVERING REPORTS WITH THE WEB FORMS VIEWER

An equivalent viewer to the Windows Forms Viewer exists for ASP.NET-based applications; it's called the *Web Forms Viewer*. This is an ASP.NET control derived from the `WebControl` class. This means that it is a server-side control that renders only HTML to the client browser. No special controls, applets, or files are required on the client in order to view reports with the Web Forms Viewer.

Like the Windows Forms Viewer, the Web Forms Viewer can be found in the Visual Studio .NET toolbox and is called CrystalReportViewer. It is found in the CrystalDecisions.Web namespace and the CrystalDecisions.Web.dll assembly. Many objects used in the Web Forms Viewer are contained in the CrystalDecisions.Shared namespace. The Web Forms Viewer has many properties and methods that control how it displays reports. This section covers these.

The first step to using the viewer is to drop it onto a Web Form from the toolbox. From there, properties can be set via the property browser or via the code-behind for the ASPX page. The first relevant property for the Web Forms Viewer is the `ReportSource` property. The nice thing is that the types of objects that can be passed into the `ReportSource` property are exactly the same as the types of objects that can be passed into the Windows Forms Viewer's `ReportSource` property. For more information on the `ReportSource` Property, refer to "The `ReportSource` Property" section earlier in this chapter.

After the `ReportSource` property is set, you can run the application. When the page is processed, the viewer is created; it processes the report specified in the report source, and then renders the output of the report page to HTML, which gets written to the response stream for the page. Figure 29.5 shows what the Web Forms Viewer looks like in action when rendering a report.

The next section describes some of the common properties used to customize the appearance and behavior of the report viewer.

CUSTOMIZING THE WEB FORMS VIEWER

The first level of customization is to show or hide the main components of the report viewer. The `DisplayGroupTree` and `DisplayToolbar` properties show and hide the group tree and toolbar, respectively. `PageToTreeRatio` is a handy property that enables you to set the

width of the group tree as a ratio to the width of the rest of the page. The default value is 6. To show or hide individual toolbar buttons, there is a collection of properties beginning with Has, such as HasExportButton and HasRefreshButton. Using these properties, you can control each button or button group on the toolbar to meet your needs. In addition, the toolbar buttons themselves are standard gif files contained in the C:\Program Files\Common Files\Business Objects\3.0\crystalreportviewers11\images\toolbar directory.

Figure 29.5
A Crystal Report is shown being displayed through the Web Forms Viewer control.

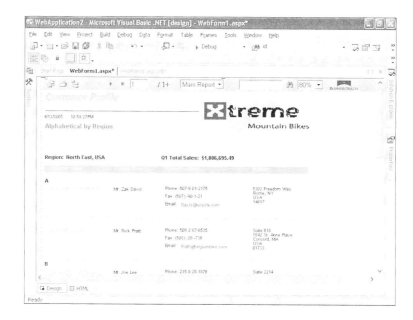

These gif files can be changed using any graphics editing program or even replaced by entirely new images assuming the filenames are kept the same. Finally, there is a style sheet associated with the Web Forms Viewer that can be overridden to change the viewer's colors, fonts, alignment, borders, and more. By default, the viewer looks for the css file in the following location:

```
/crystalreportviewers11/css/default.css
```

This location translates to the following physical path:

```
C:\Program Files\Common Files\Business
Objects\3.0\crystalreportviewers11\css\default.css.
```

You can either modify this default.css file or create multiple copies of the css files, effectively having several skins for the viewer, and dynamically point the viewer to one of the css files based on a user preference. The css file location is set via the CssFilename property of the Web Forms Viewer.

By default, the viewer renders one page of the report at a time, just like the report designer would do. However, sometimes users find that it would be easier to have all the report's content contained on a single Web page. You can do this by setting the SeparatePages property to false instead of its default value of true. When this is done, the viewer renders each page under one another, effectively producing a single Web page with the entire report's data.

DATABASE CREDENTIALS

One of the nice things about the version XI Crystal Report Viewers as opposed to previous versions is that if the report needs database credentials, it prompts the user for this information. Figures 29.6 and 29.7 show the Windows Forms and Web Forms Viewers database credential prompting.

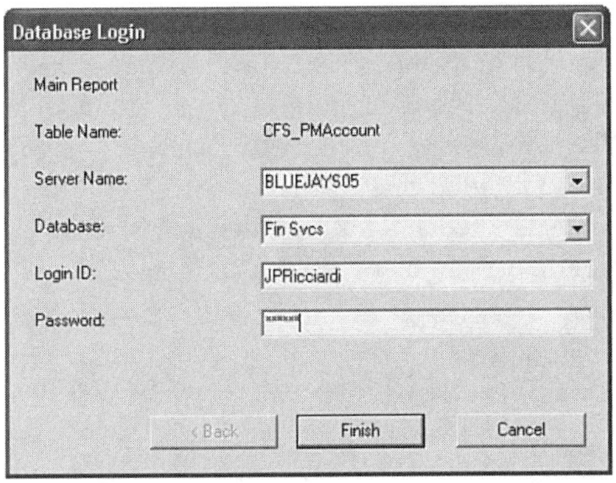

Figure 29.6
The Windows Forms Viewer prompts for database credentials.

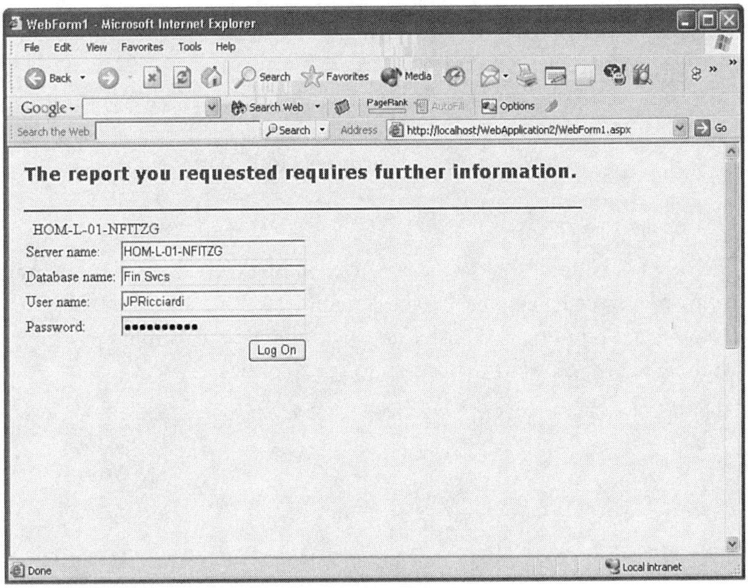

Figure 29.7
The Web Forms Viewer prompts for database credentials.

Although this is a nice feature, you will often want to suppress this and handle the database credentials themselves. The first reason to do this is to change the appearance or behavior of the database credential process. This could be as simple as customizing the look and feel of the user interface or perhaps changing the behavior in some way. For example, you could have the user prompted the first time but offer to save the credentials for later. This could be accomplished by writing the credentials to a cookie or database. The second reason for suppressing the viewer's prompting would be to set the credentials transparently behind the scenes, so the user won't need to enter them at all. The logic of the viewers is to determine whether credentials have been supplied through the viewer directly, and if not, to see if the corresponding report has them defined, and finally if not, to prompt the user. Therefore the solution to customizing or eliminating the database credential prompts is to simply set them before the report is viewed.

The easiest way to do this is to use the ReportDocument's SetDatabaseLogon method. This function is overloaded for several different argument types. There are really only two of them that you will use. The simplest version of SetDatabaseLogon accepts two strings: a username and password. Keep in mind that Crystal Reports stores the information required to connect to the database inside the RPT file, so unless you want to change the database, you only need to set the username and password. An example of this is shown in the following code:

```
Dim Report As New ReportDocument()
Report.Load("C:\Reports\Finance.rpt")
Report.SetDatabaseLogon("username", "password")
Viewer.ReportSource = Report
```

In this case, the Viewer object could be either a Windows Forms Viewer or a Web Forms Viewer because they both have the ReportSource property.

> When using the Web Forms Viewer, keep in mind that the viewer is stateless, that is, each time the ASPX page is processed, the credentials need to be set unless you are caching the ReportDocument object somewhere.

The other version of the SetDatabaseLogon method takes four string arguments: username, password, server name, and database name. This is useful for taking reports based off a test database and pointing them to a production database. Simply pass in the server name and database name you want the report to use, like this:

```
Report.SetDatabaseLogon("username", "password", "SERVER01", "SalesDB")
```

Parameter fields work almost exactly the same as database credentials. Both viewers prompt for parameters if they are required by the report but not supplied by the developer. These parameter prompting screens are shown in Figures 29.8 and 29.9.

Figure 29.8
The Windows Forms
Viewer prompting for
parameter values.

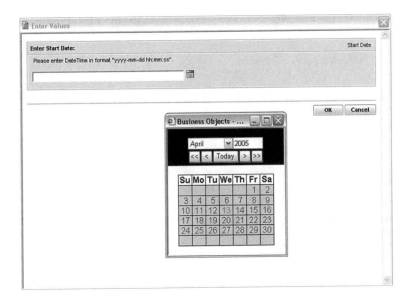

Figure 29.9
The Web Forms
Viewer prompting for
parameter values.

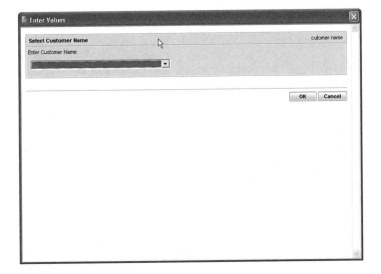

Again, the parameter prompting screens are useful but sometimes don't fit the look and feel of the application or simply need to be suppressed entirely. Another common usage of customized parameter prompting screens is to have the parameter pick list's values come directly from the database so they are always up to date. To do this you would use the ReportDocument object to set the parameters before passing it to the viewer to display. This is done via the ReportDocument's SetParameterValue method. There are three versions of this method:

- SetParameterValue(index As Integer, val As Object) is used to set a parameter value by index.

- SetParameterValue(name As String, val As Object) is used to set a parameter value by name.

- SetParameterValue(name As String, val As Object, subreport As String) is used to set a parameter for a subreport by parameter name and subreport name.

An example of this is

```
Dim Report As New ReportDocument()
Report.Load("C:\Reports\Orders.rpt")
Report.SetParameterValue("Geography", "North America")
Report.SetParameterValue("Start Date", DateTime.Now)
Viewer.ReportSource = Report
```

For parameters that accept multiple values, pass in an array of those values.

UNDERSTANDING THE REPORT APPLICATION SERVER BRIDGE

An important change has occurred to the report engine object model in version XI of Crystal Reports. In fact, you might not even have realized this change has taken place after using Crystal Reports XI for quite some time; however, it's important to understand. The object model that was previously supplied with the various .NET offerings that Business Objects has produced has talked directly to the Crystal Reports print engine. In version XI, the object model talks to the Report Application Server (a component of BusinessObjects Enterprise and Crystal Reports Server), and then in turn to the Crystal Reports engine. Although there is no immediate noticeable change to the way the engine operates, this is an important change for two key reasons:

- The Report Application Server exposes more functionality than the report engine object model discussed thus far, and this additional functionality can now be leveraged from the report engine object model.

- Because the Report Application Server is a part of the BusinessObjects Enterprise framework, any application using the Crystal Reports XI report engine object model and viewers can now be easily upgraded onto the BusinessObjects Enterprise framework.

As for the first point, the Report Application Server's API is available through the standard report engine object model. To access it, use the ReportClientDocument property of the ReportDocument object. The ReportClientDocument is the equivalent to the ReportDocument for the Report Application Server. It includes the capability to not only open and change reports, but also to create reports from scratch, add new report objects, add new data sources, and so on. For more information on the Report Application Server APIs, consult Chapter 34, "Crystal Report Creation and Modification APIs."

CREATING A CRYSTAL REPORT WEB SERVICE

Another notable facet of working in the .NET environment is the capability to create a Crystal Report that is available as a web service and that can be consumed by other applications. To highlight how simply this can be accomplished, Figure 29.10 shows Visual Studio after having added an existing sample Crystal Report (World Sales Report) to a new web service project. Enacting the Publish as Web Service function from the right-click menu creates an asmx file with the name of the report prefixing the text *service*.

Figure 29.10
Visual Studio .NET enables the quick and easy publishing of the World Sales Report as a web service.

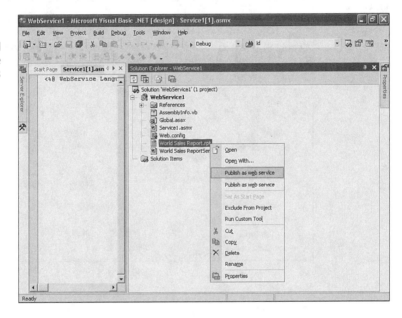

You can test this Crystal Reports web service out by setting the corresponding WorldSalesReportService.asmx file as the starting page for this web service. This option is accessed through the right-click menu of the .asmx object and can be viewed in the browser by accessing http://localhost/WebServiceName/WorldSalesReportService.asmx (see Figure 29.11). You will be presented with a list of the different operations that the report web service supports. You can view sample SOAP request-and-response information using placeholders by clicking on any of the available operations.

To use this web service from another application, you can quickly create a new ASP.NET application called ShowSalesReport (or anything you prefer) and after adding a CrystalReportViewer from the new form's toolbox, bind the ReportSource to either the web service or the involved web service's URL as follows:

```
CrystalReportViewer1.ReportSource = http://localhost/WebService1/
➥World Sales ReportService.asmx
OR
CrystalReportViewer1.ReportSource = New localhost.WorldSalesReportService
```

When adding a Crystal Reports' web service, it is recommended that you eliminate any spaces from the created .asmx web service file. You might experience problems in attempting to click through on the report operations provided by the Crystal Reports' web service when spaces have not been eliminated. Also, remember to build your solutions/projects before testing them in your browser.

Figure 29.11
Viewing the Crystal Reports web service and its associated operations.

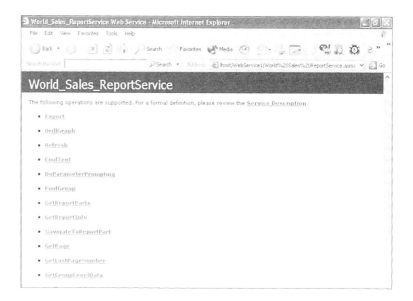

World_Sales_ReportService

The following operations are supported. For a formal definition, please review the Service Description.

- Export
- DrillGraph
- Refresh
- FindText
- DoParameterPrompting
- FindGroup
- GetReportParts
- GetReportInfo
- NavigateToReportPart
- GetPage
- GetLastPageNumber
- GetGroupLevelData

TROUBLESHOOTING

APPLICATION DEPLOYMENT WITH XCOPY

I am having problems using xcopy to deploy applications.

Although the object model is pure managed code, the underlying report engine is not. This means you can't perform a pure xcopy deployment that Microsoft likes to advertise that all .NET applications can do.

PRINTING REPORTS

I can't seem to print a report.

Sometimes when the object model is used in ASP.NET, it is running under a guest-level account, which does not have access to the machine's printers. If this is the case, you need to install and grant access to the printers for that account.

CUSTOMIZED REPORT DISTRIBUTION— USING BUSINESSOBJECTS ENTERPRISE AND CRYSTAL REPORTS SERVER

CHAPTER 30

USING THE BUSINESSOBJECTS ENTERPRISE APIS

In this chapter

OVERVIEW

As you have seen in prior chapters, Business Objects XI is a ready-to-run web-centric enterprise reporting solution that includes a self-service portal called InfoView and, with the purchase of the Application Foundation and/or the Performance Manager suite, a more advanced dashboarding capability. InfoView runs on Java application servers or on the .NET framework and requires no coding. It can be installed and configured in less than one hour. Basic customization including changing images and stylesheets can be done with minimal effort.

With the maturing of web technology over the past several years, organizations of all sizes have invested in home-grown or commercial off-the-shelf (COTS) portals. They have dabbled with single sign-on and spent sleepless nights worrying about the appropriate presentation of corporate logos and style sheets and being concerned with other usability standards. In many of these environments, InfoView might simply not fit in out of the box. It might not look right. It might not fit into the start page you have built, or perhaps, in its full, unbridled, feature-packed glory, your users are simply confused. Less is sometimes more.

This chapter will help you integrate BusinessObjects Enterprise using the SDK.

> The code samples shared in this chapter are part of a white-box portal application you can download from www.usingcrystal.com. The portal is ready to run and most of the code listed here is in a single utility class, BOEUtil.java.

CHOOSING THE RIGHT INTEGRATION APPROACH

The most flexible approach to integrating BusinessObjects Enterprise XI (or its sister product, Crystal Reports Server) is to use a software development kit (SDK) for COM, .NET, or Java. The InfoView portal and portions of the Central Management Console (CMC) are built using these SDKs. By implication, the SDKs are full-featured, and this chapter is devoted to understanding them. The Unified Web Services, described in Chapter 32, "Using the Web Service's SDK," is also very useful especially where CORBA network connectivity is not possible. However, the Web Services SDK is not full-featured.

Before continuing down the code-from-scratch/samples road, you might want to skip ahead to Chapter 31, "Using the Web Components," and see if any of the approaches described there are sufficient for your project. They include the ability to view, create, and edit reports simply by calling URLs; integrating components visually using Java Server Faces (JSF); or simply deploying prebuilt catalog browsing and viewing portlets into Microsoft SharePoint, WebSphere Portal, or any other JSR-168–compliant Java portal.

Before diving into the BusinessObjects Enterprise SDK, Table 30.1 enumerates each of the integration approaches and which platforms they support.

TABLE 30.1   SDK PLATFORM SUPPORT

SDK	Java	.NET	COM
BusinessObjects Enterprise (BOE) SDK	✓	✓	✓
Crystal Page Server/RAS Viewer SDK	✓	✓	✓
Crystal Java Runtime Control (JRC) SDK	✓	▲	▲
Crystal RAS/EROM SDK	✓	✓	✓
Web Intelligence REBean SDK	✓	†	▲
Unified Web Services (UWS) Client SDK	✓	✓	▲
Universe Designer SDK	▲	▲	✓
Application Foundation SDK	†	▲	▲
Dashboard Manager SDK	†	▲	▲

✓ Available, † Private API, ▲ Not applicable/supported

Table 30.2 shows the component integration approaches and the platforms they support.

TABLE 30.2   COMPONENT INTEGRATION PLATFORM SUPPORT

URL/Component/PIK	Java	.NET	COM
URL Reporting	✓	✓	▲
.NET Components	▲	✓	▲
Portal Integration Kits (PIKs)	✓	✓	▲
SharePoint	▲	✓	▲
WebSphere Portal	✓	▲	▲
JSR-168 Portlets	✓	▲	▲

✓ Available, † Private API, ▲ Not applicable/supported

In addition, you will want to determine the quickest and easiest way to provide the customized functionality you desire. The CMC is the 100% zero client web-based administration console that is provided out of the box with BusinessObjects Enterprise and Crystal Reports Server. This application is used in conjunction with each of the other products. Table 30.3 is a comparison matrix to help you determine what administrative functionality you may access with no custom coding.

30

Table 30.3   Out-of-the-Box Capabilities Matrix

Function	URL	PIKs	.NET Components	UWS	SDKs	CMC
Logging in/creating a session	✓	✓	✓	✓	✓	✓
Directory services/SSO support	✓	✓	✓	✓	✓	✓
Logging out	▲	✓	✓	✓	✓	✓
Catalog browsing	▲	✓	✓	✓	✓	✓
Searching for reports or other managed objects	▲	✓	✓	✓	✓	✓
View Crystal Report and thumbnails	✓	✓	✓	✓	✓	✓
Create/edit Crystal Report	▲	▲	✓	▲	✓	▲
View/drill WebI documents	✓	✓	†	✓	✓	✓
Create/edit WebI Documents	✓	✓	†	▲	✓	✓
View OLAP Intelligence documents	▲	✓	✓	▲	✓	✓
View MS Office/PDF documents	▲	✓	✓	▲	✓	✓
Manage Crystal Report notifications	▲	▲	✓	▲	✓	✓
Trigger and manage events	▲	▲	✓	▲	✓	✓
Schedule reports, optionally with events, to various destinations, including e-mail and inbox	▲	✓	✓	▲	✓	✓
Manage and monitor schedules	▲	▲	✓	▲	✓	✓
Access and manage inbox items	▲	✓	✓	▲	✓	✓
Create new objects, folders and categories	▲	✓	✓	▲	✓	✓
Manage security	▲	▲	✓	▲	✓	✓
Set user preferences	▲	✓	✓	▲	✓	▲
Manage and restrict user preferences	▲	▲	✓	▲	✓	✓
System metrics monitoring	▲	▲	✓	▲	✓	✓
Setting server properties	▲	▲	▲	▲	✓	✓
Auditing licenses and security rights	▲	▲	▲	▲	✓	✓
Universe Designer	▲	▲	▲	▲	✓	▲
Business View Manager	▲	▲	▲	▲	†	▲
Dashboard and Performance Manager	▲	▲	▲	▲	†	▲

✓ *Available,* † *Private API,* ▲ *Not applicable/supported*

THE BUSINESSOBJECTS ENTERPRISE SDK

As described in Table 30.3, the BusinessObjects Enterprise SDK provides the developer with the ability to create client and administrative applications leveraging the entire functionality of the suite. Here you'll begin to learn how to install and use the Enterprise SDK.

INSTALLING THE JAVA SDK

The BusinessObjects Enterprise Java SDK consists of a set of Java classes packaged up in a set of JAR files. These JAR files can be found in the following directory:

```
C:\Program Files\Common Files\Business Objects\3.0\java\lib
```

Most Java application servers have the following folder structure for web applications:

```
\ApplicationFolder
    \WEB-INF
        \lib
        \classes
        \src
```

To make the classes contained in these JAR files available for use, copy them to the `lib` folder of your web application.

The naming convention for the Java SDK is almost exactly the same as the COM SDK, which makes it easy for developers working on multiple development platforms. The exception to the naming is that rather than dealing with Java objects directly, interfaces are exposed. These interfaces begin with the letter *I*, for instance, IEnterpriseSession, IInfoStore, and so forth.

> **NOTE**
>
> BusinessObjects Enterprise XI represents the next generation of the Crystal Enterprise 10 infrastructure. For backward compatibility, program management decided to keep "Crystal" in existing API and package names. New packages for XI will use the "BusinessObjects" namespace.

Business Objects product documentation is actually quite good. `Deploying_webintelligence_applications.pdf` is beneficial for deployment and `customizing_webintelligence.pdf` is good for general application development. Please note that not all documentation is actually installed with the product (to make for a faster and smaller footprint install); go to the `docs` directory on the CD to find the rest! Additionally, Java developers ought to consider consulting the COM windows Help file. This format facilitates finding information fast and the API calls are quite similar to those used in Java.

INSTALLING THE .NET SDK

Business Objects has been supporting Microsoft's .NET development platform since its inception. BusinessObjects Enterprise XI provides full .NET support through COM interop assemblies. Fully managed .NET code is planned for future releases. This SDK is intended for use within Microsoft Visual Studio .NET but can also work in other tools, such as Borland C# Builder.

The .NET SDK consists of a set of .NET classes. Like Java, these classes are organized into namespaces. The BusinessObjects Enterprise .NET SDK is contained in the CrystalDecisions.Enterprise namespace. The naming of all the objects is exactly the same as the COM SDK; for instance, `SessionMgr` and `EnterpriseSession`. The .NET assemblies (`.dll` files) that make up the SDK can be found in the following folder:

`\Program Files\Common Files\Business Objects\3.0\managed`

Unlike Java, these files don't need to be copied anywhere in order to be able to program with them. A developer simply needs to bring up the Project References dialog and select which assemblies he wants to use. Although there is only a single namespace, there are multiple physical DLL files. The naming convention is `CrystalDecisions.Enterprise.Module.dll` where *Module* is one of a set of modules that comprise the full Crystal Enterprise SDK. Following are the common assemblies a developer uses:

- `CrystalDecisions.Enterprise.Framework.dll`
- `CrystalDecisions.Enterprise.InfoStore.dll`
- `CrystalDecisions.Web.dll`

`CrystalDecisions.Web.dll` does not conform to the naming convention of the other assemblies. This is because it is a shared component across Crystal Reports and Crystal Enterprise.

> The examples provided in this chapter use the Java SDK. The syntax for .NET SDK is very similar. For .NET developers, many of the snippets shown here have been translated and are available for download at www.usingcrystal.com. Before coding from scratch, .NET developers ought to investigate the .NET component libraries covered in Chapter 31 and in the excellent product documentation.

Accessing the BusinessObjects Enterprise SDK begins with the Session Manager object, `SessionMgr`, that returns a valid session. The user must authenticate against one or more directory services, including the default, built-in directory whose authentication plugin is called secEnterprise. When using the secEnterprise authentication plugin, user credentials (passwords) are stored as encrypted strings in users' respective InfoObject files in the BusinessObjects Enterprise repository. Excepting secEnterprise, authentication occurs against the directory service, and users and groups flagged for replication within the CMS are replicated on-demand with corresponding objects in the BusinessObjects Enterprise repository.

- **secEntrprise**—No external directory required
- **secLDAP**—Customizable LDAP directory adapter

- **secNT**—Under Internet Information Server (IIS)/COM/.NET, transparent Single Sign-On from the user's Windows desktop is supported
- **secAD**—Works the same way as with secNT

In step with the drive to provide transparent cross-platform Single Sign-On (SSO), BusinessObjects Enterprise XI also supports CA SiteMinder. In the future, Business Objects plans to support other vendors such as RSA ClearTrust and Tivoli WebSeal. These can be used today through simple modifications of the InfoView application using the SDK.

Additional security plugins, such as secSAP and secPeopleSoft, are installed with the various BusinessObjects Enterprise solution kits for Enterprise Resource Planning (ERP) packages.

30

> **N O T E**
>
> These authentication snippets, as well as other code listed or described in this chapter, can be found at www.usingcrystal.com in the Java SDK white-box portal. Authentication code is in a file called `_check_authentication.jsp`.

The following code logs in the user and captures her BusinessObjects Enterprise session token.

```
ISessionMgr sm = CrystalEnterprise.getSessionMgr();
IEnterpriseSession es = sm.logon( "Joe", "password", "MY_CMS_NAME",
➥ "secEnterprise" );
```

Enterprise sessions may also be recreated from a token created from an active session. Typically, such a token is created immediately after logging in the user, subsequently storing it in session or in a token, as shown in the following code.

```
ILogonTokenMgr ltm = es.getLogonTokenMgr();
logonToken = ltm.createLogonToken("", 8*60, 100);
```

The logon token can theoretically be used by anyone to access the BusinessObjects Enterprise system, so there are some controls on how long and how many times it can be used. The first argument is the number of seconds the token should live (here, 8 minutes) and the number of times it can be used to reinstantiate the session (here, 100 times). By keeping the EnterpriseSession in application server session memory, the logon token need not be used at all.

The following code shows how to log back onto BusinessObjects Enterprise with the token. This technique is especially useful when session management is on one platform (or application server context) and the BI application is on another. Additionally, as described in Chapter 31, this token can be used to view a document using openDocument without prompting for credentials.

```
IEnterpriseSession es = sm.logonWithToken(logonToken);
```

After a user is logged on using either the `logon` or `logonWithToken` methods, you need to persist the Enterprise Session in application server memory and then create and persist a logon token in a cookie.

In your application, you might not have a logon page at all. Rather, you have some kind of SSO logic that grabs a username and/or password from the environment and uses it to create a new BusinessObjects Enterprise session. If no password is available, one work-around is to reset the users' password with every logon attempt—thereby making entry through a backdoor impossible.

Retrieving Services

After logging on to the SessionMgr with a user credential, the current users' EnterpriseSession object is returned. EnterpriseSession is the key that unlocks the rest of the system. From it, several services may be instantiated by calling the getService method:

- **PSServer**—Crystal Page Server, the highest performance option for serving reports on demand
- **RASReportService**—Crystal RAS Server, most useful for introspecting report file (parameters, for example)
- **ReportEngine**—WebIntelligence Reporting Server
- **InfoStore**—The BusinessObjects Enterprise repository, which is queried using the Query method, returning InfoObjects

A best practice is to retrieve and cache these services in session during the logon routine if you intend on using them more than once in your code. Otherwise, be sure to cache the service upon creation and check for it the next time as follows:

```
IReportSourceFactory factoryPS =
(IReportSourceFactory)session.getAttribute("PSReportFactory");
 if (factoryPS==null){
        factoryPS = (IReportSourceFactory) es.getService("PSReportFactory");
        session.setAttribute("PSReportFactory",factoryPS);
 }
```

After you have created a BusinessObjects Enterprise session, the entire SDK is open for business. The EnterpriseSession created with the previous code exposes several useful getter methods for returning the PluginManager, the SystemInfo (which includes descriptive and diagnostic properties), and the current UserInfo (which contains the user profile and related information), as seen in the previous code sample.

BusinessObjects Enterprise SDK Object Model

As shown in Figures 30.1 and 30.2, the BusinessObjects Enterprise SDK object model describes relationships between top-level objects and methods in the system.

In many respects BusinessObjects Enterprise is an object-oriented SDK. However, some developers will find some of the design patterns unusual. How to interact with the objects should become clear in the following pages.

Figure 30.1
The BusinessObjects Enterprise SDK object model.

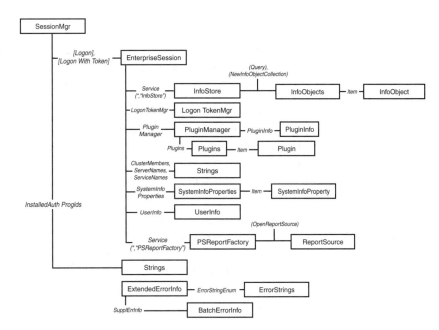

Figure 30.2
The InfoObject detail from the BusinessObjects Enterprise SDK object model.

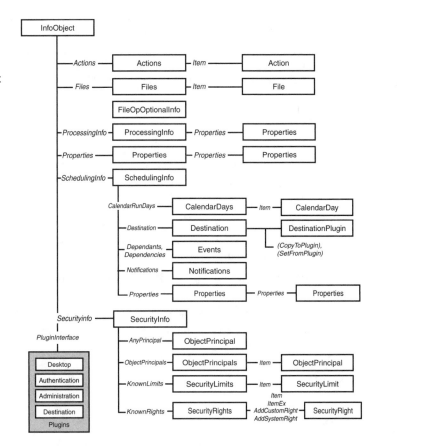

QUERYING THE INFOSTORE

For most everything else that cannot be invoked from the `EnterpriseSession` object, you need to query the InfoStore first. This includes creating objects, scheduling them, updating them, or simply retrieving them.

InfoStore objects include reports, users, groups, folders, categories, dashboards, schedules, license keys, server registrations, Universes, and Business Views—every bit of information that is presented through the portal and which the system needs to function. Regardless of type, they are all InfoObjects that implement the InfoObject interface. Every InfoObject has certain common properties, such as an ID, name, and kind. Other properties are stored as name-value pairs in a property bag datastructure.

Objects are all stored physically in the Business Objects repository database in both primitive (common properties) and composite binary fields (the rest of the bag). If you like, you can inspect the CMS_InfoObjects4 table in a database browser. The model is highly denormalized for performance. In BusinessObjects Enterprise XI, additional tables were added to speed up alias and hierarchy access associated with the inclusion of many-to-many object categorization in the design.

Did you know that the original Seagate Info had more than 20 physical tables? Its successor, Crystal Enterprise 8.0, implemented a new InfoStore service that made much greater use of binary fields in the database and eliminated reliance on database-enforced referential integrity. Smart engineers in Vancouver found that performance increased considerably and that linear scalability was now attainable.

Now that you understand that certain properties are represented physically and indexed in the database and others are buried in binary fields, please forget that there is a physical database behind InfoStore. You will never access this or any of the other tables in the system directly. Rather, you will retrieve objects using an SQL-style syntax executed against an API object called the InfoStore.

The statement below returns a list of all user-names in the system. This code snippet, like others in this chapter, assumes that valid local IInfoStore (iStore) and EnterpriseSession (es) instances have been instantiated.

```
IInfoObjects objs=iStore.query("SELECT SI_NAME FROM CI_SYSTEMOBJECTS WHERE
➡SI_KIND='USER'")
```

Under the covers, the Central Management Server (CMS) service sometimes runs a query against the physical tables, but more often it runs a query against in-memory datastructures it maintains as the system is used.

> **NOTE**
>
> If you want to speed up your InfoStore queries, you can put a loop in your application initialization code that requests a bunch of the objects from the InfoStore. There are obviously short-term performance implications in doing this.

The InfoStore functions much like an object-relational persistence tier with its own proprietary methods of accessing and updating objects. Here are some unusual characteristics that will help you understand some of the other examples in this chapter and the product documentation:

- **Everything is an IInfoObject**—The InfoStore contains many objects of many types or classes. However, they all inherit from the common IInfoObject class that permits them to be queried and persisted in a common manner and allows them to share certain common properties and methods. *Casting* is the conversion of one data type to another. When retrieving an IInfoObject object, it is sometimes necessary to cast it to a more specific object type, such as IReport. At a minimum, when iterating through IInfoObjects returned by an InfoStore query, objects must be cast to an IInfoObject.

- **Creating an object with Plugins**—When you create an object, you won't find a CreateThisTypeOfObject() method in the API. Rather, you need to look up the object type in the InfoStore and first get a reference to a system object called the Plugin interface. Similarly, if you want to schedule to a destination such as e-mail, you must get a destination plugin from the InfoStore. This design is flexible, in that new object types and destinations may be added without affecting the API, but it can be awkward to use.

- **Embedded objects**—Certain objects have what appear to be embedded objects. Job scheduling or report processing objects are accessed from their container objects through the SI_SCHEDULEINFO and SI_PROCESSINFO properties respectively. For instance, iStore.query("SELECT SI_SCHEDULEINFO FROM CI_INFOSTORE WHERE SI_NAME='World Sales Report'") will return each of the schedules created for the World Sales Report. Embedded objects, such as scheduling or processing information, must be cast before they can be accessed.

- **Committing changes to objects**—There is, in fact, no way to commit changes to one object. Every change to an InfoStore object starts with selecting *all* objects that meet certain criteria, iterating through the collection, modifying one or more InfoObject, and then committing *all* of the originally retrieved objects to the InfoStore.

Knowing what types of objects and their properties that are available for selection and/or for filtering the InfoStore will help you understand what you can do with BusinessObjects Enterprise. These topics are covered next.

BUSINESSOBJECTS ENTERPRISE CATEGORIES, KINDS, AND CASTING

InfoStore objects live virtually in one of three categories which are accessed in the FROM clause of an InfoStore query. Different types of objects belong to different categories. In fact, several objects, such as Folder, belong to *more than one* category. In BusinessObjects

Enterprise XI you no longer need to use the `CI_PROGID` identifier to find a certain type of object, but rather you use the more friendly `CI_KIND` property. Kinds can be accessed literally or through the `com.crystaldecisions.sdk.plugin.CeKinds` enumeration. Note that sometimes the enumerated constant is not the same as the literal value. The following query string will return no values:

```
IInfoObjects objs=iStore.query("SELECT TOP 1 FROM CI_INFOOBJECTS WHERE
➥ SI_KIND='CRYSTAL_REPORT'");
```

These two, however, will work:

```
IInfoObjects objs=iStore.query("SELECT TOP 1 FROM CI_INFOOBJECTS
➥WHERE SI_KIND='"+ com.crystaldecisions.sdk.plugin.CeKinds.CRYSTAL_REPORT+"'");
IInfoObjects objs=iStore.query("SELECT TOP 1 FROM CI_INFOOBJECTS
➥WHERE SI_KIND='CrystalReport'");
```

This is because the literal value `"CRYSTAL_REPORT"` is not a `SI_KIND`. However, `com.crystaldecisions.sdk.plugin.CeKinds.CRYSTAL_REPORT` evaluates to `"CrystalReport"`.

Tables 30.4–30.7 list what kinds of objects can be found in each category, as well as the interface objects to which they must be cast for all of their properties to be accessible. Certain object types specific to the Application Foundation and Performance Management suite of products are unpublished.

Although not shown, `Folder` objects can be referenced from all three table contexts.

- **CI_INFOOBJECTS**—Contains portal content

TABLE 30.4   CI_INFOOBJECTS KINDS

SI_KIND Value	CeKind Enumeration	Interface
AFDashboardPage	AFDASHBOARDPAGE	Unpublished
Analytic	ANALYTIC	Unpublished
Category	CATEGORY	ICategory
CrystalReport	CRYSTAL_REPORT	IReport
Excel	EXCEL	IExcel
FavoritesFolder	FAVORITESF	IFolder
Folder	FOLDER	IFolder
Hyperlink	HYPERLINK	IHyperlink
Inbox	INBOX	IInbox
MyInfoView	MYINFOVIEW	Unpublished
ObjectPackage	OBJECTPACKAGE	IObjectPackage
Pdf	PDF	IPDF
PersonalCategory	PERSONALCAT	ICategory
Powerpoint	POWERPOINT	IPowerpoint

SI_KIND Value	CeKind Enumeration	Interface
Program	PROGRAM	IProgram
Shortcut	SHORTCUT	IShortcut
Txt	TEXT	ITxt
Webi	WEBI	IWebi
Word	WORD	IWord

- **CI_SYSTEMOBJECTS**—Contains system objects required for the system to function and that are displayed and managed in the user interface

TABLE 30.5   CI_SYSTEMOBJECTS KINDS

SI_KIND Value	CeKind Enumeration	Interface
Calendar	CALENDAR	ICalendar
Connection	CONNECTION	IConnection
Event	EVENT	IEvent
LicenseKey	LICENSEKEY	ILicenseKey
Server	SERVER	IServer, IServerGeneralMetrics
User	USER	IUser
UserGroup	USERGROUP	IUserGroup

- **CI_APPOBJECTS**—Other objects stored in the repository but managed through client-server tools or add-ons to the system

TABLE 30.6   CI_APPOBJECTS KINDS

SI_KIND Value	CeKind Enumeration	Interface
AppFoundation	APPFOUNDATION	Unpublished
CMC	CMC	Unpublished
Designer	DESIGNER	Unpublished
Discussions	DISCUSSIONS	Unpublished
InfoView	INFOVIEW	Unpublished
StrategyBuilder	STRATEGY_BUILDER	Unpublished
Universe	UNIVERSE	IUniverse
WebIntelligence	WEBINTELLIGENCE	IWebi

Several other kinds of objects require more sophisticated query statements to access. They include destination and security plugins.

TABLE 30.7   OTHER OBJECT KINDS

SI_KIND Value	CeKind Enumeration	Interface
Destination	DESTINATION	IDestination
DiskUnmanaged	DISKUNMANAGED	IDiskUnmanaged
Ftp	FTP	IFTP
Managed	MANAGED	IManged
Overload	OVERLOAD	IOverload
Rtf	RTF	IRTF
secEnterprise	SEC_ENTERPRISE	IsecEnterprise
secLDAP	SEC_LDAP	IsecLDAP
secWinAD	SEC_WINAD	IsecWinAD
secWindowsNT	SEC_WINDOWSNT	IsecWinNT
ServerGroup	SERVER_GROUP	IServerGroup
Smtp	SMTP	ISMTP

BusinessObjects Enterprise Object Properties

Object properties are discussed next, organized first by common, indexed properties, and then by the types of objects or functions for which they are used. These properties can be found in the CePropertyID enumerated list and a complete list can be found in the SDK documentation itself. Usage notes are provided inline and several of the more commonly used ones will reappear in the sections and samples that follow.

Property Bags

All InfoObject properties—both indexed and nonindexed—are accessible from the object's property bag interface, properties(). These properties are accessed with their CePropertyID identifier as shown here:

```
//get the object
IInfoObject obj=(IInfoObject)objs.get(0);
//get the SI_INSTANCE property
int SI_INSTANCE =obj.properties().getProperty(CePropertyID.SI_INSTANCE).
➥getValue();
```

However, certain indexed properties have direct accessor methods as noted. For instance, getID() saves a few keystrokes on obj.properties().getProperty(CePropertyID.SI_ID). getValue(). Should you want to list everything in an IInfoObject, you could use call a function to recursively display the object property bags. This is such a useful function that it is provided in Listing 30.1 in its entirety.

LISTING 30.1   RECURSIVELY LISTING IINFOOBJECT PROPERTIES

```
public static String infoObjectToString(IInfoObject obj){
    return propertyBagToString(obj.properties());
}
public static String propertyBagToString(IProperties propMap) {
    return propertyBagToString(propMap,"");
}
private static String propertyBagToString(IProperties propMap,String
➥ prefix) {
    StringBuffer buff = new StringBuffer();
    buff.setLength(0);
    if ((propMap != null) && (propMap.size() > 0)) {
        Iterator iter = propMap.entrySet().iterator();
        while (iter.hasNext()) {
            Map.Entry p = (Map.Entry) iter.next();
            Integer id=(Integer)p.getKey();
            buff.append(prefix+CePropertyID.idToName(id));
            IProperty prop=(IProperty)p.getValue();
            if (prop.isContainer()){
                IProperties props=(IProperties)prop.getValue();
                buff.append("\n");

buff.append(propertyBagToString(props,prefix+CePropertyID.idToName(id)+"."));
            } else {
                buff.append("="+prop.getValue()+"\n");
            }
        }
    }
    return buff.toString();
}
```

This function returns property objects that fall into one of three categories:

- Top-level properties that contain values such as strings and integers
- Composite properties that contain other properties that require casting
- Composite properties that actually represent embedded objects with their own identifiers in the system

The SI_SCHEDINFO property, for instance, contains a collection of job objects that spawn new instances on a schedule. Listing 30.2 shows many of the properties for the Product Category report, which has not been assigned to any corporate or personal categories, scheduled, or had its default processing options modified; Microsoft Access requires none and the system default printer is assigned by default. The listing shows the output properties for the Product Catalog sample report shipping with BusinessObjects Enterprise. Properties such as SI_FILE are composite properties. There are no embedded objects in this listing as the report has not been scheduled.

LISTING 30.2   PRODUCT CATALOG REPORT PROPERTY LISTING

```
SI_APPLICATION_OBJECT=false
SI_AUTHOR=Copyright © 2004 Business Objects
SI_BUSINESSVIEWS
SI_BUSINESSVIEWS.SI_TOTAL=0
SI_CHILDREN=28
SI_COMPONENT=false
SI_CORPORATE_CATEGORIES
SI_CORPORATE_CATEGORIES.SI_TOTAL=0
SI_CREATION_TIME=Mon Dec 06 17:58:25 PST 2004
SI_CUID=AaCbu62TlMdDo60E358dydA
SI_DESCRIPTION=Product catalog, grouped by Product Class, Product Type and
➥ Product Name with Product Type picture and description. Drill down on
➥ Product Name for item numbers, sizes, etc.
SI_FILES
SI_FILES.SI_FILE1=~ce14483a4783797718.rpt
SI_FILES.SI_FILE2=~ce14483a478383d719.jpeg
SI_FILES.SI_NUM_FILES=2
SI_FILES.SI_PATH=frs://Input/a_194/024/000/6338/
SI_FILES.SI_VALUE1=728064
SI_FILES.SI_VALUE2=23015
SI_FLAGS=2050
SI_GUID=AbzQfLTci61CnFu8C6sIH3Y
SI_HASSAVEDDATA=false
SI_HASTHUMBNAIL=true
SI_HIDDEN_OBJECT=false
SI_ID=6338
SI_INSTANCE_OBJECT=false
SI_INSTANCE=false
SI_IS_SCHEDULABLE=true
SI_KIND=CrystalReport
SI_LAST_RUN_TIME=Fri Feb 18 14:25:09 PST 2005
SI_LAST_SUCCESSFUL_INSTANCE_ID=32052
SI_NAME=Product Catalog
SI_OBJECT_IS_CONTAINER=false
SI_OBTYPE=2
SI_OWNER=Administrator
SI_OWNERID=12
SI_PARENT_CUID=ARD1V.IRaKdPs3fPUzttR3k
SI_PARENT_FOLDER_CUID=ARD1V.IRaKdPs3fPUzttR3k
SI_PARENT_FOLDER=6322
SI_PARENTID=6322
SI_PERSONAL_CATEGORIES
SI_PERSONAL_CATEGORIES.SI_TOTAL=0
SI_PLUGIN_OBJECT=false
SI_PROGID=CrystalEnterprise.Report
SI_REFRESH_OPTIONS=-2
SI_RUID=AaCbu62TlMdDo60E358dydA
SI_RUNNABLE_OBJECT=false
SI_SENDABLE=true
SI_SYSTEM_OBJECT=false
SI_TABLE=0
SI_TOPIC_TOPIC_FOR_SUBJECT_GENERICENTITY
SI_TOPIC_TOPIC_FOR_SUBJECT_GENERICENTITY.SI_TOTAL=0
SI_TURNONREPOSITORY=false
SI_TURNONTHUMBNAIL=true
SI_UPDATE_TS=Fri Feb 18 14:25:09 PST 2005
```

INDEXED PROPERTIES

Every property in the property bag can be supplied in the SELECT clause (but not necessarily in the WHERE clause) of an InfoView query. Embedded object properties make no sense in the WHERE clause, but the full path to embedded object properties might. Querying for IInfoObjects WHERE SI_FILES.SI_NUM_FILES > 1 is a bogus, but valid, example. However, when querying the InfoStore, it is vital to include at least one common, indexed property to help reduce the working set. These properties exist physically in the repository database and can be queried at will without degrading system performance. Filtering exclusively on a nonindexed property forces the InfoStore API to open and examine every object in the InfoStore table to find a match. Such fields must be read, parsed, and loaded into the InfoStore memory cache before they can be used by the system, which can take time and precious CPU cycles.

NOTE

> Don't worry about the order of fields in the WHERE clause—BusinessObjects Enterprise will reorder evaluation from indexed to nonindexed properties appropriately prior to execution.

Table 30.8 lists all of the indexed properties. The boolean properties SI_HIDDEN_OBJECT, SI_NAMED_USER, and SI_PLUGINOBJECT are rarely used and have been omitted from this table. Certain job-specific properties might be null. Especially in Java, you must always test for nulls to avoid the dreaded and never specific Null Pointer Exception. Code defensively!

TABLE 30.8   INDEXED PROPERTIES

Property	Type	InfoObject Accessor Method	Description/Usage Notes
SI_ID	Integer	getID()	A sequence number unique to a single installation unless it is a common, default system object below 350. Remember that your code will not work if you hard-code an object's SI_ID and then move that object from your development to test to production environments.
SI_CUID	String	getCUID()	A string identifier, unique and consistent across all environments. Migration safe.
SI_GUID	String	getGUID()	Reserved for future use.

continues

TABLE 30.8 INDEXED PROPERTIES

Property	Type	InfoObject Accessor Method	Description/Usage Notes
SI_RUID	String	getRUID()	A string identifier that uniquely identifies an InfoObject within an object package. Outside of a package, it is equivalent to SI_CUID.
SI_NAME	String primitive	getTitle()	Object name or title. Note that instances and jobs share the same name. It is typically insufficient to query on SI_NAME alone.
SI_KIND	String	getKind()	New to BusinessObjects Enterprise XI, this property replaces SI_PROGID as the preferred method for retrieving objects of a certain type (as discussed above).
SI_DESCRIPTION	String	getDescription()	Longer description.
SI_PROGID	String	getProgID()	The internal object type identifier. For example, CrystalEnterprise. CrystalReport.
SI_OWNERID	Integer	getOwnerID()	The owner of this object. Particularly useful when trying to find a user's recurring or one-time job schedules or historical instances they have created.
SI_PARENTID	Integer	getParentID()	The parent of this object. For report templates, this refers to the parent folder. For report instances, SI_PARENTID points to the report template rather than the containing folder. The noninteger property SI_PARENT_FOLDER is the best way to finds an instance's folder.

Property	Type	InfoObject Accessor Method	Description/Usage Notes
SI_UPDATE_TS	Timestamp	Property bag	The last time any property of the object was modified. Date is returned in the format MM/DD/YYYY HH:MM:SS AM/PM. In the WHERE clause, these formats are valid: yyyy.mm.dd.hh.mm.ss, yyyy/mm/dd/hh/mm/ss, yyyy/mm/dd.hh.mm.ss, yyyy/mm/dd,hh:mm:ss. For example, `SELECT SI_ID, SI_NAME FROM CI_INFOOBJECTS WHERE SI_UPDATE_TS > '2000.01.11.18:00:00'`.
SI_INSTANCE, SI_INSTANCE_OBJECT	Boolean 1/0	Property bag	Specifies whether to retrieve the report/document or an historical instance run by the scheduler as a job.
SI_NEXTRUNTIME	Timestamp	Property bag	Nullable. The next time that one of the job servers will attempt to create an instance. See usage notes for SI_UPDATE_TS.
SI_RECURRING	Boolean 1/0	Property bag	May be null. For job/schedule embedded objects, indicates whether a job will run more than once.
SI_RUNNABLE_OBJECT	Boolean 1/0	Property bag	May be null. Crystal Reports, Web Intelligence, Program Objects, and Object Packages can be scheduled. To be runnable, such an object must actually be scheduled to run and create an instance.
SI_SCHEDULE_STATUS	Integer	Property bag	May be null. Status of a runnable object. Constantly requires decoding using the ceScheduleStatus enumeration.

COMPOSITE PROPERTIES, EMBEDDED OBJECTS

As discussed earlier, certain properties contain other properties and, in the case of SI_SCHEDINFO, have identifiers that permit individual retrieval and manipulation. A simple example is that SI_PATH, which is for folder objects, returns the property bag that includes the IDs, names, and types of every folder ancestor for the object. The function `folderBreadCrumbs(String folderID, IInfoStore iStore)` found in BOEUtil.java on www.usingcrystal.com shows how this is used.

Table 30.9 highlights some other composite properties that contain both primitive and composite values. Subproperties can be queried using dot notation. For instance, the following code retrieves the names of all the users who scheduled the World Sales Report.

```
String sql = " SELECT  SI_SCHEDULEINFO.SI_SUBMITTER FROM  CI_INFOOBJECTS
➡  WHERE  SI_NAME='World Sales Report'";
IInfoObjects objects = iStore.query(sql);
```

TABLE 30.9   COMPOSITE PROPERTIES (INCOMPLETE LIST)

Composite Property	Sample Property Values (Vary Based on Data)	Embedded Object Properties
SI_SCHEDULEINFO Returns multiple schedule (job) objects associated with an InfoObject or the schedule object itself (if accessed directly).	SI_ENDTIME=Wed Mar 16 00:00:00 PST 2005 SI_NAME=Product Catalog SI_OBJID=31747 SI_OUTCOME=0 SI_PROGRESS=1 SI_RETRIES_ALLOWED=0 SI_RETRIES_ATTEMPTED=0 SI_RETRY_INTERVAL=1800 SI_SCHED_NOW=false SI_SCHEDULE_INTERVAL_HOURS=0 SI_SCHEDULE_INTERVAL_MINUTES=0 SI_SCHEDULE_INTERVAL_MONTHS=0 SI_SCHEDULE_INTERVAL_NDAYS=0 SI_SCHEDULE_INTERVAL_NTHDAY=0 SI_SCHEDULE_TYPE=8 SI_STARTTIME=Wed Feb 16 18:13:00 PST 2005 SI_SUBMITTER=Administrator SI_SUBMITTERID=12 SI_TIMEZONE_ID=0 SI_TYPE=2 SI_UISTATUS=9	SI_DEPENDANTS SI_DEPENDENCIES SI_DESTINATION SI_RUN_ON_ TEMPLATE

Composite Property	Sample Property Values (Vary Based on Data)	Embedded Object Properties
SI_PROCESSINFO Contains report processing directives.	SI_DBNEEDLOGON=true SI_DEPENDS_ON_CIV=false SI_DEPENDS_ON_METADATA=false SI_GROUP_FORMULA= SI_HAS_DCP=false SI_NAME=Statement of Account SI_NUM_GROUPS=2 SI_OBJID=6333 SI_RECORD_FORMULA={Orders.Order Amount}>0 and {Orders.Shipped}=Yes and not {Orders.Payment Received} SI_RFSH_HITS_DB=true SI_ROW_LEVEL_SECURITY=false SI_SESSION_NEEDINFO=false SI_SESSION_USER= SI_SHARE_INTERVAL=300 SI_SHARE_SETTINGS=false SI_SHARE=true SI_USES_FILE_DB=false	SI_ALERT_INFO SI_BUSINESS_ VIEW_INFO SI_FILES SI_FORMAT_INFO SI_HYPERLINK_ INFO SI_LOGON_INFO SI_PRINTER_INFO SI_PROMPTS SI_REPOSITORY_ OBJECTS
SI_PATH Ancestor folders.	SI_FOLDER_OBTYPE1=1 SI_FOLDER_ID1=6319 SI_FOLDER_NAME1=Report Samples SI_NUM_FOLDERS=1	
SI_FILES Path to file report template and thumbnail in the File Input Server.	SI_FILE1=~ce14483a4783797718.rpt SI_FILE2=~ce14483a478383d719.jpeg SI_NUM_FILES=2 SI_VALUE1=728064 SI_VALUE2=23015	

For more information on these composite properties, consult the documentation and use the property bag recurser function to explore them yourself.

PROPERTY ENUMERATIONS

In Listing 30.3 and in ones that follow, property values are represented as numeric constants or codes. Fortunately, there is an easy way to decode these values—the static method on CePropertyID called idToName(java.lang.Integer id). This function will work for every property, although you might want to write your own based on the appropriate SDK property enumeration.

LISTING 30.3   SCHEDULE STATUS DECODER

```
public static String getScheduleStatusDescription(int status) {
    switch (status) {
        case (ISchedulingInfo.ScheduleStatus.COMPLETE):
            return "COMPLETE. Job completed successfully.";
<SNIP></SNIP>
        default:
            return "Status code not found";
    }
}
```

Other enumerations to familiarize yourself with include CeEvents, CeKind, and CeScheduleType. Enumerations in the ISchedulingInfo interface include GroupChoice, ScheduleFlags, ScheduleOutcome, and ScheduleStatus. For a complete list of enumerations, please consult the API documentation.

> The etymology of the *CI* and *SI* in table and property names might reflect the company heritage of the product, first in Seagate Software's Seagate Info, and then in Crystal Decisions, Crystal Enterprise. The *C* could also stand for *Catalog*. This kind of legacy name pollution is common in the software industry.

SYSTEM OBJECTS AND ROOT FOLDERS

As you get into more advanced SDK programming, it will help to know the addresses of well-known system objects and root folders. There are more than 100 such objects installed by default with BusinessObjects Enterprise. Only their enumerations are listed here for brevity:

- **CeSecurityID.Folder**—The IDs of the BusinessObjects Enterprise system folders.
- **CeSecurityID.Limit**—The IDs of the BusinessObjects Enterprise system security limits.
- **CeSecurityID.Right**—The IDs of the BusinessObjects Enterprise system security rights.
- **CeSecurityID.User**—Common user and group IDs.
- **CeSecurityCUID.AppConfigObject**—Identifies the unique CUIDs that are used in a query to specify the application configuration components. Remember, these are in the CI_SYSTEMOBJECTS category.
- **CeSecurityCUID.Relation**—Identifies the unique CUIDs that are used in a query to retrieve related, dynamically generated objects.

- **CeSecurityCUID.RootFolder**—Identifies the unique CUIDs that are used in a query to specify the root folder. The following SELECT statement can be used to return top level folders:

```
sql = "Select * FROM CI_INFOOBJECTS where SI_KIND = 'Folder' and
➥ SI_PARENTID="+BOEUtil.getObjectByCUID(CeSecurityCUID.RootFolder.
➥FOLDERS,"CI_INFOOBJECTS",iStore).getID();
objects = iStore.query(sql);
```

- **CeSecurityCUID.SystemObject**—Identifies the unique CUIDs that are used in a query to specify the system objects. Remember, these are in the CI_SYSTEMOB-JECTS category.

> **NOTE**
>
> Please note that the identifiers provided in these enumerations are the CUID unique identifiers, not numeric identifiers. As a result, filters such as SI_ANCESTOR that expect a numeric ID will not work.
>
> This statement fails:
>
> ```
> IInfoObjects objs=iStore.query("SELECT * CI_APPOBJECTS WHERE
> SI_ANCESTOR=" + CeSecurityCUID.RootFolder.UNIVERSES +
> ➥" AND SI_KIND='Universe' ORDER BY SI_NAME");
> ```
>
> However, this works:
>
> ```
> IInfoObjects objs=iStore.query("SELECT SI_ID CI_APPOBJECTS
> ➥WHERE SI_CUID='" + CeSecurityCUID.RootFolder.
> ➥UNIVERSES+"'");
> int UnvRootID=((IInfoObject)objs.get(0)).getID();
> System.out.println("UnvRootID:"+UnvRootID);
> IInfoObjects unvs=iStore.query("SELECT SI_ID, SI_NAME, SI_CUID
> ➥FROM CI_APPOBJECTS WHERE SI_ANCESTOR="+ UnvRootID+" AND
> ➥SI_KIND='Universe' ORDER BY SI_NAME");
> ```
>
> Remember, Universe objects are in the CI_APPOBJECTS category.

Certain system objects, unfortunately, are not in any enumeration. For instance, the only way to schedule objects to e-mail is to get a handle on an SMTP destination plugin, which is a child of the object known by its CUID as `CeSecurityCUID.SystemObject.PLUGIN`. You can iterate through these children yourself and see that the SMTP destination plugin has an ID of 29.

PERMISSIONS

Another set of constants is the rights registered for each object type. Global security rights are in the CeSecurityID.Right enumeration. Certain objects cannot be scheduled, so schedule-oriented rights naturally do not apply to those objects. System administrators will be familiar with the following enumerated rights from the CMC console:

- **CeSecurityID.Right**—ADD, COPY, DELETE, DELETE_INSTANCE, EDIT, MODIFY_RIGHTS, OWNER_DELETE, OWNER_DELETE_INSTANCE, OWNER_EDIT, OWNER_MODIFY_RIGHTS, OWNER_PAUSE_RESUME_ SCHEDULE, OWNER_RESCHEDULE, OWNER_SECURED_MODIFY_ RIGHTS,OWNER_VIEW, OWNER_VIEW_INSTANCE, PAUSE_RESUME_ SCHEDULE, PICK_MACHINES, RESCHEDULE, SCHEDULE, SCHEDULE_ON_BEHALF_OF, SECURED_MODIFY_RIGHTS, SET_ DESTINATION, VIEW, VIEW_INSTANCE
- **CeReportRightID**—DOWNLOAD, EXPORT, PRINT, REFRESH_ON_DEMAND
- **CeWebiRightID**—DOWNLOAD_FILES, EDIT_QUERY, EXPORT_REPORT_ DATA, REFRESH_LIST_OF_VALUES, RUN_AND_REFRESH_DOC, USE_LIST_ OF_VALUES, VIEW_SQL

Using the permissions model fully is very complicated because BusinessObjects Enterprise supports cascading, inherited rights on folders and from groups, as well as explicit denials. The most basic permissions (viewing a folder or report), are resolved transparently within an InfoStore query. Objects that cannot be seen by the user are not returned. However, for more advanced rights, you need to use the ISecurityInfo.checkCustomRights method. Listing 30.4 shows how to determine a user's WebI viewing rights.

LISTING 30.4 DETERMINING USER PERMISSIONS

```
// Webi app rights
IInfoObject app = getWebiAppObj(es, iStore);
if (app != null) {
    int[] rightsToCheck = new int[]{
        CeWebIntelligenceRightID.INTERACTIVEVIEW,
        CeWebIntelligenceRightID.HTMLREPORTPANEL,
        CeWebIntelligenceRightID.JAVAREPORTPANEL,
        CeWebIntelligenceRightID.DRILLMODE,
        CeWebIntelligenceRightID.CREATEDOCUMENTS};
    String kind = app.getKind();
    String[] kinds = new String[rightsToCheck.length];
    for (int i = 0; i < kinds.length; i++)
        kinds[i] = kind;
    ISecurityInfo secInfo = app.getSecurityInfo();
    boolean[] results = secInfo.checkCustomRights(rightsToCheck,
    ➥ kinds, false);
    r.setWebiInteractiveViewingAllowed(results[0]);
    r.setWebiHtmlReportPanelAllowed(results[1]);
    r.setWebiJavaReportPanelAllowed(results[2]);
    r.setWebiDrillModeAllowed(results[3]);
    r.setWebiCreateDocsAllowed(results[4]);
}
```

Rights can also be checked individually. Please consult the product documentation for more information.

SETTING CUSTOM PROPERTIES

The BusinessObjects Enterprise InfoObject is a very versatile container that easily persists properties for every type of object. The following code shows how you can add custom properties to InfoObjects. Remember the process for updating a document: query for objects, choose an object, set properties on that object, commit (all) objects.

```
public static void propertiesSet(int objID, String category, HashMap props,
➥ IInfoStore iStore) throws SDKException {
        IInfoObjects objs = iStore.query("SELECT * FROM "+category+" WHERE
        ➥ SI_ID="+objID);
        IInfoObject obj=(IInfoObject)objs.get(0);
        Iterator iter=props.entrySet().iterator();
        while (iter.hasNext()){
            Object key=(String)iter.next();
            obj.properties().setProperty(key,props.get(key));
        }
        iStore.commit(objs);
}
```

Note that custom properties cannot be accessed directly using syntax such as SI_MY_ CUSTOM_PROPERTY. To access them you must use the asterix (*) in the SELECT clause when searching for custom properties and then use the getProperty() method used in the recursive property bag lister.

USING * AND TOP N

As discussed, queries that return all properties using the asterisk operator (*) might actually return many objects. It is conceivable that a report could have 1,000 schedules associated with it. Selecting the SI_SCHEDINFO project might return 1,000 rows for 1 report alone.

Another must-know tip is how to use Top N. In BusinessObjects Enterprise, SELECT * returns an upper-limit of 1,000 objects. You can specifically ask for more or fewer objects using SELECT TOP N. You can see whether you are looking at all of the records that satisfy your query by comparing the resultInfoObjcts.getResultSize() method to the actual number of records found through the resultInfoObjcts.size() method.

QUERY EXAMPLES

Now that you understand the syntax of querying the InfoStore, some of the properties, and how they are nested, look at the following examples harvested from the documentation and the author's own BusinessObjects Enterprise projects. The example includes only the query statement itself and an explanation of what is returned by the query. The InfoStore only returns the objects that the user is permitted to view:

- Report templates in the Report Samples folder or subfolders. SI_ANCESTOR can only be used in the WHERE clause.
  ```
  SELECT SI_NAME  FROM CI_INFOOBJECTS WHERE SI_ANCESTOR=6319 AND SI_INSTANCE=0
  ```

- List of universe meta-layers.
  ```
  SELECT * FROM CI_APPOBJECTS WHERE SI_KIND='Universe' ORDER BY SI_NAME ASC
  ```

30

- Parent folder of all universes.

```
SELECT SI_ID FROM CI_APPOBJECTS WHERE SI_PARENTID=95 AND SI_NAME='Universes'
```

- Scheduled jobs submitted by WRichards for World Sales Report.

```
SELECT SI_ID FROM CI_INFOOBJECTS WHERE SI_NAME = 'World Sales Report'
➥AND SI_SCHEDULEINFO.SI_SUBMITTER = 'WRichards'
```

- Get recurring scheduled jobs owned by WRichards. SI_RECURRING will be null for non-jobs and 0 for one-time jobs.

```
SELECT * FROM CI_INFOOBJECTS WHERE SI_OWNERID='WRichards' AND SI_RECURRING=1
```

- Get all scheduled jobs owned by WRichards. Note how selecting SI_SCHEDINFO forces selection of job objects.

```
SELECT SI_SCHEDINFO FROM CI_INFOOBJECTS WHERE SI_OWNERID='WRichards'
```

- Get all objects owned by WRichards.

```
SELECT * FROM CI_INFOOBJECTS WHERE SI_OWNERID='WRichards'
```

- Get report templates owned by WRichards. SI_INSTANCE will return null for nonreport objects, 1 for report instances, and 0 for templates.

```
SELECT * FROM CI_INFOOBJECTS WHERE SI_OWNERID='WRichards' AND SI_INSTANCE=0
```

- Returns instances of report identified by 215.

```
SELECT * FROM CI_INFOOBJECTS WHERE SI_PARENTID=215 AND SI_INSTANCE=1
```

- Returns top-level report templates that have been scheduled to run.

```
SELECT * FROM CI_INFOOBJECTS WHERE SI_RUNNABLE_OBJECT=1
```

REPORT BROWSING USING INFOOBJECT QUERIES

Now that you are familiar with the structure of the InfoStore and how it is queried, you can now build portals that use it. In an effort to keep this book a manageable weight, you will need to download many of the code samples discussed here from www.usingcrystal.com. The directory.jsp page provides users with the ability to browse and drill through BusinessObjects Enterprise folders and view the reports contained therein. This file brings together several concepts: querying the InfoStore, iterating through InfoObjects, opening reports using the OpenDocument dispatcher (covered in greater depth in Chapter 31), showing Crystal Report thumbnails (Web Intelligence documents have none), and using JavaScript in your user interface.

CREATING OBJECTS AND CAPTURING THEIR IDS

As discussed earlier, creating objects using the BusinessObjects Enterprise SDK requires first instantiating an object factory called the plugin manager. In programming, a *factory* provides users a place for instantiating several types of objects. The IPluginMgr factory uses a method named getPluginInfo that takes the object's internal program ID identifier type. This is the PROG_ID property found in every object.

As noted earlier, objects may be created, but not submitted, individually to the InfoStore. An InfoObject collection must be created first and then new objects can be added to it. The ID of the object is available immediately after it is added to the collection using the standard `getID()` accessor method. Most objects require setting their title (name) and parent object identifier. Some, such as users and groups, do not. Please consult the documentation before creating new document types—many require implementing interfaces that are beyond the scope of this book. Listing 30.5 shows how to create a new folder object using the PluginMgr and capture its unique identifier.

LISTING 30.5   CREATING A FOLDER

```
//get parent folder ID using lookup function in BOEUtil class found on
//http://www.usingcrystal.com
int PARENT_ID=BOEUtil.getObjectByName("Report Samples",iStore).getID();
//instantiate plugin manager factory
IPluginMgr pluginMgr = iStore.getPluginMgr();
//choose folder plugin by its progID
IPluginInfo folderPlugin = pluginMgr.getPluginInfo("CrystalEnterprise.Folder");
//provision a new infoobject collection
IInfoObjects newInfoObjects = iStore.newInfoObjectCollection();
//add an empty infoobject to the collection
IInfoObject infoObject = newInfoObjects.add(folderPlugin);
//get the object's numeric ID
int newObjectID=infoObject.getID();
//set required properties
infoObject.setTitle(FOLDER_TITLE);
infoObject.setDescription(FOLDER_DESCRIPTION);
infoObject.setParentID(PARENT_ID);
//commit collection
iStore.commit(newInfoObjects);
//print out all properties for debuging
System.out.println(BOEUtil.infoObjectToString(infoObject));
```

DELETING OBJECTS

Deleting objects is much like creating them. The InfoStore must be queried and multiple objects (often just one) retrieved. The collection of InfoObjects is iterated or accessed using the collection's `get(index number)` accessor method. Then, the collection's `delete(IInfoObject)` method is called and, finally, the entire collection is committed.

The following function deletes a specific recurring job (or subscription) for a specific user. Supplying the user ID is optional in this case.

```
public static void deleteRecurringSchedule(IInfoStore iStore,int userID,
➥int scheduleID) throws SDKException {
    String queryString = "SELECT * " +
            " FROM CI_INFOOBJECTS WHERE SI_OWNERID=" + userID +
            " AND SI_RECURRING=1  "+
            " AND SI_ID="+scheduleID;
    IInfoObjects scheds = iStore.query(queryString);
    if (scheds.size()==1){
```

```
                    IInfoObject sched=(IInfoObject)scheds.get(0);
                    scheds.delete(sched);
            }
            iStore.commit(scheds);
    }
```

SCHEDULING REPORTS

BusinessObjects Enterprise solves three broad problem classes for Crystal Reports users: security, scalability, and distribution. The distribution capability includes the abilities to send a report once or on a recurring schedule, in any supported output format (there are deltas between Crystal Reports and Web Intelligence), and to a variety of destinations:

- **Default**—BusinessObjects Enterprise file output server. Scheduled instances will be retained according to site-wide or folder-level retention policies configurable in the CMC. Users can view these documents by retrieving the instance and using one of the export or DHTML viewers.

- **SMTP**—E-mail server. E-mailing a link or PDF document is a common use-case.

- **File**—Local or mapped file path. Publishing a PDF document to a network webserver is a common use-case.

- **FTP**—Remote FTP server that accepts an active FTP connection.

By default, these destinations are turned off in the CMC. After turning them on, it is a good idea to go into the job server configuration console and set system-wide default parameters. For instance, you could set the default SMTP server name, domain, and port number.

You will find a very powerful function `scheduleReportToEmail(IInfoStore iStore, int reportID, HttpServletRequest request, HashMap paramMap, String frequency, int periodDays, String destinationFormat, String dependentEventName, String fromEmailAddress, String toEmailAddresses, String emailSubject, String emailMessage, String emailAttachmentName)` in the BOEUtil on www.usingcrystal.com. If a schedule includes a dependent event, it will wait until the event is fired before running the job. Additionally, scheduling and formatting can be controlled with far more granularity than what you will find in this function. In the product documentation and support site, you can find code samples that more fully exercise discrete pieces of the scheduling API.

CAPTURING THE NEW SCHEDULED JOB IDENTIFIER

It is sometimes important to capture the identifier of the job as soon as it is created. This could be for status reporting or complex scheduling front-ends with their own persistence. Immediately after a job is created, its parent InfoObject will contain a property called `SI_NEW_JOB_ID` that disappears after the InfoObject falls out of scope. For a nonrecurring scheduled InfoObject, its value corresponds to the `SI_ID` of the new instance that is to be created. For a recurring, scheduled InfoObject, it refers to the `SI_ID` of the recurrence parent object.

CAPTURING PARAMETERS

Whenever most reports are displayed or scheduled, parameters need to be captured and supplied. When a report is viewed, it can be convenient to build a parameter fields collection and supply it to the viewer. Setting the parameters on the IInfoObject is the only viable approach when a report is scheduled. The getCrystalReportParameterFields(IReport report, HttpServletRequest request, HashMap paramMap, boolean bFailSilently) function captures parameter values from the request scope as well as a map object, and updates the InfoObject itself and a Fields collection. It supports multiple, range, and discrete values of any data type. The dummy function setCrystalReportParameters invokes the other and simply throws away the Fields collection. As these are quite long and complicated code listings, you will them online at www.usingcrystal.com.

For information on how to fill prompt values for scheduling a Web Intelligence document, consult customizing_webintelligence.pdf which installs in the help/language directory of BusinessObjects Enterprise (and should also be available for download from www. usingcrystal.com).

USERS AND GROUP MANAGEMENT

For customers who store users and groups in a relational database or use a nonsupported Single Sign-On (SSO) product, implementing BusinessObjects Enterprise poses the following challenges:

- **Replicating users and groups**—To fully exercise BusinessObjects Enterprise security and logging, users and groups must be replicated using batch scripts. Batch scripts themselves can be scheduled through BusinessObjects Enterprise.

- **Logging in without a password**—SSO web server plugins expect down-stream providers to accept usernames in the request header as valid and authorized. BusinessObjects Enterprise expects a password and setting it as an empty string creates a security hole. Resetting the user password every time the user logs in is one work-around.

- **Getting and setting user preferences**—Accessing user preferences and setting custom ones is easy with the getProfileString and setProfileString methods.

In BOEUtil you will find several functions that handle adding and removing users and groups; setting user properties, including arbitrary properties on the user profile; resetting user passwords; and managing group membership, including subgroups.

USING REPORTS AS A DATASOURCE

Because Crystal Reports access so many datasources and often include high-value business logic, customers increasingly request to use their Crystal Reports as datasources.

Access is provided through the RAS getRowsetController cursor. It is advisable to consult the API documentation, but here are some tips to get you started:

- **Set batch size**—Unless you have the ability to request records in batches, set the batch size to the total number of data rows in the report.

- **Rowcount is the last column in the record datastructure**—The number of columns in the metadata fields datastructure is one less column than the records datastructure. You can ignore the last column; it is just the row number.

- **Description is the only unique column**—It is possible for reports to contain many formulas and summaries. To ensure uniqueness, use the description rather than the name.

- **ADO.NET XML available**—if you prefer extracting an ADO.NET recordset, use the `resultCursor.getRowset().getXMLData()` method.

Listing 30.6 shows how to use the RowsetController to extract data from a Crystal Report.

LISTING 30.6 EXTRACTING DATA FROM A CRYSTAL REPORT

```
IInfoObject object = (IInfoObject) BOEUtil.getReportByName(reportName, iStore);
IReport report = (IReport) object;
IReportAppFactory rptAppFactory = (IReportAppFactory) es.getService("",
➡ "RASReportService");
// Get the InfoStore service from Crystal Enterprise
clientDoc = rptAppFactory.openDocument(report, 0, Locale.ENGLISH);
if (clientDoc != null) {
//create metadata structure
RowsetMetaData rowSetMetaData = new RowsetMetaData();
➡ rowSetMetaData.setDataFields(clientDoc.getDataDefinition().getResultFields());
      Fields fields = rowSetMetaData.getDataFields();
      String colName,colTypeName;
      int colType, len;
      Field field;
      HashMap colNames = new HashMap();
      HashMap colTypes = new HashMap();
      for (int i = 0; i < fields.size(); i++) {
            field = (Field) fields.get(i);
            colName =field.getDisplayName(FieldDisplayNameType.description,
            ➡ Locale.ENGLISH);
            colNames.put("COL"+i,colName);
      colType = getColTypeFromVariant(field.getType().toVariantTypeString());
      len=field.getLength();
            //Placeholder
       //add column metadata to data structure or XML
       }
      Object colValue;
      int rowCount=0;
      if (getMaxRows() != 0) {
            RowsetCursor rowsetCursor = clientDoc.getRowsetController().
            ➡createCursor(null, rowSetMetaData);
            //Setting the batch size to make sure that you get back all the
            //rows by setting the batch size.
                  clientDoc.getRowsetController().setRowsetBatchSize
                  ➡(rowsetCursor.getRowset().getTotalRecordCount());
```

```
                //Getting the Results back starting from the first row
                RowsetCursor resultCursor = clientDoc.getRowsetController().
                ►createCursor(null, rowSetMetaData);
                resultCursor.moveTo(0);
                    while (!resultCursor.isEOF()) {
                        for (int i = 0; i < fields.size(); i++) {
                                colName=(String)colNames.get("COL"+i);
                                colTypeName=(String)colTypes.get("COL"+i);
colValue=record.getValue(i);
                                //Placeholder
//add row data to data structure or XML
                        }
resultCursor.moveNext();
                    }
                }
```

WHERE TO GO FROM HERE

The BusinessObjects Enterprise SDK is the most flexible and powerful way to access
BusinessObjects Enterprise. Using the SDK, you can do create custom BI applications that
meet the look, feel, and integration requirements of your project. The focus of this chapter
was to understand the InfoStore—the object-relational repository where all BusinessObjects
Enterprise assets are persisted, related, and secured. This is the most complex and least
understood part of the API. To accelerate your development effort, please go to
www.usingcrystal.com and download the white-box sample portal, in either JSP or .NET,
which is ready-to-run and customize. After looking through the code-base, you should feel
confident and comfortable stepping out on your own.

30

CHAPTER 31

Using the Web Components

In this chapter

OVERVIEW

This chapter explores a series of rapid development options that permit you to quickly integrate BusinessObjects Enterprise XI with your enterprise applications. These include the capability to view, create, and edit reports simply by calling URLs; integrating components visually using .NET components or Java Server Faces (JSF); or simply deploying prebuilt catalog browsing and viewing portlets into Microsoft SharePoint, WebSphere Portal, or any other JSR-168–compliant Java portal.

URL REPORTING

This section of the book is vital because it covers, from an integration standpoint, the most common integration use-cases through invocation of simple URLs. To run without prompting the user for credentials, these URLs take a token parameter that represents the session token of an active BusinessObjects Enterprise session. This token is generated by using the *getToken()* method of the user's BusinessObjects Enterprise session (see Chapter 30, "Using the BusinessObjects Enterprise APIs"). These credentials expire automatically in a configurable amount of time unless they are invalidated earlier by use of the *logoff()* method.

> In this chapter, URLs are referred to as *dispatchers* or *handlers*. This means that these files dispatch or handle *other* files—in this case, *any* .rpt, .car, or .wid report file. This design pattern provides utmost flexibility by not binding the service to any one particular report.

Historically, Crystal Enterprise customers were accustomed to using the viewrpt.cwr dispatcher. Classic Business Objects customers, by contrast, were accustomed to the openAnalytic.jsp dispatcher. BusinessObjects Enterprise XI includes a new dispatcher called openDocument.jsp/aspx. OpenDocument is the most flexible of the dispatchers and moving forward, it will be the preferred approach.

VIEWING A CRYSTAL REPORT OR OLAP INTELLIGENCE DOCUMENT WITH VIEWRPT.CWR

Before discussing openDocument.jsp/aspx, please note that viewrpt.cwr has not been deprecated. Existing viewrpt.cwr users do not need to migrate their implementations. In fact, in a handful of cases, viewrpt.cwr has no analog in OpenDocument and is the only solution.

Viewrpt.cwr is a Crystal classic technology whose implementation has evolved slightly with BusinessObjects Enterprise XI. In a Java environment, viewrpt.cwr is a mapping to the viewrpt servlet. In an ASP or .NET environment, viewrpt.cwr is redirected to viewrpt.aspx or viewrpt.asp.

Although it cannot display Web Intelligence documents, viewrpt.cwr enables a variety of ways for viewing Crystal Reports that OpenDocument does not. For instance, it supports the no longer trendy but uniquely capable ActiveX and Java Applet viewers. These viewers support report streaming without page reloading. If your Crystal Report uses summarizations and formulas carefully, it is possible to begin displaying a report using these viewers before the report has finished processing.

For desktop Windows applications, there is no equal to the CRViewer1 ActiveX control, chosen by hundreds of third-party OEMs. For desktop Java applications, there is, unfortunately, no Java viewing component. Even the Java Applet viewer requires a web-based host application. Customers have had modest success by installing an application server locally and viewing reports within an embedded Java Web browser by ICEsoft (www.icesoft.com).

Additionally, viewrprt.cwr supports a powerful use case where you can programmatically push the entire reportClientDocument into the viewer via a shared session variable, identified in the URL query string.

For additional information on viewrprt.cwr, please consult the Viewers COM SDK guide.

VIEWING A CRYSTAL REPORT, WEB INTELLIGENCE DOCUMENT, OR OLAP INTELLIGENCE DOCUMENT WITH OPENDOCUMENT

OpenDocument, new to BusinessObjects Enterprise XI, provides the ability to integrate a wide variety of InfoView objects into your development projects, as well as interlink reports to one another.

Several scenarios include

- Linking from one Crystal Report to another
- Opening a managed Microsoft Office document from a custom Java or .NET application
- Drilling from an OLAP Intelligence dimension to a Web Intelligence document, passing context as a parameter
- Integrating Crystal or Web Intelligence reports with third-party web-based applications, such as ESRI ArcIMS

> **NOTE**
>
> Between Crystal Reports, report-to-report linking can also be accomplished using the built-in navigation in the Hyperlink tab of the Format Editor. This capability requires practice to master, but elegantly supports cut-and-paste report part linking.

For readers familiar with the Crystal Report viewer SDKs, OpenDocument might not seem like a big deal—implementing a custom viewer is easy. You will find a fairly robust, stand-alone Crystal Reports viewer built using the SDK on www.usingcrystal.com. Neither Web Intelligence nor OLAP Intelligence, however, has (today) a drop-in componentized viewer. You can write your own Web Intelligence viewer using instructions in the customizing_ webintelligence.pdf document that ships with the product or looking at the source code in InfoView. Be forewarned, it's fairly complicated. Using OpenDocument, you can access the InfoView viewer and do not need to write your own.

31

Now that you know *what* OpenDocument is, *when* to use it, and a bit about *why*, *how* to use OpenDocument is discussed next.

OPENDOCUMENT.JSP AND OPENDOCUMENT.ASPX

In the Java environment, the OpenDocument dispatcher is called OpenDocument.jsp and can be found at the following path:

```
http://<SERVER_NAME>:<PORT>/businessobjects/enterprise11/desktoplaunch_
/opendoc/openDocument.jsp
```

In the .NET environment, the same functionality can be found at

```
http://<SERVER_NAME>/businessobjects/enterprise11/InfoView/scripts/_
openDocument.aspx
```

QUERYSTRING SYNTAX

The OpenDocument dispatchers require parameters in the form of a URL *query string* (the part after the "?" in a URL) in order to function. Query strings are collections of ParamName/ParamValue pairs separated by equal signs ("=") and joined together by ampersands ("&").

A sample syntax for opening the World Sales Report without prompting a login is

```
http://dcakrinsky02:8080/businessobjects/enterprise11/desktoplaunch/
➡opendoc/openDocument.jsp?token=DCAKRINSKY02.CRYSTALD.NET%401901
➡JcNkdQhE3MvUpGjE1899JoLchMLcZOj03wtk&sDocType=rpt&sDocName=
➡World+Sales+Report
```

The first part of the URL refers to the machine and application server port. A default Apache Tomcat installation is run locally, so the server name is DCAKRINSKY02 and the port is 8080. The token value was captured programmatically using code discussed in Chapter 30. The sDocType parameter is the file type of the target document: wid (Web Intelligence document), rpt (Crystal Report), or car (OLAP Intelligence document). The sDocName represents the name of the object on the system. If more than one document by this name exists on the system, the first one found is used.

Table 31.1 describes each of the supported parameters and its use. For brevity, the full URL path and the token argument has been omitted from the example URLs. If a user has already logged into InfoView or a token has been provided in a prior request, the token parameter is optional because it has already been persisted in the application server session. If the Enterprise session has expired, users are redirected to the default InfoView logon page and then redirected to the requested URL. Several documented parameters, including sOutputFormat and NAII, do not work as specified and have been omitted from this table. Others that work but are not documented, such as token, have been added. Service packs and documentation updates should address these issues.

TABLE 31.1   OPENDOCUMENT URL PARAMETERS

Parameter syntax	Description of parameter	Mandatory?	Values accepted for parameter
sType or sTyp	The file type of target document or report	Yes for WebI, Crystal Reports, or OlapI documents	• wid • rpt • car
	For agnostic documents, such as Word, Excel, and Txt, the sType parameter *must* be explicitly omitted.		
sDocName or sDoc	Document name	sDocName or iDocID is mandatory	Document name
iDocID	Document identifier	One of sDocName or iDocID is mandatory	Document identifier

Example: openDocument.jsp?sType=rpt&**iDocID**=306

Parameter syntax	Description of parameter	Mandatory?	Values accepted for parameter
sIDType	Crystal object type	Yes, if the ID is not the default, numeric InfoObjectID	• CUID—Cluster identifier • GUID—Global identifier • RUID—Package identifier • ParentID—Numeric ID in cluster • InfoObjectID (default)— Numeric ID in cluster

Example:
openDocument.jsp?sType=wid&**sIDType**=CUID&iDocID=AfC7y9nvVHhMmWyZ_uiCL6E
InfoObjectID, CUID and GUID identifiers can be retrieved programmatically under the properties
SI_ID, SI_CUID, SI_GUID respectively.

Parameter syntax	Description of parameter	Mandatory?	Values accepted for parameter
sReportPart	Indicates which specific part (Object Name) of the target report to open.	No	Name of the report part object. Report parts may include field objects, charts or maps, images, cross-tabs, and text objects. They may not include subreports, among other things.

Example: openDocument.jsp?sDocType=rpt&sDocName=World+Sales+Report&**sReportPart**=
Top5CountryChart

NOTE

The Document ID is an internal integer identifier that cannot be easily determined from InfoView. You should navigate to the document in the Central Management Console. In the File Name string, you see the path within the File Input Server. Every document has its own subfolder that the document ID corresponds with the internal identifier. Here, the document ID is 306. If you click on Preview, the following URL is shown in the browser:
http://dcakrinsky02:8080/businessobjects/enterprise11/admin/en/infoobject.cwr?action=
10005&cmd=view&**id=306**

31

Figure 31.1 shows how a report part is named using the Object Name property of the Common tab of the Crystal Reports Object Format editor. Figure 31.2 shows a report part rendered using the sReportPart syntax in the previous example.

Figure 31.1
Report Part Names are set in the Crystal Report Format Editor window.

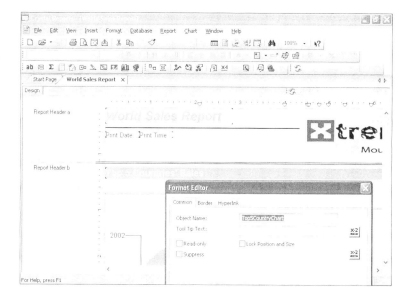

Figure 31.2
Viewing a Report Part.

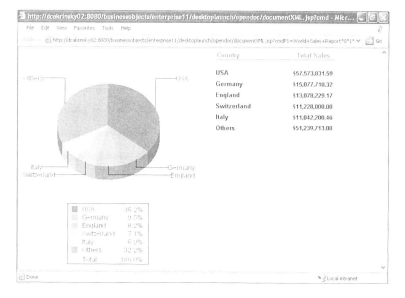

TABLE 31.1   OPENDOCUMENT URL PARAMETERS (CONTINUED)

Parameter syntax	Description of parameter	Mandatory?	Values accepted for parameter
sPartContext	In Crystal Reports, a report part is associated to a data context.	Yes, if a value is specified for sReportPart	Data context of the report part

Example: openDocument.jsp?sDocType=rpt&sDocName=World+Sales+Report&sReportPart=CountrySalesGraph&**sPartContext**=/Country[USA]

Figure 31.3 shows a particular, non top-level report part, Country, known by the dimension USA in the report group. This report part might be accessible in the top-level of a report, or might requiring drilling to reach. By default, the report part is shown in the context of its data. This is called Full mode.

Figure 31.3
Report part context in Full mode.

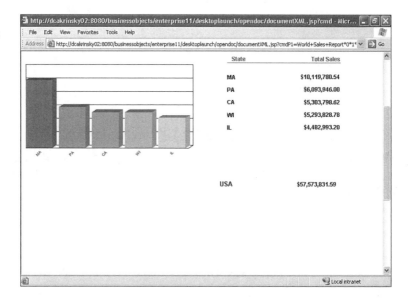

TABLE 31.1   OPENDOCUMENT URL PARAMETERS (CONTINUED)

Parameter syntax	Description of parameter	Mandatory?	Values accepted for parameter
sReportMode	For Crystal targets only, indicates whether the link should open the full target report or just the report part specified in sReportPart.	No (default is Full); only applies if a value is specified for sReportPart	• Full • Part

Example: openDocument.jsp?sDocType=rpt&sDocName=World+Sales+Report&sPartContext=/Country[USA]&**sReportMode**=Part

Figure 31.4 shows the same report part as the prior example, but without contextual data. This is called Part mode.

Figure 31.4
Report part context in
Part mode.

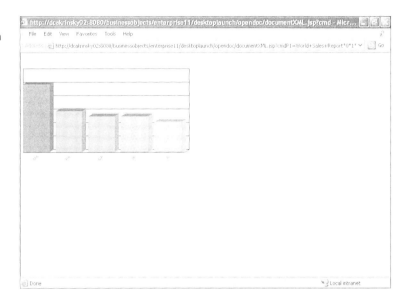

TABLE 31.1   OPENDOCUMENT URL PARAMETERS (CONTINUED)

Parameter syntax	Description of parameter	Mandatory?	Values accepted for parameter
sRefresh	Forces document refresh with prompting	No	• Y (forces the document's refresh) • N (if Refresh on Open is set to Yes in the CMC, the document is refreshed)
Example: openDocument.jsp?sDocType=rpt&sDocName=World+Sales+Report&**sRefresh**=Y			
sInstance	Indicates which specific instance of the target report to open.	No (use with sDocName and lsS[NAME])	• User—Latest instance owned by current user • Last—Latest instance for report • Param—Latest instance of report with matching parameter values
Example: openDocument.jsp?sDocType=rpt&sDocName=World+Sales+Report&**sInstance**=User			
lsS[NAME]	Specifies a value for a single prompt. [NAME] is the text of the prompt.	No	A single prompt value.
Example: openDocument.jsp?sDocType=rpt&sDocName=World+Sales+Report+ Prompted&**lsSCountry**=USA			

Parameter syntax	Description of parameter	Mandatory?	Values accepted for parameter
lsM[NAME]	Specifies multiple values for a prompt. [NAME] is the text of the prompt.	No	Multiple prompt values, separated by a comma. If the target is a Crystal report, each value must be enclosed in square brackets and separated by commas. If the target is a Web Intelligence document, multiple values must be separated by semi-colons. For more information on OLAP Intelligence parameters, please consult the product documentation. Note: To supply a single value to a Crystal Reports prompt that accepts multiple values, you must use lsS rather than the lsM.

Example: openDocument.jsp?sDocType=rpt&sDocName=World+Sales+Report+Prompted&**lsMCountries**=[USA],[Germany]

Following is a summary of differences between Web Intelligence documents and Crystal Reports accepting multiple prompt values.

Web Intelligence

For filling prompts that *accept* multiple values (in list):

- Multiple values must be specified using `lsM<PROMPTNAME>=val1;val2`
- Single values must be specified `lsM<PROMPTNAME>=val1`

Crystal Reports

For filling prompts that *accept* multiple values:

- Multiple values must be specified using `lsM<PROMPTNAME>=[val1],[val2]`
- Single values must be specified `lsS<PROMPTNAME>=val1`

TABLE 31.1   OPENDOCUMENT URL PARAMETERS (CONTINUED)

Parameter syntax	Description of parameter	Mandatory?	Values accepted for parameter
lsR[NAME]	Specifies a range of values for a prompt. [NAME] is the text of the prompt. Note: Not supported by OLAP Intelligence	No	A range of values for the prompt, separated by a double period (..). If the target is a Crystal Report, the range must be enclosed in square brackets and/or parentheses (use a square bracket next to a value to include it in the range, and parentheses to exclude it).
Example: openDocument.jsp?sType=rpt&sDocName=SalesReport&**lsRCustomer**+Order+ Count=[10..25]&lsROrder+Date+Range=[DateTime(2003,1,1,0,0,0)..DateTime(2004,12,1,0,0,0)]			
sReportName	Indicates which report to open if the target document contains multiple reports (Web Intelligence documents only)	No	Active report is opened by default
lsC	Specifies a contextual prompt if there is an ambiguity during SQL generation (Web Intelligence documents only)	No	A prompt value that resolves the ambiguity in the SQL generation.
Example: openDocument.jsp?sDocType=wid&sDocName=Ambiguous+Contexts+ Example&**lsC**=RESERVATION			

Context is a fairly complex topic covered elsewhere in this book. If there are multiple ways to resolve a SQL query, the context must be specified in order for the Universe to pass the Designer integrity check. Figure 31.5 shows how context is defined in the Universe Designer.

As shown in Figure 31.6, the end-user is prompted if a valid value for lsC is not provided.

Figure 31.5
The context definition in the Universe Designer.

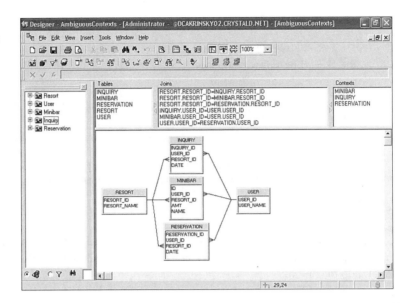

Figure 31.6
The context run-time prompt.

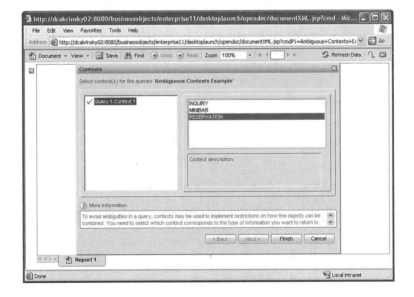

CREATING AN OPENDOCUMENT LINK IN CRYSTAL REPORTS

To open another report from Crystal Reports, use the Hyperlink tab of the Field Format Editor and follow these steps:

1. Open the source report in Crystal Reports.
2. Right-click the field in which you want to insert the OpenDocument link and select Format from the shortcut menu.

3. In the Format Editor, select the Hyperlink tab.

4. Select a website on the Internet.

5. In the Hyperlink Information area, leave the Website Address field empty and click the Format Formula Editor button.

6. In the Formula Editor, use your preferred Crystal syntax to build a context-aware OpenDocument URL link string like the following (this example also demonstrates string concatenation and the new URLEncode() function in Crystal Reports):

```
StringVar openDocURL;
openDocURL:="http://dcakrinsky02:8080/businessobjects/enterprise11/";
openDocURL:=openDocURL+"desktoplaunch/opendoc/openDocument.jsp?sDocType=rpt";
openDocURL:=openDocURL+"&sDocName="+URLEncode("World Sales Report Prompted");
openDocURL:=openDocURL+"&lsSCountry="+URLEncode({Customer.Country});
openDocURL
```

You can test the formula by creating a temporary parameter that uses the same formula and outputting it directly on your report. Click the Save and Close button in the Formula Workshop to continue.

CREATING AN OPENDOCUMENT LINK IN OLAP INTELLIGENCE

Although not the focus of this book, OLAP Intelligence is a very welcome tool in the quiver of any Business Objects customers that have deployed traditional OLAP databases. Among its more powerful features is the capability to define custom actions—a welcome addition to Crystal Analysis v.10 that also made it into XI. Prior to this enabling feature, you needed to define actions in the underlying OLAP database. Follow these steps to create a hyperlink from an OLAP Intelligence document using the openDocument.jsp/aspx dispatcher:

1. Open the source report in the OLAP Intelligence designer.

2. Click New to create a new action.

3. Enter an action name.

4. Select the area to which the action (the link) will apply.

5. Enter the OpenDocument link leveraging MDX syntax according to samples in the product documentation:

```
http://dcakrinsky02:8080/businessobjects/enterprise11/desktoplaunch/
➥opendoc/openDocument.jsp?sDocType=rpt&sDocName=Sales+Report&
➥lsSYear=[Year].[Year].&[1]
```

6. Click OK to save the link.

7. Close the Action Manager dialog box.

8. Create an Analysis button on the source report.

9. Right-click the Analysis button.

10. In the drop-down menu, select Properties and then Edit.

11. Select Launch an Action.

12. Select the action that corresponds to the OpenDocument link created in steps 3–6.

13. Click OK.

Actions for OLAP Intelligence are covered in more detail in Chapter 19, "Creating OLAP Intelligence Reports."

NOTE

> Earlier in the chapter, the token parameter was discussed from the perspective of single sign-on from a third-party application. When linking between reports, there is no way to insert the user's session token in the link. OpenDocument does not require a token if a user session is already active. If the session times out or if it's the first report link the user ever clicks, OpenDocument automatically redirects the user to a login page.

CREATING A NEW WEB INTELLIGENCE DOCUMENT

With the release of the near feature parity 0-client (IE, Netscape [Mozilla], and Safari) Web Intelligence document editor, exposing industry-leading ad hoc analysis capabilities to intranet and extranet customers is arguably the most compelling new feature in all of Business Objects XI. As a result, it was surprising to find no dispatcher that permits creation of a new Web Intelligence document with the DHTML query panel (based on a Universe identifier and a user session token). This will be rectified in the next release. In the meantime, there are two solutions that will work for XI.

First, you can call the InfoView STRUTS action that presents the user with a list of Universes and subsequently permits creating a new Web Intelligence document:

```
/businessobjects/enterprise11/desktoplaunch/InfoView/_
CrystalEnterprise_Webi/new.do
```

Figure 31.7 shows a page inside a frameset. Clicking on a Universe name in the Title column opens either the DHTML or Java query panel, depending on a user's InfoView preferences.

Figure 31.7
Creating a new
Web Intelligence
document.

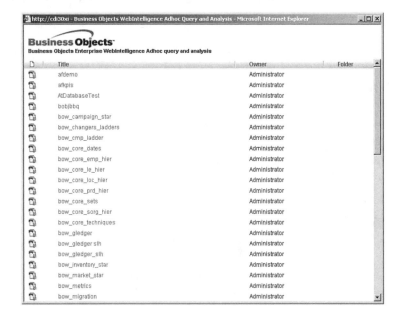

Because InfoView is likely to be rewritten and the new.do action is undocumented, this approach might break in subsequent releases. The scenarios described here will probably be fully supported through well-documented dispatchers at that time.

The second approach is to actually write dispatchers to create new WebI documents inside the DHTML and Java query panels. The code for the Java query panel actually comes from the Developer suite and is fully documented there. The code for the DHTML query panel wrappers an InfoView JSP file, openQueryPanel.jsp, that is subject to change in future releases. For both approaches, you need to first create a session token, check permissions to create Web Intelligence documents, and retrieve a list of Universes. This code is already provided in Chapter 30 and is not repeated here.

DISPLAYING A LIST OF UNIVERSES

The last chapter showed how to query the InfoStore to retrieve a list of Universes. This and code showing how to determine a user's rights vis-à-vis creating WebI documents are encapsulated in the utility function BOEUtil.java found on www.usingcrystal.com. Listing 31.1 shows how functions are used to render a list of Universes from which a user can create new WebI documents using either the DHTML or Java viewers.

LISTING 31.1   UNIVERSES.JSP

```
<SCRIPT LANGUAGE="JavaScript">
    var editor="DHTML";
    function toggleEditor(newEditor){ editor=newEditor; }
    function createWebIDoc(universeID) {
        var viewURL="webiDHTMLOpenQueryPanel.jsp?unvid="+escape(universeID)+"&
        ➥token=<%=Util.URLEncodeUTF8(logonToken)%>";
        if (editor=="JAVA"){
            viewURL="webiAppletOpenQueryPanel.jsp?unvid="+escape(universeID);
        }
    windowprops = "height=600,width=800,location=yes,scrollbars=yes,menubars=yes,
    ➥toolbars=yes,resizable=yes";
        reportWindow = window.open(viewURL,"rptWindow",windowprops);
        reportWindow.focus();
    }
</SCRIPT>
WebI Editor:
<% if (BOEUtil.isWebIDHTMLCanCreate){%>
<INPUT TYPE=RADIO NAME="editor" VALUE="DHTML" checked
➥onclick="toggleEditor('DHTML');">DHTML
<% } if (BOEUtil.isWebIJavaCanCreate) { %>
<INPUT TYPE=RADIO NAME="editor" VALUE="JAVA"
➥onclick="toggleEditor('JAVA');">Java
<% } %>
<br>Universes<hr>
<% IInfoObjects universes=null;
    IInfoObject universeObject=null;
    universes=BOEUtil.getUniverses(iStore);
    int totalUniverses = universes.size();
    if (totalUniverses>0){
        for (int i = 0; i < totalUniverses; i++) {
        universeObject = (IInfoObject) universes.get(i);
```

```
        out.print("<IMG SRC='../images/universe.gif'> __
<A HREF=\"javascript:createWebIDoc('"
➥+Util.URLEncodeUTF8(universeObject.getCUID())+"');\">"
➥+universeObject.getTitle() +"</A><br>");
        } out.print("<hr>");
    } else { out.write("<SPAN CLASS=normalText>No universes found</SPAN>");}
%> </TD></TR></TABLE>
```

CREATING A NEW WEB INTELLIGENCE DOCUMENT IN THE JAVA QUERY PANEL

You can find the complete code listing for the `webiAppletOpenQueryPanel.jsp` and the companion `webiAppletSaveDoc.jsp` files at www.usingcrystal.com. To give you a sense of what is involved, a partial code listing is shown in Listing 32.2. Remember that for the applet to work properly, you must configure the cadenza servlet in web.xml, through which the Java applet communicates with the WebIntelligence Report Engine, before samples like this will work properly.

LISTING 31.2   SNIPPETS FROM `webiAppletOpenQueryPanel.jsp`

```
var embed_size_attr = 'WIDTH="' + (self.innerWidth) + '" HEIGHT="'
➥+ (self.innerHeight-24) + '"';
out.println('<APPLET name="webiApplet"' + embed_size_attr +
' codebase="<%= contextPath %>/webiApplet/"' +
' archive="ThinCadenza.jar" ' +
' code="com.businessobjects.wp.tc.TCMain"> ' +
' <param name="Isapi" value="<%= contextPath %>/cdzServlet"></param>' +
' <param name="Server" value="<%= request.getServerName() %>"></param>' +
' <param name="Protocol" value="http"></param>' +
' <param name="Port" value="<%= request.getServerPort() %>"></param>' +
' <param name="Type" value="signed"></param>' +
' <param name="WebiSession" value="<%= strWISession %>"></param>' +
' <param name="CdzSession" value="<%= instanceID %>"></param>' +
' <param name="DocumentID" value="<%=""%>"></param>' +
' <param name="UniverseID" value="UnivCUID=<%=universeCUID%>"></param>' +
' <param name="bRobot" value="false"></param>' +
' <param name="bTraceInLogFile" value="false"></param>' +
' <param name="HelpRoot" value="<%= request.getContextPath().substring(1) %>">' +
' </param><param name="SaveAs" value="<%= request.getContextPath()%>
/javasdk/saveWebiAppletDoc.jsp?unvId=<%=universeCUID%>"></param><param name=
➥"Lang" value="<%= request.getAttribute( "lang" ) %>"></param></APPLET>');
```

CREATING A NEW WEB INTELLIGENCE DOCUMENT IN THE DHTML QUERY PANEL

The DHTML query panel is comprised of a series of JSP pages. One of them is a file called openQueryPanel.jsp that does everything you want it to do except log in the user. In order to create a new WebI document without InfoView prompting the user to enter credentials, you need to put a login page in front of openQueryPanel.jsp that logs in the user and then forwards the request to it. Place the login page in the /desktop/InfoView/viewers/cdz_adv/ directory. The full listing, webiDHTMLOpenQueryPanel.jsp, is posted on www.usingcrystal.com.

URL PARAMETER BUILDING TIPS

Conventions that apply to building any URLs apply here. Since malformed URLs are a common source of problems when building internet applications, some tips on building URLs are included in the following sections.

URL ENCODING

Because name-value pairs in a URL are delimited by = and separated from one another by &, values containing these and certain other special characters must be encoded and, when used, decoded. These are called *reserved characters* because they have a special role inside URLs. If appearing outside that role in text, they must be encoded. Other special characters are called *unsafe characters* because they can be misunderstood by the system for various reasons. These must also be encoded.

Encoded values appear as three-letter codes, starting with % and ending with the two-letter hexadecimal representation of the encoded character byte. Naturally, % is also a special character that must be encoded. Normally, this work is done by URL encoder/decoder functions in your development environment of choice. The rules for URL encoding are provided in Table 31.2.

TABLE 31.2 URL ENCODING CONVENTIONS

Acceptable Characters

The alphanumeric characters a–z, A–Z, and 0–9 remain the same.
The special characters ".", "-", "*", and "_" remain the same.

Reserved Characters		Unsafe Characters	
These characters have a special role inside URLs. If appearing outside that role in text, they must be encoded.		These characters can be misunderstood by the system for various reasons.	
Reserved	**Encoded**	**Unsafe**	**Encoded**
Ampersand ("&")	%26	Space (" ") standard	+
Dollar ("$")	%24	Space (" ") alternate	%20
Plus ("+")	%2B	Quotation marks	%22
Comma (",")	%2C	Less Than symbol ("<")	%3C
Forward slash/virgule ("/")	%2F	Greater Than symbol (">")	%3E
Colon (":")	%3A	Left curly brace ("{")	%7B
Semi-colon (";")	%3B	Right curly brace ("}")	%7D
Equals ("=")	%3D	Vertical bar/pipe ("|")	%7C
Question mark ("?")	%3F	Backslash ("\")	%5C
At symbol ("@")	%40	Caret ("^")	%5E
Pound character ("#")	%23	Tilde ("~")	%7E

Reserved	Encoded	Unsafe	Encoded
Percent character ("%")	%25	Left square bracket ("[")	%5B
		Right square bracket ("]")	%5D
		Grave accent ("`")	%60

OTHER TIPS

Here are some other tips for building URLs in Business Objects and sometimes elsewhere:

- The encoded URL cannot exceed 2,083 characters.
- Parameters in Business Objects handlers are case-sensitive.
- Strip spaces between separator characters ("=" and "&") and at the end of parameters.
- Use the new URLEncode() function in the Crystal Formula language.

JAVASERVER FACES

For years, Microsoft ASP developers debated best practices for organizing their web applications and managing interactions between the front- and back-ends. The .NET framework answered many of these questions, providing a neat methodology, system libraries, and IDE integration capability for quickly and easily wiring together stateless components into interactive web applications. In certain respects, what .NET is to ASP, JavaServer Faces (JSF) is to JSP. The similarities are so striking, in fact, that you might surmise that Redmond helped with the design. Its goal is to make rapid, consistent, and visual application development possible through a set of libraries and strict methodologies that integrated development environments (IDEs) can understand.

JSF is a follow-on to the ever-popular Apache STRUTS application development framework. Both provide an architectural design based on the Model View Controller (MVC) JSP Model 2 pattern that specifies that end-user requests are managed by a servlet that controls the flow, components are used to access and manipulate the data, and JSP is used to render content to the browser. The JSP Model 2 pattern can be difficult to understand. A simplified diagram is shown in Figure 31.8. Please Google this topic to learn more.

Figure 31.8
The JSP Model 2 MVC design pattern.

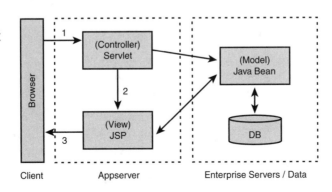

Although STRUTS had a large following, it was not a standard managed by the Java Community Process (JCP). Some critics note that the design changed frequently and tool vendors were late and inconsistent in their support. JSF, on the other hand, is a JCP standard that was designed for use inside of tools from the very beginning. As such, it is a stable specification supported by all Java tool vendors.

If JSF thrives, it is likely that you will see much more in this area from vendors such as Business Objects. In XI, Business Objects offered a taste of JSF with the Crystal Reports viewer control.

NOTE

The samples provided in Chapter 30 do not follow the JSF design methodology. Rather, they loosely follow a Model 1 architecture shown in Figure 31.9 where most computation and processing is done in Java classes and rendered through JSP scriptlets.

Figure 31.9
The JSP Model 1
design pattern.

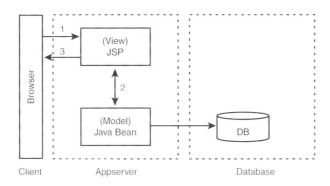

Client   Appserver   Database

NOTE

Frankly, JSF components require more effort to write, and building JSF applications requires thinking inside the JSF box, which some find cramped and uncomfortable. JSF will feel like old shoes for an MVC veteran—others might struggle at first. For large development projects involving many developers, releases, and maintenance requests, using a development framework such as STRUTS or JSF is highly recommended. For smaller endeavors, there's no shame in using simpler approaches like JSP Model 1.

JSF COMPONENT OVERVIEW

With BusinessObjects Enterprise XI, six JSF components are provided. Together, they permit logging into BusinessObjects Enterprise, changing passwords, displaying and browsing repository folders, rendering folder breadcrumbs, and viewing a Crystal Report.

Product documentation fully describes configuring and using the JSF components. The technical support team has also put together some wonderful viewlets documenting a sample development project in IBM Rational IDE that they have kindly posted at www.usingcrystal.com.

After these controls are registered with the IDE, they can be easily added to web projects. Figure 31.10 shows adding Enterprise Faces Components, Report Viewers Faces Components, and the Java Reporting Component (JRC) to a web project. Larger implementations prefer using the BusinessObjects Enterprise Page Server as a report source, eliminating the need for the JRC.

Figure 31.10
Adding JSF controls to a project.

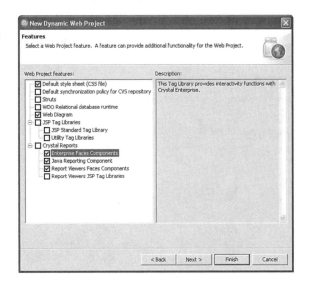

After the components are added to your project, you can drag and drop them onto your pages, set their properties, and wire them together using listeners in the code-behind pages. Figure 31.11 shows a folder-browsing and report-viewing application under construction.

Figure 31.11
JSF folder-viewing application.

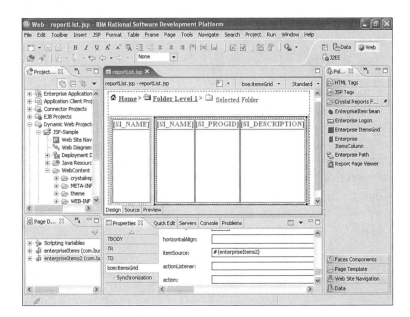

The six JSF components are as follows

- **logon**—Renders an HTML BusinessObjects Enterprise logon form
- **changePassword**—Renders an HTML BusinessObjects Enterprise change password form.
- **itemsGrid**—Renders (along with one or more itemsColumn tags) an HTML table, or grid, that displays the items from an EnterpriseItem or EnterpriseItems bean
- **itemsColumn**—Renders column within itemsGrid to display property of items from an EnterpriseItem or EnterpriseItems bean
- **path**—Renders hyperlink breadcrumb trail
- **reportPageViewer**—Renders Crystal Reports DHTML viewer

For more complete instructions for setting up and working with JSF components, please consult the product documentation and check out www.usingcrystal.com.

BUSINESSOBJECTS ENTERPRISE XI .NET SERVER CONTROLS

As always, .NET developers will be delighted by Business Objects' support for the platform. As shown in Figure 31.12, .NET support is provided through a four-tiered API stack: server controls, components, supporting API, and the underlying .NET API.

Figure 31.12
The .NET server controls for the API stack.

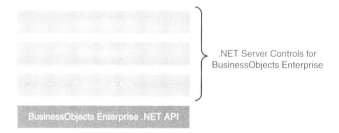

Together these APIs expose the entire BusinessObjects Enterprise infrastructure and Crystal Reports functionality. Public APIs are not provided for viewing or editing Web Intelligence and OLAP Intelligence documents. Rather, use openDocument.aspx discussed earlier in this chapter. These components are exhaustively documented in the core product. You will find examples that cover adding controls to your .NET Studio projects, setting properties, and scripting interactivity using code-behinds. This section provides a top-level glimpse of how a web developer might use the server controls to build a quick business intelligence portal.

.NET server controls are broken down into four logical categories:

- Authentication and user management
- Object listing and navigation through objects

- Scheduling of objects
- Viewing of objects

The controls included in each category and how they can help you in BusinessObjects Enterprise XI application development are discussed next.

AUTHENTICATION AND USER MANAGEMENT

This category includes two controls: logon and change password.

The *logon control* (see Figure 31.13) creates a form on your web page that allows users to authenticate themselves against the Enterprise CMS, generate a session token, and persist their entire Enterprise session for fast access on subsequent requests.

Figure 31.13
The .NET logon control.

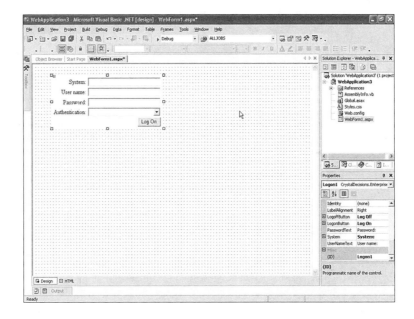

The *change password* control allows the end user to change her password when she wants to do so (see Figure 31.14).

REPOSITORY BROWSING

The *items grid control* (see Figure 31.15) allows the users to easily navigate through the folder structure inside the system and is implemented in the form of a table where columns represent the properties of each object, such as name, description, and so forth, and the rows are the items returned from the CMS. BusinessObjects Enterprise XI applies security filtering automatically.

Figure 31.14
The .NET change pass-
word control.

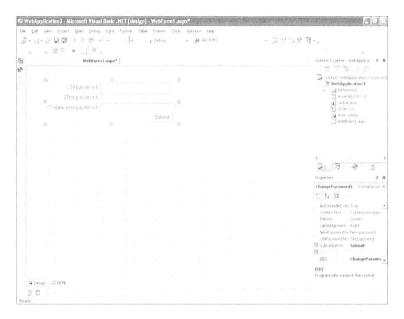

Figure 31.15
The .NET items grid
control.

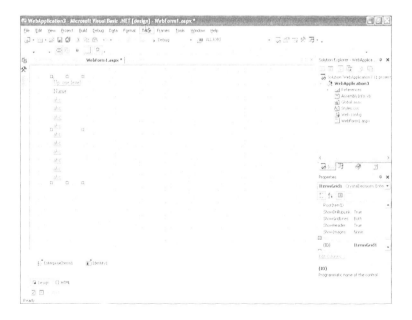

SCHEDULING

The *scheduling control* provides a nice user interface wrapper around the BusinessObjects
Enterprise XI scheduling engine (see Figure 31.16).

Figure 31.16
The .NET schedule control.

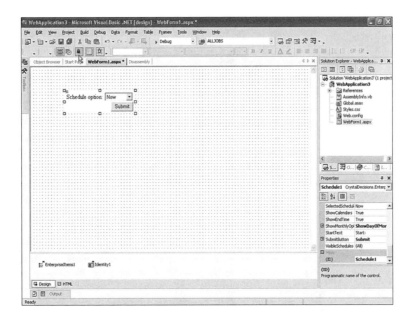

Most times, just specifying the date and time is not all that is required to schedule the report. That is why the following controls have also been implemented as part of this category:

- **Destination control**—Allows you to specify the destination for the report; for example, inbox, e-mail, FTP, file, and so forth

- **ReportFormat control**—Allows the user to specify which format the report should run; for example, Adobe Acrobat, Microsoft Word, Excel, Text, and so on

- **ReportFilters control**—Allows the user to specify the filters that should be applied when the report runs; for example, {Customer.Country}='USA'

- **ReportPrint control**—Allows the user to specify the print settings when printing the report, as well as the report layout

- **ReportDatabaseLogon control**—Allows the user to set database username and password prior to running the report

- **ReportParamters control**—Allows the user to specify the required parameter values for the particular report

Java developers ought to be rightly envious—Business Objects provides them no similar out-of-the-box control.

OBJECT VIEWING

Finally, the *viewer control* permits in-line viewing of Crystal Reports as shown in Figure 31.17.

Figure 31.17
The .NET viewer
control.

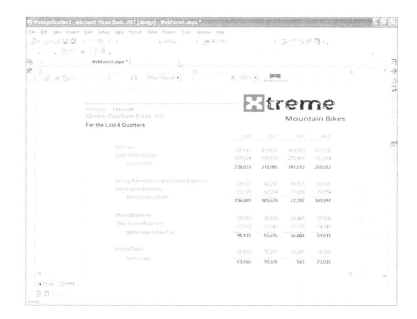

Figure 31.17
The .NET viewer
control.

EVENT HANDLING

Business Objects makes it easy for you to use server controls in your projects. All the controls share one common `AutoHandleEvents` property that allows for the forms submission to automatically perform the default action associated with the particular control. For example, when the user clicks on the Submit button on the schedule form and the `AutoHandleEvents` property is set to True, the default action is performed by the control and the specified report will be scheduled inside the BusinessObjects Enterprise XI system. You can override these events with your own logic that handles the default behavior.

Business Objects XI continues the Crystal tradition of excellent support of the .NET platform. Please consult the product documentation for more information.

PORTAL INTEGRATION KITS

Business Intelligence is a natural complement to an intranet. Most companies today have implemented custom, open-source, or commercial portals that provide a security, navigation, and layout framework for presenting corporate information assets. Products include Microsoft SharePoint, Apache Jetspeed, OpenText Livelink, and namesake portal servers by IBM, Vignette, Plumtree, BEA, SAP, and Oracle, to name but a few.

For many years, every portal product had their own API for creating, managing, and communicating between blocks in the portal, often referred to as *portlets*. In Microsoft SharePoint, these are called *web parts*. In SAP portals, they are *iViews*. Recently, Java vendors have coalesced around the JSR 168 standard that permits vendors such as Business Objects to write a single portlet implementation and deploy it in a wide variety of portal products.

Business Objects has been producing portal integration kits (PIKs) for many years. On the Crystal side, the first portlets were web parts developed for Microsoft SharePoint by Crystal veteran Craig Chaplin.

The next generation of Business Objects PIKs is modeled on the SharePoint integration and supports the JSR-168 specification. Functionality, partially shown in the following screen-shots, includes preference integration; folder browsing and management; scheduling; inbox; favorites ("subscriptions"); and personalized, parameterized viewing of Crystal Reports, Web Intelligence documents, and managed Microsoft Office/PDF files. On-report parameter support is better implemented than in the core product itself and linking between portlets on the same page (interportlet communication) is fully supported.

Light customization is possible through style sheets. Users can customize foreground and background colors themselves. If major changes are required, you can start from scratch or dig into the (somewhat complex) source code.

NOTE

Notably, security integration is *not* implemented in the JSR-168 PIK. You must present the logon portlet form to your users before the other portlets will work. In many cases, this is a show-stopper for using Business Objects portlets. Many customers choose to write their own portlets using the SDK, as shown in the previous chapter. Also, WebI documents are not shown in-line like in Crystal Reports; rather, they are popped up and leverage the openDocument.jsp handler described earlier in this chapter.

You can preview the JSR-168 portlets in the following figures below. Figure 31.18 shows navigating through the folder hierarchy and listing the reports within. Clicking on Subscribe adds a report to your personal favorites.

Figure 31.18
The JSR-168
Repository Browser
portlet.

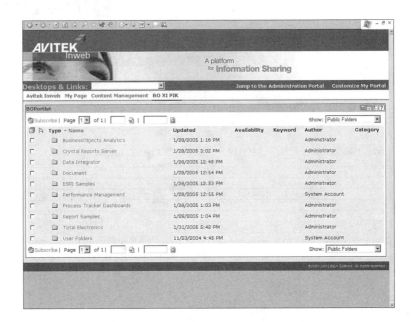

Figure 31.19 shows how the various types of objects are surfaced through the portlet and shown through a pop-up window—in this case, a Microsoft PowerPoint document.

Figure 31.19
The JSR-168 Viewer portlet, showing a hosted Microsoft Powerpoint document.

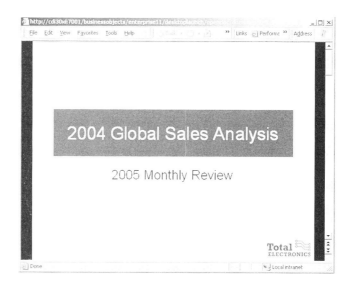

Figure 31.20 shows a Crystal Report viewer and Figure 31.21 shows a WebI document.

Figure 31.20
The JSR-168 Viewer portlet, showing a Crystal Report.

On Java platforms, portlets are packaged in a WAR archive. Instructions for configuring the BusinessObjectsPortlets.war file are provided for BEA, IBM, and Oracle application servers and IDEs in the Business Objects XI Portal Integration Kit documentation. You will be able to deploy the portlets on other J2EE application servers as well by following the methodology in the documentation.

Figure 31.21
The JSR-168 Viewer portlet, showing a WebI document.

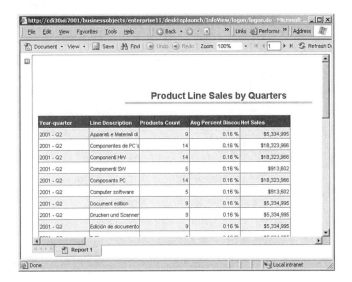

SAP PORTALS

Business Objects has invested tremendous resources in making its product stack the preeminent platform for business intelligence on SAP R/3 and BW. Crystal Reports, Web Intelligence, OLAP Intelligence, and Data Integrator all have native connectors for SAP that reduce the need for ABAP and BAPI programmers. SAP co-developed several of the solutions and bundles solely Business Objects BI products with their software. Additionally, should you want more than a limited license to the tool, SAP itself is an authorized Business Objects reseller.

Business Objects ships a collection of cross-platform iViews that deeply integrate with SAP security and provide similar capabilities as the JSR-168 portlet implementation. These iViews permit tight and fast integration of production reports, ad hoc query, and guided analysis with your SAP portal (see Figure 31.22).

More than 100 predefined reports are shipped with the SAP solution kit and there is a wizard-driven install on the Business Objects SAP BW CD-ROMs.

For more information on SAP integration, please visit www.businessobjects-sap.com.

Figure 31.22

The SAP PIK, viewing a Web Intelligence document.

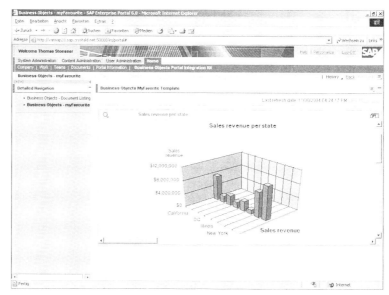

REVIEW

SDK integration, covered in Chapter 30, is the most powerful and flexible way to incorporate Business Objects functionality into your applications. However, it requires familiarity with programming and might be daunting. As described in this chapter, integrating reports using URL dispatchers, by contrast, is quick and easy—requiring only a knowledge of creating URLs. Other component integration requires some programming, but in most cases it provides more functionality in less time than writing code from scratch or cutting and pasting from samples. Beware of the little things, however. Many customers find the Java server faces development paradigm difficult to understand and the JSR-168 Business Objects PIKs do not support security integration out of the box.

CHAPTER 32

USING THE WEB SERVICE'S SDK

THE NEXT GENERATION OF WEB SERVICES

Crystal .NET developers have enjoyed the ability to publish a Crystal Report as a web service for several years. For small deployments of unmanaged reports, tightly integrated into custom .NET applications, this is an appropriate and terrific capability. For larger deployments with a separate business intelligence (BI) infrastructure and managed report repository, this approach is not satisfactory because it is not cross-platform, does not scale, is inherently insecure, and does not expose the full range of BI services.

Prior to acquiring Crystal, Business Objects was a pioneer in BI web services, permitting customers to securely expose the BI catalog and reports themselves as web services in its v.5 product. After acquiring Crystal, Business Objects soon released *Unified Web Services (UWS) 1.0*, the next-generation web services implementation, with the BusinessObjects Crystal Integration Pack. UWS bridged the Crystal Enterprise 10 and Business Objects 6.5 enterprise infrastructures, providing a single "unified" façade. The integration pack implementation carries forward to XI, with a handful of improvements:

- **Session**—Authenticate, create a session, close a session. XI adds support for LDAP authentication.

- **BI Catalog**—Navigate folders, reports, office documents, program objects, and other repository objects. XI adds support for categories and personal categories.

- **ReportEngine**—Viewing reports interactively, filling prompts and handling drilling. XI adds cluster readiness through optional use of Page Server (versus RAS).

These services follow the WS-Interoperability Basic Profile 1.0.

By the time this book goes to print, the next iteration of UWS will be nearing release. Enhancements will include

- **BI Query**—Provides full access to the BusinessObjects metalayer providing a dynamic, but secure, ad hoc query gateway directly to Enterprise BI datasources.

- **Microsoft Office sample applications**—Extraordinary sample applications for Microsoft Word and Excel have been built using the *Microsoft Visual Studio Tools for Office* (VSTO). These are designed to be extended by you, the customer and developer.

CONSUMING WEB SERVICES

Before continuing, it is important to mention that over the past year, Business Objects released a powerful XML data driver for Crystal Reports that permits writing reports off local and remote XML files. Likewise, it also parses XML documents from SOAP formatted messages returned by web services. Web service data sources are accessed through a Web Services Description Language (WSDL) endpoint—the standard format for describing a web service. After specifying a WSDL, the driver enables you to select which service, port, and method you want to use. The XML web services driver is part of the standard Crystal Reports distribution. Be sure to check for updates on the Business Objects website.

DECIDING TO USE WEB SERVICES

It is perfectly reasonable to question the utility of having a web services API. After all, Business Objects provides full-featured Java and .NET APIs. In short, web service interfaces are different from traditional APIs in the following two ways:

- **Non-Proprietary Transport**—How the application calls travel inside a machine or through the network that connects machines within your local network or wide area network to the public internet. Rather than using a proprietary network protocol and/or high or random port, web services use HTTP/SSL, typically over port 80 or 443 respectively.

- **Non-Proprietary Format**—How the information is encoded so other programs can read it. Rather than using a proprietary, binary data format, web services use SOAP-formatted XML text messages exclusively.

There are several advantages to using web services. First, there are no transport-specific limitations that could prevent API-level access outside the machine, the local network, or the wide area network. The traditional BusinessObjects Enterprise client SDKs communicate with back-end services over IIOP (Corba), using a range of ports. By default, these number some 30 ports (not including Enterprise Performance Management (EPM) services), half of which are random high-ports defined at run-time. The challenge of connecting to the BusinessObjects Enterprise cluster from client SDK applications can be made easier by setting the –request and –port command switches.

By contrast, any API in the UWS SDK can be accessed over a single configurable port using TCP/IP, like any other website in your company. Often, this port is 80 or 443. With web services, any machine on the World Wide Web internet can invoke this application—thus the name *web service*. Additionally, with UWS, there are no programming or platform-specific limitations that restrict the client application platform. Communication is accomplished by passing specially formatted text files back and forth.

32

NOTE

> Firewall issues are particularly challenging for ubiquitous client applications such as Business Objects Live Office and the Crystal Reports full client report writer. Contact Business Objects technical support for help configuring your environment to support these applications.

On the flip-side, there are a number of disadvantages with using web service SDKs generally. The most commonly cited ones are performance and security.

With web services, performance is a concern because application calls are not just traveling from one CPU register to another, but rather out to the network card, through a network cable, routers, routers, firewalls, routers, firewalls, millions of criss-crossing spam emails, and back through routers and firewalls to the machine on the other end. This is experienced every day when surfing the Web; there is a noticeable lag or latency between requests. What if every time you typed a letter in Microsoft Word, the program locked up, went out to MSN.com, looked up the word you were typing, checked to see whether it was spelled properly, and then returned a yes or no before letting you continue typing? What if it couldn't just exchange with MSN.com a tiny 1 kb binary file containing the letters of the current word and a single method such as "check spelling" represented by a single code such as "CS," but rather had to send a verbose one-page text document with a header, body, and footer, and get one back in return, which it had to open and parse using loops and regular expressions?

Converting native calls to XML documents, sending them through the networking, and deserializing them on the other end takes many CPU cycles and time. Computer people say that this is a very costly or expensive process.

On this issue of security, how does one program know that the requestor is who he says he is? Just because anyone *can* reach a web service does not mean he *should* be able to reach it. The most common approach to solving this problem is to simply require people seeking access to provide a username/password credential and to encrypt traffic through an SSL tunnel so nobody can "snoop" on it and read that information. This approach is supported by Business Objects UWS. Certificates guarantee the physical address of the receiver and/or the sender. Emerging standards might resolve this quandary issue.

SERVICE-ORIENTATED ARCHITECTURE EXPLAINED

As described above, finely grained calls to remotely hosted programs simply don't work. Microsoft would never dream of hosting the always-on Word spell checker remotely.

In fact, such approaches don't work in most distributed environments. Java programmers will remember what happened when "experts" ported their finely grained JavaBeans to EJB architectures: every getter and setter required a call over the network to the EJB server. No matter how much hardware you threw at these programs, they ran very slowly. Over time, programmers wised-up and built their objects locally before sending them over to the EJB server for processing or manipulation. Moreover, they began to bundle together objects and methods to perform on those objects so fewer network requests would be needed to get the job done. As interfaces became less object specific, they were no longer object oriented; they acted like commands of a prior generation of procedural languages.

The term *service oriented* was developed to describe this new approach generically. Service orientation is simply the idea that to facilitate efficient interoperability, especially in distributed environments, software applications should expose fewer, more functionally meaningful (but internally opaque) interfaces to other applications. Web services follow this approach and are increasingly synonymous with the service orientated architectures (SOA). Web services make their calls by passing around text messages and are therefore also called message oriented.

NOTE

> A competing BI vendor has attempted to malign Business Objects Enterprise's CORBA-based architecture as compared with its new, web service–based architecture. Although it is true that Business Objects services deployed through the Central Configuration Manager interact quite differently than do web services, the fact remains that web services are not well suited for the kinds of jobs for which BusinessObjects Enterprise uses CORBA. Although exposing an *external* web service interface makes sense, there are no compelling reasons to use web services *internally*. For inter-service communication (within the stack), the main concerns are that the engine performs quickly and reliably, is cross-platform, and scales linearly. Recent performance benchmarking emphatically validates the Business Objects architecture.

OBJECT-ORIENTED AND MESSAGE-ORIENTED APIs COMPARED

Because web service calls are so inefficient (bloated XML traveling over congested networks), API designers attempt to require a minimum number of them. Pseudo-code Table 32.1 compares (good) web services message-oriented APIs with traditional, locally accessed object-oriented APIs.

TABLE 32.1   OBJECT ORIENTED AND WEB SERVICE ORIENTED APIs COMPARED

Object-Oriented		Web Services Message-Oriented	
Local:	Create root object.	Local:	Create XML data structure.
Local:	Call function A on root object. Return object 1.	Local:	Load parameter 1 into XML element 1.
Local:	Call function B on object 1. Return object 2.	Local:	Load parameter 2 into XML element 2.
Local:	Call function C on object 2. Return object 2.	Remote:	Submit entire XML data structure in a single WS method call.
	And so on.	Local:	Parse returned XML data structure into local objects and use them.

Adapted from Business Objects, Unified Web Services Developer's Guide, p. 14

Although this approach might seem unnatural to object-oriented programmers, it cuts down the number of remote calls, thereby increasing performance.

SOAP, WSDL, AND UDDI

Web service requests are XML text provided in a standard format called *Standard Object Access Protocol* (SOAP). SOAP is a W3C standard that defines how web service messages are structured. Specifically, SOAP describes the header and footer "envelope" that surrounds the data being exchanged. *Web Services Description Language* (WSDL), also a W3C standard,

32

refers to the structure of the XML documents that describe web services so applications know what arguments their SOAP requests should contain, what data they should expect in the response, and the network address of the service.

Although showing neither the full WSDL nor SOAP documents, Figure 32.1 shows how WSDL documents describe the data SOAP requests must contain and what they should expect back from the service in return.

Figure 32.1
WSDL-SOAP relationship example highlighting common usage.

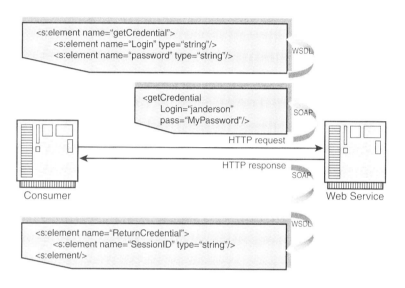

To facilitate sharing these interface specifications, WSDLs are often published to a *Universal Description, Discovery, and Integration* (UDDI) directory service that itself has a well-known interface. Obviously, not every service would be published to the outside world.

These standard-based interfaces facilitate automated discovery and invocation of web services between software applications that know nothing about one another. Web services client applications, such as Cape Clear permit users to browse UDDI directories to identify web services of interest, download their WSDL interface files, and build a simple form through which a user can invoke a web service with the arguments the service expects and see a resulting data grid.

In the current implementation of UWS, it is possible to publish the three BI services to UDDI. Used together in sequence—create a session, browse the catalog, and retrieve report data—these services do permit full access to assets in the BusinessObjects Enterprise repository. On the other hand, this implementation is like publishing a listing for the White Pages in the Yellow Pages; it's impossible to identify your BI assets from the Directory listing.

Customers might find it more useful to write a wrapper around these services that exposes a single report (including login, prompt, and formatting inputs) as a WSDL in a UDDI directory. Extend this with a publishing wizard for publishing WSDLs for all reports. With tools such as .NET Studio or Weblogic Workshop, this should not be difficult.

BI WEB SERVICES IN THE REAL WORLD

Given these interesting capabilities of a web services SDK, how are Business Objects customers actually using it? Here, two common use-cases are presented: portals and extranets, and EAI.

PORTALS AND EXTRANETS

By reducing or eliminating firewall concerns, UWS enables a wide variety of integration scenarios that were previously impossible.

Business Objects customers commonly use UWS to provide deep integration of reporting and analysis into their centrally hosted Java or .NET portals. The portal might be pulling data from BusinessObjects Enterprise servers at remote locations or even outside the company at partner locations. The other side of this coin is to offer BI services to remote and partner portals using UWS.

ENTERPRISE APPLICATION INTEGRATION (EAI)

One of the most compelling cases for deploying BI web services is for traditional application integration. Crystal Reports, for instance, makes it a trivial matter to extract data from SAP by writing complex BAPI code within its datasource adapter. In addition to providing impressive data access capabilities, including joining heterogeneous datasources, Crystal Reports permits complex business logic, including custom compiled functions, to be applied to that data. Additionally, through BusinessObjects Enterprise, Crystal Reports can be scheduled to run and archive at night, providing historical snapshots.

When exposed securely to client applications in the enterprise, Crystal Reports become the perfect connector to live and historical data from any or all enterprise data sources. Traditional application integration tools, such as SeeBeyond or WebMethods, are vastly more expensive and complex to configure than setting up a BusinessObjects Enterprise XI server and writing a few Crystal Reports!

One customer, a large defense contractor, saves approximately $10,000 per EAI flow handled through BI report versus a traditional EAI tool. The firm's CIO's office has wrapped BusinessObjects Enterprise web services with .NET code, exposing individual reports as XML data providers within their UDDI directory. Figure 32.2 highlights this usage pattern.

32

Figure 32.3
Architecture model:
Web services as EAI.

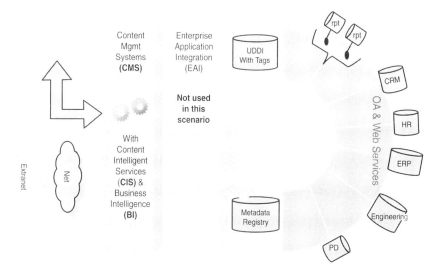

CONFIGURING THE UNIFIED WEB SERVICES (UWS) SERVER

The Unified Web Services (UWS) server component is a J2EE Web application that uses the Apache Axis web services library. Even if you are connecting to UWS from .NET, you must deploy the server component on a Java application server.

To deploy the UWS server, follow these steps:

Configure a JAVA_HOME environment variable with the operating system. Set JAVA_HOME=C:\Program Files\Business Objects\JavaSDK

Unzip C:\Program Files\Business Objects\BusinessObjects Enterprise 11\Web Services\dsws_webservice_boe\data\dswsBobjeAssembly.zip to C:\Program Files\Business Objects\. This creates a dswsBobjeAssembly directory.

Change directories to the dswsBobjeAssembly directory.

cd C:\Program Files\Business Objects\Assemble\dswsBobjeJava\

Build a WAR file by opening a CMD prompt and calling the dswsBobjeAssemblyEn batch file.

> dswsBobjeAssemblyEn.bat <MACHINE NETWORK NAME> <AXIS PORT NUMBER> <CMS NAME>

Your code might look like this example:

> dswsBobjeAssemblyEn.bat DCAKRINSKY02.crystald.net 8080 DCAKRINSKY02

A successful build will look something like the console output shown in Figure 32.3.

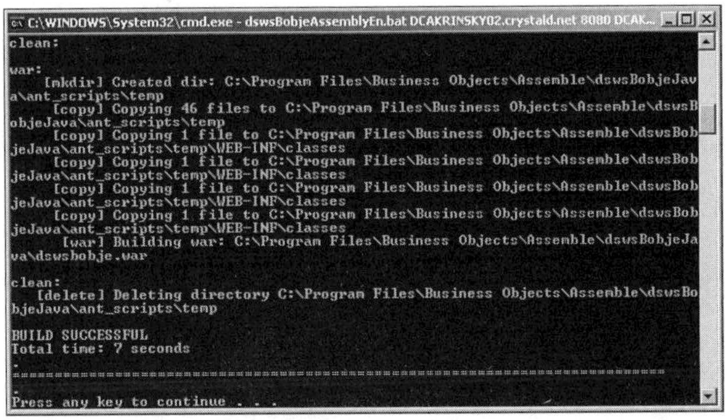

Figure 32.3
Successful UWS build
console output.

5. Copy the WAR file `C:\Program Files\Business`
   `Objects\Assemble\dswsBobjeJava\dswsboje.war` to Tomcat `C:\Program Files\Business`
   `Objects\Tomcat\webapps`. It will be deployed as an application called dswsbobje.

You can test your configuration by calling a URL such as
http://dcakrinskyo2.crystald.net:8080/dswsbobje/happydsws.jsp. At the same time, you
should test that the WSDL files deployed by the service are correct by looking in the
exploded dswsbobje\WEB-INF\classes directory under Tomcat\webapps. Search for
`soap:address` to find the URL for accessing the various services. Sometimes these services
will be on machines that differ from the initial connection URL, so you might need to
change them from the defaults. Here's the default which corresponds to the preceding
implementation:

```
<soap:address location="http://DCAKRINSKY02.crystald.net:8080/dswsbobje/
➥services/<SERVICE NAME>"/>
```

UWS may also be configured to use SSL. This requires that the client application use an
X509 public key certificate for communication. More information on setting up this configuration is not in the core documentation; look for it in a documentation update and/or on
the support site.

BUILDING UWS CLIENT APPLICATIONS

The fact that this kind of application-to-application interaction is possible at all demonstrates the flexibility of web services. Web services present a text-file interface over
HTTP(s) to any back-end service. As such, you can interact with these services directly
through HTTP(s) and XML parsing. From a programming standpoint, however, this direct
approach takes plenty of knuckle grease.

You can write the code to build XML documents, request and receive them from the web
service, and parse responses into something meaningful, if you like. Or, you can simply use
the Business Objects Java or .NET consumer SDK libraries to do the dirty work for you.
These SDKs make WSDL conformant requests to the UWS server, which in turn interacts

with BusinessObjects Enterprise XI over HTTP or SSL through a Java-based program designed for sending and receiving SOAP requests. Additionally, this SDK supports requests to clustered environments transparently by handling the state internally.

Listing 32.1 uses the Java-consumer SDK to output HTML from reportID=386.

LISTING 32.1 SIMPLE UWS REPORT VIEWER

```
String[] strBORepEngURL = boSession.getAssociatedServicesURL("ReportEngine");
//If no URLs are returned, the service is not available
if(strBORepEngURL.length > 0){
ReportEngine boRepEng = ReportEngine.getInstance(boSession,strBORepEngURL[0]);
ViewSupport htmlViewSupport = new ViewSupport();
htmlViewSupport.setOutputFormat(OutputFormatType.HTML);
htmlViewSupport.setViewType(ViewType.CHARACTER);
htmlViewSupport.setViewMode(ViewModeType.REPORT);
RetrieveCharacterView retCharView = new RetrieveCharacterView();
retCharView.setViewSupport(htmlViewSupport);
RetrieveData retBOData = new RetrieveData();
retBOData.setRetrieveView(retCharView);
DocumentInformation docInfo = boRepEng.getDocumentInformation("386",
➥null,null,null,retBOData);
docInfo = boRepEng.getDocumentInformation("386",null,null,null,retBOData);
CharacterView cv = (CharacterView)docInfo.getView();
out.print(cv.getContent());
}
```

In the snippet above, notice how output format and view mode are specified. Tables 32.2 and 32.3 show all of the retrieval options possible for Crystal Reports and WebI Documents respectively.

TABLE 32.2 UWS VIEW TYPES AND VIEW MODES SUPPORTED FOR CRYSTAL REPORTS

Crystal Reports	XLS	PDF	RTF	XML	HTML
DOCUMENT	Y	Y	Y		
REPORT				Y*	
REPORT_PAGE	Y	Y	Y		Y

XML can be returned only after patching UWS. A patch is available at www.usingcrystal.com.

TABLE 32.3 UWS VIEW TYPES AND VIEW MODES SUPPORTED FOR WEBINTELLIGENCE

Web Intelligence	XLS	PDF	RTF	XML	HTML
DOCUMENT	Y	Y			
REPORT	Y	Y		Y	Y
REPORT_PAGE				Y	Y

Because Web Intelligence supports retrieval of multiple, incongruous resultsets, WebIntelligence XML documents contain sections per resultset or data provider. With Crystal Reports, XML is returned using the RAS Rowset Controller because XML is not yet a first-class export format through the page server in this release.

BUILDING AN UWS SDK PORTAL

Now that you know how about using the web services SDK, you can now build BI portals using it. As with the samples provided for deploying the Business Objects Enterprise SDK, you can download a white-box starter portal using the web services SDKs at www. usingcrystal.com. Table 32.4 shows several of the files you will find.

TABLE 32.4   WHITE-BOX UWS SDK PORTAL JSP PAGES

JSP Page	Description
_check_authentication_uws.jsp	Checks authentication and redirects to logon page on failure.
_footer.jsp	Generic footer.
_header.jsp	Generic footer.
directory.jsp	Allows users to browse and drill through BOE folders, and view the reports contained therein.
getImage.jsp	Image call-back handler.
logon.jsp	Logon page.
logout.jsp	Logoff page.
view.jsp	For viewing a Crystal Report or WebIntelligence document. Drilling is supported for Crystal. String parameters are supported.

Portions of these pages are described in greater detail in the sections that follow.

SETTING UP A CONSUMER SDK PROJECT

Using the UWS Consumer SDKs in the Java environment requires the 1.4.2 version of the Java 2 SDK Standard Edition and a Java application server. Client jar and .NET assemblies can be found in the \Web Services\en\dsws_consumer\data directory of the installation directory. For J2EE clients, unzip the client JAR files from dswsJavaApi.zip into the WEB-INF\lib directory of your project. These files include dsws-bicatalog.jar, dsws-common.jar, dsws-reportengine.jar, dsws-session.jar, and wilog.jar. Additionally, the implementation requires these six jars that are part of the Apache Axis distribution: Axis.jar, commons-discovery.jar, Jaxrpc.jar, Saaj.jar, Wsdl4j.jar, and Jtools.jar. If you followed the previous build instructions, these files will be in the C:\Program Files\Business Objects\Assemble\dswsBobjeJava\src\WEB-INF\lib Directory. For rich Java clients, add these JAR files to your application's classpath. Note that these JARs are considerably smaller than those required to deploy the alternative CORBA-based SDK application.

32

Checking Authentication

As with the SDK portal shown in Chapter 30, "Using the BusinessObjects Enterprise APIs," every page (except for login.jsp) in the UWS portal includes a special JSP page, check_authentication_uws.jsp, that ensures that the user has logged in properly. This page can process for credentials posted from the login page or create a page-level pointer to an EnterpriseSession in application session scope. In the event that an EnterpriseSession does not exist or has timed-out, it sends a user to the login page.

Listing 32.2 contains login code from check_authentication_uws.jsp which shows how to create a new session from a username and password.

Listing 32.2 Creating a New UWS Session

```
URL boConURL = new URL(UWS_CONNECTION_URL);
Connection boConnection = new Connection(boConURL);
EnterpriseCredential boCredential = new EnterpriseCredential();
//fill in login information for both servers
boCredential.setLogin(USERNAME);
boCredential.setPassword(PASSWORD);
//create a session object using the connnection
boSession = new Session(boConnection);
//log in to the server
boSI = boSession.login(boCredential);
//cache session
session.setAttribute(UWS_SESSION, boSession);
session.setAttribute(UWS_SESSION_INFO, boSI);
session.setAttribute(UWS_USR_NAME,usr);
```

Listing 32.3 shows the login form itself, which is found in login.jsp. What is different about this login page versus the CORBA SDK code is that it does not reference a CMS name, but rather the UWS server endpoint URL. In this application, the actual URL is stored in the property file under the key UWS_CONNECTION_URL.

Listing 32.3 Simplified Logon Form

```
<form name='logonform' method='post' action='<%=returnToURL%>'>
    <input type=hidden name="returnToURL" value="<%=returnToURL%>">
    <input type=hidden name="logon_action" value="logon">
<table><tr><td class='normalText' valign='top'> User </td>
    <td><input class='normalText' type='text' size='30' name='usr'
➡value='<%=lastusr%>'></td></tr>
    <tr><td width='80' class='normalText' valign='top'> Password </td>
    <td><input class='normalText' type='password' size='30'
➡ name='pwd' value=''></td></tr>
    <tr><td width="80" class="normalText" valign="top"></td>
<td><input class="normalText" type="button" value="Logon"
➡onclick="javascript:logon();"></td></tr></table>
```

Keeping sessions alive longer than necessary may tie-up licenses and server memory. Be sure to provide a logout page that includes logic to close the Business Objects session (see Listing 32.4) and optionally invalidate the appserver session.

LISTING 32.4 LOGGING OFF

```
Session objSession = (Session)session.getAttribute(UWS_SESSION);
if (objSession!=null){
    objSession.logout();
    // first set the session state to alive
}
session.invalidate();
```

The default page is the UWS portal is `directory.jsp`. This page renders a permission-aware folder catalog. Reports can be viewed as HTML by clicking on their name and as PDF by clicking on the PDF icon. It renders a pseudo-breadcrumb at the top of the page. Portions of directory.jsp are shown in Listing 32.5.

LISTING 32.5 LISTING FOLDERS AND REPORTS

```
//get parent folder ID and name from the request scope
String catid = (String)request.getParameter("catid");
String catName = (String)request.getParameter("catName");
if (catName==null) catName="Root";
//instantiate BI catalog
BICatalog oBICatalog = BICatalog.getInstance(boSession,
➥ boSession.getAssociatedServicesURL("BICatalog")[0]);
//set sorting
SortType[] oSort = new SortType[1];
oSort[0] = SortType.NAMEASC;
//get all objects beneath root
BICatalogObject[] catItems = oBICatalog.getCatalog(catid,0,oSort,null,null,null,
➥InstanceRetrievalType.ALL);
//print pseudo bread-crumb
if (!catName.equalsIgnoreCase("Root")) out.println("<A HREF='directory.jsp'>
➥<B>Top</B></A> > ");
out.println("<b>"+catName+"</b><br>");
//write out folders and reports...
for(int i=0;i<catItems.length;i++)     {
    out.println("<br/>");
    if (catItems[i] instanceof Document)
    {
        if (catItems[i].getObjectType().equalsIgnoreCase("CrystalReport")){
            out.println("<IMG SRC='../images/report.gif'
            ➥ WIDTH=16 HEIGHT=16 BORDER=0>");
        } else {
            out.println("<IMG SRC='../images/webi.gif'
            ➥ WIDTH=16 HEIGHT=16 BORDER=0>");
        }%>
        <a href="view.jsp?docref=<%=URLEncoder.encode(catItems[i].getUID())%>
        ➥&type=html"><%=catItems[i].getName()%></a> <a href=
        ➥"view.jsp?docref=<%=URLEncoder.encode(catItems[i].getUID())%>
        ➥&type=pdf"><IMG SRC='images/pdf.gif' WIDTH=16 HEIGHT=16 BORDER=0></A>
        <%}else{%>
            <IMG SRC="images/folder.gif" WIDTH=16 HEIGHT=16 BORDER=0>
            ➥ <a href="directory.jsp?catid=<%=URLEncoder.encode(catItems[i].
            ➥getUID())%>
            ➥&catName=<%=catItems[i].getName()%>"><%=catItems[i].getName()%></a>
        <%}
    }
}
```

32

Finally, the UWS viewer page (`viewer.jsp`) is used to output a report as HTML or PDF and a second file (`getImage.jsp`) is used to render image call-backs. Drilling in CrystalReports and simple text prompts are supported. These listings are quite long and can be downloaded from usingcrystal.com.

Review

Web services are by now the most exciting new paradigm in software development. They allow disparate systems to communicate with each other over non-proprietary protocols (HTTP) using a non-proprietary data exchange format (XML text files). This flexibility comes at a cost. Performance and security are often cited. Performance issues are partially overcome through web service SDK design. Developers will notice that methods are more coarse-grained than object-oriented design patterns.

Business Objects provides a rich web services SDK for browsing folders and securely accessing Crystal Reports and WebIntelligence documents in the BOE repository. In the next release you will be able to query the Universe meta-layer directly as well. You can get started using the UWS SDK by reviewing the code in this chapter and by downloading a ready-to-run sample portal from www.usingcrystal.com.

CHAPTER 33

BusinessObjects Enterprise— Customizing the Crystal Reports Viewers

In this chapter

VIEWING REPORTS OVER THE WEB

This chapter introduces programmatic access to viewing reports over the Web through the BusinessObjects Enterprise SDKs. It is important to note that these viewers and the means to programmatically access them have been made consistent across Crystal Reports Server and BusinessObjects Enterprise Professional and Premium editions. This consistency across products enables a seamless and rapid migration through the different versions of these products as developer's application requirements grow. These SDKs are provided in Java and .NET flavors and provide rich functionality that can be integrated into both intranet and extranet targeted applications.

This chapter introduces the different Crystal Report viewer components and explains how to set them up for inclusion in your custom applications. The following topics are covered:

- Introduction to the Crystal Report viewers
- Understanding the report source
- Implementing the Page viewer and toolbar buttons
- Implementing the Part viewer
- Implementing the Interactive viewer and toolbar buttons
- Implementing the Grid viewer and toolbar buttons
- Using the Export Control

INTRODUCTION TO THE CRYSTAL REPORT VIEWERS

The Crystal Report viewers that ship with the Report Application Server break into four different categories to suit the need of a variety of applications: the DHTML Report Page viewer, Report Parts viewer, DHTML Interactive viewer, and DHTML Grid viewer. Although all four viewers offer unique capabilities, they share a common API and set of basic features. Each viewer allows the developer to indicate which report to display, supply database logon credentials, apply report parameters, and export the report. All four viewers are exposed as server-side controls and as a result, output dynamic HTML that is rendered in any web browser. No special software is required on the client's machines to view reports using any of the viewers.

Listed below is a short description about each report viewer:

- **DHTML Report Page viewer**—The standard report viewer component. It displays reports in a paginated fashion. A toolbar along the top allows access functions like page navigation, printing, exporting, zooming, and text searching.
- **Report Parts viewer**—A report viewer component that renders just individual elements of a report. This is useful for portal-style applications where only a small portion of the screen is reserved for report viewing.

- **DHTML Interactive viewer**—Looks and acts identical to the Page viewer but exposes an extra toolbar button that provides an additional user interface for doing data-level searching within the report.
- **DHTML Grid viewer**—A viewer component that just displays the data from the report in a grid without any layout or formatting applied.

The means with which all of these viewers interact with the reports themselves is a mechanism called the report source. The following section describes the report source in detail.

UNDERSTANDING THE REPORT SOURCE

Because the Crystal Report viewer components are shared across both the Crystal Reports Server and the BusinessObjects Enterprise Professional/Premium editions, there must be a common interface defined so the viewer can display reports generated using both types of report processing engines. This interface is called the report source. The report source is an object that both the Crystal Reports Server edition and Professional/Premium editions supply that the viewer in turn communicates with to render the reports to the various forms of HTML.

There are two types of report sources, the Page Server and the Report Application Server. Each type of report source offers different advantages.

WHEN TO USE A PAGE SERVER

- You want to take advantage of the Cache Server, so individual report pages are not generated every time they are requested.
- Your application delivers reports that do not need to be changed at run-time.

WHEN TO USE THE REPORT APPLICATION SERVER

- Your application needs to modify reports at run-time.
- Your application uses the DHTML Interactive viewer. The DHTML Interactive viewer requires the use of functionality only provided by the Report Application Server.
- Your application uses the DHTML Grid viewer. Since the DHTML Grid viewer does not function with a Page Server, you need to use the Report Application Server when using the DHTML grid viewer.

The Java code in Listing 33.1 illustrates the first scenario where a report source object is obtained from the standalone Report Application Server.

33

LISTING 33.1   OBTAINING A REPORT SOURCE FROM A REPORT FILE

```
//First you must create a new ReportClientDocument object
ReportClientDocument reportClientDoc = new ReportClientDocument();
//After the ReportClientDocument is created, you then need to
//specify the report file that is to be used as the report
//source:
String path = __
"C:\\Program Files\\Crystal Decisions\\Report Application Server"
+ " 10\\Reports\\Sample.rpt";
reportClientDoc.open(path, openReportOptions._openAsReadOnly);
//Finally use the openReportSource method to return the report source object
IReportSource reportSource = reportClientDoc.getReportSource();
```

All the code listings provided in this chapter are provided in JSP/Java. Although the .NET/COM and the Java flavors of the RAS SDK share identical functionality, there are obviously language nuances associated with each of them. Many code samples for additional language flavors are available for download from the www.usingcrystal.com website.

Listing 33.2 illustrates obtaining a report source when using the Report Application Server as part of BusinessObjects Enterprise. Notice that the same ReportClientDocument object is used. The difference is in how the ReportClientDocument object is obtained.

→ For more information on using the IEnterpriseSession as associated BusinessObjects Enterprise objects, see "Creating an Enterprise Session," p. 756.

LISTING 33.2   OBTAINING AN ENTERPRISESESSION OBJECT

```
//Retrieve the IEnterpriseSession object previously stored in the user's session.
IEnterpriseSession enterpriseSession = __
(IEnterpriseSession) session.getAttribute("EnterpriseSession");
//Use enterpriseSession object to retrieve the reportAppFactory object
IReportAppFactory reportAppFactory = __
(IReportAppFactory) enterpriseSession.getService("", "RASReportFactory");
//Open the report document by specifying the report ID
ReportClientDocument reportClientDoc = __
reportAppFactory.openDocument(reportID, 0, Locale.ENGLISH);
//Finally use the openReportSource method to return the report source object
IReportSource reportSource = reportClientDoc.getReportSource();
```

An alternative way to do this is shown in Listing 33.3.

LISTING 33.3   ALTERNATIVE METHOD TO OBTAIN AN ENTERPRISESESSION OBJECT

```
//Retrieve the IEnterpriseSession object.
IEnterpriseSession enterpriseSession = __
(IEnterpriseSession) session.getAttribute("EnterpriseSession");
// Use the IEnterpriseSession object's getService method to
// get an IReportAppFactory object.
```

```
IReportSourceFactory reportFactory = \
       (IReportSourceFactory) __
enterpriseSession.getService("", "RASReportFactory");
//Use IReportAppFactory object's openReportSource method, passing it
//the report ID to return the reportSource object
IReportSource reportSource = \
       reportFactory.openReportSource(reportID, Locale.ENGLISH);
```

Listing 33.4 illustrates obtaining a report source object from the Page Server service from BusinessObjects Enterprise Professional/Premium.

LISTING 33.4 UTILIZING THE PAGE SERVER TO OPEN A REPORT

```
// Retrieve the IEnterpriseSession object previously stored in __
the user's session.
IEnterpriseSession enterpriseSession =__
 (IEnterpriseSession) session.getAttribute("EnterpriseSession");
// Use the getService method of the EnterpriseSession object to
// obtain an IReportAppFactory object:
IReportSourceFactory reportFactory = \
       (IReportSourceFactory) __
enterpriseSession.getService ("", "PSReportFactory");
//Finally use the openReportSource method to return the report source object
IReportSource reportSource =__
 reportFactory.openReportSource(reportID, Locale.ENGLISH) ;
```

IMPLEMENTING THE PAGE VIEWER

The first viewer component to be covered is the Page viewer, as illustrated in Listing 33.5. To use this viewer, you will create its CrystalReportViewer object. It, along with all the other viewers, exposes a method called setReportSource that accepts a valid report source object as obtained from the description in the previous section. Finally, again like the other viewers, it has a processHttpRequest method that accepts references to the current servlet context. This method does the actual rendering to HTML.

33

LISTING 33.5 VIEWING A REPORT OVER THE WEB

```
//To create a Java report viewer you need to instantiate a CrystalReportViewer
//object. To create a CrystalReportViewer object:
CrystalReportViewer viewer = new CrystalReportViewer();
//Obtain a ReportSource object. Set the viewer's report source __
by calling its //setReportSource method.
viewer.setReportSource(reportSource);
//When you have created and initialized a Java report page viewer, __
you call//its processHttpRequest method to launch it in a web browser.
viewer.processHttpRequest(request, response, getServletContext(), null);
```

Figure 33.1 shows the output of this code.

Figure 33.1
A report being
displayed in the
DHTML Page viewer.

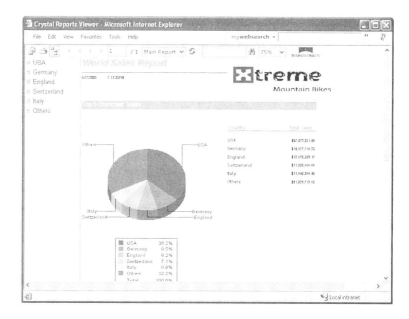

All viewers including the DHTML Page viewer share a number of toolbar elements. These properties can be programmatically toggled and are displayed in Table 33.1. All the viewer properties must be set before calling the ProcessHTTPRequest method that displays the selected report.

For example, to ensure the Business Objects logo is displayed when the involved report is viewed, the code line

```
Viewer.HasLogo(true);
```

needs to be included in the code before the processHTTPRequest method is called.

As the different viewers are introduced and discussed later in this chapter, some additional elements pertinent to the viewer being discussed will be displayed in that section's table.

TABLE 33.1   TOOLBAR ELEMENTS (DHTML PAGE VIEWER)

Property	Property Description
HasLogo	Includes or excludes the Business Objects logo when rendering the report.
HasExportButton	Includes or excludes the export button when rendering the report.
HasGotoPageButton	Includes or excludes the Go to Page button when rendering the report.
HasPageNavigationButtons	Includes or excludes the page navigation buttons when rendering the report.
HasPrintButton	Includes or excludes the Print button when rendering the report.

Property	Property Description
HasRefreshButton	Includes or excludes the Refresh button when rendering the report.
HasSearchButton	Includes or excludes the Search button when rendering the report.
HasToggleGroupTreeButton	Includes or excludes the Group Tree toggle button when rendering the report.
HasViewList	Specifies whether the viewer should display a list of previous views of the report.
SetPrintMode	Set printing to use PDF or Active X printing (0=pdf, 1=actx).
HasZoomFactorList	Specifies zoom factor for displayed report.

IMPLEMENTING THE PART VIEWER

The Part viewer works much the same way as the Page viewer—in fact, much of the code is exactly the same, except for the type of viewer object that is created. Listing 33.6 assumes that the report to be displayed has an initial report part defined in the report itself.

LISTING 33.6 VIEWING A REPORT USING THE REPORT PART VIEWER

```
//To create a Java report part viewer you need to instantiate a __
CrystalReportPartsViewer object:
CrystalReportPartsViewer viewer = new CrystalReportPartsViewer();
//Obtain a ReportSource object. Set the viewer's report source by calling
//its setReportSource method
viewer.setReportSource(reportSource);
//After you have created and initialized a Java report part viewer, you
//call its processHttpRequest method //to launch it in a web browser.
viewer.processHttpRequest(request, response, getServletContext(), null);
```

If a report part is not defined for a report, or if the default part needs to be overridden, Listing 33.7 provides code that can be used to manipulate the ReportParts collection. Figure 33.2 shows the output of this page being displayed in a web browser.

LISTING 33.7 SPECIFYING REPORT PART NODES

```
//To create a Java report part viewer you need to instantiate a
//CrystalReportPartsViewer object:
CrystalReportPartsViewer viewer = new CrystalReportPartsViewer();
//After you have created the CrystalReportPartsViewer object,
//you must specify the report parts that you want to display when the
//viewer is launched. To specify the report parts that you want the
//viewer to display Create a ReportPartsDefinition object.
ReportPartsDefinition partsDefinition = new ReportPartsDefinition();
//Get the collection of ReportPartNodes that belong to the ReportPartsDefinition.
ReportPartNodes reportPartNodes = partsDefinition.getReportPartNodes();
//Create a corresponding ReportPartNode object for each report part that
//you would like the viewer to display. Add these objects to the
```

continues

33

LISTING 33.7   CONTINUED

```
//ReportPartNodes collection. Part1 is being used here as the default
//Report Part to display
ReportPartNode node0 = new ReportPartNode();
node0.setName("Part1");
partsDefinition.getReportPartNodes().add(node0);
//Obtain a ReportSource object. Set the viewer's report source by
// calling its setReportSource method
viewer.setReportSource(reportSource);
//Call the viewer's setReportParts method,
//passing it the ReportPartsDefinition.
viewer.setReportParts(partsDefinition);
//After you have created and initialized a Java report part viewer,
//you call its processHttpRequest method //to launch it in a web browser.
viewer.processHttpRequest(request, response, getServletContext(), null) ;
```

Figure 33.2

The Report Part viewer displaying a report part.

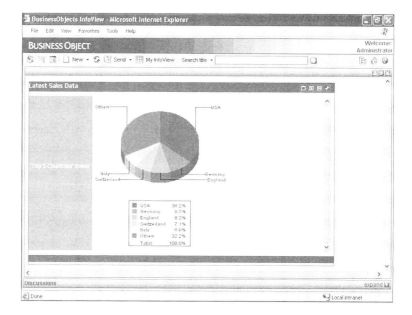

IMPLEMENTING THE INTERACTIVE VIEWER

The Interactive viewer works almost exactly like the Page viewer. In fact, the Interactive viewer component derives from the Page viewer component, so it inherits all the base functionality. What it adds is a new toolbar button that enables an advanced searching User Interface inside the viewer. This is useful for larger reports and for end users requiring advanced searches where simple text string searching is not suitable. The Interactive viewer allows the report to be filtered using a specified record selection criteria.

Listing 33.8 shows a report being viewed by the Interactive viewer. Note that the setOwnPage method is called to indicate that the viewer owns the entire page, which is generally a good thing to do when using this viewer.

LISTING 33.8 USING THE REPORT PART VIEWER IN CODE

```
//To create a Java interactive viewer you instantiate a __
CrystalReportInteractiveViewer object:
CrystalReportInteractiveViewer viewer = new CrystalReportInteractiveViewer();
//Set the viewer's report source by calling its setReportSource method
viewer.setReportSource(reportSource);
//Enable the Advanced Search Wizard.
viewer.setEnableBooleanSearch(true);
//Set the setOwnPage property to true. The setOwnPage property should always
//be set to true for the interactive viewer.
viewer.setOwnPage(true);
//After you have created and initialized a Java interactive viewer,
//you call its processHttpRequest method to launch it in a web browser.
viewer.processHttpRequest(request, response, getServletContext(), null);
```

Figure 33.3 shows a report being displayed in the Interactive viewer and the advanced searching UI being used.

Figure 33.3
The Interactive viewer in action.

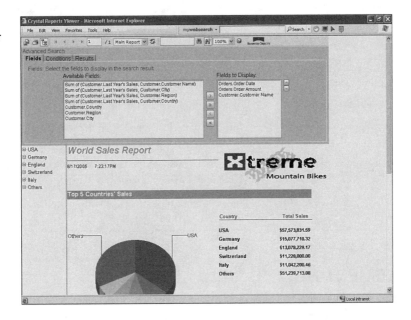

All viewers including the Interactive viewer share a number of toolbar elements. These properties can be programmatically toggled and are displayed in Table 33.2. All the viewer properties must be set before calling the ProcessHTTPRequest method that will display the selected report. For example, to ensure the Business Objects logo is displayed when the involved report is viewed, the code line

```
Viewer.HasLogo(true);
```

needs to be included in the code before the processHTTPRequest method is called.

TABLE 33.2   TOOLBAR ELEMENTS (INTERACTIVE VIEWER)

Property	Property Description
HasLogo	Includes or excludes the "Business Objects" logo when rendering the report.
HasExportButton	Includes or excludes the export button when rendering the report.
HasGotoPageButton	Includes or excludes the Go to Page button when rendering the report.
HasPageNavigationButtons	Includes or excludes the page navigation buttons when rendering the report.
HasPrintButton	Includes or excludes the Print button when rendering the report.
HasRefreshButton	Includes or excludes the Refresh button when rendering the report.
HasSearchButton	Includes or excludes the Search button when rendering the report.
HasToggleGroupTreeButton	Includes or excludes the Group Tree toggle button when rendering the report.
HasViewList	Specifies whether the viewer should display a list of previous views of the report.
SetPrintMode	Set printing to use PDF or Active X printing (0=pdf, 1=actx).
HasZoomFactorList	Specifies zoom factor for displayed report.
HasBooleanSearchButton	Includes or excludes the toggle Boolean search button when rendering the report. Unique to Interactive viewer.
HasHeaderArea	Includes or excludes the header area when rendering the report. Unique to Interactive viewer.
HasPageBottomToolbar	Includes or excludes the page bottom toolbar. Unique to Interactive viewer.

IMPLEMENTING THE GRID VIEWER

The final viewer to be covered in this chapter is the Grid viewer. The Grid viewer differs more from the other viewers in that it does not render the report's presentation onscreen. Instead it looks at the dataset associated with the report (that is, the query result after the report engine has done its magic) and displays that data in a tabular fashion. This opens up some very interesting scenarios if you use your imagination.

You can override the style of the grid table by defining a stylesheet that maps to the styles used by the grid object. Consult the documentation for more information on this.

Listing 33.9 shows a report being displayed using the Grid viewer.

LISTING 33.9   DISPLAYING A REPORT IN THE GRID VIEWER

```
//To create a Java grid viewer you need to instantiate a GridViewer object.
//To create a GridViewer object:
GridViewer viewer = new GridViewer();
//Set the viewer's report source by calling its setReportSource method
viewer.setReportSource(reportSource);
//After you have created and initialized a Java grid viewer object, you call
//its processHttpRequest method to display the results in the web page
viewer.processHttpRequest(request, response, getServletContext(), null);
```

All viewers including the Grid viewer share a number of toolbar elements. These properties can be programmatically toggled and are displayed in Table 33.3. All the viewer properties must be set before calling the ProcessHTTPRequest method that will display the selected report. For example, to ensure the Business Objects logo is displayed when the involved report is viewed, the code line

```
Viewer.HasLogo(true);
```

needs to be included in the code before the processHTTPRequest method is called.

TABLE 33.3   TOOLBAR ELEMENTS (GRID VIEWER)

Property	Property Description
HasLogo	Includes or excludes the "Business Objects" logo when rendering the report.
HasExportButton	Includes or excludes the export button when rendering the report.
HasGotoPageButton	Includes or excludes the Go to Page button when rendering the report.
HasPageNavigationButtons	Includes or excludes the page navigation buttons when rendering the report.
HasPrintButton	Includes or excludes the Print button when rendering the report.
HasRefreshButton	Includes or excludes the Refresh button when rendering the report.
HasSearchButton	Includes or excludes the Search button when rendering the report.
HasToggleGroupTreeButton	Includes or excludes the Group Tree toggle button when rendering the report.
HasViewList	Specifies whether the viewer should display a list of previous views of the report.

33

continues

TABLE 33.3   CONTINUED

Property	Property Description
SetPrintMode	Set printing to use PDF or Active X printing (0=pdf, 1=actx).
HasZoomFactorList	Specifies zoom factor for displayed report.
DisplayNavigationBar	Specifies whether the viewer should display the navigation bar at the bottom of the grid. Unique to Grid viewer.
DisplayRowNumberColumn	Specifies whether to display the row number column. Unique to Grid viewer.
DisplayToolbarFindRowButton	Includes or excludes the Find Row button when rendering the toolbar. Unique to Grid viewer.
DisplayToolbarGroupViewList	Specifies whether the viewer should display the view list. Unique to Grid viewer.
DisplayToolarSwitchViewButton	Includes or excludes the Toggle Grid View button. Unique to Grid viewer.
EnableGridToGrow	Specifies whether the viewer should enable the Grid to Grow. Unique to Grid viewer.
GridViewMode	Specifies the viewer View mode. Unique to Grid viewer.
MatchGridandToolbarWidth	Specifies whether the table should align with the toolbar. Unique to Grid viewer.
TableStyle	Specifies the style class of the table. You can apply a css style class to the grid table that shows records. You do so by stating: Gridviewer.TableStyle="cssclass"; Unique to Grid viewer.
ToolbarStyle	Specifies the style class of the toolbar. You can apply a css style class to the grid toolbar. You do so by stating: Gridviewer.ToolbarStyle="cssclass"; Unique to Grid viewer.

USING THE EXPORT CONTROL TO DELIVER REPORTS IN OTHER FORMATS

So far all the scenarios that have been discussed in this chapter have involved displaying reports in dynamic HTML format. Although this is a great report delivery method for most scenarios, there are times when reports need to be exported to various other file formats.

Although this can be accomplished by using the ReportClientDocument object model, there is an easier way to do this: using the Export control.

Listing 33.10 shows how the Export control would be used to export a report to PDF. Notice that the Export control has the concept of the report source of the processHttpRequest method.

LISTING 33.10   EXPORTING A REPORT VIA CODE

```
//Instantiate a ReportExportControl object
ReportExportControl exportControl = new ReportExportControl();
//After you have created the ReportExportControl object, you must specify the
//export format that you want to export the report to. To specify the export
//format create an ExportOptions object:
ExportOptions exportOptions = new ExportOptions();
//Specify the export format by calling the ExportOptions object's
setExportFormatType method, passing it the integer constant that
//represents the chosen format:
exportOptions.setExportFormatType(ReportExportFormat.PDF);
//To initialize an Export control in a BusinessObjects Enterprise environment set
//the control's report source by calling its setReportSource method.
exportControl.setReportSource(reportSource);
//Call the control's setExportOptions method, passing it an __
ExportOptions object exportControl.setExportOptions(exportOptions);
//You may also want to call the setExportAsAttachment method, passing it the
//Boolean value true. The Export control will then display a dialog box
//that allows users of your web application to save the exported report before
//they open it:
exportControl.setExportAsAttachment(true);
//To initialize an Export control in an unmanaged RAS environment set the
//control's report source by calling its setReportSource method and passing
//the method a reference to a report source object.
exportControl.setReportSource(reportSource);
//Call the control's setExportOptions method, passing it an ExportOptions object
exportControl.setExportOptions(exportOptions);
//You may also want to call the setExportAsAttachment method, passing it the
//Boolean value true. The Export control will then display a dialog box
//that allows users of your web application to save the exported report before
//they open it:
exportControl.setExportAsAttachment(true);
//After you have created an export control, you call its processHttpRequest
//method to complete the export.
exportControl.processHttpRequest(request, response, getServletContext(), null) ;
```

Figure 33.4 shows a report being exported to PDF.

Figure 33.4
Using the Export control to export a report to PDF.

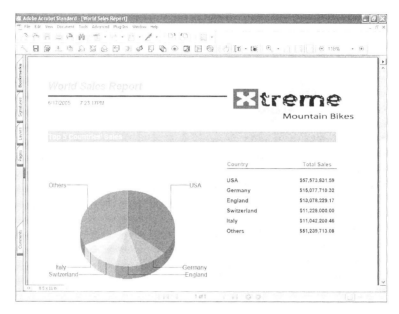

TROUBLESHOOTING

REPORT VIEWING PERFORMANCE IS SLOW

What efficiencies can I add to increase the performance of my application?

Caching a report source in the session variable allows it to be used multiple times efficiently. When a report source is not cached, the process of creating a new report source multiple times becomes fairly expensive. Furthermore, caching a report source allows reports with or without saved data to be refreshed.

Listing 33.11 shows how to store and retrieve the report source object from session state.

LISTING 33.11   CACHING A REPORT SOURCE OBJECT

```
//To store the report source in a session variable
request.getSession().settAttribute("RptSrc",reportSource);
//To retrieve the report source from a session variable
rptSrc = request.getSession().getAttribute("RptSrc");
```

THE VIEWER NEEDS TO WORK IN A PAGE WITHOUT A FORM ELEMENT

How can I control how the viewer interacts with a surrounding form?

If your web page contains only the viewer and nothing else, several things can be done that can simplify the report viewing implementation. The viewer is capable of generating complete HTML pages and can set the appropriate page properties depending on the viewing context. Setting the setOwnPage property to true provides several benefits. Allowing the viewer to handle the surrounding HTML content reduces the amount of code you need to add to your web page and allows the viewer to automatically determine certain settings. It correctly sets the content-type and charset information for the page. This ensures that pages containing international characters will be displayed correctly. When `setOwnPage` is set to true, you must use the `processHttpRequest` method to display the report instead of `getHtmlContent`. The `processHttpRequest` method must be used because using `getHtmlContent` has the same effect as setting `setOwnPage` to false, negating any of the benefits gained from setting `setOwnPage` to true. If your web page does not contain any controls that require post back, you should set the `setOwnForm` method to true. Doing so allows the viewer to handle the view state information automatically. The view state is used to perform client-side caching of information about the current state of the report. If you have other controls on the page, you must set `setOwnForm` to false and handle the view state information manually.

THE CHARACTER SET IS DISPLAYING INCORRECTLY

How can I indicate which unicode character to set should be used for the report viewing session?

To send characters from a web page to a web browser, you must use the correct encoding. Always specify the correct content-type and character set for all your web pages. If your web page returns content to a standard HTML browser, the following lines will ensure that the correct character set is defined. The contentType and charset directives let the browser know how the returned HTML page is encoded. UTF-8 is the recommended standard character set if it is available for your target client browser. For more information, consult the Release Notes or the vendor for your target client browser.

CHAPTER 34

CRYSTAL REPORT MODIFICATION AND CREATION APIs

In this chapter

INTRODUCTION

This chapter covers the capability of the Report Application Server (RAS) SDK to create and modify reports. Topics include

- RAS environments
- Loading report files
- RAS component locations
- Installing the RAS SDK
- Exception handling
- Programming with the RAS SDK

DEPLOYING RAS ENVIRONMENTS

The RAS APIS are available in two different environments—as a service of the BusinessObjects Enterprise framework or as part of Crystal Reports Server. For the remainder of the chapter, any reference to functionality being provided in BusinessObjects Enterprise automatically implies that the same functionality is available in Crystal Reports Server, unless otherwise noted.

USING RAS IN A BUSINESSOBJECTS ENTERPRISE (OR CRYSTAL REPORTS SERVER) ENVIRONMENT

BusinessObjects Enterprise provides a framework for delivering enterprise reporting. RAS adds the capability for users to modify reports stored in BusinessObjects Enterprise. In this scenario, the BusinessObjects Enterprise framework manages the RAS. Multiple instances of the RAS can be added and BusinessObjects Enterprise will load balance between them.

INSTALLING THE RAS SDK

As mentioned previously, the RAS SDK JAR files can be found in the jar folder by default. Copy the RAS and BusinessObjects Enterprise .jar files to the appropriate folder on the application server being used. If you are using Apache Tomcat, for example, move the .jar files to the Web application's WEB-INF\lib folder. Configuring a Web server to access the SDK JAR files might take additional steps, detailed in the installation help files provided with the RAS.

RAS EXCEPTION HANDLING

Options for displaying and logging exception information can also be specified. These tasks can be performed by modifying the web.xml file (located by default in the \WEB-INF\ directory of your Web application) as follows.

DISPLAYING EXCEPTIONS

Three options exist for displaying exception information to the user. Setting the `crystal_exception_info` parameter to one of the following values determines how exceptions are handled:

- **short**—The exception information is displayed without the accompanying stack trace.
- **long**—The exception information is displayed with the accompanying stack trace.
- **disable**—The exception information is not displayed; the user must handle the exception.

The following code shows an example of the exception display configuration:

```
<context-param>
   <param-name>crystal_exception_info</param-name>
   <param-value>long</param-value>
   <description> Options for displaying exception information.
      If this parameter is not set, the default value is short.
      It can be one of the following values: short, long, disable.
   </description>
</context-param>
```

The `crystal_exception_info` parameter is short by default. Modifying exception.css specifies the style and formatting of short messages.

LOGGING EXCEPTIONS

The option to turn exception logging either on or off can be set with the `crystal_exception_log_file` parameter. The exception information output to the log file will be in the long format regardless of the setting of the `crystal_exception_info` parameter. The following code shows an example of the exception logging configuration:

```
<context-param>
   <param-name>crystal_exception_log_file</param-name>
   <param-value>c:\temp\webreportingexception.log</param-valu>
   <description>
      Set this parameter to log the exception in long form
      to the file specified.
      The value is the full path of the log file.
   </description>
</context-param>
```

When setting the parameter to the desired path of the log file, by default, exceptions are not logged.

THE RAS SDK IN ACTION

This section covers the common programming tasks associated with the RAS SDK. Although the SDK provides many capabilities, some of the following tasks are common to most programming exercises and are central to the SDK.

34

INITIALIZING A RAS SESSION

Initiating a session with the RAS is the first step in programming with the RAS SDK. In this step, a specific RAS can be specified for use; otherwise, the system selects one from the RASs listed in the clientSDKOptions.xml file using a round-robin method. Initializing a RAS session by specifying a machine name at runtime is shown in the following code:

```
//Create a new Report Application Session
ReportAppSession reportAppSession = new ReportAppSession();
//Create a Report Application Server Service
reportAppSession.createService(
➡"com.crystaldecisions.sdk.occa.report.application.ReportClientDocument");
//Set the RAS server to be used for the service.
➡You can also use "localhost" if the RAS server
//is running on your local machine.
reportAppSession.setReportAppServer("MACHINE_NAME");
//Initialize RAS
reportAppSession.initialize();
//Create the report client document object
ReportClientDocument clientDoc = new ReportClientDocument();
//Set the RAS Server to be used for the Client Document
clientDoc.setReportAppServer(reportAppSession.getReportAppServer() );
```

All ReportClientDocument objects created from the same ReportAppSession communicate with the same RAS.

OPENING A REPORT

A report can be opened first by creating a new ReportClientDocument object and specifying the ReportAppServer. Then the open method can be used to open a report. This method takes two parameters:

- The absolute path and filename of the report
- A flag indicating how the file will be opened

See the OpenReportOptions class for valid report options.

> Reports are loaded from the report folder found at \Program Files\Crystal Decisions\Report Application Server 10\Reports\ by default.

The following code opens a report:

```
try
{
    reportClientDocument.open("C:\MyReports\GlobalSales.rpt", 0);
}
catch (ReportSDKException e) {
    // Handle the case where the report does not open properly.;
}
```

The previous chapter explained how to view reports using RAS. Creating and modifying those reports using the RAS SDK will be the focus of the remainder of this chapter.

ADDING FIELDS TO THE REPORT

A report can be modified after creating and opening a ReportClientDocument by using the report's controllers. The only way to modify reports and ensure that the changes are synchronized with the server is to use controllers. Although the report's fields can be accessed directly through the `DataDefinition` property, any changes made will not be committed. This section explains how to add a field to a report.

IDENTIFYING THE FIELD TO ADD

A field is usually selected by name. The DatabaseController can be used to retrieve the object that represents this field given a database field's name or its table's name. Another method of accessing a table's fields is using the ReportClientDocument's `Database` property. Here you use the DatabaseController.

The DatabaseController contains a collection of database tables that are available to the report and might be accessed using the `getDatabaseController` method of ReportClientDocument. Each table contains a collection of DBField objects.

CAUTION

> All tables and fields that are listed by DatabaseController.getDatabase() are not retrieved when the report is refreshed; that is, they are available for report design but might not actually be part of the report's data definition.

A method called `findFieldByName` is shown in the following sample code snippet. This method returns a field given its fully qualified field name in the form: <TableAlias>.<FieldName>. The table alias is used as a qualifier and it is assumed that a period is used to separate the table alias from the field name.

```
IField findFieldByName(String nameOfFieldToFind, ReportClientDocument
➥reportClientDocument)
{
    //Extracts the field name and the table name.
    int dotPosition = nameOfFieldToFind.indexOf(".");
    String tablePartName = nameOfFieldToFind.substring(0, dotPosition);
    String fieldPartName = nameOfFieldToFind.substring(dotPosition + 1,
    ➥nameOfFieldToFind.length());
    ITable table = null;
    // Uses the DatabaseController to search for the field.
    try
    {
        Tables retreivedTables = reportClientDocument.getDatabaseController().
        ➥getDatabase(). getTables();
        int tableIndex = retreivedTables.findByAlias(tablePartName);
        table = retreivedTables.getTable(tableIndex);
    }
    catch (ReportSDKException e)
    {
        return null;
    }
    // Finds the field in the table.
```

34

```
    int fieldIndex =
➥table.getDataFields().find(fieldPartName,FieldDisplayNameType.
➥fieldName,Locale.ENGLISH);
    if (fieldIndex == -1) {
       return null;
    }
    IField field = table.getDataFields().getField(fieldIndex);
    return field;
}
```

This method uses the following key methods:

- `Tables.findByAlias` finds the index of a particular table when given its alias. Given the index, the desired `Table` object can be retrieved from the collection.

- `Fields.find` finds the index of a field in a table's Fields collection when given the name of the field.

ADDING A FIELD TO THE REPORT DOCUMENT

After you obtain the `Field` object that you want to add, the field can be added to the report so that it is processed and displayed when the report is run. This is done via the DataDefController, which is used to modify the report's data definition and contains a sub-controller called the ResultFieldController. This subcontroller is used for modifying fields that have been placed on the report and that are processed at runtime. The fields that are shown on the report belong to the ResultFields collection. A new database field will be added to the ResultFields collection in this step.

> The ResultFields collection can contain other types of field objects such as parameter fields, formula fields, and summary fields in addition to DBField objects. Like DBFields, the ResultFieldController can add these fields to a report. Unlike DBFields, only the DatabaseDefController's `DataDefinition` property, and not the DatabaseDefController's `Database` property, can retrieve these fields.

A field being added to the ResultFields collection is shown by the following code:

```
/* * Because all modifications to a report must be made with a controller,
 * the resulting field controller is used to add and remove each field.*/
ResultFieldController resultFieldController = reportClientDocument.
➥getDataDefController().getResultFieldController();
// Adds fieldToAdd. -1 indicates the end of the collection.
resultFieldController.add(-1, fieldToAdd);
```

The parameter 1 indicates that the field is to be placed at the end of the collection. As a result of this code, the new field displays on the report and is processed when the report is refreshed.

DETERMINING ALL FIELDS USED IN THE REPORT

The fields that have been added to a report are stored in the ResultFields collection and can be retrieved using the following sample method:

```
Fields getUsedDatabaseFields(ReportClientDocument reportClientDocument)
{
   Fields usedFields = new Fields();
   /*
   * The DataDefinition's ResultFields collection
   * contains all the fields that have been placed
   * on the report and which will be processed
   * when the report is refreshed.
   */
   Fields resultFields = null;
   try
   {
      resultFields = reportClientDocument.getDataDefinition(). getResultFields
      ➥();
   }
   catch (ReportSDKException e)
   {
      return null;
   }
   /*
   * Because the ResultFields collection contains
   * many different kinds of fields, all fields except
   * for database fields are filtered out.
   */
   for (int i = 0; i < resultFields.size() - 1; i++)
   {
      if (resultFields.getField(i).getKind() == FieldKind.DBField)
      {
         // Adds the database field to the collection.
         usedFields.addElement(resultFields.getField(i));
      }
   }
   return usedFields;
}
```

With the full name of the field, you can use a DatabaseController to retrieve the DBField object.

REMOVING A FIELD FROM THE REPORT

When you've found the field you want to remove, use the ResultFieldController to remove it as follows:

```
// Removes fieldToDelete.
resultFieldController.remove(fieldToDelete);
```

In this code, fieldToDelete is a DBField object. After the field is removed from the result fields using this method, the report ceases to display the field.

CREATING A NEW REPORT

A new report can be created by first creating an empty ReportClientDocument as shown:

```
ReportClientDocument reportClientDocument = _

reportAppFactory.newDocument(Locale.ENGLISH);
```

34

CAUTION

> Because the `newDocument` method of ReportClientDocument is provided for deployments that use an unmanaged RAS to access report (.rpt) files, it should not be deployed when using a BusinessObjects Enterprise RAS. Instead, when deploying with BusinessObjects Enterprise, the `IReportAppFactory.newDocument` method should be used as in the previous code.

Because the report is not actually created until tables are added, after creating an empty ReportClientDocument, details such as the new report's tables and the fields used to link them should be added.

RETRIEVING A REPORT'S TABLES

However, before adding the tables to the new report, the table objects must first be retrieved from the source report. This can be accomplished in two ways: using the `DatabaseController` object and using the `Database` object, both of which are available from the `ReportClientDocument` object. The ensuing code iterates through all the tables in an open report and prints the tables' aliases:

```
Tables tables = reportClientDocument.getDatabase().getTables();
for (int i = 0; i < tables.size(); i++)
{
    ITable table = tables.getTable(i);
    out.println(table.getAlias());
}
```

ADDING TABLES TO THE REPORT

Because controllers are the only objects that can modify the report's object model, a controller must be used to add tables to a report. The following code retrieves the report's DatabaseController and adds a table.

```
DatabaseController databaseController;
try
{
    databaseController = reportClientDocument.getDatabaseController();
    databaseController.addTable(sourceTable, new TableLinks());
    databaseController.addTable(targetTable, new TableLinks());
}
catch(ReportSDKException e)
{
    throw new Exception("Error while adding tables.");
}
```

The `addTable` method of the DatabaseController adds a table to the report. The `addTable` method takes two parameters:

- The `Table` object you want to add
- A `TableLinks` object that defines how the table being added is linked with other tables

LINKING TABLES

Tables must be linked after they have been added to the report. To link two tables, first create a new `TableLink` object, set the properties of the `TableLink`, and then add the `TableLink` to the report definition.

Linking two tables using an equal join is illustrated by the following code:

```
// Create the new link that will connect the two tables.
TableLink tableLink = new TableLink();
/*
* Add the source field name and the target field name to the SourceFieldNames
* and TargetFieldNames collection of the TableLink object.
*/
tableLink.getSourceFieldNames().add(sourceFieldName);
tableLink.getTargetFieldNames().add(targetFieldName);
/*
* Specify which tables are to be linked by setting table aliases
* for the TableLink object.
*/
tableLink.setSourceTableAlias(sourceTable.getAlias());
tableLink.setTargetTableAlias(targetTable.getAlias());
// Add the link to the report. Doing so effectively links the two tables.
try
{
    databaseController.addTableLink(tableLink);
}
catch(ReportSDKException e)
{
    throw new TutorialException("Error while linking tables.");
}
```

These newly linked tables can be used as the report's data source. However there have been no visible objects added to the report, so when the report is refreshed, it will be blank.

ADDING GROUPS

To add a group, you must know which field is being grouped on. For information on working with fields, see the "Adding a Field to the Report Document" section earlier in this chapter. Because not all fields can be used to define a group, use the canGroupOn method of GroupController to check whether a field can be used for grouping. If canGroupOn returns true, the field is an acceptable field to use for grouping. The next example demonstrates a function that adds a new group to a report:

```
// Uses the sort controller to remove all the report's sorts.
Sorts sorts = dataDefController.getDataDefinition().getSorts();
SortController sortController = dataDefController.getSortController();
for (int i = 0; i < sorts.size(); i++)
{
    sortController.remove(0);
}
```

Here the group was added to the end of the Groups collection by setting the index to -1, which means that the new group becomes the innermost group. When a new group is added, a new sorting definition is also added which will sort the records according to the

34

group's condition field and group options. An additional reflection of adding the new group is the group name field appearing on the group's header. Fields added to the group header are not added to the ResultFields collection. When the group is removed, the group name field is also removed.

ADDING SORTING TO THE REPORT

Using the SortController adds a new sorting definition to a report. The SortController can add any kind of sorting definition, including a Top N sort. Adding a Top N sort requires that a summary has first been added.

Next you demonstrate how to add a sort to the report by taking a Fields collection and adding a sorting definition based on each field in the collection:

```
void addNewGroup(ReportClientDocument reportClientDocument, _
 Fields newGroupFields)
throws ExampleException
{
   try
   {
      // Create a new, empty group.
      IGroup group = new Group();
      // Iterate through every field in the given Fields collection.
      for (int i = 0; i < newGroupFields.size(); i++)
      {
         IField field = newGroupFields.getField(i);
         // Set the field that will define how data is grouped.
         group.setConditionField(field);
         GroupController groupController = reportClientDocument.
         ➥getDataDefController(). getGroupController(); groupController.
         ➥add(-1, group);
      }
   }
   // If any part of the above procedure failed, redirect the user to
   // an error page.
   catch (ReportSDKException e)
   {
      throw new ExampleException("Error while adding new groups.");
   }
}
```

When the new Sort object is added, it is added to the end of the collection, indicated by the -1 argument, which designates that the records will be sorted on this field after all other sorting definitions. The SortDirection class indicates the direction of the sort. The static objects SortDirection.ascendingOrder and SortDirection.descendingOrder are the only values that can be used for a normal sort. The other values are used for a Top N or Bottom N sort. See Adding a Top N sorting definition in the SDK documentation for additional details.

ADDING SUMMARIES TO THE REPORT

The SummaryFieldController adds a new summary field. To determine if a field can produce a summary, the SummaryFieldController's method canSummarizeOn is called. Here you add a summary to a group:

```
void setSorting(ReportClientDocument reportClientDocument, Fields fieldsToSortOn)
throws ExampleException
{
try
{
 DataDefController dataDefController = reportClientDocument
➥. getDataDefController();
// Create a new Sort object
ISort sort = new Sort();
// Iterate through the fields
for (int i = 0; i < fieldsToSortOn.size(); i++)
{
IField field = fieldsToSortOn.getField(i);
// Add the current field to the result fields.
dataDefController.getResultFieldController().add(-1, field);
// Set the field to sort on.
sort.setSortField(field);
// Define the type of sorting. Ascending here.
sort.setDirection(SortDirection.ascendingOrder);
//Get Sort Controller. SortController sortController = \
➥dataDefController.getSortController();
➥sortController.add(-1, sort);
}
}
// If any part of the above procedure failed,
//  redirect the user to an error page.
catch (ReportSDKException e)
{
throw new TutorialException("Error while setting sort.");
}
}
```

After creating a summary field, set the following properties before adding it:

- **SummarizedField**—The field used to calculate the summary.

- **Group**—The group for which the summary will be calculated.

- **Operation**—The operation used to calculate the summary. One of the static objects defined in the SummaryOperation class.

WORKING WITH FILTERS

Filters are used in record selection and group selection. The filter is initially a string written in Crystal formula syntax. The record selection formula is then parsed into an array of FilterItems stored in the Filter object's FilterItems property. The string is broken up into data components and operator components that act on the data. These components are stored as FieldRangeFilterItem and OperatorFilterItem objects respectively, which are stored in the FilterItems collection in the same order that they appear in the formula string. Re-ordering the objects in the array changes the functionality of the formula. In summary, the FieldRangeFilterItem is an expression that is joined with other expressions using an OperatorFilterItem.

34

For instance, consider a simple record selection formula such as

`{Customer.Name} = "Bashka Futbol" and {Customer.Country} = "USA".`

This results in only the records that have a name equal to "Bashka Futbol" and a country of the USA. The result is stored in the `FreeEditingText` property. After this string is parsed, the FieldRangeItems collection contains two FieldRangeFilterItem objects because there are two data items used to filter the records. The OperatorFilterItem is used to indicate how two primitive expressions are combined, so it is now equal to and.

The FieldRangeFilterItem contains three properties:

- **Operation**—This property indicates the operation performed in the primitive expression; in both cases, it is the equals operator.

- **RangeField**—The `RangeField` property indicates the comparator field used in the expression. Because not all fields are suitable to filter records and groups, use the `canFilterOn` method in the RecordFilterController and the GroupFilterController to determine whether a field can be used for a particular filter.

- **Values**—The Values property indicates the comparison values in the expression. In this example, it is the strings "USA" and "Bashka Futbol". This property has one ConstantValue object that stores "USA".

After the file is opened, and the filters parsed, the `FreeEditingText` property that stores these strings is cleared and the `FilterItems` populated. Conversely, if the formula is too complex, the `FilterItems` collection property remains empty and the `FreeEditingText` property populated. When altering a filter, you have two options: modify the `FreeEditingText` property or the `FilterItems` property.

If you use only one property to modify the filter, the other will not be automatically updated, however. For instance, you would modify the `FreeEditingText` property, but this will not necessarily be parsed again to repopulate the `FilterItems`. You should use only one of these properties per session.

Use a controller to ensure that modifications are saved. The GroupFilterController and the RecordFilterController modify the group formula and record formula respectively.

CREATING A FIELDRANGEFILTERITEM

A FieldRangeFilterItem contains a primitive comparison expression. Its most relevant properties are

- Operation
- RangeField
- Values

The `Operation` and `RangeField` properties usually contain a constant. However, the `Values` property stores either ConstantValue objects, which don't need evaluation (such as 1, 5, or

"Stringiethingie"), and ExpressionValue objects, which do need evaluation (such as "WeekToDateSinceSun," 4/2, and so on).

The following section of code defines the expression {Customer.ID > 2}. Note how it creates a new `ConstantValue` object for the number 2 and adds it to the Values collection:

```
// Create a new range filter item.
FieldRangeFilterItem fieldRangeFilterItem = new FieldRangeFilterItem();
// Assume the customerDBField has been retrieved from a table
fieldRangeFilterItem.setRangeField(customerDBField);
// Set the operation to >
fieldRangeFilterItem.setOperation(SelectionOperation.greaterThan);
fieldRangeFilterItem.setInclusive(false);
// Create a constant value and add it to the range filter item
ConstantValue constantValue = new ConstantValue();
constantValue.setValue(2);
fieldRangeFilterItem.getValues().addElement(constantValue);
// Create a filter and add the field range filter item
IFilter filter = new Filter();
filter.getFilterItems().addElement(fieldRangeFilterItem);
```

All fields cannot be used in a filter formula (for example, you can't use BLOB fields). Use the `canFilterOn` method, which is located in either the RecordFilterController or the GroupFilterController, to verify that a field can be filtered on. You must also verify that the constant data type is the same as the field. In the previous example, constantValue must not be a variant and corresponds to the data type used in the comparison.

CREATING A OPERATORFILTERITEM

The following example assumes the same expression as defined in the preceding example, but concatenates to the filter using the OR operator. Assume the filter would look like this: `{Customer.ID} > 2 OR {Customer.name} = "Arsel"`. To the code above you would add:

```
OperatorFilterItem operatorFilterItem = new OperatorFilterItem();
operatorFilterItem.setOperator("OR");
filter.getFilterItems().addElement(operatorFilterItem);
filter.getFilterItems().addElement(fieldRangeFilterItem);
```

The `filterItems` parameter is a FilterItems collection. It stores FilterItem objects. In the two examples, both a `FieldRangeFilterItem` object and an `OperatorFilterItem` object were added to this collection. Both of these objects inherit from FilterItem, making this possible.

34

ADDING A FILTER TO THE REPORT

After defining the filter, you add it to the report. Filters can be used in two places: group selection and record selection. The GroupFilterController and RecordFilterController, which can be accessed via the `DataDefController` object, modify their respective filters.

You can also obtain the filters from the `GroupFilter` and `RecordFilter` properties in the DataDefinition, although they can only be modified with a controller.

FilterController provides these methods for modifying a filter:

- **addItem**—This method adds an expression or an operator to the existing filter.
- **modify**—This method replaces the current filter with a new or modified one.
- **modifyItem**—This method modifies a filter element.
- **moveItem**—This method moves the filter element around the filter array.
- **removeItem**—This method deletes a filter element.

In the following code, the modify method is used because a new filter has already been defined. Assume that there is a ReportClientDocument object and that you have opened a report already:

```
FilterController groupFilterController = reportClientDocument.
➡getDataDefController.getGroupFilterController();
groupFilterController.modify(filter) ;
```

WORKING WITH PARAMETERS

Parameters enable end users to enter information to define the report behavior. Parameters have specific data types just like any other field: string, number, date, and so on. Parameters also are divided into two basic types: discrete and ranged. A discrete parameter value is one that represents a singular value such as 9, "Nur", 1863, True, and so on. Ranged values represent a particular span of values from one point to another such as [9..95], [4..6], ["Alpha","Omega"]. The lower bound value of the range must be smaller than the upper bound. Some parameters support more than one value: They effectively contain an array containing many values.

Parameters have default values and the user can be forced to select from them. You can also provide default parameters but allow users to enter their own values. Default values are stored in the ParameterField.DefaultValues property. Selected values are stored in the ParameterField.CurrentValues property.

Parameters support many more features than those covered here. For a complete list of features, see the ParameterField class in the SDK documentation.

READING PARAMETERS AND THEIR VALUES

The parameters are exposed in the SDK by the DataDefinition's ParameterFields class. The ParameterFields class inherits from the Fields class. For example the name of a parameter is obtained using this method:

```
Fields parameterFields = reportClientDocument.getDataDefinition()
➡. getParameterFields();
ParameterField parameterField = (ParameterField)parameterFields.getField(0);
parameterField.getDisplayName(FieldDisplayNameType.fieldName, Locale.ENGLISH);
```

The getDisplayName method is used for UI purposes and so is not a unique identifier. The getFormulaForm method can be used to retrieve a unique identifier. getDisplayName and getFormulaForm are not documented under the ParameterField class because they are inherited from Field.

Because parameter values might be either discrete or ranged, and default values might only be discrete, there are two different objects to represent these: ParameterFieldDiscreteValue and ParameterFieldRangeValue. Both of these objects inherit from ParameterField. You must understand the type of the parameter to know what kind of parameter values it contains. For example, the following code determines if the parameter is of a ranged or discrete type:

```
// Check to see if the value is range or discrete
IValue firstValue = parameterField.getCurrentValues().getValue(0);
if (firstValue instanceof IParameterFieldRangeValue)
{
IParameterFieldRangeValue rangeValue = (IParameterFieldRangeValue)firstValue;
toValueText = rangeValue.getEndValue().toString();
fromValueText = rangeValue.getEndValue().toString();
}
else
{
IParameterFieldDiscreteValue discreteValue = _
  (IParameterFieldDiscreteValue)firstValue;
discreteValueText = discreteValue.getValue().toString();
}
```

Check the parameter's type before you try to print the parameter's values. You must determine the type so you can retrieve the correct field. Trying to access the EndValue of a discrete value will cause a runtime error because no EndValue exists. The previous code example determines whether the parameter value is an instance of IParameterFieldRangeValue to determine what kind of values it will have. For parameters that support both discrete and ranged values, however, you must verify the type of the parameter by using getValueRangeKind method. The following code checks the parameter type and calls a secondary function to handle the correct type and build a table of parameters:

```
ParameterValueRangeKind kinda = parameterField.getValueRangeKind();
if (kinda == ParameterValueRangeKind.discrete)
{
table += createDiscreteParameterTableData(parameterField, key);
key += 1;
}
else if (kinda == ParameterValueRangeKind.range)
{
table += createRangeParameterTableData(parameterField, key);
key += 2;
}
else if (kinda == ParameterValueRangeKind.discreteAndRange)
{
table += createDiscreteRangeParameterTableData(parameterField, key);
key += 3;
}
else
{
table += "<td>Parameter kind not known</td>";
}
```

34

CHANGING PARAMETER VALUES

The ParameterFieldController, which can be found in the DataDefController, enables you to change parameters. To modify a parameter field in the report, you copy the field, modify the copy, and then have the controller modify the original based on changes made to the copy. For instance here you demonstrate this by changing a default discrete value:

```
ParameterField newParamField = new ParameterField();
parameterField.copyTo(newParamField, true);
newParamField.getCurrentValues().removeAllElements();
// Check the type of the parameter
ParameterValueRangeKind kinda = parameterField.getValueRangeKind();
// If it is discrete
if (kinda == ParameterValueRangeKind.discrete)
{
// Get the parameter's value
String textFieldText = request.getParameter("textField" + key);
// Convert this value to the right format
String discreteValueText = (String)convertToValidValue(newParamField,
➡ textFieldText);
// Modify the copy of the parameter field with the value above.
ParameterFieldDiscreteValue discreteValue = new ParameterFieldDiscreteValue();
discreteValue.setValue(discreteValueText);
newParamField.getCurrentValues().add(discreteValue);
key += 1;
}
```

ADDING A PARAMETER

Use the ParameterFieldController to add new parameters. You do this the same way as adding any other fields to the report: A new field is created, its fields are set, and it is added using a controller. Here you define a new, discrete, string parameter and add it using the controller:

```
IParameterField paramField = new ParameterField();
paramField.setAllowCustomCurrentValues(false);
paramField.setAllowMultiValue(false);
paramField.setAllowNullValue(false);
paramField.setDescription("Here we go dude!");
paramField.setParameterType(ParameterFieldType.queryParameter);
paramField.setValueRangeKind(ParameterValueRangeKind.discrete);
paramField.setType(FieldValueType.numberField);
paramField.setName("YourNewParameter");
reportClientDoc.getDataDefController().getParameterFieldController()
➡. add(parameterField);
```

Adding a parameter using the Parameter field controller does not place the parameter on the report, so the user is not prompted for the parameter when the report is refreshed. To prompt the user, either use it in a filter, or add it by using the ResultFieldController.

TIPS AND TRICKS FOR PARAMETER HANDLING

Handling parameters involves many important details. When using parameters keep the following points in mind:

- Parameter values must match the type of the parameter.
- Any values for the parameter should respect the parameter mask.
- Ensure that you know what type of values you are reading: Are they discrete or ranged?
- Set the bound type on a range value before adding it to the parameter.
- Ensure that the upper bound of a range value is greater than the lower bound.

Failing these tests results in a runtime error.

CHARTING OVERVIEW

The ChartObject, which represents a chart in the RAS SDK, inherits variables and methods from the ReportObject. Remember that the report that you open is represented by the ReportClientDocument, not the ReportObject.

The ChartObject's properties determine the chart's appearance and where it shows on the report.

Here you focus on three ChartObject properties:

- `ChartDefinition` indicates the chart type and the fields charted. The chart type can be a Group or Details type.
- `ChartStyle` specifies the chart style type (such as a bar chart or a pie chart) and the text that appears on the chart (such as the chart title).
- `ChartReportArea` is where the chart is located (for example, the report footer).

The following two sections show how you can use these `ChartObject` properties to create a chart. You must first specify the fields on which you want your chart to be based on. To do this, create a `ChartDefinition` object, which will then be added to the `ChartObject` with the `ChartDefinition` property.

DEFINING THE FIELDS IN A CHART

The `ChartDefinition` object determines the type of chart that appears in the report and sets the fields to be displayed. A simple, two-dimensional chart displays two types of fields:

- **ConditionFields**—The fields that determine where to plot a point on the x-axis.
- **DataFields**—The fields that determine what to plot on the y-axis.

Below the chart added is a Group type (see the `ChartType` class), so the ConditionFields and DataFields that are being charted on are group fields and summary fields respectively.

ADDING CONDITIONFIELDS

Add the first group field in the Groups collection to a Fields collection. This field is retrieved with the ChartDefinition's `getConditionFields` method.

34

```
ReportClientDocument's DataDefinition:
// Create a new ChartDefinition and set its type to Group
ChartDefinition chartDef = new ChartDefinition();
chartDef.setChartType(ChartType.group);
Fields conditionFields = new Fields();
if (!dataDefinition.getGroups().isEmpty())
{
IField field = dataDefinition.getGroups().getGroup(0).getConditionField();
conditionFields.addElement(field);
}
chartDef.setConditionFields(conditionFields);
```

Adding two groups as ConditionFields enables you to create a 3D chart. Because one value is required for the x values, the next value drives the z-axis.

ADDING DATAFIELDS

After you have added ConditionFields to the ChartDefinition, add the DataFields. In a Group type chart, the DataFields are summaries for the group fields that you added as ConditionFields.

Adding DataFields is similar to how you added ConditionFields. For example, you use the name of the summary field that the user has selected to locate the desired field in the SummaryFields collection and add this field to a Fields collection. You then accessed the summary field with the ChartDefinition's DataFields property:

```
Fields dataFields = new Fields();
for (int i = 0; i < dataDefinition.getSummaryFields().size(); i++)
{
IField summaryField = dataDefinition.getSummaryFields().getField(i);
if (summaryField.getLongName(Locale.ENGLISH).equals(summaryFieldName))
{
dataFields.addElement(summaryField);
}
}
chartDef.setDataFields(dataFields);
```

Here you use the LongName of the summary field. The LongName contains the type of summary, for example, a sum or a count, and the group field that it applies to. For example:

```
Sum of (Customer.Last Year's Sales, Customer.Country)
```

In general you will want to use a field's LongName instead of its ShortName or Name to avoid confusion as the ShortName or Name might be the same for several fields.

CREATING A CHARTOBJECT

After the fields are defined, they are added to the ChartObject with the ChartDefinition property. The following code uses the ChartObject's ChartStyle property and ChartReportArea to specify the chart style type, the chart title, and the location of the chart:

```
ChartObject chartObject = new ChartObject();
chartObject.setChartDefinition(chartDefinition);
String chartTypeString = request.getParameter("type");
String chartPlacementString = request.getParameter("placement");
String chartTitle = request.getParameter("title");
if (chartTitle.equals(""))
{
chartTitle = "no title at all!";
}
ChartStyleType chartStyleType = ChartStyleType.from_string(chartTypeString);
AreaSectionKind chartPlacement = AreaSectionKind.from_string
➥(chartPlacementString);
// Set the chart type, chart placement, and chart title
chartObject.getChartStyle().setType(chartStyleType);
chartObject.setChartReportArea(chartPlacement);
chartObject.getChartStyle().getTextOptions().setTitle(chartTitle);
// Set the width, height, and top
chartObject.setHeight(5000);
chartObject.setWidth(5000);
chartObject.setTop(1000);
```

In this example, the first chart that you add will appear 50 points below the top of the report area in which the chart is located. (These fields are measured in twips, and 20 twips = 1 font point, so 1000/20 = 50 points.) Adding another chart to the same report area places it over the first chart because the formatting for report objects is absolute. The first chart remains hidden until the second chart is removed.

ADDING A CHART TO THE REPORT

Now add the chart using the ReportObjectController's add method. This method takes three parameters: the ChartObject, the section to place it in, and the position in the ReportObjectController collection where you want to add the chart. An option of 1 for the index adds the chart to the end of the array. Return the ReportObjectController by the ReportDefController's getReportObjectController method:

```
reportDefController.getReportObjectController().add(chartObject, chartSection,
➥ 1);
```

CAUTION

> If you want to modify an existing chart, you can use the clone method to copy the chart, make the desired changes, and then call the modifyObject method using the original chart and the newly modified chart as parameters.

34

WORKING WITH SUBREPORTS

A subreport is a report within a report. It can be a free-standing or linked report in the main report. A subreport can have most of the characteristics of a report, except the followings:

- A subreport cannot stand on its own, but can be inserted as an object into a main report.

- A subreport can be placed in any section of a main report and the entire subreport will be printed in that section.

- A subreport cannot contain another subreport.

- A subreport does not have Page Header or Page Footer sections.

With RAS SDK version XI existing subreports can be modified to the same level of details as in ReportClientDocument. There two classes and one interface that define most methods and properties about subreports, they are:

- **ISubreportClientDocument**—Defined in package com.crystaldecisions.sdk.occa.report.application. Use this interface to access report data definition and controllers that are required to modify a subreport.

- **SubreportController**—Defined in package com.crystaldecisions.sdk.occa.report.application. Use this class to import a report as a subreport, to add or remove subreport links, or to retrieve the names of all of the subreports in a report.

- **SubreportObject**—Defined in package com.crystaldecisions.sdk.occa.report.definition. Use this class to access subreport properties such as layout and formatting of the subreport.

IMPORTING A SUBREPORT

From ReportClientDoccument object you call method getSubreportController() to get a SubreportController object. SubreportController class exposes two methods to import an existing report as a subreport with one setting intelligent default values for left, top, width and height of the subreport object and the other one using user-defined values for top, left, width and height.

```
try
{
//Get SubreportController object from ReportClientDocument object
SubreportController subRptController = reportClientDocument.
➥getSubreportController();
String name = "GlobalSales.rpt";
String reportURL = "C:\MyReports\GlobalSales.rpt";
//Get the section into which the subreport will be added
ISection footerSection = reportClientDocument.getReportDefController()
➥.findSectionByName("FooterSection");
//Return the imported existing report as a SubReportClientDocument object
ISubreportClientDocument subRptClientDocument = subRptController.
➥importSubreport(name, reportURL, footerSection);
}
catch (ReportSDKException e)
{
//do something here
}
```

In this example, reportURL is the URL of the report to import. The URL must be an absolute physical path accessible to the client RAS SDK. Web URLs and file paths managed by BusinessObjects Enterprise are not currently supported. If the reportURL is empty, a blank report will be imported. In this import subreport method intelligent default values for left and top are 0 in twips, that is, the relative left and top positions of the subreport to the section where it is imported are 0. The default width and height of the subreport are the width and height of the section where it is imported.

You can modify the subreport through the subRptClientDocument object by accessing the report data definition and controllers. The subreport object uses methods similar to those of the ReportClientDocument so that all controllers and properties are not different from the main document; therefore end user confusion is reduced.

ADDING SUBREPORT LINKS

A SubreportLink object specifies a link between a subreport and the enclosing main report. For example, you have customer data in a primary report and then use subreports to show the orders for each customer, to coordinate the data in the primary report with the data in the subreport so that the orders in each subreport match up with the correct customer you need to specify a field that is common to both the subreport and the primary report, such as Customer ID. A subreport link allows you to link the two common fields so that records from the primary report can be match up to those in the subreport. SubreportLinks object is a collection of SubreportLink objects.

```
SubreportLink subRptLink = new SubReportLink();
String reportFieldName = "CustomerID";
//Match up the field in the main report to that in the subreport
subRptLink.setMainReportFieldName(reportFieldName);
subRptLink.setSubreportFieldName(reportFieldName);
SubReportLinks subRptLinks = new SubReportLinks();
try
{
    //Returns true if the collection changed as a result of the method
    if(subRptLinks.add(subRptLink))
    {
        SubreportController subRptController = reportClientDocument.
        ➥getSubreportController();
        String subRptName = "Customer Orders";
        //add subreport links
        subRptController.setSubreportLinks(subRptName, subRptLinks);
    }
}
catch(ClassCastException cce)
{
    //do something here
}
Catch(NullPointerException npe)
{
    //do something here
}
catch(ReportSDKException re)
{
    //do something here
}
```

34

SERVER SIDE PRINTING

RAS SDK version XI allows server-side printing. Server-side printing allows you to print reports from machines that run the RAS SDK application server.

To print a report from the machine that runs the RAS SDK application server you need to specify print options. Use the following code:

```
PrintReportOptions printRptOptions = new PrintReportOptions();
//Set printer name
printRptOptions.setPrinterName("LaserPrinter001");
//Set paper orientation to portrait
printRptOptions.setPaperOrientation(PaperOrientation.portrait);
...
//Set printer duplex
printRptOptions.setPrinterDuplex(PrinterDuplex.horizontal);
```

Then you get PrintOutputController from ReportClientDocument. PrintOutputController is used to print a report with RAS SDK server-side printing. It also defines methods to export reports to specific format, such as RTF, editableRTF, or PDF and to modify various formatting options.

```
//Get PrintOutputController
PrintOutputController printController = _
  reportClientDocument.getPrintOutputController();
try
{
   printController.printReport(printRptOptions);
}
catch(ReportSDKPrinterException re)
{
   //do something here
}
```

PART **VIII**

WEB CHAPTERS

INDEX

B

M

maintenance phase of development, 630

managed objects. *See* object management

management

accounts. *See* **account management**

CMC for. *See* **CMC** (Central Management Console)

content. *See* **content management**

folders, 681-685

groups. *See* **groups, user**

objects. *See* **object management**

servers. *See* **server management**

manual design process steps, 45-49

Map Expert

accessing, 214

Advanced layout button, 215-218

Bar Charts, 219

blank result maps, 216

Cross-Tab layout button, 216

Data tab, 215

Dot Density type, 219

Geographic field selection, 217-218

Graduated type, 219

Group layout button, 216-217

Layout section, 215-216

Map Values field, 217

OLAP layout button, 216

On Change Of option, 216-217

Pie Charts, 219

Placement section, 215

purpose of, 214

Ranged type, 219

Rapid map Creation function, 217

Show option, 216-218

Text tab, 219-220

Type tab, 218-219

maps

advanced layout options, 215-218

Bar Charts, 219

blank result maps, 216

cross-tab layout options, 216

Dot Density type, 219

expert for. *See* **Map Expert**

Format Map dialog, 226

Geographic field selection, 217-218

Graduated type, 219

groups layout options, 216-217

layer control, 227

layout options, 215-216

MapInfo, 214

modifying properties of, 226

Navigator thumbnails, 227

OLAP based, 216, 373-374

On Change Of option, 216-217

panning, 227

Pie Charts, 219

placement control, 215

positioning, 226

Ranged type, 219

Resolve Mismatch dialog, 227

Show option, 216-218

sizing, 226

summary field creation, 217

title options, 219-220

type selection, 218-219

zooming, 227

margins, 176-177

MDX (Multi Dimensional Expressions)

Live Office Add-in with, 525

OLAP Intelligence access to SQL Server cubes, 470

Measure objects

type, 405

definitions for, 408

members, OLAP

defined, 357

drilling-down feature, 371

fields same as, 362

selector, 436

slice specification, 363-366

specifying, 362

membership settings, 653

memo fields, 308-310

menus

Chart menu, 22

Database menu, 22

Edit menu, 21

File menu, 21

Format menu, 22

Help menu, 23

Insert menu. *See* **Insert menu**

Report menu, 22

View menu, 22

Window menu, 23

Merge button, Section Expert, 190

Merge Section Below command, 199-200

metadata, CMS services for, 593-594

microcube engines

Crystal Reports lacking, 416

drilling down features, 410

multipass SQL results, 411

multiple, 411

post-query behavior rule generation, 411

projections, 410

purpose of, 410

report blocks, 410

synchronized resultsets, 411

Web Intelligence role of, 477, 496

Microsoft Access, 391

Microsoft Analysis Services, 525

Microsoft Excel. *See* **Excel, Microsoft**

Microsoft Office

Access, 391

add-in. *See* **Live Office Add-in**

Excel. *See* **Excel, Microsoft**

UWS sample applications, 812

Web Services with, 812

Word. *See* **Word, Microsoft**

Microsoft Word. *See* **Word, Microsoft**

BUSINESS OBJECTS PARTNERS

BRIDGEBUILDER

http://www.bridgebuilder.com

Founded in 1995, BridgeBuilder provides value added professional services for business intelligence (BI) and customer relationship management (CRM) solutions. By combining your company's people, processes, and technology, BridgeBuilder bridges the gap between ordinary data and meaningful business intelligence. We leverage solutions from best-of-breed companies in the BI field including Business Objects, Microsoft, Pervasive, SalesLogix, ACT!, and Salesforce.com to deliver the information you need to make the best possible strategic decisions. Contact us directly at 888-274-3432 to learn more about our services.

DATA COMPASS

www.data-compass.com

Data Compass is a group of veteran IT consultants with a proven track record of implementing enterprise reporting solutions for world-class organizations in Fortune 2000 companies, with a specialty in Financial Services, through extension of best-of-breed business intelligence products and tools.

Data Compass specializes in the design and development of highly customized enterprise reporting systems based on industry leading business intelligence technologies including the Crystal Enterprise, Crystal Reports Server, and Business Object Enterprise product lines.

FUTURE TECHNOLOGIES, INC.

www.ftiweb.com

Future Technologies, Inc. is an international technology solutions provider that offers Information Technology Consulting, Development, and Computer Training to a broad array of clients in technical and financial services industries.

INFOGAIN

www.infogain.com

Infogain is a Tier One systems integrator and business consultancy focused on driving collaboration and insight through every business relationship. By developing key technologies that support best business practices in business intelligence, integration, CRM, and portals, Infogain helps companies maximize the value of every interaction.

Our delivery centers in Europe, the US, and India improve quality of service, ensure a global footprint, and provide world class pricing structures for our clients in the global 500 as well as strong regional enterprises. At Infogain, we turn insight into knowledge and communication into collaboration.

LIQUIDHUB

www.liquidhub.com

Your organization depends on access to trusted and timely information. LiquidHub's Data Management associates employ a pragmatic and iterative approach to help you get the right information to the right people at the right time. LiquidHub is a systems integrator and technology consultancy focused on enabling the Agile Enterprise through our strategy, applications, data, and infrastructure solutions and an engagement lifecycle of planning, execution, and management.

POWERTEC SOLUTIONS

www.powertecinc.com

PowerTec has been a Business Intelligence solutions provider since 1996. As a partner of Business Objects, PowerTec specializes in providing services using the Business Objects and Crystal suite of products. For 10 years, we have worked hard to attain a solid reputation for honesty, integrity and expertise. Let us partner with you to *"Harness the Power of Information."*

VIRTUAL CONSULTING

www.virtual-consulting.net

Virtual has been a Business Objects partner since 1996 and has also worked extensively as a Consulting and Training partner. In 2002 it was voted Partner of the Year. Virtual has been involved in 75+ deployments of Crystal Enterprise and has developed thousand of reports for hundreds of customers in a variety of industries.